# Lecture Notes in Computer Scier

T0238616

*Commenced Publication in 1973*
Founding and Former Series Editors:
Gerhard Goos, Juris Hartmanis, and Jan van Leeuwen

Tat Wing Chim   Tsz Hon Yuen (Eds.)

# Information and Communications Security

14th International Conference, ICICS 2012
Hong Kong, China, October 29-31, 2012
Proceedings

 Springer

Volume Editors

Tat Wing Chim
The University of Hong Kong
Department of Computer Science
Room 519, 5/F, Haking Building, Pokfulam Road
852 Hong Kong, China
E-mail: twchim@cs.hku.hk

Tsz Hon Yuen
The University of Hong Kong
Department of Computer Science
Room 519, 5/F, Haking Wong Building, Pokfulam Road
852 Hong Kong, China
E-mail: thyuen@cs.hku.hk

ISSN 0302-9743                          e-ISSN 1611-3349
ISBN 978-3-642-34128-1                  e-ISBN 978-3-642-34129-8
DOI 10.1007/978-3-642-34129-8
Springer Heidelberg Dordrecht London New York

Library of Congress Control Number: 2012948707

CR Subject Classification (1998): E.3, D.4.6, K.6.5, K.4.4, C.2, F.2.1

LNCS Sublibrary: SL 4 – Security and Cryptology

*Typesetting:* Camera-ready by author, data conversion by Scientific Publishing Services, Chennai, India

Printed on acid-free paper

Springer is part of Springer Science+Business Media (www.springer.com)

# Preface

With the ever-increasing coverage of information technology in our daily lives, protecting confidentiality, integrity, and privacy of information via the usage of cryptography and other security technology will be an undeniable responsibility of researchers. The ICICS conference series is a well-established forum for researchers in universities, research institutes, and industry to get together to share the latest research results and exchange ideas in the areas of information and communications security. ICICS has taken place in a number of different countries including China (1997, 2001, 2003, 2005, 2007, 2009, 2011), Australia (1999), Singapore (2002), Spain (2004, 2010), USA (2006), and UK (2008). It was a memorable moment for the Center for Information Security and Cryptography (CISC), University of Hong Kong, to host the 14th International Conference on Information and Communication Security (ICICS 2012) in Hong Kong. This is because 2012 is the year that the University of Hong Kong started using the new Centennial Campus, which marks the 100th anniversary of HKU. Hosting ICICS, a renowned conference that had 13 successful past events, was a special tribute to the new campus. Participants of ICICS 2012 could use this event as a chance to visit this freshly launched new campus.

A more important attraction than visiting the new HKU Centennial Campus is to enjoy the strong technical program of ICICS. There were 101 submissions from 20 countries. A total of 23 regular papers and 26 short papers were accepted. The papers cover many important areas in information security such as privacy, security in mobile systems, software and network security, cryptanalysis, applied cryptography, as well as GPU-enabled computation. Each submission was anonymously reviewed by at least two reviewers. We would like to sincerely thank our 43 Program Committee members (from 16 countries) as well as all sub-reviewers and external referees who worked under a very tight review schedule, for their valuable time, effort, and contributions to the program.

The event of ICICS could only be made possible by the collaborating efforts of many other parties behind the scenes, including the Steering Committee Chair, local Organizing Committee members, Publication Chairs, and participants. Last, but not the least, we would like to thank also our co-organizers, the Institute of Software of Chinese Academy of Sciences (CAS), the Institute of Software and Microelectronics of Peking University, and the Information Security and Forensics Society (ISFS).

October 2012

K.P. Chow
Lucas C.K. Hui
S.H. Qing
S.M. Yiu

# Organization

## Conference Chairs

K.P. Chow        The University of Hong Kong, Hong Kong
Lucas C.K. Hui     The University of Hong Kong, Hong Kong

## Program Chairs

S.H. Qing        Chinese Academy of Sciences and Peking University, China
S.M. Yiu         The University of Hong Kong, Hong Kong

## Publication Chairs

T.W. Chim       The University of Hong Kong, Hong Kong
T.H. Yuen       The University of Hong Kong, Hong Kong

## Local Organizing Committee

Catherine K.W. Chan    The University of Hong Kong, Hong Kong (Chair)
C.B. Chan           The University of Hong Kong, Hong Kong
P.F. Chan           The University of Hong Kong, Hong Kong
Y.H. Fung          The University of Hong Kong, Hong Kong
H. Xiong           The University of Hong Kong, Hong Kong

## Program Committee

Man Ho Au        University of Wollongong, Australia
Tuomas Aura      Aalto University, Finland
Feng Bao         Institute for Infocomm Research, Singapore
Alex Biryukov      University of Luxembourg, Luxembourg
Mike Burmester     Florida State University, USA
Zhenfu Cao        Shanghai Jiaotong University, China
Chin-Chen Chang   Feng Chia University, Taiwan
Xiaolin Chang      Beijing Jiaotong University, China
Zhong Chen        Peking University, China
T.W. Chim         The University of Hong Kong, Hong Kong
Sherman S.M. Chow   University of Waterloo, Canada / Chinese University of Hong Kong, Hong Kong
Cas Cremers       ETH Zurich, Switzerland

| | |
|---|---|
| Junbin Fang | The University of Hong Kong, Hong Kong |
| Steven Furnell | University of Plymouth, UK |
| Dieter Gollmann | Hamburg University of Technology, Germany |
| Yong Guan | Iowa State University, USA |
| Shuhui Hou | University of Science and Technology, China |
| Kwangjo Kim | KAIST, Korea |
| Ming Li | Utah State University, USA |
| Joseph Liu | Institute for Infocomm Research, Singapore |
| Javier Lopez | University of Malaga, Spain |
| Di Ma | University of Michigan-Dearborn, USA |
| Mark Manulis | TU Darmstadt, Germany |
| Chris Mitchell | Royal Holloway, University of London, UK |
| Raphael Phan | Loughborough University, UK |
| Pierangela Samarati | Università degli Studi di Milano, Italy |
| Miguel Soriano | Universitat Politecnica de Catalunya, Spain |
| Willy Susilo | University of Wollongong, Australia |
| Tsuyoshi Takagi | Kyushu University, Japan |
| Wen-Guey Tzeng | National Chiao Tung University, Taiwan |
| Zhihui Wang | Dalian University of Technology, China |
| Andreas Wespi | IBM Zurich Research Laboratory, Switzerland |
| Duncan S. Wong | City University of Hong Kong, Hong Kong |
| Yang Xiang | Deakin University, Australia |
| Guomin Yang | University of Wollongong, Australia |
| Shucheng Yu | University of Arkansas at Little Rock, USA |
| T.H. Yuen | The University of Hong Kong, Hong Kong |
| Fangguo Zhang | Sun Yat-sen University, China |
| Wentao Zhang | Institute of Information Engineering, Chinese Academy of Sciences, China |
| Yuliang Zheng | University of North Carolina at Charlotte, USA |
| Jianying Zhou | Institute for Infocomm Research, Singapore |

## Additional Reviewers

| | |
|---|---|
| Duegi Aranha | Ravi Jhawar |
| Claudio Agostino Ardagna | Qingguang Ji |
| Roy Arnab | Grobschadl Johann |
| Ning Cao | Aapo Kalliola |
| Ching Bon Chan | Vadnala Praveen Kumar |
| Patrick P.F. Chan | Hyunrok Lee |
| Leurent Gaetan | Zhang Lei |
| Takuya Hayashi | Huang Lin |
| Yin Hu | Hsiao-Ying Lin |
| Xinyi Huang | Zhen Liu |
| Qiong Huang | Giovanni Livraga |
| Pustogarov Ivan | Xu Ma |

Thomas Martin
Kirill Morozov
Lan Nguyen
Takashi Nishide
Bertram Poettering
Anudath Krishna Prasad
Rodrigo Roman
Peter Schwabe
Lu Shi
Youngjoo Shin
Abdulhadi Shoufan
Xiao Tan

Boyang Wang
Weiping Wen
Jia Xu
Zhenyu Yang
Jiawei Yuan
Haibin Zhang
Mingwu Zhang
Wentao Zhang
Hui Zhang
Yao Zheng
Yan Zhu
Youwen Zhu

# Table of Contents

## Full Papers

### Applied Cryptography

Audio Steganalysis Based on Lossless Data-Compression Techniques .... 1
    *Fatiha Djebbar and Beghdad Ayad*

Enhancing the Perceived Visual Quality of a Size Invariant Visual
Cryptography Scheme ......................................... 10
    *Yang-Wai Chow, Willy Susilo, and Duncan S. Wong*

Impact of the Revocation Service in PKI Prices ..................... 22
    *Carlos Gañán, Jose L. Muñoz, Oscar Esparza,*
    *Jorge Mata-Díaz, and Juanjo Alins*

### Cryptanalysis

Cryptanalysis of Multi-Prime RSA with Small Prime Difference ........ 33
    *Hatem M. Bahig, Ashraf Bhery, and Dieaa I. Nassr*

Implicit Polynomial Recovery and Cryptanalysis of a Combinatorial
Key Cryptosystem ............................................. 45
    *Jun Xu, Lei Hu, and Siwei Sun*

Improved Related-Key Differential Attacks on Reduced-Round
LBlock ....................................................... 58
    *Shusheng Liu, Zheng Gong, and Libin Wang*

### Network Security

Countermeasures on Application Level Low-Rate Denial-of-Service
Attack........................................................ 70
    *Yajuan Tang*

Firewall Packet Filtering Optimization Using Statistical Traffic
Awareness Test ............................................... 81
    *Zouheir Trabelsi, Liren Zhang, and Safaa Zeidan*

Group Behavior Metrics for P2P Botnet Detection ................... 93
    *John Felix, Charles Joseph, and Ali A. Ghorbani*

# Optimization

Hardware Performance Optimization and Evaluation of SM3 Hash
Algorithm on FPGA .............................................. 105
    *Yuan Ma, Luning Xia, Jingqiang Lin, Jiwu Jing, Zongbin Liu, and*
    *Xingjie Yu*

# Privacy

Continual Leakage-Resilient Dynamic Secret Sharing in the Split-State
Model ........................................................... 119
    *Hao Xiong, Cong Zhang, Tsz Hon Yuen, Echo P. Zhang,*
    *Siu Ming Yiu, and Sihan Qing*

Conversion of Real-Numbered Privacy-Preserving Problems into the
Integer Domain ................................................... 131
    *Wilko Henecka, Nigel Bean, and Matthew Roughan*

Perfect Ambiguous Optimistic Fair Exchange ........................ 142
    *Yang Wang, Man Ho Au, and Willy Susilo*

Privacy-Preserving Noisy Keyword Search in Cloud Computing ........ 154
    *Xiaoqiong Pang, Bo Yang, and Qiong Huang*

# Protocols

Forward Secure Attribute-Based Signatures ......................... 167
    *Tsz Hon Yuen, Joseph K. Liu, Xinyi Huang, Man Ho Au,*
    *Willy Susilo, and Jianying Zhou*

On Constant-Round Precise Zero-Knowledge ........................ 178
    *Ning Ding and Dawu Gu*

Outsourcing Encryption of Attribute-Based Encryption with
MapReduce ....................................................... 191
    *Jingwei Li, Chunfu Jia, Jin Li, and Xiaofeng Chen*

Security Enhancement of Identity-Based Identification with
Reversibility....................................................... 202
    *Atsushi Fujioka, Taiichi Saito, and Keita Xagawa*

# Security in Mobile Systems

Coopetitive Architecture to Support a Dynamic and Scalable NFC
Based Mobile Services Architecture ............................... 214
    *Raja Naeem Akram, Konstantinos Markantonakis, and Keith Mayes*

Permission-Based Abnormal Application Detection for Android . . . . . . . .    228
  *Jiawei Zhu, Zhi Guan, Yang Yang, Liangwen Yu, Huiping Sun, and
  Zhong Chen*

Symbian Smartphone Forensics and Security: Recovery of
Privacy-Protected Deleted Data . . . . . . . . . . . . . . . . . . . . . . . . . . . . . . . . . . . .    240
  *Vrizlynn L.L. Thing and Darell J.J. Tan*

## Software Security

Detecting Encryption Functions via Process Emulation and IL-Based
Program Analysis . . . . . . . . . . . . . . . . . . . . . . . . . . . . . . . . . . . . . . . . . . . . . . . . .    252
  *Ruoxu Zhao, Dawu Gu, Juanru Li, and Hui Liu*

Taint Analysis of Security Code in the KLEE Symbolic Execution
Engine . . . . . . . . . . . . . . . . . . . . . . . . . . . . . . . . . . . . . . . . . . . . . . . . . . . . . . . . . . .    264
  *Ricardo Corin and Felipe Andrés Manzano*

## Short Papers

## Authentication

A Generic Approach for Providing Revocation Support in Secret
Handshake . . . . . . . . . . . . . . . . . . . . . . . . . . . . . . . . . . . . . . . . . . . . . . . . . . . . . . .    276
  *Yanjiang Yang, Haibing Lu, Jian Weng, Xuhua Ding, and
  Jianying Zhou*

An Efficient Single-Slow-Phase Mutually Authenticated RFID Distance
Bounding Protocol with Tag Privacy . . . . . . . . . . . . . . . . . . . . . . . . . . . . . . .    285
  *Anjia Yang, Yunhui Zhuang, and Duncan S. Wong*

Exploring Mobile Proxies for Better Password Authentication . . . . . . . . .    293
  *Nitesh Saxena and Jonathan Voris*

On Security of Universal Hash Function Based Multiple
Authentication . . . . . . . . . . . . . . . . . . . . . . . . . . . . . . . . . . . . . . . . . . . . . . . . . . .    303
  *Aysajan Abidin*

## Cryptanalysis

A New Variant of Time Memory Trade-Off on the Improvement of
Thing and Ying's Attack . . . . . . . . . . . . . . . . . . . . . . . . . . . . . . . . . . . . . . . . .    311
  *Zhenqi Li, Yao Lu, Wenhao Wang, Bin Zhang, and Dongdai Lin*

Applying Time-Memory-Data Trade-Off to Plaintext Recovery
Attack . . . . . . . . . . . . . . . . . . . . . . . . . . . . . . . . . . . . . . . . . . . . . . . . . . . . . . . . . .    321
  *Zhenqi Li, Bin Zhang, Yao Lu, Jing Zou, and Dongdai Lin*

Comparison between Side-Channel Analysis Distinguishers ............ 331
    Houssem Maghrebi, Olivier Rioul, Sylvain Guilley, and
    Jean-Luc Danger

## Multimedia Security and GPU-Enabled Computation

Acceleration of Composite Order Bilinear Pairing on Graphics
Hardware ....................................................... 341
    Ye Zhang, Chun Jason Xue, Duncan S. Wong,
    Nikos Mamoulis, and Siu Ming Yiu

Evaluating the Effect of Tolerance on Click-Draw Based Graphical
Password Scheme ................................................ 349
    Yuxin Meng and Wenjuan Li

Robust Evidence Detection of Copy-Rotate-Move Forgery in Image
Based on Singular Value Decomposition .......................... 357
    Liu Yong, Huang Meishan, and Lin Bogang

## Network Security

Cookie-Proxy: A Scheme to Prevent SSLStrip Attack ................. 365
    Sendong Zhao, Ding Wang, Sicheng Zhao, Wu Yang, and
    Chunguang Ma

Detecting and Preventing ActiveX API-Misuse Vulnerabilities in
Internet Explorer ............................................... 373
    Ting Dai, Sai Sathyanarayan, Roland H.C. Yap, and Zhenkai Liang

Endpoint Mitigation of DDoS Attacks Based on Dynamic
Thresholding .................................................... 381
    Daewon Kim, Byoungkoo Kim, Ikkyun Kim, Jeongnyeo Kim, and
    Hyunsook Cho

Parameter Pollution Vulnerabilities Detection Study Based on Tree
Edit Distance ................................................... 392
    Yan Cao, Qiang Wei, and Qingxian Wang

## Privacy

A Privacy-Preserving Path-Checking Solution for RFID-Based Supply
Chains .......................................................... 400
    Wei Xin, Huiping Sun, Tao Yang, Zhi Guan, and Zhong Chen

Efficient Attribute Proofs in Anonymous Credential Using
Attribute-Based Cryptography..................................... 408
    Yan Zhang and Dengguo Feng

$F^5P^5$: Keyword Search over Encrypted Data with Five Functions and
Five Privacy Assurances ......................................... 416
  *Huimin Shuai and Wen Tao Zhu*

Location Privacy Policy Management System........................ 427
  *Arej Muhammed, Dan Lin, and Anna Squicciarini*

Privacy Protection in Social Networks Using $l$-Diversity.............. 435
  *Liangwen Yu, Jiawei Zhu, Zhengang Wu, Tao Yang,
  Jianbin Hu, and Zhong Chen*

Selling Power Back to the Grid in a Secure and Privacy-Preserving
Manner........................................................ 445
  *Tat Wing Chim, Siu Ming Yiu, Lucas Chi Kwong Hui,
  Victor On Kwok Li, Tin Wing Mui, Yu Hin Tsang,
  Chun Kin Kwok, and Kwun Yin Yu*

## Protocols

A Key Sharing Fuzzy Vault Scheme ............................... 453
  *Lin You, Mengsheng Fan, Jie Lu, Shengguo Wang, and Fenghai Li*

A New Version of McEliece PKC Based on Convolutional Codes ....... 461
  *Carl Löndahl and Thomas Johansson*

Flexible Attribute-Based Encryption ............................. 471
  *Seiko Arita*

Non-interactive Dynamic Identity-Based Broadcast Encryption without
Random Oracles ................................................ 479
  *Yanli Ren, Shuozhong Wang, and Xinpeng Zhang*

## Software Security

A Comparative Study of Malware Family Classification .............. 488
  *Rafiqul Islam and Irfan Altas*

A Fine-Grained Classification Approach for the Packed Malicious
Code ......................................................... 497
  *Shanqing Guo, Shuangshuang Li, Yan Yu, Anlei Hu, and Tao Ban*

**Author Index** ...................................................... 505

# Audio Steganalysis
# Based on Lossless Data-Compression Techniques

Fatiha Djebbar and Beghdad Ayad

[1] UAE university, UAE
fdjebbar@uaeu.ac.ae
[2] Canadian University in Dubai, UAE
beghdadayad@gmail.com

**Abstract.** In this paper, we introduce a new blind steganalysis method that can reliably detect modifications in audio signals due to steganography. Lossless data-compression ratios are computed from the testing signals and their reference versions and used as features for the classifier design. Additionally, we propose to extract additional features from different energy parts of each tested audio signal to retrieve more informative data and enhance the classifier capability. Support Vector Machine (SVM) is employed to discriminate between the cover- and the stego-audio signals. Experimental results show that our method performs very well and achieves very good detection rates of stego-audio signals produced by S-tools4, Steghide and Hide4PGP.

**Keywords:** audio steganalysis, active speech level, lossless data-compression.

## 1 Introduction

In contrast to steganography, which is the science of hiding a message in an innocuous multimedia cover file, steganalysis is the science of detecting the presence of hidden messages. Audio steganalysis techniques have been actively investigated in the last decade. This interest is attributed to the growing number of steganography algorithms and the threats they represent. In practice, the work of a steganalyst is based on finding any unnatural modification resulting from the embedding process that might exist in the suspected audio file. To date, there is no known steganographic system that hides data in a perfect secure and undetectable way. All embedding algorithms leave a fingerprint in the stego-audio unless a very small embedding capacity is achieved. Although some research works had managed to reliably detect the presence of hidden data in audio-signals, so far all of them rely on the change of the intrinsic properties (features) of the audio signals to distinguish between stego- and cover-audio signals. Once the features are extracted, most of the steganlysis methods apply a learning process to differentiate between the cover- and the stego-audio signals. The learning process is done by training a machine learning such as a support vector machine (SVM) [1] on a dataset fed with statistical properties (features) extracted from the cover and stego-audio signals. The right choice of these features reinforce the discriminatory power between cover- and stego-audio signals.

T.W. Chim and T.H. Yuen (Eds.): ICICS 2012, LNCS 7618, pp. 1–9, 2012.

Authors in [2] presented a universal steganalysis algorithm for high quality recorded speech. In this work, a statistical model is constructed to capture the irregularities between the cover and the stego signals' spectrograms. The use of audio quality measures for audio steganalysis was proposed by [3]. The authors selected a set of nineteen perceptual and non-perceptual domain audio quality measures (i.e, Signal-to-noise ration, Log likelihood) to distinguish between the stego-signal and its de-noised version (used as an estimate to the cover-signal). ANOVA test [4] and SFS (Sequential Floating Search) [5] were used to select the most appropriate measures to better detect the presence of hidden messages. To improve the latter technique, [6] proposed a content independent distortion measures as features for the classifier design. Instead of creating a reference signal via a de-noised version of the stego-signal, they proposed to use a single reference signal that is common to all signals to be tested. The author has also minimized the set of quality measure used in [3] to only five. In [7], the features are extracted from the histograms of both statistical moments and frequency domain of the tested audio signal. The same methodology was applied by [8]. However, only higher order statistical moments of histogram and frequency histogram for both signal and its wavelet sub-bands are extracted and used as features to train an SVM classifier. The features (mean, variance, skewness, and kurtosis) wavelet coefficients are supposed to provide information about the frequency distribution of the audio signal and information about the difference between the wavelet coefficients and their linear predictive values. The same principle in selecting the features was followed by [9]. However, the signal reference used is a self-generated signal via linear predictive coding. In [10], the authors used the mean and the standard deviation as features captured from high frequencies of first, second, third and fourth order derivatives of the audio signal spectrum. A reference signal is generated by randomly modifying the least significant bits of the stego signal. The latter method was further improved in [11] by extending the features developed in [10] to include mel-cepstrum coefficients (widely used in speech recognition) [12] extracted from the second derivative and also from wavelet spectrums of the audio signal. This method is also an improvement of the work presented in [13], where mel-cepstrum coefficient were exploited for the first time in audio steganalysis and used as features to train the classifier. More recently, the same authors [14] proposed to use stream data mining for high complexity audio signals steganalysis. Their approach is based on extracting the second order derivative based Markov transition probabilities and high frequency spectrum statistics as features of the audio streams. A steganalysis method based on features extracted from the co-occurrence matrix of audio signals is presented in [15]. The statistic features are calculated from the amplitude components of audio signals. Preprocessing of principal component analysis (PCA) is performed on statistic features trained with SVM classifier. In the same perspective, [16] proposed to use Hausdorff distance [17]. Wavelet de-noising is applied on the stego-signal to create a cover-signal estimate. The Hausdorff distance measure is computed at various wavelet decomposition levels from which the statistical moments are generated. In [18], the steganalysis method is based on negative resonance phenomenon in audio signal created due to data embedding. The proposed method uses features such as mean, variance, skewness and kurtosis derived from the stego and its linear predicted value. In general, the features used in previous work are extracted from the entire tested audio-signals, a process that could dilute the hiding error effect on the stego-audio signal. To select our features, we exploit the disparities in lossless data-compression ratios between audio files with different information quantities (i.e., cover- and the stego-signals). We compute the compression rates of distinct parts of each audio signal to collect additional features to collect more informative data allowing to enhance the classifier capability. Thus, each tested signal is split into four energy level parts: noise, low, medium and high using active speech level (ASL) which is defined in ITU-T Recommendation P.56 [19]. The rational to not utilize only the entire signal for the compression process is that different energy level parts (power classes) in the audio signal could be impacted differently during the hiding process. Extra features collected from this energy parts provide more informative data allowing to enhance the classifier capability. Since the original signal will not be available during the testing stage, we need to create a reference signal for the received audio-files in order to compute the features vector. By randomly modifying the 1st LSB layer of the tested signal, a signal version is created and is used as the reference signal. We show the efficacy of our proposed algorithm on a large database of audio signals and on different steganographic algorithms such as Steghide, Stool and Hide4PGP [20,21,22]. This paper is organized as follows: the impact of lossless data-compression and ASL on cover and stego signals are presented in Section 2 and Section 3. Section 4 discusses the preprocessing steps to generate our features. In Section 5.2, classification results by SVM and evaluation study are revealed. Finally, we conclude this chapter with a summary of our work in Section 6.

## 2   Lossless Data-Compression and Signal Energy

Lossless data compression involves the compression of any type of files in a way that they can be latter recovered bit-wise identical to the original. It is based on removing redundant or "unnecessary" bits of data to reduce the file to its smallest version. When data is hidden in a cover file, the quantity of information of the file changes and so does the compression ratios. However, since the audio signal content and its energy vary as time progresses, performing lossless data-compression on distinct energy parts of the signal allows to capture all subtle changes in the audio-signal. For the compression operation, we selected three utilities (zip, rar and wavpack). These tools give distinct

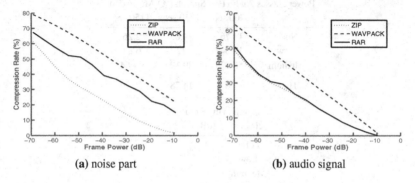

(a) noise part                    (b) audio signal

**Fig. 1.** Compression rates (1- compression ratio) for noisy part (a) and entire signal (b)

compression ratios when applied on the same audio file, which result in augmenting the detection rates of stego-audio signals as more informative data are collected. The Figures (1a) and (1b) illustrate the varying effect of lossless data-compression performed with zip, rar and wavpack utilities, on noise-only as well as an entire speech signals. The figures also describe the relation between the compression rate and the energy associated to the audio signal. More precisely, the higher are the energies the lower are compression rates of the audio signals (noise or signal). This result shows that using lossless data compression, stego and cover audio signals are more distinguishable at their lower energy parts.

## 3  Active Speech Level

ASL determines a speech activity factor ($Sp_l$) representing the fraction of time where the signal is considered to be active speech and the corresponding active level for the speech part of the signal [19]. The speech activity algorithm computes the speech energy value at each sample time (frame) and is computed using the library tool voicebox available at http://www.ee.ic.ac.uk/hp/staff/dmb/voicebox/voicebox.html . To determine which frames belong to high, medium, low and noisy (pause) power classes of active speech, $Sp_l$ (dB) is compared with a discrete set of thresholds. The thresholds set are chosen based on experimental considerations and they are specific to normalized audio files of our datasets which statistics are shown in Table 1. An example of speech-signal division process to parts with different power classes using ASL and the thresholds set is illustrated in Figure (2a). Final division result is shown in Figure (2b).

The impact of lossless data-compression on different power classes of audio signals is illustrated in Figures (3a) and (3b). These figures show that stego-audio signals are less compressible than the original audio signals (Figure 3b). In addition, the figures also indicate that the compression rates are more less important in high energy audio

**Table 1.** Statistics about the composition of the datasets in terms of different audio signal parts and thresholds set used to categorize the frames as noisy, low, medium or high

| Power classes | Audio (%) 2700 sec | Speech (%) 1550 sec | Music (%) 1150 sec |
|---|---|---|---|
| Noise | 14.76 | 24.03 | 2.26 |
| Low | 15.54 | 22 | 6.84 |
| Medium | 50.03 | 39.19 | 64.64 |
| High | 19.67 | 14.78 | 26.26 |

| Power classes | Threshold (dB) |
|---|---|
| noise | -45 |
| Low | -35 |
| Medium | -25 |
| High | -15 |

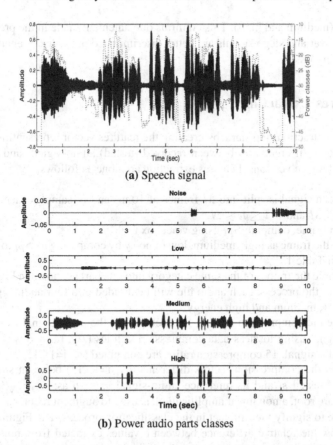

**(a)** Speech signal

**(b)** Power audio parts classes

**Fig. 2.** Speech audio-signal division based on thresholds set. The blue curve in (2a) is the temporal representation of a speech signal (left y-axis) while the red curve represents the energy in (dB) per speech signal frame (right y-axis). The energy is computed by ASL and classified to four power classes (2b) using the thresholds set presented in Table 1.

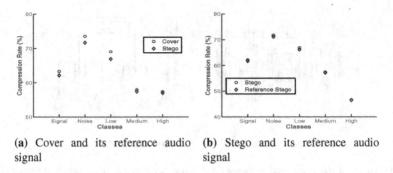

**(a)** Cover and its reference audio signal

**(b)** Stego and its reference audio signal

**Fig. 3.** Compression rates for cover- (a) and stego-signal (b) with their respective reference versions

signal parts (medium and high). This confirms our statement made in the previous section where cover and stego signals are better discriminated in the lower energetic parts of the audio signals.

## 4   Features Extraction

The features extraction step starts by creating the features vector representing the compression factors difference ($\epsilon$) between received (tested) audio-signals and their self-generated reference versions. Features extraction are done as follows:

1. The speech signal is split into $M$ frames of 10 ms and $N$ samples each, $s_t(m, n)$, $1 \le m \le M$ and $1 \le n \le N$.
2. For each frame, compute $Sp_l$ using voicebox tool.
3. Classify the frame as high, medium, low or noisy by comparing its $Sp_l$ to the values shown in Table 1.
4. Reassemble the frames of the same category into one part as shown in Figure 2b. At the end of the process, each audio file will be divided into four audio signal parts: noisy, low, medium and high energy.
5. Compute the compression ratio $\eta_i$ for each part of the audio-signal as well as the entire signal using lossless data compression utilities (zip, rar and wavpack). For each audio signal, 15 compression ratios are computed ($\eta_i$, i=1...15) .
6. Calculate the compression factors difference ($\epsilon_i$, i=1...15) between similar categories of tested $s_t$ and its reference audio-signal $s_r$ sush as: $\epsilon_i = \sqrt{|\eta_{ti} - \eta_{ri}|}$. The square root, a non linear amplification, is used to augment feeble $\eta_i$ values and therefore to signify their impact in the classification process. The Figures (4a) and (4b) show the relative difference between $\epsilon$ values extracted from noisy parts as well as entire signals.

The features vector of each audio signal contains 15 coefficients: $Features = \epsilon_1, \epsilon_2, ..., \epsilon_{15}$

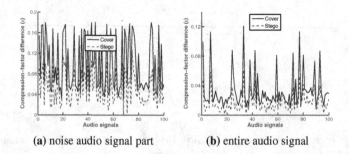

(a) noise audio signal part          (b) entire audio signal

**Fig. 4.** Variation of the compression factors difference ($\epsilon$) in noisy parts (4a) and in entire signals (4b) of 100 audio-files. The compression is performed by zip utility and the stego files are generated with Hide4PGP.

# 5    Evaluation Measures

## 5.1    Datasets

For each tested steganography algorithm, two datasets are produced: training and testing (Tr and Ts). Each dataset contains 270 stego and cover WAV audio signals of 10 s length. All signals are sampled at 44.1 kHz and quantized at 16-bits. Each training and testing dataset contains 135 positive (stego) and 135 negative (cover) audio samples. We used on-line audio files from different types such as speech signals in different languages (i.e, English, Chinese, Japanese, French, and Arabic), and music (classic, jazz, rock, blues). All stego-audio signals are generated by hiding data from different types: text, image, audio signals, video and executable files. The datasets $Tr$ and $Ts$ consist of a matrix of $\{\epsilon_i, l_i\}$,where $\epsilon_i$ refers to 15 compression-factors difference, and $l_i \in \{\pm 1\}$. The values +1 and -1 correspond to "Stego-audio" and "non Stego-audio" classes respectively. The performance of the proposed steganalysis algorithm is measured by the ability of the system to recognize and distinguish between stego and cover-audio signals. Next, we present a performance analysis of our steganalysis algorithm.

## 5.2    Results

In this section, we investigate the detection rate of our steganographic algorithm based on classification results of the SVM classifier used in conjunction with the Radial Basis Function (RBF) kernel [23]. In this study, we used SVMs library tool available at http://www.csie.ntu.edu.tw/~cjlin/libsvm. The detection rates of our algorithm are reported in Tab.2, more details are reported in the Figures 5b and 5a. The performance of the proposed steganalysis method is measured by how well the system can recognize and distinguish between the stego and the cover-audio signals. In order to analyze the evaluation measures, we firstly define the following:

- $TP$: stego-audio signal classified as stego-audio signal
- $TN$: cover-audio signal classified as cover-audio signal
- $FN$: stego-audio signal classified as cover-audio signal
- $FP$: cover-audio signal classified as stego-audio signal

In the subsequent formula, *all* represents the number of all positive and negative audio signals. The value of the above information is used to calculate the $Accuracy(AC) = \frac{TP+TN}{all}$. Following the preparation of the training and testing features vectors for for each studied steganographic tool, we use SVM classifier in conjunction with the RBF kernel for the classification process. The results of the performance evaluation study are reported in Table 2 where the accuracy of each tool is measured by the AC value. The true positive rate and false negative rates are reported in Figure 5a while in Figure 5b true-positive versus true-negative rate of the proposed steganalysis algorithm are presented. Higher AC values and ROC correspond to more accurate steganalysis detection performance. The results show that the features extracted by our method are very informative for the classification process. In addition, we only used 15 features for the classification which results shorten the computation time needed for the classification process. Most importantly, the proposed method offers very high accuracy in regards to stego-audio files detection. Stego files generated by Hide4PGP and Stools are 100% detected (Figure (5b)) versus 96% in Steghide.

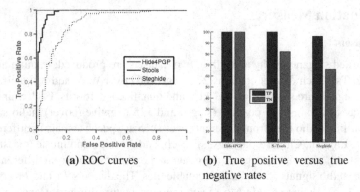

(a) ROC curves

(b) True positive versus true negative rates

**Fig. 5.** Lossless compression-based audio-steganalysis results on tested steganographic methods [20,21,22]

**Table 2.** Overall lossless data compression-based audio steganalysis

| Hiding methods | AC |
|---|---|
| Hide4PGP | 1 |
| S-Tools | 0.91 |
| Steghide | 0.81 |

## 6   Conclusion

In this paper, we proposed a simple to implement yet effective new blind audio steganalysis method. This method is based on lossless data compression techniques. To improve the detection rates of our method, more informative features are extracted from distinct energy parts of the audio signals. The proposed method have shown better accuracy rates when compared with existing landmark methods. Finally, the success of the proposed steganalysis method in detecting steganographic audio signals encouraged us to plan future investigations such as minimizing the features vector and further extending our proposed method to other steganographic applications which involve hiding small amount of data in the audio signals.

## References

1. Cristianini, N., Shawe-Taylor, J.: An introduction to Support Vector Machines Cambridge University Press (2000)
2. Johnson, K.M., Lyu, S., Farid, H.: Steganalysis of Recorded Speech. In: Proceedings of the Conference on Security, Steganography and Watermarking of Multimedia (SPIE), San Jose, USA, pp. 664–672 (January 2005)
3. Ozer, H., Avcibag, I., Sankur, B., et al.: Steganalysis of Audio Based on Audio Quality Metrics. In: Proceedings of SPIE, Santa Clara, CA, USA, pp. 55–66 (June 2003)
4. Rencher, A.C.: Methods of Multivariate Data Analysis, 2nd edn. John Wiley (2002)
5. Pudil, P., Novovicova, J., Kittler, J.: Floating Search Methods in Feature Selection. Pattern Recognition Letters, 1119–1125 (November 1994)
6. Avcibas: Audio steganalysis with content independent distortion measures. IEEE Signal Process Letter 13(2), 92–95 (2006)

7. Qi, Y., Fu, J., Yuan, J.: Wavelet domain audio steganalysis based on statistical moments of histogram. Journal of System Simulation 20(7), 1912–1914 (2008)
8. Xuan, G., Shi, Y.Q., Gao, J., et al.: Steganalysis based on multiple features formed by statistical moments of wavelet characteristic functions. In: Proceeding of Information Hiding Workshop, pp. 262–277 (2005)
9. Ru, X., Zhang, H., Huang, X.: Steganalysis of Audio: Attaching the Steghide. In: Proceeding of the Fourth International Conference on Machine Learning and Cybernetics, pp. 3937–3942 (2005)
10. Liu, Q., Sung, A., Qiao, M.: Detecting information hiding in WAV audios. In: Proceeding of 19th International Conference on Pattern Recognition, pp. 1–4 (2008)
11. Liu, Q., Sung, A.H., Qiao, M.: Temporal derivative-based spectrum and mel-cepstrum audio steganalysis. IEEE Transactions on Information Forensics and Security 4(3), 359–368 (2009)
12. Kraetzer, C., Dittmann, J.: Pros and Cons of Mel-cepstrum Based Audio Steganalysis Using SVM Classification. In: Furon, T., Cayre, F., Doërr, G., Bas, P. (eds.) IH 2007. LNCS, vol. 4567, pp. 359–377. Springer, Heidelberg (2008)
13. Kraetzer, C., Dittmann, J.: Mel-cepstrum based steganalysis for voip-steganography. In: Proceedings of SPIE, Security, Steganography, and Watermarking of Multimedia Contents IX, vol. 6505, pp. 650505.1–650505.12 (2006)
14. Liu, Q., Sung, A.H., Qiao, M.: Novel Stream Mining for Audio Steganalysis. In: Proceedings of the 17th ACM International Conference on Multimedia, Beijing, China, pp. 95–104 (October 2009)
15. Qi, Y., Wang, Y., Yuan, J.: Audio Steganalysis Based on Co-occurrence Matrix and PCA. In: International Conference on Measuring Technology and Mechatronics Automation (ICMTMA), vol. 1, pp. 433–436 (2009)
16. Liu, Y., Chiang, K., Corbett, C., Archibald, R., Mukherjee, B., Ghosal, D.: A Novel Audio Steganalysis based on Higher-Order Statistics of a Distortion Measure with Hausdorff Distance. LNCS, pp. 487–501 (September 2008)
17. Huttenlocher, D.P., Klanderman, G.A., Rucklidge, W.J.: Comparing Images using the Hausdorff Distance. IEEE Transactions on Pattern Analysis and Machine Intelligence 19(9), 850–863 (1993)
18. Ru, X., Zhang, Y., Wu, F.: Audio steganalysis based on negative resonance phenomenon caused by steganographic tools. Journal of Zhejiang 7(4), 577–583 (2006)
19. ITU-T Recommendation P56, Telephone Transmission Quality: Objective Measuring Apparatus (March 1996)
20. Steghide, http://steghide.sourceforge.net/
21. Stools Version 4.0, http://info.umuc.edu/its/online_lab/ifsm459/s-tools4/
22. Hide4PGP, http://www.heinz-repp.onlinehome.de/Hide4PGP.html
23. Vapnik, V.: Statistical Learning Theory. Wiley, Hoboken (1998)

# Enhancing the Perceived Visual Quality of a Size Invariant Visual Cryptography Scheme

Yang-Wai Chow[1], Willy Susilo[2,*], and Duncan S. Wong[3]

[1] Advanced Multimedia Research Laboratory
[2] Centre for Computer and Information Security Research,
School of Computer Science and Software Engineering,
University of Wollongong, Australia
{caseyc,wsusilo}@uow.edu.au
[3] Department of Computer Science, City University of Hong Kong, Hong Kong
duncan@cityu.edu.hk

**Abstract.** Two of the main areas of research in visual cryptography have been on improving the visual quality of the recovered image and in reducing the pixel expansion of the shares. This paper addresses both of these visual cryptography issues. First, a method to enhance the perceived visual quality of the recovered image using various image filtering techniques is presented. In particular, these image filtering techniques are used to enhance the local and global contrasts of a grayscale image. Second, a multi-pixel block size invariant visual cryptography scheme that maintains the relative density of local neighboring pixels is proposed. This method encrypts blocks of pixels based on whether the total number of black pixels within the respective blocks is above or below a certain threshold. In conjunction, these approaches effectively improve on the perceived visual quality of a recovered visual cryptography image.

**Keywords:** Visual cryptography, visual quality, image filtering, size invariant, multi-pixel encoding.

## 1 Introduction

A visual secret sharing scheme known as visual cryptography was introduced by Naor and Shamir [11] as a means of using images to conceal information. The concealed information can be decrypted by the human visual system without any need of a computer to perform decryption computations. As such, this scheme can even be decrypted by individuals who have no knowledge of cryptography.

In the $k$-out-of-$n$ Visual Cryptography Scheme (VCS) originally proposed by Naor and Shamir, a secret image is assumed to consist of a collection of black and white pixels. The secret image is used to create a set of $n$ shares, each to be printed on a separate transparency. Individually, the shares look like random black and white pixels that reveal no information about the secret image, other than the image size. When a threshold number of shares, $k$, or more are

---

* This work is supported by ARC Future Fellowship FT0991397.

T.W. Chim and T.H. Yuen (Eds.): ICICS 2012, LNCS 7618, pp. 10–21, 2012.

stacked together, the human visual system averages the black and white pixel contributions of the superimposed shares to recover the hidden information. White is usually treated as transparent in order to allow colors (i.e. black) of the other shares to pass through it when superimposed. Stacking any $k - 1$, or less, shares together does not reveal any information that can be used to recover the secret image, hence a $(k, n)$-VCS.

Since the introduction of visual cryptography, many researchers have proposed a variety of different VCSs over the years. One of the main drawbacks of traditional VCSs is the pixel expansion. In traditional VCSs, each pixel in the original secret image is represented using $m$ pixels in each of the resulting shares. The parameter $m$ is known as the pixel expansion, because the recovered image will be $m$ times larger than the secret image [3]. Pixel expansion typically increases with the number of created shares, in some cases this increase is exponential. Large pixel expansion has a number of drawbacks in terms of the quality of the recovered image and the complexity of the VCS [4]. Furthermore, it makes it inconvenient for carrying shares and wastes storage space [6]. Therefore, one of the main areas of research has been in reducing the pixel expansion. A number of researchers have proposed techniques for dealing with the pixel expansion problem in order to develop VCSs with no pixel expansion [2, 3, 6, 7, 10, 12–14]. In these size invariant VCSs, shares have the same size as the original secret image, thus $m = 1$.

In conjunction with reducing the pixel expansion, another commonly researched area has been in improving the visual quality of VCSs. Splitting the secret image into multiple shares in visual cryptography has the effect of reducing the contrast in the recovered image. Since visual cryptography relies on the human visual system to average the black and white pixel contributions of superimposed shares, the perceived visual quality of the recovered image is an extremely important issue. In general, the lower the overall contrast in the recovered image, the lower the perceived visual quality, as it becomes harder for the human mind to form a mental image of the secret image.

The issue of visual quality is even more vital in the case of size invariant VCSs, because in order to preserve the size, some information from the secret image is definitely lost. Unlike the traditional VCS, which is called deterministic because reconstruction of a secret pixel is guaranteed, size invariant VCSs give no absolute guarantee on the correct reconstruction of the original pixels. As such, it is not possible to recover the exact secret image from the shares. For the guarantee of a correct reconstruction, a certain pixel expansion must be paid in a deterministic scheme [4].

**Our Contribution.** This paper addresses both the issue of visual quality and the pixel expansion concern in visual cryptography. For grayscale images, we show that the perceived visual quality of the recovered image can be improved by using image filtering techniques prior to encrypting the secret image. It should be noted that other grayscale image VCSs can potentially benefit from the implementation of similar image filtering techniques. In addition, we also propose a size invariant VCS that maintains the relative density of local neighboring pixels in the recovered image. This is because unlike VCSs which encrypt individual pixels separately, in our proposed VCS we encrypt a block of multiple pixels based on the density of black pixels within the entire block. Together, these methods have the overall effect of enhancing the perceived visual quality of the recovered image.

## 2   Preliminaries

This section presents a brief background in relation to VCSs, including the $(k, n)$-VCS construction as defined by Naor and Shamir [11] and how it can be used for grayscale images.

### 2.1   Fundamentals of VCSs

In general, a $(k, n)$-VCS encrypts a secret image into $n$ shares. Each share contains a collection of black and white pixels that do not reveal any information about the secret image. The secret image can only be recovered by stacking together $k$ or more shares. The human visual system averages the black and white pixel contributions of the superimposed shares to recover the hidden information. No information is revealed if less than $k$ shares are stacked together.

The resulting structure can be described by two collections of $n \times m$ binary matrices, $C_0$ and $C_1$, where each row in these matrices represents the black and white subpixel configuration that are used to encrypt one share. Since each pixel in the secret image is encrypted in each share as $m$ subpixels, this represents the pixel expansion. A square is usually a good choice for the subpixel configuration because it maintains the aspect ratio. To encrypt a white pixel in the secret image, one of the matrices in $C_0$ is randomly selected, whereas to encrypt a black pixel, one of the matrices in $C_1$ is randomly selected.

Stacking shares together has the effect of 'OR'ing the $m$ subpixels of the respective matrix rows. The gray-level of the stacked shares is proportional to the Hamming weight $H(V)$ of the 'OR'ed binary vector $V$ of length $m$. This gray-level is interpreted by the human visual system as black if $H(V) \geq d$ and as white if $H(V) < d - \alpha m$ for some fixed threshold $1 \leq d \leq m$ and relative difference $\alpha > 0$ [11].

**Definition 1.** *Let* k, n, m *and* d *be non-negative integers which satisfy* $2 \leq$ k $\leq$ n *and* $1 \leq$ d $\leq$ m. *Two collections of* n×m *binary matrices,* $C_0$ *and* $C_1$, *constitute a* (k, n)-VCS *if the following conditions are satisfied:*

1. *For any S in* $C_0$, *the 'OR' operation of any* k *of the* n *rows satisfies* H(V) $< d - \alpha m$.
2. *For any S in* $C_1$, *the 'OR' operation of any* k *of the* n *rows satisfies* H(V) $\geq$ d.
3. *For any subset* $\{i_1, i_2, ..., i_q\}$ *of* $\{1, 2, ..., n\}$ *with* q < k, *the two collections of* q×m *matrices* $D_t$ *for* t $\in$ $\{1, 0\}$ *obtained by restricting each* n×m *matrix in* $C_t$ *(where* t = 0, 1*) to row* $i_1, i_2, ..., i_q$ *are indistinguishable in the sense that they contain the same matrices with the same frequencies.*

The first two conditions are known as the contrast and the third condition as the security [11]. Ateniese et al. [1] showed how general access structures can be constructed for a $(k, n)$-VCS. A $(2, 2)$-VCS can be represented by the following two collections of binary matrices, known as the basis matrices of a VCS:

$$C_0 = \{\text{all matrices obtained by permutating the columns of } \begin{bmatrix} 0 & 0 & 1 & 1 \\ 0 & 0 & 1 & 1 \end{bmatrix}\}$$

$$C_1 = \{\text{all matrices obtained by permutating the columns of } \begin{bmatrix} 0 & 0 & 1 & 1 \\ 1 & 1 & 0 & 0 \end{bmatrix}\}$$

## 2.2 VCSs for Grayscale Images

Since the secret image in the original VCS is assumed to consist of black and white pixels, for grayscale images the secret image can first be converted to an image containing only black and white pixels through a techniques known as dithering [9]. Dithering is a technique commonly used in printing applications to create an illusion of color depth in images with a limited color palette. Colors not available in the palette are approximated by a diffusion of colored pixels from within the available palette. The basic principle of the diffusion is to pack pixels with a higher density to represent darker colors and to distribute the pixels sparsely to represent lighter colors [8].

In a dithered image, the human eye perceives the diffusion as a mixture of colors within it. This means that for grayscale images, the human visual system perceives different gray levels from the distribution of black and white pixels. Figure 1 depicts this process for a $(2, 2)$-VCS. The secret image, which is a 256-level grayscale image, is shown in Figure 1(a). Figure 1(b) shows the same image after Floyd-Steinberg dithering [5]. Note that the Floyd-Steinberg dithering technique was used for all dithered images in this paper. The dithered image can then be encrypted into two shares using the basis matrices presented in the previous section. An example of the recovered image obtained by stacking the two resulting shares together is shown in Figure 1(c). The original secret image

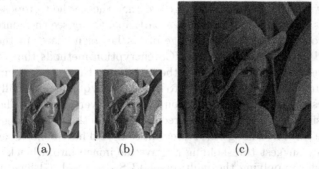

(a)                    (b)                    (c)

**Fig. 1.** Example of Naor-Shamir $(2, 2)$-VCS applied to a grayscale image by first dithering the image. (a) The secret grayscale image; (b) Dithered image; (c) Recovered image, with a pixel expansion of $m = 4$.

size was 512×512, whereas the shares and recovered image sizes are 1024×1024, hence this gives a pixel expansion of $m = 4$.

## 3   Related Work

The VCS defined in the previous section is referred to as a deterministic VCS, because reconstruction of the secret pixels is guaranteed. A probabilistic visual cryptography scheme (probVCS) was presented by Yang [14], where each pixel in the original image is represented using a single pixel in the image that is reconstructed from the shares, thus giving rise to a scheme with no pixel expansion. A similar size invariant VCS was previously proposed by Ito et al. [7].

The main characteristic of the probabilistic scheme is that there is no guarantee that each pixel in the recovered image accurately represents the actual pixel from the original secret image. This is because a black pixel in the original secret image may be incorrectly represented, with a certain probability, as a white pixel in the reconstructed image, and vice versa. This presents a trade off between pixel expansion and the accuracy of the recovered image. Cimato et al. [3] generalized Yang's [14] model and showed that it is possible to trade pixel expansion for the probability of a good reconstruction.

Chen et al. [2] proposed a method that maps a block of pixels in the original grayscale secret image into a block of the same size in each share. They presented two techniques based on histogram width-equalization and histogram depth-equalization to generate corresponding share blocks with multiple levels, each containing different black and white pixel densities, rather than just two levels as implemented in traditional visual cryptography. However, their method is only able to handle the special case of a $(n, n)$-VCS. Wu et al. [13] in turn developed a histogram approach for color images, which provides a tunable feature that allows the user to control the quality of the recovered image.

Hou and Tu [6] introduced a VCS based on a method of encoding multiple pixels simultaneously. In their approach, a number of successive white or black pixels are taken as a unit of encryption. The probability that these pixels will be encrypted as black pixels depends on the ratio of black pixels in the basis matrices. However, Liu et al. [10] suggested that the method proposed in Hou and Tu [6] has a security defect, where a participant may see the contour of the secret image only by viewing the image of his/her own share. In their paper, they proposed two other multi-pixel VCS encryption methods that attempt to improve the visual quality by reducing the variance in the recovered image. They argue that a smaller variance gives rise to better visual quality especially in terms of the evenness of the pixel distribution in the recovered image. They further suggest that since black pixels can be recovered perfectly, to obtain good visual quality for the recovered image the secret image should have a black background. Therefore, they suggest thresholding a grayscale image into a black and white image first before applying the multi-pixel VCS. Ito et al. [7] have previously made a similar observation for encrypting color images, where white pixels can perfectly be recovered.

# 4   Image Filtering

In view of the fact that the aim of visual cryptography is for the human visual system to decrypt the superimposed shares, it is conceivable that the perceived visual quality of the recovered image can be improved by performing image filtering prior to encryption. Yang and Chen [15] observed that since the contrast of a recovered image is poor, it is possible to prioritize certain 'more important' pixels during the encryption. They proposed a size reduced VCS, in which they performed edge detection on the secret image to identify important pixels, as these edge pixels give the most meaningful information about the image. Once identified, the important pixels and less important pixels are given different pixel expansions during encryption. As such, the size of the resulting shares is smaller than that of the traditional size expanded VCSs.

Instead of performing edge detection, we propose a method to enhance the perceive edges by passing the secret image through a sharpening filter. This has the effect of increasing the local contrast at discontinuities in the image, which have distinct gray-levels, hence making it easier to perceive edges in the image. To the human visual system, the resulting image appears sharper. For this we apply a Laplacian operator using a $3 \times 3$ kernel. Figure 2(a) shows the image produced by applying this sharpening filter to the secret image previously shown in Figure 1(a). The dithered image, after sharpening, is shown in Figure 2(b). This image was then encrypted using the Naor-Shamir (2, 2)-VCS into two separate shares, and the image recovered by superimposing the two shares is shown in Figure 2(c). By comparing this recovered image with the image in Figure 1(c), one can see an improvement in the perceived visual quality of the resulting image.

In addition to an image sharpening filter, which increases the local contrast at discontinuities, the global contrast of the secret image can also be enhanced using histogram equalization. In general, a grayscale image has 256 possible intensity values. An image histogram can be constructed to represent the intensity distribution of the pixels in an image over these values. Histogram equalization is a technique that can be used to spread the image intensity to cover the full $0-255$ range of values. For images that do not cover the full range of values, histogram equalization effectively increases the global contrast of an image.

The complete overall process taken to enhance the perceived visual quality of the resulting recovered image is listed as follows:

1. Perform histogram equalization
2. Pass the resulting image through a sharpening filter
3. Dither the image produced from the previous step
4. Apply a VCS

This full process is illustrated in Figure 3. Figure 3(a) shows the secret image along with its corresponding histogram. In a histogram the horizontal axis represents the intensity values and the vertical axis represents the number of pixels for each intensity value. Histogram equalization is performed on the secret image and the resulting image, and its histogram, are shown in Figure 3(b). One can

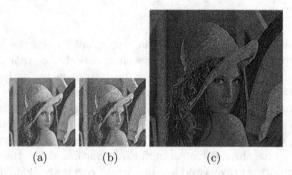

**Fig. 2.** Example of how the perceived visual quality of a VCS can be improved using an image sharpening technique. (a) Image after sharpening; (b) Dithered image; (c) Recovered image.

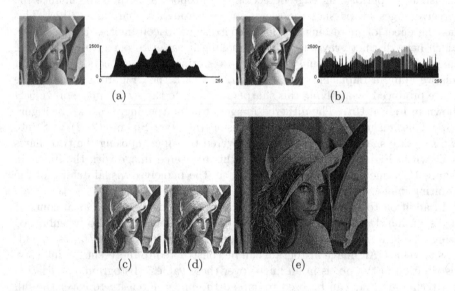

**Fig. 3.** Enhancing the perceived visual quality of a VCS via image filtering techniques. (a) Secret image and its corresponding histogram; (b) Image resulting from histogram equalization and its histogram; (c) Image produced after passing it through a sharpening filter; (d) Dithered image; (e) Recovered image.

observe the enhancement in the global image contrast. The image is then passed through a sharpening filter, resulting in the image shown in Figure 3(c). This image is then dithered to get an image with only black and white pixels, shown in Figure 3(d). The dithered image was then encrypted using the Naor-Shamir (2, 2)-VCS, and Figure 3(e) shows the image recovered by superimposing the two shares.

One can see a difference in the visual quality of the recovered image by comparing the images shown in Figure 1(c), Figure 2(c) and Figure 3(e). The details in the image can be perceived more clearly in the recovered image obtained using the described image filtering techniques. Admittedly, passing the secret image through these image filters effectively modifies the original image. Nevertheless, since the primary goal of visual cryptography is for the human visual system to be able to perceive the recovered image, enhancing the visual quality in this manner certainly achieves that objective.

# 5   Block Threshold Visual Cryptography

In this section, we propose a VCS that encrypts blocks containing multiple pixels. The aim of this approach is to preserve the relative density of local neighboring pixels in a recovered image. Probabilistic VCSs produce shares with no pixel expansion by encrypting individual pixels as either black or white in a probabilistic manner. However, since each pixel is treated independently, there is no guarantee that density of pixels within small areas in the recovered image is accurate. As such, the recovered image looks rather noisy. By proposing a scheme that encrypts blocks of pixels based on the density of the pixels within the block, this maintains the relative density of pixels within the block, thereby improving the perceived visual quality of the recovered image.

The proposed VCS is built from the same basis matrices, $C_0$ and $C_1$, as the traditional $(k, n)$-VCS. However, instead of performing encryption on a per pixel basis, in this scheme encryption is performed by taking a multi-pixel block as a unit of encryption. The block size contains the same number of pixels, $m$, as in the traditional $(k, n)$-VCS. If the total number of black pixels within the block is greater than a certain threshold, the corresponding block of pixels in the shares are encrypted using the pixel configuration representing a black pixel block, which is randomly chosen from the collection of $C_1$ matrices with equal frequencies. On the other hand, if the total number of black pixels within the block is less than, or equal to, the threshold, then the corresponding block of pixels in the shares are encrypted using the pixel configuration representing a white pixel block, which is randomly chosen from the collection of $C_0$ matrices with equal frequencies. The adopted threshold for determining whether a block should be encrypted as a white or black pixel block, is half the total number of pixels within the block, i.e. $\frac{m}{2}$. We will refer to this as the Block Threshold Visual Cryptography Scheme (BTVCS) and is defined as follows:

**Construction.** (k, n)-BTVCS. *Let* k, n, m *and* t *be non-negative integers which satisfy* $2 \leq$ k $\leq$ n *and* $0 \leq$ t $\leq$ m. *Let* $C_0$ *and* $C_1$ *be two collections of* n×m *basis matrices corresponding to white and black pixel configurations for a traditional* (k, n)-VCS, *with* n *being the number of shares and* m *being the pixel expansion. For each block of* p×q *pixels in the secret image, where the number of pixels in* p×q *is equal to* m, *let* t *be the total number of black pixels within the block. If* $t \leq \frac{m}{2}$, *encrypt the corresponding block in the* n *shares as a 'white' pixel block by randomly selecting a matrix from* $C_0$. *Otherwise, encrypt the corresponding block in the* n *shares as a 'black' pixel block by randomly selecting a matrix from* $C_1$.

Since BTVCS is built from the same basis matrices as the traditional VCS, the contrast and security conditions are also the same. In a sense, BTVCS can be seen as the image being reconstructed using large pixels (i.e. the pixel configuration obtained from the basis matrices used to represent white and black pixel blocks) as its basic building components. From an image processing point of view, this is somewhat similar to reducing the resolution of an image whilst maintaining its image size. The relative perceived density of the local neighboring pixels is maintained, whilst the image resolution is reduced.

The dimensions of the block of pixels, $p \times q$, should ideally be as close to a square as possible given the number of pixels $m$. For example, for at $(2, 2)$-BTVCS the pixel configurations can take the form of a $1 \times 2$ block using the following collections of basis matrices, where $m = 2$:

$$C_0 = \{\text{all matrices obtained by permutating the columns of } \begin{bmatrix} 0 & 1 \\ 0 & 1 \end{bmatrix}\}$$

$$C_1 = \{\text{all matrices obtained by permutating the columns of } \begin{bmatrix} 0 & 1 \\ 1 & 0 \end{bmatrix}\}$$

A $(2, 2)$-BTVCS can also be constructed using the pixel configurations obtained from the collections of basis matrices previously presented in Section 2.1, where $m = 4$. In this case, the block pixel configuration can either be a $2 \times 2$ or a $1 \times 4$ pixel block. However, using the dimensions of $2 \times 2$ will produce better visual results as shown in the section to follow.

# 6    Results and Discussions

To illustrate the end result of performing encryption using different VCSs, Figure 4 shows comparisons between the resulting recovered images for a gradient image obtained by applying various VCSs. The gradient image, where the gray-levels smoothly transition from black to white, is shown in Figure 4(a) with its corresponding dithered image shown in Figure 4(b). Figure 4(c) shows the result of Naor and Shamir's traditional $(2, 2)$-VCS which has pixel expansion. Figure 4(d) in turn shows Yang's [14] size invariant $(2, 2)$-probVCS. Figures 4(e), 4(f) and 4(g) were obtained using $(2, 2)$-BTVCS with block dimensions of $1 \times 2$, $2 \times 2$ and $1 \times 4$ respectively.

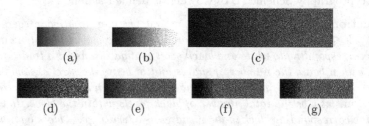

**Fig. 4.** Results of various $(2, 2)$-VCSs on a gradient image. (a) Gradient image; (b) Dithered gradient image; (c) The traditional VCS with pixel expansion; (d) probVCS; (e) BTVCS with block dimensions of 1x2; (f) BTVCS with block dimensions of 2x2; (f) BTVCS with block dimensions of 1x4.

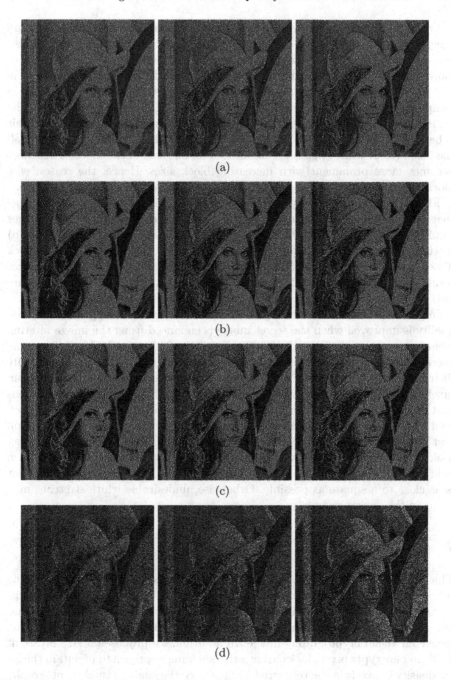

**Fig. 5.** Recovered images resulting from different techniques. Left image: with dithering only. Center image: with sharpening and dithering. Right image: with histogram equalization, sharpening and dithering. (a) (2, 2)-BTVCS with block dimensions of 1x2; (b) (2, 2)-BTVCS with block dimensions of 2x2; (c) (2, 2)-BTVCS with block dimensions of 1x4; (d) (2, 2)-probVCS.

From the figures, it can be seen that Naor and Shamir's traditional VCS and Yang's probVCS are better at capturing the overall range of intensity values. However, the former has pixel expansion and the later gives the appearance of more noise as compared to the BTVCS approach. BTVCS with block size of $m = 4$ gives rise to higher contrasting regions compared to with $m = 2$. Also, in comparing BTVCS with pixel blocks of $2 \times 2$ and $1 \times 4$, it can be seen that for the $1 \times 4$ case there are some undesirable streaks of white in the darker areas. This is because if $m$ pixels are encrypted in a single row, there will be cases where all the black (resp. white) pixels are all located on one side of the block. This effect becomes more prominent with increasing block sizes. Hence, the reason why block pixel dimensions $p \times q$, should ideally be as close to a square as possible.

Figure 5 shows the results of the size invariant schemes on the secret image that was previously shown in Figure 1(a). Figure 5(a) shows recovered images resulting from the (2, 2)-BTVCS with block dimensions of $1 \times 2$. Figure 5(b) in turn shows recovered images resulting from the (2, 2)-BTVCS with block dimensions of $2 \times 2$. This is followed by Figure 5(c) which shows recovered images resulting from the (2, 2)-BTVCS with block dimensions of $1 \times 4$. Finally, Figure 5(d) shows recovered images resulting from Yang's [14] (2, 2)-probVCS.

In general, it can be seen from the recovered images that the perceived visual quality is improved when the secret image is enhanced using the image filtering techniques, as the details in the image can be seen more clearly. In addition, the overall density of pixels in the recovered images using BTVCS are more evenly distributed and give rise to a better visual appearance, compared to the random pixel density of probVCS, which appears to be rather noisy. Similar observations that encrypting multiple pixels produce more evenly distributed pixels in recovered image have also been made in the multi-pixel schemes proposed by Hou and Tu [6] and Liu et al. [10]. Of the different BTVCS block dimensions, using a block size of $m = 4$ results in recovered images with higher contrast between light and dark regions. Also, ideally the dimensions should form a block that is as close to a square as possible. Otherwise, undesirable white stretches may occur in the darker regions.

## 7    Conclusion

This paper addresses the issue of visual quality in the recovered image and the problem of pixel expansion in the resulting shares, which are two major concerns in visual cryptography. We show that before performing dithering, the local and global contrasts of the image can first be enhanced to improve the resulting recovered visual cryptography image. In addition, we proposed a size invariant VCS that encrypts pixel blocks using a thresholding approach to maintain the local density of pixels in the recovered image. Since the goal of visual cryptography is for the human visual system to decrypt the hidden information, these image filtering techniques together with our size invariant VCS successfully enhances the resulting visual quality of the recovered image.

# References

1. Ateniese, G., Blundo, C., Santis, A.D., Stinson, D.R.: Visual cryptography for general access structures. Inf. Comput. 129(2), 86–106 (1996)
2. Chen, Y.-F., Chan, Y.-K., Huang, C.-C., Tsai, M.-H., Chu, Y.-P.: A multiple-level visual secret-sharing scheme without image size expansion. Inf. Sci. 177(21), 4696–4710 (2007)
3. Cimato, S., Prisco, R.D., Santis, A.D.: Probabilistic visual cryptography schemes. Comput. J. 49(1), 97–107 (2006)
4. Cimato, S., Yang, C.: Visual cryptography and secret image sharing. Digital Imaging and Computer Vision Series. Taylor & Francis (2011)
5. Floyd, R.W., Steinberg, L.: An adaptive algorithm for spatial greyscale. Proceedings of the Society of Information Display 17, 75–77 (1976)
6. Hou, Y.-C., Tu, S.-F.: A visual cryptographic technicque for chromatic images using multi-pixel encoding method. Journal of Research and Practice in Information Technology 37(2) (2005)
7. Ito, R., Kuwakado, H., Tanaka, H.: Image size invariant visual cryptography. IEICE Transactions on Fundamentals of Electronics, Communications and Computer Sciences 82(10), 2172–2177 (1999)
8. Leung, B.W., Ng, F.Y., Wong, D.S.: On the security of a visual cryptography scheme for color images. Pattern Recognition 42(5), 929–940 (2009)
9. Lin, C.-C., Tsai, W.-H.: Visual cryptography for gray-level images by dithering techniques. Pattern Recognition Letters 24(1-3), 349–358 (2003)
10. Liu, F., Guo, T., Wu, C.K., Qian, L.: Improving the visual quality of size invariant visual cryptography scheme. J. Visual Communication and Image Representation 23(2), 331–342 (2012)
11. Naor, M., Shamir, A.: Visual Cryptography. In: De Santis, A. (ed.) EUROCRYPT 1994. LNCS, vol. 950, pp. 1–12. Springer, Heidelberg (1995)
12. Shyu, S.J.: Image encryption by random grids. Pattern Recognition 40(3), 1014–1031 (2007)
13. Wu, X., Wong, D.S., Li, Q.: Threshold visual cryptography scheme for color images with no pixel expansion. In: Proceedings of the Second Symposium International Computer Science and Computation Technology, pp. 310–315 (2009)
14. Yang, C.-N.: New visual secret sharing schemes using probabilistic method. Pattern Recognition Letters 25(4), 481–494 (2004)
15. Yang, C.-N., Chen, T.-S.: Visual Secret Sharing Scheme: Improving the Contrast of a Recovered Image Via Different Pixel Expansions. In: Campilho, A.C., Kamel, M.S. (eds.) ICIAR 2006. LNCS, vol. 4141, pp. 468–479. Springer, Heidelberg (2006)

# Impact of the Revocation Service in PKI Prices

Carlos Gañán, Jose L. Muñoz, Oscar Esparza,
Jorge Mata-Díaz, and Juanjo Alins

Universitat Politècnica de Catalunya, Departament Enginyeria Telemàtica*
{carlos.ganan,jose.munoz,oesparza,jmata,juanjo}@entel.upc.es

**Abstract.** The ability to communicate securely is needed for many network applications. Public key infrastructure (PKI) is the most extended solution to verify and confirm the identity of each party involved in any secure transaction and transfer trust over the network. One of the hardest tasks of a certification infrastructure is to manage revocation. Research on this topic has focused on the trade-offs that different revocation mechanisms offer. However, less effort has been paid to understand the benefits of improving the revocation policies. In this paper, we analyze the behavior of the oligopoly of certificate providers that issue digital certificates to clients facing identical independent risks. We found the prices in the equilibrium, and we proof that certificate providers that offer better revocation information are able to impose higher prices to their certificates without sacrificing market share in favor of the other oligarchs. In addition, we show that our model is able to explain the actual tendency of the SSL market where providers with worst QoS are suffering loses.

**Keywords:** PKI pricing, SSL certificates, CRLs.

## 1 Introduction

Nowadays, there is a wide range of technology, products and solutions for securing electronic infrastructures. As with physical access security, the levels of security implemented should be commensurate with the level of complexity, the applications in use, the data in play, and the measurement of the overall risk at stake. A consensus has emerged among technical experts and information managers in government and industry that Public Key Infrastructure (PKI) offers the best feasible solution to these issues. PKI [1] has been a popular, yet often reviled technology since its adoption in the early nineties.

Currently deployed PKIs rely mostly on Certificate Revocation Lists (CRLs) for handling certificate revocation [2]. Although CRLs are the most widely used way of distributing certificate status information, much research effort has been put on studying other revocation distribution mechanisms in a variety of scenarios [3,4]. These studies aim to compare the performance of different revocation

---

* This work is funded by the Spanish Ministry of Science and Education under the projects CONSOLIDER-ARES (CSD2007-00004), FPU grant AP2010-0244, and TEC2011-26452 "SERVET", and by the Government of Catalonia under grant 2009 SGR 1362.

T.W. Chim and T.H. Yuen (Eds.): ICICS 2012, LNCS 7618, pp. 22–32, 2012.
© Springer-Verlag Berlin Heidelberg 2012

mechanisms in different scenarios. However, none of these studies have explicitly modeled the interaction among CAs. In this paper, we model this interaction by using a game-theoretic approach.

With the appearance of novel network environments (e.g VANET or MANET), the quantity of CAs in the SSL certificate market is becoming larger and the market concentration diminishes, but it is not simple to eliminate the oligopoly in the short-term. During the 90s, the certification market, the competition among CAs appears mainly as price competition. In this situation, malignant price competition would be detrimental to the interests of the users and lead to the CA's pay crisis. Facing the situation, the main CAs have begun to change the competitive strategies from basic price competition to price and quality of services (QoS) competition. To provide better QoS, CAs have to improve their revocation service, and specifically the freshness of the CRLs. Users will pay more for a service that issues certificate status information faster. Time-to-revocation metric is visible to costumers by checking the CA's repositories where they publicize the revocation information.

The model of this article deals with an oligopoly of CAs which compete in certificate prices and QoS, and do not know the certificate revocation probability in the next interval for sure. The assumption that the revocation probability is *ex-ante* uncertain is quite logical and intuitive. The number of revoked certificates vary with time and in a manner that cannot predictable with certainty. We show that an uncertain revocation probability introduces a systematic risk that does not decrease by selling more certificates. If CAs are risk averse, this effect relaxes price competition. The equilibrium characteristic of the certification market is found by establishing a price competition model with different QoS. We consider that there are diversities in the certification service quality, and we describe factors that affect the service quality such as the CRL lifetime. By combining the characteristics of the certification market and considering the conveniences of modeling, two key parameters are selected to measure the QoS and a duopoly price competition model with service quality differentiation is established.

## 2 Related Work

Although PKI has been a widely adopted solution for many years now, very few works have dealt with the impact of the revocation mechanism in the prices CAs offer. Most of the literature [4,5], intend to optimize the revocation mechanism to minimize the overhead or to improve the reliability. However, the most extended revocation mechanism is still CRL. Authors in [6] analyze the revocation mechanisms based on based on empirical data from a local network. They conclude that the freshness of the revocation data depends on how often the end entities retrieve the revocation information but the bandwidth cost is high if end entities retrieve the revocation lists often.

Ma *et al.* in [7] propose a series of policies that certification authorities should follow when releasing revocation information. According to this study, a CA should take different strategies when providing certificate services for a new type of certificates versus a re-serving type of certificates. Authors give the steps by which a

CA can derive optimal CRL releasing strategies and they prove that a CA should release CRLs less frequently in the case that the fixed cost is higher, the variable cost is higher, the liability cost is lower, or the issued age of certificates is shorter. Similarly authors in [8] authors address the CRL release problem through a systematic and rigorous approach which relies on a mix of empirical estimation and analytical modeling. They propose four different models which seek to exploit the variation in certificate specific properties to provide guidance to the CA in determining the optimal CRL release intervals and the associated costs. However, none of these works neither analyze the impact of CRLs releasing policies in the prices that the CA charges nor model the interaction among CAs. In this paper, we address these issues using a game theoretic approach.

## 3   Modeling the Certificate Provider Competition

To formalize our arguments we describe a model of the certificate market with profit-maximizing certification authorities and a continuum of network users. When a user requests the status of given certificate, the CA does not always provides the most updated information but a pre-signed CRL [4,5]. In this context, the CA will bear the liability cost due to any damage that may occur between the revocation of a certificate and the release of the CRL.

### 3.1   Demand for Certificates

We consider an oligopoly of $A$ CAs, indexed by $i = 1, \cdots, A - 1$, and $N$ users in the economy, where $N$ is large relative to $A$. Each user has the same strictly concave expected utility function and faces the risk to lose $l$ when using a revoked certificates. The probability $\pi$ of operating with a revoked certificate is equal for each user in the network, and conditional on $\pi$ operating with revoked certificates of different users are statistically independent. This probability is out of the user's control so that no moral hazard problem arises. Except for their probabilities of operating with revoked certificates, individuals are assumed to be identical. However, $\pi$ is not known ex-ante with certainty but is a random variable distributed on $[\underline{\pi}; \overline{\pi}]$ with cumulative density function $F(\pi)$. Each user has an initial wealth $w > 0$. When operating with a revoked certificate, users may suffer a loss. We assume that the user's wealth exceeds the potential loss, that is, $l \leq w$.

Users can purchase different certificate types from the CA with different revocation updating service. We characterize this product by the price of the certificate $P_i > 0$ and an indemnity $C_i > 0$ the CA pays to the user if it suffers from an attack and operates with another user whose certificate was revoked. Note that as CRLs are not issued each time a certificate is revoked but periodically, users will be operating with outdated information. Let $(P_i, C_i, t_i, s_i)$ be a certificate contract offered by $CA_i$ which specifies the price $P_i$ to be paid by an user and the level of coverage $C_i$ paid to the user if an attack takes place and she operates with a revoked certificate. Let $t_i$ represent the CRL updating interval, and $s_i$ represent the security level.

Let us assume that the total utility $U$ which users can get after they purchase a certificate consists of two parts. The first part is wealth utility which represented by $U_w$ the other part is QoS utility which the applicant can get after they obtained the CA's services, represented by $U_{QoS}$. The total utility $U$ is defined as:

$$U(P_i, C_i, t_i, s_i) = \alpha_1 U_w + \alpha_2 U_{QoS}, \forall \alpha_k \in [0,1] \text{ and } \sum \alpha_k = 1; \ k = 1,2. \quad (1)$$

where $\alpha_i$ represents the significance level of $U$ respectively.

On the one hand, we calculate the wealth utility. If no attack due to misuse of a revoked certificate happens after the user has purchase the service the CA, a user gains $w - P_i$, on the contrary a user gains $w - P_i + C_i$. We assume that all users have same loss with two-point distribution:

$$\mu = (w - P_i)(1 - \pi) + (w - P_i + C_i)\pi = w - P_i + \pi C_i, \quad (2)$$

$$\sigma^2 = \pi(1 - \pi)C_i^2. \quad (3)$$

Hence we can characterize the wealth utility by the mean and variance of Eq. (2) and Eq. (3) respectively. Thus, we can define $U_w$ as a mean-variance utility function:

$$U_w(P_i, C_i) = \mu - R\sigma^2, \quad (4)$$

where $R$ represents the Arrow-Pratt index of absolute risk aversion. This means that the larger $R$ is, the more risk averse the user is and the smaller $U_w$ is.

On the other hand, let $U_{QoS}$ be a linear function of the QoS that the CA offers. Thus, we define $U_{QoS}$ as:

$$U_{QoS}(t_i, s_i) = \pi\theta\left(\beta_1 s_i + \beta_2\frac{1}{t_i}\right), \forall \beta_k \in [0,1], \sum \beta_k = 1 \text{ and } \theta > 0; \ k = 1,2. \quad (5)$$

where $\theta$ represents the quality preference parameter of the user, and $\beta_1$ represents the user's preference to security level and $\beta_2$ represents the user's preference to CRL issuing interval. Note that the higher the level of security the CA provides, the larger $U_{QoS}$ is; the longer the CRL updating interval is, the smaller $U_{QoS}$ is. It is also worth noting that $\theta$ is unknown to the CAs a priori.

In order to calculate the total utility of the user, we must unify the dimension of the security level and the CRL updating interval. Thus, using (1),(4) and (5) the total utility is calculated as:

$$U(P_i, C_i, t_i, s_i) = \alpha_1[w - P_i - \pi C_i - R\pi(1 - \pi)C_i^2] + \alpha_2\left[\pi\theta\left(\beta_1 s_i + \beta_2\frac{1}{t_i}\right)\right]. \quad (6)$$

Note that according to this expression, users are willing to pay higher prices for those certificates whose issuer provides a better QoS. Note that issuing certificate status information faster, highly increases the QoS of the revocation service. Thus, certificates linked to a better revocation service provide more utility to the user.

## 3.2  Supply of Certificates

We consider an oligopoly of CAs operating in the certification market. CAs compete for users by offering certificates and CRLs. The service qualities of their CA products are also different. The level of service quality is mainly shown by the CRL updating interval and the security level[1].

When choosing a CA, a user takes into account several factors. Our goal is to gauge the impact of the revocation service on the certificate prices. However, it should be noted that, for convenience, many website owners choose the registrar's authority regardless of the price. Before issuing a certificate, the CA verifies that the person making the request is authorized to use the domain. The CA sends an email message to the domain administrator (the administrative or registrant contact, as listed in the Whois database) to validate domain control. If there is no contact information in the Whois database or the information is no longer valid, the customer may instead request a Domain Authorization Letter from his/her registrar and submit the letter to the CA as proof of his/her domain control. If the administrative/registrant contact fails to approve the certificate request, the request is denied. This authentication process ensures that only an individual who has control of the domain in the request can obtain a certificate for that domain. Therefore as CAs compete by quoting a certificate price which has associated a particular quality of service, we have Bertrand competition. The CA that quotes the lowest certificate price with the highest QoS sells to all users.

## 4  Equilibrium Certificate Providers

In this section we consider the certification industry with an oligopoly of $A$ certification authorities and analyze the competitive forces that determine equilibrium of certificate selling. Our main goal is to find the prices at which CAs obtain their maximum profit, i.e., when they reach the game equilibrium. Recall that these certificates differ in the QoS so that $\forall i, j; i \neq j, t_i \neq t_j$ and $s_i \neq s_j$ . We assume that the certification market is covered in full. Users will intend to maximize their utility, i.e.:

$$\theta^* = \arg\max_{\theta}\ U(P_i, C_i). \tag{7}$$

On the other hand, CAs will intend to minimize their costs. The CA's costs consists of fixed and variable costs. Each time a new CRL is issued, a CA incurs both fixed and variable costs. The fixed cost depends on two factors. The fix component is due to the release of a new CRL, and does not depend on the number or certificate type. The variable factor depends on the number of certificates contained in the CRL (i.e. depends on the size of the CRL) and on the type of certificate (i.e. certificate with higher security level induce higher costs). Note that in this variable cost it is included the cost of processing each certificate

---

[1] Note that additional QoS parameters could be introduced in the model. In fact, CAs distinguish themselves by offering additional value-added services (e.g. GoDaddy bundling domain registration with certificate issuance), turn-around time, etc.

revocation request. We define the service quality cost of $CA_i$ (i.e. $Q(s_i, t_i)$) as a variable that includes both fixed and variable costs associated to the QoS. The first and second derivative of $Q(s_i, t_i)$ with respect to $s_i, t_i$ are positive. Hence, we can calculate the gain function $G_i$ of any $CA_i$:

$$G_i = \theta^* P_i - Q(s_i, t_i), \tag{8}$$

where the gain function captures the overall profits of $CA_i$ for a given certificate product characterized by $(P_i, C_i)$.

We assume that the game between the two CAs is static with incomplete information, they choose the respective certificate price at the same time to maximize their profits. Now we differentiate (8) with respect to $P_i$ and $C_i$. In order to obtain the certificate price and the coverage in the equilibrium, let each derivative formula equal to zero. Solving the resulting linear system, we will obtain the price of each CA $P_i^*$ and the corresponding coverage $C_i^*$.

$$P_i^* : \frac{\partial G_i}{\partial P_i} = 0, \quad C_i^* : \frac{\partial G_i}{\partial C_i} = 0. \tag{9}$$

## 4.1   Duopoly of CAs

To better illustrate the results obtained in the previous section, we particularize the case of the oligopoly to a duopoly where only two CAs are offering certificates. This simplification, we allows us to draw some conclusion that can be easily extrapolated to the real scenario where there are more than a dozen CAs. To show that the level of service quality depends on the CA, we assume that the CA indexed by $i = 1$ offers better quality than the second CA in both QoS parameters, i.e., $t_1 < t_2$ and $s_1 > s_2$.

Following the methodology aforementioned, we have to find the prices in the equilibrium. In this situation, first we find the value of $\theta^*$ at which a user has no obvious trend between the certificates offered by different CAs.

$$\alpha_1[w - P_1 - \pi C_1 - R\pi(1 - \pi)C_1^2] + \alpha_2 \left[ \pi\theta \left( \beta_1 s_1 + \beta_2 \frac{1}{t_1} \right) \right] =$$
$$\alpha_1[w - P_2 - \pi C_2 - R\pi(1 - \pi)C_2^2] + \alpha_2 \left[ \pi\theta \left( \beta_1 s_2 + \beta_2 \frac{1}{t_2} \right) \right], \tag{10}$$

which results in:

$$\theta^* = \frac{\alpha_1 \left( P_1 - P_2 + \pi C_1(1 + RC_1 - R\pi C_1) - \pi C_2(1 - RC_2 + R\pi C_2) \right)}{\pi \alpha_2 K} \tag{11}$$

where $K = \beta_1(s_1 - s_2) + \beta_2 \left( \frac{1}{t_1} - \frac{1}{t_2} \right)$. So the market demand of $CA_2$ is $\theta^*$, and the demand of $CA_1$ is $1 - \theta^*$.

Using (8) we calculate the gain function $G_i$ of $CA_1$ and $CA_2$ :

$$G_1 = (1 - \theta^* P_1) - Q(s_1, t_1), \tag{12}$$

$$G_2 = \theta^* P_2 - Q(s_2, t_2). \tag{13}$$

We obtain the certificate price and the coverage in the equilibrium :

$$P_1^* = \frac{2\pi\,\alpha_2 K}{3\alpha_1} \qquad P_2^* = \frac{\pi\,\alpha_2 K}{3\alpha_1}, \qquad C_1^* = C_2^* = \frac{1}{2R(-1+\pi)}. \tag{14}$$

From these results we can conclude that:

- In the equilibrium, when both CAs achieve their maximum gain, $CA_1$ obtains a higher price than $CA_2$. This is mainly due to the fact that when both CAs have associated the same probability of an attack, as the QoS of the first CA is better so that $CA_1$ can set a higher price per certificate.
- In the equilibrium, the coverage that each CA should establish is the same and is inversely proportional to the risk-aversion and the probability of operating with a revoked certificate.

## 5    Analysis and Results

### 5.1    Impact of the Preference Ratio $\frac{\alpha_2}{\alpha_1}$

As the ratio between the preference of QoS utility and wealth utility of the user increases (i.e., users are more interested in a high security service and a good revocation mechanism) the prices of both CAs in the equilibrium also increase. This effect is reasonable, as the improvement of the revocation mechanism gives a higher security level which also increases the costs. This cost increment is compensated with a higher price in the equilibrium. Analyzing two CAs operating in the oligopoly such that $t_i < t_j$ and $s_i > s_j$, it is worth noting that the increment speed of $CA_i$'s QoS is faster than that of $CA_j$, so the increment speed of its certificate price is also faster than the other CA.

### 5.2    Impact of the Security Level Difference

When the level of security that a CA offers is much higher than in the others, the certificate value is also much higher. Thus, CAs that offer certificates with higher level of encryption and larger keys are able to make their certification product differentiable. For instance, SSL security levels vary depending upon the way on SSL certificate is installed on a server and the configuration used. SSL is simple to use but its security can be compromised if basic installation an configurations are not completed to a competent level, hackers are then able to decrypt the security on a badly installed SSL certificate. Once the certificates of a CA are differentiable from the other CAs, CAs do not have to use malignant prices anymore to compete. As the difference of this QoS between CAs becomes bigger, the prices that they can charge also increase. Note that if the preference extent which the user shows to the security level (i.e. $\beta_1$) increases, the differences in the certificates as products will be more apparent, thus the increase in the CA's certificate prices will also increase. The same results are expected with the increment of the interest of the users to a better service from the CAs ($\alpha_2$), that is, not higher security but also a more efficient revocation mechanism.

## 5.3    Impact of the QoS of the Revocation Mechanism

CAs that are able to offer revocation mechanisms with fresher information and high availability are able to make their certification product differentiable. Recall that this QoS increase of the revocation mechanism induces higher costs, as revocation information has to be issued more frequently. These costs are compensated with an increase of the price that CAs can charge for the certificates in the equilibrium. The reasons are the same that in the previous case, but now users pay more attention to the revocation mechanism rather than to the level of security. Analytically, that means that $\beta_2$ increases, so that the user is more interested in the efficiency of the revocation mechanism. This increase induces a proportional increase in the equilibrium prices of the CAs. Note that in this case, the increase of $CA_i$ which has higher QoS of the revocation mechanism is faster than that of $CA_j$. Again, the CA that has better service (no matter if it is higher security level or a more efficient revocation mechanism) has the advantage in competition.

## 5.4    Impact of the Revocation Probability

Logically, with an increase of the probability of operating with a revoked certificate, CAs charge more for their certificates. The reason is obvious as the CAs set they price mainly based on a forecast of this probability. An increase of $\pi$ will induce an increase of the compensation expenses that a CA will have to pay to any victim of an attack due to the misuse of a revoked certificate. Consequently, this increase will lead to a proportional increase of compensation cost and service cost so that the CAs have to increase their prices to compensate the cost increases. Note that this increase is twice faster in the case of the $CA_i$.

# 6    Case Study: SSL Providers

Finally, to corroborate the benefits of the presented model, we analyze the case of current SSL providers that issue digital certificates. An SSL certificate can be obtained from amounts as low as $43 to as high as $3000 per year. Whilst the type of encryption can be the same, the cost is determined by the rigour of the certification process as well as the assurance and warranty that the vendor can provide. Table 1 shows the prices and QoS that the leading CAs operating in the SSL Certificate market are offering. The SSL Certificate market was traditionally dominated by a small number of players, namely VeriSign and Thawte. Whilst in a monopolistic position they had the capability of charging inflated prices for a commodity product. However new providers with no necessity to hold prices high were able to offer SSL certificates at far more reasonable prices.

The SSL certificate vendors provide insurance against the misuse of certificates and this differs from one vendor to another. Verisign provides warranties of up to $250,000 while Entrust and GoDaddy offer a $10,000 warranty. The higher the insurance, the more inscription/authentication is provided by the SSL vendors.

Analyzing Table 1, it is worth noting that not always a lower price means lower quality. Therefore, it is evident that current CAs operating in this market are competing both in price and quality of service.

To test whether these factors are determinant factors for the certficate prices, we perform a multivariate regression analysis explaining the yearly price of SSL certificates. General regression investigates and models the relationship between a response (Certificate price) and predictors (Warranty, issuing interval and CRL lifetime). Note that the response of this model is continuous, but you we have both continuous and categorical predictors. You can model both linear and poly-nomial relationships using general regression. With this model we determine how the certficate price changes as a particular predictor variable changes. We use data from a survey of CAs performed in 2010 [9]. The obtained regression model is expressed in the following equations for high and low assurance certificates, respectively:

$$Price/Year(\$) = 98,4353 + 0,000220857\ W - 0,549141\ \overline{I_{time}} + 8,6116\ \frac{1}{\overline{CRL_{Lf}}},$$

$$Price/Year(\$) = 20,0405 + 0,000220857\ W - 0,5491411\ \overline{I_{time}} + 8,6116\ \frac{1}{\overline{CRL_{Lf}}},$$

where $W$ denotes the warranty, $\overline{I_{time}}$ is the mean issuing time, and $\overline{CRL_{Lf}}$ is the mean lifetime of the CRLs issued by the CA.

Note that both regression equations show that the coefficient of the predictor associated to the CRL's mean lifetime is significant. In fact, the p-value associated to this predictor is $0,008$ which indicates that is statistically significantly. Overall, the variables within the model are explaining a large portion of the variation in the certificate price. With a coefficient of determination $R^2$ above the 81%, we are capturing important drivers of certificate prices. The residuals from the analysis are normally distributed, i.e., no evidence of nonnormality, skewness, or unidentified variables exists.

**Table 1.** SSL Certificate Types and Services offered by main CAs [9]

| SSL Provider | Product Name | Price/Year($) | Warranty($) | Assurance | Mean Issuing time | Mean CRL lifetime |
|---|---|---|---|---|---|---|
| COMODO | EnterpriseSSL Plat-inum | 311.80 | 1,000,000 | High | Under 1 hour | 4 days |
| COMODO | InstantSSL Pro | 169.80 | 100,000 | High | Under 1 hour | 4 days |
| Verisign | Secure Site Pro Cert | 826.67 | 2,500,000 | High | 2-3 days | 15 days |
| Verisign | Managed PKI for SSL Std | 234.00 | 100,000 | High | 2-3 days | 15 days |
| GeoTrust | QuickSSL Premium | 118.00 | 100,000 | Low | Immediate | 10 days |
| GeoTrust | True BusinessID | 159.20 | 100,000 | High | 2 days | 10 days |
| Go Daddy | Standard SSL | 42.99 | 10,000 | Low | Immediate | 1 day |
| Go Daddy | Standard Wildcard | 179.99 | 10,000 | Low | Immediate | 1 day |
| Entrust | Advantage SSL Cer-tificates | 167.00 | 10,000 | High | 2 days | 1 week |
| Entrust | Standard SSL Cer-tificates | 132.00 | 10,000 | High | 2 days | 1 week |
| Thawte | SSL 123 | 129.80 | - | Low | Immediate | 1 month |
| Thawte | SGC Super cert | 599.80 | - | High | 2 days | 1 month |

Using the proposed model, we are able to explain these different prices and the corresponding market share and they potential evolution. First we analyze the number of revoked certificates as it will determine the probability of operating with a revoked certificate. Figure 1 shows the evolution of the daily number of revoked certificates per CA. These data were collected from different SSL CRLs that the CAs make public at their repositories. It is worth noting, that the number of revoked certificates highly varies depending on the CA. Thus, GoDaddy revokes more than 500 certificates per day on average while VerSign revokes less than 4 certificates per day on average. Therefore, the probability $\pi$ of operating with revoked certificates is higher when trusting certificates issued by GoDaddy. As our model shows, using expression (14), the probability $\pi$ directly affects the price of the certificate. Thus, as GoDaddy has a higher $\pi$, we would expect to charge less for its certificates. However, the price is quite similar to its competitors. Thus, GoDaddy is not able to sell as much certificates as the other oligarchs, and its market share is smaller.

Our model would expect GoDaddy to compete not only in prices but also in QoS to gain market share. As our model shows, the reaction of GoDaddy to compete in the oligopoly is to offer better quality of service. From table 1, we can see that GoDaddy is the CA that issues CRLs more often. Using this CRL releasing policy, users increase their utility and, at the same time, the probability of operating with a revoked certificate is also reduced. However, the variable costs increase due to this way of issuing CRLs. Similarly, Comodo intends to gain market share by decreasing the time it takes to issue a certificate and also reducing the CRL lifetime. Note that VeriSign, the leading CA, is the one who is offering the worst QoS, both in terms of CRL lifetime and time to issue a new certificate.

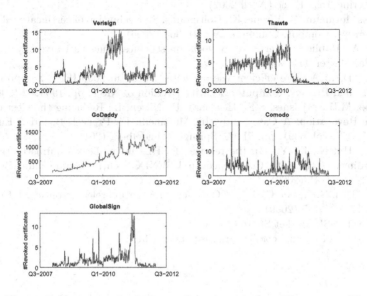

**Fig. 1.** Evolution of the daily number of revoked certificates per CA

# 7　Conclusions

The market of certificate providers can be described as an oligopoly where oligarchs compete not only in price but also in quality of service. In this paper we have modeled this oligopoly using a game theoretic approach to find the prices in the equilibrium. We have been able to capture the QoS of the products offered by a CA, by means of the timeliness of the revocation mechanism and the security level. In our model of the certification industry with profit-maximizing CAs and a continuum of individuals we showed that although the undercutting process in certification prices seems similar to the price setting behavior of firms in Bertrand competition there exists a crucial difference depending onf the QoS of the revocation service. The solution of the game for two CAs in the oligopoly that offer certificates with different QoS shows that the revenues of the CA which provides a better revocation mechanism and a higher security level are larger. Therefore, a CA when setting the prices of its certificate and the compensation expenses, it has to take into account not only the probability of operating with a revoked certificate, but also the quality of the revocation mechanism and the security level. Thus, any CA should comprehensively consider the difference in quality of its services compared with other CAs.

# References

1. Adams, C., Farrell, S.: Internet X.509 Public Key Infrastructure Certificate Management Protocols. RFC 2510, Internet Engineering Task Force (March 1999)
2. Housley, R., Polk, W., Ford, W., Solo, D.: Internet X.509 Public Key Infrastructure Certificate and Certificate Revocation List (CRL) Profile. RFC 3280, Internet Engineering Task Force (April 2002)
3. Perlines Hormann, T., Wrona, K., Holtmanns, S.: Evaluation of certificate validation mechanisms. Comput. Commun. 29, 291–305 (2006)
4. Arnes, A.: Public key certificate revocation schemes. Queen's University. Ontario, Canada. Master Thesis (2000)
5. Cooper, D.A.: A more efficient use of Delta-CRLs. In: 2000 IEEE Symposium on Security and Privacy. Computer Security Division of NIST, pp. 190–202 (2000)
6. Ofigsbø, M.H., Mjølsnes, S.F., Heegaard, P., Nilsen, L.: Reducing the Cost of Certificate Revocation: A Case Study. In: Martinelli, F., Preneel, B. (eds.) EuroPKI 2009. LNCS, vol. 6391, pp. 51–66. Springer, Heidelberg (2010)
7. Ma, C., Hu, N., Li, Y.: On the release of CRLs in public key infrastructure. In: Proceedings of the 15th Conference on USENIX Security Symposium, Berkeley, CA, USA, vol. 15 (2006)
8. Hu, N., Tayi, G.K., Ma, C., Li, Y.: Certificate revocation release policies. J. Comput. Secur. 17, 127–157 (2009)
9. WhichSSL. SSL Market Share (2010),
http://www.whichssl.com/ssl-market-share.html

# Cryptanalysis of Multi-Prime RSA with Small Prime Difference

Hatem M. Bahig, Ashraf Bhery, and Dieaa I. Nassr

Computer Science Division, Department of Mathematics,
Faculty of Science, Ain Shams University,
Cairo 11566, Egypt

**Abstract.** We show that the attack of de Weger on RSA using continued fractions extends to Multi-Prime RSA. Let $(n, e)$ be a Multi-Prime RSA public-key with private key $d$, where $n = p_1 p_2 \cdots p_r$ is a product of $r$ distinct balanced (roughly of the same bit size) primes, and $p_1 < p_2 < \ldots < p_r$. We show that if $p_r - p_1 = n^\alpha, 0 < \alpha \le 1/r, r \ge 3$ and $2d^2 + 1 < \frac{n^{2/r - \alpha}}{6r}$, then Multi-Prime RSA is insecure.

**Keywords:** continued fractions, RSA, Multi-Prime RSA, Wiener's attack, de Weger's attack.

## 1 Introduction

The RSA cryptosystem, invented by Rivest, Shamir and Adleman [18] in 1977, is one of the most important public key cryptosystems. For example, it is used by Web servers and browsers to secure Web traffic. In RSA, an integer $n = pq$ (the RSA modulus) is a product of two large distinct primes of the same bit size. The public exponent $e < \phi(n)$ and the private exponent $d < \phi(n)$ satisfy the equation $ed \equiv 1 \mod \phi(n)$, where $\phi(n) = (p-1)(q-1)$ is Euler's totient function. The public key is the pair $(n, e)$ and the private key is $d$.

Multi-prime RSA (MPRSA) is a simple extension of RSA in which the modulus has three or more distinct primes. It was patented by Compaq in 1997 [7,1]. In MPRSA with $r$ primes, the modulus is $n = p_1 \cdots p_r$, where $p_1 < p_2 < \ldots < p_r$. As with RSA, we only consider $\frac{1}{2} n^{1/r} < p_i < 2n^{1/r}$ for $1 \le i \le r$. In this case $n$ is said to be a product of distinct $r$-balanced primes. Clearly, we have

$$\frac{1}{2} n^{1/r} < p_1 < n^{1/r} < p_r < 2n^{1/r}.$$

The key generation of MPRSA is similar to RSA. It is as follows.

- Let $n$ be the product of $r$ randomly chosen distinct balanced primes $p_1, \ldots, p_r$, where $p_1 < p_2 < \ldots < p_r$.
- Compute Euler's totient function of $n$ : $\Phi(n) = \prod_{i=1}^{r} (p_i - 1)$.
- Choose an integer $e, 1 < e < \Phi(n)$, such that $\gcd(e, \Phi(n)) = 1$.
- Compute the multiplicative inverse $d = e^{-1} \mod \Phi(n)$.

T.W. Chim and T.H. Yuen (Eds.): ICICS 2012, LNCS 7618, pp. 33–44, 2012.

$n$ is called the MPRSA modulus. The public-key is $(n, e)$ and the private key is $d$.

In general, the running time of generating $(n/r)$-bits primes for MPRSA will decrease with increasing number of primes [11].

The encryption of MPRSA is identical to that of RSA. For any message $m \in Z_n$, the ciphertext is

$$c = m^e \ mod \ n.$$

The standard decryption of MPRSA is the same as standard decryption of RSA. For any ciphertext $c \in Z_n$, the plaintext is

$$m = c^d \ mod \ n.$$

When Chinese Remainder Theorem (CRT) is used in decryption, the MPRSA takes time less than in RSA. A speed-up of a factor at least $r/2$ (and at most $r^2/4$) is estimated [11]. A speed-up of 1.73 has been achieved in practice for 3-prime RSA compared to RSA using CRT with a 1024-bit modulus [5,11].

In other words, there are two practical reasons to use more than two primes.

1. The primes are smaller and key generation takes less time despite there being more of them.
2. Decryption takes less time if one uses CRT.

Many attacks on RSA are extended to MPRSA. For examples, small private exponent attacks on RSA by Wiener [24] (when the private key $d < n^{1/4}$) is extended to MPRSA by Ciet *et al.* [6] and Hinek *et al.* [12]. Boneh and Durfee attack [4] on RSA using lattice reduction technique [13] and Coppersmiths method [8] for $d < n^{0.292}$ is also extended to MPRSA by Hinek *et al.* [12]. The generalization of Blömer and May's lattice based attack for arbitrary public exponents RSA [2,16] is extended to MPRSA by Ciet *et al.* [6]. Some of the partial key exposure attacks on RSA are extended to MPRSA, see [11, Ch.9] for some details.

De Weger [23] showed that if $n = pq$ has a small difference between its prime factors $p - q = n^\beta, \frac{1}{4} \le \beta \le \frac{1}{2}$, then the private key $d = n^\delta$ of RSA can be recovered when $\delta < \frac{3}{4} - \beta$. In this paper, we show a similar result on MPRSA. Using Wiener's interval proposed by [17], we show that $d$ can be recovered when $2d^2 + 1 < \frac{n^{2/r-\alpha}}{6r} < \phi(n)$, for $r \ge 3$; and when $2d^2 + 1 < 2n^{3/2-2\alpha} + 1$, for $r = 2$ and $\phi(n) > \frac{3}{4}n$.

The paper is organized as follows. In section 2, we review some basic facts about continued fractions, and Wiener's interval. In Section 3, we cryptanalysis MPRSA with small prime difference. In Section 4, we compare between our attacks and other small private exponent attacks. An example of the cryptanalysis is given in Section 5. Finally, Section 6 includes the conclusion.

## 2   Preliminaries

In this section, we briefly recall some basic definitions and facts that will be used in the paper.

A (*finite*) continued fraction expansion (**CF** ) [19] is an $m$-tuple of integers

$$[q_1, q_2, ..., q_m]$$

with $q_2, ..., q_m > 0$, which is an abbreviation of the following rational number:

$$q_1 + \cfrac{1}{q_2 + \cfrac{1}{q_3 + ... + \frac{1}{q_m}}}.$$

Let $a, b$ be two positive integers satisfying $\gcd(a, b) = 1$ and $a < b$. The rational number $c = \frac{a}{b}$ has a unique **CF** $[q_1, q_2, ..., q_m]$ with $q_m > 1$, which can be computed in time $O(log^2 b)$ using the following algorithm [21]:

- $c_0 = c$.
- compute $c_i = \frac{1}{c_{i-1} - \lfloor c_{i-1} \rfloor}$ for $i = 1, \cdots, m$, where $m \leq 2 \log b$ is the smallest value of $i$ such that $\lfloor c_i \rfloor = c_i$.
- return $[q_1, q_2, \ldots, q_m]$, where $q_i = \lfloor c_i \rfloor$ for $i = 1, \cdots, m$.

If $c$ is an irrational number, then the computation can be continued for $m \to \infty$. In this case, we have *infinite* **CF** :

$$q_1 + \cfrac{1}{q_2 + \cfrac{1}{q_3 + ... + \frac{1}{...}}}.$$

It will be shortened to $[q_1, q_2, \ldots]$.

**Theorem 1.** (Legendre) [19] *Let $\alpha$ be a real number. If $c$ and $d$ are positive integers such that $\gcd(c, d) = 1$ and*

$$\left| \alpha - \frac{c}{d} \right| < \frac{1}{2d^2},$$

*then $\frac{c}{d}$ is a convergent of the **CF** expansion of $\alpha$.*

**Definition 1.** *[17] Let $m$ be a real number and $(n, e)$ be an RSA public key with private key $d$, where $ed - 1 = t\phi(n)$. We define a Wiener's attack on $(n, e, m)$, denoted by **WA**$(n, e, m)$, as follows:*

$$\mathbf{WA}(n, e, m) = \begin{cases} \frac{t}{d}, & \text{if } \frac{t}{d} \text{ is one of the convergents of the \textbf{CF} expansion of } \frac{e}{m}; \\ \text{failure, otherwise.} \end{cases}$$

**WA**$(n, e, m)$ *is said to be succeeds if it returns $t/d$.*

**Definition 2.** *[17] Let $(n, e)$ be an RSA public key. An interval $I \subset \Re$ (set of real numbers) is said to be a Wiener's interval for $(n, e)$ if for every $m \in I$, **WA**$(n, e, m)$ succeeds.*

The following theorem determines a Wiener's interval for an RSA public-key $(n, e)$.

**Theorem 2.** *[17] Let $(n, e)$ be an RSA public key with private exponent d. Then $I = ]\phi(n) - \frac{\phi(n)}{cd^2+1}, \phi(n) + \frac{\phi(n)}{2d^2-1}[$ is a Wiener's interval for $(n, e)$, where*

$$c = \begin{cases} 2, & \text{if } d < \sqrt{\frac{\phi(n)-1}{2}}; \\ \\ 4, & \text{if } \sqrt{\frac{\phi(n)-1}{2}} \le d < \frac{\phi(n)-1}{4}. \end{cases}$$

Theorem 2 is also true for MPRSA [17].

## 3   The Attack

In this section, we show that the result of de Weger [23] on RSA can be extended to MPRSA using Wiener's interval . By choosing $m = n - \Gamma$, where

$$\Gamma = \sum_i^r \frac{n}{n^{1/r}} - \sum_{\substack{i,j \\ i<j}}^r \frac{n}{n^{2/r}} + \sum_{\substack{i,j,k=1 \\ i<j<k}}^r \frac{n}{n^{3/r}} + \dots - (-1)^r,$$

we show that $m$ lies in Wiener's interval (Theorem 2).

Now, let

$$\Lambda = n - \phi(n) = \sum_i^r \frac{n}{p_i} - \sum_{\substack{i,j=1 \\ i<j}}^r \frac{n}{p_i p_j} + \sum_{\substack{i,j,k=1 \\ i<j<k}}^r \frac{n}{p_i p_j p_k} + \dots - (-1)^r;$$

Then we can rewrite $\Lambda$ and $\Gamma$ as follows.

$$\Lambda = \Lambda_1 - \Lambda_2 + \dots - (-1)^r \Lambda_r,$$

where

$$\Lambda_k = \sum_{\substack{i_1,\dots,i_k \\ i_1<..<i_k}}^r \frac{n}{p_{i_1} p_{i_2} \dots p_{i_k}}, \quad 1 \le k \le r.$$

And

$$\Gamma = \Gamma_1 - \Gamma_2 + \dots - (-1)^r \Gamma_r,$$

where

$$\Gamma_k = \sum_{\substack{i_1,\dots,i_k \\ i_1<..<i_k}}^{r} \frac{n}{n^{k/r}} = C_k^r n^{1-k/r},\ 1 \leq k \leq r$$

and

$$C_k^r = \frac{r!}{k!(r-k)!}(k \leq r).$$

**Lemma 1.** *Let* $n = p_1 p_2 ... p_r$ *be a product of distinct r-balanced primes and* $p_r - p_1 = n^\alpha, 0 < \alpha \leq 1/r$. *Then*

$$|\Lambda_k - \Gamma_k| < 2^k(2^k - 1)C_k^r n^{1+\alpha-\frac{k+1}{r}},$$

*where k is a positive integer such that* $k \leq r$.

*Proof*

$$|\Lambda_k - \Gamma_k| \leq \sum_{\substack{i_1,\dots,i_k \\ i_1<..<i_k}}^{r} \left| \frac{n}{p_{i_1}p_{i_2}\cdots p_{i_k}} - \frac{n}{n^{k/r}} \right|$$

$$= \sum_{\substack{i_1,\dots,i_k \\ i_1<..<i_k}}^{r} \frac{n\left| n^{k/r} - p_{i_1}p_{i_2}\cdots p_{i_k} \right|}{n^{k/r}p_{i_1}p_{i_2}\cdots p_{i_k}}$$

$$\leq \sum_{\substack{i_1,\dots,i_k \\ i_1<...<i_k}}^{r} \frac{n\left| p_r^k - p_1^k \right|}{\frac{1}{2^k}n^{2k/r}}$$

$$= \sum_{\substack{i_1,\dots,i_k \\ i_1<...<i_k}}^{r} \frac{2^k n(p_r-p_1)(p_r^{k-1}+p_r^{k-2}p_1+...+p_1^{k-1})}{n^{2k/r}}$$

$$< \sum_{\substack{i_1,\dots,i_k \\ i_1<...<i_k}}^{r} \frac{2^k n^{1+\alpha}(2^{k-1}n^{\frac{k-1}{r}}+2^{k-2}n^{\frac{k-1}{r}}+...+2^0 n^{\frac{k-1}{r}})}{n^{2k/r}}$$

$$= \sum_{\substack{i_1,\dots,i_k \\ i_1<...<i_k}}^{r} \frac{2^k n^{1+\alpha}n^{\frac{k-1}{r}}(2^{k-1}+2^{k-2}+\cdots+1)}{n^{2k/r}}$$

$$= 2^k(2^k - 1)C_k^r n^{1+\alpha-\frac{k+1}{r}}.$$

$\diamond$

**Proposition 1.** *Let* $n = p_1 p_2 \cdots p_r$ *be a product of distinct r-balanced primes and* $p_r - p_1 = n^\alpha, 0 < \alpha \leq 1/r$. *Then*

$$|\Lambda - \Gamma| < \begin{cases} \frac{1}{4}n^{2\alpha-1/2}, & \text{if } r = 2; \\ \\ 3rn^{1+\alpha-2/r}, & \text{if } r \geq 3, \text{ and } 2^k(2^k-1)C_k^r \leq \frac{n^{1/r}}{r-1}\ (2 \leq k \leq r). \end{cases}$$

*Proof*
If $r = 2$, then

$$|\Lambda - \Gamma| = |p_1 + p_2 - 1 - (2\sqrt{n} - 1)| = p_1 + p_2 - 2\sqrt{n} = \frac{(p_1 - p_2)^2}{p_1 + p_2 + 2\sqrt{n}}$$
$$< \frac{(p_1 - p_2)^2}{4\sqrt{n}} = \frac{1}{4}n^{2\alpha - 1/2}.$$

If $r \geq 3$ and $2^k(2^k - 1)C_k^r \leq \frac{n^{1/r}}{r-1}$,

$$|\Lambda - \Gamma| < |\Lambda_1 - \Gamma_1| + \sum_{k=2}^{r} |\Lambda_k - \Gamma_k|.$$

Using Lemma 1, for every $2 \leq k \leq r$, we have

$$|\Lambda_k - \Gamma_k| < 2^k(2^k - 1)C_k^r n^{1+\alpha-(k+1)/r}$$

$$\leq \frac{n^{1/r}}{r-1} n^{1+\alpha-(k+1)/r}$$

$$= \frac{n^{1+\alpha-k/r}}{r-1} \leq \frac{n^{1+\alpha-2/r}}{r-1}.$$

It follows that

$$|\Lambda - \Gamma| < 2rn^{1+\alpha-2/r} + \sum_{k=2}^{r} \frac{n^{1+\alpha-2/r}}{r-1}$$

$$= 2rn^{1+\alpha-2/r} + (r-1)\frac{n^{1+\alpha-2/r}}{r-1}$$

$$< 3rn^{1+\alpha-2/r}. \qquad \diamond$$

**Theorem 3.** *Let* $n = p_1p_2 \cdots p_r$ *be MPRSA modulus, where* $p_1, p_2, \cdots, p_r$ *are distinct* $r$-*balanced primes. If* $p_r - p_1 = n^\alpha, 0 < \alpha \leq 1/r$ *and*

$$2d^2 + 1 < \begin{cases} 2n^{3/2-2\alpha} + 1, & \text{if } r = 2 \text{ and } \phi(n) > \frac{3}{4}n; \\ \frac{n^{2/r-\alpha}}{6r}, & \text{if } r \geq 3, \text{ and } 2^k(2^k - 1)C_k^r \leq \frac{n^{1/r}}{r-1}, 2 \leq k \leq r \end{cases}$$

*then the system is insecure.*

*Proof:* Using Theorem 2, we need only to show that

$$|m - \phi(n)| < \frac{\phi(n)}{2d^2 + 1},$$

where $m = n - \Gamma$. We have

$$|m - \phi(n)| = |\Lambda - \Gamma|.$$

Thus, by Proposition 1, we have

$$|m - \phi(n)| < \begin{cases} \frac{1}{4}n^{2\alpha - 1/2}, & \text{if } r = 2; \\ \\ 3rn^{1+\alpha - 2/r}, & \text{if } r \geq 3, 2^k(2^k - 1)C_k^r \leq \frac{n^{1/r}}{r-1}, \ 2 \leq k \leq r. \end{cases}$$

We have two cases.

**Case 1:** $r = 2$. If $\phi(n) > \frac{3}{4}n$, then

$$|m - \phi(n)| < \frac{1}{4}n^{2\alpha - 1/2} = \frac{1}{4}n^{2\alpha - 3/2 + 1} = \frac{1}{4}\frac{n}{n^{3/2 - 2\alpha}}$$
$$< \frac{1}{4}\frac{n}{d^2} < \frac{\frac{4}{3}\phi(n)}{4d^2} < \frac{\phi(n)}{3d^2} < \frac{\phi(n)}{2d^2 + 1}.$$

**Case 2:** $r \geq 3$ and $2^k(2^k - 1)C_k^r \leq \frac{n^{1/r}}{r-1}$. We have

$$|m - \phi(n)| < 3rn^{1+\alpha - 2/r} = 3r\frac{n}{n^{2/r - \alpha}} < 3r\frac{2\phi(n)}{n^{2/r - \alpha}}$$

$$= \frac{\phi(n)}{\frac{n^{2/r - \alpha}}{6r}} < \frac{\phi(n)}{2d^2 + 1}. \qquad \diamond$$

*Remark 1.* 1. if $\alpha = \frac{1}{r}$, then the upper bound of $d$ is $\sqrt{\frac{n^{1/r} - 6r}{12r}}$ which is similar to the upper bound $\sqrt{\frac{n^{1/r}}{2(2r^2 - 1)}}$ in [12].

2. Since the maximum numbers of *safe* primes for MPRSA are 3, 3, 4, and 5 for 1024, 4038, 4096, and 8192 bits respectivelly [11], the condition $2^k(2^k - 1)C_k^r \leq \frac{n^{1/r}}{r-1}$ in Theorem 3 is always satisfied.

## 4   Comparison

In this section, we compare between our attack and the previous attacks.

1. For $r = 2$, and $0 < \alpha \leq \frac{1}{2}$, we have two cases:
   (a) If $0 < \alpha < \frac{1}{4}$, then Fermat's method [23] factorizes $n = p_1p_2$ in polynomial time if $p_2 - p_1 = n^\alpha$.
   (b) If $\frac{1}{4} \leq \alpha \leq \frac{1}{2}$, then de Weger's attack [23] finds $d = n^\delta$ when $p_2 - p_1 = n^\alpha$, where $\delta < \frac{3}{4} - \alpha$.
2. To the best of our knowledge, for $r \geq 3$, there is no generalization of Fermat's method for MPRSA. Our attack (Theorem 3) can be considered as an extensions of de Weger's attack since $\alpha \geq 0$ and for $r = 2$, de Weger's attack is a special case of Theorem 3.
   It is important to point that all known small private exponent attacks on MPRSA become less effective when increasing the number of primes in the modulus [11, Section 9.3].
3. When the public exponent $e$ is full sized, our attack is superior than other small private exponent attacks on MPRSA. Figure 1 shows a comparison

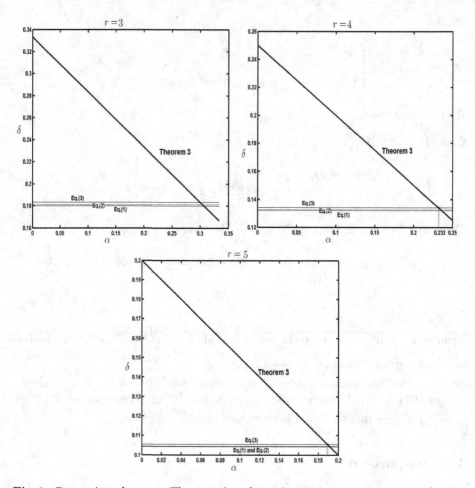

**Fig. 1.** Comparison between Theorem 3 and previous private exponent attacks on MPRSA

between our attack and attacks of Hinek *et al.* (Eqs.(1) and (2)) [11,12] and Ciet *et al.* (Eq.(3))[6,11] when $r = 3, 4$, and 5, where

$$\delta < \frac{1}{3r}(4r - 1 - 2\sqrt{(r-1)(4r-1)}) - \epsilon, \ \epsilon > 0 \tag{1}$$

$$\delta < \frac{1}{5r}(6 - 4r + 2\sqrt{4r^2 - 7r + 4}) - \epsilon, \ \epsilon > 0 \tag{2}$$

$$\delta < (r - \sqrt{r(r-1)})/r - \epsilon, \ \epsilon > 0 \tag{3}$$

# 5    Numerical Example

In this section we give an example for the presented attack. We used Shoup's package [20] NTL in the implementation.

Let $n = p_1 p_2 p_3 p_4$ be a product of four primes each of size 100 decimal digits such that $p_4 - p_1 \leq n^{0.19}$. Thus, $\alpha = 0.19$ and $\delta = 0.15$.

Suppose that $e$ of size 400 decimal digits.

$n = 25573763889872927537617615777695651985936974831528660360885069448895 7\backslash$
$13240873561141263153256675011291710696981355151597274521278492940446 57\backslash$
$08310744010276679704862894640223344687429432593752204272004537285252 67\backslash$
$61909319087570432256645683464670571033014357021713074121467159222772 87\backslash$
$20142528841621833611993102873657868395542500974683107511901381914226 5\backslash$
$046330193730129013231484126392267563403208765626567.$

$e = 12826145240584271570621841656548046666862027139453531607165614567116 62\backslash$
$14400477970874371504503861100686991120228942885371691652375440581552 30\backslash$
$69892604327625491593782689356669556162952379150674089128644648923560 07\backslash$
$21785147253950635172743190949148724984942092596724798858791922007239 26\backslash$
$35516490877868205804737002779941001636650813971269269387752182110198 08\backslash$
$3817715573291743326052915381042542189796320310450\,1.$

Now, we compute $m = n - \Gamma$.

$m = 25573763889872927537617615777695651985936974831528660360885069448895 57\backslash$
$13240873561141263153256675011147861984280940468198992057360325443793 21\backslash$
$45582639838523183762367859610857277295984254393206641278060230076748 83\backslash$
$48674569437522275918954110104822367211853537337312799778335814054922 08\backslash$
$92707297274099290970525439023098990024040746265715839794074250643833 16\backslash$
$948756268405057909316894888299002927706691737584 08.$

and **CF** $(e/m) =$

[0, 1, 1, 162, 2, 1, 63, 1, 4, 5, 2, 1, 1, 1, 1, 9, 2, 1, 1, 2, 1, 5, 1, 1, 278, 1, 10, 3, 2,
1, 3, 1, 1, 1, 1, 2, 1, 7, 3, 11, 7, 15, 1, 1, 1, 17, 4, 5, 2, 2, 2, 8, 1, 2, 3, 1, 6, 1, 1,
1, 1, 4, 2, 2, 1, 1, 2, 3, 1, 1, 14, 1, 2, 7, 1, 1, 3, 2, 2, 1, 1, 1, 2, 5, 143, 1, 2, 1, 1,
1, 10, 1, 7, 18, 1, 4, 3, 1, 1, 101, 1, 8, 2, 1, 32, 1, 6, 2, 8, 1, 2, 53, 11, 3, 3, 1, 1, 1,
1, 1, 2, 1, 1646332861278020346917835445367, 1, 6, 3, 1, 1, 4, 1, 2, 1, 11, 1, 4, 3,
1, 2, 1, 1, 1, 7, 2, 5, 5, 1, 1, 1, 1, 2, 1, 1, 2, 2, 1, 5, 1, 2, 1, 4, 1, 2, 1, 5, 10, 1, 7,
1, 4, 1, 4, 2, 1, 1, 1, 1, 3, 154, 5, 2, 11, 2, 23, 7, 1, 2, 1, 6, 5, 1, 9, 1, 6, 1, 8, 1, 3,
3, 1, 1, 8, 2, 1, 6, 1, 1, 2, 9, 2, 3, 1, 1, 3, 1, 1, 2, 1, 1, 7, 1, 6, 2, 1, 2, 1, 7, 2, 71,
2, 1, 5, 2, 1, 97, 4, 1, 1, 1, 1, 3, 1, 2, 6, 2, 1, 5, 1, 33, 15, 1, 1, 5, 1, 1, 19, 2, 1, 6,
5, 2, 8, 1, 1, 14, 1, 1, 1, 2, 1, 2, 12, 1, 2, 3, 3, 133, 3, 6, 12, 3, 14, 1, 3, 29, 3, 5, 3,
4, 1, 1, 1, 2, 4, 15, 2, 15, 1, 1, 3, 6, 1, 2, 2, 1, 5, 3, 1, 6, 18, 1, 1, 1, 2, 1, 1, 1, 1,
1, 1, 69, 399, 4, 1, 6, 1, 3, 3, 1, 1, 1, 6, 1, 7, 1, 3, 8, 1, 2, 50, 3, 1, 1, 11, 2, 62, 1,
5, 5, 1, 1, 1, 3, 1, 1, 1, 6, 1, 2, 3, 1, 2, 1, 1, 1, 12, 5, 1, 22, 2, 36, 1, 1, 1, 3, 4, 1,

4, 15, 1, 3, 1, 3, 2, 1, 1, 1, 3, 1, 5, 2, 2, 1, 1, 17, 1, 16, 1, 2, 1, 1, 6, 6, 27, 3, 1, 4,
2, 2, 10, 2, 1, 2, 3, 2, 1, 1, 4, 4, 11, 2, 3, 1, 10, 1, 1, 2, 1, 1, 2, 20, 13, 1, 2, 1, 3, 3,
1, 1, 1, 1, 11, 3, 1, 1, 97, 1, 4, 12, 3, 6, 2, 73, 1, 1, 1, 1, 3, 1, 1, 16, 8, 4, 5, 1, 2,
60, 1, 1, 10, 1, 3, 2, 1, 1, 2, 20, 1, 1, 1, 2, 1, 61, 1, 3, 1, 44, 2, 13, 1, 1, 6, 3, 4, 1,
3, 1, 2, 202, 1, 4, 1, 9, 1, 2, 2, 1, 40, 1, 8, 2, 6, 99, 3, 2, 3, 1, 10, 2, 22, 1, 4, 1, 3,
4, 1, 3, 1, 15, 2, 10, 5, 1, 1, 1, 427, 1, 3, 1, 2, 3, 2, 2, 91, 1, 1, 1, 2, 1, 1, 2, 1, 23,
1, 3, 12, 6, 2, 13, 1, 16, 1, 1, 8, 4, 1, 2, 44, 1, 2, 22, 2, 1, 1, 4, 1, 3, 27, 1, 2, 3, 1,
2, 7, 1, 6, 1, 1, 1, 6, 5, 1, 1, 1, 1, 1, 1, 5, 4, 1, 1, 15, 2, 1, 4, 18, 1, 1, 1, 2, 2, 3, 2,
4, 13, 4, 1, 9, 3, 1, 2, 11, 1, 1, 6, 30, 2, 2, 2, 11, 17, 1, 1, 1, 1, 1, 2, 7, 7, 1, 2, 2,
1, 2, 1, 3, 7, 31, 1, 3, 1, 2, 452, 1, 19, 9, 11, 1, 2, 1, 1, 2, 6, 1, 28, 10, 4, 1, 2, 3,
2, 5, 2, 1, 15, 1, 3, 2, 42, 5, 1, 1, 2, 1, 1, 4, 1, 1, 9, 2, 1, 3, 8, 6, 32, 1, 3, 2, 12, 1,
4, 1, 11, 2, 1, 41, 4, 1, 6, 2, 1, 1, 48, 2, 2, 3, 2, 2, 4, 2, 4, 4, 10, 1, 12, 14, 4, 1, 2, 92].

Thus, we can conclude that

$$d = 189877018016769650162234978064222550351916979376481456967901.$$

$p_1 = 71112944731410736200936098026102194286183896202223461645293266435374\backslash$
$\quad 24133992279467748393278156440741.$

$p_2 = 71112944731410736200936161704354259548674079134065376681839091861977\backslash$
$\quad 764920543470207538471074910420 31.$

$p_3 = 71112944731410736200936135161274092520974419744378917664439975869666\backslash$
$\quad 144717031836034662717839370173 79.$

$p_4 = 71112944731410736200936153839445191771143086686623743978164216730335\backslash$
$\quad 75558876657813072394314100437063.$

## 6    Conclusion and Futures Work

Let $n = p_1 p_2 \cdots p_r$, and $p_r - p_1 = n^\alpha$. Based on Wiener's Interval , we have
showed that MPRSA is insecure if $2d^2 + 1 < \frac{n^{2/r-\alpha}}{6r} < \phi(n)$, for $r \geq 3$; and
$2d^2 + 1 < 2n^{3/2-2\alpha} + 1$, for $r = 2$ and $\phi(n) > \frac{3}{4}n$.

Many interesting questions arise from the work presented above. For examples:

1. The possibility to generalize Fermat's method to MPRSA. It seems that
   $p_r - p_1 = n^\alpha$, $\alpha = \frac{1}{r}$.
2. Uses of lattice instead of CF.
3. Improve the condition $2d^2 + 1 < \frac{n^{2/r-\alpha}}{6r}$.

# References

1. Alison, C., Paixão, M.: An efficient variant of the RSA cryptosystem, http://eprint.iacr.org/2003/159
2. Blömer, J., May, A.: A Generalized Wiener Attack on RSA. In: Bao, F., Deng, R., Zhou, J. (eds.) PKC 2004. LNCS, vol. 2947, pp. 1–13. Springer, Heidelberg (2004)
3. Boneh, D.: Twenty years of attacks on the RSA cryptosystem. Notices of the American Mathematical Society 46(2), 203–213 (1999)
4. Boneh, D., Durfee, G.: Cryptanalysis of RSA with private key d less than $N^{0.292}$. IEEE Trans. on Information Theory 46(4), 1339–1349 (2000)
5. Boneh, D., Shacham, H.: Fast Variants of RSA. CryptoBytes 5(1), 1–9 (2002)
6. Ciet, M., Koeune, F., Laguillaumie, F., Quisquater, J.-J.: Short private exponent attacks on fast variants of RSA. UCL Crypto Group Technical Report Series CG-2003/4, Universite Catholique de Louvain (2003)
7. Collins, T., Hopkins, D., Langford, S., Sabin, M.: Public key cryptographic apparatus and method. US patent #5, 848, 149 (January 1997)
8. Coppersmith, D.: Small solutions to polynomial equations and low exponent vulnerabilities. Journal of Cryptology 10(4), 223–260 (1997)
9. Durfee, G., Nguyen, P.: Cryptanalysis of the RSA Schemes with Short Secret Exponent from Asiacrypt 99. In: Okamoto, T. (ed.) ASIACRYPT 2000. LNCS, vol. 1976, pp. 14–29. Springer, Heidelberg (2000)
10. Hinek, M.J.: On the security of multi-prime RSA. Journal of Mathematical Cryptology 2(2), 117–147 (2008)
11. Hinek, M.J.: Cryptanalysis of RSA and its variants. Chapman & Hall/CRC (2010)
12. Hinek, M.J., Low, M.K., Teske, E.: On Some Attacks on Multi-prime RSA. In: Nyberg, K., Heys, H.M. (eds.) SAC 2002. LNCS, vol. 2595, pp. 385–404. Springer, Heidelberg (2003)
13. Lenstra, A.K., Lenstra, H.W., Lovasz, L.: Factoring polynomials with rational coefficients. Mathematische Annalen 261, 513–534 (1982)
14. Lim, S., Kim, S., Yie, I., Lee, H.: A Generalized Takagi-Cryptosystem with a Modulus of the Form $p^r q^s$. In: Roy, B., Okamoto, E. (eds.) INDOCRYPT 2000. LNCS, vol. 1977, pp. 283–294. Springer, Heidelberg (2000)
15. Maitra, S., Sarkar, S.: Revisiting Wiener's Attack – New Weak Keys in RSA. In: Wu, T.-C., Lei, C.-L., Rijmen, V., Lee, D.-T. (eds.) ISC 2008. LNCS, vol. 5222, pp. 228–243. Springer, Heidelberg (2008)
16. May, A.: New RSA Vulnerabilities using Lattics Reduction Methods. Ph.D. Dissertation. University of Paderborn (2003)
17. Nassr, D., Bahig, H.M., Bhery, A., Dauod, S.: A New RSA Vulnerability Using Continued Fractions. In: Proceeding of the Sixth IEEE/ACS International Conference on Computer Systems and Applications (Security and Information Assurance Track), April 31- May 4, pp. 694–701 (2008)
18. Rivest, R., Shamir, A., Adleman, L.: A method for obtaining digital signatures and public-key cryptosystems. Communication of ACM 21, 120–126 (1978)
19. Rosen, K.H.: Elementary Number Theory. Addison-Wesley, Reading Mass (1984)
20. Shoup, V.: NTL: A Library for doing Number Theory, http://www.shoup.net/ntl/index.html
21. Steinfeld, R., Contini, S., Pieprzyk, J., Wang, H.: Converse Results to the Wiener Attack on RSA. In: Vaudenay, S. (ed.) PKC 2005. LNCS, vol. 3386, pp. 184–198. Springer, Heidelberg (2005)

22. Verheul, E.R., van Tilborg, H.C.A.: Cryptanalysis of 'less short' RSA secret exponents. Applicable Algebra in Engineering, Communication and Computing 8, 425–435 (1997)
23. de Weger, B.: Cryptanalysis of RSA with small prime difference. Applicable Algebra in Engineering, Communication and Computing 13(1), 17–28 (2002)
24. Wiener, M.: Cryptanalysis of short RSA secret exponents. IEEE Transactions on Information Theory 36, 553–558 (1990)

# Implicit Polynomial Recovery and Cryptanalysis of a Combinatorial Key Cryptosystem

Jun Xu[1,2], Lei Hu[1], and Siwei Sun[1]

[1] State Key Laboratory of Information Security,
Institute of Information Engineering, Chinese Academy of Sciences,
Beijing 100093, China
[2] Graduate University of Chinese Academy of Sciences, Beijing 100049, China
{jxu,hu,swsun}@is.ac.cn

**Abstract.** A public key cryptosystem based on factoring and a combinatorial problem of matrices over $\mathbb{Z}_N$ proposed in 2010 is analyzed in this paper. We propose an efficient partial private key recovery attack on it by solving a problem of recovering implicit polynomials with small coefficients given their large roots and deriving the large roots from the public key. From the partial information of private key, we can decrypt any ciphertext of the cryptosystem by a simple computation. Our implicit polynomial recovery is an application of lattice basis reduction.

**Keywords:** Public Key Cryptography, Combinatorial Cryptosystem, Implicit Polynomial Recovery, Lattice, LLL Algorithm.

## 1 Introduction

Many asymmetric encryption schemes have been proposed after the discovery of public key cryptography, including the well known ones based on number theoretic problems like RSA and ElGamal. It is important for public key cryptography to research secure and fast asymmetric encryption cryptosystems relying on other hard mathematical problems such as lattice problems (e.g., Atjai-Dwork [1], GGH [5] and NTRU [6] public key cryptosystems) and combinatorial problems (e.g., knapsack trapdoors [8]).

Recently, a new combinatorial public key cryptosystem mixed with integer factorization problem were presented [13]. The authors of [13] thought that the security of the system is not dependent on the intractability of integer factorization but on a hard combinatorial problem involving matrices. Some attacks, especially lattice attacks and private key recovery attacks, were stressed and extensively discussed in [13], and the authors concluded that the lattice reduction algorithms do not work for this cryptosystem.

In this paper, we propose a partial private key recovery attack on the above cryptosystem [13] by using the means of lattice. We observe that a secret matrix $A$ in the private key of the cryptosystem has relatively small entries compared with the RSA modulus $N$. By analyzing the relations between the public and secret matrices in the system, we derive elements in $\mathbb{Z}_N$ which are roots of

T.W. Chim and T.H. Yuen (Eds.): ICICS 2012, LNCS 7618, pp. 45–57, 2012.

some polynomials modulo $N$ with the entries of $A$ as their coefficients. Then we can construct some lattices and run the well known LLL algorithm [7] to recover the relatively small coefficients. This problem of recovering an implicit polynomial with small coefficients given its large roots is a dual of the problem of finding small roots of a polynomial with large coefficients, which is solved by Coppersmith in his seminal paper [3] in 1996. With the recovered matrix $A$, we can find out the factorization of $N$ and partially recover information on the other secret matrices $D$ and $F$ in the private key. With this partially private key information, an attacker can recover the plaintext of any ciphertext by a very simple computation.

The paper is organized as follows. In Section 2 we give a description for the cryptographic system in [13]. We present our cryptanalysis on it in Section 3. The last section is the conclusion.

## 2    Description of the Public Key Encryption System

In this section we review the public key encryption scheme proposed in [13].

**Key Generation:** This cryptosystem involves $n \times n$ matrices over $\mathbb{Z}_N$, where $n$ is an even integer and $N = pq$ is a random 1024-bit RSA modulus with two primes $p$ and $q$ of length of 512 bits. The authors of [13] suggest $n$ is chosen as 2 or 4. Let $\Gamma$ be the set of all $n \times n$ matrices over $\mathbb{Z}_N$ such that each entry in odd-numbered rows is multiples of $p$ and each entry in the even-numbered rows is multiples of $q$. Define two $n \times n$ permutation matrices $P_1$ and $P_2$ as follows:

$$P_1 = \begin{bmatrix} 0 \cdots 0\,1 \\ 0 \cdots 1\,0 \\ \cdots \\ 1 \cdots 0\,0 \end{bmatrix}, P_2 = \begin{bmatrix} 0 \cdots 0\,1 \\ 1 \cdots 0\,0 \\ \cdots \\ 0 \cdots 1\,0 \end{bmatrix}.$$

Four matrices $C, D, E, F \in \mathbb{Z}^{n \times n}$ are chosen such that

$$C + EP_1 \in \Gamma, \quad D + FP_2 \in \Gamma. \tag{1}$$

Randomly generate an $n \times n$ invertible matrix $A$ over $\mathbb{Z}$ whose all entries have "short" binary length of 59 bits, then generate another matrix $A' \in \mathbb{Z}_N^{n \times n}$ such that $A' - A \in \Gamma$. Randomly choose two invertible matrices $D$ and $F$ in $\mathbb{Z}_N^{n \times n}$, and compute

$$\begin{cases} B \equiv D^{-1}A' \pmod{N}, \\ G \equiv D^{-1}C \pmod{N}, \\ H \equiv F^{-1}E \pmod{N}. \end{cases} \tag{2}$$

**Public Key:** The RSA modulus $N$ and three matrices $B$, $G$ and $H$.
**Private Key:** The primes $p$, $q$ and the matrices $D$, $F$ and $A$.
**Encryption:** The plaintext $m$ is coded into an $n$-dimensional column vector $(m_1, \cdots, m_n)^t$, where each entry $m_i$ is of length of 450 bits. The sender randomly

chooses two $n$-dimensional vectors $r = (r_1, \cdots, r_n)^t$ and $s = (s_1, \cdots, s_n)^t$ over $\mathbb{Z}_N$. The ciphertext is a 2-tuple $(u, v)$ given as follows:

$$\begin{cases} u \equiv Bm + Gr + s \pmod{N}, \\ v \equiv HP_1r + P_2s \pmod{N}. \end{cases} \tag{3}$$

**Decryption:** Given a ciphertext $(u, v)$, the receiver computes the plaintext $m$ as follows:

$$\begin{cases} t = (t_1, \ldots, t_n)^t \equiv Du + Fv \pmod{N}, \\ w_i = t_i \bmod p \quad \text{when } i \text{ is odd}, \\ w_i = t_i \bmod q \quad \text{when } i \text{ is even}, \\ m = A^{-1}(w_1, \ldots, w_n)^t. \end{cases}$$

## 3   Attack on the Public Key Encryption Scheme

In this section we present a partial private key recovery attack on the scheme including: (i) revealing the primes $p$ and $q$ and the secret matrix $A$ by using a lattice basis reduction method. This is done by implicit polynomials recovery; and (ii) getting partial information of the secret matrices $D$ and $F$. With such partial private key information in hand, a ciphertxet-only attacker can decrypt any ciphertext of this cryptosystem by a simple operation only like the decryption process.

### 3.1   Recovering Relations on Secret Matrices and Factoring the RSA Modulus

From Formulas (1) and (2) in the key generation, we have

$$DG + FHP_1 \equiv C + EP_1 \pmod{N}, \text{and} \quad DG + FHP_1 \in \Gamma. \tag{4}$$

Let $D_i$ and $F_i$ denote the $i$-th rows of $D$ and $F$ respectively. Then

$$\begin{cases} D_iG + F_iHP_1 \equiv 0 \pmod{p} \quad \text{for odd } i, \\ D_iG + F_iHP_1 \equiv 0 \pmod{q} \quad \text{for even } i. \end{cases} \tag{5}$$

Since $D + FP_2 \in \Gamma$ by (1), we have

$$\begin{cases} D_iP_2^{-1} + F_i \equiv 0 \pmod{p} \quad \text{for odd } i, \\ D_iP_2^{-1} + F_i \equiv 0 \pmod{q} \quad \text{for even } i. \end{cases} \tag{6}$$

By the two above equalities we obtain

$$\begin{cases} D_i(G - P_2^{-1}HP_1) \equiv 0 \pmod{p} \quad \text{for odd } i, \\ D_i(G - P_2^{-1}HP_1) \equiv 0 \pmod{q} \quad \text{for even } i. \end{cases} \tag{7}$$

**Structure of the Matrix $G - P_2^{-1}HP_1$:**

Let $m = n/2$. Clearly, $W := G - P_2^{-1}HP_1$ is a matrix which any attacker can know from the public key. By the first relation of (7), since $D \pmod{p}$ is invertible over $\mathbb{Z}_p$ and chosen at random, and $p$ is a large prime of 512 bits, with a probability very close 1 the remainder of $W$ modulo $p$ has rank $m$ and its first $m$ rows are linearly independent over $\mathbb{Z}_p$. Thus, with this probability we assume

$$W \equiv \begin{pmatrix} W_1 \\ T_1 W_1 \end{pmatrix} \pmod{p}, \tag{8}$$

where $W_1 \in \mathbb{Z}_p^{m \times n}$ is of rank $m$ over $\mathbb{Z}_p$ and $T_1 \in \mathbb{Z}_p^{m \times m}$. Similarly, with a probability very close 1 we have

$$W \equiv \begin{pmatrix} W_2 \\ T_2 W_2 \end{pmatrix} \pmod{q}, \tag{9}$$

where the rank of $W_2 \in \mathbb{Z}_q^{m \times n}$ is $m$ over $\mathbb{Z}_q$ and $T_2 \in \mathbb{Z}_q^{m \times m}$.

By the Chinese remainder theorem, there is an $m \times n$ matrix $\widetilde{W}$ over $\mathbb{Z}_N$ such that $\widetilde{W} = W_1 \pmod{p}$ and $\widetilde{W} = W_2 \pmod{q}$, and there is also an $m \times m$ matrix $T$ over $\mathbb{Z}_N$ such that $T = W_1 \pmod{p}$ and $T = W_2 \pmod{q}$. Then from (8) and (9), we get

$$G - P_2^{-1} H P_1 \equiv \begin{pmatrix} \widetilde{W} \\ T\widetilde{W} \end{pmatrix} \pmod{N}. \tag{10}$$

### Relations on the Secret Matrix $D$:

Consider the block submatrices of $D$. Let $P_3$ denote an $n \times n$ permutation matrix which transforms a column vector $(x_1, x_2, \cdots, x_n)^t$ into $(x_1, x_3, \cdots, x_{n-1},$ $x_2, x_4, \cdots, x_n)^t$, and $\Delta$ be the set of all $n \times n$ matrices over $\mathbb{Z}_N$ such that all entries in the first $m$ rows are multiples of $p$ and all entries in the last $m$ rows are multiples of $q$. Then, an $n \times n$ matrix $D'$ over $\mathbb{Z}_N$ is in $\Gamma$ if and only if $P_3 D' \in \Delta$.

By (7),

$$P_3 D(G - P_2^{-1} H P_1) \in \Delta. \tag{11}$$

Evenly partition $P_3 D$ into

$$P_3 D = \begin{pmatrix} D^{(1)} & D^{(2)} \\ D^{(3)} & D^{(4)} \end{pmatrix},$$

where $D^{(1)}, D^{(2)}, D^{(3)}, D^{(4)}$ are four $m \times m$ matrices over $\mathbb{Z}_N$. Plugging (10) into (11), we have

$$\begin{pmatrix} D^{(1)} & D^{(2)} \\ D^{(3)} & D^{(4)} \end{pmatrix} \begin{pmatrix} \widetilde{W} \\ T\widetilde{W} \end{pmatrix} \in \Delta,$$

and in other words,

$$\begin{cases} (D^{(1)} + D^{(2)}T)\widetilde{W} \equiv 0 \pmod{p}, \\ (D^{(3)} + D^{(4)}T)\widetilde{W} \equiv 0 \pmod{q}. \end{cases}$$

Since $\widetilde{W}(\mathrm{mod}\ p)$ and $\widetilde{W}(\mathrm{mod}\ q)$ are both of rank $m$, we have

$$\begin{cases} D^{(1)} \equiv -D^{(2)}T \ (\mathrm{mod}\ p), \\ D^{(3)} \equiv -D^{(4)}T \ (\mathrm{mod}\ q). \end{cases} \tag{12}$$

## Relations Related on the Secret Matrix $A$:

By the key generation, we have $DB - A = A' - A \in \Gamma$ and

$$P_3 DB - P_3 A \in \Delta.$$

Let

$$P_3 A = \begin{pmatrix} A^{(1)} & A^{(2)} \\ A^{(3)} & A^{(4)} \end{pmatrix}, B = \begin{pmatrix} B^{(1)} & B^{(2)} \\ B^{(3)} & B^{(4)} \end{pmatrix}$$

be the even partitions of matrices. The above relation says that

$$\begin{pmatrix} D^{(1)} & D^{(2)} \\ D^{(3)} & D^{(4)} \end{pmatrix} \begin{pmatrix} B^{(1)} & B^{(2)} \\ B^{(3)} & B^{(4)} \end{pmatrix} - \begin{pmatrix} A^{(1)} & A^{(2)} \\ A^{(3)} & A^{(4)} \end{pmatrix} \in \Delta,$$

and equivalently,

$$\begin{cases} D^{(1)}B^{(1)} + D^{(2)}B^{(3)} \equiv A^{(1)} \ (\mathrm{mod}\ p), \\ D^{(1)}B^{(2)} + D^{(2)}B^{(4)} \equiv A^{(2)} \ (\mathrm{mod}\ p), \\ D^{(3)}B^{(1)} + D^{(4)}B^{(3)} \equiv A^{(3)} \ (\mathrm{mod}\ q), \\ D^{(3)}B^{(2)} + D^{(4)}B^{(4)} \equiv A^{(4)} \ (\mathrm{mod}\ q). \end{cases} \tag{13}$$

Plugging (12) into (13), we have

$$\begin{cases} D^{(2)}(B^{(3)} - TB^{(1)}) \equiv A^{(1)} \ (\mathrm{mod}\ p), \\ D^{(2)}(B^{(4)} - TB^{(2)}) \equiv A^{(2)} \ (\mathrm{mod}\ p), \\ D^{(4)}(B^{(3)} - TB^{(1)}) \equiv A^{(3)} \ (\mathrm{mod}\ q), \\ D^{(4)}(B^{(4)} - TB^{(2)}) \equiv A^{(4)} \ (\mathrm{mod}\ q). \end{cases} \tag{14}$$

Again with a probability very close to 1, $A^{(1)}$ and $A^{(2)}$ are invertible over $\mathbb{Z}_p$ and over $\mathbb{Z}_q$.

Let $K = (B^{(3)} - TB^{(1)})^{-1}(B^{(4)} - TB^{(2)}) \ (\mathrm{mod}\ N)$, which is an $m \times m$ matrix and can be computed from the public key $N, G, H, B$. Then the relations in (14) lead to:

$$\begin{cases} A^{(2)} \equiv A^{(1)}K \ (\mathrm{mod}\ p), \\ A^{(4)} \equiv A^{(3)}K \ (\mathrm{mod}\ q). \end{cases} \tag{15}$$

These are implicit relations related on the secret matrix $A$ and the secret primes $p$ and $q$.

Now we go to recover these implicit relations by using the fact that $A$ is a relatively small matrix, and then find the secret primes. To simplify the notations and illustrate the principle, below we first consider the simplest case that $n = 2$.

The method is similar for other cases of $n$ but involves higher dimensional lattices and further skills.

**Recovering $A$ and Factoring $N$ when $n = 2$:**

For $n = 2$, $P_3$ is the identity matrix,

$$P_3 A = \begin{pmatrix} A^{(1)} & A^{(2)} \\ A^{(3)} & A^{(4)} \end{pmatrix} = A = \begin{pmatrix} a_{11} & a_{12} \\ a_{21} & a_{22} \end{pmatrix}, P_3 B = \begin{pmatrix} B^{(1)} & B^{(2)} \\ B^{(3)} & B^{(4)} \end{pmatrix} = B = \begin{pmatrix} b_{11} & b_{12} \\ b_{21} & b_{22} \end{pmatrix},$$

and $K = (b_{21} - Tb_{11})^{-1}(b_{22} - Tb_{12}) \pmod{N}$. From the pair of relations modulo $p$ and $q$ in (15), we get a relation modulo $N$ as $(a_{12} - Ka_{11})(a_{22} - Ka_{21}) \equiv 0 \pmod{N}$, which is

$$a_{11}a_{21}K^2 - (a_{11}a_{22} + a_{12}a_{21})K + a_{12}a_{22} \equiv 0 \pmod{N}. \qquad (16)$$

Note that the $a_{ij}$ are of length of not exceeding 59 bits, the sizes of the coefficients in (16) (namely $a_{11}a_{21}, a_{11}a_{22} + a_{12}a_{21}, a_{12}a_{22}$) are not more than 119 bits, which are relatively small integers compared with the 1024-bit modulus $N$. This is a problem of recovering an implicit polynomial with small coefficients given its large roots. See Appendix A for its general description and a solution. It can be regarded as a dual of the problem of finding small roots of a polynomial with large coefficients, which had been solved by Coppersmith in his seminal paper [3] in 1996 by the well known lattice basis reduction method. For our problem, we can recover the small coefficients also by the lattice means as follows.

Construct a matrix as

$$\begin{pmatrix} 1 & 0 & -K^2 (\bmod N) \\ 0 & 1 & K \\ 0 & 0 & N \end{pmatrix}$$

and let $L_1$ be the three-dimensional lattice spanned by its rows. Run the LLL lattice basis reduction algorithm and get a short lattice vector $(a, b, c)$ in the lattice. Obviously, all lattice vectors $(a, b, c)$ satisfy that $aK^2 - bK + c \equiv 0 \pmod{N}$. Since the lattice is of very low dimension like 3, we almost always obtain the shortest vector $(a, b, c)$ in $L_1$.

Note that $a_{12}/a_{11} \pmod{N}$ and $a_{22}/a_{21} \pmod{N}$ are two roots of (16), from this we know that $(a_{11}a_{21}, a_{11}a_{22} + a_{12}a_{21}, a_{12}a_{22})$ and $(a, b, c)$ are proportional modulo $N$. They are relatively very small with respect to $N$, so they must be proportional in the usual sense. Assume that $(a_{11}a_{21}, a_{11}a_{22} + a_{12}a_{21}, a_{12}a_{22}) = t(a, b, c)$. This $t$ is a small integer, we can exhaust to search it. In fact, $t = 1$ holds with a probability of about 39 percent (see the corollary in Appendix B).

For each small searched value of $t$ such that $ta, tb, tc$ are of length of not exceeding 119 bits, factor $ta$ and $tc$ as $ta = x_1 x_3$ and $tc = x_2 x_4$ with $x_1, \cdots, x_4$ of no more than 59 bits. We note that integers of lengths of less than two hundreds bits like 119 bits are very easy to factor by using the open source software like Shoup's number theoretical library NTL [11] or Magma [2]. From the complete decomposition of $ta$ and $tc$, there may be several choices for these $x_i$, and hence we test whether $x_1 x_4 + x_2 x_3 = tb$ holds or not. If yes, we let $(a_{11}, a_{12}, a_{21}, a_{22}) = (x_1, x_2, x_3, x_4)$ and compute $\gcd(a_{12} - Ka_{11}, N)$. This will generally get $p$ by $\gcd(a_{12} - Ka_{11}, N) = p$.

**Experimental Result for $n = 2$:** We have implemented the above attack with the LLL algorithm on a PC with Intel(R) Core(TM) Quad CPU (2.83GHz, 3.25GB RAM, Windows XP). For $n = 2$, our experiment always successfully outputs the shortest vector $(a, b, c)$, and amongst 100 instances randomly generated, there are 40 times that $t$ is equal to 1. The time complexity is very low, all work including the lattice computation and decomposition test can be finished within ten seconds.

**Recovering $A$ and Factoring $N$ when $n = 4$:**

For $n = 4$, let

$$K = \begin{pmatrix} k_1 & k_2 \\ k_3 & k_4 \end{pmatrix}, A^{(i)} = \begin{pmatrix} a_i & b_i \\ a_i' & b_i' \end{pmatrix}, 1 \leq i \leq 4.$$

The relations in (15) then become:

$$\begin{cases} k_1 a_1 + k_3 b_1 - a_2 \equiv 0 \pmod{p}, \\ k_2 a_1 + k_4 b_1 - b_2 \equiv 0 \pmod{p}, \\ k_1 a_3 + k_3 b_3 - a_4 \equiv 0 \pmod{q}, \\ k_2 a_3 + k_4 b_3 - b_4 \equiv 0 \pmod{q}. \end{cases} \quad (17)$$

From the pair of relations modulo $p$ and $q$ in (17), we get relations modulo $N$ as

$$\begin{cases} k_1^2(a_1 a_3) + k_3^2(b_1 b_3) + k_1 k_3(a_1 b_3 + a_3 b_1) \\ \quad -k_1(a_1 a_4 + a_2 a_3) - k_3(a_2 b_3 + a_4 b_1) + a_2 a_4 \equiv 0 \pmod{N}, \\ k_2^2(a_1 a_3) + k_4^2(b_1 b_3) + k_2 k_4(a_1 b_3 + a_3 b_1) \\ \quad -k_2(a_1 b_4 + a_3 a_2) - k_4(b_2 b_3 + b_1 b_4) + b_2 b_4 \equiv 0 \pmod{N}. \end{cases} \quad (18)$$

Obviously, we can get the same relations on $a_i'$, $b_i'$ ($1 \leq i \leq 4$) as (18) from

$$\begin{cases} k_1 a_1' + k_3 b_1' - a_2' \equiv 0 \pmod{p}, \\ k_2 a_1' + k_4 b_1' - b_2' \equiv 0 \pmod{p}, \\ k_1 a_3' + k_3 b_3' - a_4' \equiv 0 \pmod{q}, \\ k_2 a_3' + k_4 b_3' - b_4' \equiv 0 \pmod{q}. \end{cases} \quad (19)$$

Construct two six-dimensional lattices $L_2$ and $L_3$ which are generated by the rows of the matrices

$$\begin{pmatrix} 1 & & & & & -k_1^2 \pmod{N} \\ & 1 & & & & -k_3^2 \pmod{N} \\ & & 1 & & & -k_1 k_3 \pmod{N} \\ & & & 1 & & k_1 \\ & & & & 1 & k_3 \\ & & & & & N \end{pmatrix} \text{ and } \begin{pmatrix} 1 & & & & & -k_2^2 \pmod{N} \\ & 1 & & & & -k_4^2 \pmod{N} \\ & & 1 & & & -k_2 k_4 \pmod{N} \\ & & & 1 & & k_2 \\ & & & & 1 & k_4 \\ & & & & & N \end{pmatrix}$$

respectively. Running the LLL algorithm, we get a reduced basis of $L_2$, $\{\alpha_1, \cdots, \alpha_6\}$, and a reduced basis of $L_3$, $\{\beta_1, \cdots, \beta_6\}$ (the vectors in a basis are listed in the increasing length order).

Note that the following vectors which we desire to find

$$\begin{cases} (a_1a_3, b_1b_3, a_1b_3 + a_3b_1, a_1a_4 + a_2a_3, a_2b_3 + a_4b_1, a_2a_4) \in L_2, \\ (a_1a_3, b_1b_3, a_1b_3 + a_3b_1, a_1b_4 + b_2a_3, b_2b_3 + b_4b_1, b_2b_4) \in L_3, \\ (a_1'a_3', b_1'b_3', a_2'b_3' + a_3'b_1', a_1'a_4' + a_2'a_3', a_2'b_3' + a_4'b_1', a_2'a_4') \in L_2, \\ (a_1'a_3', b_1'b_3', a_2'b_3' + a_3'b_1', a_1'b_4' + b_2'a_3', b_2'b_3' + b_4'b_1', b_2'b_4') \in L_3 \end{cases} \quad (20)$$

are of sizes less than $2^{118} \cdot \sqrt{3 \cdot 1^2 + 3 \cdot 2^2} < 2^{120}$, which are relatively very short vectors compared with most vectors in $L_2$ and $L_3$ with 1024-bit components.

Let

$$\begin{cases} (a_1a_3, b_1b_3, a_1b_3 + a_3b_1, a_1a_4 + a_2a_3, a_2b_3 + a_4b_1, a_2a_4) = x_1\alpha_1 + \cdots + x_6\alpha_6, \\ (a_1a_3, b_1b_3, a_1b_3 + a_3b_1, a_1b_4 + b_2a_3, b_2b_3 + b_4b_1, b_2b_4) = y_1\beta_1 + \cdots + y_6\beta_6, \end{cases} \quad (21)$$

where $x_i, y_i \in \mathbb{Z}$, $1 \le i \le 6$. In our experiment (see below), we observe that to search short vectors $x_1\alpha_1 + \cdots + x_6\alpha_6$ and $y_1\beta_1 + \cdots + y_6\beta_6$ in the lattices, only the first three or four coefficients in the two tuples of coefficients, $x_1, \cdots, x_6$ and $y_1, \cdots, y_6$ are not zero and they are always very small integers like ones with absolute values less than 50. This is reasonable because under the increasing length order, the last two vectors, $\alpha_5$ and $\alpha_6$, or $\beta_5$ and $\beta_6$, are obviously much longer than the first several vectors $\alpha_1, \alpha_2, \alpha_3, \alpha_4$ and $\beta_1, \beta_2, \beta_3, \beta_4$. Do an exhaust lexicographical-like search for the integral coefficient vector $(x_1, \cdots, x_6)$ with $x_6$ and $x_5$ being set to 0 prior and all other components starting from 0 to a small number like 50 (in absolute value sense), and find all linear combinations $x_1\alpha_1 + \cdots + x_6\alpha_6$ of length less than $2^{120}$. More precisely, we require that the first, second and last components of these vectors are all of length not exceeding 118 bits and the other components are of length not exceeding 119 bits.

Further, note that for the desired two vectors in (21), let $(c_1 \cdots, c_6)$ be either one of them, then $c_3^2 - 4c_1c_2 = (a_1b_3 + a_3b_1)^2 - 4a_1a_3b_1b_3 = (a_1b_3 - a_3b_1)^2$ and similarly $c_4^2 - 4c_1c_6, c_5^2 - 4c_2c_6$ are complete square numbers over integers. If one of $c_3^2 - 4c_1c_2, c_4^2 - 4c_1c_6, c_5^2 - 4c_2c_6$ is not a complete square number, then the vector $(c_1 \cdots, c_6)$ is not a desired vector of the form (21). Otherwise, by continuing to find square roots of the completely square numbers, we get the intended values for $a_1b_3$ and $a_3b_1$ from the values of $a_1b_3 + a_3b_1$ and $a_1b_3 - a_3b_1$, and similarly get the intended values for $a_1a_4, a_3a_2, b_1a_4, b_3a_2, a_1b_4, a_3b_2, b_1b_4, b_3b_2$. All these values obtained should be of length not exceeding 118 bits, if any one of such requirements invalidates, then the vector $(c_1 \cdots, c_6)$ can not be a desired vector of the form (21).

Search all linear combinations $x_1\alpha_1 + \cdots + x_6\alpha_6$ satisfying all requirements mentioned above, and let them form a set $S_2$. Similarly in the lattice $L_3$, search all vectors $y_1\beta_1 + \cdots + y_6\beta_6$ with the same restrictions and then form a set $S_3$. Typically in our experiment, the cardinalities of $S_2$ and $S_3$ are less than 500.

Now for the desired two vectors in (21), the first three components are pairwisely identical. This tells us that by simply finding "projective collisions" of $S_2$

and $S_3$, we will find all vectors in $S_2$ such that their first three components are equal to the corresponding components of some vectors in $S_3$. In our experiment, there are typically less than 200 such collisions. For any one of such three dimensional vectors, if it is a desired one which can be the projection of the vectors in (21), then the values obtained for $a_1a_3, b_1b_3, a_2a_4, b_2b_4$ and the intended values obtained for $a_1b_3, a_3b_1, a_1a_4, a_3a_2, b_1a_4, b_3a_2, a_1b_4, a_3b_2, b_1b_4, b_3b_2$ should satisfy many division relations like the following

$$a_1a_3 |\gcd(a_1b_3, a_1a_4, a_1b_4) \cdot \gcd(b_1a_3, a_2a_3, b_2a_3).$$

If any one of such relations invalidates, then we discard the collision. Otherwise, we can further try to find the values for $a_1, \cdots, a_4, b_1, \cdots, b_4$ as follows.

By using the fact that $a_1$ divides $\gcd(a_1a_3, a_1b_3, a_1a_4, a_1b_4)$ and many similar relations hold, factoring some of 14 products for

$$a_1a_3, b_1b_3, a_2a_4, b_2b_4, a_1b_3, a_3b_1, a_1a_4, a_3a_2, b_1a_4, b_3a_2, a_1b_4, a_3b_2, b_1b_4, b_3b_2,$$

which are all of lengths not exceeding 118 bits and are easy to factor as shown in the previous subsection about the case of $n = 2$, we will get at once the values for $a_1, \cdots, a_4, b_1, \cdots, b_4$ and distill out improper candidates that the values for $a_1, \cdots, a_4, b_1, \cdots, b_4$ are not less than $2^{59}$. Finally, we get all proper candidates for $a_1, \cdots, a_4, b_1, \cdots, b_4$. In our experiment, there are typically less than 100 such candidates.

Now we have found out all candidate tuples for $(a_1, a_2, a_3, a_4, b_1, b_2, b_3, b_4)$. From any such tuple, we get the factorization of $N$ by computing $p = \gcd(k_1a_1 + k_3b_1 - a_2, N)$. These candidate tuples are also suitable for $(a'_1, a'_2, a'_3, a'_4, b'_1, b'_2, b'_3, b'_4)$ since they both satisfy the completely same requirements, and they can not be distinguished. However, fortunately, there are only few such candidate tuples (let the number of candidate tuples be $l$), and that means there are at most $l(l - 1)$ choices for the invertible matrix $A$. In our experiment, $l$ is always less than 30. Thus, we have recovered the secret matrix $A$ in the sense that we limit it into a small range. The $l(l - 1)$ possibilities for $A$ can be further removed out or namely we can further fix the choice after doing one or few proper ciphertect-only decryptions, see Subsection 3.3 below.

As mentioned in the case of $n = 2$, if the entries of the original $(a_1, a_2, a_3, a_4, b_1, b_2, b_3, b_4)$ are small and this vector has a multiple whose all entries are of length not exceeding 59 bits, then there may be several candidates for $A$, however, this happens with a much lower probability than in the case of $n = 2$ (See the proposition of Appendix B).

**Experimental Result for $n = 4$:** In the search of short vectors in $L_2$, the last two coefficients of the integral linear combinations $x_1\alpha_1 + \cdots + x_6\alpha_6$, $x_5$ and $x_6$, are always zero, and in many cases $x_4$ is also zero. While for other coefficients, they are always less than 50 in absolute values. A similar situation happens for $L_3$. The whole computation time for finding the $(a_1, a_2, a_3, a_4, b_1, b_2, b_3, b_4)$ including lattice computing and factorization is within two hours.

## 3.2   Partial Information Recovery of Secret Matrices $D$ and $F$

When $n = 2$, $p$ and $q$ are factored out and the matrix $A$ is found, the secret matrix $D$ can be partially recovered as

$$\begin{cases} (D^{(1)}, D^{(2)}) \equiv (A^{(1)}, A^{(2)})B^{-1} \pmod{p}, \\ (D^{(3)}, D^{(4)}) \equiv (A^{(3)}, A^{(4)})B^{-1} \pmod{q}, \end{cases} \tag{22}$$

by (16). Although we do not completely know what is $D$, we have gotten its half information by (22). The similarity does for $F$ by the fact that $D + FP_2 \in \Gamma$, and this suffices to mount a ciphertext-only attack. See Subsection 3.3.

For $n = 4$, $p$ and $q$ are revealed and there are at most $l^2 - l$ possibilities for $A$, recall the process of key generation, we have

$$\begin{cases} D_i \equiv A_i B^{-1} \pmod{p} \quad \text{when } i \text{ is odd}, \\ D_i \equiv A_i B^{-1} \pmod{q} \quad \text{when } i \text{ is even}. \end{cases} \tag{23}$$

Once we select some possibility for $A$, we can get half information of $D$ by (23). Similarly, since $D + FP_2 \in \Gamma$, we can also obtain its half information of $F$.

## 3.3   Ciphertext-Only Attack

Recall the decryption process,

$$\begin{cases} t = (t_1, \dots, t_n)^t \equiv Du + Fv \pmod{N}, \\ w_i = t_i \bmod p \quad \text{when } i \text{ is odd}, \\ w_i = t_i \bmod q \quad \text{when } i \text{ is even}. \end{cases}$$

When $n = 2$, we have

$$\begin{cases} w_i = \big((D_i \bmod p) u + (F_i \bmod p) v\big) \pmod{p} \quad \text{when } i \text{ is odd}, \\ w_i = \big((D_i \bmod q) u + (F_i \bmod q) v\big) \pmod{q} \quad \text{when } i \text{ is even}, \end{cases}$$

so the plaintext is completely recovered as $m = (m_1, \cdots, m_n)^t = A^{-1}(w_1, \dots, w_n)^t$.

For $n = 4$, although there are probably $l(l - 1)$ choices for the secret matrix $A$ and for the partial information of $D$ and $F$, we can try each possibility to decrypt the plaintext. If a meaningful information for the plaintext is recovered, then we find out a proper choice for the secret matrices $A$, $D$ and $F$. Thus, by doing one or few proper ciphertext-only decryptions, we in fact recover the secret matrix $A$ and fix the choice.

## 4   Conclusion

In this paper, we proposed an efficient partial private key recovery on the combinatorial public key cryptosystem recently proposed in [13]. The partial information recovery of private key is sufficient to decrypt any ciphertext of the cryptosystem in a simple computation.

We recover the partial information of private keys in the cryptosystem by solving a problem of recovering implicit polynomials with small coefficients given their large roots, and the large roots are derived from the public key. The problem of recovering an implicit polynomial with small coefficients can be regarded as a dual of the problem of finding small roots of a polynomial with large coefficients, and these two problems were solved respectively by Coppersmith in [3] in 1996 and in this paper by the lattice basis reduction method.

**Acknowledgements:** The work of this paper was supported by the National Natural Science Foundation of China (Grants 61070172 and 10990011), the Strategic Priority Research Program of Chinese Academy of Sciences under Grant XDA06010702, NBRPC 2011CB302400, and the State Key Laboratory of Information Security, Chinese Academy of Sciences.

# References

1. Ajtai, M., Dwork, C.: A public-key cryptosystem with worst-case/average-case equivalence. In: Proceedings of the Twenty-Ninth Annual ACM Symposium on Theory of Computing, pp. 284–293 (1997)
2. Bosma, W., Cannon, J., Playoust, C.: The Magma Algebra System I: The user language. Journal of Symbolic Computation 24, 235–265 (1997)
3. Coppersmith, D.: Finding a Small Root of a Univariate Modular Equation. In: Maurer, U.M. (ed.) EUROCRYPT 1996. LNCS, vol. 1070, pp. 155–165. Springer, Heidelberg (1996)
4. Coppersmith, D., Franklin, M., Patarin, J., Reiter, M.: Low-Exponent RSA with Related Messages. In: Maurer, U.M. (ed.) EUROCRYPT 1996. LNCS, vol. 1070, pp. 1–9. Springer, Heidelberg (1996)
5. Goldreich, O., Goldwasser, S., Halvei, S.: Public-Key Cryptosystems from Lattice Reduction Problems. In: Kaliski Jr., B.S. (ed.) CRYPTO 1997. LNCS, vol. 1294, pp. 112–131. Springer, Heidelberg (1997)
6. Hoffstein, J., Pipher, J., Silverman, J.H.: NTRU: A Ring-Based Public Key Cryptosystem. In: Buhler, J.P. (ed.) ANTS 1998. LNCS, vol. 1423, pp. 267–288. Springer, Heidelberg (1998)
7. Lenstra, A.K., Lenstra Jr., H.W., Lovász, L.: Factoring polynomials with rational coefficients. Mathematische Annalen 261, 515–534 (1982)
8. Merkle, R.C., Hellman, M.E.: Hiding Information and Signatures in Trapdoor Knapsack. IEEE Transaction on Information Theory 24, 525–530 (1978)
9. Nguyen, P.Q., Stern, J.: Cryptanalysis of the Ajtai-Dwork Cryptosystem. In: Krawczyk, H. (ed.) CRYPTO 1998. LNCS, vol. 1462, pp. 223–242. Springer, Heidelberg (1998)
10. Odlyzko, A.M.: The rise and fall of knapsack cryptosystems. Cryptology and Computational Number Theory 42, 75–88 (1990)
11. Shoup, V.: A library for doing number theory, http://www.shoup.net/ntl
12. Wang, B., Hu, Y.: Diophantine Approximation Attack on a Fast Public Key Cryptosystem. In: Chen, K., Deng, R., Lai, X., Zhou, J. (eds.) ISPEC 2006. LNCS, vol. 3903, pp. 25–32. Springer, Heidelberg (2006)
13. Wang, B., Hu, Y.: A Novel Combinatorial Public Key Cryptosystem. Informatica 21(4), 611–626 (2010)
14. Zwillinger, D.(editor in chief): CRC Standard Mathematical Tables and Formulae, 30th edn. CRC Press, Boca Raton (1996)

## A   Recovering Implicit Polynomials with Small Coefficients

**Problem.** Assume $f(x_1, \cdots, x_n) \in \mathbb{Z}[x_1, \cdots, x_s]$ is a polynomial with unknown coefficients and absolute values of these coefficients are relatively small compared to some large integer $N$. Given $a_1, \cdots, a_s \in \mathbb{Z}_N$ such that $f(a_1, \cdots, a_s) \equiv 0 \pmod{N}$. We expect to recover $f(x_1, \cdots, x_s)$.

**Solution:**   Let $f(x_1, \cdots, x_s) = \sum\limits_{(k_1, \cdots, k_s)} c_{k_1, \cdots, k_s} x_1^{k_1} \cdots x_s^{k_s}$. Then we have $\sum c_{k_1, \cdots, k_s} a_1^{k_1} \cdots a_s^{k_s} \equiv 0 \pmod{N}$. Construct a lattice $L$ which is generated by the rows of the matrix $\begin{pmatrix} I & \alpha \\ 0 & N \end{pmatrix}$, where $I$ is the identity matrix whose numbers of rows and columns are equal to the number of nonzero coefficients $c_{k_1, \cdots, k_s}$ with $(k_1, \cdots, k_s) \neq (0, \cdots, 0)$, and $\alpha$ is a column vector whose entry at the position labeled by $(k_1, \cdots, k_s)$ is equal to $a_1^{k_1} \cdots a_s^{k_s} \pmod{N}$. A lattice vector $(\cdots, \tilde{a}_{k_1, \cdots, k_s}, \cdots, \tilde{a}_{0, \cdots, 0})$ in $L$ satisfies $\sum_{(k_1, \cdots, k_s) \neq (0, \cdots, 0)} \tilde{a}_{k_1, \cdots, k_s} a_1^{k_1} \cdots a_s^{k_s} \equiv \tilde{a}_{0, \cdots, 0} \pmod{N}$, it results in a solution for the problem. Running the LLL algorithm for $L$, we may find out a small solution for the problem.

## B   Probability That Several Random Integers Are Coprime

**Proposition.** Let $N$ be a large positive integer and $l \geq 2$ be an integer. The probability that $l$ integers which are chosen uniformly at random and independently in the interval $[1, N]$ are coprime is about $\prod\limits_{\text{prime } r \leq N} (1 - \frac{1}{r^l})$, where the product is taken over all primes $r$ not exceeding $N$. If $l = 2$, then this probability is about 0.6181. If $l = 8$, this probability is about 0.9959.

**Proof:** Set $S_N = \{1, 2, \cdots, N\}$ and let $S_N^l = S_N \times \cdots \times S_N$ be the Descartesian product of $l$ copies of $S_N$. Then the set $S_N^l - \{(a_1, \cdots, a_l) \in S_N^l : \gcd(a_1, \cdots, a_l) = 1\}$ is equal to $\bigcup\limits_{2 \leq k \leq N} (k S_{[\frac{N}{k}]})^l$. We restrict the index $k$ in the union is square-free, that is, $k$ is a product of distinct primes. For such integers, define $\rho_k = (-1)^u$ if $k$ is a product of $u$ distinct primes. By the inclusion-exclusion principle, the cardinality of the above union is equal to $\sum_{2 \leq k \leq N} (-\rho_k) \left[ \frac{N}{k} \right]^l$, and hence, the number of pairs of coprime integers in $S_N$ is equal to

$$N^l + \sum_{2 \leq k \leq N} \rho_k \left[ \frac{N}{k} \right]^l \approx \sum_{1 \leq k \leq N} \rho_k \left( \frac{N}{k} \right)^l$$
$$\approx N^l (1 - \frac{1}{2^l} - \frac{1}{3^l} - \frac{1}{5^l} + \frac{1}{6^l} - \frac{1}{7^l} + \cdots)$$
$$\approx N^l \prod_{\text{prime } r \leq N} (1 - \frac{1}{r^l}) \approx N^l \prod_{\text{prime } r} (1 - \frac{1}{r^l}).$$

When $l = 2$, $\prod_{\text{prime } r} (1 - \frac{1}{r^l}) \approx 0.6181$. When $l = 8$, $\prod_{\text{prime } r} (1 - \frac{1}{r^l}) \approx 0.9959$.

**Corollary.** For a random matrix with integral entries independently and uniformly chosen in a large interval $[1, N]$, the probability that its two entries in each row are coprime is about $0.6181^2 \approx 0.3821$.

# Improved Related-Key Differential Attacks on Reduced-Round LBlock*

Shusheng Liu, Zheng Gong, and Libin Wang

School of Computer Science,
South China Normal University. 510631 Guangzhou, China
{liushusheng914,cis.gong,lbwang}@gmail.com

**Abstract.** At ACNS 2011, Wu and Zhang proposed a new lightweight block cipher which is named LBlock. The design rationale of LBlock considers the trade-offs between security against cryptanalyses and performance in low-resource implementations. In this paper, we present new attacks on reduced-round LBlock using related-key differential cryptanalysis. Firstly, we construct a new related-key boomerang distinguishing attack on 16-round LBlock. Secondly, we construct a key recovery attack on 22-round LBlock based on a 16-round related-key truncated differential. In contrast to the published cryptanalysis results of reduced-round LBlock, our attacks have advantages on data and computational complexities.

**Keywords:** Lightweight block cipher, Differential analysis, Related-key boomerang attack, LBlock.

## 1 Introduction

Due to a growing requirement of ciphers suited for constrained environment, the design and analysis of lightweight block cipher have received a lot of attention. Many lightweight block ciphers have been proposed such as PRESENT [4], KLEIN [6], LED [7], LBlock [14], Piccolo [11] and KATAN & KTANTAN [5].

LBlock is a lightweight block cipher with the Feistel structure, which is proposed by Wu and Zhang at ACNS 2011 [14,15]. The components of LBlock represent the trade-off between fast diffusion and performance in resource-constrained environment. For the differential analysis, The authors of LBlock proved that the probability of 15-round characteristic can be lower than $2^{-64}$ [14]. For the impossible differential analysis, a 14-round impossible differential is used to mount a key recovery attack on 20-round LBlock [14]. For the integral attack, a 15-round integral distinguisher is used to mount a key recovery attack on 20-round LBlock [14]. Although Shibutani et al.'s paper mentioned they can break 22-round LBlock using integral analysis [12], the details of the attack has not been publicly verifiable yet. Thus the complexities of Shibutani et al.'s attack are described as "?" in Table 1. Recently, a key recovery attack on 22-round LBlock is presented in [9], which takes advantage of a 14-round related-key impossible differential. Table 1 includes the existing attacks of LBlock.

---

* The authors are supported by NSFC 61100201 and Foundation for distinguished Young Talents in Higher Education of Guangdong (LYM11053), China.

T.W. Chim and T.H. Yuen (Eds.): ICICS 2012, LNCS 7618, pp. 58–69, 2012.
© Springer-Verlag Berlin Heidelberg 2012

In this paper, we present new related-key differential attacks on reduced-round LBlock. We first propose a 16-round related-key boomerang distinguishing attack, which has a successful probability of $2^{-60}$. The distinguisher exploits two 8-round related-key characteristics. Then we present a key recovery attack on 22-round LBlock, which uses a 16-round related-key truncated differential. The time and data complexities of our key recovery attack are $2^{67}$ and $2^{64.1}$ respectively, which are better than the previous attacks on 22-round LBlock.

**Table 1.** Summary of the existing attacks on LBlock

| Rounds | Time | Data | Type | Reference |
|--------|------|------|------|-----------|
| 13 | $2^{53}$ | - | related-key differential distinguisher | [14] |
| 16 | $2^{60}$ | - | related-key boomerang distinguisher | this paper |
| 20 | $2^{63.7}$ | $2^{63.7}$ | integral key recovery | [14] |
| 22 | ? | ? | integral attack | [12] |
| 22 | $2^{70}$ | $2^{68}$ | related-key impossible key recovery | [9] |
| 22 | $2^{67}$ | $2^{64.1}$ | related-key differential key recovery | this paper |

## 2   Preliminary

In this section, we first list some notions and notation which will be used in the following analysis. Next, a brief description of LBlock is presented. Finally, the method of the related-key boomerang attack is recalled in short.

### 2.1   Notations

1. $V_i$ is a 64-bit word, which denotes the input of round i. Moreover, $V_{i,l}$ and $V_{i,r}$ are 32-bit words, where $V_i = V_{i,l} \| V_{i,r}$.
2. $K$ denotes the 80-bit master key and $subkey_i$ is 32-bit subkey of round i. Furthermore, $subkey_i^j$ is the j-th nibble of $subkey_i$ and $subkey_i^{j,k}$ is the k-th bit of $subkey_i^j$.
3. For $0 \le i \le 9$, $s_i$ denotes a 4-bit input-output S-box, and $s_i^{-1}$ is its inverse.
4. $\Delta x$ denotes the difference between two values of x. X denotes an active nibble with an uncertain difference.
5. $\lll 8$ denotes an 8-bit cyclic left rotation, $\oplus$ denotes the bitwise exclusive-or (XOR) operation, and $\|$ is the concatenation of two binary strings.

### 2.2   A Brief Description of LBlock

The first introduction of the LBlock proposal was described by Wu and Zhang at ACNS 2011 [14]. In [15], some literal flaws of the initial proposal were fixed. Here we briefly recall the illustration of LBlock. The i-th round of the LBlock is shown in the left of Fig. 1, and the F function is shown in the right of Fig. 1. The block length of LBlock is 64-bit, and the key length is 80-bit. Where $V_i = V_{i,l} \| V_{i,r}$ is the input of round i. The round function F first computes $V_{i,l} \oplus subkey_i$, then applies eight different 4-bit S-boxes. The round function F finally applies a permutation P, which exchanges the places of the eight nibbles.

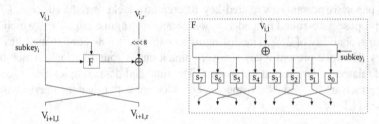

**Fig. 1.** Left of the figure is the i-th round of LBlock and right of the figure is the $F$ function

The key schedule stores an 80-bit master key $K$ in key register, which is denoted by $K = k_{79}k_{78}k_{77}k_{76} \cdots \cdots k_1 k_0$. It repeats the following operations for $i = 1$ to 32:

1. Output the leftmost 32 bits of current register $K$ as $subkey_i$.
2. $K \lll 29$
3. $[k_{79}k_{78}k_{77}k_{76}] = s_9[k_{79}k_{78}k_{77}k_{76}]$,  $[k_{75}k_{74}k_{73}k_{72}] = s_8[k_{75}k_{74}k_{73}k_{72}]$
4. $[k_{50}k_{49}k_{48}k_{47}k_{46}] = [k_{50}k_{49}k_{48}k_{47}k_{46}] \oplus [i]_2$

where $s_8$ and $s_9$ are two 4-bits S-boxes and $[i]_2$ is a binary counter.

### 2.3   The Related-Key Boomerang Attack

The related-key attack was first introduced by Biham in [1]. The attack allows adversary to encrypt plaintexts and decrypt ciphertexts under multiple secret keys, but the relation between the secret keys is known to (or even chosen by) the adversary. The boomerang attack was introduced by Wagner in [13]. By extending the boomerang attack in the

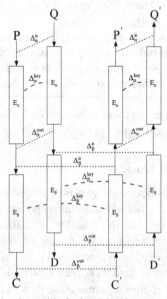

**Fig. 2.** A schematic of related-key boomerang attack

related-key model [2], Biham *et al.* proposed the related-key boomerang attack. As shown in Fig. 2, the related-key boomerang attack views a cipher $E$ as a decomposition into two sub-ciphers, such that $E = E_\alpha \circ E_\beta$. In each of two sub-ciphers, there exists a high probability related-key differential for constructing a boomerang attack. Based on the boomerang technique, algorithms can be built to distinguishing a "weak" block cipher from an ideal cipher. The examples of boomerang distinguishing attacks can be found in [3,8].

If the probability of the $E_\alpha$ differential $(\Delta_\alpha^{in}, \Delta_\alpha^{out}, \Delta_\alpha^{key})$ is $p$ and the probability of the $E_\beta$ differential $(\Delta_\beta^{in}, \Delta_\beta^{out}, \Delta_\beta^{key})$ is $q$, it was proven that the probability of the corresponding related-key boomerang attack is close to $(p \cdot q)^2$.

## 3    Related-Key Boomerang Attack on 16-Round LBlock

In [9], Minier and Naya-Plasencia found that ones are able to construct subkey differences with a very low general weight. Thus, here we consider a related-key boomerang distinguisher, which exploits the weakness of key scheduling.

Let $E$ denote the 16 rounds of LBlock and $E_\alpha$ denote the first eight rounds (1 to 8) of $E$. $E_\beta$ is viewed as the sub-cipher of the following 8 rounds (9 to 16). In this section, we first introduce the subkey differences that are used in our boomerang attack. Then we present an 8-round related-key characteristic of $E_\alpha$ and $E_\beta$, separately. Finally, we propose the related-key boomerang distinguishing attack on 16-round LBlock.

### 3.1    The Subkey Differences

The following differences $\Delta_\alpha^{key}$ and $\Delta_\beta^{key}$ are selected for constructing the 8-round related-key differential of $E_\alpha$ and $E_\beta$, respectively.

$$\Delta_\alpha^{key} = 0x0000020000000000000000, \quad \Delta_\beta^{key} = 0x0000c000000000000000000$$

According to the key schedule of LBlock, the subkey differences of $E_\alpha$, which can be obtained from $\Delta_\alpha^{key}$, have probability 1. The subkey differences of $E_\alpha$ are given in the left of Table 2. According to the key schedule of LBlock, the equation $s_9(0x3) = 0x8$ in *subkey*$_7$ is satisfied with a probability of $2^{-2}$. Thus, the subkey differences of $E_\beta$, which are obtained from $\Delta_\beta^{key}$, have a probability of $2^{-2}$. The subkey differences of $E_\beta$ are given in the right of Table 2.

**Table 2.** The subkey differentials for the related-key boomerang distinguishing attack

| $\Delta_\alpha^{key}$ :00000200000000000000 | $\Delta_\beta^{key}$ :0000c0000000000000000 | |
|---|---|---|
| $\Delta$ *subkey*$_1$ : 0 0 0 0 0 2 0 0 | $\Delta$ *subkey*$_1$ : 0 0 0 0 c 0 0 0 | $\Delta$ *subkey*$_9$ : 0 0 0 0 0 2 0 0 |
| $\Delta$ *subkey*$_2$ : 0 0 0 0 0 0 0 0 | $\Delta$ *subkey*$_2$ : 0 0 0 0 0 0 0 0 | $\Delta$ *subkey*$_{10}$ : 0 0 0 0 0 0 0 0 |
| $\Delta$ *subkey*$_3$ : 0 0 0 0 0 0 0 0 | $\Delta$ *subkey*$_3$ : 0 0 0 0 0 0 0 0 | $\Delta$ *subkey*$_{11}$ : 0 0 0 0 0 0 0 0 |
| $\Delta$ *subkey*$_4$ : 0 0 0 1 0 0 0 0 | $\Delta$ *subkey*$_4$ : 0 0 6 0 0 0 0 0 | $\Delta$ *subkey*$_{12}$ : 0 0 0 1 0 0 0 0 |
| $\Delta$ *subkey*$_5$ : 0 0 0 0 0 0 0 0 | $\Delta$ *subkey*$_5$ : 0 0 0 0 0 0 0 0 | $\Delta$ *subkey*$_{13}$ : 0 0 0 0 0 0 0 0 |
| $\Delta$ *subkey*$_6$ : 0 0 0 0 0 0 0 0 | $\Delta$ *subkey*$_6$ : 0 0 0 0 0 0 0 1 | $\Delta$ *subkey*$_{14}$ : 0 0 0 0 0 0 0 0 |
| $\Delta$ *subkey*$_7$ : 0 0 8 0 0 0 0 0 | $\Delta$ *subkey*$_7$ : 8 0 0 0 0 0 0 0 | $\Delta$ *subkey*$_{15}$ : 0 0 8 0 0 0 0 0 |
| $\Delta$ *subkey*$_8$ : 0 0 0 0 0 0 0 0 | $\Delta$ *subkey*$_8$ : 0 0 0 0 0 0 0 0 | $\Delta$ *subkey*$_{16}$ : 0 0 0 0 0 0 0 0 |

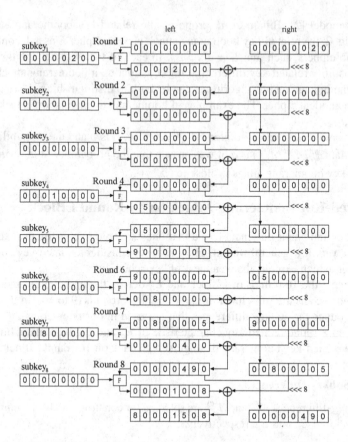

**Fig. 3.** An 8-round related-key characteristic of $E_\alpha$. The 8-round related-key characteristic of $E_\beta$ is the same as $E_\alpha$. In other words, the difference $\Delta subkey_i$ of $E_\beta$ is equal to the difference $\Delta subkey_{i-8}$ of $E_\alpha$ and the difference of round i of $E_\beta$ is equal to the difference of round i-8 of $E_\alpha$, for $9 \le i \le 16$.

## 3.2  The 16-Round Related-Key Boomerang Distinguisher

The 8-round related-key characteristic of $E_\alpha$ shown in Fig. 3 works for the subkey differences of $\Delta_\alpha^{key}$. It contains seven active S-boxes, and the probability of the seven active S-boxes are equal to $2^{-2}$. Therefore the 8-round related-key characteristic of $E_\alpha$ has probability $2^{-14}$.

We choose $\Delta_\beta^{key}$ to ensure the $\Delta subkey_i$ of $\Delta_\beta^{key}$ equals the $\Delta subkey_{i-8}$ of $\Delta_\beta^{key}$, for $9 \le i \le 16$. Thus, we can reuse the 8-round related-key characteristic of $E_\alpha$ as the related-key characteristic of $E_\beta$. As a result, we obtain an 8-round related-key characteristic of $E_\beta$, which has a probability of $2^{-16}$.

Based on the related-key differential of $E_\alpha$ and $E_\beta$, the corresponding differences in Fig. 2 are derived as follows.

$$\Delta_\alpha^{in} = 0x0000000000000020 \quad \Delta_\alpha^{out} = 0x8000150800000490$$
$$\Delta_\beta^{in} = 0x0000000000000020 \quad \Delta_\beta^{out} = 0x8000150800000490$$

The related-key differential of $E_\alpha$ ($\Delta_\alpha^{in}, \Delta_\alpha^{out}, \Delta_\alpha^{key}$) has a probability of $2^{-14}$, and the one of $E_\beta$ ($\Delta_\beta^{in}, \Delta_\beta^{out}, \Delta_\beta^{key}$) has a probability of $2^{-16}$. Thus, the related-key boomerang distinguisher of 16-round LBlock succeeds with a probability of $(2^{-14} \times 2^{-16})^2 = 2^{-60}$. As a result, the boomerang distinguisher works as follows.

1. Chooses a random message $P$ and calculates $Q = P \oplus \Delta_\alpha^{in}$.
2. Encrypts $P$ and $Q$, obtain $C = E_k(P)$ and $D = E_{k \oplus \Delta_\alpha^{key}}(Q)$.
3. Selects $C' = C \oplus \Delta_\beta^{out}$ and $D' = D \oplus \Delta_\beta^{out}$.
4. Decrypts $C'$ and $D'$, obtains $P' = E_{k \oplus \Delta_\beta^{key}}^{-1}(C')$ and $Q' = E_{k \oplus \Delta_\alpha^{key} \oplus \Delta_\beta^{key}}^{-1}(D')$.
5. Checks if $P' \oplus Q' = \Delta_\alpha^{in}$.

For ideal ciphers with 64-bit block size, the probability of the final equation $P' \oplus Q' = \Delta_\alpha^{in}$ must be $2^{-64}$. On the other hand, the final equation is expected to hold with a probability of $(2^{-14} \times 2^{-16})^2 = 2^{-60}$ in the related-key boomerang distinguisher, which is apparently lower than exhaustive search. Therefore, an adversary can distinguish 16-round LBlock and an ideal cipher by executing the above boomerang attack.

## 4   Related-Key Differential Attack on 22-Round LBlock

In [9], a related-key impossible attack, which exploits the weakness of the key schedule, was presented on reduced-round LBlock. Since the key schedule of LBlock does not provide a fast diffusion [9], it is possible to construct a 16-round related-key truncated differential. In this section, a new key-recovery attack on 22-round is proposed by exploiting a 16-round related-key truncated differential.

### 4.1   The Subkey Differences

The difference $\Delta K = 0x0000001000000000000000$ is selected for constructing the 16-round related-key truncated differential, which will be described in the next subsection. According to the key schedule, we obtain a subkey differences in the first 22 round from $\Delta K$, which is shown in Table 3. Since the equation $s_8(0x2) = 0x2$ in $subkey_{10}$ is satisfied with probability $2^{-2}$, the subkey differences has probability $2^{-2}$ as well.

**Table 3.** The subkey differences in the first 22 round of LBlock

| $\Delta_K$ : 0000001000000000000000 | | |
|---|---|---|
| $\Delta subkey_1$ : 0 0 0 0 0 0 1 0 | $\Delta subkey_8$ : 0 0 0 0 0 0 0 0 | $\Delta subkey_{15}$ : 0 0 0 0 0 4 0 0 |
| $\Delta subkey_2$ : 0 0 0 0 0 0 0 0 | $\Delta subkey_9$ : 0 0 0 0 0 0 0 0 | $\Delta subkey_{16}$ : 0 0 0 0 0 0 0 0 |
| $\Delta subkey_3$ : 0 0 0 0 0 0 0 0 | $\Delta subkey_{10}$ : 0 2 0 0 0 0 0 0 | $\Delta subkey_{17}$ : 0 0 0 0 0 0 0 0 |
| $\Delta subkey_4$ : 0 0 0 0 0 8 0 0 | $\Delta subkey_{11}$ : 0 0 0 0 0 0 0 0 | $\Delta subkey_{18}$ : 0 0 0 2 0 0 0 0 |
| $\Delta subkey_5$ : 0 0 0 0 0 0 0 0 | $\Delta subkey_{12}$ : 0 0 0 0 0 0 0 8 | $\Delta subkey_{19}$ : 0 0 0 0 0 0 0 0 |
| $\Delta subkey_6$ : 0 0 0 0 0 0 0 0 | $\Delta subkey_{13}$ : 0 0 0 0 0 0 0 0 | $\Delta subkey_{20}$ : 0 0 0 0 0 0 0 0 |
| $\Delta subkey_7$ : 0 0 0 4 0 0 0 0 | $\Delta subkey_{14}$ : 0 0 0 0 0 0 0 0 | $\Delta subkey_{21}$ : 0 X 0 0 0 0 0 0 |
| | | $\Delta subkey_{22}$ : 0 0 0 0 0 0 0 0 |

## 4.2    The 16-Round Related-Key Truncated Differential

The detail of the 16-round related-key truncated differential is depicted in Fig. 4, which is used for our 22-round key recovery attack. In Fig. 4, numeral represents a nibble with this specific difference. Such as, a numeral 1 in the $subkey_1$ denotes that this nibble has difference 1. Zero-difference nibbles are represented by 0. The active nibbles $(\overline{X}, \underline{X}, \widehat{4})$ represent three different conditions on their differences, which are described as follows.

- One active nibble $\overline{X}$ xor the other active nibble $\overline{X}$ produces difference 0 with probability $1/15 \approx 2^{-3.9}$. We call it *vanished condition*.
- One active nibble $\underline{X}$ xor the other active nibble $\underline{X}$ produces a non-zero difference with probability $14/15 \approx 2^{-0.1}$. We call it *unvanished condition*.
- A specific difference 4 marked by $\widehat{4}$ in Fig. 4 is a input difference of S-box. The equation $s_2(4) = 1$ satisfies with probability $2^{-2}$. We call it *S-box condition*.

The 16-round related-key truncated differential in Fig. 4 has 14 vanished conditions, 1 S-box condition and 3 unvanished conditions. Based on the probabilities of the subkey differences, the 16-round related-key truncated differential has a probability of about $((1/15)^{14} \times 2^{-2} \times (14/15)^3 \times 2^{-2}) > 2^{-59}$.

## 4.3    The Key Recovery Attack for 22 Rounds

Combing our 16-round related-key truncated differential, we can mount a key recovery attack for 22 rounds. Our key recovery attack is based on the following observation. In the round function of LBlock, every 4-bit nibble in the underlying subkey only affects itself. In key-recovery procedure, one can guess one nibble of subkey each time, and then partially decrypts the corresponding nibble of ciphertext pairs. By checking the difference of the decrypted nibble, we rule out some ciphertext pairs. Therefore, the time complexity of the key recovery attack can be reduced.

Our key recovery attack is derived from the related-key truncated differential shown in Fig. 5. The key-recovery differential requests one vanished and two unvanished conditions. Thus a difference $\Delta_1 = (000X0000, 00000000)$ from round 17 to round 22 verifies the key-recovery differential with a probability of $(1/15) \times (14/15)^2 \approx 2^{-4.1}$. Since the 16-round related-key truncated differential has a probability of $2^{-59}$. After the 22-th round, the output difference is $\Delta_2 = (V_{22,l}, V_{22,r}) = (XXXXXXX0, XX00XX0X)$ with a probability $2^{-59} \times 2^{-4.1} = 2^{-63.1}$. Therefore, there exist one pair of plaintexts verifies the 16-round related-key truncated differential and the key-recovery differential, when $2^{63.1}$ pairs of plaintexts with difference $\Delta_3 = (00000010, 00000004)$ are encrypted.

Without loss of generality, a pair satisfies the truncated difference $\Delta_2$ with a probability of about $(15/16)^{12} \times (1/16)^4 \approx 2^{-17.1}$. Therefore, there exist about $2^{46}$ pairs satisfy the truncated difference $\Delta_2$ after 22 rounds, when $2^{63.1}$ pairs of plaintexts with difference $\Delta_3$ are encrypted. One pair of 22-round ciphertexts, which has a difference $\Delta_2$, satisfies the key-recovery differential whit a probability of $((1/15)^{12} \times (14/15)^2 \approx 2^{-47}$, when decrypted from round 22 to round 17. If the subkeys are wrong, there exist one pair of 22-round ciphertexts satisfies the key-recovery differential with a probability of $2^{-1}$, when the $2^{46}$ pairs of 22-round ciphertexts are decrypted from round 22 to round 17.

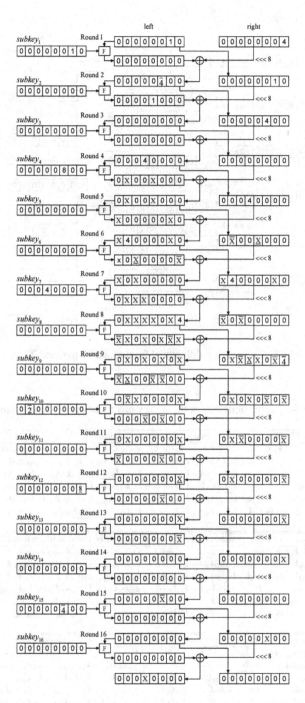

**Fig. 4.** A 16-round truncated differential path for the key recovery attack. The active nibbles ($\overline{X}$, $\underline{X}$, 4) represent vanished, unvanished and S-box conditions on their differences, respectively.

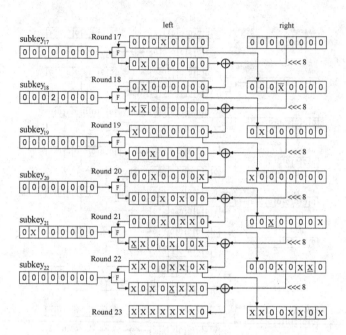

**Fig. 5.** A related-key differential from round 17 to round 22

**Table 4.** The relations among the subkey bits in the partial decryptions

| The underline bits of $subkey_i$ can be obtained from the underline bits of $subkey_{22}$, where $17 \leq i \leq 21$ |
|---|
| $subkey_{17}$ $k_{15}k_{14}k_{13}k_{12}$ $k_{11}k_{10}k_9k_8$ $k_7k_6k_5k_4$ $k_3\underline{k_2}k_1\underline{k_0}$ $k_{79}k_{78}k_{77}k_{76}$ $k_{75}k_{74}k_{73}k_{72}$ $k_{71}k_{70}k_{69}k_{68}$ $k_{67}k_{66}k_{65}k_{64}$ |
| $subkey_{18}$ $k_{66}k_{65}k_{64}k_{63}$ $k_{62}k_{61}k_{60}k_{59}$ $k_{58}k_{57}k_{56}k_{55}$ $k_{54}k_{53}k_{52}k_{51}$ $k_{50}k_{49}k_{48}k_{47}$ $k_{46}k_{45}k_{44}k_{43}$ $k_{42}k_{41}k_{40}k_{39}$ $k_{38}k_{37}k_{36}k_{35}$ |
| $subkey_{19}$ $k_{37}k_{36}k_{35}k_{34}$ $k_{33}k_{32}k_{31}k_{30}$ $k_{29}k_{28}k_{27}k_{26}$ $k_{25}k_{24}k_{23}k_{22}$ $k_{21}k_{20}k_{19}k_{18}$ $k_{17}k_{16}k_{15}k_{14}$ $\underline{k_{13}}\underline{k_{12}}k_{11}k_{10}$ $k_9k_8k_7k_6$ |
| $subkey_{20}$ $k_8k_7k_6k_5$ $k_4k_3k_2k_1$ $\underline{k_0}k_{79}k_{78}k_{77}$ $k_{76}k_{75}k_{74}k_{73}$ $k_{72}k_{71}k_{70}k_{69}$ $k_{68}k_{67}k_{66}k_{65}$ $k_{64}k_{63}k_{62}k_{61}$ $k_{60}k_{59}k_{58}k_{57}$ |
| $subkey_{21}$ $k_{59}k_{58}k_{57}k_{56}$ $k_{55}k_{54}k_{53}k_{52}$ $k_{51}k_{50}k_{49}k_{48}$ $k_{47}k_{46}k_{45}k_{44}$ $k_{43}k_{42}k_{41}k_{40}$ $k_{39}k_{38}k_{37}k_{36}$ $k_{35}k_{34}k_{33}k_{32}$ $k_{31}k_{30}k_{29}k_{28}$ |
| $subkey_{22}$ $k_{30}k_{29}\underline{k_{28}}k_{27}$ $k_{26}k_{25}k_{24}k_{23}$ $k_{22}k_{21}k_{20}k_{19}$ $k_{18}k_{17}k_{16}k_{15}$ $k_{14}\underline{k_{13}}\underline{k_{12}}\underline{k_{11}}$ $\underline{k_{10}}k_9k_8k_7$ $k_6k_5k_4k_3$ $\underline{k_2}k_1\underline{k_0}\underline{k_{79}}$ |

| The underline bits of $subkey_i$ can be obtained from the underline bits of $subkey_{21}$, where $17 \leq i \leq 20$ |
|---|
| $subkey_{17}$ $k_{15}k_{14}k_{13}k_{12}$ $k_{11}k_{10}k_9k_8$ $k_7k_6k_5k_4$ $k_3k_2k_1k_0$ $k_{79}k_{78}k_{77}k_{76}$ $k_{75}k_{74}k_{73}k_{72}$ $k_{71}k_{70}k_{69}k_{68}$ $k_{67}k_{66}k_{65}k_{64}$ |
| $subkey_{18}$ $k_{66}k_{65}k_{64}k_{63}$ $k_{62}k_{61}k_{60}k_{59}$ $k_{58}k_{57}k_{56}k_{55}$ $k_{54}k_{53}k_{52}k_{51}$ $k_{50}k_{49}k_{48}k_{47}$ $k_{46}k_{45}k_{44}k_{43}$ $k_{42}k_{41}k_{40}k_{39}$ $k_{38}k_{37}k_{36}k_{35}$ |
| $subkey_{19}$ $\underline{k_{37}}k_{36}\underline{k_{35}}\underline{k_{34}}$ $k_{33}k_{32}k_{31}k_{30}$ $k_{29}k_{28}k_{27}k_{26}$ $k_{25}k_{24}k_{23}k_{22}$ $k_{21}k_{20}k_{19}k_{18}$ $k_{17}k_{16}k_{15}k_{14}$ $k_{13}k_{12}k_{11}k_{10}$ $k_9k_8k_7k_6$ |
| $subkey_{20}$ $k_8k_7k_6k_5$ $k_4k_3k_2k_1$ $k_0k_{79}k_{78}k_{77}$ $k_{76}k_{75}k_{74}k_{73}$ $k_{72}k_{71}k_{70}k_{69}$ $k_{68}k_{67}k_{66}k_{65}$ $k_{64}k_{63}k_{62}k_{61}$ $k_{60}k_{59}k_{58}k_{57}$ |
| $subkey_{21}$ $k_{59}k_{58}k_{57}k_{56}$ $k_{55}k_{54}k_{53}k_{52}$ $k_{51}k_{50}k_{49}k_{48}$ $k_{47}k_{46}k_{45}k_{44}$ $k_{43}k_{42}k_{41}k_{40}$ $k_{39}k_{38}\underline{k_{37}}k_{36}$ $\underline{k_{35}}k_{34}k_{33}k_{32}$ $k_{31}k_{30}k_{29}k_{28}$ |
| $subkey_{22}$ $k_{30}k_{29}k_{28}k_{27}$ $k_{26}k_{25}k_{24}k_{23}$ $k_{22}k_{21}k_{20}k_{19}$ $k_{18}k_{17}k_{16}k_{15}$ $k_{14}k_{13}k_{12}k_{11}$ $k_{10}k_9k_8k_7$ $k_6k_5k_4k_3$ $k_2k_1k_0k_{79}$ |

| The underline bits of $subkey_i$ can be obtained from the underline bits of $subkey_{20}$, where $17 \leq i \leq 19$ |
|---|
| Round 17 $k_{15}k_{14}k_{13}k_{12}$ $k_{11}k_{10}k_9k_8$ $k_7k_6k_5k_4$ $k_3k_2k_1k_0$ $k_{79}k_{78}k_{77}k_{76}$ $k_{75}k_{74}k_{73}k_{72}$ $k_{71}k_{70}k_{69}k_{68}$ $k_{67}k_{66}k_{65}k_{64}$ |
| Round 18 $k_{66}k_{65}k_{64}k_{63}$ $k_{62}k_{61}\underline{k_{60}}k_{59}$ $k_{58}k_{57}k_{56}k_{55}$ $k_{54}k_{53}k_{52}k_{51}$ $k_{50}k_{49}k_{48}k_{47}$ $k_{46}k_{45}k_{44}k_{43}$ $k_{42}k_{41}k_{40}k_{39}$ $k_{38}k_{37}k_{36}k_{35}$ |
| Round 19 $k_{37}k_{36}k_{35}k_{34}$ $k_{33}k_{32}k_{31}\underline{k_{30}}$ $k_{29}k_{28}k_{27}k_{26}$ $k_{25}k_{24}k_{23}k_{22}$ $k_{21}k_{20}k_{19}k_{18}$ $k_{17}k_{16}k_{15}k_{14}$ $k_{13}k_{12}k_{11}k_{10}$ $k_9k_8k_7k_6$ |
| Round 20 $k_8k_7k_6k_5$ $k_4k_3k_2k_1$ $k_0k_{79}k_{78}k_{77}$ $k_{76}k_{75}k_{74}k_{73}$ $k_{72}k_{71}k_{70}k_{69}$ $k_{68}k_{67}k_{66}k_{65}$ $k_{64}k_{63}k_{62}k_{61}$ $\underline{k_{60}}k_{59}k_{58}k_{57}$ |
| Round 21 $k_{59}k_{58}k_{57}k_{56}$ $k_{55}k_{54}k_{53}k_{52}$ $k_{51}k_{50}k_{49}k_{48}$ $k_{47}k_{46}k_{45}k_{44}$ $k_{43}k_{42}k_{41}k_{40}$ $k_{39}k_{38}k_{37}k_{36}$ $k_{35}k_{34}k_{33}k_{32}$ $\underline{k_{31}}k_{30}k_{29}k_{28}$ |
| Round 22 $k_{30}k_{29}k_{28}k_{27}$ $k_{26}k_{25}k_{24}k_{23}$ $k_{22}k_{21}k_{20}k_{19}$ $k_{18}k_{17}k_{16}k_{15}$ $k_{14}k_{13}k_{12}k_{11}$ $k_{10}k_9k_8k_7$ $k_6k_5k_4k_3$ $k_2k_1k_0k_{79}$ |

If the subkeys are guessed correctly, there exist one pair of 22-round ciphertexts satisfies the key-recovery differential, when the $2^{46}$ pairs of 22-round ciphertexts are decrypted from round 22 to round 17.

In the procedure of our key recovery, the adversary can partially decrypt one nibble each time. For better understanding, the relations among the subkey bits in the partial decryptions are described in Table 4. The procedure of the attack is described as follows.

1. encrypt $2^{63.1}$ pairs of plaintexts with a difference of $\Delta_3$.
2. For the $2^{63.1}$ pairs of output, the adversary chooses the pairs that satisfy difference $\Delta_2$. Without loss of generality, one pair satisfies $\Delta_2$ with a probability of $(15/16)^{12} \times (1/16)^4 \approx 2^{-17.1}$. Thus, there remain $2^{46}$ pairs satisfy difference $\Delta_2$.
3. The partial decryption of round 22 involves $subkey_{22}^0$, $subkey_{22}^2$, $subkey_{22}^3$, $subkey_{22}^4$, $subkey_{22}^5$, $subkey_{22}^6$, $subkey_{22}^7$.
   (a) For every guess of $subkey_{22}^0$, the adversary partially decrypts the 2-th nibble of $V_{23,l}$ of the $2^{46}$ pairs of 22-round ciphertexts and verifies if the difference of the decrypted nibbles equal to zero. Since this verification has one vanished condition, there remain $2^{46} \times 2^{-3.9} = 2^{42.1}$ pairs.
   (b) In similar, the partial decryption of the 1,5,7-th nibble of $V_{23,l}$ require three vanished condition. Consequently, there remain $2^{42.1} \times 2^{-3.9 \times 3} = 2^{30.4}$ pairs.
   (c) For every guess of 12 bits ($subkey_{22}^2$, $subkey_{22}^4$, $subkey_{22}^5$), the adversary partially decrypts the 3,4,6-th nibbles of $V_{23,l}$ of the $2^{30.4}$ pairs and verify whether the differences of the decrypted nibbles not equal to zero. Since this verification has one unvanished condition, there remain $2^{30.4} \times 2^{-0.1} = 2^{30.3}$ pairs.
   After the partial decryption of round 22, there remain about $2^{30.3}$ pairs of 21-round ciphertexts, which satisfy $(\Delta V_{22,l}, \Delta V_{22,r}) = (XX00XX0X\ 000X00XX0)$.
4. The partial decryption of round 21 involves $subkey_{21}^0$, $subkey_{21}^1$, $subkey_{21}^2$, $subkey_{21}^4$, $subkey_{21}^6$. As shown in Table 4, the three subkey bits ($subkey_{21}^{0,0}$, $subkey_{21}^{0,1}$, $subkey_{21}^{0,2}$) can be obtained from $subkey_{22}^7$. Thus, the adversary needs to guess 17 bits in $subkey_{21}$. Similar to the decryption of round 22, the decryption of round 21 partially decrypt the 0,3,6-th nibbles of $V_{22,l}$. It requires three vanished condition. Then the adversary partially decrypts other nibbles in the decryption of round 21. Since this step has three vanished conditions and one unvanished condition, there remain about $2^{30.3} \times 2^{-11.8} = 2^{18.5}$ pairs of 20-round outputs after this verification, which satisfy $(\Delta V_{21,l}, \Delta V_{21,r}) = (000X0XX0\ 00X0000X)$.
5. The partial decryption of round 20 involves $subkey_{20}^0$, $subkey_{20}^3$, $subkey_{20}^5$. As shown in Table 4, the two subkey bits ($subkey_{20}^{5,3}$, $subkey_{20}^{5,2}$) can be obtained from $subkey_{22}^{0,1}$, $subkey_{22}^{0,0}$. Thus, the adversary needs to guess 10 bits in $subkey_{20}$. Similar to the decryption of round 22, the adversary partially decrypts the 2,4-th nibble of $V_{21,l}$. It requires two vanished condition, and then the decryption of round 20 partially decrypts the 1-th nibble of $V_{21,l}$. Since this step has two vanished conditions, there remain $2^{18.5} \times (2^{-3.9})^2 = 2^{10.7}$ pairs of 19-round outputs after this verification, which satisfy $(\Delta V_{20,l}, \Delta V_{20,r}) = (00X0000X\ X0000000)$.
6. The partial decryption of round 19 involves $subkey_{19}^1$ and $subkey_{19}^7$. As shown in Table 4, $subkey_{19}^1$ can be obtained from ($subkey_{22}^{3,2}$, $subkey_{22}^{3,1}$, $subkey_{22}^{3,0}$, $subkey_{22}^{2,3}$) and $subkey_{19}^7$ can be obtained from ($subkey_{21}^{2,1}$, $subkey_{21}^{2,0}$, $subkey_{21}^{1,3}$, $subkey_{21}^{1,2}$) directly. Thus, no subkey nibbles need to be guessed.

After the partial decryption of round 19, the adversary verifies if the pairs of 18-round outputs satisfy $(\Delta V_{19,l}, \Delta V_{19,r}) = (X0000000, 0X000000)$. Since this step requires one vanished conditions, there remain $2^{10.7} \times 2^{-3.9} = 2^{6.8}$ pairs of 18-round outputs after this verification.

7. The partial decryption of round 18 involves $subkey_{18}^4$ and $subkey_{18}^6$. As shown in Table 4, $subkey_{18}^{6,1}$ can be obtained from $subkey_{20}^{0,3}$ and $subkey_{18}^{6,0}$ can be obtained from $subkey_{20}^{0,2}$ directly. Thus, the adversary needs to guess 6 bits of $subkey_{18}$.

Similar to the decryption of round 22, the decryption of round 18 partially decrypt the 7-th nibble of $V_{19,l}$. It requires one vanished condition and the decryption of round 18 partially decrypt the 6-th nibble of $V_{19,l}$. Since this step requires one vanished conditions, there remain $2^{6.8} \times 2^{-3.9} = 2^{2.9}$ pairs of 17-round outputs after this verification, which satisfy $(\Delta V_{18,l}, \Delta V_{18,r}) = (0X000000, 000X0000)$.

8. the partial decryption of round 17 involves $subkey_{17}^4$. As shown in Table 4, $(subkey_{17}^{4,2}, subkey_{17}^{4,1}$ and $subkey_{17}^{4,0})$ can be obtained from $(subkey_{22}^{0,3}, subkey_{22}^{0,2}, subkey_{22}^{0,1})$. Thus, the adversary needs to guess 1 bit of $subkey_{17}$.

For every guess of the 1-bit subkey partially decrypt round 17 to verify if the pairs of 16-round outputs satisfy $\Delta_1 = (\Delta V_{17,l}, \Delta V_{17,r}) = (000X0000, 00000000)$. Since this step has one vanished conditions, there exists one pair of 16-round outputs that satisfies difference $\Delta_1$ with a probability of $2^{2.9} \times 2^{-3.9} = 2^{-1}$.

9. After the decryption of round 17, if there exists one pairs of 16-round outputs satisfy $\Delta_1$, the adversary knows he has successfully recovered 62 subkey bits. The left 18 bits of the master key can be recovered by exhaustive searches.

Considering the equation of $s_8(0x2) = 0x2$ in $subkey_{10}$ has been satisfied, the adversary just needs to guess $2^2$ pairs of $subkey_{18}^4$. According to the key schedule of LBlock, the $2^2$ pairs of $subkey_{18}^4$ are obtained from the equation of $s_8(0x2) = 0x2$. In similar, the adversary only needs to guess $2^3$ pairs of $subkey_{21}^6$.

The time complexity of the above partial decryption is about $2^{67}$. Therefore, the 80-bit master key can be recovered with the time complexity of about $2^{67} + 2^{64} + 2^{18} \approx 2^{67}$. Since $2^{63.1}$ pairs of ciphertexts need to be stored during the attack, the data complexity of our key recovery attack is about $2^{64.1}$. Although the whole codebook is $2^{64}$ for a 64-bit cipher, the related-key pairs allow the attacker access $2 * 2^{64}$ pairs of plaintext and ciphertext. After the partial decryption of round 17, there exists one pair with a probability of $2^{-1}$. Thus the success probability of our key recovery attack is $2^{-1}$.

## 5   Conclusions

In this paper, we have proposed new related-key differential attacks on the reduced-round LBlock. First we constructed a boomerang distinguishing attack on 16-round LBlock, which exploits the slow diffusion of the key schedule. Then we presented a key recovery attack on 22-round LBlock by using the 16-round related-key truncated differential. Compares to the known results, the time and data complexities of our key recovery attack are both reduced. Although our attacks do not threaten the practical security of LBlock, future work may seek to extend the existing attacks to more rounds LBlock based on our related-key differentials.

# References

1. Biham, E.: New types of cryptanalytic attacks using related keys. J. Cryptology 7(4), 229–246 (1994)
2. Biham, E., Dunkelman, O., Keller, N.: Related-Key Boomerang and Rectangle Attacks. In: Cramer, R. (ed.) EUROCRYPT 2005. LNCS, vol. 3494, pp. 507–525. Springer, Heidelberg (2005)
3. Biryukov, A., Nikolic, I., Roy, A.: Boomerang Attacks on BLAKE-32. In: Joux, A. (ed.) FSE 2011. LNCS, vol. 6733, pp. 218–237. Springer, Heidelberg (2011)
4. Bogdanov, A., Knudsen, L.R., Leander, G., Paar, C., Poschmann, A., Robshaw, M.J.B., Seurin, Y., Vikkelsoe, C.: PRESENT: An Ultra-Lightweight Block Cipher. In: Paillier, P., Verbauwhede, I. (eds.) CHES 2007. LNCS, vol. 4727, pp. 450–466. Springer, Heidelberg (2007)
5. De Cannière, C., Dunkelman, O., Knežević, M.: KATAN and KTANTAN — A Family of Small and Efficient Hardware-Oriented Block Ciphers. In: Clavier, C., Gaj, K. (eds.) CHES 2009. LNCS, vol. 5747, pp. 272–288. Springer, Heidelberg (2009)
6. Gong, Z., Nikova, S., Law, Y.W.: KLEIN: A New Family of Lightweight Block Ciphers. In: Juels, A., Paar, C. (eds.) RFIDSec 2011. LNCS, vol. 7055, pp. 1–18. Springer, Heidelberg (2012)
7. Guo, J., Peyrin, T., Poschmann, A., Robshaw, M.J.B.: The led block cipher. In: Preneel and Takagi [10], pp. 326–341
8. Lamberger, M., Mendel, F.: Higher-order differential attack on reduced sha-256. IACR Cryptology ePrint Archive, 37 (2011)
9. Minier, M., Naya-Plasencia, M.: A related key impossible differential attack against 22 rounds of the lightweight block cipher lblock. Inf. Process. Lett. 112(16), 624–629 (2012)
10. Preneel, B., Takagi, T. (eds.): CHES 2011. LNCS, vol. 6917, pp. 2011–2013. Springer, Heidelberg (2011)
11. Shibutani, K., Isobe, T., Hiwatari, H., Mitsuda, A., Akishita, T., Shirai, T.: Piccolo: An ultra-lightweight blockcipher. In: Preneel and Takagi [10], pp. 342–357
12. Suzaki, S.M.T., Minematsu, K., Kobayashi, E.: Twine: A lightweight, versatile block cipher. In: ECRYPT Workshop on Lightweight Cryptography (2011)
13. Wagner, D.: The Boomerang Attack. In: Knudsen, L.R. (ed.) FSE 1999. LNCS, vol. 1636, pp. 156–170. Springer, Heidelberg (1999)
14. Wu, W., Zhang, L.: LBlock: A Lightweight Block Cipher. In: Lopez, J., Tsudik, G. (eds.) ACNS 2011. LNCS, vol. 6715, pp. 327–344. Springer, Heidelberg (2011)
15. Wu, W., Zhang, L.: Lblock: A lightweight block cipher *. Cryptology ePrint Archive, Report 2011/345 (2011), http://eprint.iacr.org

# Countermeasures on Application Level Low-Rate Denial-of-Service Attack*

Yajuan Tang

Department of Electronic Engineering, Shantou University
yjtang@stu.edu.cn

**Abstract.** Low-Rate Denial-of-Service (LRDoS) attack is an emerging
threat to Internet because it can evade detection and defense schemes for
flooding based attacks. LRDoS attack at application level is particularly
difficult to counteract as it mimics legitimate client. Although there are
several approaches proposed to mitigate LRDoS attacks, they are limited
to particular protocols, target systems, or attack patterns that they are
not able to detect this threat at application level. In this paper, we propose a nonparametric detection algorithm and a hybrid defense system to
mitigate LRDoS attacks at application level. Our extensive experiments
have confirmed the effectiveness of the detection and defense system.

## 1 Introduction

Denial-of-Service (DoS) attack is one of the most serious security concerns in
the Internet as they prevent legitimate users from using Internet services. DoS
attack is also known as flooding attack due to the fact that it sends out high
rate requests or packets to consume resources. However, high rate traffic is statistically abnormal to legitimate traffic that it is easy to be detected [1]. On the
contrary, Low-Rate Denial-of-Service (LRDoS) attack can evade detection and
defense methods designed for flooding-based attacks, therefore attracts more and
more interests in literature.

LRDoS attack is typically illustrated by ON/OFF traffic pattern because
it sends out intermittent pulses of malicious packets or requests to a target
[2–5]. It was originally designed to attack TCP mechanism [2,3,5] and later was
generalized to application level by exploiting vulnerability of feedback control
based Internet services [4].

In this paper, we focus on application level LRDoS attacks because they make
detection and defense more difficult than network level attacks do. The difficulty
lies in two major reasons. First, application level LRDoS attacks send requests
following the same characteristic of legitimate clients such that it is difficult to
distinguish attack requests from legitimate requests. Second, there is a variety of
LRDoS attacks that exploit application specific knowledge to launch an attack,

---

* This work is supported by the National Natural Science Foundation of China
(60903185) and Industry-Universities-Research Institutes Collaboration Foundation
of Guangdong (cgzhzd0717).

T.W. Chim and T.H. Yuen (Eds.): ICICS 2012, LNCS 7618, pp. 70–80, 2012.

which requires a general countermeasure approach without knowing particular vulnerability the attack exploits. For example, approaches [2, 5–13] have been proposed to detect and defend LRDoS attacks. However, they are limited either to particular protocols and target victim or to specific attack patterns that are not able to protect Internet services. [2, 5, 6, 12] rely on specific features of TCP; [7,10] assume the attack is periodic; [11] is designed for the specific LRDoS attack proposed in [14] that needs to estimate victim's service time.

Motivated by these aspects, we provide a detection algorithm and a defense system to mitigate LRDoS attacks at application level. Our detection algorithm has two distinct features: (1) unlike most existing detection mechanisms, it can detect both periodic and non-periodic LRDoS attacks; (2) it exploits the feature directly affected by LRDoS attacks and uses nonparametric sequential test. To do this, it adopts a nonparametric method to identify the anomalies in admission rate resulted from LRDoS attacks. Admission rate is a parameter that determines whether a request is accepted or not. It is widely used in Internet services for the provision of guaranteed QoS. More importantly, it relies on no protocols or applications which makes our algorithm general for detecting application layer LRDoS attacks. Simulation and testbed results show our detection algorithm can effectively discover LRDoS attacks in various attack scenarios. In the testbed experiments, the attack can be found just after the arrival of the first pulse.

We propose a defense algorithm to quickly restore service immediately after detecting an attack. Our defense algorithm is a combination of rate-based and queue-length based method. It proactively drops requests according to a dropping probability before requests reach the admission controller. By doing so, our defense system overcomes slow reaction time of admission controller and also helps the victim to achieve a utilization level close to the desired value. Our experiments show the defense system can quickly restore system performance as soon as an attack is detected.

The remainder of this paper is organized as follows. The next section reviews related works. The nonparametric approach is presented in Section 3, followed by an introduction for the defense system in Section 4. Section 5 details the LRDoS attack simulation and testbed results. Section 6 concludes this paper.

## 2   Related Works

Since an LRDoS attack has ON/OFF traffic pattern, it can evade the detection schemes targeting at flooding-based DoS attacks and therefore motivates the design of several new countermeasure approaches [2, 5–13]. However, these approaches cannot mitigate LRDoS attacks at application level because of two reasons. First, since all of these approaches aim at LRDoS attacks on TCP or particular systems (e.g., wireless network, P2P network, etc.), they rely on features specific to TCP or those systems. For example, Luo et al. proposed a detection scheme that exploits anomalies in incoming TCP data traffic and outgoing TCP ACK traffic [5]. Shevtekar et al. regarded a TCP flow as malicious if its period is equal to the fixed minimal retransmission timeout (RTO) and its burst length is no less than other connections' RTTs [9]. Maciá-Fernández et al. [11] established the defense goal as reducing service queue positions seized by the attacker and discussed some possible defense techniques. To detect distributed LRDoS attacks, Xiang et al. [13] used generalized entropy and information distance to quantify the anomalies in packets. Their solution requires to control all routers in the network.

Second, the majority of previous work focuses on the Shrew attack [2] that has a fixed attack period equal to TCP's minimal RTO. For example, spectral-analysis approaches rely on the spectrum difference between Shrew attack flows and normal flows [7,8,10]. Sun et al. suggested using autocorrelation and dynamic time warping (DTW) to detect Shrew attacks, because its traffic bursts are the same and have fixed period [6]. However, LRDoS attacks are not necessarily periodic. Our detection method makes no assumption of periodic attacks that it is more general than these approaches.

Although some mechanisms have been proposed to detect application level DoS attacks, they could not effectively detect LRDoS attacks because their assumptions and detection features are usually not applicable to LRDoS attacks. For example, Ranjan et al. [15] assumed that inter-arrival time of requests decreases over time and requests also ask for specific resources that could overload the server. LRDoS attacks dispatch requests following the ON/OFF pattern and need not send specific requests that could lead to severer damage. Xie and Yu proposed a hidden semi-Markov model to represent normal user's browsing behaviors [16]. Although their method may notice a high request rate when an LRDoS attack sends request, it may miss the attack when the attacker dispatches nothing because it has difficulty in distinguishing high request rate caused by an LRDoS attack from a flash crowd. Moreover, such parametric method depends on the accuracy of the model. Our detection scheme employs suitable feature and nonparametric method to uncover LRDoS attacks, thus it avoids the disadvantages of existing detection mechanisms.

## 3   Detecting LRDoS Attacks

We propose a new detection scheme to identify LRDoS attacks, which distinguishes itself from other detection mechanisms against LRDoS attacks in two aspects. First, it aims at both periodic and non-periodic LRDoS attacks while the majority of existing detection mechanisms focuses on periodic LRDoS attacks. Second, for the sake of effectiveness and efficiency, it exploits the feature directly affected by LRDoS attacks and uses nonparametric sequential test. More precisely, our scheme employs admission rate for the detection, because an LRDoS attack intends to force the victim server to drop normal requests by throttling its admission rate [17]. Admission rate can detect both periodic and non-periodic LRDoS attacks because it does not rely on LRDoS attack's frequency character. Moreover, we adopt a nonparametric CUSUM algorithm [18] and light-weight detection algorithm to avoid unrealistic assumptions on arrival patterns of legitimate requests and to achieve online detection.

As the CUSUM method assumes that the mean value of the variable changes from negative to positive when a change occurs, we define the detection measure as

$$Z(t) = d(t) - median(d_n) - \nu \times IQR(d_n), \tag{1}$$

where $d(t) = 1 - \alpha(t)$, $\alpha(t)$ is admission rate, $d_n$ is the training dataset obtained in the absence of LRDoS, and $\nu$ is a parameter adjusted by the user. To avoid noise in the training dataset, we adopt robust statistics [19] in the design of $Z(t)$. That is, we use median instead of mean and employ interquartile range (IQR) defined as the difference between the third and the first quartiles [19] to replace standard deviation.

Let $T^{det}$ be the detection time for $Z(t)$ when

$$y_{z(t)} > C_{cusum} = 0, \tag{2}$$

where $y_{z(t)}$ is the CUSUM value of $Z(t)$ and $C_{cusum}$ is the threshold of CUMSUM that is defined as the mean of sequence $d_n - median(d_n)$. The detection system reports the existence of an LRDoS attack when (2) holds.

To make it sequential, we update $y_{z(k)}$, $k \in \mathbb{Z}^+$ every time unit as

$$y_{z(k)} = \begin{cases} y_{z(k-1)} + Z(k) \ k \in \mathbb{Z}^+, \\ 0 \qquad\qquad k = 0. \end{cases} \tag{3}$$

Let $T^{att}$ be the start time of an LRDoS attack, and the detection delay $\tau^{delay}$ is

$$\tau^{delay} = T^{att} - T^{det}. \tag{4}$$

The averaged detection delay (ADD) and false alarm rate (FAR) are denoted as [20]

$$ADD(T^{det}) = E(T^{det} - T^{att}), \tag{5}$$

$$FAR(T^{det}) = \frac{1}{E_0 T^{det}}, \tag{6}$$

where $E(\cdot)$ is the expectation function and $E_0$ is the expectation of $y_{z(k)}$, $k \in \mathbb{Z}^+$, before the attack. As our target of detection is a sequence of pulses, we define averaged detection pulse (ADP) instead of ADD as the performance metric. ADP is defined as number of pulses before the detection alarm is raised. For example, suppose the attack sequence starts at $t = 0$ with $\tau = 1$ second. If the algorithm reports at $t = 3.2$ second that an attack is present, $ADP = 3$ as three pulses are passed before the alarm.

## 4    Defending against LRDoS Attacks

In this section we present a defense scheme. As the attack traffic exhibits ON/OFF pattern, we could drop packets adaptively according to the packet arrival rate. This can be done through a virtual queue [21] whose virtual capacity is updated by the change in the arrival rate. However, our defense mechanism not only needs to be sensitive to rate changes, but also needs to regulate the queue length to a target value such that the Internet service has a high utilization rate.

A queue-length based algorithm can achieve the goal of regulating traffic. For example, Queue Regulated Virtual Queue (QRVQ) scheme [22] updates the virtual capacity according to the deviation of the queue length from its target value. QRVQ is reported to be more robust under various traffic situations at the cost of slow adaptation to changes of arrival rate.

Recognizing the complementary strengths of rate-based and queue-based algorithms, we propose a hybrid algorithm for our defense system that maintains a *virtual target arrival rate*, denoted by $\lambda_v$, and *a virtual queue* that has a capacity of $C_v$ requests per second. $C_v$ and $\lambda_v$ are updated according to

$$\begin{cases} \dot{C}_v(t) = K_1(\lambda_v(t) - \lambda(t)), \\ \dot{\lambda}_v(t) = K_2(q^* - q(t)), \end{cases} \quad (7)$$

where $q(t)$ is the queue length, $q^*$ is the target queue length, $K_1$ and $K_2$ are constants, and $\lambda(t)$ is the arrival rate of the requests. Therefore, when $q(t) > q^*$, $\lambda_v$ is reduced. Consequently, $C_v$ also decreases, which results in rejecting more requests. The dropping probability is defined as

$$\pi(t) = (\lambda(t) - C_v(t))/\lambda(t). \quad (8)$$

This new algorithm has two advantages. First, it updates $C_v$ directly based on traffic rates, which allows for a fast response to traffic changes. Second, by maintaining a target queue length, the traffic rate is more predictable than rate-based one.

Our defense scheme is summarized in Algorithm 1.

---

**Algorithm 1.** Hybrid Algorithm Framework

---

**Input:** capacity of defense system $C$,
      arrival rate to the defense system $\lambda$,
      virtual capacity $C_v$,
      virtual queue $\lambda_v$.
**Output:** drop rate $\pi$
 1: **for** each arrived request **do**
 2:    $q(t) = q(t) - C \times \Delta t + \lambda(t)\Delta t$, update queue size;
 3:    $\pi = (\lambda(t) - C_v)/\lambda(t)$, update drop rate;
 4:    update $C_v$ and $\lambda_v$ according to (7);
 5:    drop packet in real queue according to $\pi$;
 6: **end for**

---

## 5    Evaluation

### 5.1    Target Victim

In this section we adopt a web server [4] as targeted victim whose model is given in Figure 1. Details of the server please refer to [4]. In the presence of attack, the server evolves through three different stages before returning to the steady state: saturation, recovery I, and recovery II. Figure 2(a) shows how the admission rate and the system utilization behave during these three stages. We have proven that according to various attack periods, the sequence of these stages forms three general cases as shown in Figure 2(b). Details please refer to [23]. In the following experiments, we will investigate the performance of our proposed scheme in these three cases. It is worth noting that examining this web server is just an example of our methodology that can be applied to investigate the effect of detection and defense system on other Internet services.

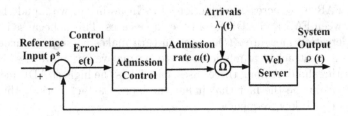

**Fig. 1.** Structure of the web server used in this section

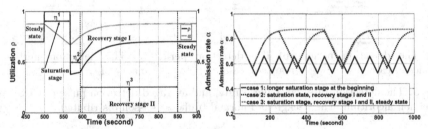

(a) The effect of one attack pulse at $t =$ (b) The effect of a sequence of attack
0 on admission rate and utilization.    pulses on admission rate.

**Fig. 2.** The effects of the attack on the admission rate. $\eta^1$, $\eta^2$ and $\eta^3$ are time elapsed between different stages, respectively.

## 5.2   Simulation Results

This subsection presents MATLAB simulation results to evaluate the performance of detection algorithm and defense system. We use the parameters from [4]: $A = 0.00267$, $B = 0.2$, $C = 0.024$, $D = -1.4$, $\ell = 75$, $K = 0.01$, $\mu = 90$, and $\rho^* = 0.7$. Details of these parameters please refer to [4].

When evaluating the performance of the detection algorithm, we generated three kinds of background traffic [24–26]: log-normal, pareto and poisson distributed traffic. The parameters of the distributions were set such that for each of the distribution the mean arrival rate was 100 requests per second. We also generated periodic and random attack sequences in the simulation. Due to paper limit, we only present poisson distributed background traffic and periodic attack as illustrations, the others can be found in the supplementary [27].

Figure 3 shows the detection rate (DET), FAR and ADP for case 1, 2, and 3. The background traffic was poisson distributed; $\nu$ varied from 0 to 2. We found for all the three cases, our detection algorithm is effective as $DET \geq 0.996$, $FAR \leq 0.024$ when $\nu = 1.8$. In case 3, the detection rate decreases as $\nu$ increases. This can be explained as follows. The period of case 3 is larger than the period of case 1 and 2, as shown in [28] and Figure 2(b). Therefore the oscillation of admission rate due to attack in case 3 has a low frequency than that in case 1 and 2. This low oscillation results in a low detection rate as increased $\nu$ means detection algorithm is tolerant to deviations. Also due to the fact that increased $\nu$ means normal oscillations of admission rate are likely to be classified as normal, FAR is a decreasing function of $\nu$. In addition, we found there is a tradeoff between FAR and ADP for all the three cases. This is because increased $\nu$ reduces detection measure $Z(t)$, which in turn makes it longer to accumulate the deviation of attacked admission rate to normal value before the deviation exceeds the threshold. Among three cases, case 3 has the highest ADP in general. This results from the the fact that it has the largest attack periods that yields an oscillation with low frequency.

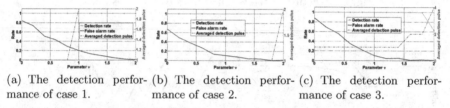

(a) The detection perfor-    (b) The detection perfor-    (c) The detection performance of case 1.    mance of case 2.    mance of case 3.

**Fig. 3.** The detection rate, false alarm rate, and averaged detection pulse of CUSUM detection algorithm. The background normal traffic is poisson distributed.

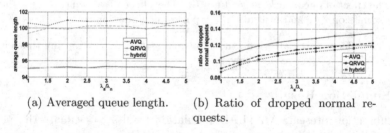

(a) Averaged queue length.    (b) Ratio of dropped normal requests.

**Fig. 4.** Defense scheme comparison for periodic attacks

To evaluate the performance of our defense system, we compared it with AVQ [21] and QRVQ [22] by considering the average queue length and ratio of dropped normal requests to total normal requests. In our simulation, $q^* = 100$ requests, $K_1 = 0.8$, $K_2 = 0.5$, and the attack pulses are periodic. We also conducted random attacks, whose results can be found in the supplementary [27]. Figure 4 presents the results, which shows our hybrid approach achieves a good performance. Figure 4(a) illustrates the averaged queue length versus $\lambda_a/\lambda_n$, where $\lambda_a$ and $\lambda_n$ are arrival rate of attack and normal requests, respectively. It can be seen that the queue length regulation achieved by AVQ is low because it is a pure rate based scheme. On the other hand, our hybrid scheme and QRVQ both regulate the queue length very closely to the predefined target value. The averaged queue length of our hybrid scheme is similar to that of QRVQ, however, they differ in the ratio of dropped normal requests to total normal requests, as shown in Figure 4(b). Figure 4(b) demonstrates that the hybrid scheme drops less normal requests than QRVQ. This is because the hybrid approach responds quickly to arrival rate changes, thus can accept more requests.

### 5.3   Testbed Results

A testbed was set up to emulate the attack scenarios and to evaluate the detection and defense algorithms. Figure 5 shows the diagram of the testbed. The target was a web server running `Minihttpd` 1.9 [29], which was equipped with a proportional-integral (PI) controller to perform admission control. A legitimate client generated HTTP requests continuously using `Httperf` [30] with an arrival rate of 100 requests per second. There were also seven attack zombies, each of which generated attack traffic at a rate of 100 requests per second. These zombies were synchronized by the network time protocol.

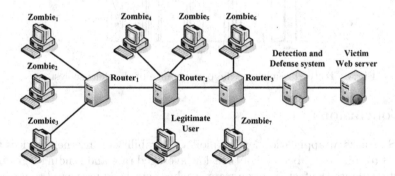

**Fig. 5.** The testbed topology

To evaluate the effectiveness of our detection method, we used it for the traces collected from the testbed. We wanted to know whether the algorithm we evaluated in simulation can still work in real situations. More importantly, whether the impact of $\nu$ is the same for DET, FAR and ADP in actual environment. Thus we let the detection parameters be the same as the ones used for simulation. We conducted 16 experiments, each one contained an attack period varied from 29.3 seconds to 249 seconds, covered all the three cases. We repeated each experiment 4 times and obtained the mean of each performance metric. The results are shown in Table 1. We found the impact of $\nu$ is the same as the simulation

**Table 1.** Detection performance on testbed

| | case 1 | | | case 2 | | | case 3 | | |
|---|---|---|---|---|---|---|---|---|---|
| | DET | FAR | ADP | DET | FAR | ADP | DET | FAR | ADP |
| $\nu = 0$ | 1 | 0.14 | 1 | 1 | 0.33 | 1 | 1 | 0.25 | 1 |
| $\nu = 1$ | 1 | 0.14 | 1 | 1 | 0.12 | 1 | 1 | 0 | 1 |
| $\nu = 2$ | 1 | 0.09 | 1 | 1 | 0 | 1 | 1 | 0 | 1 |

results. That is, detection rate is 1 for all $\nu$; increased $\nu$ causes small FAR. ADP equals 1 for all the three cases. These results show that the proposed CUSUM detection scheme can effectively discover LRDoS attacks.

The performance of the defense system was also assessed. Figures 6 illustrates how the defense system can mitigate the effects of an attack. It shows the arrival rates at the defense system and the resulting arrival rates at the server. The peaks in the request arrival rate caused by LRDoS attacks are clearly smoothed out by the defense system.

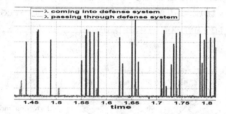

**Fig. 6.** Testbed results for the performance of the defense system

## 6    Conclusions

LRDoS attacks at application level exploit vulnerability of Internet services and are hard to counteract because of their low averaged rate and sending legitimate requests. Despite the fact that some approaches have been presented to mitigate LRDoS attacks, they are limited to certain protocols, system or attack patterns. Therefore, it is important to address the security issues and threats to these Internet services.

In this paper we restrict our attention to the countermeasures on LRDoS attacks at the application level. We have designed a nonparametric sequential test and an adaptive queue management algorithm to quickly restore system performance. Extensive simulation and testbed experiments have been carried out to validate the results.

## References

1. Kuzmanovic, A., Knightly, E.: Low-rate TCP-targeted Denial-of-Service attacks and counter strategies. IEEE/ACM TON 14(4), 683–696 (2006)

2. Kuzmanovic, A., Knightly, E.: Low-rate TCP-targeted Denial-of-Service attacks: The shrew vs. the mice and elephants. In: ACM SIGCOMM (2003)
3. Guirguis, M., Bestavros, A., Matta, I., Zhang, Y.: Exploiting the transients of adaptation for RoQ attacks on Internet resources. In: IEEE ICNP (2004)
4. Guirguis, M., Bestavros, A., Matta, I., Zhang, Y.: Reduction of quality RoQ attacks on Internet end-systems. In: IEEE INFOCOM (2005)
5. Luo, X., Chang, R.: On a new class of Pulsing Denial-of-Service attacks and the defense. In: ISOC NDSS (2005)
6. Sun, H., Lui, J., Yau, D.: Defending against low-rate TCP attacks: dynamic detection and protection. In: IEEE ICNP (2004)
7. Chen, Y., Kwok, Y., Hwang, K.: Filtering Shrew DDoS attacks using a new frequency-domain approach. In: IEEE WoNS (2005)
8. Chen, Y., Hwang, K.: Collaborative detection and filtering of Shrew DDoS attacks using spectral analysis. JPDC 66(9), 1137–1151 (2006)
9. Shevtekar, A., Anantharam, K., Ansari, N.: Low rate TCP Denial-of-Service attack detection at edge routers. IEEE Communication Letters 9, 363–365 (2005)
10. Thatte, G., Mitra, U., Heidemann, J.: Detection of low-rate attacks in computer networks. In: IEEE Global Internet Symposium (2008)
11. Maciá-Fernández, G., Rodriguez-Góomez, R., Diaz-Verdejo, J.: Defense techniques for low-rate DoS attacks against application servers. Computer Networks 54(15), 2711–2727 (2010)
12. Chang, C., Lee, S., Lin, B., Wang, J.: The taming of the shrew: mitigating low-rate TCP-targeted attack. IEEE TNSM 7(1), 1–13 (2010)
13. Xiang, Y., Li, K., Zhou, W.: Low-rate DDoS attacks detection and traceback by using new information metrics. IEEE TIFS 6(2), 426–437 (2011)
14. Maciá-Fernández, G., Díaz-Verdejo, J., Garcia-Teodoro, P., Toro-Negro, F.: LoR-DAS: A Low-Rate DoS Attack against Application Servers. In: Lopez, J., Hämmerli, B.M. (eds.) CRITIS 2007. LNCS, vol. 5141, pp. 197–209. Springer, Heidelberg (2008)
15. Ranjan, S., Swaminathan, R., Uysal, M., Knightly, E.: DDoS-resilient scheduling to counter application layer attacks under imperfect detection. In: IEEE INFOCOM (2006)
16. Xie, Y., Yu, S.: A large-scale hidden semi-Markov model for anomaly detection on user browsing behaviors. IEEE/ACM TON 17(1), 54–65 (2009)
17. Guirguis, M., Bestavros, A., Matta, I., Zhang, Y.: Reduction of quality (RoQ) attacks on dynamic load balancers: Vulnerability assessment and design tradeoffs. In: IEEE INFOCOM (2007)
18. Brodsky, B., Darkhovsky, B.: Non-Parametric Statistical Diagnosis Problems and Methods. Kluwer Academic Publishers (2000)
19. Rousseeuw, P., Hubert, M.: Robust statistics for outlier detection. Wiley Interdisciplinary Reviews: Data Mining and Knowledge Discovery 1(1), 73–79 (2011)
20. Tartakovsky, A., Rozovskii, B., Blazek, R., Kim, H.: A novel approach to detection of intrusions in computer networks via adaptive sequential and batch-sequential change-point detection methods. IEEE TOSP 54(9), 3372–3382 (2006)
21. Kunniyur, S., Srikant, R.: Analysis and design of an adaptive virtual queue (AVQ) algorithm for active queue management. In: ACM SIGCOMM (2001)
22. Deng, X., Yi, S., Kesidis, G., Das, C.: Stabilized virtual buffer (SVB) - an active queue management scheme for internet Quality-of-Service. In: IEEE Globecom (2002)

23. Tang, Y., Luo, X., Hui, Q., Chang, R.K.: Understanding the vulnerability of feedback-control based internet services to low-rate DoS attacks (manuscript for publication)
24. Karagiannis, T., Molle, M., Faloutsos, M., Broido, A.: A nonstationary Poisson view of internet traffic. In: IEEE INFOCOM (2004)
25. Park, K., Kim, G., Crovella, M.: On the effect of traffic self-similarity on network performance. In: SPIE PCNS (1997)
26. Downey, A.: Evidence for long-tailed distributions in the internet. In: ACM IMW (2001)
27. Tang, Y.: Supplementary to "countermeasures on application level low-rate Denial-of-Service attack"
28. Tang, Y., Luo, X., Chang, R.K.C.: Protecting internet services from low-rate DoS attacks. In: CIP (2007)
29. mini_httpd, http://www.acme.com/software/mini_httpd/
30. httperf, http://www.hpl.hp.com/research/linux/httperf/

# Firewall Packet Filtering Optimization
# Using Statistical Traffic Awareness Test

Zouheir Trabelsi, Liren Zhang, and Safaa Zeidan

Faculty of Information Technology
UAE University
Al-Ain, UAE
{trabelsi,lzhang,safaa.z}@uaeu.ac.ae

**Abstract.** In this paper, we present a mechanism that utilizes network traffic behavior and packet filtering statistics to improve firewall performance. The proposed mechanism allows optimizing the filtering rules order and their corresponding fields order upon certain threshold qualification following the divergence of the traffic behavior. The current and previous traffic windows statistics are used to check the system stability using Chi-Square Test. The achieved gain in processing time compared to related mechanisms is due to minimizing the overhead corresponding to the frequency of updating the security policy rule/field structures.

**Keywords:** Packet Classification, Rule Order, Rule-fields Order, System Stability, Chi-square Test.

## 1    Introduction

In this paper, we propose a mechanism to optimize firewall early acceptance path as well as early rejection path. Based on traffic statistics, a decision is made regarding whether or not there is a need to reorder the rules and/or rule-fields orders. The proposed mechanism is based on the following three optimization levels: 1) Filtering rules are reordered in a descending manner according to their packet matching histograms. This will yield to faster packet filtering time for the next similar traffic (optimization in the acceptance path). 2) Rule-fields are reordered in a descending manner according to their packet not matching histograms. This will reduce the time needed for tuple comparison (optimization in the rejection path). 3) The firewall will continue filtering packets using certain rule and rule-fields orders under a certain threshold qualification (the system stability decision). This will reduce the time needed for the reordering process and updating the firewall security policy structure. The three optimization levels will minimize the total packet filtering time and therefore the firewall performance will be improved significantly.

The paper is organized as follows: Section 2 discusses the related work. Section 3 presents the mathematical model of the proposed mechanism. Section 4 evaluates the

T.W. Chim and T.H. Yuen (Eds.): ICICS 2012, LNCS 7618, pp. 81–92, 2012.
© Springer-Verlag Berlin Heidelberg 2012

firewall performance against the proposed mechanism. Finally, Section 5 concludes the paper.

## 2     Related Work

The most early research works on firewall focus on the improvement of packet searching times using various mechanisms including hardware-based solutions [6, 7], specialized data structures [8, 9, 5, 10, 11, 12], and heuristics [5].  Research works in [17, 23, 4, 13 and 14] focus on the statistical filtering schemes to improve the average packet filtering time. The structure of searching by taking into account the packet flow dynamics is introduced in [3, 14, 15, 16].

The idea of firewall optimization through early packet rejection was introduced in [1, 2, 23, 21and 18]. In [1] early packet rejection is done through rule- fields ordering. In [2] early packet rejection is done through multilevel filtering process including field and intersection filtering modules. In [23] a new approach named FVSC is proposed to optimize the rejection path. PBER technique in [18] is considered as a generalization of FVSC [23] it finds short cuts for both accepted and rejected packets. In [21] a binary search on prefix length algorithm is applied to every policy filtering field along with the property of splaying the search tree nodes while maintaining the min-node at high level for early packet rejection.

The most relative to this paper is research work dealing with rules reordering which falls into two categories: Rules reordering including dependency as in[16, 23,] these research work give an approximation of the optimal rules order. Disjoint Rules reordering as in [24, 25]. Up to our knowledge all research work done in the field of firewall optimization through rule reordering, emphasis on the importance of rule field reordering in early packet rejection. In [1] we were the first to propose the idea of rule-field reordering and focus on its major effect in reducing the overall packet processing time.

## 3     Proposed Work

In this paper, we use the Firewall Decision Tree Tool (FDT) described in [26]. FDT tool releases the dependency relation between rules. As a result, the filtering rules can be reordered according to their matching frequencies.

The mathematical model in this paper is based on rule and rule-fields histograms proposed in [1]. A mechanism named Dynamic Rule and Rule-Fields Ordering (DR-RFO) is proposed in [1]. In which the reordering process is carried out at the end of each network traffic window. Thus, in this paper we propose a mechanism named Dynamic Rule and Rule-Fields Ordering with Decision Test (DR-RFOD) to organize the reordering process according to the system stability test.

Since the proposed work in this paper uses the rule and rule-fields histograms, we will describe them in more details in the following section. Then we will discuss the decision regarding the rule/rule-fields reordering processes.

## 3.1    Mathematical Model

**Histogram of Rule Matching Probability and Field not Matching Probability**
Considering that packet matching test in firewall is based on a security policy with N rules, excluding the default "Deny" rule. Each rule consists of a maximum number of M fields, excluding the action field. A N×M matrix vector F(i,j) represents the security policy, that is:

$$F(i,j) = \begin{bmatrix} R(1) \\ ... \\ R(i) \\ ... \\ R(N) \end{bmatrix} = \begin{bmatrix} F(1,1) ... F(1,j) ... F(1,M_1) \\ ... \\ F(i,1) ... F(i,j) ... F(i,M_i) \\ ... \\ F(N,1) ... F(N,j) ... F(N,M_N) \end{bmatrix} \tag{1}$$

Where $i \in \{1,2,...,N\}$ and $j \in \{1,2,...,M_i\}$ are the indices for rule and field respectively.

Let $a_{w,s}(i,j)_l$ and $b_{w,s}(i,j)_l$ represent the status of the $l^{th}$ packet matching and not matching an active field $F(i,j)$ in rule $R(i)$, respectively. Where $w$ ($w \in \{1,2,...,W\}$), $s$ ($s \in \{1,2,...,S\}$) and $l$($l \in \{1,2,...,L\}$) are the window, segment and packet indices, respectively. During the process, when the $l^{th}$ packet matches the field $F(i,j)$ in the rule $R(i)$, the state value of $a_{w,s}(i,j)_l$ is incremented by "1", while $b_{w,s}(i,j)_l$ remains no change. That is:

$$\begin{cases} a_{w,s}(i,j)_l = a_{w,s}(i,j)_{l-1} + 1 \\ b_{w,s}(i,j)_l = b_{w,s}(i,j)_{l-1} \end{cases} \tag{2}$$

By contrast, when the $l^{th}$ packet does not match the field $F(i,j)$in the rule $R(i)$, the state of $b_{w,s}(i,j)_l$ is incremented by "1",   while $a_{w,s}(i,j)_l$ remains no change. That is:

$$\begin{cases} a_{w,s}(i,j)_l = a_{w,s}(i,j)_{l-1} \\ b_{w,s}(i,j)_l = b_{w,s}(i,j)_{l-1} + 1 \end{cases} \tag{3}$$

Note that if the $l^{th}$ packet is not tested for the field $F(i,j)$ in the rule $R(i)$, the state value of $a_{w,s}(i,j)_l$ and $b_{w,s}(i,j)_l$ remain no change. That is:

$$\begin{cases} a_{w,s}(i,j)_l = a_{w,s}(i,j)_{l-1} \\ b_{w,s}(i,j)_l = b_{w,s}(i,j)_{l-1} \end{cases} \tag{4}$$

Let $C_{w,s}(i)=a_{w,s}(i,M_i)$ and $D_{w,s}(i,j)=b_{w,s}(i,j)$ present the number of packets in the $s^{th}$ segment matching rule $R(i)|_{i=1,2,...,N}$ and not matching field $F(i,j)|_{j=1,2,...,Mi}$ contained in $R(i)$ on segment basis, respectively.

Therefore, the probability of packet matching rule $R(i)$ on segment basis can be defined as:

$$P_r\left(C_{w,s}(i)\right) = \frac{C_{w,s}(i)}{L} \quad \text{for} 1 \le i \le N \tag{5}$$

Likewise, the probability of packet not matching field $F(i,j)|_{j=1,2,...,Mi}$ in the rule $R(i)$ on segment basis can be defined as:

$$P_r\big(D_{w,s}(i,j)\big)=\begin{cases} \dfrac{D_{w,s}(1,1)}{L} & \text{for } i=1, j=1 \\[2ex] \dfrac{D_{w,s}(1,j)}{L-\sum\limits_{k=1}^{j-1} D_{w,s}(1,k)} & \text{for } i=1, 2\le j\le M_1 \\[3ex] \dfrac{D_{w,s}(i,1)}{\sum\limits_{k=1}^{M_{i-1}} D_{w,s}(i-1,k)} & \text{for } 2\le i\le N, j=1 \\[3ex] \dfrac{D_{w,s}(i,j)}{\sum\limits_{k=1}^{M_{i-1}} D_{w,s}(i-1,k)-\sum\limits_{k=1}^{j-1} D_{w,s}(i,k)} & \text{for } 2\le i\le N, 2\le j\le M_i \end{cases} \qquad (6)$$

More explanation can be found in [1].

At the end of each window there will be an average probability for each rule and field which give us a further indication of the importance of that rule or field, that is:

$$\overline{P}_r\big(R(i)\big)_w = \frac{\sum\limits_{s=1}^{S} P_r\big(C_{w,s}(i)\big)}{S} \qquad \text{for } 1\le i\le N \qquad (7)$$

$$\overline{P}_r\big(F(i,j)_{R(i)}\big)_w = \frac{\sum\limits_{s=1}^{S} P_r\big(D_{w,s}(i,j)\big)}{S} \qquad \text{for } 1\le i\le N, 1\le j\le M_i \qquad (8)$$

Where $\overline{P}_r\big(R(i)\big)_w$ and $\overline{P}_r\big(F(i,j)_{R(i)}\big)_w$ are the average probabilities for $R(i)$ and $F(i,j)$ in $R(i)$ in the $w^{th}$ window, respectively.

### Reordering Decision

*A-Statistical rules reordering decision*
Assume that the firewall consists of $N$ filtering Rules with certain order in the previous window $(w-1)^{th}$. We want to know if this order will be changed or not in the $w^{th}$ window. First let us introduce some notations to be used in Table 1.

**Table 1.** Previous and current situations for policy filtering Rules

| State←k← | $R_1$ | $R_2$ | ... | $R_N$ | Total |
|---|---|---|---|---|---|
| Previous(w-1) | $n_{(w-1),1}$ $E_{(w-1),1}$ | $n_{(w-1),2}$ $E_{(w-1),2}$ | | $n_{(w-1),N}$ $E_{(w-1),N}$ | $T_{(w-1)}$ |
| Current(w) | $n_{w,1}$ $E_{w,1}$ | $n_{w,2}$ $E_{w,2}$ | | $n_{w,N}$ $E_{w,N}$ | $T_w$ |
| Total | $C_1$ | $C_2$ | | $C_N$ | $T$ |

Let $n_{(w-1),i}$ and $n_{w,i}$ (observed values) are the number of matched packets by Rule $R(i)$ in the $(w-1)^{th}$ and $w^{th}$ windows, respectively. To know if there is a significant difference between the observed and expected values we use the Chi-square test to test the equality of two multinomial distributions. That is:

$$\chi^2(Rules(N)) = \sum_{k=(w-1)}^{w} \sum_{i=1}^{N} \frac{(n_{k,i} - E_{k,i})^2}{E_{k,i}} \tag{9}$$

where $E_{k,i}$ is the expected number of packets to be matched by $R(i)$ in the current or previous window. That is:

$$E_{k,i} = \frac{T_k C_i}{T} \quad \text{for } k = \{w, (w-1)\} \tag{10}$$

If p_value ($\chi^2(Rules(N))$ ,dF)<α → The system is not stable and there is a need to reorder the security policy rules according to histograms of packet matching $R(i)$ on window basis in descending order. The new rule distribution will be computed using the following equation, where $\delta = 1 - (P\_value)$:

$$\overline{P}_r(R(i))_w = \delta \, \overline{P}_r(R(i))_w + (1-\delta)\overline{P}_r(R(i))_{w-1} \tag{11}$$

Otherwise, if p_value ($\chi^2(Rules(N))$ ,dF)>α → The system is stable, no need to reorder the rules. The same previous rule order will be used for the next window and the rules histograms will be renewed using the above equation.

The probability of the current window is given more weight. By doing this the behavior of the traffic in the previous window will not be ignored and will have relatively less effect than the traffic behavior in the current window. As a result the new computed average probabilities would allow producing a better optimized rules ordering for the next window traffic. This procedure will be followed for each rule fields.

*B) Statistical policy rule-fields reordering decision*
Here, we discuss whether to decide to reorder the policy rules fields or not using the number of packets non-matching field $F(i,j)$ in rule $R(i)$ Where $i \in \{1,2,...,N\}$, $j \in \{1,2,...,M_i\}$ . So the same concept of chi-square used in the previous section will be applied for fields of each rule in the security policy as shown in table 2. That is:

$$\chi^2(F(i,j))_{R(i)} = \sum_{k=(w-1)}^{w} \sum_{j=1}^{Mi} \frac{(m_{k,j} - E_{k,j})^2}{E_{k,j}} \tag{12}$$

Where $m_{k,j}$ (observed) is the number of non-matched packets by $F(i,j)$ in $R(i)$, $k$ refers to the current or previous situation. $E_{k,j}$ is the expected number of packets non matching $F(i,j)$ in $R(i)$ in the current or previous window. That is:

$$E_{k,j} = \frac{T_k C_j}{T} \quad \text{for } k = \{w, (w-1)\} \tag{13}$$

**Table 2.** Previous and current situations for policy filtering Fields for Rule $R_i$

| State($k$) | $F_{b1}$ | $F_{b2}$ | ... | $F_{bMi}$ | Total |
|---|---|---|---|---|---|
| Previous($w$-1) | $m_{(w-1),1}$ $E_{(w-1),1}$ | $m_{(w-1),2}$ $E_{(w-1),2}$ | | $m_{(w-1),Mi}$ $E_{(w-1),Mi}$ | $T_{(w-1)}$ |
| Current($w$) | $m_{w,1}$ $E_{w,1}$ | $m_{w,2}$ $E_{w,2}$ | | $m_{w,Mi}$ $E_{w,Mi}$ | $T_w$ |
| Total | $C_1$ | $C_2$ | | $C_{Mi}$ | T |

If $p\_value$ ($\chi^2(F(i,j))_{R(i)}$,dF)<α → There is a need to reorder the fields in $R(i)$ according to histograms of packet non matching $F(i,j)$ in $R(i)$ on window basis in descending order. The new $F(i,j)$ distribution in $R(i)$ will be computed using the following equation, where $\delta = 1 - (P\_value)$.

$$\overline{P}_r\big(F(i,j)_{R(i)}\big)_w = \delta\overline{P}_r\big(F(i,j)_{R(i)}\big)_w + (1-\delta)\overline{P}_r\big(F(i,j)_{R(i)}\big)_{w-1} \qquad (14)$$

Otherwise, if $p\_value$ ($\chi^2(F(i,j))_{R(i)}$,dF)>α → no need to reorder the fields in $R(i)$. Rules and rule-fields reordering processes are independent of each other. Depending on $\chi^2(Rules(N))$ and $\chi^2(F(i,j))_{R(i)}$ tests, the system may change the rules order without changing the fields order and vice versa or changing only some rule fields order.

The following algorithms show the main operation of the statistical module. In Algorithm 1 the buildup of the candidate rule list that are independent and equivalent to the original security policy using FDT tool takes place as well as getting the initial rule and rule-field probabilities to start with after training the system $S_0$ segments. Algorithm 2 is responsible for packet filtering process using function $tuple\_comparasion(l)$. Then it computes rule and rule-fields statistics (Lines 12-13)

---

**Algorithm 1.** Startup Phase

---

```
1:    <SP>←FDT(Policy Rules)
2:s₀←1
3:l₀←1
4:repeat
5:       inisialize(a₀,b₀)
6:       while l₀<=L₀ do
7:              l_s₀←get_pak(f_s₀)
8:              tuple_comparasion(l_ws)
9:              l₀←l₀+1
10:      end while
11:      no_mat_R_s←last_Field(a)
12:      no_nonmat_F_rs←r_Field(b)
13:      pR_s ←prob_Rule_s(no_mat_R_s)
14:      pField_rs ←prob_Field(no_nonmat_F_rs)
15:      s₀← s₀ +1
16:   until s₀=S₀
17:      avgpR₀ ←avg(sum(pR_s₀)_s₀=1:S0)
18:      avgpField_r₀ ←avg(sum(pField_rs₀)_s₀=1:S0)
19:      previous_R₀ ←sum(no_mat_R_s₀)_s₀=1:S0
20:      previous_RField_r₀ ←sum(no_nonmat_F_rs₀)_s₀=1:S0
21:      previous_avgpR₀← avgpR₀
22:      previous_avgpField_r₀ ← avgpField_r₀
```

---

**Algorithm 2.** System Stability

---

1: $w \leftarrow 1$
2: $s \leftarrow 1$
3: **repeat**
4:     $l \leftarrow 1$
5:     **repeat**
6:             inisialize(a,b)
7:             **while** $l <= L$ **do**
8:                     $l_{ws} \leftarrow \text{get\_pak}(f_{ws})$
9:                     tuple_comparasion($l_{ws}$)
10:                     $l \leftarrow l+1$
11:             **end while**
12:             no_mat_$R_s \leftarrow$ last_Field(a)
13:             no_nonmat_$F_{rs} \leftarrow$ r_Field(b)
14:             $pR_s \leftarrow$ prob_Rule$_s$(no_mat_$R_s$)
15:             $p\text{Field}_{rs} \leftarrow$ prob_Field(no_nonmat_$F_{rs}$)
16:             $s \leftarrow s+1$
17:     **until** $s=S$
18:     avgpR $\leftarrow$ avg(sum($pR_s$)$_{s=1:S}$ )
19:     avgpField$_r \leftarrow$ avg(sum($p\text{Field}_{rs}$)$_{s=1:S}$ )
20:     //*current state*//
21:     current_R $\leftarrow$ sum(no_mat_$R_s$)$_{s=1:S}$
22:     current_RField$_r \leftarrow$ sum(no_nonmat_$F_{rs}$) $_{s=1:S}$
23:     current_avgpR $\leftarrow$ avgpR
24:     current_avgpField$_r \leftarrow$ avgpField$_r$
25: //*Rule-Fields stability test*//
26:     **foreach** $r \in R$
27:             p_value$_r \leftarrow$ chi_square(previous_RField$_r$ ,
            current_RField$_r$)
28:             $\delta_r \leftarrow 1-$ p_value$_r$
29:             current_avgpField$_r \leftarrow (1- \delta_r)*$
                    current_avgpField$_r + \delta_r *$
                    previous_avgpField$_r$
30:             **if** p_value$_r < \alpha$
31:                     Rule$_r \leftarrow$ reorder(rule$_r$,
            current_avgpField$_r$)
32:             **end if**
33:     **end for**
34: //*Rules stability test*//
35:     p_value$_R \leftarrow$ chi_square(previous_R, current_R)
36:     current_avgpR $\leftarrow (1- \delta_r)*$ current_avgpR +
$\delta_r *$ previous_     avgpR
37:     **if** p_value$_R < \alpha$
                reorder(R, current_avgpR)
38:     **end if**
39: /*update the previous state*/
40:     previous_R $\leftarrow$ current_R
41:     previous_RField$_r \leftarrow$ current_RField$_r$
42:     previous_avgpR $\leftarrow$ current_avgpR
43:     previous_avgpField$_r \leftarrow$ current_avgpField$_r$
44:     $w \leftarrow w+1$
45: **until** $w=W$

---

and calculate the corresponding segment probabilities (Lines 14-15). Lines (18-19) compute the average rule and rule-fields probability on window basis. $\chi^2(F(i,j))_{R(i)}$ and $\chi^2(Rules(N))$ are computed in (Lines 25-38). Also, the re-ordering process for rule-fields and rules is done in a descending manner according to current average probability based on if statement in lines 30 and 37. The current rule-fields and rule average probability are computed in (Lines 29 and 36). In (Lines 38-42) the previous state variables are updated to be used in the next traffic window.

# 4    Evaluation

## 4.1    DR-RFOD vs DR-RFO

In order to evaluate the performance of the proposed mechanism, an algorithm that dynamically changes the order of the rules and rule-fields according to system stability has been implemented using MATLAB programming environment. This experiment is done using 20 filtering rules and 200 traffic windows each of 1000 packets. These numbers are used just to make it easy to trace the rules and fields ordering position process using both DR-RFO and DR-RFOD mechanisms.

**DR-RFOD vs DR-RFO According to Rules Reordering Process**
The algorithms in DR-RFO and DR-RFOD mechanisms start optimizing the rule positions after treating the second window. In DR-RFO mechanism positions of the rules are updated dynamically after treating each window. On the other hand, in DR-RFOD mechanism positions of the rules are updated dynamically according to eq. (9) and eq. (11) after system stability test. Fig.1 compares the evolution in R1 as an example using DR-RFO and DR-RFOD mechanisms. The horizontal constant lines in the figure shows the corresponding windows for DR-RFOD mechanism where the system was stable according to eq. (9) and no rule reordering process is done.

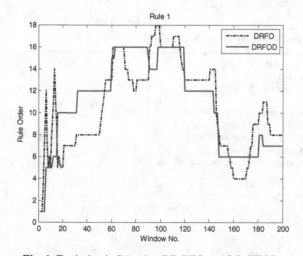

**Fig. 1.** Evolution in R1 using DR-RFO and DR-RFOD

**DR-RFOD vs DR-RFO According to Rule-Fields Reordering Process**
The same concept used in rules reordering process will be used in rule-fields reordering process. In DR-RFO mechanism positions of the rule-fields are updated dynamically after treating each window. On the other hand, in DR-RFOD mechanism positions of the rule-fields are updated dynamically according to eq. (12) and eq. (14) after system stability test. Fig.2 compares the evolution for field Source-IP in R1 as an example using DR-RFO and DR-RFOD mechanisms.

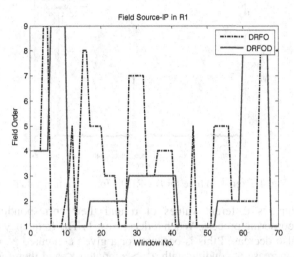

**Fig. 2.** Evolution in Field Source-Port in R1 using DR-RFO and DR-RFOD

Fig. 3 shows the cumulative processing time for DR-RFO and DR-RFOD for different values of $\alpha$. For $\alpha=0.005$, the gain for using DR-RFOD for 200 traffic windows is 9.1119(s), while for $\alpha=0.05$ the gain is18.2855(s).

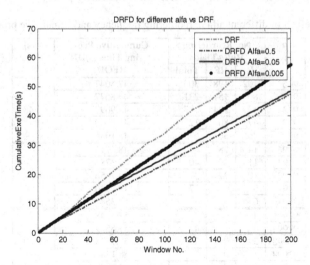

**Fig. 3.** Cumulative processing time for DR-RFOD vs DR-RFO for different $\alpha$ values

## 4.2    The Effect of Error Precision (α) on DR-RFOD Mechanism

This experiment studies the effect of different α values in the cumulative execution time and the number of rule/rule-fields reordering process. Fig.4 gives an idea about the execution time needed for each of the 200's windows for different α values.

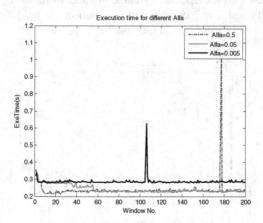

**Fig. 4.** Execution time for DR-RFOD for different α values

Table 3 compares different values of α and their corresponding number of rule/rule-field reordering process. When α decreases: 1) The frequency of the reordering process is also decreased this is because for a given computed $\chi^2$, decreasing the value of α will increase $\chi^2_\alpha$ ending with $\chi^2_\alpha$ >computed $\chi^2$ and therefore no need for reordering. 2) The cumulative execution time increases. This is because in fact when we decide not to reorder we might keep the system running with a non-efficient configuration (order) for longer time and therefore it might take longer execution time than when we reorder often especially if the cost of re-ordering is small and this depends on the number of rules and rule-fields in the security policy.

**Table 3.** The effect of different alfa in reordering frequency and cumulative processing time

| α | No. Reordering Rules/Fields | | | Cumulative Processing Time (s)DR-RFOD | ≈ (s) |
|---|---|---|---|---|---|
| | R | RF | Total | | |
| O⊳5 | 102 | 198 | 300 | 47.4047 | |
| O⊳4 | 80 | 151 | 231 | 47.8677 | |
| O⊳3 | 63 | 124 | 187 | 47.9697 | 47-48 |
| O⊳2 | 47 | 80 | 127 | 48.0900 | |
| O⊳1 | 26 | 36 | 62 | 48.1036 | |
| O⊳05 | 14 | 28 | 42 | 48.3715 | |
| O⊳04 | 11 | 29 | 40 | 49.3784 | |
| O⊳03 | 10 | 27 | 37 | 49.7656 | 48-57 |
| O⊳02 | 9 | 18 | 27 | 49.9930 | |
| O⊳01 | 6 | 3 | 9 | 57.3541 | |
| O⊳005 | 4 | 0 | 4 | 57.5448 | |
| O⊳004 | 4 | 0 | 4 | 57.5537 | |
| O⊳003 | 3 | 0 | 3 | 57.7527 | 57-60 |
| O⊳002 | 1 | 0 | 1 | 58.1344 | |
| O⊳001 | 1 | 0 | 1 | 60.5990 | |

# 5    Conclusion

In this paper, we have proposed a mechanism to improve firewall packet filtering time through optimizing the order of security policy filtering rules and rule-fields. The proposed mechanism is based on reordering rules and rule-fields according to packet matching and non-matching histograms, respectively. The current and previous traffic windows statistics are used to check the system stability using Chi-Square Test. If the system stability test indicates that the firewall is stable the same current rule and/or rule-fields orders are used for filtering the next traffic window. Otherwise, an update of the rule and/or rule-fields order structures is required for filtering the next traffic window. The proposed mechanism gives better cumulative execution time compared to DR-RFO mechanism. Also, the effect of α on the cumulative processing time and on the frequency of the reordering process has been discussed. In future work, we intend to investigate the effect of dynamically changing the traffic window size, and improve the proposed mathematical model to take into consideration security policy with dependent rules.

**Acknowledgment.** The authors acknowledge the support of NRF Foundation and Emirates Foundation through researches grants 21T023 and 2009/161, respectively.

# References

1. Trabelsi, Z., Zhang, L., Zeidan, S.: Packet Flow Histograms to Improve Firewall Efficiency. In: ICICS (December 2011)
2. Trabelsi, Z., Zeidan, S.: Multilevel Early Packet Filtering Technique based on Traffic Statistics and Splay Trees for Firewall Performance Improvement. In: ICC (June 2012)
3. Lan, K., Heidemann, J.: On the correlation of internet flow characteristics. Technical Report ISI-TR-574, USC/ISI (2003)
4. El-Atawy, A., Samak, T., Al-Shaer, E., Li, H.: Using online traffic statistical matching for optimizing packet filtering performance. In: IEEE INFOCOM 2007, pp. 866–874 (2007)
5. Gupta, P., McKeown, N.: Algorithms for packet classification. IEEE Network 15(2), 24–32 (2001)
6. Baboescu, F., Varghese, G.: Scalable packet classification. In: ACM SIGCOMM 2001 (2001)
7. McAulay, A.J., Francis, P.: Fast routing table lookup using CAMs. In: IEEE INFOCOM 1993 (March 1993)
8. Srinivasan, V., Suri, S., Varghese, G.: Packet classification using tuple space search. In: Computer ACM SIGCOMM Communication Review, pp. 135–146 (October 1999)
9. Feldmann, A., Muthukrishnan, S.: Tradeoffs for packet classification. In: IEEE INFOCOM 2000 (March 2000)
10. Gupta, P., McKeown, N.: Packet classification using hierarchical intelligent cuttings. In: Interconnects VII (August 1999)
11. Cohen, E., Lund, C.: Packet classification in large isps: design and evaluation of decision tree classifiers. In: SIGMETRICS 2005: Proceedings of the 2005 ACM SIGMETRIC International Conference on Measurement and Modeling of Computer Systems, pp. 73–84. ACM Press, New York (2005)

12. Woo, T.Y.C.: A modular approach to packet classification: Algorithms and results. In: IEEE INFOCOM 2000, pp. 1213–1222 (March 2000)
13. Gupta, P., Prabhakar, B., Boyd, S.: Near optimal routing lookups with bounded worst case performance. In: IEEE INFOCOM 2000 (2000)
14. Kencl, L., Schwarzer, C.: Traffic-adaptive packet filtering of denial of service attacks. In: WOWMOM 2006: The 2006 International Symposium on on World of Wireless, Mobile and Multimedia Networks, Washington, DC, USA, pp. 485–489 (2006)
15. Acharya, S., Abliz, M., Mills, B., Znati, T.F.: Optwall: a hierarchical traffic-aware fire-wall. In: Proceedings of 14th Annual Network & Distributed System Security Symposium (NDSS), San Diego, US (February 2007)
16. Hamed, H., Al-shear, E.: Dynamic Rule-ordering optimization for High-speed Firewall Filtering. In: ASIACCs 2006, Tuipei, Taiwam, March 21-24 (2006)
17. Hamed, H., El-Atawy, A., Al-Shaer, E.: On Dynamic Optimization of Packet Matching in High-Speed Firewalls. IEEE Journal on Selected Areas in Communications 24(10) (October 2006)
18. Al-Shear, E., El-Atawy, A., Tran, T.: Adaptive Early Packet filtering for Defending firewalls against DoS Attack. In: Proceeding of IEEE INFOCOM, pp. 1–9 (2009)
19. Waldvogel, M., Varghese, G., Turner, J., Plattner, B.: Scalable High Speed IP Routing Lookups. In: Proceedings of the ACM SIGCOMM (SIGCOMM 1997), pp. 25–36 (1997)
20. Sleator, D., Tarjan, R.: Self Adjusting Binary Search Trees. Journal of the ACM 32(3), 652–686 (1985)
21. Neji, N., Bouhououla, A.: Dynamic Scheme for Packet Classification Using Splay trees. Information Assurance and Security, 1–9 (2009)
22. Hamed, H., El-Atawy, A., Al-Shaer, E.: Adaptive statistical optimization techniques for firewall packet filtering. In: IEEE INFOCOM 2006 (April 2006)
23. Mothersole, I., Reed, M.: Optimizing Rule Order for a Packet Filtering Firewall. In: SAR-SSI (2011)
24. Wang, W., Chen, H., Chen, J., Liu, B.: Firewall rule Ordering based on statistical Model. In: International Conference on Computer Enginnering and Technology (2009)
25. Wang, W., Ji, R., Chen, W., Chen, B., Li, Z.: Firewall Rules Sorting Baseb on Markov Model. In: Procedings of the International Symposium on Data Privacy and E-Comerce (2007)
26. Liu, A., Gouda, M.: Complete Redundancy Detection in Firewalls. In: Jajodia, S., Wijesekera, D. (eds.) Data and Applications Security 2005. LNCS, vol. 3654, pp. 193–206. Springer, Heidelberg (2005)

# Group Behavior Metrics for P2P Botnet Detection

John Felix, Charles Joseph[1], and Ali A. Ghorbani[2]

University of New Brunswick,
Fredericton NB, Canada
`johnfelixc@gmail.com, ghorbani@unb.ca`

**Abstract.** Botnet is becoming the biggest threat to the integrity of Internet and
its resources. The advent of P2P botnets has made detection and prevention of
botnets very difficult. In this paper, we propose a set of metrics for efficient botnet detection. The proposed metrics captures the unique group behavior that is
inherent in bot communications. Our premise for proposing group behavior metrics for botnet detection is that, group behavior observed in botnets are unique
and this unique group behavior property is inherent in the botnet architecture.
The proposed group behavior metrics uses three standard network traffic characteristics, namely, topological properties, traffic pattern statistics and protocol
sequence and usage to derive the proposed metrics. We derive six group behavior metrics and illustrate the efficiency of botnet detection using these metrics. It
was observed that, group behavior metrics offers a promising solution for botnet
detection.

## 1   Introduction

Malicious botnets has become a major security threat to the integrity of Internet [19]. A
bot is an autonomous software agent which is programmed to perform some designated
tasks automatically. A network formed by a set of bots residing in different hosts is
referred to as a botnet. Though the concept of botnet was initially designed for benign
purposes, its current usage in Internet serves for more malicious causes [3].

Peer to Peer (P2P) botnets [16] is new generation botnets which have replaced the
old centralized IRC/HTTP based botnets [8]. P2P botnets are more stealthy and hard to
detect. Due to the distributed and autonomous network structure of P2P systems, it is
almost impossible to shutdown a botnet [6]. Attackers have become aware to strengths
of P2P botnets and there has been steady increase in bot malwares that use P2P protocol
for malicious botnets.

In this paper, we propose a set of metrics that capture group behavior among hosts to
detect botnets. Our premise for proposing group behavior metrics for botnet detection
is that, group behavior observed in botnets are unique and this unique group behavior
property is inherent in the botnet architecture. As bots are software agents and follow
a fixed protocol, their communication patterns are similar. In our work, we exploit this
property of bot behavior to detect them. The proposed work uses topological properties,
traffic pattern statistics and protocol based signatures for identifying hosts which have

T.W. Chim and T.H. Yuen (Eds.): ICICS 2012, LNCS 7618, pp. 93–104, 2012.

similar communication patterns. In evaluating the group behavior metrics for botnet detection, we found that the metrics deliver accurate and precise detection of bots in the traffic.

The paper is organized as follows. The succeeding section discusses the relevant work with respect to group behavior based botnet detection. Section 3 gives an overview on the inherent group behavior of botnets. The derivation of the proposed group behavior metrics is presented in section 4. The group behavior metrics is evaluated for accuracy on detecting P2P botnets in section 5. Section 6 concludes the paper by summarizing the contribution of the work and brief comments on future work.

## 2   Related Work

Botnet detection is a non-trivial problem [5]. Experience with respect to centralized IRC/HTTP based botnet detection and mitigation will prove that[19]. Now, the challenge of botnet detection has become harder due to the advent of P2P botnets. Research is yet to provide standard and efficient system for botnet detection [12]. Existing botnets detection methodologies suffer from the tactics used by attackers to thwart detection. Just like software, the bot malware is constantly updated and new revised versions are released, periodically. With P2P technology, this update process is distributed and autonomous, which make botnet resilient to detection and mitigation.

Existing work on group behavior based detection of botnets are very few [2,1,18]. Group behavior is often looked due to the intuitive belief that presence of groups of bots within the same subnet is highly unlikely. However, a look at the traffic through an ISP gateway will prove otherwise. Due to bot propagation mechanism, it is highly likely that more than few bots exist in the traffic of a subnet.

Choi.H et al [2] proposed BotGAD, a framework for capturing group activity in network traffic for botnet detection. They provided a comprehensive overview of current climate in botnet detection research and the usefulness of group behavior as a measure for botnet. Chang.S and Daniels [1] proposed a set of schemes to detect C&C channel of P2P botnets. In this work, the authors characterize a host behavior by jointly considering the spatial and temporal correlations within the traffic. These correlations essentially capture the group behavior of hosts within the network traffic. Hosseinpour and Borazjani [18] proposed a botnet detection framework that uses Artificial Immune System (AIS) to detect common network behavior in the traffic. This approach primarily focuses on detecting spam messages and port scan activity of infected hosts. Spamming and port scanning activities exhibits strong group behaviour among the infected hosts and this property of the malicious behaviour is used to detect them.

## 3   Group Behavior in P2P Botnets

The generic development cycle of a malicious botnet consists of three primary stages [13] , as shown in figure 1. First, the malicious bot is made to install on an end-user machine by various techniques such as, social engineering, spamming, etc. This process is referred to as *bot infection or initial infection*. In the second stage of botnet development cycle, the bot searches and connects to bots that reside in other infected hosts.

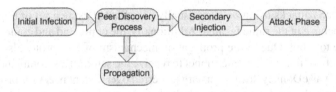

**Fig. 1.** Bot Development Cycle

Thus, the malicious botnet is formed. This stage also establishes a command and control (C&C) channel for the botmaster (attacker) to control the bot. Additionally, bots try to propagate itself to hosts in the infected host's network neighborhood. Bots are generally equipped with propagation mechanisms which will spread the bot malware to hosts which are connected to the infected host. At the third stage, the bot downloads infection vectors through C&C channel which will program the bot for future malicious tasks. This process is referred to as *secondary injection*. After the three stages, the bots and botnet is ready for malicious attacks controlled by the botmaster.

As mentioned earlier, group behavior among bots is inherent due to the botnet architecture. After the initial infection, each phase in the development cycle of the malicious botnet adds strong group behavior properties to the bot behavior.

Once a host is being infected with the malicious bot code, the bot tries to propagate itself to other hosts that are connected to the infected host. Through this process, the bot infects other neighboring hosts with the same bot code. As the hosts that are infected using the propagation mechanism are infected with the same bot code, the bots' network behavior is completely identical. However, this identical network behavior is often difficult to notice, as this behavior is hidden within the hosts' network traffic generated by other benign applications within the infected host. The proposed group metrics in this paper aim to capture the bots' identical network behavior that is hidden within the infected hosts' benign traffic.

In the second stage of botnet development cycle, the malicious bot installed in the infected host tries to connect to other bots (peers). This process in P2P terminology is referred to as peer discovery process [11]. This peer discovery process causes a bot to exhibit strong group behavior with respect to common network connectivity. In most bots, the peer discovery process starts by trying to connect to a set of peers whose IP addresses are hard-coded within the bot code. This property causes the bots to have high common connectivity, as bots infected with the same malware will connect to the same list of peers. Even between different versions of bot malware, large number of peers in the hard-coded peer list remains unchanged. After the peers in the hard-coded peer list are connected, the bot downloads a list of active peers in the botnet through the successfully connected peers. This downloaded peer list is almost the same for different bots in the botnet. This further strengthens the common network connectivity among the bots. Thus, the similarity between the network topology among bots is inherent. If the attacker tries to hide this similarity by randomizing and sub-grouping the peer list, thus formed botnet will be disconnected and hard to manage for the attacker. Thus, similarity in network topology is key feature for detecting group behavior in bots.

During the attack phase of a botnet, bots exhibit strong group behavior. This is primary due to the fact that attacks are coordinated using a set of bots. For example, Denial of Service (DoS) attacks using bots are usually coordinated using a set of bots. Hence, bots tend to behave in the same fashion. Additionally, the command and control channel is not unique to a bot. Due to the propagation mechanism of P2P protocols, there is a high probability of bots in the same subnet to receive the same attack commands. In P2P networks, such as eDonkey, local peers are preferred over distant peers for propagation. This property of the botnet system make the bots to exhibit strong group behavior in terms of network connectivity, traffic pattern and protocol sequence and usage.

## 4   Group Behavior Metrics

The group behavior metrics for hosts in the network are derived using three network traffic characteristics, namely, topology, traffic pattern and protocol usage. The process of deriving the group behavior metrics from the network traffic is illustrated in figure 2. The process comprises of five stages. In the succeeding sections, we discuss each stage of deriving the group behavior metrics.

For each of three network traffic characteristics, we use features that capture group behavior in network behavior. Common connectivity among hosts is derived from the topological properties of the network and is used for capturing the group connectivity. Similarity in packet sizes and frequency is used to measure the group behavior in traffic patterns. Similarity in protocol sequence exhibited by hosts in their network traffic is used to measure the group behavior in protocol usage. Thus, the process uses the three primary characteristics of network traffic to derive the group behavior metrics.

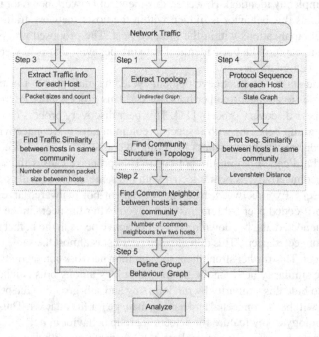

**Fig. 2.** Group Behavior Metrics

## 4.1 Topological Properties

In the first step, the topology of the network that is represented in the network is extracted, as shown in figure 2. A directional graph $G_{IP}(V, E)$ is used to represent the topology, with vertices $(V)$ being the set of unique host IPs found in the network traffic and edges $(E)$ represent the communication links between source IP and destination IP found in the packet header. Similarly, a directional graph $G_{IP/PORT}(V, E)$ is used to represent the topology that considers both IP address and port numbers. The vertices in graph $G_{IP/PORT}(V, E)$ is a set of unique host IP address and port number pairs found in the network traffic and edges (E) represent the link between source IP / source port and destination IP / destination port.

After the topology graphs $G_{IP}(V, E)$ and $G_{IP/PORT}(V, E)$ are defined, each topology is divided into groups based on the connectivity between the hosts. Sub-graphs are defined for each graphs $G_{IP}(V, E)$ and $G_{IP/PORT}(V, E)$. These sub-graphs are formed by considering the connectivity of hosts in the graph, such that strongly connected hosts are formed into sub-graphs. The process of deriving this sub-graphs is discussed later in this section.

The purpose of dividing the topology into sub-graphs is to reduce the complexity of deriving the group behavior metrics. Without grouping, deriving the group behavior metric for each host with all remaining hosts in the topology is almost impossible due to computational complexity. In this case, for deriving the group behavior metric, each host's network behavior has to be compared with the remaining hosts in the network. Such a process has computational complexity in the order of $O(N^2)$, where $N$ is the number of hosts in the network. By dividing the topology into groups, the group behavior is evaluated for hosts only within the sub-graphs of the topology. This reduces the complexity of the group behavior metric computation, significantly.

To find the groups of strongly connected hosts in the topology, we use community detection algorithm [4]. The fundamental idea behind community detection algorithms is that, the nodes of a network can be formed into groups based on the connectivity between them. Newman [10], in his seminal work proposed the notion of modularity which is used as a measure to group nodes in a network. Modularity is a benefit function which quantifies the quality of grouping a certain set of nodes in the network based on connectivity. Modularity [10] is high for set of nodes which have a high degree of connectivity between them but less to nodes with few connections. Hence, in other words, modularity aims to maximize the number links within the group and minimize the links between the groups. We use the community detection algorithm proposed by Schuetz and Caflisch [14].

Community detection algorithm aim to group strongly connected nodes. The outcome from the community detection algorithm is a group index to each host in the topology. The nature of strong connectivity among bots will be preserved by the community structure detection algorithm. In community detection terminology, groups or clusters are referred to as communities. Therefore, hereinafter, the terms communities and groups will be used interchangeably.

At stage two, the group behavior within the topological properties of the network is evaluated. For each graph, $G_{IP}(V, E)$ and $G_{IP/PORT}(V, E)$, the common connectivity [9] of nodes is derived by computing the number of common neighbors between two hosts within the community. The common neighbor for every node pairs in the sub-graphs is computed. The property of bot to have high common connectivity is captured using this metric.

## 4.2  Traffic Pattern Statistics

As discussed in section III, bots exhibit a common traffic pattern. However, this traffic pattern similarity is often hidden within the network traffic generated by the benign ap-plications in the infected host. Typical features of network traffic statistics [15] include,

- Aggregated number of incoming packets
- Aggregated number of incoming bytes
- Aggregated number of outgoing packets
- Aggregated number of outgoing bytes

The above four features are most common used traffic statistics features in existing detection systems. It should be noted here that, the four features represent only the incoming and outgoing bandwidth of a specific host communication. Traffic patterns, however, cannot be perceived using the above four features. Furthermore, the aggre-gation of packet and byte count for host traffic allows the bot traffic properties to be hidden within the benign traffic. Thus, the conventional features of traffic statistics are inadequate for deriving group behavior.

For representing the traffic pattern, we primarily use packet size feature of the net-work traffic. At stage three, we extract the traffic information for each host in the net-work. For each host, we record different packet sizes that are observed within the host's network traffic. Additionally, the frequency of packet sizes within the host's commu-nication is also extracted. Hence, for $i^{th}$ host in the network, the traffic information is represented as $\left(P_E^I, F_E^I\right)$, where $P^I$ is the set of packet sizes observed for the $i^{th}$ host, $F^I$ is the set of frequency of corresponding packet size and $S$ is the number of unique packet sizes observed within the host's network traffic.

After the traffic pattern is extracted, the common traffic pattern is evaluated for every two hosts within every group in the topology. Similarity in traffic pattern using the packet size representation is computed as follows:

$$P_{Common}^{I,J} = P^I \cap P^J \ \forall I \in C \ and \ \forall J \in C \tag{1}$$

$$F_{Common}^{I,J} = \sum_{K=P_{Common}} min\left(F_K^I, F_K^I\right) \tag{2}$$

Equation 1 finds common packet sizes observed between $i^{th}$ and $j^{th}$ host in the topol-ogy community $C$. The number of packets $\left(F_{Common}^{I,J}\right)$ between $i^{th}$ and $j^{th}$ host that have similar packet size is computed in equation 2. The two features namely, $F_{Common}^{I,J}$ and number of elements in $P_{Common}^{I,J}$ are used to represent the group behavior in traffic pattern between the $i^{th}$ and $j^{th}$ host. Similarly, traffic pattern similarity is computed for all hosts pairs within the different topology communities.

### 4.3    Protocol Sequence Signature

Protocol usage is an important property for botnet detection. This feature is more important in group behavior metrics, as the protocol among the bots is fixed and the protocol sequence exhibited by bot traffic is highly similar. This phenomenon in bots is further illustrated in the results section of the paper, where we discuss the efficiency of this particular metric. Protocol sequence of a host represents the different protocols and protocol states of the host network behavior and also the various protocol state transitions exhibited by the host's network communications.

At stage four, the protocol usage and sequence is extracted from the network traffic. First, we identify the protocol of each packet in the network traffic by using wireshark's protocol dissectors. The wireshark's protocol dissectors identifies the protocol and also the type of protocol message, for example, HTTP get request, eDonkey protocol's kademlia hello request/response, etc. The wireshark dissectors searches the packet payload for keywords to identify protocol message type of the packet. For each packet, the protocol state is defined in the following format: $<$*Network Layer Protocol*$>$ . $<$*Transport Layer Protocol*$>$ . $<$*Application Layer Protocol*$>$ . $<$*Application Layer Message Type*$>$ . $<$*Application Layer Message sub-type*$>$. Hence, a protocol state definition looks like "$ip.tcp.edonkey.helloreq$".

After protocol analysis, for each host, the sequence of protocol communication is captured in a state graph. For every $i^{th}$ host in the network, a state graph $(S^I)$ represents the protocol sequence of host's network traffic. In the state graph, the different unique protocol states observed in the host's traffic is defined. The sequence of protocol usage is represented as state transitions in the state graph.

With the protocol sequence state graphs defined for all hosts in the network, we then compute the similarity in protocol sequence between every two hosts in a network topology community. The similarity between state graphs of two hosts is used to compute the common behavior in protocol sequence and usage. For measuring the similarity between two state graphs, we use two different similarity measures, namely, Levenshtein distance [17] and Jaccard similarity [7]. Levenshtein distance is most commonly used approach for comparing DNA sequences in bio-sciences. The distance measure computes the number of minimum steps necessary to change a graph/sequence A to another graph/sequence B. The computed number of steps represents the Levenshtein distance between graph A and B. The Jaccard similarity is a more generic similarity measure that computes the ratio of number of common elements between graph A and B with the total number of unique elements in A and B.

$$PS^{I,J}_{Levenshtein} = L\left(S^I, S^J\right), \forall I \in C \ \ and \ \ \forall J \in C \tag{3}$$

$$PS^{I,J}_{Jaccard} = \frac{\left(S^I \cup S^J\right) - \left(S^I \cap S^J\right)}{S^I \cup S^J} \forall I \in C \ \ and \ \ \forall J \in C \tag{4}$$

Equation 3 computes the Levenshtein distance between protocol sequence state graphs of every $i^{th}$ and $j^{th}$ host in the topology community $C$. The algorithm for computing the Levenshtein distance function $L()$ can be found here [17]. Similarly, equation (4) computes the Jacobian similarity measure between state graphs and of every $i^{th}$ and $j^{th}$ host in the topology community, respectively.

### 4.4   Group Behavior Graph

The metrics derived from the above three group behavior properties is used to define a group behavior graph. The features used include,

- $CN_{IP}^{I,J}$ – Number of Common Neighbors between two hosts in graph $G_{IP}(V, E)$
- $CN_{IP/PORT}^{I,J}$ – Number of Common Neighbors between two hosts in graph $G_{IP/PORT}(V, E)$
- $P_{Common}^{I,J}$ – Number of Similar Packet Size
- $F_{Common}^{I,J}$ – Frequency of Similar Packet Size
- $PS_{Levenshtein}^{I,J}$ – - Levenshtein Distance between protocol sequence
- $PS_{Jaccard}^{I,J}$ – Jaccard Similarity measure between protocol sequence of two hosts.

Host pairs, which have non-zero values for all the above six group behavior features are added to group behavior graph. That is, if the derived six group behavior metrics are non-zero for $I^{th}$ and $J^{th}$ host, then the host $I$ and $J$ are added to the group behavior graph as vertices and the added vertices are connected using an edge. Thus, all hosts which exhibit strong common behavior are captured in the group behavior graph.

In order to filter hosts which exhibit benign group behavior, we define a threshold $(T)$ for each of the above group behavior features. Hence, hosts which has group behavior feature values below the threshold are removed from the group behavior graph. We propose to train the threshold value for the six group behavior features using known bot group behavior. In the next section, we illustrate that finding the threshold is not difficult and can be statically defined.

After the threshold based filtering, the group behavior graph consists only of infected hosts and the botnet topology is represented by this graph.

## 5   Results and Evaluation

In this section, the proposed group behavior metrics is evaluated for accuracy in detection of botnets. Furthermore, the properties of the observed group behavior with respect to the three network traffic characteristics, namely, topology, traffic pattern and protocol usage are discussed.

The results using the group behavior metrics is summarized in Table 1. The threshold for filtering hosts in group behavior graph is trained as a simple Bayesian classifier. The trained threshold is listed in Table 1.

### 5.1   Experimental Setup

Among our research community, real botnet traffic is a scarce resource. Due to the sensitive nature of the content in network traffic traces, ISPs are reluctant to share their traffic captures. It is even more difficult to obtain network traffic traces that contain few bots in the traffic. To evaluate the efficiency of group metrics, we needed a traffic data that has few bots in the traffic. Thus, we had to build our own network traffic data.

**Table 1.** Detection Accuracy

| Number of Hosts in Benign Traffic | | | 42456 | | |
|---|---|---|---|---|---|
| Number of Hosts in Benign Traffic with Group Behavior | | | 8556 | | |
| **Threshold for Group Behavior Graph** | | | | | |
| $CN_{IP}^{I,J}$ | $CN_{IP/PORT}^{I,J}$ | $P_{Common}^{I,J}$ | $F_{Common}^{I,J}$ | $PS_{Levenshtein}^{I,J}$ | $PS_{Jaccard}^{I,J}$ |
| 143 | 59 | 15 | 2964 | 62 | 0.7 |
| Bots used for Training Threshold | | | 6 | | |
| Bots used for Testing | | | 4 | | |
| Detected Bots | | | 4 | | |
| Detection Accuracy | | | 100% | | |

Initially, we collected from various sources, bot traffic captures from different versions of the same bot malware. We were able to collect network traffic generated by 10 different versions of Stormbot [13]. The malware network traffic is captured using honeypots which ran different versions of the Stormbot.

To create the network setup, we use traffic captured from an ISP's gateway. The captured network traffic is real-world traffic data, thus, gives a realistic network setup. We select the 10 IPs from the ISP traffic data and map the IP addresses to the 10 different Stormbot attack traffic data. Once the IP address in the attack traces are modified, we merge and synchronize the 10 attack traffic data with the ISP traffic dataset. Now, the merged network traffic data comprises of 10 bots that run different versions of Stormbot. Using this network data, we evaluate the efficiency of botnet detection using group behavior metrics.

For testing the detection accuracy of the proposed group behavior metrics, two network traffic datasets are built using the above technique. The first traffic dataset comprises of 6 bots within traffic, that is merged using 6 bots and ISP traffic data. ISP traffic data acts as the background traffic for the network setup. This dataset is used for training the threshold (T) that is used to filter the group behavior graph. Similarly, the second dataset, comprises of 4 bots within traffic. This dataset is used for testing the detection accuracy of the proposed group behavior metrics.

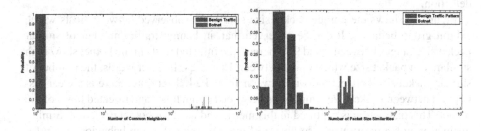

**Fig. 3.** (a) Group Behavior in Topology (b) Group Behavior in Traffic Pattern

## 5.2   Group Behavior in Topology

In this section, we discuss the topology properties that were observed in normal topology and P2P botnet topology. Analyzing the structure of groups identified by the community detection algorithm, it was found that the topological properties within and between groups of normal and P2P botnet topology differs significantly.

In normal topology, communities are evenly and sparsely connected, whereas, in botnet topology, communities are strongly connected with many intra community links. Density of links within communities is relatively high in P2P botnet topology, whereas, in normal P2P, hosts and links are evenly distributed within communities.

The most notable observation in the group structure is that, in normal topology, the hosts are connected in one-to-many connectivity configuration (tree structure) within the community. In most cases, communities have one or two central host to which all other hosts in the community are connected. Due to the above intra community structure, most of the hosts within the community have one common neighbor. On the other hand, in P2P botnet communities, the hosts are connected in many-to-many connectivity configuration. Botnet communities are very strongly connected. Due to many-to-many connectivity, infected hosts have many common neighbors (mostly $> 150$ and $< 400$). This is shown in Figure 3a. It can be clearly observed from Figure 3a, that number of common neighbors observed is different between normal topology and P2P botnet topology. In normal topology, 99.56% of hosts in the network have less than two common neighbors. Whereas, in botnets, number of common neighbors ranges between 236 and 396.

Thus, the number of common neighbors between hosts found within the community is efficient to be used for botnet detection and it is key feature describing the group behavior of hosts.

## 5.3   Group Behavior in Traffic Pattern

Packet size and frequency of packet size within traffic of a specific host is used in our approach to represent the traffic pattern. This is a unique way of representing the traffic pattern and these features truly captures the traffic pattern of network behavior. In this section, we discuss the efficiency of using similarities between packet size and frequency of packet size to compute group behavior of hosts for botnet detection.

Figure 3b shows the unique packet size similarities observed between hosts which exhibit group behavior. It can be observed that, in benign traffic, number of similar packet size ranges between 0 and 9. Whereas, the infected hosts in the botnet show high similarity in packet size which range between 16 and 24. In other words, the number of similar packet size between bots is between 16 and 24. Therefore, there is a clear distinction between packet size similarities between benign hosts and infected hosts of the botnet. This distinction is captured in this metric and used for botnet detection. Similar distinction in similarity was also observed over the second group behavior metric for traffic pattern - frequency of packet size.

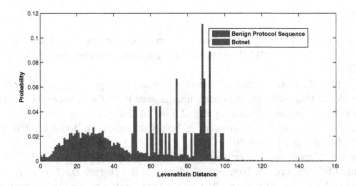

**Fig. 4.** Group Behavior in Protocol Sequence

### 5.4   Group Behavior in Protocol Sequence

Using protocol sequence as a feature for botnet detection is an unprecedented approach. As mentioned earlier in the paper, the Levenshtein distance and Jaccard distance is used to represent the protocol sequence similarity between hosts in the network community. Figure 4 shows the Levenshtein distance observed between protocol sequence of benign hosts and botnets.

Similarity in protocol sequence between bots and benign hosts are not completely different. The probability distribution of Levenshtein distance observed from figure 4 shows that the two distributions overlap. Hence, protocol sequence similarity is not a distinct metric as observed in group behavior metrics derived using topology and traffic pattern characteristics. However, though distributions overlap in Figure 4, the distributions are not completely similar. The center of distributions lies far apart. Protocol sequence similarity measure is still efficient for botnet group behavior detection.

Inferring from Figure 4, Levenshtein distance observed for protocol sequence between infected hosts range between 49 and 98. Within this range, 22% of the hosts that exhibit group behavior in benign traffic are observed. As 21% of the uninfected hosts in the network exhibit group behavior, the false positives using only this metric for botnet detection is $\bar{4}$ % and the true positives is 100%. This illustrates the strength of group behavior metrics for botnet detection. With better protocol analysis techniques, the false positives can still reduce further.

## 6   Conclusion

In this paper, we have presented a set of group behavior metrics which are efficient for botnet detection. The property of bots to exhibit similar communication patterns is exploited to derive these metrics. Three network properties, namely, topological characteristics, traffic statistics and protocol usage sequence is used to derive the group behavior for each host in the network. It is observed that, group behavior of bots is distinctly captured by these metrics.

# References

1. Chang, S., Daniels, T.E.: P2p botnet detection using behavior clustering & statistical tests. In: Proceedings of the 2nd ACM Workshop on Security and Artificial Intelligence, pp. 23–30. ACM (2009)
2. Choi, H., Lee, H., Kim, H.: Botgad: detecting botnets by capturing group activities in network traffic. In: Proceedings of the Fourth International ICST Conference on Communication System Software and Middleware, pp. 2:1–2:8. ACM (2009)
3. Dagon, D., Gu, G., Lee, C.: A taxonomy of botnet structures. In: Botnet Detection, vol. 36, pp. 143–164. Springer US (2008)
4. Fortunato, S., Castellano, C.: Community structure in graphs, pp. 1141–1163 (2009)
5. Grizzard, J.B., Sharma, V., Nunnery, C., Kang, B.B., Dagon, D.: Peer-to-peer botnets: overview and case study. In: Proceedings of the First Conference on First Workshop on Hot Topics in Understanding Botnets, p. 1. USENIX Association (2007)
6. Ha, D.T., Yan, G., Eidenbenz, S., Ngo, H.Q.: On the effectiveness of structural detection and defense against p2p-based botnets. In: IEEE/IFIP International Conference on Dependable Systems Networks, pp. 297–306 (2009)
7. Honov, S.A., Ivchenko, G.I.: On the jaccard similarity test. Journal of Mathematical Sciences 88(6), 789–794 (1998)
8. Kang, B., Nunnery, C.: Decentralized peer-to-peer botnet architectures. Advances in Information and Intelligent Systems 251, 251–264 (2009)
9. Choi, S., Kang, Y.: Common Neighborhood Sub-graph Density as a Similarity Measure for Community Detection. In: Leung, C.S., Lee, M., Chan, J.H. (eds.) ICONIP 2009, Part I. LNCS, vol. 5863, pp. 175–184. Springer, Heidelberg (2009)
10. Newman, M.E.J.: Fast algorithm for detecting community structure in networks. Physical Review E - Statistical, Nonlinear, and Soft Matter Physics 69(62), 066133-1–066133-5 (2004)
11. Rossi, D., Sottile, E., Veglia, P.: Black-box analysis of internet p2p applications. In: Peer-to-Peer Networking and Applications, pp. 1–19 (2010)
12. Van Ruitenbeek, E., Sanders, W.H.: Modeling peer-to-peer botnets. In: Proceedings of the 2008 Fifth International Conference on Quantitative Evaluation of Systems, pp. 307–316. IEEE Computer Society (2008)
13. Stover, J.H.S., Dittrich, D., Dietrich, S.: Analysis of the storm and nugache trojans: P2p is here (2007)
14. Caflisch, A., Schuetz, P.: Efficient modularity optimization by multistep greedy algorithm and vertex mover refinement. Physical Review E - Statistical, Nonlinear, and Soft Matter Physics 77(4) (2008)
15. Strayer, W., Lapsely, D., Walsh, R., Livadas, C.: Botnet detection based on network behavior. In: Botnet Detection, vol. 36, pp. 1–24. Springer US (2008)
16. Wang, P., Wu, L., Aslam, B., Zou, C.C.: A systematic study on peer-to-peer botnets. In: International Conference on Computer Communications and Networks, pp. 1–8 (2009)
17. Bo, L., Yujian, L.: A normalized levenshtein distance metric. IEEE Transactions on Pattern Analysis and Machine Intelligence 29(6), 1091–1095 (2007)
18. Borazjani, P.N., Zeidanloo, H.R., Hosseinpour, F.: Botnet detection based on common network behaviors by utilizing artificial immune system(ais) 1, V121–V125 (2010)
19. Kadobayashi, Y., Zhang, Z.: A holistic perspective on understanding and breaking botnets: Challenges and countermeasures. Journal of the National Institute of Information and Communications Technology 55(2-3), 43–59 (2008)

# Hardware Performance Optimization and Evaluation of SM3 Hash Algorithm on FPGA

Yuan Ma[1,2,*], Luning Xia[1], Jingqiang Lin[1], Jiwu Jing[1],
Zongbin Liu[1], and Xingjie Yu[1,2]

[1] State Key Laboratory of Information Security,
Institute of Information Engineering, CAS, Beijing, China
[2] Graduate University of Chinese Academy of Sciences, Beijing, China
{yma,halk,linjq,jing,zbliu,xjyu}@lois.cn

**Abstract.** Hash algorithms are widely used for data integrity and authenticity. Chinese government recently published a standard hash algorithm, SM3, which is highly recommended for commercial applications. However, little research of SM3 implementation has been published. We find that the existing optimization techniques cannot be adopted to SM3 efficiently, due to the complex computation and strong data dependency. In this paper, we present our novel optimization techniques: shift initialization and SRL-based implementation. Based on the techniques, we propose two architectures: compact design and high-throughput design, both of which significantly improve the performance on FPGA. As far as we know, our work is the first one to evaluate SM3 hardware performance. The evaluation result suggests that SM3 with low area and high efficiency is suitable for hardware implementations, especially for those resource-limited platforms.

**Keywords:** SM3, hash algorithm, FPGA, optimization, hardware performance evaluation.

## 1 Introduction

At present, the performance in hardware has been demonstrated to be an important factor in the evaluation of cryptographic algorithms. The ASIC (Application-Specific Integrated Circuit) and FPGA (Field-Programmable Gate Array) are two common hardware devices for cryptographic implementations. FPGA implementation has become more and more popular recently since it is reconfigurable and relatively flexible.

Hash algorithms that compute a fixed-length message digest from arbitrary length messages are widely used for many purposes in information security. SM3 hash algorithm [1] was published by Chinese Commercial Cryptography Administration Office in December, 2010. As the only standard hash algorithm of China

* This work was supported by National Natural Science Foundation of China (Grant No. 70890084/G021102, 61003274 and 61003273) and Strategy Pilot Project of Chinese Academy of Sciences, Sub-Project XDA06010702.

T.W. Chim and T.H. Yuen (Eds.): ICICS 2012, LNCS 7618, pp. 105–118, 2012.
© Springer-Verlag Berlin Heidelberg 2012

and the replacement of other hash algorithms, SM3 is being integrated into most commercial security products in China.

Up to now, there are no results for hardware implementation of SM3 in literature. As far as we know, our work is the first one to evaluate SM3 hardware performance. Although SM3 can be implemented in a similar way as SHA-1 and SHA-256 which have a similar structure, the common optimization techniques cannot be efficiently applied for SM3 implementations, due to the complex computation and strong data-dependency in the iteration. Furthermore, when SM3 is implemented in FPGA without specific optimizations, we find that the use of registers and LUTs (Look-Up Tables) is not balanced. Much more registers are used than LUTs. So the number of registers will determine the number of occupied slices. Apparently, the imbalance increases the area and reduces the resource utilization.

Our goal is to propose new optimization techniques for SM3 implementation, either to minimize the area or to maximize the throughput. The paper makes two contributions as follows.

**1.** We propose a very compact architecture for processing one message.
Compared with the "standard" (defined in Section 5) SM3 implementation, the compact one only occupies 60% area with no degradation of throughput. The compact architecture is based on our novel optimization techniques – shift initialization and SRL (Shift Register LUT) based implementation, which are based on the following observations.

- There is a unique characteristic in SM3 algorithm. For processing one data block, the message expansion takes 68 clock cycles, while the iteration takes 64 rounds. It indicates that in the first four cycles, the iteration module is idle.
- Some area-saving optimization can be done by utilizing the idle four cycles, which means trading time for space.
- The initialization circuit occupies substantial registers and LUTs. Instead of initializing in one cycle, the circuit can complete the process in the additional four clock cycles.
- SRL is helpful to balance registers and LUTs in FPGA.

**2.** We propose a high-throughput architecture for processing two concurrent messages alternatingly.
Our optimization techniques are more efficient for the two-message architecture. Compared with the stand implementation, the high-throughput one improves the throughput by 69%, and also saves 17% area. Compared with the compact implementation, the high-throughput one also achieves a 68% throughput improvement with only a 40% area increase, resulting in that the ratio of throughput to area increases by 20%. The high-throughput architecture is inspired by the following observations.

- By inserting registers in the critical path, the strong data dependency can be avoided for processing two independent message. And the throughput will significantly increase.

- The two messages can share the same computation unit for compression and expansion in an alternative form. Thus, the LUT resources are reused.
- However, the registers for variable storage have to be doubled for processing two messages. Fortunately, the shift initialization structure and SRL-based implementation can provide a good means to minimize the register consumption.

The rest of this paper is organized as follows. Section 2 presents the SM3 hash algorithm. Section 3 analyzes the critical path and describes our optimization techniques and the compact architecture. Section 4 proposes the high-throughput architecture. Section 5 defines the standard implementation and presents the implementation and comparison results. Section 6 presents related works. Section 7 concludes the paper.

## 2   Preliminary: SM3 Hash Algorithm

The SM3 hash algorithm processes a message of length $l$ ($l < 2^{64}$) bits to produce a final digest message of 256 bits after padding and compressing. The message, which is composed of multiple blocks of 512 bits each after padding, is expanded and fed to the 64 cycles of the compression function in words of 32 bits each.

### 2.1   Message Padding and Parsing

The binary message of length $l$ to be processed is appended with a '1' and padded with zeros of length $k$ until $(l + k + 1) \equiv 448 \bmod 512$. And the resultant padded message is parsed into $N$ 512-bit blocks, denoted $B(1), B(2), ..., B(N)$. These $B(i)$ message blocks are fed individually to the message expander.

### 2.2   Message Expansion

The functions in the SM3 algorithm operate on 32-bit words, so each 512-bit block $B(i)$ from the padding stage is viewed as 16 32-bit blocks denoted $B_j^{(i)}, 0 \leq j \leq 15$. The message expander takes each $B(i)$ and expands it to form 68 32-bit blocks $W_j$ and 64 32-bit blocks $W_j'$, according to the equations:

$$P_1(X) = X \oplus (X \lll 15) \oplus (X \lll 23) \tag{1}$$

$$W_j = \begin{cases} B_j^{(i)}, & 0 \leq j \leq 15; \\ P_1(W_{j-16} \oplus W_{j-9} \oplus (W_{j-3} \lll 15)) \oplus (W_{j-13} \lll 7) \oplus W_{j-6}, & 16 \leq j \leq 67. \end{cases} \tag{2}$$

$$W_j' = W_j \oplus W_{j+4} \tag{3}$$

where $x \lll n$ denotes a circular rotation of $x$ by $n$ positions to the left. All additions in the SM3 algorithm are modulo $2^{32}$.

## 2.3    Message Compression

The $W_j$ and $W_j'$ words from the message expansion stage are then passed to the SM3 compression function. The function utilizes 8 32-bit working variables labeled $A, B, C, D, E, F, G, H$, which are initialized to predefined values $V_0^{(0)}, \ldots, V_7^{(0)}$ at the start of each call to the hash function. Sixty-four iterations of the compression function are then performed, given by:

$$
\begin{aligned}
SS1 &= ((A \lll 12) + E + (T_j \lll j)) \lll 7 \\
SS2 &= SS1 \oplus (A \lll 12) \\
TT1 &= FF_j(A, B, C) + D + SS2 + W_j' \\
TT2 &= GG_j(E, F, G) + H + SS1 + W_j \\
D &= C \qquad\qquad C = B \lll 9 \\
B &= A \qquad\qquad A = TT1 \\
H &= G \qquad\qquad G = F \lll 19 \\
F &= E \qquad\qquad E = P_0(TT2)
\end{aligned}
\tag{4}
$$

where

$$
T_j = \begin{cases} 79cc4519, & 0 \le j \le 15; \\ 7a879d8a, & 16 \le j \le 63. \end{cases}
\tag{5}
$$

and the functions denoted $FF_j$, $GG_j$ and $P_0$ are given by:

$$
FF_j(X, Y, Z) = \begin{cases} X \oplus Y \oplus Z, & 0 \le j \le 15; \\ (X \wedge Y) \vee (X \wedge Z) \vee (Y \wedge Z), & 16 \le j \le 63. \end{cases}
\tag{6}
$$

$$
GG_j(X, Y, Z) = \begin{cases} X \oplus Y \oplus Z, & 0 \le j \le 15; \\ (X \wedge Y) \vee (\neg X \wedge Z) \vee (Y \wedge Z), & 16 \le j \le 63. \end{cases}
\tag{7}
$$

$$
P_0(X) = X \oplus (X \lll 9) \oplus (X \lll 17)
\tag{8}
$$

where $\oplus$ represents the bitwise $XOR$ operation, $\vee$ the bitwise $OR$ operation, $\wedge$ the bitwise $AND$ operation and $\neg$ the bitwise $NOT$ operation.

After 64 iterations of the compression function, an intermediate hash value $V^{(i)}$ is calculated:

$$
V_0^{(i)} = A \oplus V_0^{(i-1)}, V_1^{(i)} = B \oplus V_1^{(i-1)}, \ldots, V_7^{(i)} = H \oplus V_1^{(i-1)}
\tag{9}
$$

The SM3 compression algorithm then repeats and begins processing another 512-bit block from the message padder. After all $N$ data blocks have been processed, the final 256-bit output, $V^{(N)}$, is formed by concatenating the final hash values:

$$
V^{(N)} = V_0^{(N)} V_1^{(N)} \ldots V_7^{(N)}
\tag{10}
$$

## 3    Proposed Compact Architecture

In this section, based on the analysis of the critical path, we find that the fixed critical path limits the maximum frequency and the throughput. Then we turn to minimize the area to improve the ratio of throughput to area. We propose a shift initialization structure to reuse hardware resources, and the SRL-based implementation to balance registers and LUTs. Based on them, the compact architecture is proposed.

### 3.1    Critical Path

The critical path refers to the one which creates the longest delay, and it limits the maximum working frequencies of systems. From Equations (4), it can be observed that the SM3 round computation is oriented towards the $A$ and $E$ value calculations. The remaining values do note require any computation, aside from the rotations of $B$ and $F$. The values of A and E are both computed from $SS1$, which depends on the previous values of $A$ and $E$, as depicted in Equations (11)-(13).

$$SS1 = (A \lll 12 + E + T_j \lll j) \lll 7 \tag{11}$$

$$A = FF_j(A, B, C) + D + W_j' + SS1 \oplus (A \lll 12) \tag{12}$$

$$E = P_0(GG_j(E, F, G) + H + W_j + SS1) \tag{13}$$

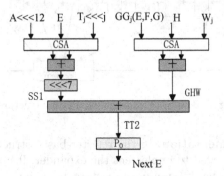

**Fig. 1.** The critical path of SM3

Note that the rotation operation does not require additional resources in hardware, and $SS1 \oplus (A \lll 12)$ can be synthesized with the addition to one-stage LUTs in FPGA. Thus, Equation (13), $E$ path, is longer than Equation (12) by a delay of one-stage LUTs . The additional LUTs are used to implement function $P_0$. For $E$ path, the computations of $SS1$ and $GG_j + H + W_j$ that are both the addition of three numbers can be processed simultaneously. The structure of the critical path of SM3 algorithm is depicted in Figure 1.

The additions of three numbers are optimized by CSA (Carry Save Adder), which separates the sum and carry paths and minimizes the delay caused by traditional carry propagation. The rotation $\lll 7$ sets up a major barrier for optimizing the critical path, because it isolates the additions of $SS1$ from others. Thus $SS1$ has to be computed separately. Pre-computing $H + W_j$ is useless for shortening the critical path, as the computation of $SS1$ is still in the critical path. Further more, both $A$ and $E$ depend on their values of the previous round. Thus, the critical path is almost fixed, due to the strong data dependency. Thus, the throughput is hardly improved due to such a critical path. For the SM3 implementation, in order to improve the ratio of throughput to area, our optimization goal is to minimize the resource consumption.

## 3.2   Message Expansion

The input data block expansion described in Equations (1)-(3), can be implemented with registers and XOR operations. The output value is selected between the original data block, for the first 16 rounds, and the computed values, for the remaining rounds. Figure 2 depicts the implemented structure. In order to eliminate this expansion computation from the critical path, both $W$ and $W'$ are the outputs of registers.

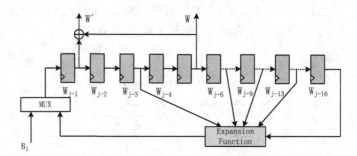

**Fig. 2.** The SM3 message expansion structure

**SRL-Based Implementation.** In the register-based structure, sixteen 32-bit width registers are needed to implement the expander. It can be observed that most of them are only used to temporarily store data, so we use SRLs to replace the shift register for area saving.

In FPGA, LUTs can also be configured as 16-bit shift registers, as shown in Figure 3. One SRL can implement a 1-bit wide, 16-bit long shift register. Thus, SRL used to reduce registers provides a way to balance registers and LUTs. The input $CE$ is used to control data shift, and $Addr$ is used to change the length of the shift register dynamically. In addition, the SRL contents can be initialized by designers.

In SM3 message expansion, the registers used to create the temporal delay of $W_j$ can be replaced by SRLs, as shown in Figure 4, where SRL-x represents a

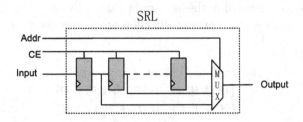

**Fig. 3.** The Shift Register LUT structure

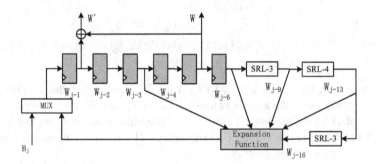

**Fig. 4.** SRL-based message expansion structure

32-bit wide, x-bit long shift register. Only $6 \times 32$ registers and $3 \times 32$ SRLs are used to implement the 32-bit 16-length shift registers.

It should be noticed that $W_j' = W_j \oplus W_{j+4}$ implying that the first $W_0'$ will not be obtained until $j = 4$. Due to this fact, the compressor starts to iterate 64 rounds after its input $W_0'$ is generated at the 4th clock round. Therefore, the SM3 module takes 68 cycles to process one 512-bit chunk of data with the additional 4 clock cycles for initializing $W_j'$. In fact, our optimization techniques are inspired by the additional four cycles.

### 3.3 SIS-Based Compact Architecture

**Shift Initialization Structure (SIS).** Before every 64-round iteration, variables $A$ to $H$ should be initialized using intermediate hash values $V_0$ to $V_7$. And after the computation of a given data block, the finial values of internal variables $A$ to $H$ are XORed to the current intermediate hash values $V_0$ to $V_7$. Especially, for the first message block, $V_0$ to $V_7$ are initialized by constants $IV$. If these operations were implemented in a straightforward manner, eight multiplexers and eight XOR gates would be required. In this section, we propose a shift initialization structure that can efficiently completes the initialization and XOR operation with a low area.

When the message expander is initializing $W_j'$ in the first four clock cycles, the compressor is idle. Therefore, instead of completing XOR in one clock cycle, we use shifted registers to operate that in the four cycles. The SIS is based on

Equations (14), as presented in the most right part of Figure 5. Furthermore, using shift registers has another advantage, allowing us to replace the 256 registers $V_0$ to $V_7$ with only 64 SRLs.

$$
\begin{aligned}
&\text{for } j = 0 \text{ to } j = 3 \text{ do}\\
&\quad \{D, C, B, A\} = \{C, B, A, V_3 \oplus D\}\\
&\quad \{H, G, F, E\} = \{G, F, E, V_7 \oplus H\}\\
&\text{endfor}\\
\\
&\text{for } j = 0 \text{ to } j = 4 \text{ do}\\
&\quad \{V_3, V_2, V_1, V_0\} = \{V_2, V_1, V_0, A\}\\
&\quad \{V_7, V_6, V_5, V_4\} = \{V_6, V_5, V_4, E\}\\
&\text{endfor}
\end{aligned}
\tag{14}
$$

When configured, the SRLs for $V_0$ to $V_7$ are initialized using the constant $IV$. For the first message block, the values of $V_0$ to $V_7$ are derived from $IV$, and the values of $A$ to $H$ are set to zero. After the shift initialization, both $V_0$ to $V_7$ and $A$ to $H$ equal the value of XOR zero to $IV$, i.e. $IV$, meaning that the initialization properly complete.

**Proposed Compact Architecture.** Based on SIS, we propose a very compact SM3 architecture, depicted in Figure 5 which is approximately symmetrical. Three CSAs are used to reduce the path delay, followed by five 32-bit adders that can be implemented conveniently by Carry Propagate Adders (CPAs) in FPGAs.

The shift initialization, as shown in the most right part of Figure 5, also allows us to remove many multiplexers. For variables $B,D,F$ and $H$ the multiplexers are saved, because whenever in the first four cycles or in the next 64-round iterations the assignments for them are not changing. But for $C$ and $G$, the multiplexers are needed as the rotation operation exists. Notice that the XOR gate and multiplexer used for $E$ in the right part of Figure 5 don't increase the resource consumption and the critical path, because they can be synthesized to one-stage LUTs of six inputs with the function $P_0$. That is why we do not use the output of XOR gates to update $V_0$ and $V_4$, as the XOR gates can be synthesized with the multiplexers.

In this architecture, only 160 LUTs, that divided into 5 groups of 32, are required for the whole round implementation on the basis of the iteration structure. Two groups are used for the two multiplexers of $C$ and $G$, two for the SRL-4's, and the last one for the multiplexer and XOR gate of $A$.

**Efficient Shift Output.** We use the SRL-based implementation for a efficient reading of the final hash values. $Addr$, the input of SRL which acts as a RAM, can be used to dynamically change the length of shift register. That means we can control $Addr$ to obtain any register value in the SRL as long as we know the right address of that register. Thus, when $CE$ is low, we successively increase $Addr$ from 2-bit 00 to 2-bit 11 to obtain $V_0$ to $V_3$ and $V_4$ to $V_7$ sequentially.

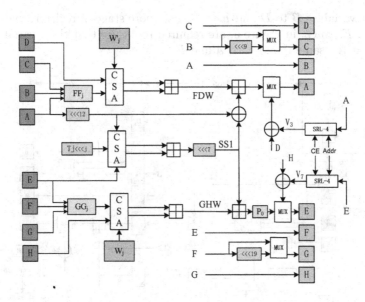

**Fig. 5.** The proposed compact SM3 architecture

# 4    Proposed High-Throughput Architecture

In this section, in order to further improve resource utilization, we propose a high-throughput architecture that can processes two independent messages alternatingly. That is motivated by the long and symmetrical critical path in SM3. We split the critical path in half by inserting registers to increase the maximum frequency and throughput. Meanwhile, the iteration and expansion LUT circuits are reused in our high-throughput architecture. Furthermore, the SRL optimization technique can be used more efficiently for registers saving in the architecture, yielding a higher throughput/area.

## 4.1    High-Throughput Architecture

We propose a high-throughput architecture that processes two independent messages alternatingly, as shown in Figure 6 where $FDW$, $SS1$ and $GHW$ are the inserted registers. The computation of these register variables are presented in Equations (15), which are all three-number additions, labeled *Stage* 1 in Figure 6. The additions are implemented by CSA that consists of one-stage LUT and one 32-bit CPA. For the path after the registers labeled *Stage* 2 in Figure 6, either for $A$ or $E$, the calculating path is also one 32-bit CPA and one-stage LUT. Thus, The critical path is shorten by half.

$$
\begin{aligned}
FDW &= FF_j(A, B, C) + D + W_j{}' \\
SS1 &= (A \lll 12 + E + T_j \lll j) \lll 7 \\
GHW &= GG_j(E, F, G) + H + W_j
\end{aligned}
\tag{15}
$$

For other variables $B$ to $D$ and $F$ to $H$, one more stage of registers, named $A_r$ to $C_r$ and $E_r$ to $G_r$ in Figure 6, are required to ensure that these variables are updated at the same round with $A$ and $E$.

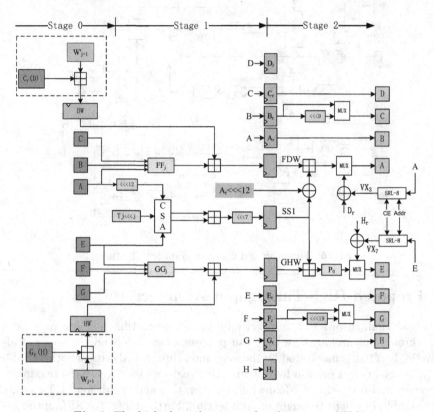

**Fig. 6.** The high-throughput round architecture of SM3

**SIS-Based Implementation.** SIS can be embedded efficiently in the architecture, as depicted in the most right part of Figure 6. In the architecture, the shift initialization for two messages runs according to Equations (16). The initialization process here is similar to that in the compact architecture, except for processing two messages alternatingly.

$$\text{for } j = 0 \text{ to } j = 7 \text{ do}$$
$$\{D_r, D, C_r, \ldots, A_r, A\} = \{D, C_r, C, \ldots, A, VX_3 \oplus D_r\}$$
$$\{H_r, H, G_r, \ldots, E_r, E\} = \{H, G_r, G, \ldots, E, VX_7 \oplus H_r\}$$
$$\text{endfor}$$

$$\text{for } j = 0 \text{ to } j = 8 \text{ do}$$
$$\{VX_3, VY_3, VX_2, \ldots, VX_0, VY_0\} = \{VY_3, VX_2, VY_2, \ldots, VY_0, A\}$$
$$\{VX_7, VY_7, VX_6, \ldots, VX_4, VY_4\} = \{VY_7, VX_6, VY_6, \ldots, VY_4, E\}$$
$$\text{endfor}$$

Instead of two SRL-4's in the compact architecture, two SRL-8's are needed to store eight intermediate values $VX$ and $VY$ for $X$ and $Y$ alternatingly. More precisely, the first SRL-8 stores intermediate values in order of $\{VX_3, \ldots, VY_0\}$, and the second SRL-8 $\{VX_7, \ldots, VY_4\}$. Notice that this change does not increase LUT consumption, because SRL-4 and SRL-8, the difference of which is the length of shift register, are both implemented by 32 LUTs. Furthermore, $D_r$ and $H_r$ used to temporarily store $D$ and $H$ are needed for executing XOR with $VX_3$ and $VX_7$ in Figure 6.

**Adding Additional Pipeline.** We add additional pipeline named *Stage* 0 for keeping the critical path as expected, as labeled in the two dotted frames of Figure 6. One-stage LUTs are not enough to implement the CSA for $FDW$, because the total number of input variables is seven, as shown Equations (15) where $W_j' = W_j \oplus W_{j+4}$. Thus we compute the additions $D + W_j'$ and $H + W_j$ in the previous round. *Stage* 0 pre-computes the additions using $C_r + W'_{j+1}$ and $G_r + W_{j+1}$ of the previous round.

With this pipeline, an additional clock cycle is required for each block. The additional cycle, however, can be hidden in the initialization of $A$ to $H$. Therefore, each 512-bit chunk of the two messages can be processed within 136 clock cycles, 68 cycles for each message.

## 4.2   Message Expansion

Similar to the message expansion in the compact architecture, the expander for two alternative messages are implemented using SRL, as shown in Figure 7. Only $6 \times 32$ registers and $7 \times 32$ SRLs are used to implement the 32-bit 32-length shift registers, which store the expanded messages for $X$ and $Y$ alternatingly. With the registers shifting, the expansion function circuit is reused for the alternative messages.

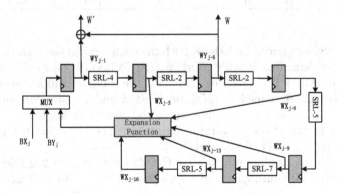

**Fig. 7.** The SRL-based message expansion structure for two messages

# 5   Hardware Performance Evaluation

As there is no hardware implementation of SM3 in literature, we provide a standard SM3 implementation as a baseline for our optimized implementations. Honestly, we do not intentionally make it slower or larger. The standard implementation is defined as follows.

- The message padding module is not included. As the message padding is performed once to the end of the message, and has no significant cost when implemented in software. This is consistent with majority of other hash cores.
- The message expansion module is implemented based on the structure as shown in Figure 2, which is a common implementation in other hash algorithms such as SHA-1.
- The iteration process works as follows. Variables $A$ to $H$ are initialized with $IV$ for the first message block. The iteration module is idle in the first four cycles waiting for $W_0'$. In the iteration, The assignments of $A$ and $E$ are implemented according to Figure 1. At the last iteration round, besides the iteration operation, $A$ to $H$ performs XOR operation with $V_0$ to $V_7$.
- The intermediate value $V_0$ to $V_7$ are assigned as follows. For the first message block, $V_0$ to $V_7$ are also initialized with $IV$. For the subsequent blocks, $V_0$ to $V_7$ are assigned by $A$ to $H$ at the first iteration round.

**Table 1.** Hardware Performance of SM3 and SHA-256 implementations

| Name | Devices | Slices | Max Freq. (MHz) | Bits/cycle | ThrPut. (Mbps) | ThrPut/Slice |
|------|---------|--------|-----------------|------------|----------------|--------------|
| *Standard-SM3* | Virtex-5 | 384 | 214 | 7.53 | 1611 | **4.20** |
| *C-SM3* | Virtex-5 | 234 | 215 | 7.53 | 1619 | **6.92** |
| *T-SM3* | Virtex-5 | 328 | 362 | 7.53 | 2726 | **8.31** |
| SHA-256[2] | Virtex-5 | 319 | 221 | 7.76 | 1714 | **5.37** |

In order to evaluate our SM3 designs, both the compact and the high-throughput designs are implemented on Xilinx Virtex-5 (XC5VLX110T-3) FPGA, and Place and Route by Xilinx ISE 13.2. For simplicity, the compact and high-throughput implementations are named *C-SM3* and *T-SM3*, and the standard one named *Standard-SM3*. Table 1 shows the comparison results of implementation performance in terms of slices, working frequency, bits processed per cycle and throughput per slice (ThrPut/Slice).

Implementation results indicate that *C-SM3* only occupies 234 Slices and *P-SM3* achieves a high throughput of 2.7 Gbps on Virtex-5. In addition, both the two implementations achieve a high ratio of throughput to area.

Compared with *Standard-SM3*, *C-SM3* only occupies 61% area with no degradation of throughput, resulting in that the Throughput/Slice increases 65%.

Also, compared with *Standard-SM3*, *T-SM3* improves the throughput by 69%, and also saves 17% area. When compared with the compact implementation, the high-throughput one also achieves a 68% throughput improvement with only a 40% area increase, resulting in that the ratio of throughput to area increases by 20%. The comparison result suggests that our optimization techniques are not only effective for the one-message architecture, but more efficient for the two-message architecture.

When compared with the best SHA-256 implementation[2], our *C-SM3* occupies 73% slices, while achieving a 29% improvement to ThrPut/Slice. This means that our SM3 implementation can occupy much smaller area with a competitive throughput.

# 6   Related Work

Several techniques have been proposed to improve the FPGA implementations of hash algorithms, such as using CSAs, using embedded memories, pipelining, unrolling and rescheduling.

CSA techniques are used to improve the partial additions [3,4]. We also use CSAs in the standard and optimized implementations. The rotation operation $\lll 7$, however, limits further optimization for shortening the critical path.

The usage of embedded memories such as block RAMs to store the required constants can save resources [3,4,5]. The technique is useless for SM3 implementation, as there are not substantive constants need to be stored.

Pipelining techniques are helpful to achieve higher working frequencies [3,5,6]. These technique, however, can hardly improve the maximum frequency in SM3 implementations, due to the rotation operation $\lll 7$ in $SS1$ and the strong dependency of variables $A$ and $E$. The details have been explained in Section 3.1. Unrolling techniques optimize the data dependency [4,6,7,8,9], while they may significantly increase the required hardware resources .

The pipeline architecture for multiple messages is also useful to achieve a high throughput for multiple independent messages [7,8,10]. The main idea of the techniques is reusing the calculation logic to decrease the area and processing multiple messages simultaneously to increase the throughput. Nonetheless, the register resources are duplicated several times. Our optimization techniques provide a good means to minimize the registers in the multiple-message architecture.

Rescheduling and hardware reutilization techniques can improve hardware realizations both in speed and in area [3,5]. The rescheduling technique can not be applied in SM3 implementation directly, due to the ROL operations $\lll 9$ for $B$ and $\lll 19$ for $F$ in the iteration of SM3. Instead of the finalization operation within the 64-round iteration in the techniques, our finalization operation is completed before the iteration begins, which allows us to remove many multiplexers for the variables $A$ to $H$.

# 7    Conclusion

This paper optimizes and evaluates the hardware performance of SM3 hash algorithm on FPGA for the first time. We propose novel techniques to optimize the SM3 implementation, since common optimization techniques are not applicable. Implementation results clearly indicate that our techniques allow a substantial reduction on reconfigurable resources, either in the compact architecture or in the high-throughput architecture. Thus, SM3 with higher efficiency is suitable for hardware implementations, especially for the resource-limited hardware platforms. In fact, our optimization techniques can also be used for the implementations of other hash algorithms, such as SHA-2. We will work on this issue in the next stage.

# References

1. Chinese Commercial Cryptography Administration Office: Sepecification of SM3 Cryptographic Hash Function (2010) (in Chinese),
   http://www.oscca.gov.cn/UpFile/20101222141857786.pdf
2. HELION: Fast SHA-256 core for xilinx FPGA (2011), http://www.helion.com/
3. Chaves, R., Kuzmanov, G., Sousa, L., Vassiliadis, S.: Improving SHA-2 Hardware Implementations. In: Goubin, L., Matsui, M. (eds.) CHES 2006. LNCS, vol. 4249, pp. 298–310. Springer, Heidelberg (2006)
4. McEvoy, R.P., Crowe, F.M., Murphy, C.C., Marnane, W.P.: Optimisation of the SHA-2 Family of Hash Functions on FPGAs. In: IEEE Computer Society Annual Symposium on Emerging VLSI Technologies and Architectures (ISVLSI), pp. 317–322 (2006)
5. Chaves, R., Kuzmanov, G., Sousa, L., Vassiliadis, S.: Cost-Efficient SHA Hardware Accelerators. IEEE Transactions on Very Large Scale Integration (VLSI) Systems 16(8), 999–1008 (2008)
6. Macchetti, M., Dadda, L.: Quasi-Pipelined Hash Circuits. In: IEEE Symposium on Computer Arithmetic, pp. 222–229 (2005)
7. Michail, H.E., Kakarountas, A.P., Selimis, G.N., Goutis, C.E.: Optimizing SHA-1 Hash Function for High Throughput with a Partial Unrolling Study. In: Paliouras, V., Vounckx, J., Verkest, D. (eds.) PATMOS 2005. LNCS, vol. 3728, pp. 591–600. Springer, Heidelberg (2005)
8. Lee, E.H., Lee, J.H., Park, I.H., Cho, K.R.: Implementation of High-Speed SHA-1 Architecture. IEICE Electronics Express 6(16), 1174–1179 (2009)
9. Sklavos, N., Koufopavlou, O.: Implementation of the SHA-2 Hash Family Standard Using FPGAs. The Journal of Supercomputing 31(3), 227–248 (2005)
10. Kakarountas, A.P., Michail, H., Milidonis, A., Goutis, C.E., Theodoridis, G.: High-Speed FPGA Implementation of Secure Hash Algorithm for IPSec and VPN Applications. The Journal of Supercomputing 37(2), 179–195 (2006)

# Continual Leakage-Resilient Dynamic Secret Sharing in the Split-State Model

Hao Xiong[1], Cong Zhang[1], Tsz Hon Yuen[1,*], Echo P. Zhang[1],
Siu Ming Yiu[1], and Sihan Qing[2,**]

[1] The University of Hong Kong, Hong Kong
{hxiong,czhang2,thyuen,pzhang2,smyiu}@cs.hku.hk
[2] Chinese Academy of Sciences and Peking University, China
qsihan@ss.pku.edu.cn

**Abstract.** Traditional secret sharing assume the absolute secrecy of the private shares of the uncorrupted users. It may not hold in the real world due to the side-channel attacks. Leakage-resilient cryptography is proposed to capture this situation. In the continual leakage model, the attacker can continuously leak the private value owned by the user with the constraint that the information leaked should be less than $\ell$ between updates. We propose continual leakage-resilient dynamic secret sharing under split-state model in this paper. After a preprocessing stage, the dealer is able to dynamically choose a set of $n$ users and to allow a threshold of $t$ users to reconstruct different secrets in different time instants, by using the same broadcast message. The secrets are protected even if an adversary corrupts up to $t - 1$ users and obtains continual leakage from the rest of them. Our scheme can provide the security for secret sharing under continual leakage model while at the same time allowing the users to join and quit the scheme dynamically.

## 1 Introduction

Secret sharing is an important cryptographic primitive that a dealer shares a secret value between a group of users $\mathcal{P}$. Any set of $t$ (threshold) users from $\mathcal{P}$ can jointly recover the secret value. However, the collusion of any $t - 1$ or less users cannot obtain any information about the secret value. Secret sharing was firstly proposed by Shamir [13]. This type of secret sharing is sometimes referred as *threshold secret sharing*, in contrast with the secret sharing with general access structure. In this paper, we will focus on the threshold secret sharing. Secret sharing is useful in applications that require a collaboration like the management of cryptographic keys and secure multi-party computation.

Dynamic secret sharing has the feature that the dealer enables different sets of users (based on different access structures) to recover different secrets in different

* Supported by the HKU Small Project Funding No. 201109176192.
** Supported by the National Natural Science Foundation of China Grant No. 60970135 and 61170282.

T.W. Chim and T.H. Yuen (Eds.): ICICS 2012, LNCS 7618, pp. 119–130, 2012.

time instants simply by sending the same broadcast message to all of them. It was firstly formalized by Blundo *et al.* [3]. In the sense of threshold secret sharing, the dealer can choose different sets of users to recover different secrets, but a threshold of them is sufficient to recover a secret. It is fully dynamic since anyone can join or leave the system at any time, and the authorized set (to recover the secret) can be chosen at the time of generating the broadcast message (instead of the user share generating phase). In practical application, consider the example of the board of directors of a company. A threshold of the directors can sign a contract on behalf of the company. However, the members of the board of directors may change from time to time. Furthermore, it is favorable that only the directors of the related departments is capable to sign on certain projects. Therefore, dynamic (threshold) secret sharing is useful in this kind of situation.

Traditional secret sharing schemes assume the absolute secrecy of the user shares. Like many cryptosystems, such assumption may not hold in the real world due to the side-channel attacks, such as the timing attack, power analysis, etc. These attacks capture partial information about the private user shares and their internal states through various physical attributes of a computation device. Therefore, traditional security model can no longer provide security guarantee under the side-channel attack. Hence, leakage-resilient cryptography is proposed to capture this scenario in recent years. The relative leakage model was firstly introduced by Akavia et al. [1] which allows the attacker to learn at most $\ell$-bits information about the internal state of the system. Later on, the continual leakage model [9] describes that the secret key is updated periodically and the attacker can learn information continually, with the constraint that at most $\ell$-bits leakage of internal state is allowed between update.

**Our Contribution.** Our main result is to construct a dynamic secret sharing scheme under the continual leakage model (CLM-DSS). In our scheme, the attacker can continually learn the share owned by each user with the constraint that the total information leaked is less than $\ell$-bits between update. The random number used to update the share can also be leaked. Our scheme will guarantee the privacy of the secret value even up to $t-1$ parties are corrupted (where $t$ is threshold) and information owned by other parties are partially leaked. Moreover, the user can dynamically join and leave the secret sharing scheme. For different secret values, we can set different authorized set and threshold for each of them.

We model the leak function in our security model as the split-state model in [7]. Davì *et al.* [7] assumed that the memory of a system can be divided into two parts, and each of them is accessed independently by different process and different time interval. Therefore, when there is side-channel attack on the memory, the attacker can only obtain leakage from one part only. Therefore in the security model, the leak oracle is modeled in a way that the leak function can only leak on one part of the memory at one time, but not leak on both parts simultaneously.

**Our Techniques.** Our construction is based on the dynamic threshold encryption by Delerablée and Pointcheval [8]. Our construction begins with generating the master key and the public key as in [8]. Instead of sending a share directly to each user as in [8], the dealer encrypts it and sends the corresponding ciphertext and decryption key to the user. We use the Continual-Leakage-Resilient Sharing (CLRS)-friendly encryption scheme in [6] to provide the leakage-resilient property as well as the update protocol. Therefore, we can update the ciphertext and the secret key asynchronously to protect the secret value under the continual leakage model.

We have a few restrictions imposed on our security model due to the building blocks we used. Firstly, we use the split-state model for leakage since the ciphertext and the secret key of the CLRS-friendly encryption scheme is leaked independently in [6]. Secondly, we use the non-adaptive adversary and corruption model to handle the corruption of users which is inherited from the dynamic threshold encryption in [8]. Finally, we assume that the secret value to be shared and the master key of the dealer is leak-free, or else we can continuously leak on them and thus get the exact value of them. This is a common assumption in leakage-resilient cryptography, such as [5,11][1].

**Related Work.** It is useful to compare our scheme with other primitives from the literature. Firstly, standard secret sharing scheme [13] provides security when some subset of the shares are fully compromised which others are fully secure. Laih *et al.* [10] gave the first dynamic threshold secret sharing such that different secrets can be shared by different broadcast messages. Blakley *et al.* [2] introduced the user disenrollment to the dynamic threshold secret sharing. Their security models also assume full security of the uncorrupted users. In our security model, the shares that are not fully compromised can be partially leaked.

In leakage-resilient secret sharing, Boyle *et al.* [5] introduced a (non-dynamic) secret sharing which guarantees the privacy of the secret value only under the bounded leakage model; while we provide the security under the continual leakage model. The continual leakage-resilient secret sharing scheme for general access structure proposed by Dodis *et al.* [9] mainly focus on two parties and when it extends to more than two parties, the user cannot dynamically join and leave the scheme.

## 2   Security Model

Our goal is to give the definition of dynamic threshold secret sharing scheme under continual leakage model. We require that any user can dynamically join the secret sharing system. For each secret, the dealer can dynamically choose the share group $\mathcal{P}$ and the threshold value $t$. Finally, the secret share stored in each device may be continuously leaked by the attacker.

Our security is modified from the model of dynamic secret sharing in [3], by changing from monotone access structure to threshold access structure, and adding the update and leak oracle for the continual leakage model.

---

[1] There exist cryptosystems that allow leakage of the master secret key, such as identity-based encryption in [14].

## 2.1  Security Notion

A dynamic threshold secret sharing scheme is a tuple of algorithms CLR_DSS = (Setup, SharePreprocess, Update, MsgGen, Reconstruct) as follows:

- Setup($1^\lambda$): On input a security parameters $1^\lambda$, it outputs (MK, PK), where MK is the master secret key of the dealer and PK is the corresponding public key. PK may include the maximal size of an authorized set $m$, and a list of participants L.
- SharePreprocess(MK,PK,$S$,$\mathcal{P}$): On input MK, PK, the space of possible secrets $S$ and a set of participants $\mathcal{P} = (ID_1, \ldots, ID_n)$, it outputs the corresponding shares $a_1, \ldots, a_n$ for each participant, and may update L.
- MsgGen(PK,$s$,$t$,$\mathcal{P}'$,$(a_1, \ldots, a_n)$): On input PK, a secret $s \in S$, a threshold $t$, a set of participants $\mathcal{P}'$ with corresponding shares $(a_1, \ldots, a_n)$, it outputs the broadcast message $M$.
- Update(PK, $a_i$): On input PK, each user updates his share $a_i$ to protect the privacy of the secret share against continual leakage from the attacker. It outputs the updated share $a_i'$.
  In this model, we also assume that the share $a_i$ is split into two parts and they are updated and accessed independently. Denote them as $sh_1$ and $sh_2$, and define Update$_b$ ($b = 1, 2$) as follows (we omit the input PK for simplicity): Update$_b(sh_b) \rightarrow sh_b'$: The randomized update algorithm takes the index $b$ and the current version of the share $sh_b$ and outputs an update version $sh_b'$. The notation Update$_b^k(sh_b)$ denote the operation of updating the share $sh_b$ successively $k$ times in a row so that Update$_b^0(sh_b) = sh_b$, Update$_b^{k+1}(sh_b) =$ Update$_b$(Update$_b^k(sh_b)$).
- Reconstruct(PK, $(a_1, \ldots, a_t)$, $M$): On input PK, the secret shares $(a_1, \ldots, a_t)$ and a broadcast message $M$, it outputs the secret value $s$.

## 2.2  Security Model

First we will define what information can be leaked and what the leakage function should be in the split-state model. As described before, user $i$ will have a secret share $a_i$ which is stored in two parts $sh_1$ and $sh_2$. The leak function $f$ (which is an input to the Leak oracle) is a function of $a_i$ and the random value used. We denote $state_b = (sh_b, R_b)$ for $b \in \{1, 2\}$, where $R_b$ is the randomness used for $sh_b$. We can see that the attacker only leaks on the information on each user's share and randomness since other information are either leak-free or published. There is one restriction to the leak function $f$ as specified in [7]. For each user $i$, the leak oracle can only be applied on either $state_1$ or $state_2$, but it cannot be applied on both of them at the same time.

**Correctness:** It consists of two parts:

- *Update Correctness:* Notice that the update of $sh_1$ and $sh_2$ can be asynchronous, which means that for any sequence of $i \geq 0$, $j \geq 0$, $sh_1' \leftarrow$ Update$_1^i(sh_1)$, $sh_2' \leftarrow$ Update$_2^j(sh_2)$, the updated shares $(sh_1', sh_2')$ can be viewed as a valid share $a$ used for reconstruction.

– *Reconstruct Correctness*: If $M \leftarrow \mathsf{MsgGen}(\mathsf{PK}, s, t, \mathcal{P}', (a_1, \ldots, a_n))$ and $(a'_1, \ldots, a'_t)$ is a (updated) subset of the shares $(a_1, \ldots, a_n)$, then $s \leftarrow \mathsf{Reconstruct}(\mathsf{PK}, (a'_1, \ldots, a'_t), M)$.

**Privacy:** For any secret $s$ shared by a set $\mathcal{P}$ of registered users with a threshold $t$, any collusion that contains less than $t$ users from this authorized set and the bounded leakage from the uncorrupted users cannot learn any information about the secret $s$.

We formally define the above privacy notion, under the classical semantic security notion and under various attacks, using a game between the adversary $\mathcal{A}$ and the challenger $\mathcal{C}$. Both the adversary and the challenger are given as input a security parameter $1^\lambda$. The restriction we impose are:

– $\mathcal{A}$ cannot get any leakage about the master secret key and secret value.
– $\mathcal{A}$ has to decide the challenge set $\mathcal{P}^*$ of users, the challenge threshold $t^*$, and the identities set $\mathcal{I}$ that he will corrupt at the beginning of the game. This restriction is called non-adaptive adversary and corruption model(NAA-NAC). We restrict that $|\mathcal{P}^* \bigcap \mathcal{I}| \leq t^* - 1$.
– $\mathcal{A}$ cannot get leakage of more than $\ell$ bits between updates.

We now define our game CorruptLeak which consists of the following phases:

1. **Setup:** The adversary $\mathcal{A}$ sends to the challenger $\mathcal{C}$ the challenge set $\mathcal{P}^*$ of users, the challenge threshold $t^*$, and the identities set $\mathcal{I}$ that he will corrupt. $\mathcal{C}$ runs $\mathsf{Setup}(1^\lambda)$ to obtain the set of parameters param $= (\mathsf{MK}, \mathsf{PK})$. The public key $\mathsf{PK}$ is given to $\mathcal{A}$. Denote the secret space as $S$. $\mathcal{C}$ stores an initially empty list $\mathcal{L}$ of the form $(ID, b, sh_b, \ell_b, rand_b)$, which stores a part of the share $sh_b$ (b=1/2) for a user $ID$, the leaked bits, and the randomness used for the next update.

2. **Query Phase 1:** The adversary $\mathcal{A}$ adaptively issues queries:
   – **Join** query: on input an identity $ID$, $\mathcal{C}$ runs the $a = (sh_1, sh_2) \leftarrow \mathsf{SharePreprocess}(\mathsf{MK}, \mathsf{PK}, S, ID)$ to create a new user in the system. $\mathcal{C}$ chooses the randomness $rand_1$ and $rand_2$ used for the next update for $sh_1$ and $sh_2$ respectively. $\mathcal{C}$ stores $(ID, 1, sh_1, 0, rand_1)$ and $(ID, 2, sh_2, 0, rand_2)$ in the list $\mathcal{L}$.
   – **Corrupt** query: on input an identity $ID \in \mathcal{I}$, $\mathcal{C}$ retrieves $(ID, 1, sh_1, \cdot, \cdot)$ and $(ID, 2, sh_2, \cdot, \cdot) \in \mathcal{L}$ and returns $a = (sh_1, sh_2)$ to $\mathcal{A}$.
   – **Leak** query: on input an identity $ID \in \mathcal{I} \cup \mathcal{P}^*$, a leakage function $f : \{0, 1\}^* \rightarrow \{0, 1\}$ and $b = 1/2$, $\mathcal{C}$ retrieves $(ID, b, sh_b, \ell_b, rand_b) \in \mathcal{L}$. If $\ell_b \leq \ell$, then $\mathcal{C}$ responds with $f(sh_b, rand_b)$ and increases the counter $\ell_b = \ell_b + 1$ in the list $\mathcal{L}$. Otherwise returns $\perp$.
   – **Update** query: on input an identify $ID$ and $b = 1/2$, $\mathcal{C}$ retrieves $(ID, b, sh_b, \ell_b, rand_b) \in \mathcal{L}$ and computes $sh'_b = \mathsf{Update}_b(sh_b; rand_b)$. It samples fresh random number $rand'_b$ and updates $(ID, b, sh'_b, 0, rand'_b) \in \mathcal{L}$.

3. **Challenge:** $\mathcal{A}$ submits a secret value $s^* \in S$ to $\mathcal{C}$. $\mathcal{C}$ sets $s^*_0 = s^*$ and $s^*_1$ to be a random number. $\mathcal{C}$ retrieves $(ID^*_j, b, sh^*_{j,b}, \cdot, \cdot) \in \mathcal{L}$ for all $ID_i \in \mathcal{P}^*$ where $b = 1/2$. Denote $a^*_j = (sh^*_{j,1}, sh^*_{j,2})$. $\mathcal{C}$ flips a uniform coins $b' \xleftarrow{\$} \{0, 1\}$, generates $M^* = \mathsf{MsgGen}(\mathsf{MK}, s^*_{b'}, t^*, \mathcal{P}^*, \{a^*_j\})$ and sends it to $\mathcal{A}$.

4. **Query Phase 2:** $\mathcal{A}$ adaptively issues **Join, Corrupt** and **Leak** queries as in phase 1 , but the constraint is that the total number of identities $ID \in \mathcal{P}^*$ asked in **Corrupt** queries is less that $t^* - 1$ (which is $\mathcal{P}^* \cap \mathcal{I} \le t^* - 1$) and the **Leak** queries in phase 2 cannot be executed in the target set of users $\mathcal{P}^* - \mathcal{P}^* \cap \mathcal{I}$.

5. **Guess:** Finally, $\mathcal{A}$ outputs a bit $b^* \leftarrow \{0,1\}$ and wins the game if $b^* = b'$.

The advantage of $\mathcal{A}$ is defined as $Adv_\mathcal{A}(\lambda) = |\mathbf{Pr}[b' = b] - \frac{1}{2}|$.

**Definition 1.** *A dynamic threshold secret sharing scheme is $\ell$-continual leakage resilient if for all PPT adversaries $\mathcal{A}$, $Adv_\mathcal{A}(\lambda) \le negl(\lambda)$.*

# 3    Notation and Preliminaries

**Bilinear Maps.** Let $\mathbb{G}_1, \mathbb{G}_2$ and $\mathbb{G}_T$ be three cyclic groups of prime order $p$. A map $\hat{e} : \mathbb{G}_1 \times \mathbb{G}_2 \to \mathbb{G}_T$ is bilinear if for any generators $g_1 \in \mathbb{G}_1, g_2 \in \mathbb{G}_2$ and $a, b \in \mathbb{Z}_p$, $\hat{e}(g_1^a, g_2^b) = \hat{e}(g_1, g_2)^{ab}$. Let $\mathcal{G}$ be a pairing generation algorithm which takes as input a security parameter $1^\lambda$ and outputs $(p, \mathbb{G}_1, \mathbb{G}_2, \mathbb{G}_T, \hat{e}) \leftarrow \mathcal{G}(1^\lambda)$. The generators of the groups may also be given. All group operations as well as the bilinear map $\hat{e}$ are efficiently computable.

**The Symmetric External Diffie-Hellman Assumption (SXDH) [12].** The SXDH assumption is that the DDH assumption holds in $\mathbb{G}_1$ and $\mathbb{G}_2$.

**The Multi-Sequence of Exponents Diffie-Hellman Assumption (MSE-DDH) [8].** We now give the following decisional problem $(\ell, m, t)$-MSE-DDH introduced by Delerablée and Pointcheval [8]. Let $(p, \mathbb{G}_1, \mathbb{G}_2, \mathbb{G}_T, \hat{e}) \leftarrow \mathcal{G}(1^\lambda)$ be a bilinear map generator and let $\ell$, $m$ and $t$ be three integers. Let $g_0$ be a generator of $\mathbb{G}_1$ and $h_0$ a generator of $\mathbb{G}_2$. Given two random coprime polynomials $f$ and $g$, of respective orders $\ell$ and $m$, with pairwise distinct roots $-x_1, \ldots, -x_\ell$ and $-y_1, \ldots, -y_m$ respectively, as well as several sequences of exponentiations of some random and hidden $\alpha, \gamma \in \mathbb{Z}_p$:

$$g_0, g_0^\gamma, \ldots, g_0^{\gamma^{\ell+t-2}}, g_0^{\alpha \cdot \gamma}, \ldots, g_0^{\alpha \cdot \gamma^{\ell+t}}, g_0^{k \cdot \gamma \cdot f(\gamma)}$$
$$h_0, h_0^\gamma, \ldots, h_0^{\gamma^{m-2}}, h_0^{\alpha \cdot \gamma}, \ldots, h_0^{\alpha \cdot \gamma^{2m-1}}, h_0^{k \cdot g(\gamma)},$$

and $T \in \mathbb{G}_T$, decide whether $T$ is equal to $e(g_0, h_0)^{k \cdot f(\gamma)}$.

Delerablée and Pointcheval [8] showed that this problem belongs to the general Diffie-Hellman exponent problem due to Boneh *et al.* [4]. Therefore, the generic security of the assumption follows the result from [4]. We emphasize on the fact that, whereas the assumption has several parameters, it is non-interactive, and thus falsifiable.

**Continual Leakage-Resilient Sharing (CLRS) and CLRS-Friendly Encryption.** We review the two user continual leakage-resilient sharing (2-CLRS) in [6]. It is constructed from an updatable encryption. An updatable encryption [6] is a standard public key encryption scheme (KeyGen, Encrypt, Decrypt) with two additional procedures:

- SKUpdate: On input a secret key sk, it outputs an updated key $sk'$.
- CTUpdate: On input a ciphertext ct, it outputs an updated ciphertext $ct'$.

The 2-CLRS in [6] is constructed as follows (without the share preprocess phase):

- Setup: On input a security parameter $1^\lambda$, it samples $(\mathsf{pk}, \mathsf{sk}) \leftarrow \mathsf{KeyGen}(1^\lambda)$ and outputs the public key pk.
- MsgGen: On input a secret $s$, it calculates $\mathsf{ct} \leftarrow \mathsf{Encrypt}_{\mathsf{pk}}(s)$ and outputs two shares $sh_1 = \mathsf{sk}$ and $sh_2 = \mathsf{ct}$.
- Update: On input a share $sh_1$ or $sh_2$, it outputs $\mathsf{SKUpdate}(\mathsf{sk})$ or $\mathsf{CTUpdate}(\mathsf{ct})$.
- Reconstruct: On input $sh_1$ and $sh_2$, it outputs $s \leftarrow \mathsf{Decrypt}_{\mathsf{sk}}(\mathsf{ct})$.

We say that an updatable encryption scheme is an $\ell$-CLRS-friendly encryption if the corresponding 2-CLRS is correct and $\ell$-continual leakage resilient. The details of the construction of the $\ell$-CLRS-friendly encryption is in [6].

# 4 Our Construction

In this section, we will describe how to construct dynamic secret sharing scheme under continual leakage model (CLM-DSS).

Our construction is inspired from the threshold encryption scheme by Delerablée and Pointcheval [8]. In order to allow leakage of secret shares of different users, we adopt the CLRS-friendly encryption scheme described in [6]. It is composed of (KeyGen, Encrypt, Decrypt, SKUpdate, CTUpdate). Then the secret share of each user is composed of two parts: (1) the secret key of the CLRS-friendly encryption [6], and (2) the ciphertext which is the encryption of the secret key of the threshold encryption [8]. By [6], both parts can be updated and leaked independently in the security proof.

## 4.1 CLM-DSS Scheme

Setup($1^\lambda$) : Given the security parameter $1^\lambda$, it runs $(p, \mathbb{G}_1, \mathbb{G}_2, \mathbb{G}_T, \hat{e}) \leftarrow \mathcal{G}(1^\lambda)$. Also, two generators $g \in \mathbb{G}_1$ and $h \in \mathbb{G}_2$ are randomly selected as well as two secret values $\gamma, \alpha \in \mathbb{Z}_p^*$. Finally, a set $\mathcal{D} = \{d_i\}_{i=1}^{m-1}$ of values in $\mathbb{Z}_p^*$ is randomly selected, where $m$ is the maximal size of an authorized set. This corresponds to a set of dummy users, that will be used to complete a set of authorized users. It computes $u = g^{\alpha\gamma}$, $v = \hat{e}(g, h)^\alpha$. Denote $H : \mathbb{G}_1 \to \mathbb{G}_T$ be an efficiently computable function and its inverse $H^{-1}$ is also efficiently computable. The list of users L is initially empty. It sets

$$\mathsf{PK} = (m, u, v, h, h^\alpha, \{h^{\gamma^i}\}_{i=1}^{m-2}, \{h^{\alpha\gamma^i}\}_{i=1}^{2m-1}, \mathcal{D}, H, H^{-1}, \mathsf{L}), \quad \mathsf{MK} = (g, \gamma, \alpha).$$

SharePreprocess(MK, PK, $S, \mathcal{P}$) : Given MK,PK and a set of users $\mathcal{P}$ (our scheme supports the secret space $S = \mathbb{G}_T$), for each identity $ID_i \in \mathcal{P}$, it randomly chooses a new and distinct $x_i \in \mathbb{Z}_p^*$ such that $x_i$ should be different from all previous one, including the dummy users in $\mathcal{D}$. It runs $(\mathsf{pk}_i, \mathsf{sk}_i) \leftarrow \mathsf{KeyGen}(1^\lambda)$ and $\mathsf{ct}_i \leftarrow \mathsf{Encrypt}_{\mathsf{pk}_i}(H(g^{\frac{1}{\gamma+x_i}}))$ of the CLRS-friendly encryption of [6]. It generates the share $a_i = (\mathsf{sk}_i, \mathsf{ct}_i)$ for user $ID_i$. The value $(x_i, ID_i)$ is published by putting it into L.

$\mathsf{MsgGen}(\mathsf{PK}, s, t, \mathcal{P}, (a_1, \ldots, a_n))$ : Given PK, the secret $s$, a threshold $t$ and a set of users $\mathcal{P} = (ID_1, \ldots, ID_n)$, it first finds the corresponding $x_i$ for $ID_i$ from L. Denote the set $\bar{P}$ be the set of all $x_i$. It randomly picks $k \in \mathbb{Z}_p^*$ and a random subset $\bar{\mathcal{D}} \subseteq \mathcal{D}$ of size $m+t-n-1$. It outputs the broadcast message $M = (C_1, C_2, C_3, \bar{\mathcal{D}})$, where:

$$C_1 = u^{-k}, \quad C_2 = h^{k \cdot \alpha \cdot \Pi_{x_i \in \bar{P}}(\gamma + x_i) \cdot \Pi_{x \in \bar{\mathcal{D}}}(\gamma + x)}, \quad C_3 = s \cdot v^k.$$

$\mathsf{Update}(\mathsf{PK}, a_i)$ : For a share $a_i = (\mathsf{sk}_i, \mathsf{ct}_i)$, it can either update the first or the second part. For $\mathsf{Update}_1(\mathsf{sk}_i)$, it calls the function $\mathsf{SKUpdate}(\mathsf{sk}_i)$. For $\mathsf{Update}_2(\mathsf{ct}_i)$, it calls the function $\mathsf{CTUpdate}(\mathsf{ct}_i)$.

$\mathsf{Reconstruct}(\mathsf{PK}, (a_1, \ldots, a_t), M)$ : Given PK, a broadcast message $M = (C_1, C_2, C_3, \bar{\mathcal{D}})$, and shares $a_i = (\mathsf{sk}_i, \mathsf{ct}_i)$ for $i = 1 \ldots, t$, denote $T = (x_1, \ldots x_t)$ be the corresponding value in L. It first calls the function $usk_i \leftarrow H^{-1}(\mathsf{Decrypt}_{\mathsf{sk}_i}(\mathsf{ct}_i))$, where we can get $usk_i = g^{\frac{1}{\gamma + x_i}}$. We can compute

$$\sigma_i = \hat{e}(usk_i, C_2) = e(g, h)^{\frac{k \cdot \alpha \cdot \Pi_{x_i \in \bar{P} \cup \bar{\mathcal{D}}}(\gamma + x_i)}{\gamma + x}}.$$

Denote $\Omega$ as the set of $\{\sigma_1, \ldots \sigma_t\}$. Finally, it can recover the secret $s$:

$$s = \frac{C_3}{(\hat{e}(C_1, h^{p(T, \bar{P})(\gamma)}) \cdot \mathbf{Aggregate}(\mathbb{G}_T, \Omega))^{\frac{1}{c(T, \bar{P})}}},$$

where $h^{p(T, \bar{P})(\gamma)}$ is computed from PK since

$$p(T, \bar{P})(\gamma) = \frac{1}{\gamma} \cdot \left( \prod_{x \in \bar{P} \cup \bar{\mathcal{D}} - T} (\gamma + x) - c(T, \bar{P}) \right),$$

$$c(T, \bar{P}) = \prod_{x \in \bar{P} \cup \bar{\mathcal{D}} - T} x,$$

$$\mathbf{Aggregate}(\mathbb{G}_T, \Omega) = \mathbf{Aggregate}(\mathbb{G}_T, \{\hat{e}(g, C_2)^{\frac{1}{\gamma + x}}\}_{x \in T})$$

$$= \hat{e}(g, C_2)^{\frac{1}{\Pi_{x \in T}(\gamma + x)}} = \hat{e}(g, h)^{k \cdot \alpha \cdot \Pi_{x_i \in \bar{P} \cup \bar{\mathcal{D}} - T}(\gamma + x_i)}.$$

The $\mathbf{Aggregate}$ algorithm computes $\hat{e}(g, C_2)^{\frac{1}{(\gamma + x_1) \cdots (\gamma + x_t)}}$ given $\Omega = \{\sigma_j = \hat{e}(g, C_2)^{\frac{1}{\gamma + x_j}}\}_{j=1}^t$. The detail of $\mathbf{Aggregate}$ can be found in [8].

**Correctness.** Assuming that $\Omega$ is correct, we have

$$\hat{e}(C_1, h^{p(T, \bar{P})(\gamma)}) \cdot \mathbf{Aggregate}(\mathbb{G}_T, \Omega)$$

$$= \hat{e}(g^{-k \cdot \alpha \cdot \gamma}, h^{p(T, \bar{P})(\gamma)}) \cdot \hat{e}(g, C_2)^{\frac{1}{\Pi_{x \in T}(\gamma + x)}}$$

$$= \hat{e}(g, h)^{-k \cdot \alpha \cdot \gamma \cdot p(T, \bar{P})(\gamma)} \cdot \hat{e}(g, h)^{k \cdot \alpha \cdot \Pi_{x \in \bar{P} \cup \bar{\mathcal{D}}_{m+t-s-1} - T}(\gamma + x)}$$

$$= \hat{e}(g, h)^{k \cdot \alpha \cdot c(T, \bar{P})} = (v^k)^{c(T, \bar{P})}.$$

## 4.2   Security

**Hybrid Game Definitions.** We first define several hybrid games. The main part of the proof is to show statistical indistinguishability between these games. The output of each game consists of the view of the adversary $\mathcal{A}$ as well as a bit $b$ chosen by the challenger $\mathcal{C}$ representing its choice of which challenge secret $s_0^*, s_1^*$ to be shared. Denote Q as $|\mathcal{P}^*| - t^* + 2$, where $|\mathcal{P}^*|$ is the size of the challenge set of users and $t^*$ is the threshold. We describe the games in details below.

- **GameReal:** This is the original "CorruptLeak" game.
- **Game $i$:** In Game $i$, for Leak queries on the first $i$ uncorrupted identities from $\mathcal{P}^*$, the challenger $\mathcal{C}$ will answer the query using a random number, and for the rest of the identities, $\mathcal{C}$ answers it using the valid key.
- **GameFinal:** It is the same as **Game $Q$**, except that instead of sharing the challenge secret value $s_b^*$, we just share a random number. More specifically, in **GameFinal**, the secret shares used in the LeakOracle are all random and the broadcast message is just a random number. Thus, the view of the adversary in **GameFinal** is independent of the challenger's bit $b$.

**Theorem 1.** For $z \geq 6$, $n \geq 3z - 6$, our secret sharing scheme is $\ell_{SK}$-continual leakage-resilient under the SXDH assumption and the $(l, m, t)$-MSE-DDH assumption, for $\ell_{SK} \leq \min(z/6 - 1, n - 3z + 6)\log(p) - \omega(\log(\lambda))$, $\mathcal{P}^* \cap \mathcal{I} \leq t - 1$, $l = \mathcal{I} - \mathcal{P}^* \cap \mathcal{I}$ and $m = \max |\mathcal{P}^*|$.

*Proof.* In order to prove that our secret sharing scheme is $\ell_{SK}$-continual leakage secure, we will build several games to simulate the different cases and show that those games are indistinguishable under the SXDH, MSE-DDH assumption and the following lemma.

**Lemma 1.** Let $z \geq 6$, $n \geq 3z - 6$. Given $(p, \mathbb{G}_1, \mathbb{G}_2, \mathbb{G}_T, \hat{e})$, an efficiently computable function $H : \mathbb{G}_1 \rightarrow \mathbb{G}_T$, the CLRS-friendly encryption [6] algorithm Encrypt with corresponding public key pk, secret key sk and the sequences:

$$x_1, x_2, \ldots, x_{l+1};\ g^{\frac{1}{\gamma+x_1}}, g^{\frac{1}{\gamma+x_2}}, \ldots, g^{\frac{1}{\gamma+x_l}};\ \{h^{\alpha \cdot \gamma^i}\}_{i=0}^{2m-1}, \{h^{\gamma^i}\}_{i=0}^{m-2}, g^{\alpha \cdot \gamma}, \hat{e}(g, h)^{\alpha}.$$

For simplicity, we denote the above mentioned sequences as D. Let $(sh_1, sh_2) = (\text{sk}, \text{Encrypt}_{pk}(H(g^{\frac{1}{\gamma+x_{l+1}}})))$ and $(sh_1', sh_2') = (\text{sk}, \text{Encrypt}_{pk}(R))$ where $R$ is randomly chosen from the message space. Then under the SXDH assumption:

$$(D, f_1(sh_1), f_2(sh_2)) \stackrel{stat}{\approx} (D, f_1(sh_1'), f_2(sh_2')),$$

as long as the function $f_1$ and $f_2$ have the output size $|f_1|, |f_2| \leq \min(z/6 - 1, n - 3z + 6)\log(p) - \omega(\log(\lambda))$.

*Proof.* According to the security of the CLRS-Friendly Encryption in [6], no PPT adversary can distinguish the ciphertext of $H(g^{\frac{1}{\gamma+x_{l+1}}})$ from a random number, as long as $|f_1|, |f_2| \leq \min(z/6 - 1, n - 3z + 6)\log(p) - \omega(\log(\lambda))$, even given the value $H(g^{\frac{1}{\gamma+x_{l+1}}})$. Therefore, given the sequence $D$, no PPT adversary can distinguish these two distributions under the SXDH assumption.     □

**Lemma 2.** *GameReal* $\overset{stat}{\approx}$ *Game 0.*

It is easy to see that **GameReal** is the same as **Game 0**.

**Lemma 3.** *For $i = 0, \ldots, Q - 1$, under the SXDH assumption with $z \geq 6, n \geq 3z-6, \ell_{SK} \leq \min(z/6-1, n-3z+6)\log(p) - \omega(\log(\lambda))$, Game $i \overset{stat}{\approx}$ Game $i+1$.*

*Proof.* If there exists an adversary $\mathcal{A}$ who has a non-negligible advantage in distinguishing **Game** $i$ and **Game** $i+1$, we will create a PPT algorithm $\mathcal{B}$ which will distinguish between $(D, f_1(sh_1), f_2(sh_2))$ and $(D, f_1(sh'_1), f_2(sh'_2))$ from Lemma 1 with non-negligible probability. This will yield a contradiction, since these distributions have a negligible statistical distance if the CLRS-friendly encryption scheme [6] is secure.

$\mathcal{B}$ simulates either **Game** $i$ or **Game** $i + 1$ with $\mathcal{A}$ as follows. It starts by running the Setup algorithm by itself and giving $\mathcal{A}$ the public parameters by using the **Lemma** 1's instances. By the notion of the **Lemma** 1, $\mathcal{B}$ can create enough valid keys and responds to all the $\mathcal{A}$'s queries.

For the Join queries on the $(i + 1)$-th uncorrupted identity from $\mathcal{P}^*$, $\mathcal{B}$ just responds by putting $x_{l+1}$ in L. When $\mathcal{A}$ issues the Leak query on the $(i + 1)$-th identity, $\mathcal{B}$ will encode the leakage $\mathcal{A}$ asks for this key in **Phase 1** as a single polynomial time computable function $f$. It can do this by fixing the values of all other keys and fixing all other variables involved in the challenge key. $\mathcal{B}$ then receives a sample $\langle D, f_1(SH_1), f_2(SH_2)\rangle$(where $SH_i$ is either distributed as $sh_i$ or $sh'_i$ using the notation of the **Lemma** 1). $\mathcal{B}$ will use $f_1(SH_1), f_2(SH_2)$ to answer $\mathcal{A}$'s Leak query for the $(i + 1)$-th identity by implicitly defining the challenge key as $(SH_1, SH_2)$.

At some point, $\mathcal{A}$ declares the challenge secret value, and $\mathcal{B}$ flips a coin $b$ and produces the challenge broadcast message $M^*$. Since $M^*$ is independent of the queries above, the ciphertext is well-distributed. The **Phase 2** is the same as the **Phase 1** except the forbiddance of the Leak queries.

If $SH_2$ is the ciphertext of $H(g^{\frac{1}{\gamma+x_{l+1}}})$, then $\mathcal{B}$ responds with the correct leak query, so $\mathcal{B}$ properly simulates **Game** $i$. If $SH_2$ is the ciphertext of a random number, it correctly simulates **Game** $i + 1$.   $\square$

**Lemma 4.** *If the $(l, m, t)$-MSE-DDH assumption holds, where $t - 1 \geq \mathcal{P}^* \cap \mathcal{I}$, $l = \mathcal{I} - \mathcal{P}^* \cap \mathcal{I}$, $m = \max |\mathcal{P}^*|$, then Game $Q \overset{stat}{\approx}$ GameFinal.*

*Proof.* Initially, the attacker output a target set $\mathcal{P}^* = \{ID_1^*, \ldots, ID_{|\mathcal{P}^*|}^*\}$ of identities that he wants to attack (the target authorized set), and a set $\mathcal{I}$ of identities that he wants to corrupt, with $|\mathcal{I}| \leq l + t - 1$ and $|\mathcal{P}^* \cap \mathcal{I}| \leq t - 1$. Given the $(l, m, t)$-MSE-DDH instance with the bilinear group $(p, \mathbb{G}_1, \mathbb{G}_2, \mathbb{G}_T, \hat{e})$, two coprime polynomials $f$ and $g$ of respective orders $l$ and $m$ with their pairwise distinct roots $(-x_1, \ldots, -x_l)$ and $(-x_{l+t}, \ldots, -x_{l+t+m-1})$, and given:

$$g_0, g_0^\gamma, \ldots, g_0^{\gamma^{\ell+t-2}}, g_0^{\alpha \cdot \gamma}, \ldots, g_0^{\alpha \cdot \gamma^{\ell+t}}, g_0^{k \cdot \gamma \cdot f(\gamma)}$$

$$h_0, h_0^\gamma, \ldots, h_0^{\gamma^{m-2}}, h_0^{\alpha \cdot \gamma}, \ldots, h_0^{\alpha \cdot \gamma^{2m-1}}, h_0^{k \cdot g(\gamma)}, T,$$

where $T$ is either equal to $\hat{e}(g_0, h_0)^{k \cdot f(\gamma)}$ or a random elements from $\mathbb{G}_T$. We can randomly choose $x_{l+1}, \ldots, x_{l+t-1}$ from $\mathbb{Z}_p^*$ (different from other $x_i$'s) and write $f$, $g$ and an additional function $q$ as:

$$f(X) = \prod_{i=1}^{l}(X + x_i), \quad q(X) = \prod_{i=l+1}^{l+t-1}(X + x_i), \quad g(X) = \prod_{i=l+t}^{l+t+m-1}(X + x_i).$$

The polynomial $f$ corresponds to a set of $l$ users not in the target set that can be corrupted. The polynomial $q$ corresponds to a set of $t - 1$ users of the target set that can be corrupted. The polynomial $g$ corresponds to the $|\mathcal{P}^*| - t + 1$ users of the target set and the rest dummy keys used in the challenge phase, and the users of the target set can be leaked by the leakage function specified by the attacker. For $i \in [1, l + t - 1]$, we set $f_i(\gamma) = \frac{f(\gamma) \cdot q(\gamma)}{\gamma + x_i}$.

**Setup:** To generate the system parameters, the simulator $\mathcal{B}$ calculates $g = g_0^{f(\gamma) \cdot q(\gamma)}$ and sets

$$h = h_0, \quad u = g_0^{\alpha \cdot \gamma \cdot f(\gamma) \cdot q(\gamma)} = g^{\alpha \cdot \gamma}, \quad v = e(g_0, h_0)^{\alpha \cdot f(\gamma) \cdot q(\gamma)} = e(g, h)^{\alpha}.$$

The two latter formula can be computed from the MSE-DDH instance input, since $f \cdot q$ is a polynomial of degree $l + t - 1$. $\mathcal{B}$ then sets the set $\mathcal{D} = \{d_i\}_{i=1}^{m-1}$ corresponding to dummy users:

- $\mathcal{D}^* = \{d_i\}_{i=1}^{m+t-|\mathcal{P}^*|-1}$ is a subset of $\{x_i\}_{l+t}^{l+t+m-1}$. This subset corresponds to the dummy users included to complete the target set in the challenge phase as mentioned above.
- $\{d_i\}_{m+t-|\mathcal{P}^*|}^{m-1}$ is a set of random elements in $\mathbb{Z}_p^*$.

Finally, $\mathcal{B}$ sets PK as the definition in the previous section.

**Query:** For each Join query with input $ID_i$, $\mathcal{B}$ puts $(x, ID_i) \in L$ where:

- if $ID_i \in \mathcal{I} \cap \mathcal{P}^*$, $\mathcal{B}$ sets $x$ as an "unused" element in $\{x_i\}_{l+1}^{l+t-1}$.
- if $ID_i \in \mathcal{I} - \mathcal{I} \cap \mathcal{P}^*$, $\mathcal{B}$ sets $x$ as an "unused" element in $\{x_i\}_{1}^{l}$.
- if $ID_i \in \mathcal{P}^* - \mathcal{I} \cap \mathcal{P}^*$, $\mathcal{B}$ sets $x$ as an "unused" element in $\{x_i\}_{l+t}^{l+t+m-1}$.
- if $ID_i \notin \mathcal{I} \cup \mathcal{P}^*$, $\mathcal{B}$ randomly picks a $x \notin \{x_i\}_{i=1}^{l+t+m-1}$ in $\mathbb{Z}_p$.

When comes to the Leak query, $\mathcal{B}$ answers it using a random number. When receiving the Corrupt query for $x_i$, $\mathcal{B}$ computes the valid key $g^{\frac{1}{\gamma + x_i}} = g_0^{f_i(\gamma)}$ using the MSE-DDH problem instance and gives it to $\mathcal{A}$.

**Challenge:** $\mathcal{B}$ picks a random bit $b$ and generates a broadcast message for the secret $s_b^*$ for a dummy set $\mathcal{D}^*$:

$$C_1^* = g_0^{-k \cdot \gamma \cdot f(\gamma)} = u^{-k'}, \quad C_2^* = h_0^{k \cdot g(\gamma)} = h^{k' \cdot \alpha \cdot \prod_{x_i \in \mathcal{P}^* \cup \mathcal{D}^*}(\gamma + x)}, \quad C_3^* = T \cdot s_b^*,$$

where $k' = \frac{k}{\alpha \cdot q(\gamma)}$. $\mathcal{B}$ returns $(C_1^*, C_2^*, C_3^*, \mathcal{D}^*)$ to $\mathcal{A}$.

The definition of **GameFinal** is the same as **Game Q** except for that instead of sending $v^{k'} \cdot s_b^*$ to $\mathcal{A}$, $\mathcal{B}$ sends $v^{k'} \cdot R$ to the attacker, where $R$ is a random number. If $T = e(g_0, h_0)^{k \cdot f(\gamma)}$, then $C_3^* = v^{k'} \cdot s_b^*$ which is the simulation of **Game Q**. If $T$ is a random number in $\mathbb{G}_T$, then $C_3^*$ is random in $\mathbb{G}_T$. Therefore $\mathcal{B}$ simulates the **GameFinal**. $\qquad \square$

**Putting Them All Together.** Following the above lemmas, we can easily get **GameReal** $\overset{stat}{\approx}$ **GameFinal**. Recall that the output of each game includes the view of $\mathcal{A}$ at the end of experiment along with the challenger's choice bit $b$, since $\mathcal{A}$'s guess $b'$ at the end of the game can be efficiently computed from the output of each game. In the **GameFinal**, the view of $\mathcal{A}$ is independent of the random bit $b$. Hence we have $\Pr[\mathcal{A} \text{ wins}] = \frac{1}{2}$ since the two games are indistinguishable under the SXDH assumption the MSE-DDH assumption. □

# References

1. Akavia, A., Goldwasser, S., Vaikuntanathan, V.: Simultaneous Hardcore Bits and Cryptography against Memory Attacks. In: Reingold, O. (ed.) TCC 2009. LNCS, vol. 5444, pp. 474–495. Springer, Heidelberg (2009)
2. Blakley, B., Blakley, G.R., Chan, A.H., Massey, J.L.: Threshold Schemes with Disenrollment. In: Brickell, E.F. (ed.) CRYPTO 1992. LNCS, vol. 740, pp. 540–548. Springer, Heidelberg (1993)
3. Blundo, C., Cresti, A., De Santis, A., Vaccaro, U.: Fully Dynamic Secret Sharing Schemes. In: Stinson, D.R. (ed.) CRYPTO 1993. LNCS, vol. 773, pp. 110–125. Springer, Heidelberg (1994)
4. Boneh, D., Boyen, X., Goh, E.-J.: Hierarchical Identity Based Encryption with Constant Size Ciphertext. In: Cramer, R. (ed.) EUROCRYPT 2005. LNCS, vol. 3494, pp. 440–456. Springer, Heidelberg (2005)
5. Boyle, E., Goldwasser, S., Kalai, Y.T.: Leakage-Resilient Coin Tossing. In: Peleg, D. (ed.) Distributed Computing. LNCS, vol. 6950, pp. 181–196. Springer, Heidelberg (2011)
6. Brakerski, Z., Kalai, Y.T., Katz, J., Vaikuntanathan, V.: Overcoming the hole in the bucket: Public-key cryptography resilient to continual memory leakage. In: FOCS, pp. 501–510. IEEE Computer Society (2010)
7. Davì, F., Dziembowski, S., Venturi, D.: Leakage-Resilient Storage. In: Garay, J.A., De Prisco, R. (eds.) SCN 2010. LNCS, vol. 6280, pp. 121–137. Springer, Heidelberg (2010)
8. Delerablée, C., Pointcheval, D.: Dynamic Threshold Public-Key Encryption. In: Wagner, D. (ed.) CRYPTO 2008. LNCS, vol. 5157, pp. 317–334. Springer, Heidelberg (2008)
9. Dodis, Y., Lewko, A.B., Waters, B., Wichs, D.: Storing secrets on continually leaky devices. In: Ostrovsky, R. (ed.) FOCS, pp. 688–697. IEEE (2011)
10. Laih, C.-S., Harn, L., Lee, J.-Y., Hwang, T.: Dynamic Threshold Scheme Based on the Definition of Cross-Product in an N-dimensional Linear Space. In: Brassard, G. (ed.) CRYPTO 1989. LNCS, vol. 435, pp. 286–298. Springer, Heidelberg (1990)
11. Lewko, A.B., Rouselakis, Y., Waters, B.: Achieving Leakage Resilience through Dual System Encryption. In: Ishai, Y. (ed.) TCC 2011. LNCS, vol. 6597, pp. 70–88. Springer, Heidelberg (2011)
12. Scott, M.: Authenticated id-based key exchange and remote log-in with simple token and pin number. Cryptology ePrint Archive, Report 2002/164 (2002), http://eprint.iacr.org/
13. Shamir, A.: How to share a secret. Commun. ACM 22(11), 612–613 (1979)
14. Yuen, T.H., Chow, S.S.M., Zhang, Y., Yiu, S.M.: Identity-Based Encryption Resilient to Continual Auxiliary Leakage. In: Pointcheval, D., Johansson, T. (eds.) EUROCRYPT 2012. LNCS, vol. 7237, pp. 117–134. Springer, Heidelberg (2012)

# Conversion of Real-Numbered Privacy-Preserving Problems into the Integer Domain

Wilko Henecka, Nigel Bean, and Matthew Roughan

School of Mathematical Sciences, University of Adelaide, Australia
{wilko.henecka,nigel.bean,matthew.roughan}@adelaide.edu.au

**Abstract.** Secure Multiparty Computation (SMC) enables untrusting parties to jointly compute a function on their respective inputs without revealing any information but the outcome. Almost all techniques for SMC support only integer inputs and operations. We present a *secure scaling* protocol for two parties to map real number inputs into integers without revealing any information about their respective inputs. The main component is a novel algorithm for privacy-preserving random number generation. We also show how to implement the protocol using Yao's garbled circuit technique.

## 1 Introduction

For the last 30 years the field of privacy-preserving techniques for distributed computation, also called *Secure Multiparty Computation* (SMC), has been growing. It offers solutions for multiple parties to compute functions without revealing their respective inputs to each other. These techniques have come a long way from the first theoretical ideas to practical solutions for problems such as electronic voting, auctions, data mining, network management and optimisation.

Almost all secure multiparty computation techniques have a message space consisting of a finite set of integers and the operations they provide are only defined over the integers. What if you want to engage in a privacy preserving protocol with real numbers, or floating point approximations? You can either extend a SMC technique to support fixed-point [1] or floating-point [2,3] arithmetic, or you create a mapping from the inputs into the integer space and then use conventional SMC [4–6]. The first approach introduces more complexity and limits the choice of techniques to just a few, the latter raises an interesting privacy question: *How do you agree on a mapping without revealing information about the inputs?*

In this paper we present the first secure scaling protocol for two parties. It enables them to agree on a mapping (by scaling) in a privacy-preserving manner. The key building block for this protocol is a novel algorithm for privacy-preserving random number generation. We also provide an efficient implementation of the protocol.

T.W. Chim and T.H. Yuen (Eds.): ICICS 2012, LNCS 7618, pp. 131–141, 2012.
© Springer-Verlag Berlin Heidelberg 2012

## 2    Secure Multiparty Computation

Secure Multiparty Computation (SMC) protocols enable parties to carry out distributed computation tasks without having to reveal their inputs to each other. The most famous example is the *millionaires problem*: Two millionaires want to find out who is richer without revealing their actual wealth to each other. When SMC was introduced in 1982 by Yao [7], he used this example as a motivation.

**Yao's Garbled Circuits.** The earliest generic solution for SMC was proposed by Yao in 1986 [8]. It is a constant-round protocol for securely computing a two-party function while at the same time keeping the inputs private. Let Alice and Bob be two parties holding the inputs $x^{(A)}$ and $x^{(B)}$ respectively and $f$ be a polynomial-time function. The first step is to view $f$ as a Boolean circuit $C$.

*Boolean Circuit:* A Boolean circuit consists of wires and gates. The wires transmit a value $\{0,1\}$ and the gates compute a Boolean function on their input wires, and output the result to another wire. This wire may then be connected to the input of another gate or be an output value of the circuit (Figure 1). Mathematically we describe a circuit by a series of functions $g_i(\alpha, \beta)$, $\alpha, \beta \in \{0,1\}$, $g_i : \{0,1\}^n \to \{0,1\}$.

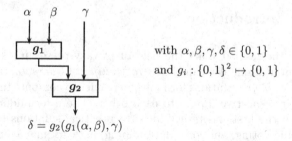

$$\delta = g_2(g_1(\alpha, \beta), \gamma)$$

with $\alpha, \beta, \gamma, \delta \in \{0,1\}$
and $g_i : \{0,1\}^2 \mapsto \{0,1\}$

**Fig. 1.** A Boolean circuit consisting of 2 two-input gates

Once the input wires to a gate are given values $\alpha, \beta$, it is possible to compute $g_1(\alpha, \beta)$ and assign it to the output wire which becomes an input to $g_2(\cdot, \cdot)$, etc. The output of the circuit is given by the values of the output wires of the circuit. Thus, computing the circuit $C$ is essentially just allocating appropriate Boolean values to all wires of the circuit.

*Privacy:* The values for some wires are provided by Alice, and others by Bob. These represent private inputs that should not be leaked to the other party. Likewise all intermediate values have to remain hidden, since they could reveal information about the inputs. The only values learned should be the outputs. The protocol works by having one party (say Alice) first generate a *garbled* version of the circuit and then send it to Bob. To create the garbled circuit Alice first assigns random labels for the 0 and 1 states of all wires. She then uses these labels as keys to encrypt the truth-tables of the gates and finally sends the encrypted values to Bob. In this form it doesn't leak any information to Bob. However, he can obtain the output of the circuit by decrypting it, using the labels given to him by Alice. In order to ensure that Bob learns nothing more than the output itself, Bob is only given the labels for the actual input values (not all possible inputs). He receives the labels for his input by running an oblivious transfer protocol with Alice (See [9] for further details).

*Security Model:* Yao's protocol for SMC is secure in the *semi-honest* model, *i.e.,* parties are assumed to correctly follow the protocol, and there is no efficient adversary that can extract more information from the transcript of the protocol execution than is revealed by that party's private input and the result of the function. There are also extensions to the protocol which are secure against certain types of active adversaries: (See Lindell and Pinkas [9] and the citations therein).

*Practicality:* Recent contributions [10, 11] improved the efficiency of implementations of Yao's protocol significantly.

Over the past few years several implementations for generic secure two-party computation using garbled circuits have been developed [11–14]. They differ in abstraction level, supported optimisation techniques and efficiency. We use [14] because it allows construction of dynamic loops.

There are other protocols for secure multiparty computation, varying in assumptions, security guaranties, number of supported parties, performance and supported operations (see [15] for an overview). However, our protocol translates naturally into a Boolean circuit.

## 3    Secure Scaling

Almost all secure multiparty computation techniques support only integers as inputs and operations on the integers. To engage in a privacy preserving protocol having real numbers, or floating point approximations, as inputs, you can define a mapping from the real inputs into the integer space and then use conventional SMC.

The obvious trivial approach to map real numbers to integers is scaling and quantisation. Let $r \in \mathbb{R}$ be the real number input. Then $i = \lceil s \cdot r \rfloor$ is the mapping from $r$ to $i$, where $\lceil \cdot \rfloor$ is the function that rounds to the nearest integer, and $s$ is a scaling factor the parties agree on.

It is easy to see that the scaling factor leaks information about the inputs, since it has to be chosen such that all inputs are mapped into the finite set and are still distinguishable. Each party can support a different set of scaling factors, depending on their respective inputs. Revealing these sets to each other leaks information. They want to agree on a scaling factor without having to reveal any information about their supported sets other than they contain the chosen scaling factor.

We propose a *Secure Scaling* protocol to pick a scaling factor at random out of the intersection of ranges given by two parties. The basic idea is to first compute a secure set intersection and then, without revealing the intersection, pick an element at random (see Section 4.4). While secure set intersection protocols are readily available we propose the first protocol we know of to draw a random number from a private range.

# 4  Drawing Random Numbers from a Private Range

We don't want to reveal the range of the scaling factors, once it is computed with the privacy-preserving set-intersection protocol. Instead we keep it in the encrypted space and use it as the input to the random number algorithm. The goal of this algorithm is to pick an element uniformly at random out of the range without giving the participants any more information than the randomly drawn element itself.

We first show the simple case where the range starts with 0 and has a power of two elements. Then we allow for an arbitrary number of elements, still starting with 0, and finally we present the algorithm where both bounds of the range are arbitrary values.

## 4.1  Range $N_{2^m-1} = \{0, 1, 2, \ldots, 2^m - 1\}$

The set $N_{2^m-1} = \{0, 1, 2, \ldots, 2^m-1\}$ is the set of integers that can be represented by an $m$-bit number. If we choose $m$ random bits, each with probability $1/2$, the binary number denoted by these bits will be uniformly distributed over $N_{2^m-1}$. The algorithm combines random bits chosen by both parties, and then chooses $m$ of these.

Let the private input $m$ come from a finite set $I = \{0, 1, \ldots, n\}$, which is agreed on by both parties, and, $N_{2^n-1} = \{0, 1, \ldots, 2^n - 1\}$ be the set of all $n$-bit integers. Now both parties choose $r^{(A)}, r^{(B)} \in_R N_{2^n-1}$, respectively, where $\in_R$ means chosen uniformly at random from the set. The algorithm first combines the random $n$-bit inputs by the bitwise exclusive OR operation (XOR) to get $r$, and then selects the $m$ least significant bits of $r$ by computing the output $x = r \bmod 2^m$.

---

**Algorithm 1.** *urandom1:* Drawing $x$ randomly from $\{0, 1, 2, \ldots, 2^m - 1\}$

---

**Inputs:** (private) $m \in I$
**Outputs:** $x = \text{urandom1}(\{0, 1, \ldots, 2^m - 1\})$
    $r \leftarrow r^{(A)} \text{ XOR } r^{(B)}$   $\{r^{(A)}, r^{(B)} \in_R N_{2^n-1}, \text{ where } r^{(i)} \text{ is provided by party } i\}$
    $x \leftarrow r \bmod 2^m$
    **return** $x$

---

*Correctness:* It is easy to see that $x \in \{0, 1, \ldots, 2^m - 1\}$ since that is exactly the co-domain of $r \bmod 2^m$. We also have to show that $x$ is a uniformly distributed random variable over that range.

**Lemma 1.** *If at least one of $r^{(A)}$ and $r^{(B)}$ is chosen uniformly at random out of $N_{2^n-1} = \{0, 1, \ldots, 2^n - 1\}$ then $r = r^{(A)} \, \text{XOR} \, r^{(B)}$ is a random number uniformly distributed over $N_{2^n-1}$.*

*Proof.* Let $N_{2^n-1} = \{0, 1, 2, \ldots, 2^n - 1\}$ be the set of all integers that can be represented by $n$ bits. If $r^{(A)}$ is a random variable on $N_{2^n-1}$, then there exists a unique random vector $(r_1^{(A)}, \ldots, r_n^{(A)})$ on $\{0,1\}^n$ such that $r^{(A)} = \sum_{i=1}^{n} 2^{i-1} r_i^{(A)}$. If $r^{(A)}$ is uniformly distributed over $N_{2^n-1}$ then the $r_i^{(A)}$'s are mutually independent Bernoulli random variables with parameter $1/2$. $r = r^{(A)} \, \text{XOR} \, r^{(B)}$ can now be written as $r = \sum_{i=1}^{n} 2^{i-1} r_i$ with $r_i = r_i^{(A)} \, \text{XOR} \, r_i^{(B)}$. Note that the XOR operation returns 1 iff both arguments are different.

Assume that $r^{(A)}$ is uniformly distributed. Therefore

$$\Pr[r_i = 1 | r_i^{(B)} = 0] = \Pr[r_i^{(A)} = 1] = 1/2$$
$$\Pr[r_i = 1 | r_i^{(B)} = 1] = \Pr[r_i^{(A)} = 0] = 1/2.$$

Note that the value of $r_i^{(B)}$ has no influence on $\Pr[r_i = 1]$. Thus $\Pr[r_i = 1] = \Pr[r_i = 0] = 1/2$. XOR is a bitwise operation and the $r_i$ are mutually independent and thus $r$ is uniformly distributed over $N_{2^n-1}$. □

Now $x = r \bmod 2^m$ can be rewritten as $x = \sum_{i=1}^{m} 2^{i-1} r_i$ since the $\bmod 2^m$ operation selects the $m$ least significant bits of $r$. The $r_i$ are mutually independent Bernoulli random variables with parameter $1/2$, hence $x$ is a random variable uniformly distributed over $\{0, 1, \ldots, 2^m - 1\}$.

*Security:* We want to keep the input $m$ private. We will ensure that the parties don't learn it using the garbled circuit technique (see Section 5). What's left to show is that neither party can choose their input to manipulate the output. A successful attack would distort the uniform distribution of the output. However, we know from Lemma 1 that the output is uniformly distributed as long as at least one input is uniformly distributed. So even if party A (or party B) deviates from the protocol and deliberately chooses a specific value for $r^{(A)}$ (or $r^{(B)}$) the output will remain uniformly distributed.

## 4.2   Range $N_q = \{0, 1, \ldots, q\}$

In this section, we relax the restriction that the size of the range must be an exact power of two. Now we allow any range $N_q = \{0, 1, \ldots, q\}$ with $q \in \mathbb{N}$. The number of elements in that range is not necessarily a power of two and therefore we can't directly apply Algorithm 1.

We use the acceptance-rejection method to constructing a Las Vegas type algorithm that uses Algorithm 1 repeatedly until it produces a value in the required range. To do this, we extend $N_q$ to $N_{2^m-1}$ so that it is of the form of Algorithm 1. That is, we choose the unique $m \in \mathbb{N}$ with $2^{m-1} - 1 < q \le 2^m - 1$, and then run the algorithm as described in Algorithm 2. This approach translates naturally into a compact circuit with a number of gates that is linear in the input size.

---

**Algorithm 2.** *urandom2:* Drawing $x$ randomly from $\{0, 1, \ldots, q\}$

---

**Inputs:** (private) $q \in N_{2^n-1}$
**Outputs:** $x = \text{urandom2}(\{0, 1, \ldots, q\})$
  $m \leftarrow \lfloor log_2(q) + 1 \rfloor$
  **repeat**
    $x \leftarrow \text{urandom1}(\{0, 1, \ldots, 2^m - 1\})$
  **until** $x \le q$
  **return** $x$

---

*Correctness:* When the algorithm terminates $x \in_R \{0, 1, \ldots, q\}$ since the exit condition ensures $x \le q$, and *urandom1* produces non-negative numbers, and $x$ is uniformly distributed since acceptance-rejection sampling of a subset of a uniform distribution is again uniformly distributed.

The number of iterations of the loop follows a geometric distribution. Let $X$ be a random variable describing how many iterations Algorithm 1 takes to get a valid result. The probability that $X \le k$ with $k \in \mathbb{N}$ is

$$\Pr[X \le k] = 1 - (1 - \Pr[x \le q])^k.$$

The probability that the exit condition is fulfilled in one iteration is

$$\Pr[x \le q] \ge \frac{2^{m-1} + 1}{2^m} > \frac{1}{2},$$

because $2^{m-1} - 1 < q \le 2^m - 1$, and so $\Pr[X \le k] > 1 - (1/2)^k$.

That means that even in the worst case the expected number of iterations is less than 2, and the probability of less than 10 iterations is greater than 99.9%. We illustrate the performance in Section 5.2.

*Security:* Again, neither party can distort the uniform distribution of the random value by the same argument as for Algorithm 1.

### 4.3   Range $N_{p,q} = \{p, p + 1, \ldots, q\}$

In the most general case where the range is arbitrary we first shift it to zero and then use Algorithm 2 to compute a random value and finally shift it back to the initial range (See Algorithm 3 for details).

**Algorithm 3.** *urandom3:* Drawing $x$ randomly from $\{p, p+1, \ldots, q\}$

**Inputs:** (private) $p, q \in N_{2^n}$
**Outputs:** $x = \text{urandom3}(\{p, p+1, \ldots, q\})$
$\quad m \leftarrow \lfloor \log_2(q-p) + 1 \rfloor$
$\quad$ **repeat**
$\quad\quad s \leftarrow \text{urandom1}(\{0, 1, \ldots, 2^m - 1\})$
$\quad$ **until** $s \leq q - p$
$\quad$ **return** $x = s + p$

*Correctness and Security:* Correctness and security follow from the same arguments as for Algorithm 2.

### 4.4 Secure Scaling

Once we have a random number generator, we can build an efficient solution for the secure scaling problem.

Both parties input their smallest $(p^{(A)}, p^{(B)})$ and biggest $(q^{(A)}, q^{(B)})$ possible scaling factors. The first step is to determine the intersection of these ranges by computing the boundaries of the intersection as $p = \max(p^{(A)}, p^{(B)})$ and $q = \min(q^{(A)}, q^{(B)})$. In the second step we use the random number generator to select an element out of $\{p, p+1, \ldots, q\}$.

**Algorithm 4.** The Secure Scaling algorithm

**Inputs:** $p^{(A)}, q^{(A)}, p^{(B)}, q^{(B)} \in N_{2^n - 1}$
**Outputs:** $s \in_R \{p^{(A)}, p^{(A)} + 1, \ldots, q^{(A)}\} \cap \{p^{(B)}, p^{(B)} + 1, \ldots, q^{(B)}\}$
$\quad p \leftarrow \max(p^{(A)}, p^{(B)})$
$\quad q \leftarrow \min(q^{(A)}, q^{(B)})$
$\quad s \leftarrow \text{urandom3}(\{p, p+1, \ldots, q\})$
$\quad$ **return** $s$

*Correctness and Security:* Correctness and security follow from the same arguments as for Algorithm 2. In the following section we show how to implement all of the steps needed in Algorithm 4 using garbled circuits.

## 5 Secure Scaling with Boolean Circuits

We compute the secure scaling algorithm with Yao's garbled circuit technique by expressing it as a Boolean circuit. Boolean circuits are easily combined, so we will show the subcircuits corresponding to the elementary operations in the algorithm.

We will describe the complexity of each subcircuit by the number of non-linear two-input gates in relation to the number of bits $l$ needed to represent the inputs $p^{(A)}, p^{(B)}, q^{(A)}, q^{(B)}$. A linear input gate has an even number of zeros and ones in the truth table. The linear gates for a constant output or the (negated) identity of an input wire can be trivially optimised away, e.g. XOR gates can be evaluated essentially for free [16], therefore the dominating factor for efficiency of the circuits is the number of non-linear gates.

- $(\min(q^{(A)}, q^{(B)}), \max(p^{(A)}, p^{(B)}))$: To compute these we use the integer comparison circuit described by Kolesnikov *et al.* [17], it has a complexity of $l$ non-linear gates.
- $(m \leftarrow \lfloor \log_2(q-p) + 1 \rfloor)$: In this step we don't actually have to compute $m$, because all we need later on is a bit mask to select the $\lfloor \log_2(q-p) + 1 \rfloor$ least significant bits. Therefore we first compute $t = q - p$ with the integer subtraction circuit described in [17] and then we use a chain of OR-gates (see Figure 2) to calculate the mask $2^{\lfloor (\log_2(t)+1) \rfloor} - 1$. This circuit consists of $l - 1$ non-linear gates.

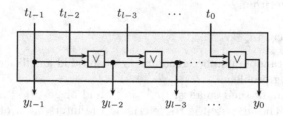

**Fig. 2.** A chain of OR gates to compute $y = 2^{\lfloor \log_2(t)+1 \rfloor} - 1$

- $(r = r^{(A)} \, \text{XOR} \, r^{(B)})$: $r$ is just a bitwise XOR between $r^{(A)}$ and $r^{(B)}$. Therefore the complexity is 0 non-linear gates.
- $(s = r \bmod 2^m)$: Computing modulo a power of two is the special case where we just want to select the $m$ least significant bits of $r$. We can achieve this by computing a bitwise AND between $r$ and $2^m - 1$, the bit-mask with the $m$ least significant bits set to 1. This is exactly the bit-mask we computed before. The complexity is $l$ non-linear gates.
- (repeat until $s \leq q - p$): Note that this loop has an unknown number of iterations, therefore it is impossible to generate the whole circuit to compute the loop beforehand. However, in this case, where the exit condition of the loop does not reveal any sensitive information, we can use a step-by-step approach. That is, the creator generates the circuit for one round of the loop and then the evaluator evaluates the circuit and reveals the result of the exit condition. Depending on that result the creator then generates either another round of the loop or goes on with the rest of the algorithm. Note that the disclosure of the result of the exit condition gives neither party an advantage in inferring the other parties input as long as their random inputs are kept private. This privacy is guaranteed by the garbled circuit technique.
  For the exit condition we can reuse $q - p$ which we computed before. Thus we only need an integer comparison circuit [17] which has a complexity of $l$ non-linear gates.
- $(x = s + p)$: We use the addition circuit of [17] to compute this sum. Again, the complexity is $l$ non-linear gates.

*Overall Complexity:* Let $X$ describe the number of iterations of the repeat-until loop in Algorithm 2. Then the number of non-linear gates add up to $2l + 2l - 1 + X(2l) + l = 5l - 1 + 2lX$. Since $X$ follows a geometric distribution with success probability $1/2 < p \leq 1$, we know that $1 \leq \mathbb{E}[X] < 2$, thus the expected overall complexity is less than $9l$.

## 5.1    Implementation

We chose the EFSFE framework of Henecka and Schneider [14] to implement our example of the random scaling factor. Amongst other optimisation techniques used in this framework the following are particularly useful for our application:

- Pipelined circuit execution: The circuit generation and evaluation processes are overlapped in time [11] thereby removing the need to construct the complete circuit before the evaluation, which is useful here because we cannot build the circuit in advance, since the number of iterations is dynamic.
- Oblivious-transfer extension: In [18], Ishai *et al.* show how to efficiently extend Oblivious transfer. You first have to execute a certain amount of conventional OTs and then by using this result you can generate a virtually unlimited number of very efficient OTs. (The initial OTs take $\sim 0.5$ s, and then every additional OT takes only 3.5 $\mu s$).

The EFSFE framework contains a library of circuits for common arithmetic which can be easily combined to describe the desired function. You can combine circuits from and add circuits to the library by extending the *CompositeCircuit* class. For example, the implementation of the chain of OR-gates circuit as shown in Figure 2 is done by defining subcircuits and connecting them with wires as follows:

```
public class NextBitMask extends CompositeCircuit {
  protected void createSubCircuits() throws Exception {
    for(int i=0; i<l-1; i++){
      subCircuits[i] = OR_2_1.newInstance();
    }
    super.createSubCircuits();
  }
  protected void connectWires() throws Exception {
    for(int i=0; i<l-1; i++){
      inputWires[i].connectTo(subCircuits[i].inputWires, 0);
    }
    inputWires[l-1].connectTo(subCircuits[l-2].inputWires, 1);
    for(int i=0; i<l-2; i++){
      subCircuits[i+1].outputWires[0].connectTo(
                            subCircuits[i].inputWires, 1);
    }
  }
  protected void defineOutputWires() { ... }
```

## 5.2   Measurements

All our measurements were run on an iMac with a Core i3 3Ghz processor, running Mac OS X 10.6.8 and Java 1.6.0_31. We ran measurements for four different input sizes (10, 100, 1000 and 10000 bits). For each size we ran the secure scaling algorithm 10000 times with inputs $(p^{(A)}, p^{(B)}, q^{(A)}, q^{(B)})$ generated uniformly at random from the set of non-negative integers able to be represented by the given number of bits. The resolution of the measurements is 1 ms, therefore the data points for the 10 bit input size are not very precise and only included in the graph to underline the overall trend. Figure 3 shows the distributions of the runtimes for the different input sizes. The single red line denotes the median, the blue box include the data points from the 25th to the 75th percentile and the whiskers include all points up to 1.5 times the size of the blue box. The linear circuit complexity with respect to input bit lengths is clear. Note also the very strong right skewness of the data.

Figure 4 shows the complementary cumulative distribution functions of the number of iterations for different input sizes. That is the probability that a run has more than $X$ iterations. We also added the worst case scenario for 1000 bit inputs, that is the inputs are chosen such that the private range is $2^{999}$ and therefore the probability that the exit condition of the loop is fulfilled is $(2^{999} + 1)/2^{1000} \approx 1/2$. We see that the input size has little effect on the distribution. Even for the worst case the probability for a high number of iterations drops rapidly.

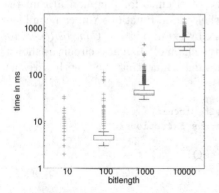 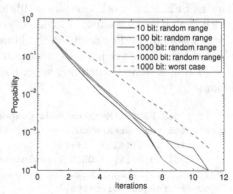

**Fig. 3.** Runtime distributions of the secure scaling algorithm for different input sizes

**Fig. 4.** Complementary cumulative distribution functions of the number of iterations for different input sizes

## 6   Conclusions

This paper presents a protocol to solve the secure scaling problem. Its main component is, to our knowledge, the first privacy-preserving random number generator. We believe that it might be a useful component for other privacy-preserving protocols. We show the practicality of our solution by an implementation of the protocol.

**Acknowledgement.** The authors would like to acknowledge the support of an Adelaide Scholarship International, a supplementary Scholarship of the Defence Systems Innovation Centre, and Australian Research Council grant DP0985063.

# References

1. Catrina, O., Saxena, A.: Secure Computation with Fixed-Point Numbers. In: Sion, R. (ed.) FC 2010. LNCS, vol. 6052, pp. 35–50. Springer, Heidelberg (2010)
2. Fouque, P., Stern, J., Wackers, G.: Cryptocomputing with Rationals. In: Blaze, M. (ed.) FC 2002. LNCS, vol. 2357, pp. 136–146. Springer, Heidelberg (2003)
3. Franz, M., Deiseroth, B., Hamacher, K., Jha, S., Katzenbeisser, S., Schroeder, H.: Secure computations on Non-Integer values. Technical report (2010)
4. Nguyen, H., Roughan, M.: Multi-Observer privacy preserving hidden markov models. In: IEEE/IFIP NOMS, pp. 514–517 (2012)
5. Blanton, M., Aliasgari, M.: Secure computation of biometric matching. Technical Report CSE Technical Report 2009-03, University of Notre Dame (April 2009)
6. Bianchi, T., Piva, A., Barni, M.: On the implementation of the discrete fourier transform in the encrypted domain. IEEE Transactions on Information Forensics and Security, 86–97 (March 2009)
7. Yao, A.C.: Protocols for secure computations. In: Proceedings of the 23rd Annual Symposium on Foundations of Computer Science, pp. 160–164 (1982)
8. Yao, A.C.: How to generate and exchange secrets. In: 27th Annual Symposium on Foundations of Computer Science, pp. 162–167. IEEE (October 1986)
9. Lindell, Y., Pinkas, B.: An Efficient Protocol for Secure Two-Party Computation in the Presence of Malicious Adversaries. In: Naor, M. (ed.) EUROCRYPT 2007. LNCS, vol. 4515, pp. 52–78. Springer, Heidelberg (2007)
10. Pinkas, B., Schneider, T., Smart, N.P., Williams, S.C.: Secure Two-Party Computation Is Practical. In: Matsui, M. (ed.) ASIACRYPT 2009. LNCS, vol. 5912, pp. 250–267. Springer, Heidelberg (2009)
11. Huang, Y., Evans, D., Katz, J., Malka, L.: Faster secure two-party computation using garbled circuits. In: USENIX Security Symposium (2011)
12. Malkhi, D., Nisan, N., Pinkas, B., Sella, Y.: Fairplay - a secure two-party computation system. In: USENIX Security Symposium (2004)
13. Henecka, W., Kögl, S., Sadeghi, A.R., Schneider, T., Wehrenberg, I.: TASTY: tool for automating secure two-party computations. In: Proceedings of the 17th ACM Conference on Computer and Communications Security, CCS 2010, pp. 451–462 (2010)
14. Henecka, W., Schneider, T.: EFSFE: Even faster secure function evaluation (submission, 2012)
15. Frikken, K.: Secure multiparty computation. In: Algorithms and Theory of Computation Handbook, 2nd edn., pp. 1–16. Chapman & Hall/CRC (2009)
16. Kolesnikov, V., Schneider, T.: Improved Garbled Circuit: Free XOR Gates and Applications. In: Aceto, L., Damgård, I., Goldberg, L.A., Halldórsson, M.M., Ingólfsdóttir, A., Walukiewicz, I. (eds.) ICALP 2008, Part II. LNCS, vol. 5126, pp. 486–498. Springer, Heidelberg (2008)
17. Kolesnikov, V., Sadeghi, A., Schneider, T.: Improved Garbled Circuit Building Blocks and Applications to Auctions and Computing Minima. In: Garay, J.A., Miyaji, A., Otsuka, A. (eds.) CANS 2009. LNCS, vol. 5888, pp. 1–20. Springer, Heidelberg (2009)
18. Ishai, Y., Kilian, J., Nissim, K., Petrank, E.: Extending Oblivious Transfers Efficiently. In: Boneh, D. (ed.) CRYPTO 2003. LNCS, vol. 2729, pp. 145–161. Springer, Heidelberg (2003)

# Perfect Ambiguous Optimistic Fair Exchange

Yang Wang, Man Ho Au, and Willy Susilo*

Centre for Computer and Information Security Research
School of Computer Science and Software Engineering
University of Wollongong, Australia
yw990@uowmail.edu.au, {aau,wsusilo}@uow.edu.au

**Abstract.** Protocol for fair exchange of digital signatures is essential in many applications including contract signing, electronic commerce, or even peer-to-peer file sharing. In such a protocol, two parties, Alice and Bob, would like to exchange digital signatures on some messages in a fair way. It is known that a trusted arbitrator is necessary in the realization of such a protocol.

We identify that in some scenarios, it is required that prior to the completion of the protocol, no observer should be able to tell whether Alice and Bob are conducting such an exchange. Consider the following scenario in which Apple engages Intel in an exchange protocol to sign a contract that terminates their OEM agreement. The information would be of value to a third party (such as the stock broker, or other OEM companies). If the protocol transcript can serve as an evidence that such a communication is in progress, any observer of this communication, including the employees of both companies, would be tempted to capture the transcript and sell it to outsiders.

We introduce a new notion called *perfect ambiguous optimistic fair exchange* (PAOFE), which is particularly suitable to the above scenario. PAOFE fulfils all traditional requirements of cryptographic fair exchange of digital signatures and, in addition, guarantees that the communication transcript cannot be used as a proof to convince others that the protocol is in progress. Specifically, we formalize the notion of PAOFE and present a rigorous security model in the multi-user setting under the chosen-key attack. We also present a generic construction of PAOFE from existing cryptographic primitives and prove that our proposal is secure with respect to our definition in the standard model.

## 1 Introduction

Consider a scenario in which Apple engages Intel in a fair exchange protocol to sign a contract that pays an amount of money for the early termination of the use of Intel technology in the next generation of Macbook and iMac desktop computers. In this situation, reveal of the contract, or leakage of the information about this contract, prior to its effective date will be potentially harmful to the companies. For instance, Apple may be reluctant to expose prematurely the

---

* This work is supported by ARC Future Fellowship FT0991397.

changes it is introducing to its next generation products, which may possibly affect the sales of the current generation of the products. On the other hand, the potential termination of cooperation with Apple may lead to a decline of Intel's shares value. Therefore, it is necessary that the fair exchange protocol should not leak any information about the signatures being exchanged.

To the best of our knowledge, ambiguous optimistic fair exchange (AOFE) [9] is the closest cryptographic solution to the above problem. An AOFE protocol comprises three parties, namely, signer Alice, verifier Bob, and a semi-trusted third party known as the "arbitrator". In a typically execution of an AOFE protocol, Alice delivers a "commitment" of her signature, called ambiguous partial signature, to Bob. Upon successful verification of the ambiguous partial signature, Bob delivers his full signature to Alice. After verifying the full signature from Bob, Alice sends to Bob her own full signature. This completes the protocol.

Bob can approach the arbitrator for assistance in the situation in which Alice refuses to send her full signature at the end of the exchange protocol. The ambiguous partial signature is designed in such a way that the arbitrator can turn it into Alice's full signature, which is indistinguishable to a "real" signature created by Alice. In this way, as long as the arbitrator is trusted to carry out its duty, Bob can always be assured he can obtain a full signature from Alice, either from Alice or the arbitrator. In addition, the arbitrator is not required to take part in typical executions of the protocol.

AOFE differs from traditional optimistic fair exchange (OFE) schemes, for example [1, 3, 5–8, 10–12, 14], in the sense that the ambiguous partial signature does not reveal the identity of its creator. Specifically, in OFE, everyone can verify that Alice has created a commitment of her signature in the first step. This may create an unfair situation to Alice as Bob can simply use Alice's commitment as a mean to his advantage. For instance, if Alice's signature represents her contract tender for Bob's service, Bob can use Alice's commitment as a way to ask for a higher price from another party. On the other hand, the ambiguous partial signature in AFOE has the extra property that it can be created by either Alice or Bob. Thus, while Bob can be assured that this is Alice's commitment of her signature, he cannot convince anybody that this is Alice's commitment since he could have been the creator of the ambiguous partial signature as well. Nonetheless, in AOFE, the arbitrator knows who is the creator of the ambiguous signature.

Unfortunately, AOFE is inadequate to the aforementioned problem we raised earlier. If AOFE is employed in the above scenario, Apple will transmit the ambiguous partial signature to Intel on the contract of the termination of the use of Intel technology in its next generation of computers as the first step of the exchange. This ambiguous partial signature itself leaks sufficient information to be valuable. The reason is that in this scenario, it does not matter who is the signer of this contract. The valuable information to an outsider is that these two companies are discussing about a potential termination, which is the partial signature. The ambiguous partial signature created by Apple or Intel is sufficient evidence to prove the authenticity of the information. At the first sight, one may think that providing a secure channel between the parties would be sufficient in the above scenario. Nevertheless, this approach has a huge drawback. To build a secure channel between any two parties is known to be extremely expensive, and therefore, this approach will not be feasible in practice.

One key observation about the existing exchange protocol is that the ambiguous partial signature in AOFE, as well as the regular partial signature in OFE, is indeed publicly verifiable. This is not strictly a necessary functional requirement of an exchange protocol. In fact, this may have an undesirable effect as illustrated in our case earlier. In general, if Bob is known to be trustworthy, for example, if Bob is a government department, then malicious observer Oven who obtains an ambiguous partial signature submitted to Bob knows the intention of Alice. Besides, we make the observation that the arbitrator in AOFE knows who the creator of an ambiguous partial signature is, and is capable of converting it into a full signature. A high level of trust has to be placed on the arbitrator.

Hence, we introduce a new notion, called *Perfect Ambiguous Optimistic Fair Exchange* (PAOFE), as a practical cryptographic solution to the aforementioned scenario. Indeed, our solution builds on top of AOFE and it also fulfills all the security requirements of an AOFE. In addition, PAOFE enjoys a new property called *Perfect Ambiguity* in which the equivalent of an "ambiguous partial signature" leaks no information about the actual signer, intended recipient and the signature itself, and not even in the view of the arbitrator. Thus, no outsider can tell if an exchange is in progress.

## 1.1  Our Contributions

In this paper we make the following contributions.

1. We propose the notion of *Perfect Ambiguous Optimistic Fair Exchange*, which allows a signer Alice to generate a partial signature in such a way that no outsider, not even the arbitrator, is able to infer any useful information about the signature. Indeed, a partial signature in PAOFE generated by the signer Alice with Bob being the receiver is indistinguishable to a random bit string chosen from the signature space. In other words, any partial signature is indistinguishable to a partial signature on a random message with respect to a random signer and receiver. To realize this notion, Bob's secret key is required in the verification of the partial signature in PAOFE. Thus, only Bob is able to verify the partial signature, and an outsider gains nothing about the transaction. Both the identities of the signer and receiver and the content of an transaction are perfectly hidden.

2. We define a security model for PAOFE in the multi-user setting under chosen-key attack. Our model captures the existing security requirements for AOFE, namely, signer ambiguity, resolution ambiguity, security against signers, security against verifiers and security against the arbitrator. In addition, PAOFE covers an additional requirement: *perfect ambiguity*. It is required that any user can generate a partial signature whose distribution is indistinguishable from that of a partial signatures generated by Alice. In

other words, a specific partial signature generated by Alice with recipient Bob is indistinguishable from a partial signature uniformly randomly chosen from the whole signature space.

3. We propose a generic construction of PAOFE from two well established cryptographic primitives, namely, AOFE and key-private encryption and provide the security proof of our proposal in the proposed model. Our generic construction works in the standard model and does not involve any extra assumptions.

## 1.2  Paper Organization

In the next section, we review the notions and security models of public key encryption and AOFE respectively. In Section 3, a formal definition of PAOFE, together with the security model in the multi-user and chosen key setting is proposed. Then, we propose a generic construction of PAOFE and also provide the security proof of our scheme under our model in Section 4. Finally, we conclude the paper in Section 5.

# 2  Building Blocks

Throughout the paper, the following notations are used. For a finite set $\mathcal{S}$, $s \leftarrow \mathcal{S}$ denotes that an element is randomly chosen from $\mathcal{S}$. By $y \leftarrow A^O(x)$, we mean the algorithm $A$, on input $x$ and having access to oracle $O$, outputs $y$. By $x := y$, we mean variable $x$ is assigned with the value of $y$. We use $[A_1(\mathsf{in}_1) \rightarrow \mathsf{out}_1] \stackrel{\mathbf{P}}{\Longleftrightarrow} [A_2(\mathsf{in}_2) \rightarrow \mathsf{out}_2]$ to denote that two PPT algorithms $A_1$ and $A_2$ outputs $\mathsf{out}_1$ and $\mathsf{out}_2$ respectively upon the completion of the protocol $\mathbf{P}$ in which $A_1$ takes as input $\mathsf{in}_1$ and $A_2$ takes as input $\mathsf{in}_2$.

## 2.1  Encryption

A public key encryption scheme $\mathcal{E}$ consists of three algorithms: $\mathcal{E} = (\mathsf{Kg}, \mathsf{Enc}, \mathsf{Dec})$. We consider *indistinguishability of encryptions against adaptive chosen ciphertext attacks*, denoted by IE-CCA [2]. It is identical to the more widely used notion IND-CCA [4]. Here we just adopt the notion IE-CCA, as the authors did in [2]. We define the adversary's advantage IE-Adv$_{\mathcal{A}}^{\mathcal{E}}(k)$ as

$$\left| \Pr \left[ b = \tilde{b} \, \middle| \, \begin{array}{l} (ek, dk) \leftarrow \mathsf{Kg}(1^\kappa), \ (m_0, m_1, \alpha) \leftarrow \mathcal{A}^{O_{\mathsf{Dec}}}(ek, \mathsf{find}), \\ b \leftarrow \{0,1\}, \ c_b \leftarrow \mathsf{Enc}_{ek}(m_b), \ \tilde{b} \leftarrow \mathcal{A}^{O_{\mathsf{Dec}}}(c_b, \alpha, \mathsf{guess}) \end{array} \right] - \frac{1}{2} \right|.$$

$\mathcal{E}$ is said to be IE-CCA secure if the function IE-Adv$_{\mathcal{A}}^{\mathcal{E}}(k)$ is negligible for any PPT adversary $\mathcal{A}$.

To hide the information about the public key under which an encryption is conducted, we consider *indistinguishability of keys under adaptive chosen ciphertext attacks*, denoted by IK-CCA [2]. For an efficient algorithm $\mathcal{A}$, we define the adversary's advantage IK-Adv$_{\mathcal{A}}^{\mathcal{E}}(k)$ as

$$\left| \Pr \left[ b = \tilde{b} \middle| \begin{array}{l} (ek_0, dk_0) \leftarrow \mathsf{Kg}(1^\kappa),\ (ek_1, dk_1) \leftarrow \mathsf{Kg}(1^\kappa), \\ (m, \alpha) \leftarrow \mathcal{A}^{\mathcal{D}_{dk_0}(\cdot), \mathcal{D}_{dk_1}(\cdot)}(ek_0, ek_1, \mathsf{find}),\ b \leftarrow \{0,1\}, \\ c_b \leftarrow \mathsf{Enc}_{ek_b}(m),\ \tilde{b} \leftarrow \mathcal{A}^{\mathcal{D}_{dk_0}(\cdot), \mathcal{D}_{dk_1}(\cdot)}(c_b, \alpha, \mathsf{guess}) \end{array} \right] - \frac{1}{2} \right|.$$

$\mathcal{E}$ is said to be IK-CCA secure if the function IK-$\mathsf{Adv}_{\mathcal{A}}^{\mathcal{E}}(k)$ is negligible for any PPT adversary $\mathcal{A}$.

To guarantee both the message-privacy and key-privacy properties at the same time, we combine the above two security notions into one.

**Definition 1.** *An encryption scheme $\mathcal{E}$ consisting of three algorithms $\mathcal{E} = (\mathsf{Kg},$ Enc, Dec) is said to be IE-IK-CCA secure if for any probabilistic polynomial-time algorithm $\mathcal{A}$, the advantage of $\mathcal{A}$ $\mathsf{Adv}_{\mathcal{A}}^{\mathsf{IE\text{-}IK}}(\kappa)$ is negligible in $\kappa$, where $\mathsf{Adv}_{\mathcal{A}}^{\mathsf{IE\text{-}IK}}(\kappa)$ is defined as*

$$\left| \Pr \left[ b = \tilde{b} \middle| \begin{array}{l} (ek, dk) \leftarrow \mathsf{Kg}(1^\kappa), (m, \alpha) \leftarrow \mathcal{A}^{O_{\mathsf{Dec}}}(ek, \mathsf{find}),\ b \leftarrow \{0,1\}, \\ c_b \leftarrow \begin{cases} \mathsf{Enc}_{ek}(m) \ if\ b = 0 \\ c' \leftarrow \mathcal{C} \quad\ if\ b = 1 \end{cases},\ \tilde{b} \leftarrow \mathcal{A}^{O_{\mathsf{Dec}}}(c_b, \alpha, \mathsf{guess}) \end{array} \right] - \frac{1}{2} \right|.$$

*where $\mathcal{C}$ is the whole ciphertext space with respect to any message and any public key, and $\mathcal{A}$ is allowed invoke the decryption oracle $O_{\mathsf{Dec}}(\cdot)$ at any point with the only restriction of not querying $c_b$ during the* guess *stage.*

It is easy to see that any public key encryption scheme that is both IE-CCA secure and IK-CCA secure will be IE-IK-CCA secure. Since Cramer-Shoup encryption scheme [4] is both IE-CCA secure and IK-CCA secure [2], it is IE-IK-CCA secure.

## 2.2  Ambiguous Optimistic Fair Exchange

We review the notion and security model of the ambiguous optimistic fair exchange protocol introduced in [9].

**Definition 2.** *An ambiguous optimistic fair exchange scheme involves the users (signers and verifiers) and the arbitrator, and consists of the following (probabilistic) polynomial-time algorithms:*

- PMGen: *On input $1^\kappa$ where $\kappa$ is a security parameter, it outputs a system parameter $PM$.*
- Setup$^{\mathsf{TTP}}$: *On input $PM$, the algorithm generates a secret key $ASK$, and a public key $APK$ of the arbitrator.*
- Setup$^{\mathsf{User}}$: *On input $PM$ and (optionally) $APK$, it outputs a secret/public key pair $(SK, PK)$. For a user $U_i$, we use $(SK_i, PK_i)$ to denote the user's key pair.*
- Sig and Ver: $\mathsf{Sig}(M, SK_i, PK_i, PK_j, APK)$, *outputs a (full) signature $\sigma$ on $M$ of user $U_i$ with the designated verifier $U_j$, where message $M$ is chosen by user $U_i$ from the message space $\mathcal{M}$ defined under $PK_i$, while $\mathsf{Ver}(M, \sigma, PK_i, PK_j, APK)$ outputs $\top$ or $\bot$, indicating $\sigma$ is $U_i$'s valid full signature on $M$ with the designated verifier $U_j$ or not.*

- PSig *and* PVer: *These are partial signing and verification algorithms respectively.* PSig$(M, SK_i, PK_i, PK_j, APK)$ *outputs a partial signature* $\sigma_P$, *while* PVer$(M, \sigma_P, \mathbf{PK}, APK)$ *outputs* $\top$ *or* $\bot$, *where* $\mathbf{PK} = \{PK_i, PK_j\}$.
- Res: *This is the resolution algorithm.* Res$(M, \sigma_P, ASK, \mathbf{PK})$, *where* $\mathbf{PK} = \{PK_i, PK_j\}$, *outputs a full signature* $\sigma$, *or* $\bot$ *indicating the failure of resolving a partial signature.*

*Resolution ambiguity property states that any "resolved signature"* Res$(M,$ PSig $(M, SK_i, PK_i, PK_j, APK)$, $ASK$, $\{PK_i, PK_j\})$ *is computationally indistinguishable from the "actual signature"* Sig$(M, SK_i, PK_i, PK_j, APK)$.

The security of an AOFE scheme consists of four aspects: signer ambiguity, security against signers, security against verifiers, and security against the arbitrator.

SIGNER AMBIGUITY. We require that any PPT distinguisher $D$ succeeds with at most negligible probability greater than $1/2$ in the following experiment.

$$PM \leftarrow \mathsf{PMGen}(1^k)$$
$$(ASK, APK) \leftarrow \mathsf{Setup}^{\mathsf{TTP}}(PM)$$
$$(M, (SK_0, PK_0), (SK_1, PK_1), \delta) \leftarrow D^{O_{\mathsf{Res}}}(APK)$$
$$b \leftarrow \{0, 1\}$$
$$\sigma_P \leftarrow \mathsf{PSig}(M, SK_b, PK_b, PK_{1-b}, APK)$$
$$b' \leftarrow D^{O_{\mathsf{Res}}}(\sigma_P, \delta)$$
$$\text{success of } A := [b' = b$$
$$\wedge (M, \sigma_P, \{PK_0, PK_1\}) \notin Query(D, O_{\mathsf{Res}})]$$

where $\delta$ is $D$'s state information, oracle $O_{\mathsf{Res}}$ takes as input a valid partial signature $\sigma_P$ of user $U_i$ on message $M$ with respect to verifier $U_j$ (i.e. $(M, \sigma_P, PK_i, PK_j)$ such that PVer$(M, \sigma_P, \{PK_i, PK_j\}, APK) = \top$), and outputs a full signature $\sigma$ on $M$ under $PK_i, PK_j$, and $Query(D, O_{\mathsf{Res}})$ is the set of valid queries $D$ issued to the resolution oracle.

SECURITY AGAINST SIGNERS. We require that any PPT adversary $\mathcal{A}$ succeeds with at most negligible probability in the following experiment.

$$PM \leftarrow \mathsf{PMGen}(1^k)$$
$$(ASK, APK) \leftarrow \mathsf{Setup}^{\mathsf{TTP}}(PM)$$
$$(SK_B, PK_B) \leftarrow \mathsf{Setup}^{\mathsf{User}}(PM, APK)$$
$$(M, \sigma_P, PK_A) \leftarrow \mathcal{A}^{O_{\mathsf{PSig}}^B, O_{\mathsf{Res}}}(APK, PK_B)$$
$$\sigma \leftarrow \mathsf{Res}(M, \sigma_P, ASK, \{PK_A, PK_B\})$$
$$\text{success of } \mathcal{A} := [\mathsf{PVer}(M, \sigma_P, \{PK_A, PK_B\}, APK) = \top$$
$$\wedge \mathsf{Ver}(M, \sigma, PK_A, PK_B, APK) = \bot$$
$$\wedge (M, PK_A) \notin Query(\mathcal{A}, O_{\mathsf{PSig}}^B)]$$

where oracle $O_{\mathsf{Res}}$ is described in the previous experiment, oracle $O_{\mathsf{PSig}}^B$ takes as input $(M, PK_i)$ and outputs a signature on $M$ with respect to $PK_i$ and $PK_B$

generated using $SK_B$, and $Query(\mathcal{A}, O^B_{\mathsf{PSig}})$ is the set of queries made by $\mathcal{A}$ to oracle $O^B_{\mathsf{PSig}}$.

SECURITY AGAINST VERIFIERS. We require that any PPT adversary $\mathcal{A}$ succeeds with at most negligible probability in the following experiment.

$$PM \leftarrow \mathsf{PMGen}(1^k)$$
$$(ASK, APK) \leftarrow \mathsf{Setup}^{\mathsf{TTP}}(PM)$$
$$(SK_A, PK_A) \leftarrow \mathsf{Setup}^{\mathsf{User}}(PM, APK)$$
$$(M, \sigma, PK_B) \leftarrow \mathcal{A}^{O_{\mathsf{PSig}}, O_{\mathsf{Res}}}(APK, PK_A)$$
$$\text{success of } \mathcal{A} := [\mathsf{Ver}(M, \sigma, PK_A, PK_B, APK) = \top$$
$$\wedge \, (M, \cdot, \{PK_A, PK_B\}) \notin Query(\mathcal{A}, O_{\mathsf{Res}})]$$

where oracle $O_{\mathsf{Res}}$ is described in the experiment of signer ambiguity, $Query(\mathcal{A}, O_{\mathsf{Res}})$ is the set of queries made by $\mathcal{A}$ to oracle $O_{\mathsf{Res}}$, and oracle $O_{\mathsf{PSig}}$ takes as input $(M, PK_j)$ and outputs a signature on $M$ with respect to $PK_A$ and $PK_j$ generated using $SK_A$.

SECURITY AGAINST THE ARBITRATOR. We require that any PPT adversary $\mathcal{A}$ succeeds with at most negligible probability in the following experiment.

$$PM \leftarrow \mathsf{PMGen}(1^k)$$
$$(APK, ASK^*) \leftarrow \mathcal{A}(PM)$$
$$(SK_A, PK_A) \leftarrow \mathsf{Setup}^{\mathsf{User}}(PM, APK)$$
$$(M, \sigma, PK_B) \leftarrow \mathcal{A}^{O_{\mathsf{PSig}}}(ASK^*, APK, PK_A)$$
$$\text{success of } \mathcal{A} := [\mathsf{Ver}(M, \sigma, PK_A, PK_B, APK) = \top$$
$$\wedge \, (M, PK_B) \notin Query(\mathcal{A}, O_{\mathsf{PSig}})]$$

where $ASK^*$ is $\mathcal{A}$'s state information, which might not be the corresponding private key of $APK$, oracle $O_{\mathsf{PSig}}$ is described in the previous experiment, and $Query(\mathcal{A}, O_{\mathsf{PSig}})$ is the set of queries made by $\mathcal{A}$ to oracle $O_{\mathsf{PSig}}$.

## 3    Perfect Ambiguous Optimistic Fair Exchange

In a PAOFE scheme, we require that given a partial signature, no outsider should be able to learn any information about it. Specifically, the message on which the partial signature was generated, in addition to the identities of both the signer and the receiver should be completely hidden. To achieve this, we require that the verification algorithm in PAOFE to involve the secret key of the receiver, rather than the case that the partial signature is publicly verifiable in AOFE. Besides, we extend the resolution algorithm in AOFE to the resolution protocol in PAOFE. Since an algorithm can be seen as a non-interactive protocol, our model is more general and could capture a larger class of schemes.

**Definition 3.** *A perfect ambiguous optimistic fair exchange scheme involves the users (signers and verifiers) and the arbitrator, and consists of the following (probabilistic) polynomial-time algorithms/protocols:*

- **PMGen**: *On input $1^\kappa$ where $\kappa$ is a security parameter, this algorithm outputs a system parameter* PM.
- **Setup$^{\text{TTP}}$**: *On input* PM, *the algorithm generates a secret key* ASK, *and a public key* APK *of the arbitrator.*
- **Setup$^{\text{User}}$**: *On input* PM *and (optionally)* APK, *it outputs a secret/public key pair* (SK, PK). *For a user $U_i$, we use* $(\text{SK}_i, \text{PK}_i)$ *to denote the user's key pair.*
- **Sig** *and* **Ver:** $\text{Sig}(M, \text{SK}_i, \text{PK}_i, \text{PK}_j, \text{APK})$, *outputs a (full) signature $\sigma$ on message $M$ of user $U_i$ with the designated verifier $U_j$, while* $\text{Ver}(M, \sigma, \text{PK}_i, \text{PK}_j, \text{APK})$ *outputs $\top$ or $\bot$, indicating $\sigma$ is $U_i$'s valid full signature on $M$ with the designated verifier $U_j$ or not.*
- **PSig** *and* **PVer:** *These are partial signing and verification algorithms respectively.* $\text{PSig}(M, \text{SK}_i, \text{PK}_i, \text{PK}_j, \text{APK})$, *run by a signer $U_i$, outputs a partial signature $\sigma_P$, while* $\text{PVer}(M, \sigma_P, \text{SK}_j, \text{PK}_i, \text{PK}_j, \text{APK})$, *run by a verifier $U_j$, outputs $\top$ or $\bot$.*
- **Res:** *This is a resolution protocol between the verifier $U_j$ and the arbitrator, involving a pair of interactive algorithms* $(\text{Res}_v, \text{Res}_\tau)$. $\text{Res}_v(M, \sigma_P, \text{SK}_j, \text{PK}_i, \text{PK}_j, \text{APK})$, *run by the verifier, outputs a full signature $\sigma$, or $\bot$ indicating the failure of resolving a partial signature.*

*Resolution ambiguity property states that any "resolved signature"* $\text{Res}_v(M, \textbf{PSig}$ $(M, \text{SK}_i, \text{PK}_i, \text{PK}_j, \text{APK}), \text{SK}_j, \text{PK}_i, \text{PK}_j, \text{APK})$ *is computationally indistinguishable from the "actual signature"* $\textbf{Sig}(M, \text{SK}_i, \text{PK}_i, \text{PK}_j, \text{APK})$.

### 3.1  PAOFE Models

- **Perfect Ambiguity:** Intuitively, we require that no outsiders, even the arbitrator, should be able to learn any information about a partial signature such as the content of the message or the identities of the signer and receiver. This ensures the privacy for both the signer and the receiver. To achieve this property, we require that in the view of an outsider, the partial signature is indistinguishable to a signature randomly sampled from the signature space. Formally, we require no PPT distinguisher $\mathcal{A}$ succeeds with non-negligible probability in the following experiment:

$$\text{PM} \leftarrow \textbf{PMGen}(1^k)$$
$$(\text{APK}, \text{ASK}^*) \leftarrow \mathcal{A}(\text{PM})$$
$$(\text{SK}_B, \text{PK}_B) \leftarrow \textbf{Setup}^{\text{User}}(\text{PM}, \text{APK})$$
$$(M, (\text{SK}_A, \text{PK}_A), \Upsilon) \leftarrow \mathcal{A}^{O^B_{\text{PSig}}, O^B_{\text{FakePSig}}, O^B_{\text{PVer}}}(\text{ASK}^*, \text{APK}, \text{PK}_B)$$
$$b \leftarrow \{0, 1\}$$

$$\sigma_P \leftarrow \begin{cases} \mathbf{PSig}(M, \mathsf{SK}_A, \mathsf{PK}_A, \mathsf{PK}_B, \mathsf{APK}) \text{ if } b = 0 \\ \sigma'_P \leftarrow \mathcal{S} \text{ if } b = 1 \end{cases}$$

$$b' \leftarrow \mathcal{A}^{O^B_{\mathbf{PSig}}, O^B_{\mathbf{FakePSig}}, O^B_{\mathbf{PVer}}}(\sigma_P, \Upsilon)$$

$$\text{success of } \mathcal{A} := [b' = b$$
$$\wedge (M, \sigma_P, \mathsf{PK}_A) \notin Query(\mathcal{A}, O^B_{\mathbf{PVer}})]$$

where $\Upsilon$ is $\mathcal{A}$'s state information, $\mathcal{S}$ is the whole partial signature space, oracle $O^B_{\mathbf{PSig}}$ takes as input $(M, \mathsf{PK}_j)$ and outputs a partial signature of $\mathsf{PK}_B$'s on $M$ with the receiver's public key being $\mathsf{PK}_j$, oracle $O^B_{\mathbf{FakePSig}}$ takes as input $(M, \mathsf{PK}_i)$ and returns a fake partial signature of user $U_i$'s generated using $\mathsf{SK}_B$ on $M$ with the receiver's public key being $\mathsf{PK}_B$, oracle $O^B_{\mathbf{PVer}}$ takes as input a partial signature $\sigma_P$ of user $\mathsf{PK}_i$'s on message $M$ with the verifier being $\mathsf{PK}_B$, i.e., $(M, \sigma_P, \mathsf{PK}_i)$, and outputs $\top$ or $\bot$, and $Query(\mathcal{A}, O^B_{\mathbf{PVer}})$ is the set of queries $\mathcal{A}$ issued to oracle $O^B_{\mathbf{PVer}}$. Note that in previous ambiguous optimistic fair exchange models, the partial verification oracle $O^B_{\mathbf{PVer}}$ was not provided, as a partial signature is publicly verifiable. To cope with the change in PAOFE that partial signature is no longer publicly verifiable, we provide a partial signature verification oracle to the adversary in the security model.

- **Signer Ambiguity:** Informally, *signer ambiguity* means that $B$ may forge partial signatures that look indistinguishable from those generated by $A$. Formally, we require no PPT distinguisher $\mathcal{A}$ succeeds with non-negligible probability in the following experiment:

$$\mathsf{PM} \leftarrow \mathbf{PMGen}(1^k)$$
$$(\mathsf{ASK}, \mathsf{APK}) \leftarrow \mathbf{Setup}^{\mathsf{TTP}}(\mathsf{PM})$$
$$(M, (\mathsf{SK}_0, \mathsf{PK}_0), (\mathsf{SK}_1, \mathsf{PK}_1), \Upsilon) \leftarrow \mathcal{A}^{O_{\mathbf{Res}}}(\mathsf{APK})$$
$$b \leftarrow \{0, 1\}$$
$$\sigma_P \leftarrow \begin{cases} \mathbf{PSig}(M, \mathsf{SK}_0, \mathsf{PK}_0, \mathsf{PK}_1, \mathsf{APK}), b = 0 \\ \mathbf{FakePSig}(M, \mathsf{SK}_1, \mathsf{PK}_0, \mathsf{PK}_1, \mathsf{APK}), b = 1 \end{cases}$$
$$b' \leftarrow \mathcal{A}^{O_{\mathbf{Res}}}(\sigma_P, \Upsilon)$$
$$\text{success of } \mathcal{A} := [b' = b$$
$$\wedge (M, \mathsf{PK}_0, \mathsf{PK}_1) \notin Query(\mathcal{A}, O_{\mathbf{Res}})$$

where $\Upsilon$ is $\mathcal{A}$'s state information, oracle $O_{\mathbf{Res}}$ takes an input $(M, \mathsf{PK}_i, \mathsf{PK}_j)$ and starts an execution of the **Res** protocol with the adversary running the interactive algorithm $\mathsf{Res}_{\mathcal{R}}$, algorithm $\mathbf{FakePSig}$ is a fake partial signature signing algorithm and $\mathbf{FakeSig}(M, \mathsf{SK}_j, \mathsf{PK}_i, \mathsf{PK}_j, \mathsf{APK})$ outputs a forged partial signature $\sigma_P$ on $M$ of user $U_i$ with the designated verifier $U_j$ generated using $\mathsf{SK}_j$, and $Query(\mathcal{A}, O_{\mathbf{Res}})$ is the set of queries $\mathcal{A}$ issued to the resolution oracle $O_{\mathbf{Res}}$.

- **Security against Signers:** We require that any PPT adversary $\mathcal{A}$, who models a dishonest signer, succeeds with at most negligible probability in the following experiment:

$$\mathsf{PM} \leftarrow \mathbf{PMGen}(1^k)$$

$$(\mathsf{ASK}, \mathsf{APK}) \leftarrow \mathbf{Setup}^{\mathsf{TTP}}(\mathsf{PM})$$

$$(\mathsf{SK}_B, \mathsf{PK}_B) \leftarrow \mathbf{Setup}^{\mathsf{User}}(\mathsf{PM}, \mathsf{APK})$$

$$(M, \sigma_P, \mathsf{PK}_A) \leftarrow \mathcal{A}^{O_{\mathbf{PSig}}^B, O_{\mathbf{FakePSig}}^B, O_{\mathbf{PVer}}^B, O_{\mathbf{Res}}}(\mathsf{APK}, \mathsf{PK}_B)$$

$$\mathsf{Input}_{\mathcal{T}} := (M, \mathsf{ASK}, \mathsf{PK}_A, \mathsf{PK}_B)$$

$$\mathsf{Input}_{\mathcal{V}} := (M, \sigma_P, \mathsf{SK}_B, \mathsf{PK}_A, \mathsf{PK}_B, \mathsf{APK})$$

$$[\mathsf{Res}_{\mathcal{T}}(\mathsf{Input}_{\mathcal{T}}) \rightarrow \mathsf{state}_{\mathcal{T}}] \overset{\mathbf{Res}}{\Longleftrightarrow} [\mathsf{Res}_{\mathcal{V}}(\mathsf{Input}_{\mathcal{V}}) \rightarrow \sigma]$$

$$\text{success of } \mathcal{A} := [\mathbf{PVer}(M, \sigma_P, \mathsf{SK}_B, \mathsf{PK}_A, \mathsf{PK}_B, \mathsf{APK}) = \top$$

$$\wedge \mathbf{Ver}(M, \sigma, \mathsf{PK}_A, \mathsf{PK}_B, \mathsf{APK}) = \perp$$

$$\wedge (M, \mathsf{PK}_A) \notin Query(\mathcal{A}, O_{\mathbf{FakePSig}}^B)]$$

where all the four oracles are described in the previous experiments, $Query(\mathcal{A}, O_{\mathbf{FakePSig}}^B)$ is the set of queries made by $\mathcal{A}$ to oracle $O_{\mathbf{FakePSig}}^B$. Note that the adversary is not allowed to corrupt $\mathsf{PK}_B$, otherwise it can easily success in the experiment by simply using $\mathsf{SK}_B$ to produce a fake partial signature under public keys $\mathsf{PK}_A$, $\mathsf{PK}_B$ and outputting it.

- **Security against Verifiers:** We require that any PPT adversary $\mathcal{A}$, who models a dishonest verifier, succeeds with at most negligible probability in the following experiment:

$$\mathsf{PM} \leftarrow \mathbf{PMGen}(1^k)$$

$$(\mathsf{ASK}, \mathsf{APK}) \leftarrow \mathbf{Setup}^{\mathsf{TTP}}(\mathsf{PM})$$

$$(\mathsf{SK}_A, \mathsf{PK}_A) \leftarrow \mathbf{Setup}^{\mathsf{User}}(\mathsf{PM}, \mathsf{APK})$$

$$(M, \sigma, \mathsf{PK}_B) \leftarrow \mathcal{A}^{O_{\mathbf{PSig}}, O_{\mathbf{FakePSig}}, O_{\mathbf{PVer}}, O_{\mathbf{Res}}}(\mathsf{APK}, \mathsf{PK}_A)$$

$$\text{success of } \mathcal{A} := [\mathbf{Ver}(M, \sigma, \mathsf{PK}_A, \mathsf{PK}_B, \mathsf{APK}) = \top$$

$$\wedge (M, \mathsf{PK}_A, \mathsf{PK}_B) \notin Query(\mathcal{A}, O_{\mathbf{Res}})]$$

where oracle $O_{\mathbf{Res}}$ is described in the previous experiments, oracle $O_{\mathbf{PSig}}$ takes as input $(M, \mathsf{PK}_j)$ and outputs a partial signature of $\mathsf{PK}_A$'s on $M$ with the receiver's public key being $\mathsf{PK}_j$ generated using $\mathsf{SK}_A$, oracle $O_{\mathbf{FakePSig}}$ takes as input $(M, \mathsf{PK}_i)$ and returns a fake partial signature of user $U_i$'s generated using $\mathsf{SK}_A$ on $M$ with the receiver's public key being $\mathsf{PK}_A$, oracle $O_{\mathbf{PVer}}$ takes as input a partial signature $\sigma_P$ of user $U_i$'s on message $M$ with the receiver's public key being $\mathsf{PK}_A$, i.e., $(M, \sigma_P, \mathsf{PK}_i)$, and outputs $\top$ or $\perp$, and $Query(\mathcal{A}, O_{\mathbf{Res}})$ is the set of queries $\mathcal{A}$ issued to the resolution oracle.

- **Security against the Arbitrator:** We require that any PPT adversary $\mathcal{A}$, who models a dishonest arbitrator, succeeds with at most negligible probability in the following experiment:

$$\mathsf{PM} \leftarrow \mathbf{PMGen}(1^k)$$

$$(\mathsf{APK}, \mathsf{ASK}^*) \leftarrow \mathcal{A}(\mathsf{PM})$$

$$(\mathsf{SK}_A, \mathsf{PK}_A) \leftarrow \mathbf{Setup}^{\mathsf{User}}(\mathsf{PM}, \mathsf{APK})$$

$$(M, \sigma, \mathsf{PK}_B) \leftarrow \mathcal{A}^{O_{\mathrm{PSig}}, O_{\mathrm{FakePSig}}, O_{\mathrm{PVer}}}(\mathsf{ASK}^*, \mathsf{APK}, \mathsf{PK}_A)$$

$$\text{success of } \mathcal{A} := [\mathbf{Ver}(M, \sigma, \mathsf{PK}_A, \mathsf{PK}_B, \mathsf{APK}) = \top$$

$$\wedge \, (M, \mathsf{PK}_B) \notin \mathit{Query}(\mathcal{A}, O_{\mathrm{PSig}})]$$

where all the three oracles are described in the previous experiment, $\mathsf{ASK}^*$ is $\mathcal{A}$'s state information, which might not be the corresponding secret key of $\mathsf{APK}$, and $\mathit{Query}(\mathcal{A}, O_{\mathrm{PSig}})$ is the set of queries $\mathcal{A}$ issued to oracle $O_{\mathrm{PSig}}$.

## 4  Generic Construction

In this section, we will present a generic construction of PAOFE. Let $\Gamma = (\mathsf{PMGen}, \mathsf{Setup}^{\mathsf{TTP}}, \mathsf{Setup}^{\mathsf{User}}, \mathsf{Sig}, \mathsf{Ver}, \mathsf{PSig}, \mathsf{PVer}, \mathsf{Res})$ be an ambiguous optimistic fair exchange scheme. Let $\mathcal{E} = (\mathsf{Kg}, \mathsf{Enc}, \mathsf{Dec})$ be a public key encryption scheme that is IE-IK-CCA secure.

A perfect ambiguous optimistic fair exchange can be constructed as follows:

- **PMGen:** This algorithm calls $\Gamma.\mathsf{PMGen}(1^\kappa) \to PM$ where $\kappa$ is a security parameter, and outputs $\mathsf{PM} := PM$.
- **Setup$^{\mathsf{TTP}}$:** The arbitrator runs $\Gamma.\mathsf{Setup}^{\mathsf{TTP}}(\mathsf{PM}) \to (ASK, APK)$, and sets $(\mathsf{ASK}, \mathsf{APK}) := (ASK, APK)$.
- **Setup$^{\mathsf{User}}$:** Each user $U_i$ runs $\Gamma.\mathsf{Setup}^{\mathsf{User}}(\mathsf{PM}, APK) \to (SK_i, PK_i)$ and $\mathcal{E}.\mathsf{Kg}(1^\kappa) \to (ek_i, dk_i)$ respectively, and sets $(\mathsf{SK}_i, \mathsf{PK}_i) := ((SK_i, dk_i), (PK_i, ek_i))$.
- **PSig:** To partially sign a message $M$ with the verifier $U_j$, $U_i$ runs $\Gamma.\mathsf{PSig}(M\|$ $\mathsf{PK}_i\| \mathsf{PK}_j, SK_i, PK_i, PK_j, APK) \to \sigma'_P$ and then encrypts it under $U_j$'s public encryption key $ek_j$ by running $c = \mathcal{E}.\mathsf{Enc}_{ek_j}(\sigma'_P)$. The partial signature is set as $\sigma_P := c$.
- **PVer:** On receiving a partial signature $\sigma_P$ on message $M$ from the signer $U_i$, user $U_j$ decrypts it using its own decryption key $dk_j$, i.e., $\sigma'_P = \mathcal{E}.\mathsf{Dec}_{dk_j}(\sigma_P)$, and then checks if $\Gamma.\mathsf{PVer}(M\|\mathsf{PK}_i\|\mathsf{PK}_j, \sigma'_P, PK_i, PK_j, APK) = \top$. If so, it accepts; otherwise, it rejects.
- **Sig:** To fully sign a message $M$ for the verifier $U_j$, $U_i$ calls $\Gamma.\mathsf{Sig}(M\| \mathsf{PK}_i\| \mathsf{PK}_j, SK_i, PK_i, PK_j, APK) \to \sigma$ and sends $\sigma$ to $U_j$.
- **Ver:** On receiving a full signature $\sigma$ from $U_i$, $U_j$ outputs $\Gamma.\mathsf{Ver}(M\| \mathsf{PK}_i\| \mathsf{PK}_j, \sigma, PK_i, PK_j, APK)$.
- **Res:** Given a partial signature $\sigma_P$ on message $M$ from the signer $U_i$, user $U_j$ decrypts it using its own decryption key $dk_j$, i.e., $\sigma'_P = \mathcal{E}.\mathsf{Dec}_{dk_j}(\sigma_P)$, and sends $(M, \sigma'_P, \mathsf{PK}_i, \mathsf{PK}_j)$ to the arbitrator. The arbitrator first checks the validity of $\sigma'_P$ by running $\Gamma.\mathsf{PVer}(M\| \mathsf{PK}_i\| \mathsf{PK}_j, \sigma'_P, PK_i, PK_j, APK)$. If it's invalid, it returns $\bot$ to $U_j$. Otherwise, it returns $\Gamma.\mathsf{Res}(M\| \mathsf{PK}_i\| \mathsf{PK}_j, \sigma'_P, ASK, PK_i, PK_j)$ to $U_j$.

### 4.1  Security Analysis

Our generic construction is secure according to the model in Section 3.1. Detailed security analysis is presented in the full version of this paper [13].

# 5  Conclusion

We proposed the notion of perfect ambiguous optimistic fair exchange, and gave a formal security model. We then proposed a generic construction of PAOFE, and proved its security under the proposed model in the standard model.

Our generic construction involves an encryption and an AOFE scheme and thus, it is bounded to be less efficient than AOFE. We leave it as our future work to construct more efficient PAOFE schemes, probably without directly using any encryption scheme.

# References

1. Asokan, N., Schunter, M., Waidner, M.: Optimistic Protocols for Fair Exchange. In: ACM CCS, pp. 7–17 (1997)
2. Bellare, M., Boldyreva, A., Desai, A., Pointcheval, D.: Key-Privacy in Public-Key Encryption. In: Boyd, C. (ed.) ASIACRYPT 2001. LNCS, vol. 2248, pp. 566–582. Springer, Heidelberg (2001)
3. Boneh, D., Gentry, C., Lynn, B., Shacham, H.: Aggregate and Verifiably Encrypted Signatures from Bilinear Maps. In: Biham, E. (ed.) EUROCRYPT 2003. LNCS, vol. 2656, pp. 416–432. Springer, Heidelberg (2003)
4. Cramer, R., Shoup, V.: A Practical Public Key Cryptosystem Provably Secure against Adaptive Chosen Ciphertext Attack. In: Krawczyk, H. (ed.) CRYPTO 1998. LNCS, vol. 1462, pp. 13–25. Springer, Heidelberg (1998)
5. Dodis, Y., Lee, P.J., Yum, D.H.: Optimistic Fair Exchange in a Multi-user Setting. In: Okamoto, T., Wang, X. (eds.) PKC 2007. LNCS, vol. 4450, pp. 118–133. Springer, Heidelberg (2007)
6. Dodis, Y., Reyzin, L.: Breaking and Repairing Optimistic Fair Exchange from PODC 2003. In: Digital Rights Management Workshop, pp. 47–54 (2003)
7. Heidarvand, S., Villar, J.L.: A Fair and Abuse-Free Contract Signing Protocol from Boneh-Boyen Signature. In: Camenisch, J., Lambrinoudakis, C. (eds.) EuroPKI 2010. LNCS, vol. 6711, pp. 125–140. Springer, Heidelberg (2011)
8. Huang, Q., Wong, D.S., Susilo, W.: Group-oriented Fair Exchange of Signatures. Inf. Sci. 181(16), 3267–3283 (2011)
9. Huang, Q., Yang, G., Wong, D.S., Susilo, W.: Ambiguous Optimistic Fair Exchange. In: Pieprzyk, J. (ed.) ASIACRYPT 2008. LNCS, vol. 5350, pp. 74–89. Springer, Heidelberg (2008)
10. Huang, Q., Yang, G., Wong, D.S., Susilo, W.: Efficient Optimistic Fair Exchange Secure in the Multi-user Setting and Chosen-Key Model without Random Oracles. In: Malkin, T. (ed.) CT-RSA 2008. LNCS, vol. 4964, pp. 106–120. Springer, Heidelberg (2008)
11. Micali, S.: Simple and Fast Optimistic Protocols for Fair Electronic Exchange. In: PODC, pp. 12–19 (2003)
12. Wang, G.: An Abuse-free Fair Contract Signing Protocol Based on the RSA Signature. In: WWW 2005, pp. 412–421 (2005)
13. Wang, Y., Au, M.H., Susilo, W.: Perfect ambiguous optimistic fair exchange. International Association for Cryptographic Research (IACR) ePrint Archive: Report 2012/462 (2012)
14. Zhang, J., Mao, J.: A Novel Verifiably Encrypted Signature Scheme Without Random Oracle. In: Dawson, E., Wong, D.S. (eds.) ISPEC 2007. LNCS, vol. 4464, pp. 65–78. Springer, Heidelberg (2007)

# Privacy-Preserving Noisy Keyword Search in Cloud Computing*

Xiaoqiong Pang[1,2], Bo Yang[3], and Qiong Huang[1]

[1] South China Agricultural University, Guangzhou 510642, China
[2] North University of China, Taiyuan 030051, China
[3] Shaanxi Normal University, Xi'an 710062, China
pxqiong@126.com, byang@snnu.edu.cn, csqhuang@alumni.cityu.edu.hk

**Abstract.** We consider the following problem: a user with either limited resources or limited expertise wants to outsource its private documens, which are associated with noisy keywords, to an untrusted cloud server in a private manner, while maintaining the ability to retrieve the stored data in a fault-tolerant manner. For example, the organization of homeland security wishes to outsource its private criminal database comprised of a set of criminal dossiers to the cloud server in encrypted form and hopes to retrieve encrypted dossiers by biometrics.

In this paper, we first present a general framework for searching on private-key encrypted data by noisy keywords in a fault-tolerant manner. Then we propose a concrete scheme which is proved secure against an adaptive adversary under well-defined security definition. It achieves search in two rounds of communication, and requires an amount of work from the server that is linear in the number of noisy keywords.

**Keywords:** Noisy Keyword, Searchable Encryption, Storage Outsourcing.

## 1 Introduction

Consider a cloud data system: a user with either limited resources or limited expertise wishes to outsource its private data to an untrusted cloud server in a private manner, while maintaining the ability to retrieve the stored data. The informal security requirement for this system claims that the cloud server should not learn any useful information about the data that it stores for the user and the queried words. A feasible solution to preserve privacy is to design a searchable encryption scheme such that: 1) the records are stored in disguised/encrypted form. 2) the key employed to encrypt the data is kept secret from the cloud server. 3) the records can be searched for securely and efficiently[21].

Motivated by the practical relevance of this problem, the research community has mainly considered two models for searching with privacy (see the related work for a detailed description) quite extensively and presented a number of techniques

---

* This work is supported by the National Natural Science Foundation of China under Grants 60973134, 61173164, 61272436 and 61103232.

T.W. Chim and T.H. Yuen (Eds.): ICICS 2012, LNCS 7618, pp. 154–166, 2012.
© Springer-Verlag Berlin Heidelberg 2012

that vary in costs and the levels of security guarantees, e.g. [1–7, 14, 15, 17, 19–21]. Unfortunately, except[14, 5] all of solutions above that only support exact keyword search do not apply to the situation where the keywords associated with the records are noisy data. For example, the organization of homeland security wishes to outsource its private criminal database comprised of a set of criminal dossiers to the cloud server in encrypted form and hopes to retrieve encrypted dossiers by biometrics whenever. As we know, biometric traits are the deciding factors to recognize a person's identity by using special features such as face, finger-prints, iris, voice, DNA, and so on. However, biometric data are noisy, even two readings of the same biometric source are rarely identical. Therefore, exact-match search over biometric data does not work. It seems that searching on encrypted fuzzy data in a private manner is much more difficult. To address this problem we present a solution for privacy-preserving noisy-keyword-based search on remote encrypted data in a fault-tolerant manner.

## 1.1 Related Work

Various methods have been proposed for searching on encrypted data. The existing solutions can be divided into two classes according to the models of searching on encrypted data with privacy.

*Searching on private-key encrypted data.* In this setting, the user itself encrypts the database and uploads it to the server so that only somebody holding the private key can obtain the records it retrieves. Solution in this model can be realized with optimal security by using the work of Goldreich and Ostrovsky about oblivious RAM in [12], which hides the identities of the data items being accessed from a remote server. Because of the overwhelming cost of the oblivious RAM protocol (see the analyse in [18]), it was always quoted as a theoretical solution that was clearly infeasible in practice. Compared with the method of [12], Song et al.[20] presented a solution with little communication in one round of interaction. However, their construction is not secure against statistical analysis. In [6], Chang and Mitzenmacher proposed a scheme based on index. In their scheme, the overhead required for a query is proportional to the number of files. In [7], Curtmola et al. presented two solutions, in which the server's search time is optimal but updates to the index are inefficient. The authors also considered adaptive security of their schemes. Li et al. [14] provided a solution for privacy-preserving fuzzy search on encrypted data. To achieve fuzzy search, the user constructs a wildcard-based fuzzy keyword set for each keyword according to some edit distance before outsourcing data, which incurs extra large storage. There also exists other solutions in this model, however, almost all of existing solutions except [14] do not apply to the situation where the keywords associated with the records are noisy data. Our goal is to design an efficient and secure noisy-keyword-based searchable encryption scheme in a fault-tolerant manner under this model.

*Searching on public-key encrypted data.* In this setting, the party who searches over the data can be different from the party that generates it. In other words, anyone with access to a party's public key can add encrypted data to the database, but only the party holding the decryption key can decrypt and retrieve. As far as we know, solution in this model was proposed for the first time by Boneh et al. in [2]. The scheme in [2] reveals the users access pattern. In [3], Boneh et al. presented a solution that guarantees the complete privacy of queries by sacrificing efficiency. Bellare et al.[1] proposed fast search schemes in the random oracle model. Since the encryption algorithm they utilized is deterministic, their constructions provide weak security guarantees. Bringer et al.[5] described a primitive called Public Key Error-Tolerant Searchable Encryption and applied it to biometric identification. In addition, some works about more complex search have been studied such as range queries[4, 19], join queries[15] and conjunctive searches[17, 4].

## 1.2 Our Contribution

We propose a general framework for noisy-keyword-based searchable private-key encryption in a fault-tolerant manner. This general scheme allows to search on encrypted/disguised data with a noisy keyword. In addition, different from all the previous schemes, which use the same private key to encrypt all documents, our scheme utilizes the fuzzy extractor, which can extract a uniformly random string $k_i$ from each noisy keywords $w_i$ in a noise-tolerant way. The extracted $k_i$ is used to encrypt the documents which are associated with noisy keyword $w_i$. The advantage follows the fact that our scheme does not store the extracted $k_i$. Instead, the noisy keyword itself effectively acts as the key, and only when the "correct keyword" is presented will the documents be decrypted. Therefore, if a $k_i$ is leaked for some reason, the privacy of the documents that are not labeled with $w_i$ is still preserved. Another important notion we employ is secure sketch, which can be used to construct the fuzzy extractor.

In accordance with the simulation-based security definition presented in [7] and the real condition in noisy-keyword-based search, we present a notion named match pattern, and use it in security proof. Compared with the notion of search pattern, which refers to the information whether searches are for the same word or not[7], match pattern indicates how well the queried words match the noisy keywords.

We present a concrete scheme which is proved secure against an adaptive adversary under the simulation-based security definition presented in [7]. It achieves search in two rounds of interaction, and requires an amount of work from the server that is linear in the number of noisy keywords. Our idea comes from the **SSO/Approx/Squ** protocol proposed by Du and Atallah in [10], where they address the problem that a user, who outsources its database comprised of $N$ keywords to the server, wants to know which keyword in the database is closest to the query string $x$. We use this protocol as a building block in our concrete scheme.

**Organization.** The remainder of this paper is structured as follows. In Section 2 we introduce the notions of secure sketch and fuzzy extractor. In Section 3 we present a general framework for noisy-keyword-based searchable private-key encryption and describe its security requirement. Section 4 describes a concrete scheme, argues its correctness and security. We consider performance issues in Section 5. Finally, Section 6 concludes the paper.

## 2 Useful Tools

### 2.1 Preliminaries

If $X$ is a random variable, we denote the probability distribution over the range of the variable by $X$ for simplicity. We denote the uniform distribution over binary strings of length $l$ by $U_l$. For a set $A$, the notation $a \leftarrow_r A$ means $a$ is chosen uniformly at random from $A$. For a matrix $\mathbf{B}$, the rank of $\mathbf{B}$ is denoted by $\mathsf{Rank}(\mathbf{B})$.

The Hamming distance between two strings of equal length is the number of positions at which the corresponding symbols are different. The edit distance between two strings is the number of operations required to transform one string into the other. The set difference between two sets is the size of the symmetric difference of the two sets.

The *min-entropy* $\mathbf{H}_\infty(X)$ of a random variable $X$ is $-\log(\max_x \Pr(X = x))$. A random variable with min-entropy at least $m$ is called an $m$-source. We define *average min-entropy* of $X$ given $Y$ to be the logarithm of the average probability of the most likely value of $X$ given $Y$, namely $\widetilde{\mathbf{H}}_\infty(X|Y) = -\log(E_{y \leftarrow Y}[2^{-\mathbf{H}_\infty(X|Y)}])$. The statistical distance between two probability distributions $X$ and $Y$ is defined as $\mathsf{SD}[X, Y] = \frac{1}{2} \sum_v |P[X = v] - P[Y = v]|$. We use $X \approx_\varepsilon Y$ to denote that $X$ and $Y$ are at distance at most $\varepsilon$.[9]

### 2.2 Secure Sketch and Fuzzy Extractor

The following descriptions and definitions are based on [9, 8]. Let $\mathcal{M}$ be a metric space with distance function dis. $t$ is a threshold value. Informally, a secure sketch allows precise reconstruction of a noisy input $w \in \mathcal{M}$ from any $w'$ close to $w$ without revealing much about $w$.

**Definition 1.** *An $(m, m', t)$-secure sketch is a pair of efficient randomized procedures* (SS,Rec) *such that the following hold:*

*1. The sketching procedure* SS *on input $w \in \mathcal{M}$ returns a string $s \in \{0,1\}^*$. The recovery procedure* Rec *takes as input an element $w' \in \mathcal{M}$ and $s \in \{0,1\}^*$.*

*2. Correctness: If $\mathsf{dis}(w, w') \leq t$, then $\mathsf{Rec}(w', \mathsf{SS}(w)) = w$.*

*3. Security: For any $m$-source over $\mathcal{M}$, the min-entropy of $W$ given $s$ is high: For any $(W,E)$, if $\widetilde{\mathbf{H}}_\infty(W|E) \geq m$, then $\widetilde{\mathbf{H}}_\infty(W|\mathsf{SS}(W), E) \geq m'$.*

Next we present the definition of fuzzy extractor. As opposed to secure sketch, the goal of fuzzy extractor is not to recover the original noisy input, but to extract a close-to-uniform string $R$ from $w$ and then reproduce $R$ exatcly from any $w'$ that is close to $w$. The reproduction is done with the help of the helper string $P$ that is generated during the initial extraction procedure.

**Definition 2.** *An $(m, l, t, \varepsilon)$-fuzzy extractor is a pair of efficient randomized procedures* (Gen,Rep) *such that the following hold:*

*1. Given $w \in \mathcal{M}$,* Gen *outputs an extracted string $R \in \{0, 1\}^l$ and a helper string $P \in \{0, 1\}^*$.* Rep *takes as input an element $w' \in \mathcal{M}$ and a string $P \in \{0, 1\}^*$.*

*2. Correctness: If* $\operatorname{dis}(w, w') \leq t$ *and* $(R, P) \leftarrow$ Gen$(w)$, *then* Rep$(w', P) = R$.

*3. Security: For all m-sources $W$ over $\mathcal{M}$, the string $R$ is nearly uniform even given $P$; that is, if $\widetilde{\mathbf{H}}_\infty(W|E) \geq m$, then $(R, P, E) \approx_\varepsilon (U_l, P, E)$.*

A secure sketch can be used to construct a fuzzy extractor that extracts a key by combining the sketch with a strong randomness extractor, such as the universal hash functions which extract well even from conditional min-entropy.

**Lemma 1.** *Suppose we compose an $(m, m', t)$-secure sketch* (SS,Rec) *for a space $\mathcal{M}$ and a universal hash function* Ext: $\mathcal{M} \to \{0, 1\}^l$ *as follows: In* Gen, *choose a random $i$ and let $P = (\text{SS}(w), i)$ and $R = \text{Ext}(w; i)$; let* Rep$(w', (s, i)) =$ Ext$(\text{Rec}(w', s), i)$. *The result is an $(m, l, t, \varepsilon)$-fuzzy extractor with $l = m' + 2 - 2\log(1/\varepsilon)$.*

*Remark.* It is noting that: 1)There exist many concrete constructions of secure sketch and fuzzy extractor for the Hamming distance, set difference, edit distance and other notions of distance, e.g. [9, 16]. 2) The concrete constructions of secure sketch and fuzzy extractor are not our goal, we use them as building blocks to construct our scheme. 3)In our general framework we do not assume any particular metrics to measure the closeness between $w'$ and $w$.

# 3    General Framework

## 3.1    Definition for Noisy-Keyword-Based Searchable Private-Key Encryption

We begin by defining a general framework for searching on encrypted data by noisy keywords in a fault-tolerant manner. A user owns a private document set $\mathbf{D} = \{D_1, \cdots, D_N\}$, each document is associated with corresponding noisy keyword. We consider an honest-but-curious server in the sense that it correctly follows the protocol specification while it attempts to derive as much information as possible from user's queries and access patterns.

In the following definitions, we use $\operatorname{id}(D_i)$ to denote the identifier of the document $D_i$, and *threshold* to denote the predetermined threshold value. Let $\delta(\mathbf{D})$ denote the set of all noisy keywords in $\mathbf{D}$. If $\operatorname{dis}(x, w_i) \leq threshold$, we refer to $x$ and $w_i$ as synonyms. W.l.o.g, we assume that for a noisy keyword $w_i \in \delta(\mathbf{D})$, if $x$ is a synonym of $w_i$, then $x$ is not synonymous with all the other noisy keywords in $\delta(\mathbf{D})$, furthermore, it is evident that $\operatorname{dis}(x, w_i) = \min_{j=1}^{|\delta(\mathbf{D})|} \operatorname{dis}(x, w_j)$. We use $\mu(w_i)$ to denote the set of all the synonyms of $w_i$, and $\delta'(\mathbf{D})$ to denote $\bigcup_{i=1}^{|\delta(\mathbf{D})|} \mu(w_i)$. Let $\mathbf{D}(w_i)$ be the set of identifiers of documents in $\mathbf{D}$ that are labeled with noisy keyword $w_i$. For some queried word $x_i \in \delta'(\mathbf{D})$, if $x_i$ is synonymous with $w_j$, then $\mathbf{D}(x_i) = \mathbf{D}(w_j)$. We denote the set of ciphertexts of all documents in $\mathbf{D}$ by $\mathbf{C}=(c_1, \cdots, c_N)$ and the set of ciphertexts of documents in $\mathbf{D}$ that are associated with noisy keyword $w_i$ by $\mathbf{C}_{w_i}$.

**Definition 3.** *A Noisy-Keyword-based Searchable Private-key Encryption scheme* NKSPE= (KeyGen, Document-Storage, Search) *consists of three phases:*

1. KeyGen($1^k$): *given a security parameter k as input, output a secret key K.*
2. Document-Storage($K, \mathbf{D}$) : *given a document set* $\mathbf{D} = \{D_1, \cdots, D_N\}$ *and a secret key K as input, output a secure index I and a series of ciphertexts* $\mathbf{C}=(c_1, \cdots, c_N)$. *For each $D_j$ associated with noisy keyword $w_i$, the ciphertexts are produced by employing a fuzzy extractor and a private-key encryption scheme as follows:*
   Gen($w_i$) : *given $w_i \in \delta(\mathbf{D})$ as input, output an extracted string $k_i$ and a helper string $P_i$.*
   Enc($D_j, k_i$) : *given $D_j$ and $k_i$ (extracted from $w_i$) as input, output ciphertext $c_j$ under private key $k_i$ .*
3. Search($I, x$) *is an interactive two party protocol between the user and the server. For any query $x \in \delta'(\mathbf{D})$, the user generates corresponding* **trapdoor** *t under secret key K. Given the trapdoor t and index I, the server can find the $w_i$ which is synonymous with x and the user will get encrypted documents* $\mathbf{C}_{w_i}$. *Then the decryption procedure utilizing fuzzy extractor is as follows:*
   Rep($x, P_i$) : *given x and $P_i$ as input, reproduce the decryption key $k_i$.*
   Dec($\mathbf{C}_{w_i}, k_i$) : *given $\mathbf{C}_{w_i}$ and $k_i$ as input, output corresponding documents.*

We now define correctness for such an NKSPE scheme.

**Definition 4.** *For all $k \in \mathbb{N}$, for all K output by* KeyGen($1^k$), *for all $(I, \mathbf{C})$ output by* Document-Storage($K, \mathbf{D}$), *for all $w_i \in \delta(\mathbf{D})$, for all $x \in \delta'(\mathbf{D})$, if* dis$(x, w_i) \leq threshold$ *and $(k_i, P_i) \leftarrow$ Gen($w_i$), then*

$$\mathbf{C}_{w_i} \leftarrow \text{Search}(I, x) \wedge k_i \leftarrow \text{Rep}(x, P_i) \wedge \text{Dec}(k_i, c_j) = D_j, \text{ for all } c_j \in \mathbf{C}_{w_i}.$$

*We say the* NKSPE *scheme is correct.*

## 3.2   Security Definition

In this paper, we will follow the security definitions presented in [7]. The security requirement for searchable encryption is typically characterized as one that nothing should be leaked except the result of a search, which is referred to as access pattern. However, except for oblivious RAMs, there exists no practical construction that satisfies this requirement, all existing exact-match schemes also disclose whether queries are for the same keyword or not, which is referred to as search pattern. Curtmola et al.[7] analyzed two existing security definitions that had been used for searching on private-key encrypted data: IND2-CKA(Indistinguishability against Chosen-Keyword Attacks) in [11] and a simulation-based definition in [6]. They pointed out that IND2-CKA was not strong enough to ensure that an index could be safely employed to construct a searchable private-key encryption scheme. For the simulation-based definition in [6], they pointed out that even an insecure scheme would satisfy this definition and this definition was inherently non-adaptive. In [7], Curtmola et al. proposed more accurate security definitions for searchable private-key encryption scheme under non-adaptive and adaptive adversarial models [1]respectively. In next section we will present an adaptively secure NKSPE scheme under security definitions in [7].

Next we introduce four auxiliary notions we will use in security definition. Except Definition 7, the following descriptions and definitions are based on [7].

**Definition 5.** (History) *Let* $\mathbf{D}$ *be a set of* $N$ *documents. A* $q$-*query* history over $\mathbf{D}$ *is a tuple* $H = (\mathbf{D}, \boldsymbol{x})$ *that consists of the document set* $\mathbf{D}$ *and a vector of* $q$ *query keywords* $\boldsymbol{x} = (x_1, \cdots, x_q)$, *where* $x_i \in \delta'(\mathbf{D})$, *for all* $i \in [1, q]$.

**Definition 6.** (Access pattern) *The access pattern induced by a* $q$-*query history* $H = (\mathbf{D}, \boldsymbol{x})$ *is a tuple* $\alpha(H) = (\mathbf{D}(x_1), \cdots, \mathbf{D}(x_q))$.

Compared with the notion of search pattern in exact-match scenario, we present a notion termed match pattern in noisy-keyword-based search scenario, which indicates how well the queried words match the noisy keywords.

**Definition 7.** (Match pattern) *The match pattern induced by a* $q$-*query history* $H = (\mathbf{D}, \boldsymbol{x})$ *is a matrix* $\beta(H) = (\mathbf{b}_1, \cdots, \mathbf{b}_q)$, *where* $\mathbf{b}_i = (b_i^1, \cdots, b_i^{|\delta(\mathbf{D})|})^\top$ *and* $b_i^j$ *indicates the closeness degree[2] between queried word* $x_i$ *and noisy keyword* $w_j$, *where* $i \in [1, q]$ *and* $j \in [1, |\delta(\mathbf{D})|]$.

Next, we present the definition of the trace of a history, which can be considered as the information the user would like to leak about the history to the server. This should include document size and identifier, the number of keywords used in all documents , access pattern and match pattern.

**Definition 8.** (Trace) *Let* $\mathbf{D}$ *be a set of* $N$ *documents. The trace induced by a* $q$-*query history* $H = (\mathbf{D}, \boldsymbol{x})$ *is a sequence* $\tau(H) = (\mathrm{id}(D_1), \cdots, \mathrm{id}(D_N), |D_1|, \cdots, |D_N|, |\delta(\mathbf{D})|, \alpha(H), \beta(H))$ *consisting of sizes and identifiers of the documents in* $\mathbf{D}$, *the number of noisy keywords, the access and match patterns induced by* $H$.

We now present the adaptive simulation-based security definition, where we require that the view of an adversary(including the index, the trapdoors and the ciphertexts) generated from an adversarially and adaptively chosen history be simulatable given only the trace.

---

[1] Non-adaptive adversaries make queries without considering previous trapdoors and search outcomes while adaptive ones make queries according to previous trapdoors and search results.

[2] The actual closeness degree depends on the particular metric in concrete scheme.

**Definition 9.** (Adaptive semantic security) *Let* NKSPE=(KeyGen, Document-Storage, Search) *be a Noisy-Keyword-based Searchable Private-key Encryption scheme, $k \in \mathbb{N}$ be the security parameter, $\mathcal{A} = (\mathcal{A}_0, \cdots, \mathcal{A}_q)$ be an adversary such that $q \in \mathbb{N}$ and $\mathcal{S} = (\mathcal{S}_0, \cdots, \mathcal{S}_q)$ be a simulator and consider the following probabilistic experiments* $\mathbf{Real}_{\mathsf{NKSPE},\mathcal{A}}(k)$ *and* $\mathbf{Sim}_{\mathsf{NKSPE},\mathcal{A},\mathcal{S}}(k)$:

| $\mathbf{Real}_{\mathsf{NKSPE},\mathcal{A}}(k)$ | $\mathbf{Sim}_{\mathsf{NKSPE},\mathcal{A},\mathcal{S}}(k)$ |
|---|---|
| $K \leftarrow \mathsf{KeyGen}(1^k)$ | $(\mathbf{D}, st_\mathcal{A}) \leftarrow \mathcal{A}_0(1^k)$ |
| $(\mathbf{D}, st_\mathcal{A}) \leftarrow \mathcal{A}_0(1^k)$ | $(I, \mathbf{C}, st_\mathcal{S}) \leftarrow \mathcal{S}_0(\tau(\mathbf{D}))$ |
| $(I, \mathbf{C}) \leftarrow \mathsf{Document\text{-}Storage}(K, \mathbf{D})$ | $(x_1, st_\mathcal{A}) \leftarrow \mathcal{A}_1(st_\mathcal{A}, I, \mathbf{C})$ |
| $(x_1, st_\mathcal{A}) \leftarrow \mathcal{A}_1(st_\mathcal{A}, I, \mathbf{C})$ | $(t_1, st_\mathcal{S}) \leftarrow \mathcal{S}_1(st_\mathcal{S}, \tau(\mathbf{D}, x_1))$ |
| *generate trapdoor $t_1$ from $K$ and $x_1$* | *for* $2 \leq i \leq q$ |
| *for* $2 \leq i \leq q$ | $\quad (x_i, st_\mathcal{A}) \leftarrow \mathcal{A}_i(st_\mathcal{A}, I, \mathbf{C}, t_1, \cdots, t_{i-1})$ |
| $\quad (x_i, st_\mathcal{A}) \leftarrow \mathcal{A}_i(st_\mathcal{A}, I, \mathbf{C}, t_1, \cdots, t_{i-1})$ | $\quad (t_i, st_\mathcal{S}) \leftarrow \mathcal{S}_i(st_\mathcal{S}, \tau(\mathbf{D}, x_1, \cdots, x_i))$ |
| $\quad$ *generate trapdoor $t_i$ from $K$ and $x_i$* | *let* $\boldsymbol{t} = (t_1, \cdots, t_q)$ |
| *let* $\boldsymbol{t} = (t_1, \cdots, t_q)$ | *output* $\mathbf{v} = (I, \mathbf{C}, \boldsymbol{t})$ *and* $st_\mathcal{A}$ |
| *output* $\mathbf{v} = (I, \mathbf{C}, \boldsymbol{t})$ *and* $st_\mathcal{A}$ | |

*We say that* NKSPE *is adaptively semantically secure if for all polynomial-size adversaries $\mathcal{A} = (\mathcal{A}_0, \cdots, \mathcal{A}_q)$ such that $q = \mathsf{poly}(k)$, there exists a non-uniform polynomial-size simulator $\mathcal{S} = (\mathcal{S}_0, \cdots, \mathcal{S}_q)$, such that for all polynomial-size distinguisher $\mathcal{D}$,*

$$| \Pr[\mathcal{D}(\mathbf{v}, st_\mathcal{A}) = 1 : (\mathbf{v}, st_\mathcal{A}) \leftarrow \mathbf{Real}_{\mathsf{NKSPE},\mathcal{A}}(k)]$$

$$- \Pr[\mathcal{D}(\mathbf{v}, st_\mathcal{A}) = 1 : (\mathbf{v}, st_\mathcal{A}) \leftarrow \mathbf{Sim}_{\mathsf{NKSPE},\mathcal{A},\mathcal{S}}(k)]| \leq \mathsf{negl}(k)$$

*where $st_\mathcal{A}$ is a string that captures $\mathcal{A}$'s state, and the probabilities are taken over the random coins of* KeyGen, Document-Storage *and trapdoor.*

## 4    Efficient and Secure Noisy-Keyword-Based Searchable Private-Key Encryption

In this section we present our concrete NKSPE construction, and argue its correctness and security according to the definitions in section 3. The concrete scheme is described in Fig.1.

Different noisy data, such as different biometric information, has different error patterns[3]. In our concrete construction, we consider $\sum_{k=1}^{n}(w_{ik} - x_k)^2$ as metric to measure the closeness between binary strings $x = x_1 \cdots x_n$ and $w_i = w_{i,1} \cdots w_{i,n}$. In fact, the value $\sum_{k=1}^{n}(w_{ik} - x_k)^2$ is the same with the Hamming distance between $x = x_1 \cdots x_n$ and $w_i = w_{i,1} \cdots w_{i,n}$.

---

[3] Biometric measurements usually have to be processed before they fall under a suitable metric space; For example, techniques such as IrisCode transform images of irises into strings in the Hamming space. This procedure is itself a research area. Transformations of biometric feature vectors into binary strings have been discussed in [13].

1. KeyGen($1^k$): sample $K_1 \leftarrow_r \{0,1\}^k$ and invertible matrix $\mathbf{Q} \leftarrow_r \mathbf{M}_{n+3,n+3}(\mathbb{F})$, where $\mathbf{M}_{n+3,n+3}(\mathbb{F})$ is a predetermined finite integral matrix group consisting of invertible $(n+3) \times (n+3)$ matrices over field $\mathbb{F}$. output $K = (K_1, \mathbf{Q})$.

2. Document-Storage($K, \mathbf{D}$) :
   - Init($\mathbf{D}$) :
     1) scan ($\mathbf{D}$) and generate the set $\delta(\mathbf{D})$
     2) for all $w_i \in \delta(\mathbf{D})$, output $\mathbf{D}(w_i)$
   - BuildIndex($K, \delta(\mathbf{D}), \{\mathbf{D}(w_i)|w_i \in \delta(\mathbf{D})\}$) :
     3) $R \leftarrow_r \mathbb{F}$
     4) for $1 \leq i \leq |\delta(\mathbf{D})|$, creat index $I_{w_i} = (\mathbf{A}_{w_i}, B_{w_i})$
        4.1) for each $w_i = w_{i,1} \cdots w_{i,n} \in \delta(\mathbf{D})$, $R_i \leftarrow_r \mathbb{F}$, let $\mathbf{w}_i = (\sum_{k=1}^n w_{ik}^2 + R - R_i, w_{i1}, \cdots, w_{in}, 1, R_i)$, then compute $\mathbf{A}_{w_i} = \mathbf{Q}\mathbf{w}_i^\top$
        4.2) compute EXT.Gen($w_i$), output an extracted string $k_i$ and a helper $P_i$
        4.3) compute $B_{w_i} = \pi_{K_1}(\mathbf{D}(w_i)||P_i)$
   - Data-Storage($\mathbf{D}$) :
     5) for each $D_j$ associated with noisy keyword $w_i(1 \leq j \leq N, 1 \leq i \leq |\delta(\mathbf{D})|)$, compute SKE.Enc($D_j, k_i$), output ciphertext $c_j$ under private key $k_i$

3. Search($I, x$):
   - for any query $x = x_1 \cdots x_n$, $R_A \leftarrow_r \mathbb{F}$, the user constructs a vector $\mathbf{x} = (1, -2x_1, \cdots, -2x_n, R_A, 1)$, then generates trapdoor $\mathbf{t} = \mathbf{x}\mathbf{Q}^{-1}$ under secret key $\mathbf{Q}$. The user sends $\mathbf{t}$ to the server.
   - for $1 \leq i \leq |\delta(\mathbf{D})|$, the server computes $\mathbf{t} \times \mathbf{A}_{w_i} = \mathbf{x}\mathbf{Q}^{-1}\mathbf{Q}\mathbf{w}_i^\top = \mathbf{x}\mathbf{w}_i^\top$, gets $dis' = \mathbf{min}_{i=1}^{|\delta(\mathbf{D})|}\mathbf{x}\mathbf{w}_i^\top$ and the corresponding $i$. The server then returns $(dis', B_{w_i})$ to the user.
   - the user computes $\mathsf{dis}(x, w_i) = dis' + \sum_{k=1}^n x_k^2 - R - R_A$. If $\mathsf{dis}(x, w_i) > threshold$, it implies that there exists no matched record with overwhelming probability. Otherwise, the user computes $\pi^{-1}(K_1, B_{w_i})$, gets $\mathbf{D}(w_i)$ and $P_i$. The user then sends search result, i.e. $\mathbf{D}(w_i)$, to the server.
   - the server returns $\mathbf{C}_{w_i}$ to the user.
   - the user computes EXT.Rep($x, P_i$) to reproduce the decryption key $k_i$, then outputs SKE.Dec($\mathbf{C}_{w_i}, k_i$).

**Fig. 1.** An adaptively secure NKSPE scheme

We assume that each helper string is a $l$-bit string. Each $w_i \in \delta(\mathbf{D})$ is associated with at most $m$ documents, The identifier of each document can be represented as an $h$-bit string. $\pi : \{0,1\}^k \times \{0,1\}^{l+m*h} \to \{0,1\}^{l+m*h}$ is a pseudorandom permutation. Let SKE=(Enc,Dec) be a PCPA-secure symmetric encryption scheme (refer to [7], Appendix A). Let EXT=(Gen,Rep) be a fuzzy extractor.

We observe that, for a queried word $x$, the match pattern is $\mathbf{b} = (b^1, \cdots, b^{|\delta(\mathbf{D})|})^\top$, where $b^j = \mathbf{t} \times \mathbf{A}_{w_j}$. Next, we analyze the correctness of our concrete scheme.

**Theorem 1.** *The* NKSPE *scheme described in Fig.1 is correct (i.e. satisfies Definition 4).*

*Proof.* For query string $x = x_1 \cdots x_n \in \delta'(\mathbf{D})$, let $\mathbf{x} = (1, -2x_1, \cdots, -2x_n, R_A, 1)$. For each $w_i = w_{i,1} \cdots w_{i,n} \in \delta(\mathbf{D})$, let $\mathbf{w}_i = (\sum_{k=1}^n w_{ik}^2 + R - R_i, w_{i1}, \cdots, w_{in}, 1, R_i)$. Thus,

$$\mathbf{x}\mathbf{Q}^{-1}\mathbf{Q}\mathbf{w}_i^\top = \mathbf{x}\mathbf{w}_i^\top = (\sum_{k=1}^n w_{ik}^2 + R - R_i) - 2(x_1 w_{i1} + \cdots + x_n w_{in}) + R_A + R_i$$

$$= \sum_{k=1}^n (w_{ik} - x_k)^2 - \sum_{k=1}^n x_k^2 + R_A + R$$

Therefore,

$$\sum_{k=1}^n (w_{ik} - x_k)^2 = \mathbf{x}\mathbf{w}_i^\top + \sum_{k=1}^n x_k^2 - R_A - R$$

Since $\sum_{k=1}^n x_k^2 - R_A - R$ is a constant, the server can use $\mathbf{x}\mathbf{w}_i^\top$ to compute the closest match and return corresponding $(dis', \pi_{K_1}(\mathbf{D}(w_i)||P_i))$. It is evident that $\mathrm{dis}(x, w_i) = dis' + \sum_{k=1}^n x_k^2 - R - R_A \leq threshold$ ($x$ is a synonym of $w_i$). After receiving $\mathbf{D}(w_i)$, the server returns $\mathbf{C}_{w_i}$ to the user. The user then computes $\mathrm{Rep}(x, P_i)$ to reproduce the decryption key $k_i$. Therefore, the user can decrypt $\mathbf{C}_{w_i}$ correctly. This completes the proof.

## 4.1   The Proof of Security

In this subsection, we analyze the security of our concrete scheme.

**Theorem 2.** *The proposed scheme is adaptively secure (i.e. satisfies Definition 9) assuming that the private-key encryption scheme SKE is PCPA-secure and $\pi$ is a pseudorandom permutation.*

*Proof.* What we need to do is to construct a simulator $\mathcal{S} = (\mathcal{S}_0, \cdots, \mathcal{S}_q)$ such that for the adversary $\mathcal{A} = (\mathcal{A}_0, \cdots, \mathcal{A}_q)$, the outputs of $\mathbf{Real}_{\mathsf{NKSPE},\mathcal{A}}(k)$ and $\mathbf{Sim}_{\mathsf{NKSPE},\mathcal{A},\mathcal{S}}(k)$ are computationally indistinguishable. We construct a simulator $\mathcal{S} = (\mathcal{S}_0, \cdots, \mathcal{S}_q)$ that adaptively produces a string $\mathbf{v}' = (I', \mathbf{C}', t') = (I', c_1', \cdots, c_N', t_1', \cdots, t_N')$ as follows:

1. $\mathcal{S}_0(1^k, \tau(\mathbf{D}))$ : it constructs a simulated index $I'$ by making a table comprised of entries $(\mathbf{A}_i, B_i)$, for $i = 1, \cdots, |\delta(\mathbf{D})|$, where $\mathbf{A}_i \leftarrow_r \mathbf{M}_{n+3,1}(\mathbb{F})$ and $B_i \leftarrow_r \{0,1\}^{l+m*h}$, such that for the matix $\mathbf{A}_{|\delta(\mathbf{D})| \times (n+3)} = (\mathbf{A}_1^\top, \cdots, \mathbf{A}_{|\delta(\mathbf{D})|}^\top)^\top$, $\mathrm{Rank}(\mathbf{A}) = \min(|\delta(\mathbf{D})|, n+3)$. $\mathcal{S}_0$ then includes $I'$ in $st_\mathcal{S}$ and outputs $(I', \mathbf{C}', st_\mathcal{S})$, where $c_i' \leftarrow_r \{0,1\}^{|D_i|}$.
   We now claim that $I'$ is indistinguishable from a real index, i.e. the tuples $(\mathbf{A}_i, B_i)$ are indistinguishable from tuples $(\mathbf{A}_{w_i}, B_{w_i})$. It is evident that the distributions over $\mathbf{A}_i$ and $\mathbf{A}_{w_i}$ are identical, and that $B_i$ is indistinguishable from $B_{w_i} = \pi(\mathbf{D}(w_i)||P_i)$ since $\pi$ is a pseudorandom permutation. Furthermore, since the private-key encryption scheme is PCPA-secure, each $c_i'$ is indistinguishable from a real ciphertext.

2. $S_1(st_S, \tau(\mathbf{D}, x_1))$ : it solves system of linear equations $\mathbf{Ax} = \mathbf{b}_1$. Note that it knows $\mathbf{b}_1$ from the trace of $(\mathbf{D}, x_1)$. We denote a solution of $\mathbf{Ax} = \mathbf{b}_1$ by $\mathbf{t}^*$ (if there exists solution). Let $\mathbf{t}'_1 = \mathbf{t}^{*\top}$ that is indistinguishable from a real trapdoor $\mathbf{t}_1$, since $\mathbf{t}_1 \times \mathbf{A}_{w_i} = \mathbf{t}'_1 \times \mathbf{A}_i$ holds for all $i \in [1, |\delta(\mathbf{D})|]$. $S_1$ then includes $\mathbf{t}'_1$ in $st_S$ and outputs $(\mathbf{t}'_1, st_S)$.

3. $S_i(st_S, \tau(\mathbf{D}, x_1, \cdots, x_i))$ : $S_i$ generates a trapdoor $\mathbf{t}'_i$ in the same way that $S_1$ does, i.e. by solving the system of linear equations $\mathbf{Ax} = \mathbf{b}_i$. $S_i$ then includes $\mathbf{t}'_i$ in $st_S$ and outputs $(\mathbf{t}'_i, st_S)$. It is evident that $\mathbf{t}'_i$ is indistinguishable from a real trapdoor $\mathbf{t}_i$. This completes the proof.

*Remark.* Note that in our security proof if $|\delta(\mathbf{D})| \leq n + 3$, then $\mathsf{Rank}(\mathbf{A}) = \mathsf{Rank}(\mathbf{A}, \mathbf{b}_i) = |\delta(\mathbf{D})| \leq n+3$ which guarantees that $\mathbf{Ax} = \mathbf{b}_i$ must have solution. Otherwise, for a randomly selected matrix $\mathbf{A}$ in advance, it is hard to guarantee $\mathsf{Rank}(\mathbf{A}) = \mathsf{Rank}(\mathbf{A}, \mathbf{b}_i) \leq n + 3$. A solution to this problem is to divide $|\delta(\mathbf{D})|$ noisy keywords into $\lceil \frac{|\delta(\mathbf{D})|}{n+3} \rceil$ groups. There are at most $n + 3$ noisy keywords in each group. The user selects and stores different secret keys for each group.

# 5    Performance

## 5.1    Exact Efficiency of the Proposed Scheme

For each query, the number of rounds of communication is exactly 2. The user computes 1 matrix multiplication, the server performs $|\delta(\mathbf{D})|$ vector inner product operations. Regarding storage, the user must have a long-term storage for private key $K = (K_1, \mathbf{Q})$ and a random number $R$. The server stores an index $I$ comprised of $|\delta(\mathbf{D})|$ entries (each entry includes a matrix of dimensions $(n + 3) \times 1$ and a $(l + m * h)$-bit string) and $N$ encrypted documents.

## 5.2    Comparison

In this subsection, we highlight the differences between the fuzzy keyword search scheme in [14] and ours in Table1.

**Metric.** In [14], edit distance is used to measure the similarity, while Hamming distance is considered when the input can be represented as a binary string in our concrete scheme.

**Security.** The scheme in [14] was proved secure against IND2-CKA, however, it is not adaptively secure. The reason is that for a query $(w, k)$, the simulator has no idea how many simulated trapdoors it should compute even if given the trace of $(\mathbf{D}, (w, k))$[4]. While our scheme is proven secure against adaptive adversary.

**Efficiency.** The scheme in [14] requires two rounds of communication for each query. Assume that the length of all keywords is polynomial in $n$. For a query $(w, k)$, the user computes the trapdoor set of size $O(n^k)$, the server compares this trapdoor set with the index table. Regarding the server's storage, except for $N$ encrypted documents, the size of index is $O(Mn^k)$, where $M$ is the number of distinct keywords in document set and $k$ is the edit distance.

---

[4] To search with $(w, k)$, the user computes a trapdoor set $T$ of size $O(n^k)$, where $w$ is a fuzzy query with edit distance $k$ and $n$ is the length of $w$.

**Table 1.** Performance (per query) and properties comparison between the scheme in [14] and ours

| Performance and Properties | [14] | ours |
|---|---|---|
| metric | edit distance | Hamming distance |
| security | IND2-CKA | adaptively secure |
| server computation | $O(Mn^{2k})$ | $O(M)$ |
| server's extra storage (index) | $O(Mn^k)$ | $O(M)$ |
| user computation | $O(n^k)$ | $O(1)$ |
| user storage | $O(1)$ | $O(1)$ |
| number of rounds | 2 | 2 |

# 6 Conclusion and Future Work

In this paper, we presented a general framework for noisy-keyword-based searchable private-key encryption in a fault-tolerant manner. Under this framework, we proposed a concrete scheme which is proved adaptively secure according to the simulation-based security definition presented in [7]. The keyword search finishes in two rounds of interaction bewteen the user and the server, and requires an amount of work from the server that is linear in the number of noisy keywords. Finally, we compared the scheme in [14] and ours both in properties and efficiency.

In our model, only the owner of the document set can search on encrypted documents by noisy keywords. The next problem we will address is a natural extension where a group of authorized parties other than the owner can submit search queries. On the other hand, we will consider other notions of distance such as set difference, edit distance and so on in concrete NKSPE schemes.

# References

1. Bellare, M., Boldyreva, A., ONeill, A.: Efficiently-searchable and deterministic asymmetric encryption. Tech. rep., Citeseer (2006)
2. Boneh, D., Di Crescenzo, G., Ostrovsky, R., Persiano, G.: Public Key Encryption with Keyword Search. In: Cachin, C., Camenisch, J. (eds.) EUROCRYPT 2004. LNCS, vol. 3027, pp. 506–522. Springer, Heidelberg (2004)
3. Boneh, D., Kushilevitz, E., Ostrovsky, R., Skeith, W.: Public Key Encryption That Allows PIR Queries. In: Menezes, A. (ed.) CRYPTO 2007. LNCS, vol. 4622, pp. 50–67. Springer, Heidelberg (2007)
4. Boneh, D., Waters, B.: Conjunctive, Subset, and Range Queries on Encrypted Data. In: Vadhan, S. (ed.) TCC 2007. LNCS, vol. 4392, pp. 535–554. Springer, Heidelberg (2007)
5. Bringer, J., Chabanne, H., Kindarji, B.: Error-tolerant searchable encryption. In: IEEE International Conference on Communications, ICC 2009, pp. 1–6. IEEE (2009)
6. Chang, Y., Mitzenmacher, M.: Privacy Preserving Keyword Searches on Remote Encrypted Data. In: Ioannidis, J., Keromytis, A., Yung, M. (eds.) ACNS 2005. LNCS, vol. 3531, pp. 442–455. Springer, Heidelberg (2005)

7. Curtmola, R., Garay, J., Kamara, S., Ostrovsky, R.: Searchable symmetric encryption: Improved definitions and efficient constructions. Journal of Computer Security 19(5), 895–934 (2011)
8. Dodis, Y., Reyzin, L., Smith, A.: Fuzzy Extractors: How to Generate Strong Keys from Biometrics and Other Noisy Data. In: Cachin, C., Camenisch, J. (eds.) EUROCRYPT 2004. LNCS, vol. 3027, pp. 523–540. Springer, Heidelberg (2004)
9. Dodis, Y., Reyzin, L., Smith, A.: Fuzzy extractors. Security with Noisy Data, 79–99 (2007)
10. Du, W., Atallah, M.: Protocols for secure remote database access with approximate matching. In: E-Commerce Security and Privacy, pp. 87–111. Springer (2001)
11. Goh, E.: Secure indexes. An early version of this paper first appeared on the Cryptology ePrint Archive, pp. 1–18 (October 7, 2003)
12. Goldreich, O., Ostrovsky, R.: Software protection and simulation on oblivious rams. Journal of the ACM (JACM) 43(3), 431–473 (1996)
13. Kevenaar, T.: Protection of biometric information. Security with Noisy Data, 169–193 (2007)
14. Li, J., Wang, Q., Wang, C., Cao, N., Ren, K., Lou, W.: Fuzzy keyword search over encrypted data in cloud computing. In: 2010 Proceedings IEEE INFOCOM, pp. 1–5. IEEE (2010)
15. Ma, S., Yang, B., Li, K., Xia, F.: A Privacy-Preserving Join on Outsourced Database. In: Lai, X., Zhou, J., Li, H. (eds.) ISC 2011. LNCS, vol. 7001, pp. 278–292. Springer, Heidelberg (2011)
16. Monrose, F., Reiter, M., Li, Q., Wetzel, S.: Cryptographic key generation from voice. In: 2001 IEEE Symposium on Security and Privacy, S&P 2001. Proceedings, pp. 202–213. IEEE (2001)
17. Park, D., Kim, K., Lee, P.: Public Key Encryption with Conjunctive Field Keyword Search. In: Lim, C., Yung, M. (eds.) WISA 2004. LNCS, vol. 3325, pp. 73–86. Springer, Heidelberg (2005)
18. Pinkas, B., Reinman, T.: Oblivious RAM Revisited. In: Rabin, T. (ed.) CRYPTO 2010. LNCS, vol. 6223, pp. 502–519. Springer, Heidelberg (2010)
19. Shi, E., Bethencourt, J., Chan, T., Song, D., Perrig, A.: Multi-dimensional range query over encrypted data. In: IEEE Symposium on Security and Privacy, SP 2007, pp. 350–364. IEEE (2007)
20. Song, D., Wagner, D., Perrig, A.: Practical techniques for searches on encrypted data. In: Proceedings of IEEE Symposium on Security and Privacy, S&P 2000, pp. 44–55. IEEE (2000)
21. Van Liesdonk, P., Sedghi, S., Doumen, J., Hartel, P., Jonker, W.: Computationally Efficient Searchable Symmetric Encryption. In: Jonker, W., Petkovic, M. (eds.) SDM 2010. LNCS, vol. 6358, pp. 87–100. Springer, Heidelberg (2010)

# Forward Secure Attribute-Based Signatures

Tsz Hon Yuen[1], Joseph K. Liu[2], Xinyi Huang[3,*], Man Ho Au[4],
Willy Susilo[4], and Jianying Zhou[2]

[1] University of Hong Kong, Hong Kong
thyuen@cs.hku.hk
[2] Institute for Infocomm Research, Singapore
{ksliu,jyzhou}@i2r.a-star.edu.sg
[3] School of Mathematics and Computer Science,
Fujian Normal University, China
xyhuang81@gmail.com
[4] School of Computer Science and Software Engineering,
University of Wollongong, Australia
{aau,wsusilo}@uow.edu.au

**Abstract.** Attribute-Based Signatures (ABS) is a versatile primitive
which allows an entity to sign a message with fine-grained control over
identifying information. A valid ABS only attests to the fact that "A
single user, whose attributes satisfy the predicate, has endorsed the
message". While ABS has been well investigated since its introduction, it is unfortunate that key exposure–an inherent weakness of digital
signatures–has never been formally studied in the scenario of ABS. We
fill this gap by proposing a new notion called forward secure ABS, its
formal security models and a generic (also the first) design based on well
established crypto primitives.

## 1 Introduction

Attribute-Based Signatures [13,15] (or, ABS for short) is a primitive proposed to
provide signer anonymity. An ABS allows an entity to sign a message with fine-
grained control over identifying information. A valid ABS signature attests to the
fact that "A single user, whose attributes satisfy the predicate, has endorsed the
message". Ring signatures [18,5,19] and group signatures [9,3,6] are comparable
to special cases of ABS, in which the only allowed predicates are disjunctions over
the universe of attributes (identities). In ABS, each entity possesses a set of attributes and a key-authority generates the associated private keys, with which one
can sign a message with a predicate satisfied by his/her attributes. The signature
reveals no more than the fact that a single user with some set of attributes satisfying the predicate has attested to the message. In particular, ABS does not provide
any information on the particular set of attributes used to satisfy the predicate.
For example, an "(Engineer, Department A)" or an "(Engineer, Department B)"
can independently generate an ABS to assure the recipient that the signature was

---

* Corresponding author.

T.W. Chim and T.H. Yuen (Eds.): ICICS 2012, LNCS 7618, pp. 167–177, 2012.

produced by an "Engineer" without disclosing the department information. Furthermore, users of ABS cannot collude to pool their attributes together (which separates ABS from mesh signatures): It is never possible for an "(Engineer, Department A)" and an "(Auditor, Department B)" to collude and generate an ABS satisfying the predicate "(Auditor, Department A)".

## 1.1   Key Exposure Problem

Ordinary digital signatures have a fundamental limitation: If the private key of a signer is compromised, all the signatures of that signer become worthless. This may become quite a realistic threat since if the private key is compromised, any message can be forged. All future signatures are invalidated as a result of such a compromise, and more importantly, no previously issued signatures can be trusted. Once a leakage has been identified, there may exist some key revocation mechanism to be involved immediately in order to prevent the generation of any signature using the compromised private key. However, this does not solve the problem of forgeability for past signatures. It is not possible to ask the signer to re-issue all previous signatures due to many physical and practical limitations. The problem of key exposure in ABS is more serious. In ABS, if a user's secret key is exposed to an adversary, the adversary can generate not only ABS for any documents, but can also sign any documents on behalf of any users with the same attributes. The exposure of one user's secret key not only requires changing the attribute name for the whole group, but also renders all previously obtained ABS invalid, because one cannot distinguish whether a signature is generated by an adversary after it has obtained one of the secret keys or by a legitimate user before key exposure.

FORWARD SECURE SIGNATURE. Forward-secure signature schemes are designed to resolve the key exposure: a fundamental limitation of digital signature. The goal of a forward-secure signature scheme is to preserve the validity of past signatures even if the current secret key has been compromised. The concept was first suggested by Anderson [2], and solutions were designed by Bellare and Miner [4]. The idea is that even a compromise of the present secret key does not enable an adversary to forge signatures pertaining to the past. This can be achieved by the key evolution paradigm: dividing the total time of the validity of the public key into $T$ time periods, and using a different secret key in each time period while the public key remains the same. Each subsequent secret key is computed from the current secret key via an update algorithm, while any past secret key cannot be computed by the current one. The time period during which a message is signed becomes part of the signature as well. The property of forward security means that even if the current secret key is compromised, a forger cannot forge signatures for past time periods. In other words, the forger can only forge signatures for documents pertaining to time periods after the exposure but not before. The integrity of documents signed before the exposure remains intact.

## 1.2 Contribution

We propose a new notion called *Forward Secure Attribute-Based Signatures (FS-ABS)*. It is similar to a normal ABS but providing forward security. That is, even when a secret key is compromised, previously generated signatures remain valid and do not need to be re-generated. It can greatly reduce the damage of exposure of any secret key of users in the environment. We formally define the security of FSABS, provide a generic design of FSABS and suggest some efficient instantiations.

## 2 Preliminaries

This section briefly reviews the preliminaries required in our scheme.

### 2.1 Monotone Span Programs

Let $\Upsilon : \{0,1\}^n \to \{0,1\}$ be a monotone boolean function. A monotone span program for $\Upsilon$ over a field $\mathbb{F}$ is an $\ell \times t$ matrix $\mathbf{M}$ with entries in $\mathbb{F}$, along with a labeling function $a : [\ell] \to [n]$ that associates each row of $\mathbf{M}$ with an input variable of $\Upsilon$, that for every $(x_1, ..., x_n) \in \{0,1\}^n$, satisfies the following:

$$\Upsilon(x_1, ..., x_n) = 1 \iff \exists v \in \mathbb{F}^{1 \times \ell} : \; v\mathbf{M} = [1, 0, 0, ..., 0], \text{ and}$$
$$(\forall i : x_{a(i)} = 0 \Rightarrow v_i = 0).$$

In other words, $\Upsilon(x_1, ..., x_n) = 1$ if and only if the rows of $\mathbf{M}$ indexed by $\{i | x_{a(i)} = 1\}$ span the vector $[1, 0, 0, ..., 0]$. We call $\ell$ the length and $t$ the width of the span program, and $\ell + t$ the size of the span program.

### 2.2 NIWI Proof of Knowledge

We give a brief overview of the non-interactive witness-indistinguishable (NIWI) proof of knowledge. We refer the reader to [10,11] for detailed definitions.

Let $R$ be an efficiently computable ternary relation. For triplets $(gk, x, w) \in R$ we call $gk$ the setup, $x$ the statement and $w$ the witness. Given some $gk$ we let $L$ be the language consisting of statements in $R$. A non-interactive proof system for a relation $R$ comprised of the following algorithms:

- Setup: Outputs a setup $(gk, sk)$.
- CRSGen: On input $(gk, sk)$, outputs a reference string crs.
- Prove: On input $(gk, \mathsf{crs}, x, w)$, where $(gk, x, w) \in R$, outputs a proof $\pi$.
- Verify: On input $(gk, \mathsf{crs}, x, \pi)$, outputs 1 if the proof is acceptable and 0 if rejecting the proof.

We call (Setup, CRSGen, Prove, Verify) a non-interactive proof system for $R$ with Setup if it has the completeness and soundness properties described below.

- The *perfect completeness* requirement is that for all adversaries $\mathfrak{A}$ we have

$$\Pr[(gk, sk) \leftarrow \mathsf{Setup}(1^\lambda); \mathsf{crs} \leftarrow \mathsf{CRSGen}(gk, sk); (x, w) \leftarrow \mathfrak{A}(gk, \mathsf{crs});$$
$$\pi \leftarrow \mathsf{Prove}(gk, \mathsf{crs}, x, w) : \mathsf{Verify}(gk, \mathsf{crs}, x, \pi) = 1 \text{ if } (gk, x, w) \in R] = 1.$$

- The *perfect soundness* requirement is that for all adversaries $\mathfrak{A}$ we have

$$\Pr[\quad (gk, sk) \leftarrow \mathsf{Setup}(1^\lambda); \quad \mathsf{crs} \leftarrow \mathsf{CRSGen}(gk, sk);$$
$$(x, \pi) \leftarrow \mathfrak{A}(gk, \mathsf{crs}) : \mathsf{Verify}(gk, \mathsf{crs}, x, \pi) = 0 \text{ if } x \notin L] = 1.$$

A non-interactive proof is *composable witness indistinguishable* if there is a probabilistic polynomial time simulator CRSSim, such that for all non-uniform polynomial time adversaries $\mathfrak{A}$ we have

$$\Pr[(gk, sk) \leftarrow \mathsf{Setup}(1^\lambda); \mathsf{crs} \leftarrow \mathsf{CRSGen}(gk, sk) : \mathfrak{A}(gk, \mathsf{crs}) = 1]$$
$$\approx \Pr[(gk, sk) \leftarrow \mathsf{Setup}(1^\lambda); \mathsf{crs} \leftarrow \mathsf{CRSSim}(gk, sk) : \mathfrak{A}(gk, \mathsf{crs}) = 1],$$

and for all adversaries $\mathfrak{A}$ we have:

$$\Pr[(gk, sk) \leftarrow \mathsf{Setup}(1^\lambda); \mathsf{crs} \leftarrow \mathsf{CRSSim}(gk, sk);$$
$$(x, w_0, w_1) \leftarrow \mathfrak{A}(gk, \mathsf{crs}); \pi \leftarrow \mathsf{Prove}(gk, \mathsf{crs}, x, w_0) : \mathfrak{A}(\pi) = 1]$$
$$= \Pr[(gk, sk) \leftarrow \mathsf{Setup}(1^\lambda); \mathsf{crs} \leftarrow \mathsf{CRSSim}(gk, sk);$$
$$(x, w_0, w_1) \leftarrow \mathfrak{A}(gk, \mathsf{crs}); \pi \leftarrow \mathsf{Prove}(gk, \mathsf{crs}, x, w_1) : \mathfrak{A}(\pi) = 1],$$

where we require $(gk, x, w_0), (gk, x, w_1) \in R$.

A non-interactive proof is a proof of knowledge (*perfect knowledge extraction*) if there is a probabilistic polynomial time knowledge extractor $(\mathsf{Ext}_1, \mathsf{Ext}_2)$, such that for all non-uniform polynomial time adversaries $\mathfrak{A}$ we have

$$\Pr[(gk, sk) \leftarrow \mathsf{Setup}(1^\lambda); \mathsf{crs} \leftarrow \mathsf{CRSGen}(gk, sk) : \mathfrak{A}(gk, \mathsf{crs}) = 1]$$
$$\approx \Pr[(gk, sk) \leftarrow \mathsf{Setup}(1^\lambda); (\mathsf{crs}, \tau) \leftarrow \mathsf{Ext}_1(gk, sk) : \mathfrak{A}(gk, \mathsf{crs}) = 1],$$

and for all adversaries $\mathfrak{A}$ we have:

$$\Pr[(gk, sk) \leftarrow \mathsf{Setup}(1^\lambda); (\mathsf{crs}, \tau) \leftarrow \mathsf{Ext}_1(gk, sk); (x, \pi) \leftarrow \mathfrak{A}(gk, \mathsf{crs});$$
$$w \leftarrow \mathsf{Ext}_2(gk, \mathsf{crs}, \tau, x, \pi) : \mathsf{Verify}(gk, \mathsf{crs}, x, \pi) = 0 \text{ or } (gk, x, w) \in R] = 1.$$

**Definition 1.** *A non-interactive proof system is a perfect non-interactive witness indistinguishable (NIWI) proof of knowledge if it has perfect completeness, perfect soundness, composable witness indistingushable and perfect knowledge extraction.*

## 3   Security Models

We give our security models of forward secure attributed-based signatures and define relevant security notions.

## 3.1   Syntax of Forward Secure Attribute-Based Signatures

Let $\mathbb{A}$ be the universe of possible attributes. A *claim-predicate* over $\mathbb{A}$ is a monotone boolean function, whose inputs are associated with attributes of $\mathbb{A}$. We say that an attribute set $\mathcal{A} \subseteq \mathbb{A}$ satisfies a claim-predicate $\Upsilon$ if $\Upsilon(\mathcal{A}) = 1$ (where an input is set to be true if its corresponding attribute is present in $\mathcal{A}$).

**Definition 2.** *A forward secure attribute-based signature scheme is a tuple of six algorithms parameterized by a universe of possible attributes $\mathbb{A}$, a total number of time period $T$ and a message space $\mathbb{M}$:*

- FSABS.TSetup (to be run by a trustee): On input the security parameter $1^\lambda$, generates public reference information $TPK$.
- FSABS.ASetup (to be run by an attribute-issuing authority): On input the security parameter $1^\lambda$, generates a key pair $(APK, ASK)$.
- FSABS.AttrGen: On input $(ASK, \mathcal{A} \subseteq \mathbb{A})$, outputs an assoicated signing key $sk_{\mathcal{A},0}$.
- FSABS.Update: On input $sk_{\mathcal{A},i}$ and a time period $j$ (where $i < j \leq T$), outputs an assoicated signing key $sk_{\mathcal{A},j}$.
- FSABS.Sign: On input $(PK = (TPK, APK), sk_{\mathcal{A},t}, m \in \mathbb{M}, \Upsilon, t)$, where $\Upsilon(\mathcal{A}) = 1$ and $t$ is the time period, outputs a signature $\pi$.
- FSABS.Verify: On input $(PK = (TPK, APK), m, \Upsilon, \pi, t)$, outputs accept or reject.

**Correctness.** FSABS schemes must satisfy that signatures signed according to specification are accepted during verification.

## 3.2   Notions of Security of Forward Secure Attribute-Based Signatures

Security of forward secure attributed-based signature schemes has unforgeability and privacy.

1. <u>UNFORGEABILITY.</u>
   The unforgeability for forward secure attributed-based signature schemes is defined in the following game between the Challenger $\mathfrak{C}$ and the Adversary $\mathfrak{A}$ in which $\mathfrak{A}$ is given access to oracles $\mathcal{JO}, \mathcal{CO}$ and $\mathcal{SO}$:
   (a) $\mathfrak{C}$ generates

   $$TPK \leftarrow \text{FSABS.TSetup}(1^\lambda) \text{ and } (APK, ASK) \leftarrow \text{FSABS.TSetup}(1^\lambda).$$

   $\mathfrak{C}$ gives $\mathfrak{A}$ the public information $PK = (TPK, APK)$.
   (b) $\mathfrak{A}$ may query the following oracles according to any adaptive strategy.
   - $sk_{\mathcal{A},t} \leftarrow \mathcal{GO}(\mathcal{A}, t)$. The AttrGen Oracle, on input an attribute set $\mathcal{A}$ and a time period $t$, returns the corresponding secret key $sk_{\mathcal{A},t} \leftarrow$ FSABS.Update(LABS.AttrGen($ASK, \mathcal{A}$), $t$). We require for the same $(i, \mathcal{A}, t)$ as input, the same $sk_{\mathcal{A},t}$ is the output.

- $\sigma \leftarrow \mathcal{SO}(\mathcal{A}, t, m, \Upsilon)$. The Sign Oracle, on input an attribute set $\mathcal{A}$, a time period $t$, a message $m$ and a claim-predicate $\Upsilon$ where $\Upsilon(\mathcal{A}) = 1$, returns a valid signature $\sigma \leftarrow$ FSABS.Sign$(PK, sk_{\mathcal{A},t} \leftarrow$ FSABS.Update(FSABS.AttrGen$(ASK, \mathcal{A}), t), m, \Upsilon, t)$.

(c) $\mathfrak{A}$ gives $\mathfrak{C}$ a time period $t^*$, a claim-predicate $\Upsilon^*$, a message $m^*$ and a signature $\pi^*$.

$\mathcal{B}$ wins the game if:

(1) FSABS.Verify$(PK, m^*, \Upsilon^*, \pi^*, t^*)$=accept ;
(2) $(\cdot, t^*, m^*, \Upsilon^*)$ is not a query input to $\mathcal{SO}$ ; and
(3) $\Upsilon^*(\mathcal{A}) = 0$ for all $(\mathcal{A}, t)$ queried to $\mathcal{GO}$ with $t \leq t^*$.

We denote by

$$\mathbf{Adv}_{\mathfrak{A}}^{unf} = \Pr[\mathfrak{A} \text{ wins the game }].$$

**Definition 3 (Unforgeability).** *A Forward Secure Attribute-Based Signature scheme is unforgeable if for all PPT adversary* $\mathfrak{A}$, $\mathbf{Adv}_{\mathfrak{A}}^{unf}$ *is negligible.*

The unforgeability ensures that a valid signature must be signed by a user with attributes satisfying the predicate in the current time period.

2. PRIVACY.

In order to protect privacy, forward secure ABS must hide the attributes used during signature generation. This is defined in the following game between the Challenger $\mathfrak{C}$ and the Adversary $\mathfrak{A}$ in which $\mathfrak{A}$ is given the $ASK$. $\mathfrak{A}$ does not need to query any oracle since it can generate the signing keys by himself.

(a) $\mathfrak{C}$ generates

$$TPK \leftarrow \text{FSABS.TSetup}(1^\lambda) \text{ and } (APK, ASK) \leftarrow \text{FSABS.TSetup}(1^\lambda).$$

$\mathfrak{C}$ gives $\mathfrak{A}$ the public information $PK = (TPK, APK)$ and also $ASK$.

(b) $\mathfrak{A}$ sends $\mathfrak{C}$ $(\mathcal{A}_0, \mathcal{A}_1, m, t, \Upsilon)$, where $\Upsilon(\mathcal{A}_0) = \Upsilon(\mathcal{A}_1) = 1$.
(c) $\mathfrak{C}$ chooses a random bit $b \in \{0, 1\}$ and generates

$$sk_{\mathcal{A}_b, t} \leftarrow \text{FSABS.Update}(\text{FSABS.AttrGen}(ASK, \mathcal{A}_b), t).$$

It generates the signature $\pi_b \leftarrow$ FSABS.Sign$(PK, sk_{\mathcal{A}_b, t}, m, \Upsilon, t)$ and sends $\sigma_b$ to $\mathfrak{A}$.

(d) $\mathfrak{A}$ outputs a bit $b'$.

$\mathfrak{A}$ wins the game if $b' = b$. We denote by

$$\mathbf{Adv}_{\mathfrak{A}}^{Anon} = \left| \Pr[ \mathfrak{A} \text{ wins the game }] - \frac{1}{2} \right|.$$

**Definition 4 (Privacy).** *A Forward Secure Attribute-Based Signature scheme is private if for all PPT adversary* $\mathfrak{A}$, $\mathbf{Adv}_{\mathfrak{A}}^{Anon}$ *is negligible.*

The privacy property ensures that it is hard to distinguish between two signatures, each associated with different attributes, which both satisfy the claim-predicate.

# 4 Our Generic Forward Secure Attribute-Based Signature Scheme

Our scheme is motivated by the attribute-based signature scheme from [15].

## 4.1 Forward Secure Credential Bundle

We extend the *credential bundle* primitive in [15] with forward security.

**Definition 5 (Forward Secure Credential Bundle).** *A forward secure credential bundle scheme is parameterized by a message space $\mathcal{M}$ and a time period $T$, and consists of the following four algorithms.*

- CB.Setup: *On input a security parameter $1^\lambda$, outputs a verification key $vk$ and a secret key $sk$.*
- CB.Gen: *On input $sk$ and a set of messages $\{m_1, \ldots, m_n\} \subseteq \mathcal{M}$, outputs a credential $c_0$ (of time 0), which consists of a tag $\tau_0$ and values $\sigma_{1,0}, \ldots, \sigma_{n,0}$.*
- CB.Update: *On input a credential $c_{t_1}$ of time $t_1$ and a new time period $t_2$ (with $t_1 < t_2 \le T$), outputs a new credential $c_{t_2}$.*
- CB.Ver: *On input $vk$, a message $m$, a time period $t$ and a credential $(\tau, \sigma)$, outputs 1 for* accept *and 0 for* reject.

*The scheme is* correct *if for all $(vk, sk) \leftarrow$ CB.Setup$(1^\lambda)$, $c_0 = (\tau_0, \sigma_{1,0}, \ldots, \sigma_{n,0})$ $\leftarrow$ CB.Gen$(sk, (m_1, \ldots, m_n))$ and $c_t = (\tau_t, \sigma_{1,t}, \ldots, \sigma_{n,t}) \leftarrow$ CB.Update$(c_0, t)$, we have* CB.Ver$(vk, m_i, t, (\tau_t, \sigma_{i,t})) = 1$ *for all $i \in [1, n]$.*

Observe that one can generate a new bundle on a subset of attributes. Our security definition below requires that taking a subset of a single bundle and update is the only way to obtain a new bundle in time $t_2$ from existing bundles at time $t_1 \le t_2$. In particular, attributes from several bundles cannot be combined; and credentials of the present time cannot be used to find credentials of the past.

**Definition 6.** *A credential bundle scheme is forward secure if the success probability of any polynomial-time adversary in the following experiment is negligible:*

1. *Run $(vk, sk) \leftarrow$ CB.Setup$(1^\lambda)$, and give $vk$ to the adversary.*
2. *The adversary is given access to an extract oracle with input $(t, (m_1, \ldots, m_n))$. It obtains $c_t \leftarrow$ CB.Update$(c_0, t)$, where $c_0 \leftarrow$ CB.Gen$(sk, (m_1, \ldots, m_n))$.*
3. *Finally the adversary outputs $(t^*, \tau^*, (m_1^*, \sigma_1^*), \ldots, (m_{n^*}^*, \sigma_{n^*}^*))$.*

*We say the adversary succeeds if* CB.Ver$(vk, m_i^*, t^*, (\tau^*, \sigma_i^*)) = 1$ *for all $i \in [1, n^*]$, and if no superset of $(m_1^*, \ldots, m_{n^*}^*)$, was ever queried (in a single query) to the extract oracle with time $t \le t^*$.*

**Instantiation.** From any plain forward secure digital signature scheme (e.g. [12,1,16,8,7,14]) we can easily construct a credential bundle scheme in which the bundle is a collection of signatures of messages "$\tau||m_i$", where each $m_i$ is the name of an attribute and $\tau$ is an identifier that is unique to each user. Conversely, when a credential bundle scheme is restricted to singleton sets of messages, its forward security definition is equivalent to normal forward secure digital signature.

## 4.2   Forward Secure ABS Construction

Let $\mathbb{A}$ be the desired universe of ABS attributes. Let $\mathbb{A}'$ denote a space of pseudo-attributes, where $\mathbb{A} \cap \mathbb{A}' = \emptyset$. For every message $m$ and claim-predicate $\Upsilon$ we associate a psuedo-attribute $a_{m,\Upsilon} \in \mathbb{A}'$. Let CB be a secure credential bundle scheme, with message space $\mathbb{A} \cap \mathbb{A}'$, and let (NIWI.Setup, NIWI.CRSGen, NIWI.Prove, NIWI.Verify) be a perfect NIWI proof of knowledge scheme. Our ABS construction is as follows:

FSABS.TSetup: Let $\lambda$ be a security parameter. The signature trustee runs $(gk, sk)$ $\leftarrow$ NIWI.Setup$(1^\lambda)$, crs $\leftarrow$ NIWI.CRSGen$(gk, sk)$ as well as $(tvk, tsk) \leftarrow$ CB.Setup $(1^\lambda)$ and publishes $TPK = (gk, \text{crs}, tvk)$.

FSABS.ASetup: The attribute-issuing authority runs $(avk, ask) \leftarrow$ CB.Setup$(1^\lambda)$ and publishes $APK = avk$ and sets $ASK = ask$.

FSABS.AttrGen: The key generation algorithm takes as input a subset of attributes $\mathcal{A} \subset \mathbb{A}$ and the secret key $ASK$. Ensure that $\mathcal{A}$ contains no pseudo-attributes. Then output the result of $sk_{\mathcal{A},0} \leftarrow$ CB.Gen$(ASK, \mathcal{A})$.

FSABS.Update: On input a signing key $sk_{\mathcal{A},i}$ for attribute $\mathcal{A}$ and new time period $j$, if $i < j \leq T$ the user updates the secret key by $sk_{\mathcal{A},j} \leftarrow$ CB.Update$(sk_{\mathcal{A},i}, j)$.

FSABS.Sign: The signing algorithm takes as input the public keys $TPK$, $APK$, a signing key $sk_{\mathcal{A},i}$ for attribute $\mathcal{A}$ and current time period $j$, a message $m$ and a claim-predicate $\Upsilon$. Assume $\Upsilon(\mathcal{A}) = 1$. Parse $sk_{\mathcal{A},j}$ as $(\tau, \{\sigma_{a,j} | a \in \mathcal{A}\})$. Define $\tilde{\Upsilon} := \Upsilon \vee a_{m,\Upsilon}$, where $a_{m,\Upsilon} \in \mathbb{A}'$ is the pseudo-attribute associated with $(m, \Upsilon)$. Thus, we still have $\tilde{\Upsilon}(\mathcal{A}) = 1$. Let $\{a_1, \ldots a_n\}$ denote the attributes appearing in $\tilde{\Upsilon}$. Let $vk_i$ be $avk$ if attribute $a_i$ is a pseudo-attribute, and $tvk$ otherwise. Finally, let $\Phi[vk, m, \Upsilon, j]$ denote the following boolean expression:

$$\exists \tau, \sigma_1, \ldots, \sigma_n : \tilde{\Upsilon} \left( \{a_i | \text{CB.Ver} \left( vk_i, a_i, j, (\tau, \sigma_i) \right) = 1\} \right) = 1$$

For each $i$, set $\hat{\sigma}_{i,j} = \sigma_{a_i,j}$ from $sk_{\mathcal{A},i}$ if it is present, and to any arbitrary value otherwise. Compute $\pi \leftarrow$ NIWI.Prove(crs, $\Phi[vk, m, \Upsilon, j], (\tau, \hat{\sigma}_{1,j}, \ldots, \hat{\sigma}_{n,j}))$. Output $\pi$ as the ABS signature.

FSABS.Verify: The verification algorithm takes as input a message $M$, a signature $\pi$, a time period $j$, a signing policy $\Upsilon$ and the public keys $TPK$, $APK$. Output the result of NIWI.Verify(crs, $\Phi[vk, m, \Upsilon, j], \pi$).

### Security of the Generic Construction

**Theorem 1.** *The scheme is private if the NIWI is composable witness indistinguishable.*

The privacy follows directly from the composable witness indistinguishable property of the NIWI.

**Theorem 2.** *The scheme is unforgeable if the NIWI has knowledge extraction and the* CB *is forward secure.*

*Proof.* If the NIWI scheme is sound, we can show that any adversary $A$ that violates ABS unforgeability can be used to construct an algorithm $B$ that breaks the security of the underlying credential bundle scheme, with non-negligible probability. Suppose $B$ receives $vk$ from the challenger $C$ of the CB security experiment. Let $B$ flips a random coin $b = 0/1$ and perform one of the following two simulations:

Simulation 0: $B$ runs $(gk, sk) \leftarrow \text{NIWI.Setup}(1^\lambda)$, $(\text{crs}, \tau) \leftarrow \text{NIWI.Ext}_1(gk, sk)$ and sets $tvk = vk$. Note that $A$ cannot distinguish a real CRS from a simulated CRS by the security of the NIWI proof system. $B$ gives $TPK = (gk, \text{crs}, tvk)$ to $A$. $B$ runs $(APK, ASK) \leftarrow \text{FSABS.ASetup}(1^\lambda)$ honestly and gives $APK$ to $A$.

When $A$ makes a query $\mathcal{A} \subseteq \mathbb{A}$ to the FSABS.AttrGen Oracle, $B$ computes the response honestly using $ASK$. When $A$ makes a query $(\mathcal{A}, t, m, \Upsilon)$ to the FSABS.Sign Oracle, $B$ requests from $C$ the CB.Gen Oracle a singleton bundle for the pseudo-attribute associated with $(m, \Upsilon)$ and time $t$. $B$ uses the result as a witness to generate a NIWI proof of $\Phi[vk, m, \Upsilon, t]$ to use as the simulated ABS signature.

Finally $A$ outputs a valid forgery $(m^*, \Upsilon^*, \pi^*, t^*)$, $B$ uses NIWI.Ext$_2$ with the trapdoor $\tau$ to extract a witness for $\Phi[vk, m^*, \Upsilon^*, t^*]$. Extraction succeeds with overwhelming probability, thus we obtain a bundle that contains the pseudo-attribute associated with $(m^*, \Upsilon^*)$ and time $t^*$, or sufficient attributes to satisfy $\Upsilon^*$. If the bundle contains the pseudo-attribute, then it represents a forgery against $tvk = vk$ from the experiment with $C$, since $B$ has never requested $(t^*, (m^*, \Upsilon^*))$ from the CB.Gen Oracle.

Simulation 1: Similar to above, except that $B$ sets $avk = vk$ instead of $tvk$. $B$ honestly generates $tvk$ as in FSABS.TSetup. $B$ gives simulated ABS signatures to $A$ by generating bundle signatures on the pseudo-attribute. $B$ forwards all of $A$'s queries on its FSABS.AttrGen Oracle to the CB.Gen Oracle provided by $C$. Finally $A$ outputs an ABS forgery and $B$ uses NIWI.Ext$_2$ with the trapdoor $\tau$ to extract a witness. If the extracted bundle satisfies $\Upsilon^*$ (rather than contains the associated pseudo-attribute), then $B$ returns the bundle as a forgery in the experiment with $C$.

The above simulations are identical from the view of $A$. Any valid forgery by $A$ must be extracted to give a forgery suitable for one of the two simulations. Therefore, we can see that the advantage of one of the two simulations in its unforgeability game is comparable to that of $A$ in the ABS forgery game (losing only a factor of $1/2$). □

**Instantiation.** We can instantiate our generic construction using the CB scheme is section 4.1 and the NIWI proof of Groth and Sahai [11]. Note that the Groth and Sahai's proof (for the SXDH and DLIN instantiation) only has a knowledge extractor for the group elements, but not the exponent elements [17]. Observe that the private keys of our CB scheme only consist of the group elements. Therefore, we simply use the SXDH or DLIN instantiation of the Groth and Sahai's proof together with our CB scheme.

## 5    Conclusion

Key exposure is a fundamental limitation of ordinary digital signatures: If the secret key of a signer is compromised, all the signatures of that signer become worthless. This issue can be properly addressed using forward-secure techniques, which ensures that past signatures remain valid even if the current secret key is leaked. While the notion of attributed-based signatures was introduced in 2008 and many variants have been proposed, the issue of key exposure in ABS has never been formally studied. We filled this gap by giving a generic (also the first) design of forward-secure attributed-based signatures with provable security. We believe the result presented in this paper will draw the attention of cryptographers and anticipate more efficient designs of forward-secure attributed-based signatures.

**Acknowledgement.** Joseph K. Liu, Xinyi Huang and Jianying Zhou are supported by the EMA project SecSG-EPD090005RFP(D). Willy Susilo is supported by the ARC Future Fellowship (FT0991397).

## References

1. Abdalla, M., Reyzin, L.: A New Forward-Secure Digital Signature Scheme. In: Okamoto, T. (ed.) ASIACRYPT 2000. LNCS, vol. 1976, pp. 116–129. Springer, Heidelberg (2000)
2. Anderson, R.: Two remarks on public-key cryptology. Manuscript, September 2000. Relevant material presented by the author in an invited lecture at the Fourth ACM Conference on Computer and Communications Security (1997)
3. Bellare, M., Micciancio, D., Warinschi, B.: Foundations of Group Signatures: Formal Definitions, Simplified Requirements, and a Construction Based on General Assumptions. In: Biham, E. (ed.) EUROCRYPT 2003. LNCS, vol. 2656, pp. 614–629. Springer, Heidelberg (2003)
4. Bellare, M., Miner, S.: A Forward-Secure Digital Signature Scheme. In: Wiener, M. (ed.) CRYPTO 1999. LNCS, vol. 1666, pp. 431–448. Springer, Heidelberg (1999)
5. Bender, A., Katz, J., Morselli, R.: Ring Signatures: Stronger Definitions, and Constructions Without Random Oracles. In: Halevi, S., Rabin, T. (eds.) TCC 2006. LNCS, vol. 3876, pp. 60–79. Springer, Heidelberg (2006)
6. Boneh, D., Boyen, X., Shacham, H.: Short Group Signatures. In: Franklin, M. (ed.) CRYPTO 2004. LNCS, vol. 3152, pp. 41–55. Springer, Heidelberg (2004)
7. Boyen, X., Shacham, H., Shen, E., Waters, B.: Forward-secure signatures with untrusted update. In: ACM Conference on Computer and Communications Security, pp. 191–200. ACM (2006)
8. Camenisch, J., Koprowski, M.: Fine-grained forward-secure signature schemes without random oracles. Discrete Applied Mathematics 154(2), 175–188 (2006)

9. Chaum, D., van Heyst, E.: Group Signatures. In: Davies, D.W. (ed.) EUROCRYPT 1991. LNCS, vol. 547, pp. 257–265. Springer, Heidelberg (1991)

10. Groth, J.: Simulation-Sound NIZK Proofs for a Practical Language and Constant Size Group Signatures. In: Lai, X., Chen, K. (eds.) ASIACRYPT 2006. LNCS, vol. 4284, pp. 444–459. Springer, Heidelberg (2006)

11. Groth, J., Sahai, A.: Efficient Non-interactive Proof Systems for Bilinear Groups. In: Smart, N.P. (ed.) EUROCRYPT 2008. LNCS, vol. 4965, pp. 415–432. Springer, Heidelberg (2008)

12. Krawczyk, H.: Simple forward-secure signatures from any signature scheme. In: ACM Conference on Computer and Communications Security, pp. 108–115. ACM (2000)

13. Li, J., Au, M.H., Susilo, W., Xie, D., Ren, K.: Attribute-based signature and its applications. In: Feng, D., Basin, D.A., Liu, P. (eds.) ASIACCS, pp. 60–69. ACM (2010)

14. Libert, B., Quisquater, J.-J., Yung, M.: Forward-secure signatures in untrusted update environments: efficient and generic constructions. In: ACM Conference on Computer and Communications Security, pp. 266–275. ACM (2007)

15. Maji, H.K., Prabhakaran, M., Rosulek, M.: Attribute-Based Signatures. In: Kiayias, A. (ed.) CT-RSA 2011. LNCS, vol. 6558, pp. 376–392. Springer, Heidelberg (2011)

16. Malkin, T., Micciancio, D., Miner, S.K.: Efficient Generic Forward-Secure Signatures with an Unbounded Number of Time Periods. In: Knudsen, L.R. (ed.) EUROCRYPT 2002. LNCS, vol. 2332, pp. 400–417. Springer, Heidelberg (2002)

17. Meiklejohn, S.: An extension of the groth-sahai proof system. Master's thesis, Brown University (2009)

18. Rivest, R.L., Shamir, A., Tauman, Y.: How to Leak a Secret. In: Boyd, C. (ed.) ASIACRYPT 2001. LNCS, vol. 2248, pp. 552–565. Springer, Heidelberg (2001)

19. Shacham, H., Waters, B.: Efficient Ring Signatures Without Random Oracles. In: Okamoto, T., Wang, X. (eds.) PKC 2007. LNCS, vol. 4450, pp. 166–180. Springer, Heidelberg (2007)

# On Constant-Round Precise Zero-Knowledge

Ning Ding and Dawu Gu

Department of Computer Science and Engineering
Shanghai Jiao Tong University, China
{dingning,dwgu}@sjtu.edu.cn

**Abstract.** Precise zero-knowledge, introduced by Micali and Pass [STOC'06], captures the idea that a view of any verifier can be *indifferently* reconstructed. Though there are some constructions of precise zero-knowledge, constant-round constructions are unknown to exist. This paper is towards constant-round constructions of precise zero-knowledge. The results of this paper are as follows.

- We propose a relaxation of precise zero-knowledge that captures the idea that with a probability *arbitrarily polynomially* close to 1 a view of any verifier can be *indifferently* reconstructed, i.e., there exists a simulator (without having $q(n), p(n, t)$ as input) such that for *any* polynomial $q(n)$, there is a polynomial $p(n, t)$ satisfying with probability at least $1 - \frac{1}{q(n)}$, the view of any verifier in every interaction can be reconstructed in $p(n, T)$ time by the simulator whenever the verifier's running-time on this view is $T$. Then we show the impossibility of constructing constant-round protocols satisfying our relaxed definition with all the known techniques.
- We present a constant-round precise zero-knowledge argument for any language in **NP** with respect to our definition, assuming the existence of collision-resistant hash function families (against all $n^{O(\log \log n)}$-size circuits).

## 1 Introduction

(*Question.*) Zero-knowledge proofs were introduced by Goldwasser, Micali and Rackoff [6]. Their definition essentially states that an interactive proof of $x \in L$ provides zero (additional) knowledge if, for any efficient verifier $V$, the view of $V$ in the interaction can be "indistinguishably reconstructed" by an efficient simulator $S$-interacting with no one- on just input $x$. Since efficiency is formalized as polynomial-time, a worst-case notion, zero-knowledge too automatically becomes a worst-case notion. Micali and Pass [7] argued that this worst-case definition of zero-knowledge may not suffice to characterize that the view can be reconstructed *indifferently*. For instance, taking part in an interaction to gain a view only requires $n$ steps while the simulator may need $n^{10}$ steps to reconstruct this view. It is hard to say $n$ and $n^{10}$ are indifferent.

Hence [7] put forward a notion of *precise zero-knowledge*, which augments the definition of zero-knowledge by presenting an additional precision requirement

T.W. Chim and T.H. Yuen (Eds.): ICICS 2012, LNCS 7618, pp. 178–190, 2012.

that a prover provides a zero-knowledge proof of $x \in L$ if the view $v$ of any verifier in an interaction with the prover about $x$ can be reconstructed in the same time within a constant/polynomial factor.

To construct precise zero-knowledge protocols [7] developed a method, called the "cut-off" technique. A simulator with the "cut-off" technique still adopts the rewind strategy, but in the first run it records the verifier's running-time and then in the second run if the verifier cannot output the message within this recorded time then the simulator cancels this rewind. Though its success probability (in extracting secret) in each rewind becomes smaller, after $\omega(1)$ or $\omega(\log n)$ rewinds the simulator can succeed with overwhelming probability, achieving polynomial or linear precision respectively. Recently, [3] proposed a notion of precise time and space simulatable zero-knowledge which strengthes the notion of precise zero-knowledge by requiring that a view of any verifier in each interaction with a prover can be reconstructed in the same time and space simultaneously. Then it adopted an improved "cut-off" technique to construct some precise time and space simulatable zero-knowledge protocols.

Also, [8] presented a slightly relaxed notion of *weak-precise zero-knowledge* that requires the precision requirement holds with overwhelming probability. This paper does not distinguish the two notions for concision of statement.

There are also some negative results. [7] showed there don't exist black-box precise zero-knowledge protocols for any non-trivial language, and [8] showed Barak's non-black-box zero-knowledge argument [1] are imprecise due to the imprecise simulation strategy.

As the known precise zero-knowledge protocols use at least $\omega(1)$ rounds, a natural question arose at that time *if there exist constant-round precise zero-knowledge proofs or arguments*. As we will point out later, it seems unhopeful to adopt the known simulation strategies to realize precise simulation in constant-round constructions. So a feasible way towards this question is to present a slight but meaningful relaxation and then construct constant-round precise zero-knowledge protocols with respect to this relaxation. In this paper we will investigate the question in this way and attempt to present an answer to it.

### 1.1    Our Results

Recall that precise zero-knowledge requires that with probability $1 - \mathsf{neg}(n)$ a view of any verifier can be reconstructed in $p(n, T)$ time whenever the verifier's running-time on this view is $T$. We consider a relaxation that for a protocol to be precise zero-knowledge, there is a strict polynomial-time simulator (without having $q(n), p(n, t)$ as input) such that for *any* polynomial $q(n)$, there is a precision $p(n, t)$ satisfying with probability $1 - \frac{1}{q(n)}$ the simulator's running-time in outputting a view is bounded by $p(n, T)$ whenever a verifier's running-time on this view is $T$. Namely, we slightly relax the satisfiable probability from $1 - \mathsf{neg}(n)$ to $1 - \frac{1}{q(n)}$ where $q(n)$ can be an arbitrarily large polynomial.

Though a precise zero-knowledge protocol w.r.t. the standard definition in [7,8] of course satisfies our relaxation, our focus in this work is constant-round constructions. As we will show later, all known constant-round zero-knowledge protocols do not satisfy the relaxation. We will also point out that it seems still unhopeful to adopt the known simulation techniques to construct constant-round zero-knowledge protocols satisfying the relaxation.

Our main contribution in this paper is a constant-round construction of precise zero-knowledge protocols for any language in **NP** satisfying the relaxation. Formally, we achieve the following result.

**Theorem 1.** *Assume the existence of hash function families which collision-resistance hold against all $n^{O(\log\log n)}$-size circuits. Then there exists a constant-round precise zero-knowledge argument for each language in **NP** with respect to our relaxation.*

**Our Technique.** Notice that using the "cut-off" technique, we can achieve the following result that for any $q(n)$, a simulator with the "cut-off" technique can extract secret information (in one rewind interval) with probability $1 - \frac{1}{q(n)}$ and thus the simulation satisfies a precision related to $p(n, t)$. Note that $q(n)$ should be known to the simulator in advanced. However, for any other polynomial $q'(n)$ this simulator may not achieve a precision (related to $q'(n)$) with probability $1 - \frac{1}{q'(n)}$.

Our idea for going beyond this barrier is to rewind the verifier sufficiently large polynomial (less than $n^{\log\log n/5}$) times such that for any polynomial $q(n)$, we can always be ensured that the extraction can succeed with probability at least $1 - \frac{1}{q(n)}$, while on the same time the whole simulation is still of strict polynomial-time (not super-polynomial-time).

To realize this idea, we combine the constructions of Barak's protocol [1] and ordinary zero-knowledge protocols to propose a desired protocol. The protocol consists of two phases. Phase 1 adopts a mixed structure of Barak's protocol and ordinary zero-knowledge protocols. Phase 2 is a constant-round zero-knowledge universal argument (ZKUA) of the statement that $x \in L$ or the transcript $\tau$ of phase 1 is in a language $\Lambda$. Basically, $\tau$ consists of the verifier's description and those messages generated in the ordinary run of one rewind interval. The language $\Lambda$ consists of those $\tau$'s, in which if we perform at most $n^{\log\log n/5}$ rewinding runs with "cut-off" techniques at the verifier, it can output a correct secret information. (This actually means that we relegate all rewinds to the verification of $\tau \in \Lambda$.)

Our simulator for this protocol is an extension of Barak's simulator. That is, our simulator commits to (the oblivious machine of) the verifier's code and the auxiliary input bits *really accessed* by the verifier (not the entire auxiliary input) as well as performs other computation in phase 1. We remark that it is due to this strategy of committing only to accessed auxiliary bits that we can bypass the imprecision of Barak's simulator shown in [8]. In phase 2, the simulator employs a parallel simulation strategy which adopts the honest prover with the witness to interact with the verifier and in parallel calls the simulator of ZKUA. $S$ finally adopts the output generated in that one of the two parallel simulation which first finishes as the simulated view of phase 2. We will show the simulator can achieve our definition indeed.

## 1.2   Organizations

The rest of the paper is arranged as follows. We assume familiarity with the notations and notions used throughout this paper. Section 2 analyzes the barriers for constructing constant-round precise zero-knowledge protocols. Section 3 formalizes our relaxation and demonstrates the impossibility of constructing constant-round protocols satisfying the relaxation with the known techniques. Section 4 presents our constant-round protocol and shows it is an argument for any language in **NP**. Section 5 presents a novel precise simulator for the protocol and proves that the protocol is precise zero-knowledge with respect to this relaxation. Section 6 concludes the paper.

# 2   Barriers for Constructing Constant-Round Precise Zero-Knowledge

In this section we introduce the notion of precise zero-knowledge in [7,8] and review the know constructions and lastly point out the barriers that all the known constructions and simulation strategies cannot realize constant-round precise zero-knowledge protocols.

## 2.1   Precise Zero-Knowledge

**Counting Steps.** If $M$ is a probabilistic machine, denote by $M_r$ the deterministic one obtained by fixing the content of $M$'s random tape to $r$, by $\text{STEPS}_{M_r(x)}$ the number of computational steps taken by $M_r$ on input $x$.

Assume $(P, V)$ uses $u$-round prover's messages. In an execution of $(P, V)$, for any $V^*$ with an auxiliary input aux, denote by $v = (x, \text{aux}, (m_1, m_2, ..., m_u))$ the view of $V^*$, where $m_i$ is the $i$th prover's message (w.l.o.g, assume $V^*$ is deterministic). Then denote by $\text{STEPS}_{V^*}(v)$ the number of computational steps taken by $V^*$ running on view $v$, i.e. $V^*$'s running-time on input $x$ and auxiliary input aux and letting the $i$th message received be $m_i$. In counting steps, we assume that an algorithm $A$, given the code of a second algorithm $B$ and an input $x$, can simulate the computation of $B$ on input $x$ with linear-time slowdown [7]. (This assumption is inessential and we can use the logarithmic slowdown instead. Actually, for Turing machines and Random Access Machines, logarithmic slowdown is achieved.)

**Definition 1.** *(Precise Zero-Knowledge [7,8]) Let $(P, V)$ be an interactive proof or argument system for a language $L$, $p : N \times N \to N$ be a monotonically increasing 2-variate polynomial. We say that $(P, V)$ is a zero-knowledge proof or argument with precision $p$ if there exists a probabilistic algorithm $S$ such that for every polynomial-time $V^*$ and every auxiliary input $\text{aux} \in \{0, 1\}^*$ for $V^*$:*

1. *The view of $V^*$ in an interaction with $P$, where the public input is $x$ and $P$ has a witness $w$ for $x \in L$, is computationally indistinguishable from the output of $S(x, V^*, \text{aux})$.*

2. *For sufficiently long random coins $r \in \{0,1\}^*$, let $v$ be the view generated by $S_r(x, V^*, aux)$. Then $\Pr[\text{STEPS}_{S_r(x,V^*,aux)} \leq p(n, \text{STEPS}_{V^*}(v))] = 1 - neg(n)$.*

*We refer to $S$ as above as a precise simulator. We say that $(P, V)$ has polynomial precision or linear precision if $p(n, t)$ is a polynomial or linear function in $t$.*

*Remark 1.* The original definition in [7,8] requires it holds with probability 1 that $\text{STEPS}_{S_r(x,V^*,aux)} \leq p(n, \text{STEPS}_{V^*}(v))$. Definition 1 is actually the definition of weak precise zero-knowledge in [8]. As said before, we don't distinguish the two notions in this paper.

## 2.2    Barriers for Achieving Constant-Round Constructions

Though there exist some constructions of precise zero-knowledge, constant-round constructions are unknown to exist. We now review the reasons that the known constructions cannot achieve the constant-round property and polynomial precision simultaneously.

**Confliction Between "Cut-off" Simulation and Constant-Round Requirements.** The known constructions of precise zero-knowledge in [7,8,3] employ "cut-off" simulation techniques. One such simulator counts the verifier's running-time in the first run and then in each rewinding run it uses the counted time to bound the verifier's computation, which finally ensures the simulation time is no more than a polynomial of the verifier's running-time. As shown in e.g. [8], the simulator's successful probability in extracting the secret information is at most $1 - 1/\text{poly}(n)$ in a rewind interval. Thus to make the success probability overwhelming, a precise zero-knowledge protocol should use at least $\omega(1)$ rewind intervals. Thus it seems impossible to construct constant-round protocols with the "cut-off" techniques.

**Imprecision of Barak's Non-black-box Simulator.** One may ask if we can modify the known constant-round non-black-box zero-knowledge protocols to obtain precise zero-knowledge. However, the current situation is that the only known construction paradigm of constant-round non-black-box zero-knowledge is Barak's protocol [1]. However, as shown in [8], Barak's protocol is also imprecise. Recall that Barak's protocol consists of two phases. In phase 1, the verifier sends a random hash function $h$ to the prover, which then responds with a commitment $c$ to the 0-string. Then the verifier sends back a random string $r$. Let $\tau$ denote $(h, c, r)$. In phase 2, the prover proves to the verifier via a WI universal argument that either $x \in L$ or $\tau \in \Lambda$ for a well-defined language $\Lambda \in \textbf{Ntime}(n^{\log \log n})$. We now show the simulator for this protocol is imprecise.

Given access a verifier's code, Barak's protocol can be simulated without making use of rewinding: To perform simulation, the simulator commits to the hash of the verifier's message function including the auxiliary input (instead of committing to zeros). The verifier's next message function is then a program whose output, on input $c$, is $r$. This provides the simulator a valid witness to use in phase 2. However, consider a verifier $V^*$ that has a very long auxiliary

input, but most of the time only accesses a small portion of it. The simulator
will always commit to the hash of whole description of $V^*$ (including the whole
auxiliary input) and will thus always take long time, while $V^*$ might run fast a
large portion of the time. Hence the simulation strategy is imprecise.

## 3 Our Relaxation

In this section we present a slight relaxation on the precision requirement
and then point out that the known techniques cannot achieve this relaxation
and the constant-round property simultaneously. A constant-round precise zero-
knowledge protocol satisfying the relaxation will be introduced in next section.

### 3.1 The Relaxed Definition

Definition 1 requires that the precision $p$ holds for all verifiers with probability
$1 - \mathsf{neg}(n)$. Thus a slight relaxation is to require that with a probability *arbitrarily
polynomially* close to 1, there exists a precision $p$ which holds for all verifiers.
Namely, we only relax the satisfiable probability from $1 - \mathsf{neg}(n)$ to $1 - 1/q(n)$
where $q(n)$ can be an arbitrarily large polynomial. The formal definition is as
follows.

**Definition 2. (The relaxation.)** *Let $(P, V)$ be an interactive proof or argument system for a language $L$. We say that $(P, V)$ is a precise zero-knowledge
proof or argument, if there exists a strict PPT algorithm $S$ satisfying the following conditions:*

1. *For every poly-time $V^*$ and every auxiliary input $\mathsf{aux} \in \{0,1\}^*$ to $V^*$, the
   output of $S(x, V^*, \mathsf{aux})$ is computationally indistinguishable from $V^*$'s real
   view interacting with $P(x, w)$.*
2. *For any polynomial $q(n)$, there is a monotonically increasing 2-variate polynomial $p : N \times N \to N$ such that for each poly-time $V^*$ and each auxiliary
   input $\mathsf{aux} \in \{0,1\}^*$ to $V^*$, for sufficiently long random coins $r \in \{0,1\}^*$,
   letting $v$ be the view generated by $S_r(x, V^*, \mathsf{aux})$, $\Pr[\mathrm{STEPS}_{S_r(x,V^*,\mathsf{aux})} \leq
   p(n, \mathrm{STEPS}_{V^*}(v))] \geq 1 - \frac{1}{q(n)}$.*

### 3.2 Limitations of the Known Techniques

At this moment one may ask if the known techniques for constructing precise
zero-knowledge can achieve our relaxation and the constant-round property simultaneously. Unfortunately, we now point out that the known construction
techniques cannot do this job indeed.

Let us first consider the known precise zero-knowledge protocols and the "cut-
off" simulation techniques sketched in Section 2.2. As shown there, a simulator
can succeed in extraction in each rewind interval with probability $1 - \frac{1}{\mathrm{poly}(n)}$. For
any polynomial $q(n)$, this success probability can be instantiated with $1 - \frac{1}{q(n)}$.

Thus we have there is a polynomial $p(n, T)$ such that with probability $1 - \frac{1}{q(n)}$, the simulation is precise. However, in this construction $q(n)$ should be known to the simulator in advanced. That means for any larger polynomial $q'(n)$ this simulator cannot achieve any precision related to $q'(n)$ with probability $1 - \frac{1}{q'(n)}$. This shows Definition 2 cannot be satisfied by this construction.

Let us then consider Barak's protocol and his simulator. It can be seen that the barrier shown in Section 2.2 still exists w.r.t. out relaxation. That is, for a $V^*$, any $q(n)$ and $p$, there exists an aux of length more than $p(n, T)$ where $T$ denotes $V^*$'s running-time. Since Barak's simulator needs to compute a commitment to $V^*$'s next message function which contains aux, its running-time is more than $p(n, T)$, contradicting condition 2 of Definition 2. So Barak's simulator is still imprecise with respect to Definition 2.

# 4    The Protocol

In this section we present a constant-round zero-knowledge argument. In Section 4.1 we give a high-level overview of the protocol. In Section 4.2 we present the actual construction and prove it is an interactive argument for **NP**.

## 4.1    The Overview

Our protocol consists of two phases. Phase 1 adopts a mixed structure of Barak's protocol and ordinary zero-knowledge protocols. The adopted structure of ordinary zero-knowledge protocols is a commitment-challenge-response paradigm. That is, the verifier first sends the prover $n$ commitments to random strings which then responds with a random challenge indicating that some commitments should be revealed, and lastly the verifier opens the corresponding commitments.

The adopted structure of Barak's protocol is that in the above step of sending a challenge, the prover additionally sends the verifier a commitment to the 0-string and after the verifier opens some commitments, the prover sends the verifier a commitment to the hash of the 0-string. The goal of this strategy is for using Barak's non-black-box simulation strategy.

In phase 2, the prover proves to the verifier that it knows a witness for $x \in L$ or the transcript of phase 1 is in a language $\Lambda$. The definition of $\Lambda$ requires that a transcript is in $\Lambda$ iff what are committed by the prover in phase 1 are actually a program and some auxiliary input bits such that the program on given the auxiliary input bits and a challenge, can output the value of one unrevealed commitment by the verifier in phase 1.

## 4.2    Our Language $\Lambda$ and Protocol

In this subsection we present our protocol, which uses the following cryptographic primitives:

- Let $\{\mathcal{H}_n\}_{n \in N}$, in which each $h \in \mathcal{H}_n$ maps $\{0,1\}^*$ to $\{0,1\}^n$, denote a hash function family which collision resistance holds against all $n^{O(\log \log n)}$-size circuit.
- Let HCom denote a two-round perfectly-hiding commitment scheme, BCom denote a one-round (or two-round) perfectly-binding commitment scheme. For simplicity of statement we always use $C$ or $Z$ to denote a perfectly-hiding or perfectly-binding commitment (while ignoring the possible first message of HCom and BCom).
- Let PRG denote a pseudorandom generator which admits the following properties. On input an $n$-bit random seed $r$, PRG$(r)$ can iteratively generate arbitrarily polynomial pseudorandom bits. That is, it generates a fixed polynomial pseudorandom bits in each iteration, and then when run iteratively, PRG$(r)$ can output an arbitrarily polynomial pseudorandom bits. [4] presented one construction of such PRGs. PRG will be used in our definition of language $\Lambda$. In the verification of membership in $\Lambda$, PRG will be run iteratively. That is, the verification sets up a repetition process and in each repetition PRG$(r)$ is run once to output a fixed polynomial bits iteratively based on the internal state generated in the previous iterations.
- Let CoinToss denote a constant-round coin-tossing protocol, which runs as follows. The verifier first adopts HCom to compute a commitment to a random $n$-bit string and sends it to the prover, which responds with an independent $n$-bit strings. Then the verifier opens the commitment. Then the XOR of the two strings are the final coins.
- Let ZKUA denote a constant-round zero-knowledge universal argument for any language in **NE** defined in [2] and its simulator runs in strict polynomial-time. Note that [2] already presented a construction of ZKUA, but its simulator runs in expected polynomial-time. We can easily adapt it to our requitement. The ZKUA in [2] consists of two phases, where phase 1 is an "encrypted" commitment-challenge-commitment construction and phase 2 is an ordinary zero-knowledge protocol of knowledge, aiming at proving that the committed messages in phase 1 are consistent and satisfy the requirement of a PCP verification. Due to the call to the simulator of the ordinary zero-knowledge protocol in simulation, the simulator of this ZKUA runs in expected polynomial-time.

  Now we replace the zero-knowledge protocol in phase 2 by Barak's zero-knowledge protocol in [1] (note that phase 2 itself of Barak's protocol is a WI universal arument). Thus we can see the new ZKUA owns a strict polynomial-time simulator and still satisfies the weak proof of knowledge property. Thus the new ZKUA is a desired universal argument.

Now we present a definition of $\Lambda$ in Definition 3. Assume $L$ is an arbitrary **NP** language and our argument for $L$ is shown in Protocol 1.

**Definition 3.** *(Language $\Lambda$). We define $\Lambda$ as follows: $\tau = (h, \sigma, U, Z_1, Z_2, r) \in \Lambda$ iff there exist a program $\Pi \in \{0,1\}^n$, a string $y$ (as auxiliary input to $\Pi$) and coins $(s_1, s_2)$ such that the following conditions can be verified within $n^{\log \log n}$ steps:*

---

**Public input:** $x \in \{0,1\}^n$ (statement to be proved is "$x \in L$");
**Prover's auxiliary input:** $w$ (a witness that $x \in L$).

---

1. $V \rightarrow P$: Verifier selects $h \leftarrow_R \mathcal{H}_n$. Choose $u_i \leftarrow_R \{0,1\}^n$ and compute $C_i \leftarrow$ HCom$(u_i)$ for $1 \leq i \leq n$. Send $h$ and $C_i, 1 \leq i \leq n$, to prover.
2. $P \rightarrow V$: Prover selects a random $\sigma \in \{0,1\}^n$ and computes $Z_1 \leftarrow_R$ BCom$(0^n)$. Send $\sigma$ and $Z_1$ to verifier.
3. $V \rightarrow P$: For each $i$ satisfying that the $i$th bit of $\sigma$ is 0, open all these $C_i$ to prover.
4. $P \rightarrow V$: Prover computes $Z_2 \leftarrow_R$ BCom$(h(0^n))$ and sends $Z_2$ to verifier.
5. $V \rightarrow P$: For all $i$ satisfying the $i$th bit of $\sigma$ is 1, send these $u_i$'s to prover. Let $U$ denote the set consisting of these $u_i$'s. Then prove to prover via a constant-round zero-knowledge protocol of that these $u_i$'s are the committed messages in the corresponding $C_i$'s.
6. $P \leftrightarrow V$: Prover and verifier execute CoinToss to agree with random $r \in \{0,1\}^n$.

---

Let $\tau$ denote $(h, \sigma, U, Z_1, Z_2, r)$.

---

$P \rightarrow V$: Prover proves to verifier using its input $w$ via ZKUA that $x \in L$ or $\tau \in \Lambda$.

**Protocol 1.** *Our precise zero-knowledge argument for $L$*

1. $Z_1 = $ BCom$(\Pi; s_1)$ and $Z_2 = $ BCom$(h(y); s_2)$, where $s_1, s_2$ denote the randomness in commitments.
2. Run the following repetitions at most $n^{\log \log n / 5}$ times. In the $j$th repetition, $j > 0$, do the following:
   (a) Iteratively run PRG$(r)$ based on its existing internal state generated in the previous $(j-1)$ runs (if $j = 1$, PRG has no internal state) to generate sufficient pseudorandom bits, denoted $(\sigma_j, r_j)$ (where $\sigma_j \in \{0,1\}^n$ and $r_i$ is used as randomness in BCom, which length is a fixed polynomial that we omit specifying for clearness of statement);
   (b) Compute $Z_j^* \leftarrow$ BCom$(\Pi; r_j)$;
   (c) Run $\Pi(\sigma_j, Z_j^*, y)$ ($y$ as auxiliary input) and during this running if $\Pi$ needs an additional auxiliary input bit beyond $y$, cancel the running and denote by $\perp$ $\Pi$'s output, else let $U_j^*$ denote $\Pi$'s output. In the case $\Pi$'s output is $U_j^*$, if there exists at least one string in $U_j^*$ (viewed as a set) such that it is in $U$, the verification of this condition succeeds. In other cases, continue the repetitions.

A witness $w$ for $\tau \in \Lambda$ is a tuple of $(\Pi, y, s_1, s_2)$ satisfying Definition 3.

**Theorem 2.** *Assume the existence of hash function families which collision-resistance hold against all $n^{O(\log \log n)}$-size circuits. Then Protocol 1 is an interactive argument for $L$.*

Due to the hiding property of the commitments, any prover in the ordinary run cannot know the value of any unrevealed commitment and the committed program and auxiliary input by the prover are independent of the values in the unrevealed commitments. So the program cannot output any unrevealed message. Thus the transcript cannot belong to $\Lambda$, which leads to the soundness. We remark that the full proof of Theorem 2 employs the simulator of the zero-knowledge protocol in Step 5 to show the soundness. Due to short of space we omit the full proof.

## 5  The Precise Simulator

In this section we will prove the following result.

**Theorem 3.** *Protocol 1 is precise zero-knowledge with respect to Definition 2.*

In Section 5.1 we present the overview and actual description of our precise simulator. In Section 5.2 we show this simulator satisfies all requirements in Definition 2 and complete the proof of Theorem 3.

### 5.1  The Description

Let $V^*$ denote any verifier of length $\{0,1\}^{n/2}$, aux be an arbitrarily long auxiliary input to $V^*$, $S$ denote our simulator. Basically, $S$ behaves like Barak's simulator, which runs as a prover interacting with $V^*$, tries to obtain a witness for the transcript $\tau$ of phase 1 and lastly uses this witness for the combined statement in phase 2. Informally, in phase 1 $S$ commits to $V^*$'s next message function excluding aux in Step 2. W.l.o.g. let $\Pi \in \{0,1\}^n$ denote this committed program (more precisely, $S$ first computes $V^*$'s next message program and then generates $\Pi$ as an *oblivious machine* of this program). Notice that in Step 3 $V^*$ (i.e. $\Pi$) may access some positions in aux. Thus $S$ emulates $\Pi$'s computation on input $S$'s message of Step 2 as well as aux to generate an output, and at the same time records those auxiliary input bits $\Pi$ really accesses. Let $y$ denote the auxiliary bits. Then $S$ commits to the hash of $y$ in Step 4.

In phase 2 $S$ adopts a parallel simulation strategy, in which it uses $(\Pi, y)$ (as well as some coins used in commitments) as a witness for the transcript in $\Lambda$ to interact with $V^*$, and in parallel, it employs the simulator of ZKUA to generate a view. $S$ finally adopts that view generated in the one of the two parallel simulation which first finishes as the simulated view of phase 2.

**Oblivious Machines.** We outline some facts on obvious machines to help understand the execution of $\Pi$. A machine is oblivious if the sequence in which it accesses memory locations is equivalent for any two inputs with the same running time, e.g. oblivious Turing Machines (TM) and oblivious Random Access Machines (RAM). If an oblivious machine accesses more memory locations, it consumes more running-time. W.l.o.g. we assume a machine can be emulated by an oblivious machine with polynomial slowdown (for any unspecified appropriate computational model used for verifiers and the simulator). For instance, [9] showed how to emulate an arbitrary one-tape TM by a two-tape oblivious TM

---

**Input:** $x \in \{0,1\}^n$ (statement to be proved is "$x \in L$");
**Verifier's code:** $V^* \in \{0,1\}^{n/2}$; $V^*$**'s auxiliary input:** aux $\in \{0,1\}^*$.

---

1. $V^* \to S$: $S$ emulates $V^*$ to output $h$ and $C_i$ for $1 \leq i \leq n$.
2. $S \to V^*$: Compute the oblivious machine corresponding to $V^*$'s next message function (excluding aux), denoted $\Pi \in \{0,1\}^n$. $S$ selects a random $\sigma \in \{0,1\}^n$ and random coins $s_1$. Compute $Z_1 \leftarrow \mathsf{BCom}(\Pi; s_1)$ and send $(\sigma, Z_1)$ to $V^*$.
3. $V^* \to S$: $S$ emulates $\Pi$ to output some $u_i$'s. During the emulation, $S$ records those bits in aux accessed by $\Pi$. Denote by $y$ these accessed bits. (Also run $V^*$ to finish this step.)
4. $S \to V^*$: $S$ chooses random coins $s_2$ and computes $Z_2 \leftarrow \mathsf{BCom}(h(y); s_2)$. Send $Z_2$ to $V^*$.
5. $V^* \to S$: $S$ emulates $V^*$ to output the remainder $u_i$'s and interacts with $V^*$ in the following zero-knowledge proof. Let $U$ denote the set consisting of these $u_i$'s.
6. $S \leftrightarrow V^*$: $S$ and $V^*$ run CoinToss to agree with coins $r \in \{0,1\}^n$.

---

Let $\tau$ denote $(h, \sigma, U, Z_1, Z_2, r)$.

---

$S \to V^*$: $S$ adopts the following parallel simulation strategy. It adopts the honest prover's strategy with witness $(\Pi, y, s_1, s_2)$ to prove to $V^*$ via ZKUA that $x \in L$ or $\tau \in \Lambda$, and in parallel it calls the simulator of ZKUA to generate a simulated view. $S$ halts whenever an arbitrary one of the two parallel simulations finishes, and adopts the view in the finished one as the simulated view in phase 2.

---

**Algorithm 1.** *The precise simulator $S$*

with a logarithmic slowdown, and [5] showed how to emulate an arbitrary RAM by an oblivious RAM with a poly-logarithmic slowdown.

In our simulation, $\Pi$ is an oblivious machine corresponding to the verifier's next message function. Thus in an execution of $\Pi$, more auxiliary input bits $\Pi$ accesses, more running-time $\Pi$ consumes. Thus that $\Pi$ accesses more auxiliary input bits is equivalent to that $\Pi$ consumes more running-time. So in the verification of $\tau \in \Lambda$, the condition that the execution of $\Pi(\cdots, y)$ should be canceled if $\Pi$ needs to access more auxiliary input bits than $y$ is equivalent to that the execution of $\Pi(\cdots, y)$ should be canceled if $\Pi$'s running-time is more than (the poly-logarithmic overhead of) $V^*$'s running-time. This fact will be used to establish the precision property of $S$ in next subsection.

The actual construction of the simulator is shown in Algorithm 1.

## 5.2   Analysis

In this subsection we present the following three claims to show that $S$ can provide precise zero-knowledge property with respect to Definition 2. We also sketch the proofs of them but omit the full details due to short of space.

**Claim 4.** *For any polynomial $q(n)$, with probability at least $1-\frac{1}{q(n)}$ $(\Pi,y,s_1,s_2)$ is a witness for $\tau \in \Lambda$ and on the occurrence of this the membership of $\tau \in \Lambda$ can be verified with $(\Pi,y,s_1,s_2)$ in $O(q(n)\omega(\log n)T)$ time, where $T$ denotes the running-time of $\Pi(\sigma,Z_1,y)$.*

*Proof.* (sketch) Let $\Pi(\cdots,y)$ denote $\Pi$ with $y$ hardwired. We need to show the conditions in Definition 3 can be satisfied. In the verification of $\tau \in \Lambda$, first assume each prover's message $(\sigma_j,Z_j^*)$ is truly random. If in the execution of $\Pi(\sigma_j,Z_j^*,y)$ $\Pi$ doesn't need to access any auxiliary bit beyond $y$, $\Pi(\sigma_j,Z_j^*,y)$ can output some decommitments to those in the verifier's message of Step 1. Since $\sigma_j$ equals the real challenge with probability $2^{-n}$, there is a commitment which was not revealed in the real interaction, but is revealed in the output of $\Pi(\sigma_j,Z_j^*,y)$. Thus the membership of $\tau \in \Lambda$ can be verified. Thus all that is left is to show $\Pi$ doesn't need any auxiliary input bit beyond $y$ in one repetition with high probability. In fact, it is true that within $2q(n)\omega(\log n)$ repetitions, the desired event occurs with probability at least $1 - \frac{1}{2q(n)} - \mathsf{neg}(n)$. Now replacing each $(\sigma_j,Z_j^*)$ by the pseudorandom strings output by $\mathsf{PRG}(r)$, the probability is at least $1 - \frac{1}{q(n)}$. So the claim holds.                                    □

**Claim 5.** *For any pair $(x,w)$ such that $w$ is the witness for $x \in L$, the view of $V^*$ in an interaction with the honest prover of Protocol 1 holding $(x,w)$ is computationally indistinguishable from $S$'s output on input $(x,V^*,\mathsf{aux})$.*

*Proof.* (sketch) We use $S_1$ (resp. $S_2$) to denote $S$'s strategy with the first (resp. second) strategy used in phase 2. We have both $S_1$'s and $S_2$'s outputs are indistinguishable from the real view of $V^*$. In particular, over any noticeable sub probability space, $S_1$'s output is indistinguishable from $S_2$'s. We then show $S$'s output is indistinguishable from $S_1$'s. If there is only an negligible probability that $S$'s strategy in phase 2 equals $S_2$, the fact holds. Otherwise, let $B$ denote the noticeable event that $S$'s strategy in phase 2 equals $S_2$. So on the occurrence of $\overline{B}$, $S$ is actually $S_1$. Then for any $D$, $|\Pr[D^S(n) = 1]-\Pr[D^{S_1}(n) = 1]| \leq \Pr[\overline{B}]|\Pr[D^S(n) = 1|\overline{B}] - \Pr[D^{S_1}(n) = 1|\overline{B}]| + \Pr[B]|\Pr[D^S(n) = 1|B] - \Pr[D^{S_1}(n) = 1|B]| \leq |\Pr[D^S(n) = 1|B] - \Pr[D^{S_1}(n) = 1|B]|$. Since $|\Pr[D^S(n) = 1|B] - \Pr[D^{S_1}(n) = 1|B]| = \mathsf{neg}(n)$, $S$'s output is indistinguishable from $S_1$'s. The claim holds.                                    □

**Claim 6.** *$S$ satisfies condition 2 of Definition 2.*

*Proof.* (sketch) Choose a random sufficiently long coins *rand* for $S$. Let $T'$ denote $\mathsf{STEPS}_{V_{\mathsf{aux}}^*}(v)$, where $V_{\mathsf{aux}}^*$ denotes $V^*$ with the auxiliary input aux. We now analyze the running-time of $S$. First, $S$ runs in strict polynomial-time. $S$'s running-time for emulating $V_{\mathsf{aux}}^*$ is $O(T'+T)$. Due to Claim 4 and the relatively efficient prover property of ZKUA, $S$'s running-time in phase 2 is $O(n^{c_0}T^c)$ for some constant $c_0,c$ (where $c_0,c$ are independent of $T,T'$). So we have there exists a polynomial $p(n,T')$ such that $S$'s running-time is less than $p(n,T')$ with probability $1 - \frac{1}{q(n)}$. The claim holds.                                    □

Combining the three claims, we complete the proof of Theorem 3. Then combining it with Theorem 2, we also complete the proof of Theorem 1.

# 6 Conclusions

In this paper we investigate the question of how to construct constant-round precise zero-knowledge protocols. Since there are some barriers in solving this question that cannot be go beyond with all the known techniques, we look for a meaningful relaxation for precise zero-knowledge and a candidate constant-round construction with respect to the relaxation.

As a result, we propose one such relaxation that requires that with a probability arbitrarily polynomially close to 1, there exists a precision $p$ such that the simulator can reconstruct all verifiers' views satisfying the requirement $p$. Then we show the impossibility of constructing constant-round protocols satisfying our relaxed definition with all the known techniques, which makes the relaxation meaningful with respect to constant-round constructions. The main contribution of this work is a constant-round precise zero-knowledge argument for **NP** satisfying the relaxation.

**Acknowledgments.** The authors are grateful to the reviewers of ICICS 2012 for their useful comments. This work is supported by the National Natural Science Foundation of China (61100209) and Shanghai Postdoctoral Scientific Program (11R21414500).

# References

1. Barak, B.: How to go beyond the black-box simulation barrier. In: FOCS, pp. 106–115 (2001)
2. Barak, B., Goldreich, O.: Universal arguments and their applications. In: IEEE Conference on Computational Complexity, pp. 194–203 (2002)
3. Ding, N., Gu, D.: Precise Time and Space Simulatable Zero-Knowledge. In: Boyen, X., Chen, X. (eds.) ProvSec 2011. LNCS, vol. 6980, pp. 16–33. Springer, Heidelberg (2011)
4. Goldreich, O., Micali, S.: Increasing the expansion of pseudorandom generators (1996), http://www.wisdom.weizmann.ac.il/oded/papers.html
5. Goldreich, O., Ostrovsky, R.: Software protection and simulation on oblivious rams. J. ACM 43(3), 431–473 (1996)
6. Goldwasser, S., Micali, S., Rackoff, C.: The knowledge complexity of interactive proof systems. SIAM J. Comput. 18(1), 186–208 (1989)
7. Micali, S., Pass, R.: Local zero knowledge. In: Kleinberg, J.M. (ed.) STOC, pp. 306–315. ACM (2006)
8. Pass, R.: A precise computational approach to knowledge. Tech. rep., Ph. D. thesis, MIT. Available (2006)
9. Pippenger, N., Fischer, M.J.: Relations among complexity measures. J. ACM 26(2), 361–381 (1979)

# Outsourcing Encryption of Attribute-Based Encryption with MapReduce

Jingwei Li[1], Chunfu Jia[1], Jin Li[2], and Xiaofeng Chen[3]

[1] College of Information Technical Science, Nankai University
lijw@mail.nankai.edu.cn,
cfjia@nankai.edu.cn
[2] School of Computer Science, Guangzhou University
lijin@gzhu.edu.cn
[3] State Key Laboratory of Integrated Service Networks, Xidian University
xfchen@xidian.edu.cn

**Abstract.** Attribute-based encryption (ABE) is a promising crypto-graphic tool for fine-grained access control. However, the computational cost in encryption commonly grows with the complexity of access policy in existing ABE schemes, which becomes a bottleneck limiting its application. In this paper, we formulize the novel paradigm of outsourcing encryption of ABE to cloud service provider to relieve local computation burden. We propose an optimized construction with MapReduce cloud which is secure under the assumption that the master node as well as at least one of the slave nodes is honest. After outsourcing, the computational cost at user side during encryption is reduced to approximate four exponentiations, which is constant. Another advantage of the proposed construction is that the user is able to delegate encryption for any policy.

## 1 Introduction

Recently, much attention has been attracted by a new public-key primitive called attribute-based encryption (ABE). ABE achieves flexible one-to-many encryption instead of one-to-one, which has significant advantage over the traditional public key primitives. ABE thus is envisioned as an important tool for addressing the problem of secure and fine-grained data sharing and access control on un-trusted server in cloud computing. Until now, there are two kinds of ABE having been proposed: key-policy attribute-based encryption (KP-ABE) and ciphertext-policy attribute-based encryption (CP-ABE). In KP-ABE, the access policy is assigned in private key, whereas, in CP-ABE, it is specified in ciphertext.

However, one of the main efficiency drawbacks of ABE is that the computational cost in encryption phase grows with the complexity of the access formula. Thus, before ABE can be widely deployed in cloud computing for the purpose of providing secure access control, there is an increasing need to improve its efficiency. To address this problem, outsourced ABE, which provides a way to outsource encryption or/and decryption to third party service providers without revealing data or private keys, was introduced [17][28]. Outsourced ABE has a

T.W. Chim and T.H. Yuen (Eds.): ICICS 2012, LNCS 7618, pp. 191–201, 2012.

wide range of applications. For example, in the cloud computing environment which has mobile devices or sensors as information collection nodes, user terminal (e.g. mobile device) has constrained computation ability to independently finish basic encryption or decryption to protect sensitive data residing in public cloud. Outsourced ABE allows user to perform heavy encryption or/and decryption through "borrowing" the computation resources from a third party service provider. Therefore, with this paradigm computation/storage intensive tasks can be performed even by resource-constrained users.

## 1.1 Contribution

In this paper, concerning on outsourcing encryption of ABE, we formulize the security definition for this novel paradigm. We propose an outsourced ABE construction with delegated encryption. In this construction, user is to control the trival policy while a two-leveled MapReduce paradigm is utilized to produce a partial ciphertext for the user specified policy. The proposed construction is secure under the assumption that the master node as well as at least one of the slave nodes in MapReduce cloud is honest. This assumption is weaker than those assumptions in previous work which require all the nodes in the cloud are honest. Furthermore, we state that another advantage of our construction is that through introducing trivial policy, it is able to delegate encryption for any policy, while in previous work [28], user is required to specify a hybrid one connected by an AND gate.

## 1.2 Related Work

The notion of ABE, which was introduced as fuzzy identity-based encryption in [25], was firstly dealt with by Goyal et al. [16]. Two different and complementary notions of ABE were defined. In KP-ABE, each ciphertext is labeled with a set of attributes and each key is associated with an access structure. On the contrary, In CP-ABE, each private key is identified by a set of attributes and each ciphertext is labeled with an access structure. A construction of KP-ABE was provided in the same paper [16], while the first CP-APE construction supporting tree-based structure in generic group model is presented by Bethencourt et al. [5]. Subsequently, a number of variants of ABE schemes have been proposed since its introduction [8][22][27][20][26][21][24]. However, almost all of them requires a large number of exponentiations at user side during encryption.

To reduce the load at local, it always desires to deliver expensive computational tasks outside. Actually, the problem that how to securely outsource different kinds of expensive computations has drew much attention from theoretical computer science community [3][2][4][1]. But they are not suitable for reliving ABE computational overhead of exponentiations at user side. To achieve this goal, the traditional approach is to utilize server-aided techniques [6][19][18][7]. However, previous server-aided techniques are oriented to accelerating the speed of exponentiation using untrusted servers. Directly utilizing these techniques in ABE will not work efficiently.

Another approach might be to leverage recent general outsourcing technique or delegating computation [15][13][12][9][14] based on fully homomorphic encryption or interactive proof systems. However, Gentry [14] has shown that even for weak security parameters on "bootstrapping", the operation of homomorphic encryption would take at least 30 seconds on a high performance machine. Therefore, even if the privacy of the inputs and outputs can be preserved by utilizing these general techniques, the computational overhead is still huge and impractical.

Another two related work similar to us are [17] and [28]. In [17], a novel paradigm for outsourcing decryption of ABE is provided while in [28] the authors presented the PP-CP-ABE (privacy preserving cipher policy attribute-based encryption) which allows to securely outsource both decryption and encryption to third party service providers. Comparing with our work, i) the former has a different goal aiming at partial decryption delegation but we consider on outsourcing encryption of ABE; ii) the latter is the inspiration of this paper. Based on Zhou's work [28], we formulize the notion of outsourcing encryption of ABE and propose an optimized construction to enhance Zhou's scheme [28] in both security and functionality.

### 1.3 Organization

This paper is organized as follows. In Section 2 we describe the system model of our scheme. The construction and its security analysis are presented in Section 3. Finally, we draw conclusion in Section 4.

## 2 System Model

### 2.1 MapReduce

A two-leveled MapReduce [10] which is a software framework for supporting data-intensive computing, comprises a set of slave computer nodes and a master computer node. We now give an overview of MapReduce's workflow as follows.

- **Upload Phase.** User contacts with the master node to get knowledge which slave nodes are free. Then, he/she goes on to upload a set of data and "operations", i.e. complied Java classes, to these slave nodes to produce partially encrypted ABE ciphertext.
- **Map Phase.** After data and implementations have been uploaded, the MapReduce is triggered. Each involved slave node becomes a "mapper" node, which scans the information uploaded on it to obtain the key-value pair. Furthermore, the mapper node takes the key-value pair as input and executes the map function to generate an intermediate key-value pair. The phase can be denoted as $\mathsf{Map}(k, v) \rightarrow (k', v')$.
- **Reduce Phase.** After each slave node finishes its assigned task, MapReduce starts the "Reduce" phase, in which the master node is selected as the reducer. The reducer executes reduce function on the set of intermediate pairs $(k', v')$ with the same key and outputs the final result. The phase can be denoted as $\mathsf{Reduce}(\{(k', v')\}) \rightarrow Output$.

## 2.2    System Model

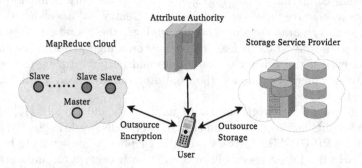

**Fig. 1.** System Model for Outsourcing Encryption of ABE

We present proposed system model for outsourcing encryption of ABE scheme in Fig. 1. Comparing with that for traditional ABE, a MapReduced cloud is involved to execute the delegated ABE encryption task.

With the custom in [17], we denote $(I_{\text{enc}}, I_{\text{key}})$ as the input to encryption and key generation in ABE. Therefore, in CP-ABE, $(I_{\text{enc}}, I_{\text{key}}) = (\mathbb{A}, \omega)$ while that is $(\omega, \mathbb{A})$ in KP-ABE, where $\omega$ and $\mathbb{A}$ are attribute set and access structure respectively. Then, based on the proposed system model, we provide algorithm definitions as follows.

- **Setup**$(\lambda)$ : The setup algorithm takes as input – a security parameter $\lambda$. It outputs the public key PK and the master key MK.
- **KeyGen**$(I_{\text{key}}, \text{MK})$ : For each user's private key request on $I_{\text{key}}$, the key generation algorithm takes as input – an access structure (or attribute set) $I_{\text{key}}$ and the master key MK. It outputs the private key SK.
- **Encrypt**$_{\text{U}}(I_{\text{enc}}, \text{M})$ : The encryption algorithm at user side takes as input – an attribute set (or access structure) $I_{\text{enc}}$ and the message M. It outputs the partially encrypted ciphertext at local $\text{CT}_{\text{U}}$ and the set of outrourcing encryption keys $\{\text{OEK}_i\}_{i=1}^n$ where $n$ is the number of slave nodes in MapReduce cloud to be assigned.
- **Encrypt**$_{\text{MR}}(I_{\text{enc}}, \{\text{OEK}_i\}_{i=1}^n)$ : The delegated encryption algorithm at the MapReduce cloud takes as input – an attribute set (or access structure) $I_{\text{enc}}$ and the set of outsourcing encryption keys $\{\text{OEK}_i\}_{i=1}^n$. It outputs the partially encrypted ciphertext at MapReduce $\text{CT}_{\text{MR}}$.
- **Decrypt**$(\text{CT}, \text{SK})$ : The decryption algorithm takes as input – a ciphertext $\text{CT} = (\text{CT}_{\text{U}}, \text{CT}_{\text{MR}})$ which was assumed to be encrypted under the attribute set (or access structure) $I_{\text{enc}}$ and the private key SK for access structure (or attribute set) $I_{\text{key}}$. It outputs the message M if $\gamma(I_{\text{key}}, I_{\text{enc}}) = 1$, otherwise outputs $\perp$, where $\gamma$ is a predicate predefined.

## 2.3   Adversary Model

In the system, we assume that the master node as well as at least one of the slave nodes in MapReduce cloud is "honest-but-curious". Specifically, they will follow our proposed protocol but try to find out as much private information as possible based on their possession. We note that this adversary model is weaker than that in [28], which requires the whole encryption service provider is "honest-but-curious".

Therefore, two types of adversaries are considered: i) The MapReduce service provider, who can potentially access all the information including encrypted message, the outsourcing encryption keys, etc; ii) A curious user, who can obtain his individual private key and share his authentication with others.

Having such intuition, we will follow the replayable chosen-ciphertext attack (RCCA) security in [17] and define RCCA security for our setting.

**Setup.** The challenger runs setup algorithm and gives the public key PK to the adversary.

**Phase 1.** The challenger initializes an empty set $D_{\text{key}}$. Proceedingly, adversary is allowed to make the following queries for several times.

- *Private key query.* Upon receiving $I_{\text{key}}$, challenger runs key generation algorithm on $I_{\text{key}}$ to obtain SK and returns SK after setting $D_{\text{key}} = D_{\text{key}} \cup \{I_{\text{key}}\}$.
- *Encryption query.* Upon receiving M, $j$ and $I_{\text{enc}}$, challenger runs encryption algorithm totally to obtain CT and $\{\text{OEK}_i\}_{i=1}^{n}$. But only return CT and $\{\text{OEK}_i\}_{i=1,i\neq j}^{n}$ to adversary.
- *Decryption query.* Upon receiving CT encrypted under $I_{\text{enc}}$, challenger generates SK for $I_{\text{key}}$ and performs decryption on CT to obtain M. Finally return M.

**Challenge.** Adversary submits two messages $M_0$ and $M_1$. In addition the adversary gives $I_{\text{enc}}^{*}$ satisfying that $\gamma(I_{\text{key}}, I_{\text{enc}}^{*}) = 0$ for all $I_{\text{key}} \in D_{\text{key}}$. Challenger flips a random coin $b$ and encrypts $M_b$ under $I_{\text{enc}}^{*}$ totally. Finally return the resulting ciphertext CT*.

**Phase 2.** Phase 1 is repeated with the restrictions: i) Adversary cannot issue *private key query* on $I_{\text{key}}$ where $\gamma(I_{\text{key}}, I_{\text{enc}}^{*}) = 1$. ii) *Decryption query* will be answered normally except that the response would be either $M_0$ or $M_1$, then challenger responds with a special message instead.

**Guess.** Adversary outputs a guess $b'$ of $b$.

**Definition 1.** *A CP-ABE or KP-ABE scheme with outsourced encryption is secure against replayable chosen-ciphertext attack if all polynomial time adversaries have at most a negligible advantage in the game defined above.*

Finally, beyond the RCCA security, we also specify that i) An ABE with delegated encryption is CPA-secure (or secure against chosen-plaintext attack) if no polynomial time adversary has non-negligible advantage in a modified game, in which the *decryption query* in both phase 1 and phase 2 is removed; ii) An ABE with delegated encryption is secure in selective model if no polynomial time adversary has non-negligible advantage in a modified game, in which the $I_{enc}^*$ submission is advanced to an additional stage before setup.

# 3   Proposed Construction

## 3.1   Access Structure

In the proposed construction, private keys will be identified with a set $\omega$ of descriptive attributes, while the encryption policy is specified as an access tree $\mathcal{T}$. We will briefly review the concept of access tree in [5] as well as [28] before providing our construction.

Let $\mathcal{T}$ be a tree representing an access structure, in which each interior node is a threshold gate (i.e. AND gate or OR gate) while the leaves are associated with attributes. A user is able to decrypt a ciphertext with a given key if and only if there is an assignment of attributes from the private key to leaf nodes of the tree such that the tree is satisfied.

To facilitate working with the access tree, we define a few notations and functions as follows.

- $num_x$ is the number of children of an interior node $x$. In order to uniquely identify each child, an ordering between the children of every node is defined, that is, the children of node $x$ is numbered from 1 to $num_x$. Therefore, if assuming $y$ is the child of node $x$, we could denote index($y$) as such number associated with the node $y$.
- $k_x$ is the threshold value of an interior node $x$, specifically, when $k_x = 1$, the threshold gate at $x$ is OR gate and when $k_x = num_x$, that is an AND gate. We note that if $x$ is a leaf node it is described by an attribute and a threshold value $k_x = 1$.
- The function parent($x$) returns the parent of the node $x$ in the tree. attr($x$) returns the attribute associated with the leaf node $x$.

## 3.2   Our Construction

We utilize the MapReduce paradigm to split the secret $s$ used in ciphertext into $n$ pieces and each of them is dealt by slave node separately. Another trick used is to introduce a trival policy $\mathcal{T}_\theta$ consisting of a single leaf node $\theta$ to improve [28]. Specifically, our scheme supports to delegate encryption with any generic tree-based access policy.

Before providing construction, we define some basic tools used later.

**Definition 2 (Bilinear Map).** *Suppose* $\mathbb{G}, \mathbb{G}_T$ *be cyclic groups of prime order* $q$, *writing the group action multiplicatively.* $g$ *is a generator of* $\mathbb{G}$. *Let* $e : \mathbb{G} \times \mathbb{G} \to \mathbb{G}_T$ *be a map with the following properties:*

- *Bilinearity:* $e(g_1^a, g_2^b) = e(g_1, g_2)^{ab}$ for all $g_1, g_2 \in \mathbb{G}$, and $a, b \in_R \mathbb{Z}_q$;
- *Non-degeneracy: There exists* $g_1, g_2 \in \mathbb{G}$ *such that* $e(g_1, g_2) \neq 1$, *in other words, the map does not send all pairs in* $\mathbb{G} \times \mathbb{G}$ *to the identity in* $\mathbb{G}_T$;

We also define the Lagrange coefficient $\Delta_{i,S}$ for $i \in \mathbb{Z}_q$ and a set $S$ of elements in $\mathbb{Z}_q$ :

$$\Delta_{i,S} = \prod_{j \in S, j \neq i} \frac{x - j}{i - j}$$

Then, the proposed construction in detail is shown as follows.

- **Setup**$(\lambda)$ : The setup algorithm is executed by authority. Select a bilinear group $\mathbb{G}$ of prime order $q$ with generator $g$ and two random integers $\alpha, \beta \in \mathbb{Z}_q$, and define a hash function $H : \{0,1\}^* \to \mathbb{G}$ modeled as a random oracle. Finally, output the public key PK $= (\mathbb{G}, H(\cdot), g, h = g^\beta, e(g,g)^\alpha)$ and the master key MK $= (\beta, g^\alpha)$.
- **KeyGen**$(\omega, \text{MK})$ : For each user's private key request, the authority runs the key generation algorithm. Choose $r \in_R \mathbb{Z}_q$ and $r_j \in_R \mathbb{Z}_q$ for each attribute $j \in \omega \cup \{\text{attr}(\theta)\}$. Finally compute and output the private key as SK $= (d = g^{\frac{\alpha+r}{\beta}}, \{d_{j0} = g^r \cdot H(j)^{r_j}, d_{j1} = g^{r_j}\}_{j \in \omega \cup \{\text{attr}(\theta)\}})$.
- **Encrypt**$_U(\mathcal{T}_U, M)$ : To encrypt a message M with access policy $\mathcal{T}_U$, firstly pick an integer $s \in_R \mathbb{Z}_q$ and randomly select a 1-degree polynomial $q_R(\cdot)$ such that $q_R(0) = s$. Furthermore, let $s_1 = q_R(1)$ and $s_2 = q_R(2)$. Then, make an $n$-splits on $s_1$ by randomly selecting $s_{11}, \ldots, s_{1n} \in \mathbb{Z}_q$ with $s_{11} + \ldots + s_{1n} = s_1$ and set OEK$_i = s_{1i}$ for $i = 1, \ldots, n$. Finally, it outputs the partially encrypted ciphertext at local CT$_U = (\mathcal{T}_U \wedge \mathcal{T}_\theta, \tilde{E} = \text{M}e(g,g)^{\alpha s}, E = h^s, (E_{\theta 0} = g^{s_2}, E_{\theta 1} = H(\text{attr}(\theta))^{s_2}))$ and the set of outsourcing keys $\{\text{OEK}_i\}_{i=1}^n$.
- **Encrypt**$_{\text{MR}}(\mathcal{T}_U, \{\text{OEK}_i\}_{i=1}^n)$ : The delegated encryption algorithm is executed by the MapReduce cloud. As described in Section 2.1, user uploads $(\mathcal{T}_U, \text{OEK}_i)$ which is scaned as the key-value pair to the $i$-th slave node. Then the MapReduce is triggered.
  - **Map.** The slave node $i$ finishes the "partial encryption" task by choosing a $(k_x - 1)$-degree polynomial $q_x^{(i)}(\cdot)$ for each node $x$ (including the leaves) in the tree $\mathcal{T}_U$ in a top-down manner. The selected polynomial $q_x^{(i)}(\cdot)$ must satisfy the restriction that $q_x^{(i)}(0) = s_{1i}$ if $x$ is the root node in $\mathcal{T}_U$, otherwise $q_x^{(i)}(0) = q_{\text{parent}(x)}^{(i)}(\text{index}(x))$. Let $Y_U$ denote the set of leaf nodes in $\mathcal{T}_U$, then the partially encrypted ciphertext at slave node $i$ is computed as CT$_{\text{MR}}^{(i)} = (\{E_{y0}^{(i)} = g^{q_y^{(i)}(0)}, E_{y1}^{(i)} = H(\text{attr}(y))^{q_y^{(i)}(0)}\}_{y \in Y_U})$. The map function for outsourced encryption is described as $\text{Map}(\mathcal{T}_U, \text{OEK}_i) \to (\mathcal{T}_U, \text{CT}_{\text{MR}}^{(i)})$.
  - **Reduce.** Let $q_y(x) = \sum_{i=0}^n q_y^{(i)}(x)$ for $y \in Y_U$. The master node is selected as the reducer. Then, after gathering all the intermediate key-value pairs $\{(\mathcal{T}_U, \text{CT}_{\text{MR}}^{(i)})\}_{i=1}^n$ sent from the other slave nodes, reducer

computes $\text{CT}_{\text{MR}} = (\{E_{y0} = \prod_{i=1}^{n} E_{y0}^{(i)} = g^{q_y(0)}, E_{y1} = \prod_{i=1}^{n} E_{y1}^{(i)} = H(\text{attr}(y))^{q_y(0)}\}_{y \in Y_U})$. The reduce function for outsourced encryption can be described as $\text{Reduce}(\{(\mathcal{T}_U, \text{CT}_{\text{MR}}^{(i)})\}_{i=1}^{n}) \rightarrow \text{CT}_{\text{MR}}$.
Finally, such ciphertext $\text{CT}_{\text{MR}}$ is sent back to user.

- **Decrypt**$(\text{CT}, \text{SK})$ : The recursive decryption algorithm is executed by user. Suppose $\text{CT} = (\text{CT}_U, \text{CT}_{\text{MR}})$ is encrypted under the policy corressponding to SK, then the decryption is followed in a down-top manner.

  - For each leaf node $y$ in the hybrid access tree $\mathcal{T}_U \wedge \mathcal{T}_\theta$, let $i = \text{attr}(y)$ and the decryption is presented as follows.

$$F_y = \frac{e(E_{y0}, d_{i0})}{e(d_{i1}, E_{y1})} = \frac{e(g^{q_y(0)}, g^r H(i)^{r_i})}{e(g^{r_i}, H(\text{attr}(y))^{q_y(0)})} = e(g, g)^{r q_y(0)}$$

  - For each interior node $y$, let $S_y$ be an arbitrary $k_y$-sized set of child nodes $z$ such that $F_z \neq \perp$. If no such set exists then the node is not satisfied and the function returns $\perp$. Then, the decryption is presented as follows.

$$\begin{aligned} F_y &= (\prod_{z \in S_y} F_z)^{\Delta_{i,S_y}(0)} \\ &= (e(g,g)^{\sum_{z \in S_y} r q_z(0)})^{\Delta_{i,S_y}(0)} = e(g,g)^{\sum_{z \in S_y} r q_{\text{parent}(z)}(\text{index}(z)) \Delta_{i,S_y}(0)} \\ &= e(g,g)^{r \sum_{z \in S_y} q_y(i) \Delta_{i,S_y}(0)} \\ &= e(g,g)^{r q_y(0)} \end{aligned}$$

Finally, we are able to decrypt the root node by computing $F_R = e(g,g)^{r q_R(0)} = e(g,g)^{rs}$. Then, the ciphertext can be decrypted by computing

$$M = \frac{\widetilde{E}}{\frac{e(E,d)}{F_R}} = \frac{Me(g,g)^{\alpha s}}{\frac{e(h^s, g^{\frac{\alpha+r}{\beta}})}{e(g,g)^{rs}}}$$

### 3.3   Security Analysis

**Theorem 1.** *The proposed construction is CPA-secure under the assumption that the master node as well as at least one of the slave nodes in MapReduce cloud is "honest-but-curious" in the generic group model.*

*Proof.* We observe that in the security game shown in Section 2.3, the challenge ciphertext has a component $\widetilde{E}$ which is randomly either $M_0 e(g,g)^{\alpha s}$ or $M_1 e(g,g)^{\alpha s}$. We can instead consider a modified game in which $\widetilde{E}$ is either $e(g,g)^{\alpha s}$ or $e(g,g)^{\nu}$, where $\nu$ is selected uniformly at random from $\mathbb{Z}_q$, and the adversary must decide which is the case. It is clear that any adversary has advantage $\epsilon$ in the origianl game can be transformed into an adversary that has advantage at least $\frac{\epsilon}{2}$ in the modified game. Then, we would like to bound the adversary's advantage in the modified game.

Then, we are to denote $\phi_0 : \mathbb{Z}_q \to \{0,1\}^{\log q}$ as a random encoding for the group operation $g^x \in \mathbb{G}$ and $\phi_1 : \mathbb{Z}_q \to \{0,1\}^{\log q}$ as a random encoding for $e(g,g)^x \in \mathbb{G}_T$. Let $g = \phi_0(1)$.

At setup time, simulator chooses $\alpha, \beta \in_R \mathbb{F}_q$. Note that if $\beta = 0$ which happens with probability $\frac{1}{q}$, then setup is aborted. Finally, publish public parameters $h = g^\beta$ and $e(g,g)^\alpha$ to adversary.

When the adversary calls for the evaluation of $H$ on any string $i$, simulator maintains a list $\mathcal{L}$ to store the response to hash query. Upon receiving a string $i$, if the entry $(i, g^{t_i})$ exists in $\mathcal{L}$, straightforwardly return $g^{t_i}$. Otherwise, pick $t_i \in_R \mathbb{F}_q$ and return $g^{t_i}$ after adding the entry $(i, g^{t_i})$ into $\mathcal{T}$.

When the adversary makes its $j$-th private key request on $\omega_j$ of attributes, challenger picks $r^{(j)} \in_R \mathbb{F}_q$ and comptutes $d = g^{\frac{\alpha + r^{(j)}}{\beta}}$ and we have $d_{i0} = g^{r^{(j)} + t_i r_i^{(j)}}$ and $d_{i1} = g^{r_i^{(j)}}$ for $i \in \omega_j \cup \{\mathsf{attr}(\theta)\}$ and $r_i^{(j)} \in_R \mathbb{Z}_q$.

When the adversary makes encryption request on M, $j$ as well as $\mathcal{T}_U$, the simulator chooses $s \in_R \mathbb{F}_q$. Then it splits $s$ into $s_1$ and $s_2$ with linear secret sharing. i) For $s_1$, the simulator continues to split it into $s_{11}, \ldots, s_{1n}$ and uses the linear secret sharing scheme associated with $\mathcal{T}_U$ to construct shares $\lambda_i^{(j)}$ of $s_{1j}$ ($j = 1, \ldots, n$) for all relevant attributes $i$. Then, the simulator makes a reduce by computing $E_{i0} = g^{\sum_{j=1}^k \lambda_i^{(j)}}$ and $E_{i1} = g^{t_i \sum_{j=1}^k \lambda_i^{(j)}}$ for each relevant attribute $i$. ii) For $s_2$, the simulation perform computation like Section 3.2 to obtain $E_{\theta 0} = g^{s_2}$ and $E_{\theta 1} = g^{t_\theta s_2}$. Finally, these values along with $\widetilde{E} = Me(g,g)^{\alpha s}, E = g^s$ and $\{s_{1i}\}_{i=1, i \neq j}^n$ are sent to adversary.

When adversary asks for challenge on $M_0, M_1$ and $\mathcal{T}^*$, simulator's action is identical to the response to encryption query, except that it picks $u \in_R \mathbb{Z}_q$ and constructs the encryption as follows: $\widetilde{E} = e(g,g)^u$ and $E = h^s$. For each relevant attribute $i$, $E_{i0} = g^{\lambda_i}$ and $E_{i1} = g^{t_i \lambda_i}$.

Subsequently, the response to the group operation is identical to that in [5]. Therefore, using the generic bilinear group model, it is able to be shown that with probability $1 - O(\frac{p^2}{q})$ taken over the randomness of the choice of variable values in the simulation, adversary's view in this simulation is identically distributed to what its view would have been if it had been given $\widetilde{E} = e(g,g)^{\alpha s}$, where $p$ is the bound on the total number of group elements received from queries to hash functions, group $\mathbb{G}, \mathbb{G}_T$ and the bilinear map $e$, and from its interaction with security game. Therefore, the proposed construction is secure in the proposed model.

In our construction, the reduce operation is run by the master node which is honest. Moreover, a further split on $s_1$ is performed to "map" the "partial encryption" task onto $n$ slave nodes to allow for concurrent execution. Since at least one of the slave nodes is honest, they are not able to recover $s_1$ to fake access policy even if $n - 1$ slave nodes collude.

Finally, we specify that though the proposed construction is secure against chosen-plaintext attack, it is allowed to be extended to the stronger RCCA-security guarantee by using simulation-sound NIZK proofs [23]. Alternatively, if we are willing to use random oracle, then we can use standard techniques such as the Fujisaki-Okamoto transformation [11].

## 4   Conclusion

In this paper, we formulize the paradigm of outsourcing encryption of ABE in cloud computing. We utilize MapReduce to propose a security enhanced construction which is secure under the assumption that the master node as well as at least one of the slave nodes in cloud is honest. Another advantage of the proposed construction is that it is able to delegate encryption for any access policy, instead of a special hybrid access policy. With our proposed outsourcing method, the computational cost at user side in encryption algorithm is reduced to four exponentiations, which is constant and does not grow with the number of attributes included in the ciphertext.

**Acknowledgements.** This work is supported by the National Natural Science Foundation of China (Nos. 61272423, 60973141, 61100224 and 60970144), Specialized Research Fund for the Doctoral Program of Higher Education of China (No. 20100031110030), Natural Science Foundation of Guangdong Province (No. 10451009101004573), and Foundation for Distinguished Young Talents in Higher Education of Guangdong Province (No. LYM10106).

## References

1. Atallah, M.J., Frikken, K.B.: Securely outsourcing linear algebra computations. In: Proceedings of the 5th ACM Symposium on Information, Computer and Communications Security, ASIACCS 2010, pp. 48–59. ACM, New York (2010)
2. Atallah, M.J., Li, J.: Secure outsourcing of sequence comparisons. International Journal of Information Security 4, 277–287 (2005)
3. Atallah, M.J., Pantazopoulos, K., Rice, J.R., Spafford, E.E.: Secure outsourcing of scientific computations. In: Zelkowitz, M.V. (ed.) Trends in Software Engineering. Advances in Computers, vol. 54, pp. 215–272. Elsevier (2002)
4. Benjamin, D., Atallah, M.J.: Private and cheating-free outsourcing of algebraic computations. In: Proceedings of the 2008 Sixth Annual Conference on Privacy, Security and Trust, PST 2008, pp. 240–245. IEEE Computer Society, Washington, DC (2008)
5. Bethencourt, J., Sahai, A., Waters, B.: Ciphertext-policy attribute-based encryption. In: IEEE Symposium on Security and Privacy 2007, pp. 321–334 (May 2007)
6. Bicakci, K., Baykal, N.: Server Assisted Signatures Revisited. In: Okamoto, T. (ed.) CT-RSA 2004. LNCS, vol. 2964, pp. 143–156. Springer, Heidelberg (2004)
7. Chen, X., Li, J., Ma, J., Tang, Q., Lou, W.: New Algorithms for Secure Outsourcing of Modular Exponentiations. In: Foresti, S., Yung, M., Martinelli, F. (eds.) ESORICS 2012. LNCS, vol. 7459, pp. 541–556. Springer, Heidelberg (2012)
8. Cheung, L., Newport, C.: Provably secure ciphertext policy abe. In: Proceedings of the 14th ACM Conference on Computer and Communications Security, CCS 2007, pp. 456–465 (2007)
9. Chung, K.M., Kalai, Y., Liu, F.H., Raz, R.: Memory Delegation. In: Rogaway, P. (ed.) CRYPTO 2011. LNCS, vol. 6841, pp. 151–168. Springer, Heidelberg (2011)
10. Dean, J., Ghemawat, S.: Mapreduce: simplified data processing on large clusters. Commun. ACM 51(1), 107–113 (2008)
11. Fujisaki, E., Okamoto, T.: Secure Integration of Asymmetric and Symmetric Encryption Schemes. In: Wiener, M. (ed.) CRYPTO 1999. LNCS, vol. 1666, pp. 537–554. Springer, Heidelberg (1999)

12. Gennaro, R., Gentry, C., Parno, B.: Non-interactive Verifiable Computing: Outsourcing Computation to Untrusted Workers. In: Rabin, T. (ed.) CRYPTO 2010. LNCS, vol. 6223, pp. 465–482. Springer, Heidelberg (2010)

13. Gentry, C.: Fully homomorphic encryption using ideal lattices. In: Proceedings of the 41st Annual ACM Symposium on Theory of Computing, STOC 2009, pp. 169–178. ACM, New York (2009)

14. Gentry, C., Halevi, S.: Implementing Gentry's Fully-Homomorphic Encryption Scheme. In: Paterson, K.G. (ed.) EUROCRYPT 2011. LNCS, vol. 6632, pp. 129–148. Springer, Heidelberg (2011)

15. Goldwasser, S., Kalai, Y.T., Rothblum, G.N.: Delegating computation: interactive proofs for muggles. In: Proceedings of the 40th Annual ACM Symposium on Theory of Computing, STOC 2008, pp. 113–122. ACM, New York (2008)

16. Goyal, V., Pandey, O., Sahai, A., Waters, B.: Attribute-based encryption for fine-grained access control of encrypted data. In: Proceedings of the 13th ACM Conference on Computer and Communications Security, pp. 89–98 (2006)

17. Green, M., Hohenberger, S., Waters, B.: Outsourcing the decryption of abe ciphertexts. In: Proceedings of the 20th USENIX Conference on Security, SEC 2011, p. 34. USENIX Association, Berkeley (2011)

18. Hohenberger, S., Lysyanskaya, A.: How to Securely Outsource Cryptographic Computations. In: Kilian, J. (ed.) TCC 2005. LNCS, vol. 3378, pp. 264–282. Springer, Heidelberg (2005)

19. Jakobsson, M., Wetzel, S.: Secure Server-Aided Signature Generation. In: Kim, K.-C. (ed.) PKC 2001. LNCS, vol. 1992, pp. 383–401. Springer, Heidelberg (2001)

20. Lewko, A., Okamoto, T., Sahai, A., Takashima, K., Waters, B.: Fully Secure Functional Encryption: Attribute-Based Encryption and (Hierarchical) Inner Product Encryption. In: Gilbert, H. (ed.) EUROCRYPT 2010. LNCS, vol. 6110, pp. 62–91. Springer, Heidelberg (2010)

21. Li, J., Ren, K., Zhu, B., Wan, Z.: Privacy-Aware Attribute-Based Encryption with User Accountability. In: Samarati, P., Yung, M., Martinelli, F., Ardagna, C. (eds.) ISC 2009. LNCS, vol. 5735, pp. 347–362. Springer, Heidelberg (2009)

22. Ostrovsky, R., Sahai, A., Waters, B.: Attribute-based encryption with non-monotonic access structures. In: Proceedings of the 14th ACM Conference on Computer and Communications Security, CCS 2007, pp. 195–203. ACM, New York (2007)

23. Sahai, A.: Non-malleable non-interactive zero knowledge and adaptive chosen-ciphertext security. In: 40th Annual Symposium on Foundations of Computer Science, pp. 543–553 (1999)

24. Sahai, A., Seyalioglu, H., Waters, B.: Dynamic Credentials and Ciphertext Delegation for Attribute-Based Encryption. In: Safavi-Naini, R., Canetti, R. (eds.) CRYPTO 2012. LNCS, vol. 7417, pp. 199–217. Springer, Heidelberg (2012)

25. Sahai, A., Waters, B.: Fuzzy Identity-Based Encryption. In: Cramer, R. (ed.) EUROCRYPT 2005. LNCS, vol. 3494, pp. 457–473. Springer, Heidelberg (2005)

26. Waters, B.: Dual System Encryption: Realizing Fully Secure IBE and HIBE under Simple Assumptions. In: Halevi, S. (ed.) CRYPTO 2009. LNCS, vol. 5677, pp. 619–636. Springer, Heidelberg (2009)

27. Waters, B.: Ciphertext-Policy Attribute-Based Encryption: An Expressive, Efficient, and Provably Secure Realization. In: Catalano, D., Fazio, N., Gennaro, R., Nicolosi, A. (eds.) PKC 2011. LNCS, vol. 6571, pp. 53–70. Springer, Heidelberg (2011)

28. Zhou, Z., Huang, D.: Efficient and secure data storage operations for mobile cloud computing. Cryptology ePrint Archive, Report 2011/185 (2011)

# Security Enhancement
# of Identity-Based Identification with Reversibility

Atsushi Fujioka[1], Taiichi Saito[2], and Keita Xagawa[1]

[1] NTT Secure Platform Laboratories,
3-9-11 Midori-cho, Musashino-shi, Tokyo 180-8585, Japan
{fujioka.atsushi,xagawa.keita}@lab.ntt.co.jp
[2] Tokyo Denki University,
5 Senju Asahi-cho, Adachi-ku, Tokyo 120-8551, Japan
taiichi@c.dendai.ac.jp

**Abstract.** In this paper, we discuss security enhancement for a natural class of identity-based identification (IBI) protocols.

We first introduce *reversible $\Sigma$-type* IBI protocol, which is an extension of reversible identification protocol by Kurosawa and Heng.

We next propose a transformations from a reversible IBI protocol secure against static-identity and passive attacks to another one secure against adaptive-identity and (active and) concurrent attacks. The transformation requires no other cryptographic primitives and no additional number-theoretic assumptions, and the security proof is accomplished without the random oracles.

**Keywords:** identity-based identification, reversible $\Sigma$-type identification, impersonation under active and concurrent attacks.

## 1 Introduction

Identification is an important research topic in information and communication security, and *identity-based identification* (IBI) provides functionality of identification in *identity-based setting* [15]. The functionality is realized with a protocol between a *prover* and a *verifier*, where the prover wants to show the identity to the verifier, and the verifier needs not to have any other information related to the prover except the prover's identity. For engaging the protocol, IBI requires a *private key generator* (PKG) as other identity-based cryptographic primitives do so. The PKG publishes a public parameter to setup an identification system. It generates a secret key corresponding to a given identity of an entity, and gives the secret key to the entity. The entity performs identification with the given secret key. Thus, this concludes that IBI has three phases: SETUP, EXTRACT, and IDENTIFICATION.

Security of IBI protocols is defined by an experiment of an adversary who acts as (cheating) verifiers to gather much knowledge in the *learning phase* after the *setup phase* and then acts as a (cheating) prover to impersonate some entity in the *challenge phase*. We say that the protocol is secure when the probability that, in the experiment, the adversary succeeds in impersonation is negligible.

T.W. Chim and T.H. Yuen (Eds.): ICICS 2012, LNCS 7618, pp. 202–213, 2012.

The first security formulation for IBI was given by Kurosawa and Heng [11], and Bellare, Namprempre, and Neven provided formal descriptions of IBI [2].

A strong security notion of IBI protocols is defined as *security against impersonation under concurrent attacks* [3]. Roughly speaking, an adversary in the security model against impersonation under passive attacks (called imp-pa *model* [3]) is only allowed to eavesdrop communications in identification, though an adversary in the security model against impersonation under active attacks (called imp-aa *model* [3]) is allowed to *sequentially* access entities who prove their identities. If an identification protocol is secure against an adversary is allowed to *concurrently* access entities who prove their identities, it is said to be secure against impersonation under concurrent attacks (imp-ca *secure* [3]).

In addition, the security notions of IBI protocols are classified depending on selection of identities. The imp-atk security is also called *security against impersonation under adaptive-identity attacks* (adapt-id-imp-atk *security*) [2,14], where atk denotes a type of attacks such that atk $\in \{$pa, aa, ca$\}$. We can consider a weak version of the adapt-id-imp-atk security such that an adversary requests secret keys of identities only at the beginning of the learning phase, which is called *security against impersonation under static-identity attacks* (stat-id-imp-atk *security*) [14].

**Security Enhancement of Identity-Based Identification.** Along with these formulations, a few security enhancement techniques have been investigated [7,14]. A well-known OR-proof technique [7] enhances the security of standard identification protocols from the passive security to the concurrent security. Moreover, it is applicable also to IBI protocols, if the underlying IBI protocol is $\Sigma$-*type* [8], which is a similar property to $\Sigma$-*protocol* [6]. Furthermore, Rückert proposed another security enhancement technique which can convert a stat-id-imp-atk secure IBI protocol to an imp-atk secure IBI protocol where atk denotes a type of attacks such that atk $\in \{$pa, aa, ca$\}$ [14]. The technique is applicable to any IBI protocols, however, it needs a chameleon hash function [10] as an additional cryptographic primitive.

Though both the techniques do not require the random oracles [4] for their security proofs, a chameleon hash function is still necessary when we convert a stat-id-imp-pa secure IBI protocol to an adapt-id-imp-ca secure one combining the OR-proof technique and the Rückert technique. To the best of our knowledge, there is no security enhancement transformation from a stat-id-imp-pa secure IBI protocol to an adapt-id-imp-ca secure one without an additional primitive.

**Our Contributions.** We first introduce *reversible $\Sigma$-type* IBI protocol, which is an extension of reversible identification protocol by Kurosawa and Heng [12]. When we apply the identity-based construction [2] to a reversible identification [12], we obtain a reversible $\Sigma$-type IBI protocol. We also note that many IBI protocols from signature schemes in [11] are reversible $\Sigma$-type.

We next propose a transformations from a stat-id-imp-pa secure reversible IBI protocol to another adapt-id-imp-ca secure one. The transformation requires no other cryptographic primitives and no additional number-theoretic assumptions, and the security proof is accomplished without the random oracles.

**Organization.** We give a definition of identity-based identification and a related notion in **Section 2**. **Section 3** provides a security enhancement technique, its security proof and discussions with the related works.

## 2   Definitions

In this section, we present a definition of identity-based identification (IBI) protocols and introduce a property similar to $\Sigma$-type [8]. We adopt the definition of IBI protocols in [2].

**Identity-Based Identification.** We adopt the definition of IBI protocols in [2]. Let IBI = (SetUp, KG, P, V) be an IBI protocol, where SetUp is the master-key-generation algorithm that on input $1^\kappa$ outputs $mpk$ and $msk$, KG is the user-key-generation algorithm that on input $(mpk, msk, id)$ outputs $sk_{id}$, P is the prover algorithm that, taking inputs $mpk$, $id$ and $sk_{id}$, interacts with V, and V is the verifier algorithm that, taking inputs $mpk$ and $id$, interacts with P and finally outputs $dec \in \{accept, reject\}$.

The PKG uses SetUp to generate master public key $mpk$ and secret key $msk$, publicizes $mpk$ and keeps $msk$ secret. It also uses KG to generate a secret key $sk_{id}$ for the entity of an identity $id$. The entity having $id$ uses P, as a prover. The prover interacts with another entity who uses V as a verifier to convince the verifier that the identity is $id$. If both the entities correctly follows the protocol, V outputs $accept$.

We describe the formal definitions of security of IBI based on the following experiments $\mathbf{Exp}_{\mathsf{IBI},\mathcal{I}}^{\mathsf{adapt\text{-}id\text{-}imp\text{-}atk}}(\kappa)$ between a challenger and an impersonator $\mathcal{I} = (\mathsf{CV}, \mathsf{CP})$, where atk denotes a type of attacks such that atk $\in \{\mathsf{pa}, \mathsf{aa}, \mathsf{ca}\}$.

**Experiment $\mathbf{Exp}_{\mathsf{IBI},\mathcal{I}}^{\mathsf{adapt\text{-}id\text{-}imp\text{-}atk}}(\kappa)$:**

   **Setup Phase:** The challenger obtains $(mpk, msk) \leftarrow \mathsf{SetUp}(1^\kappa)$ and initializes $HU, CU, TU, PS \leftarrow \emptyset$, where $HU$, $CU$, and $TU$ denote the sets of honest users, corrupted users, and target users, respectively, and $PS$ denotes the set of provers' sessions. The impersonator CV is given the security parameter $1^\kappa$ and the master public key $mpk$.

   **Learning Phase:** The impersonator CV can query to the oracles INIT, CORR and CONV when atk = pa, and also to PROV when atk = {aa, ca}. Note that $id \notin HU \setminus TU$ means that $id$ is target user, corrupted user, or non-initiated user.

   - The oracle INIT receives input $id$. If $id \in HU \cup CU \cup TU$, then INIT returns $\perp$. Otherwise, it obtains $sk_{id} \leftarrow \mathsf{KG}(mpk, msk, id)$, adds $id$ to $HU$, and provides CV with $id$.
   - The oracle CORR receives input $id$. If $id \notin HU \setminus TU$, then CORR returns $\perp$. Otherwise, it adds $id$ to $CU$, deletes $id$ from $HU$, and returns $sk_{id}$ to CV.

- The oracle CONV receives input $id$. If $id \notin HU$, then CONV returns $\perp$. Otherwise it returns a transcript of a transaction between the prover with identity $id$ and a verifier.
- (only when atk = aa) The oracle PROV receives inputs $id$, $s$, and $M_{in}$. If $id \notin HU \setminus TU$, then PROV returns $\perp$. Otherwise if $PS = \emptyset$, it sets $PS = \{(id, s)\}$, picks a random coin $\rho$, and sets a state of the prover $st_{\mathsf{P}}[(id, s)] \leftarrow (mpk, sk_{id}, \rho)$. Next, it obtains $(M_{out}, st_{\mathsf{P}}[(id, s)]) \leftarrow \mathsf{P}(M_{in}, st_{\mathsf{P}}[(id, s)])$. Finally, it returns $M_{out}$. If $M_{out}$ is the final message of the protocol, PROV sets $PS \leftarrow \emptyset$.
- (only when atk = ca) The oracle PROV receives inputs $id$, $s$, and $M_{in}$. If $id \notin HU \setminus TU$, then PROV returns $\perp$. If $(id, s) \notin PS$, then it adds $(id, s)$ to $PS$, picks a random coin $\rho$, and sets a state of the prover $st_{\mathsf{P}}[(id, s)] \leftarrow (mpk, sk_{id}, \rho)$. Next, it obtains $(M_{out}, st_{\mathsf{P}}[(id, s)]) \leftarrow \mathsf{P}(M_{in}, st_{\mathsf{P}}[(id, s)])$. Finally, it returns $M_{out}$.

**Challenge Phase:** CV outputs a target identity $id^*$ and $st_{\mathsf{CP}}$. If $id^*$ is not in $HU$ then the challenger outputs 0 and halts. Otherwise, the challenger sets $TU \leftarrow \{id^*\}$, and gives $st_{\mathsf{CP}}$ to CP. CP can query to the oracles INIT, CORR, and CONV, (and PROV when atk = aa or ca) as in the learning phase. Finally, the challenger obtains $(tr, dec) \leftarrow \mathbf{Run}[\mathsf{CP}(st_{\mathsf{CP}})^{\mathrm{INIT},\mathrm{CORR},\mathrm{CONV}(,\mathrm{PROV})} \leftrightarrow \mathsf{V}(mpk, id^*)]$ and outputs $dec$.

In the case of atk = aa, the PROV oracle allows only a single session at a time. On the other hand, in the case of atk = ca, it allows multiple sessions at the same time.

**Definition 2.1.** *Let* $\mathsf{IBI} = (\mathsf{SetUp}, \mathsf{KG}, \mathsf{P}, \mathsf{V})$ *be an IBI protocol and* $\mathcal{I} = (\mathsf{CV}, \mathsf{CP})$ *an impersonator. Let* $\kappa$ *be a security parameter. The advantage of* $\mathcal{I}$ *in attacking* $\mathsf{IBI}$ *is defined by*

$$\mathbf{Adv}_{\mathsf{IBI},\mathcal{I}}^{\mathsf{adapt\text{-}id\text{-}imp\text{-}atk}}(\kappa) := \Pr\left[\ \mathbf{Exp}_{\mathsf{IBI},\mathcal{I}}^{\mathsf{adapt\text{-}id\text{-}imp\text{-}atk}}(\kappa) = accept\ \right].$$

*We say that an IBI protocol,* $\mathsf{IBI}$, *is* secure against impersonation under adaptive-identity and concurrent attacks (adapt-id-imp-ca secure) *if* $\mathbf{Adv}_{\mathsf{IBI},\mathcal{I}}^{\mathsf{adapt\text{-}id\text{-}imp\text{-}ca}}(\kappa)$ *is negligible for every polynomial-time impersonator* $\mathcal{I}$, *is* secure against impersonation under adaptive-identity and active attacks (adapt-id-imp-aa secure) *if* $\mathbf{Adv}_{\mathsf{IBI},\mathcal{I}}^{\mathsf{adapt\text{-}id\text{-}imp\text{-}aa}}(\kappa)$ *is negligible for every polynomial-time impersonator* $\mathcal{I}$, *and is* secure against impersonation under adaptive-identity and passive attacks (adapt-id-imp-pa secure) *if* $\mathbf{Adv}_{\mathsf{IBI},\mathcal{I}}^{\mathsf{adapt\text{-}id\text{-}imp\text{-}pa}}(\kappa)$ *is negligible for every polynomial-time impersonator* $\mathcal{I}$.

According to [14], we also describe a weaker security definition of IBI based on the following experiments $\mathbf{Exp}_{\mathsf{IBI},\mathcal{I}}^{\mathsf{stat\text{-}id\text{-}imp\text{-}atk}}(\kappa)$ (atk $\in \{\mathsf{pa}, \mathsf{aa}, \mathsf{ca}\}$) between a challenger and an impersonator $\mathcal{I} = (\mathsf{CV}, \mathsf{CP})$.

**Experiment** $\mathbf{Exp}_{\mathsf{IBI},\mathcal{I}}^{\mathsf{stat\text{-}id\text{-}imp\text{-}atk}}(\kappa)$:

**Setup Phase:** At the beginning of this phase, the impersonator CV issues a single corruption query $(id_1, \ldots, id_t)$ to the challenger before seeing master public key. The challenger is given the security parameter $1^\kappa$, obtains $(mpk, msk) \leftarrow \mathsf{SetUp}(1^\kappa)$, and computes $sk_{id_i} \leftarrow \mathsf{KG}(mpk, msk, id_i)$ for all $i$ $(1 \leq i \leq t)$. It sets $CU \leftarrow \{id_1, id_2, \ldots, id_t\}$ and then returns $(sk_{id_1}, \ldots, sk_{id_t})$ to $\mathsf{CV}$. The challenger initializes $HU$, $TU$, $PS \leftarrow \emptyset$. The impersonator $\mathsf{CV}$ is given the security parameter $1^\kappa$ and the master public key $mpk$.

**Learning and Challenge Phases:** The learning and challenge phases are defined as the same way as those in the experiments $\mathbf{Exp}_{\mathsf{IBI},\mathcal{I}}^{\mathsf{adapt\text{-}id\text{-}imp\text{-}atk}}(\kappa)$, except that the impersonator $\mathcal{I}$ is not allowed to additional queries to CORR during these phases.

**Definition 2.2.** *Let* $\mathsf{IBI} = (\mathsf{SetUp}, \mathsf{KG}, \mathsf{P}, \mathsf{V})$ *be an IBI protocol and* $\mathcal{I} = (\mathsf{CV}, \mathsf{CP})$ *an impersonator. Let* $\kappa$ *be a security parameter. The advantage of* $\mathcal{I}$ *in attacking* $\mathsf{IBI}$ *is defined by*

$$\mathbf{Adv}_{\mathsf{IBI},\mathcal{I}}^{\mathsf{stat\text{-}id\text{-}imp\text{-}atk}}(\kappa) := \Pr\left[\ \mathbf{Exp}_{\mathsf{IBI},\mathcal{I}}^{\mathsf{stat\text{-}id\text{-}imp\text{-}atk}}(\kappa) = accept\ \right].$$

*We say that* $\mathsf{IBI}$ *is* secure against impersonation under static-identity and concurrent attacks (stat-id-imp-ca secure) *if* $\mathbf{Adv}_{\mathsf{IBI},\mathcal{I}}^{\mathsf{stat\text{-}id\text{-}imp\text{-}ca}}(\kappa)$ *is negligible for every polynomial-time* $\mathcal{I}$, *is* secure against impersonation under static-identity and active attacks (stat-id-imp-aa secure) *if* $\mathbf{Adv}_{\mathsf{IBI},\mathcal{I}}^{\mathsf{stat\text{-}id\text{-}imp\text{-}aa}}(\kappa)$ *is negligible for every polynomial-time* $\mathcal{I}$, *and is* secure against impersonation under static-identity and passive attacks (stat-id-imp-pa secure) *if* $\mathbf{Adv}_{\mathsf{IBI},\mathcal{I}}^{\mathsf{stat\text{-}id\text{-}imp\text{-}pa}}(\kappa)$ *is negligible for every polynomial-time* $\mathcal{I}$.

**Reversible $\Sigma$-Type IBI Protocol.** We define an analogue of $\Sigma$-protocols in the context of IBI protocols. Let $\mathsf{IBI} = (\mathsf{SetUp}, \mathsf{KG}, \mathsf{P}, \mathsf{V})$ be an identity-based identification protocol.

Suppose that communication between $\mathsf{P}$ and $\mathsf{V}$ is realized by the following three-move protocol through which five polynomial-time algorithms ($\Sigma_{\mathsf{ibi\text{-}gnc}}$, $\Sigma_{\mathsf{ibi\text{-}cmt}}$, $\Sigma_{\mathsf{ibi\text{-}clg}}$, $\Sigma_{\mathsf{ibi\text{-}rsp}}$, $\Sigma_{\mathsf{ibi\text{-}chk}}$) are used, and that $\Sigma_{\mathsf{ibi\text{-}cmt}}$, $\Sigma_{\mathsf{ibi\text{-}rsp}}$, and $\Sigma_{\mathsf{ibi\text{-}chk}}$ are deterministic.

$\mathsf{P} \to \mathsf{V}$: $\mathsf{P}$ computes $r \leftarrow \Sigma_{\mathsf{ibi\text{-}gnc}}(mpk, id)$, $x = \Sigma_{\mathsf{ibi\text{-}cmt}}(mpk, id, r)$ and sends $x$ to $\mathsf{V}$.
$\mathsf{V} \to \mathsf{P}$: $\mathsf{V}$ computes $c \leftarrow \Sigma_{\mathsf{ibi\text{-}clg}}(mpk, id)$ and sends $c$ to $\mathsf{P}$.
$\mathsf{P} \to \mathsf{V}$: $\mathsf{P}$ computes $y = \Sigma_{\mathsf{ibi\text{-}rsp}}(mpk, id, sk_{id}, r, c)$ and sends $y$ to $\mathsf{V}$.
$\mathsf{V}$: $\mathsf{V}$ outputs $accept$ if $x = \Sigma_{\mathsf{ibi\text{-}chk}}(mpk, id, c, y)$ holds, and, $reject$ otherwise.

Let $\mathrm{RND}_{(mpk,id)}$ denote a set $\{r \mid r \leftarrow \Sigma_{\mathsf{ibi\text{-}gnc}}(mpk, id)\}$, and assume that $r$ is uniformly distributed over $\mathrm{RND}_{(mpk,id)}$.

We call this type of three-move IBI protocols *canonical*, and moreover, we call an IBI protocol $\mathsf{IBI}$ *reversible $\Sigma$-type* if it is canonical and satisfies three properties: *y-uniformity*, *special soundness*, *special commitment*, and *special response*.

**$y$-Uniformity:** Let $\mathrm{RES}_{(mpk,id)}$ be a set $\{y \mid y \leftarrow \Sigma_{\mathsf{ibi\text{-}rsp}}(mpk, id, sk_{id}, r, c), c \leftarrow \Sigma_{\mathsf{ibi\text{-}clg}}(mpk, id), r \in \mathrm{RND}_{(mpk,id)}\}$. For any fixed $(mpk, id, sk_{id}, c)$,

$y = \Sigma_{\text{ibi-rsp}}(mpk, id, sk_{id}, r, c)$ is uniformly distributed over $\text{RES}_{(mpk,id)}$ if $r$ is uniformly distributed over $\text{RND}_{(mpk,id)}$.

**Special Soundness:** We can compute the user secret key $sk_{id}$ for an identity $id$ from $mpk$, $id$ and two accepting transcripts $(x, c, y)$ and $(x, \tilde{c}, \tilde{y})$ such that $c \neq \tilde{c}$. That is, there is a polynomial-time algorithm $\Sigma_{\text{ibi-ext}}$ that takes as inputs $mpk$, $id$ and two transcripts $(x, c, y)$ and $(x, \tilde{c}, \tilde{y})$ satisfying $x = \Sigma_{\text{ibi-chk}}(mpk, id, c, y) = \Sigma_{\text{ibi-chk}}(mpk, id, \tilde{c}, \tilde{y})$ and $c \neq \tilde{c}$, and outputs $sk_{id}$.

**Special Commitment:** We can compute $r$ from $mpk$, $id$, $sk_{id}$, $c$, $y$ such that $\Sigma_{\text{ibi-cmt}}(mpk, id, r) = \Sigma_{\text{ibi-chk}}(mpk, id, c, y)$. That is, there is a polynomial-time algorithm $\Sigma_{\text{ibi-rvs}}$ that takes as inputs $mpk$, $id$, $sk_{id}$, $c$, and $y$, and outputs $r$.

**Special Response:** We can generate $y$ only from $mpk$ and $id$ such that for some $r$ and $c$, $\Sigma_{\text{ibi-cmt}}(mpk, id, r) = \Sigma_{\text{ibi-chk}}(mpk, id, c, y)$ holds, and the generated $y$ is randomly and uniformly distributed over $\text{RES}_{(mpk,id)}$. That is, there is a polynomial-time algorithm $\Sigma_{\text{ibi-gnr}}$ that takes as inputs $mpk$ and $id$, and outputs $y$.

Note that the $y$-uniformity and special response properties imply the following *special zero-knowledge* property.

**Special Zero-Knowledge:** We can obtain an accepting transcript from a challenge $c$, $mpk$ and $id$. That is, there is a polynomial-time algorithm $\Sigma_{\text{ibi-sim}}$ that takes on inputs $mpk$, $id$ and $c$ such that $c \leftarrow \Sigma_{\text{ibi-clg}}(mpk, id)$, runs $y \leftarrow \Sigma_{\text{ibi-gnr}}(mpk, id)$ and $x \leftarrow \Sigma_{\text{ibi-chk}}(mpk, id, c, y)$, and outputs $(x, y)$. The distribution of transcripts generated by $\Sigma_{\text{ibi-clg}}$ and $\Sigma_{\text{ibi-sim}}$ is indistinguishable from that of real transcripts.

# 3 Proposed Security Enhancement Transformations

## 3.1 Description

Here we propose a generic transformation that converts any stat-id-imp-pa secure reversible $\Sigma$-type IBI protocol into an adapt-id-imp-ca secure IBI one. We note that, in conversion, $x$ and $id$ are treated as challenges. Our transformation modifies a three-move transaction $(x, c, y)$ of the underlying protocol into another three-move one $((X', Y', X''), c, (x, y, Y''))$ such that $Y' \leftarrow \Sigma_{\text{ibi-gnr}}(mpk, \tilde{id})$, $X' = \Sigma_{\text{ibi-chk}}(mpk, \tilde{id}, id, Y')$, $Y'' \leftarrow \Sigma_{\text{ibi-gnr}}(mpk, \tilde{id})$, and $X'' = \Sigma_{\text{ibi-chk}}(mpk, \tilde{id}, x, Y'')$, where $\tilde{id}$ is a fixed string called *master identity* and is a part of master public key for the constructed IBI protocol.

Let $\text{IBI}' = (\text{SetUp}', \text{KG}', \text{P}', \text{V}')$ be a reversible $\Sigma$-type IBI protocol, where $(\text{P}', \text{V}')$ is realized by $(\Sigma'_{\text{ibi-gnc}}, \Sigma'_{\text{ibi-cmt}}, \Sigma'_{\text{ibi-clg}}, \Sigma'_{\text{ibi-rsp}}, \Sigma'_{\text{ibi-chk}})$ and the $y$-uniformity, special soundness, and special commitment properties are shown by $(\Sigma'_{\text{ibi-gnr}}, \Sigma'_{\text{ibi-ext}}, \Sigma'_{\text{ibi-rvs}})$.

From this $\Sigma$-type IBI protocol $\text{IBI}'$, we construct another IBI protocol $\text{IBI} = (\text{SetUp}, \text{KG}, \text{P}, \text{V})$ as follows.

**SetUp:** It takes as input $1^\kappa$, runs $(mpk', msk') \leftarrow \text{SetUp}'(1^\kappa)$, $(mpk'', msk'') \leftarrow \text{SetUp}'(1^\kappa)$, chooses a master identity $\tilde{id}$, and outputs $(mpk, msk) = ((mpk', mpk'', \tilde{id}), msk')$.

KG: It takes as input $(mpk, msk, id)$, parses $mpk$ and $msk$ as $mpk = (mpk', mpk'', \tilde{id})$ and $msk = msk'$, respectively, runs $Y'_{id} \leftarrow \Sigma'_{\text{ibi-gnr}}(mpk'', \tilde{id})$, $X'_{id} = \Sigma'_{\text{ibi-chk}}(mpk'', \tilde{id}, id, Y'_{id})$, $sk'_{id} \leftarrow \text{KG}'(mpk', msk', X'_{id})$ and outputs $sk_{id} = (sk'_{id}, X'_{id}, Y'_{id})$.

P: P takes as input $(mpk, id, sk_{id})$, and parses $mpk$ and $sk_{id}$ as $mpk = (mpk', mpk'', \tilde{id})$ and $sk_{id} = (sk'_{id}, X'_{id}, Y'_{id})$, respectively.

V: V takes as input $(mpk, id)$, and parses $mpk$ as $mpk = (mpk', mpk'', \tilde{id})$.

P → V: P computes $r \leftarrow \Sigma'_{\text{ibi-gnc}}(mpk', X'_{id})$, $x = \Sigma'_{\text{ibi-cmt}}(mpk', X'_{id}, r)$, $Y'' \leftarrow \Sigma'_{\text{ibi-gnr}}(mpk'', \tilde{id})$, $X'' = \Sigma'_{\text{ibi-chk}}(mpk'', \tilde{id}, x, Y'')$, and sends $(X'_{id}, Y'_{id}, X'')$ to V.

V → P: V computes $c \leftarrow \Sigma'_{\text{ibi-clg}}(mpk', X'_{id})$ and sends $c$ to P.

P → V: P computes $y = \Sigma'_{\text{ibi-rsp}}(mpk', X'_{id}, sk'_{id}, r, c)$ and sends $(x, y, Y'')$ to V.

V: V outputs $accept$ if $x = \Sigma'_{\text{ibi-chk}}(mpk', X'_{id}, c, y)$, $X'_{id} = \Sigma'_{\text{ibi-chk}}(mpk'', \tilde{id}, id, Y'_{id})$ and $X'' = \Sigma'_{\text{ibi-chk}}(mpk'', \tilde{id}, x, Y'')$ hold, and, $reject$ otherwise.

SETUP

| $\text{SetUp}(1^\kappa)$ |
| --- |
| $(mpk', msk') \leftarrow \text{SetUp}'(1^\kappa)$ |
| $(mpk'', msk'') \leftarrow \text{SetUp}'(1^\kappa)$ |
| choose a master identity $\tilde{id}$ |
| output $(mpk, msk) = ((mpk', mpk'', \tilde{id}), msk')$ |

EXTRACT

| $\text{KG}(mpk, msk, id)$ |
| --- |
| $mpk = (mpk', mpk'', \tilde{id})$ |
| $msk = msk'$ |
| $Y'_{id} \leftarrow \Sigma'_{\text{ibi-gnr}}(mpk'', \tilde{id})$ |
| $X'_{id} = \Sigma'_{\text{ibi-chk}}(mpk'', \tilde{id}, id, Y'_{id})$ |
| $sk'_{id} \leftarrow \text{KG}'(mpk', msk', X'_{id})$ |
| outputs $sk_{id} = (sk'_{id}, X'_{id}, Y'_{id})$ |

IDENTIFICATION

| $\text{P}(mpk, id, sk_{id})$ | | $\text{V}(mpk, id)$ |
| --- | --- | --- |
| $mpk = (mpk', mpk'', \tilde{id})$ | | $mpk = (mpk', mpk'', \tilde{id})$ |
| $sk_{id} = (sk'_{id}, X'_{id}, Y'_{id})$ | | |
| $r \leftarrow \Sigma'_{\text{ibi-gnc}}(mpk', X'_{id})$ | | |
| $x = \Sigma'_{\text{ibi-cmt}}(mpk', X'_{id}, r)$ | | |
| $Y'' \leftarrow \Sigma'_{\text{ibi-gnr}}(mpk'', \tilde{id})$ | | |
| $X'' = \Sigma'_{\text{ibi-chk}}(mpk'', \tilde{id}, x, Y'')$ | $\xrightarrow{(X'_{id}, Y'_{id}, X'')}$ | |
| | $\xleftarrow{\quad c \quad}$ | $c \leftarrow \Sigma'_{\text{ibi-clg}}(mpk', X'_{id})$ |
| $y = \Sigma'_{\text{ibi-rsp}}(mpk', X'_{id}, sk_{id}, r, c)$ | | |
| | $\xrightarrow{(x, y, Y'')}$ | check $x = \Sigma'_{\text{ibi-chk}}(mpk', X'_{id}, c, y)$, |
| | | $X'_{id} = \Sigma'_{\text{ibi-chk}}(mpk'', \tilde{id}, id, Y'_{id})$, and |
| | | $X'' = \Sigma'_{\text{ibi-chk}}(mpk'', \tilde{id}, x, Y'')$ |
| | | output $accept$ if all hold; |
| | | otherwise, output $reject$ |

**Fig. 1.** Proposed Transformation

## 3.2   Security

In this section, we show that the proposed transformation can enhance the security of reversible $\Sigma$-type IBI protocols from the security against impersonation under static-identity and passive attacks (i.e., stat-id-imp-pa security) to the security against impersonation under adaptive-identity and (active and) concurrent attacks (i.e., adapt-id-imp-ca security).

**Theorem 3.1.** *If there exists a* stat-id-imp-pa *secure reversible $\Sigma$-type IBI protocol, then there exists an* adapt-id-imp-ca *secure IBI protocol.*

*Proof (Sketch).* Suppose that there exists an adapt-id-imp-ca impersonator, $\mathcal{I} =$ (CV, CP), against IBI. We construct a stat-id-imp-pa impersonator, $\mathcal{I}' =$ (CV', CP'), against IBI'. Here we outline the construction.

Suppose that $\mathcal{I}'$ obtains two accepting transcripts $((X'_{id^*}, Y'_{id^*}, X''), c, (x, y, Y''))$ and $((X'_{id^*}, Y'_{id^*}, X''), \tilde{c}, (\tilde{x}, \tilde{y}, \tilde{Y}''))$ by rewinding $\mathcal{I}$. There are two cases that (A) $x \neq \tilde{x}$ or (B) $x = \tilde{x}$. We call the impersonator $\mathcal{I}$ that makes the former and latter transcripts a type A and type B impersonator, respectively.

**From Type A Impersonator:** We first describe the case that $\mathcal{I}$ is a type A impersonator, because it is easier. In the setup phase of the static-identity experiment, $\mathcal{I}'$ issues no corruption query to its stat-id-imp-pa challenger. $\mathcal{I}'$ receives $mpk_e$ from the challenger. It generates $(mpk_s, msk_s) \leftarrow$ SetUp'$(1^\kappa)$, chooses $\tilde{id}$, and sets $mpk' = mpk_s$, $mpk'' = mpk_e$, and $mpk = (mpk', mpk'', \tilde{id})$. $\mathcal{I}'$ starts the experiment with the impersonator $\mathcal{I}$ by feeding $mpk$.

In the learning phase, since $\mathcal{I}'$ has $msk'$, it can generate $sk'_{id}$ and then $sk_{id}$. Thus, $\mathcal{I}'$ can perfectly simulate the oracles.

In the challenge phase, $\mathcal{I}$ declares the target identity $id^*$, and then, $\mathcal{I}'$ declares $\tilde{id}$ as the target identity. $\mathcal{I}'$ rewinds $\mathcal{I}$ and obtains two transcripts $((X'_{id^*}, Y'_{id^*}, X''), c, (x, y, Y''))$ and $((X'_{id^*}, Y'_{id^*}, X''), \tilde{c}, (\tilde{x}, \tilde{y}, \tilde{Y}''))$. We can classify the transcripts into two cases: If $X'_{id^*}$ has already been generated for a distinct identity $id \neq id^*$, then $\mathcal{I}'$ obtains two accepting transcripts under $mpk''$ and $\tilde{id}$, that is, $(X'_{id^*}, id^*, Y'_{id^*})$ and $(X'_{id}, id, Y'_{id})$ with $X'_{id^*} = X'_{id}$. $\mathcal{I}'$ can extract $sk_{\tilde{id}}$ from the two transcripts due to the special soundness property, and wins the stat-id-imp-pa experiment. Otherwise, it has the transcripts for distinct $x$ and $\tilde{x}$. It extracts $sk_{\tilde{id}}$ from the two accepting transcripts, $(X'', x, Y'')$ and $(X'', \tilde{x}, \tilde{Y}'')$ under $mpk''$ and $\tilde{id}$ due to the special soundness property, and wins the stat-id-imp-pa experiment.

**From Type B Impersonator:** We next consider the case that $\mathcal{I}$ is a type B impersonator. Let $Q$ be an upperbound of the number of the INIT queries from $\mathcal{I}$. In the setup phase of the static-identity experiment, $\mathcal{I}'$ generates $(mpk_s, msk_s) \leftarrow$ SetUp'$(1^\kappa)$, chooses $\tilde{id}$, and sets $mpk'' = mpk_s$. $\mathcal{I}'$ then guesses $i^* \in \{1, \ldots, Q\}$ such that in the $i^*$-th INIT query, $\mathcal{I}$ initializes the target identity $id^*$. Next, $\mathcal{I}'$ generates $sk''_{\tilde{id}} \leftarrow$ KG'$(mpk'', msk'', \tilde{id})$. $\mathcal{I}'$ generates $Q$ random identities $id'_i$ $(1 \leq i \leq Q)$, converts $id'_i$ to $X'_i$ with $\hat{Y}_i$ using $mpk''$, and issues a corruption query $(X'_1, \ldots, X'_{i^*-1}, X'_{i^*+1}, \ldots, X'_Q)$ to the challenger. Then $\mathcal{I}'$ receives the secret keys $(sk'_1, \ldots, sk'_{i^*-1}, sk'_{i^*+1}, \ldots, sk'_Q)$ for $(X'_1, \ldots, X'_{i^*-1},$

$X_{i^*+1}, \ldots, X'_Q)$ and the master public key $mpk_e$. It sets $mpk' = mpk_e$ and sets $mpk = (mpk', mpk'', \tilde{id})$ (see Fig. 2). $\mathcal{I}'$ starts the experiment with $\mathcal{I}$ by feeding $mpk$.

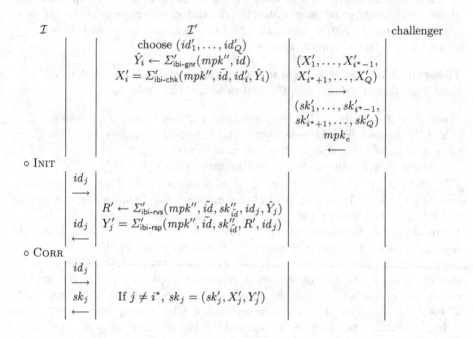

**Fig. 2.** Sketch of INIT and CORR oracle simulation

In the learning phase, $\mathcal{I}'$ answers the oracle queries as follows: On an INIT query $id_j$, $\mathcal{I}$ computes $Y'_j$ such that $X'_j = \Sigma'_{\text{ibi-chk}}(mpk'', \tilde{id}, id_j, Y'_j)$ by using $\Sigma'_{\text{ibi-rvs}}$ and $\Sigma'_{\text{ibi-rsp}}$. On a CORR query $id$, if $id = id_{i^*}$ then $\mathcal{I}$ aborts. Otherwise, since $id = id_j$ for $j \neq i^*$, $\mathcal{I}$ can return $sk_{id} = (sk'_j, X'_j, Y'_j)$ (see Fig. 2).

On a PROV query $id_i$ ($id_i \neq id_{i^*}$), $\mathcal{I}$ answers the query by using $sk_{id} = (sk'_i, X'_i, Y'_i)$. The problem arises on $id_{i^*}$, since $\mathcal{I}'$ does not have $sk'_{i^*}$. Even in this case, $\mathcal{I}'$ can simulate $id_{i^*}$ by using $sk''_{id}$. Given $id_{i^*}$ with a session $s$, then it simulates the conversation $(\hat{x}, \hat{c}, \hat{y})$ and the commitment $X''$ of $\hat{x}$, and returns $(X'_{i^*}, Y'_{i^*}, X'')$. On the query $(id_{i^*}, s, c)$, it newly generates the conversation $(x, c, y)$ and computes a decommitment $Y''$ by using $sk''_{id}$ and $x$. Then, it returns $(x, y, Y'')$ (see Fig. 3).

In the challenge phase of the inner experiment, $\mathcal{I}$ declares the target identity $id^*$. We see that $id^* = id_{i^*}$ occurs with probability $1/Q$. Otherwise, $\mathcal{I}'$ aborts. $\mathcal{I}'$ randomly chooses two challenges $c$ and $\tilde{c}$ and obtains two transcripts $((X'_{id^*}, Y'_{id^*}, X''), c, (x, y, Y''))$ and $((X'_{id^*}, Y'_{id^*}, X''), \tilde{c}, (\tilde{x}, \tilde{y}, \tilde{Y}''))$. Suppose that both transcripts are accepted. If $X'_{id^*}$ equals to $X'_i$ for $i \neq i^*$, then $\mathcal{I}'$ aborts. If $x \neq \tilde{x}$ then $\mathcal{I}'$ aborts. Otherwise, $\mathcal{I}'$ obtains two accepting transcripts $(x, c, y)$ and $(x, \tilde{c}, \tilde{y})$ under $mpk'$ and $X'_{id^*} = X'_{i^*}$. Due to the special soundness, $\mathcal{I}'$

$$
\begin{array}{c|l}
\mathcal{I} & \mathcal{I}' \\
\circ \text{ PROV} & \\
\end{array}
$$

$$
\begin{array}{ccl}
& \xrightarrow{\ id_{i*}\ } & \hat{c} \leftarrow \Sigma'_{\text{ibi-clg}}(mpk', X'_{i*}) \\
& & \hat{y} \leftarrow \Sigma'_{\text{ibi-gnr}}(mpk', X'_{i*}) \\
& & \hat{x} = \Sigma'_{\text{ibi-chk}}(mpk', X'_{i*}, \hat{c}, \hat{y}) \\
& & \hat{Y} \leftarrow \Sigma'_{\text{ibi-gnr}}(mpk'', \tilde{id}) \\
& \xleftarrow{\ (X'_{i*}, Y'_{i*}, X'')\ } & X'' = \Sigma'_{\text{ibi-chk}}(mpk'', \tilde{id}, \hat{x}, \hat{Y}) \\[2mm]
& \xrightarrow{\ c\ } & y \leftarrow \Sigma'_{\text{ibi-gnr}}(mpk', X'_{i*}) \\
& & x \leftarrow \Sigma'_{\text{ibi-chk}}(mpk', X'_{i*}, c, y) \\
& & R \leftarrow \Sigma'_{\text{ibi-rvs}}(mpk'', \tilde{id}, sk''_{\tilde{id}}, x, \hat{Y}) \\
& \xleftarrow{\ (x, y, Y'')\ } & Y'' = \Sigma'_{\text{ibi-rsp}}(mpk'', \tilde{id}, sk''_{\tilde{id}}, R, x) \\
\end{array}
$$

**Fig. 3.** Sketch of PROV oracle simulation on $id_{i*}$

can extract $sk_{i*}$. Then, $\mathcal{I}'$ declares $X'_{i*}$ as the target identity and can win the stat-id-imp-pa experiment.                                                             □

Due to page limitation, the proof of Theorem 3.1 is given in the final version of this paper.

### 3.3   Discussions

**On Reversible $\Sigma$-Type Protocols.** Kurosawa and Heng [12] defined a *reversible* property for identification protocols, and showed the conversion of the reversible identification protocol to trapdoor commitment scheme and vice versa. They also constructed an online/offline signature scheme, directly combining a signature scheme and a reversible identification protocol [12, Section 5]. The constructed scheme has smaller size of public keys than that of a scheme based on the Shamir-Tauman construction [16], which simply combines a signature scheme and a trapdoor commitment scheme.

Canetti et al. [5] defined *augmented $\Sigma$-protocol*, which is an extension of $\Sigma$-protocol for proving knowledge for some relation and has a property similar to "reversible" for standard identification. They then construct an identity-based trapdoor commitment scheme [1] from any signature scheme with an augmented $\Sigma$-protocol.

From a *reversible $\Sigma$-type* IBI protocol, which is an extension of reversible identification protocol [12], we can construct a trapdoor commitment scheme. In addition, we can construct a multi-trapdoor commitment [9], identity-based trapdoor commitment [1], simulation-sound trapdoor commitment [13], and non-malleable trapdoor commitment [13] from it.

We observe that many IBI protocols fall into reversible $\Sigma$-type. Kurosawa and Heng [12] noted that many practical identification protocols have the reversible property. Applying to the reversible identification protocol the certificate-based construction by Bellare, Namprempre, and Neven [2], which constructs an IBI protocol from an identification protocol and a digital signature scheme, we obtain a reversible $\Sigma$-type IBI protocol. We also note that the Kurosawa-Heng construction [11] can convert a signature scheme with an augmented $\Sigma$-protocol into a reversible $\Sigma$-type IBI protocol.

**On Security Enhancements.** It is known that a trapdoor commitment scheme enhances the security of IBI protocol from the static-identity setting to the adaptive-identity setting [14]. Consequently we may apply the constructed trapdoor commitment to the IBI protocol in order to enhance its security.

However, we present a transformation that converts a stat-id-imp-pa secure IBI protocol to an adapt-id-imp-ca secure one. In this transformation, an instance of an underlying IBI protocol is directly combined with another instance of the same IBI protocol, instead of constructing multi-trapdoor commitment and simply combining it with IBI protocol. The obtained IBI protocol attains more efficiency than the one by simple combination of the underlying IBI protocol with the multi-trapdoor commitment schemes, as well as we see in the construction of online/offline signature schemes in [12].

Yang et al. [17] presented a construction of IBI protocols secure under weak-selective-identity attacks in the standard model. In this paper, we discuss only security under adaptive-identity and static-identity attacks (adapt-id-imp-atk and stat-id-imp-atk), not weak-selective-identity attacks. In [8], it is shown that security under weak-selective-identity attacks is not stronger than stat-id-imp-atk security, and stat-id-imp-atk security is not stronger than adapt-id-imp-atk security.

## 4    Conclusion

We introduced *reversible $\Sigma$-type* IBI protocol, which is an extension of reversible identification protocol by Kurosawa and Heng [12]. Then, we proposed a security enhancement technique for reversible $\Sigma$-type identity-based identification protocols. The proposed transformation can convert a stat-id-imp-pa secure IBI protocol to an adapt-id-imp-ca secure one. It requires no other cryptographic primitives and no additional assumptions, and the security proof is done without the random oracles.

## References

1. Ateniese, G., de Medeiros, B.: Identity-Based Chameleon Hash and Applications. In: Juels, A. (ed.) FC 2004. LNCS, vol. 3110, pp. 164–180. Springer, Heidelberg (2004)
2. Bellare, M., Namprempre, C., Neven, G.: Security proofs for identity-based identification and signature schemes. Journal of Cryptology 22(1), 1–61 (2009); A preliminary version appeared in EUROCRYPT 2004 (2004)

3. Bellare, M., Palacio, A.: GQ and Schnorr Identification Schemes: Proofs of Security against Impersonation under Active and Concurrent Attacks. In: Yung, M. (ed.) CRYPTO 2002. LNCS, vol. 2442, pp. 162–177. Springer, Heidelberg (2002)
4. Bellare, M., Rogaway, P.: Random oracle are practical: A paradigm for designing efficient protocols. In: CCS 1993, pp. 62–73. ACM (1993)
5. Canetti, R., Dodis, Y., Pass, R., Walfish, S.: Universally Composable Security with Global Setup. In: Vadhan, S.P. (ed.) TCC 2007. LNCS, vol. 4392, pp. 61–85. Springer, Heidelberg (2007), http://eprint.iacr.org/2006/432
6. Cramer, R.: Modular Design of Secure, yet Practical Cryptographic Protocols. PhD thesis, University of Amsterdam (1996)
7. Feige, U., Shamir, A.: Witness indistinguishable and witness hiding protocols. In: STOC 1990, pp. 416–426. ACM (1990)
8. Fujioka, A., Saito, T., Xagawa, K.: Security Enhancements by OR-Proof in Identity-Based Identification. In: Bao, F., Samarati, P., Zhou, J. (eds.) ACNS 2012. LNCS, vol. 7341, pp. 135–152. Springer, Heidelberg (2012)
9. Gennaro, R.: Multi-trapdoor Commitments and Their Applications to Proofs of Knowledge Secure Under Concurrent Man-in-the-Middle Attacks. In: Franklin, M.K. (ed.) CRYPTO 2004. LNCS, vol. 3152, pp. 220–236. Springer, Heidelberg (2004)
10. Krawczyk, H., Rabin, T.: Chameleon signatures. In: NDSS 2000, pp. 143–154. Internet Society (2000)
11. Kurosawa, K., Heng, S.-H.: From Digital Signature to ID-based Identification/Signature. In: Bao, F., Deng, R.H., Zhou, J. (eds.) PKC 2004. LNCS, vol. 2947, pp. 248–261. Springer, Heidelberg (2004)
12. Kurosawa, K., Heng, S.-H.: The power of identification schemes. International Journal of Applied Cryptography (IJACT) 1(1), 60–69 (2008); A preliminary version appeared in PKC 2006 (2006)
13. MacKenzie, P., Yang, K.: On Simulation-Sound Trapdoor Commitments. In: Cachin, C., Camenisch, J.L. (eds.) EUROCRYPT 2004. LNCS, vol. 3027, pp. 382–400. Springer, Heidelberg (2004)
14. Rückert, M.: Adaptively Secure Identity-Based Identification from Lattices without Random Oracles. In: Garay, J.A., De Prisco, R. (eds.) SCN 2010. LNCS, vol. 6280, pp. 345–362. Springer, Heidelberg (2010)
15. Shamir, A.: Identity-Based Cryptosystems and Signature Schemes. In: Blakely, G.R., Chaum, D. (eds.) CRYPTO 1984. LNCS, vol. 196, pp. 47–53. Springer, Heidelberg (1985)
16. Shamir, A., Tauman, Y.: Improved Online/Offline Signature Schemes. In: Kilian, J. (ed.) CRYPTO 2001. LNCS, vol. 2139, pp. 355–367. Springer, Heidelberg (2001)
17. Yang, G., Chen, J., Wong, D.S., Deng, X., Wang, D.: A new framework for the design and analysis of identity-based identification schemes. Theoretical Computer Science 407(1-3), 370–388 (2008); A preliminary version appeared ACNS 2007 (2007)

# Coopetitive Architecture to Support a Dynamic and Scalable NFC Based Mobile Services Architecture

Raja Naeem Akram[1,2], Konstantinos Markantonakis[1], and Keith Mayes[1]

[1] ISG Smart Card Centre, Royal Holloway, University of London Egham,
Surrey, United Kingdom
[2] School of Computing, Edinburgh Napier University, Edinburgh, United Kingdom
R.Akram@napier.ac.uk,
{K.Markantonakis,Keith.Mayes}@rhul.ac.uk

**Abstract.** Near Field Communication (NFC) has reinvigorated the multi-application smart card initiative. The NFC trials are relying on an extension of Issuer Centric Smart Card Model (ICOM) referred as Trusted Service Manager (TSM) architecture, which may create market segregation. Where the User Centric Smart Card Ownership Model (UCOM) takes an opposite approach of delegating the smart card ownership to its users. Therefore, to reconcile these two approaches we proposed the Coopetitive Architecture for Smart Cards (CASC) that avoids market segregation, increase revenue generation, and provide flexibility, robustness, and scalability. To support the CASC framework in this paper, we propose an application installation protocol that provides entity authentication, trust assurance and validation, mutual key and contractual-agreement generation. The protocol is compared with existing protocols on its performance, stated security, and operational goals. Furthermore, CasperFDR is used to provide a mechanical formal analysis of the protocol.

## 1 Introduction

In late 1990s, the multi-application smart card initiative enabled heterogeneous applications to co-exist and share resources in a secure and reliable manner [1]. At the time, it was envisioned that diverse organisations would converge with their services on a single device [2]; however, the reality has been different.

The issues related to the card ownership, marketing potential of the card surface, customer loyalty, and potential revenue stream, hindered any meaningful collaboration effort [3]. In addition, there were other voices mainly concerned with the security implication [4]. The enthusiasm died quickly until a new technology termed as Near Field Communication (NFC) emerged that enables a mobile phone to emulate a contact-less smart card [5]. Since 2007, NFC based mobile services with applications like banking, telecom, and transports are in trial around 38 countries [6]. In these trials, the smart card management architecture is based on the framework that has been deployed in the smart card

T.W. Chim and T.H. Yuen (Eds.): ICICS 2012, LNCS 7618, pp. 214–227, 2012.
© Springer-Verlag Berlin Heidelberg 2012

industry since its inception, namely Issuer Centric Smart Card Ownership Model (ICOM). In the ICOM, smart cards are issued and controlled by a centralised authority known as a card issuer. Application providers require prior-authorisation from the card issuers to install their applications. The extension of the ICOM deployed in the NFC based trials is termed as Trusted Service Manager (TSM) architecture [7]. The TSM is an entity that can be either a card issuer or an independent third party. It manages the card platform, and relationship with individual stakeholders.

In contrast, User Centric Smart Card Ownership Model (UCOM) [3] is based on the citizen ownership architecture. In this model, cardholders (users) own smart cards, and they have the choice to install or delete any application. To reconcile between the UCOM and TSM, we proposed the Coopetitive Architecture for Smart Card (CASC)[1] that merges the TSM and UCOM frameworks, thus increasing the overall scalability of the multi-application smart card architecture, and possibly provide more revenue-generating opportunities than the TSM can individually achieve.

## 1.1 Contributions

In this paper, based on the CASC architecture, we propose a trusted and secure entity authentication, key generation, and contractual-agreement protocol for application download referred as Application Acquisition and Contractual Agreement Protocol (ACAP). The contractual-agreement guarantees to the participating entities that they have executed the protocol and as a successful outcome, an application is installed (and the application is operational).

## 1.2 Organisation

In section two, we provide a brief motivation behind the coopetitive architecture. A succinct discussion on the smart card architecture that supports the CASC framework is provided in section three. In this section we only discuss elements of the smart card design that is required to support the proposed protocol. These two sections set the background on which we base the security and operational requirements of the proposed protocol. Next in section four, the description of the ACAP is provided. Section five analyse the ACAP to see whether it meets the stated goals and requirements in comparison to existing protocols. In addition, we discuss the implementation experience and performance measurement of the ACAP along with formal analysis based on the CasperFDR. Finally, in section six we provide concluding remarks and list future research directions.

## 2  Motivation for Coopetitive Architecture

The TSM architecture, in a simplistic form, is illustrated in figure 1. In such an environment, a customer of a Mobile Network Operator (MNO) that has a

---

[1] To facilitate the blind reviewing process, references to CASC are removed.

relationship with the TSM-1 will only be able to have applications from Card Issuing Bank (CIB), Transport Service Provider (TSO) and leisure centres that are associated with the TSM-1. However, if the respective customer $C_A$ does banking with the $CIB_2$ that is associated with the TSM-2 (figure 1) then either she has to acquire a new smart card from the TSM-2 or change bank. Therefore, in such a scheme, there is a potential for the segmentation of the market.

One possible option is to have all application providers maintain relationships with all or most of the TSMs. For example, in figure 1, the $CIB_1$ of TSM-1 should also have a relationship with the TSM-2. Another possible option is to create a syndicated scheme in which multiple TSMs participate.

Therefore, any application provider affiliated with one TSM will be able to issue its application to a customer of any syndicated TSM. Both scenarios can be argued to be workable, but they also suffer from limited scalability, flexibility, and ubiquity of the framework.

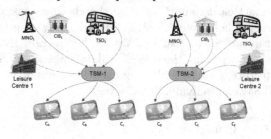

**Fig. 1.** Trusted Service Manager Architecture

The limited scalability roots from: (a) not all application providers could establish or manage relationships with every possible TSM, and (b) not all TSMs would be part of a single syndicated TSM. In addition, to be part of a collaborative scheme a TSM might require subscription fee from application providers. Therefore, small or medium-scale organisations like local libraries, universities, and health centres, etc., may not be able to afford it. We consider that such a barrier to enter the scheme reduces its flexibility. Furthermore, it lacks true ubiquity as different countries might opt for having their own independent TSMs. Thereby, tourists or business travellers would face difficulty in acquiring applications (e.g. TSO's application) in a foreign country. These issues are on top of the ones that are discussed in [4] including ownership privileges, customer loyalty and relationship management, card surface marketing, and revenue generation [3].

In the UCOM, most of the issues discussed above are not present [3]. We consider that UCOM itself will be a preferable solution, but it is difficult to conceive that it can have a widespread acceptance in the business community. Therefore, a compromise between the TSM and UCOM is referred as Coopetitive Architecture for Smart Cards (CASC).

The coopetitive architecture focuses on the core competences of individual companies and leaves other areas to the organisations that have expertise in them. For example, an MNO in the coopetitive architecture can be a TSM and even have the ability to form alliance with other companies to provide their services via the respective smart cards. In addition, it also enables the users to download applications they like from any of the application providers of their choice. The main stake the MNO has is to generate maximum revenue out of its investment in the secure element, and its security. Therefore, if there is a way in which an application can be securely downloaded onto a smart card that does not have any prior relationship with the particular application provider and the MNO charges the customer for acquiring the application. Then in such a model, there is a probability that customers would actually generate higher revenue for the respective card issuer or TSM than in the traditional architecture based on the ICOM.

## 3   Coopetitive Architecture for Smart Cards

In this section, first we discuss the coopetitive architecture and then briefly describe the multi-application smart card architecture to support it.

### 3.1   Smart Card Architecture Overview

A generic architecture is illustrated in figure 2, for brevity we will only discuss those components that are related to this paper. On top of the hardware layer is the Trusted Environment & Execution Manager (TEM), which is discussed in the next section.

Above TEM is the smart card runtime environment that might conform to any of the smart card platforms or operating systems (e.g. Java Card [8] or Multos [9]). The smart card firewall manages the inter-application communication and access to the platform services (i.e. APIs). The top most layer is partitioned into three sections separated by the firewall mechanism: namely the Platform's, TSM's, and Cardholder's space. The Platform's space holds the platform APIs, where application related to individual entities (e.g. TSM and cardholder) are in their respective spaces.

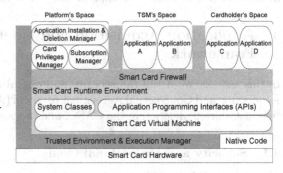

**Fig. 2.** Generic Smart Card Architecture for Coopetitive Framework

### 3.2   Trusted Environment and Execution Manager (TEM)

A TEM provides a platform independent dynamic, runtime, and remote – security and reliability assurance mechanism for the UCOM based smart cards. In a naive manner, we can term it as a trusted platform base for the smart cards; however, TEM's functionality differs from the traditional Trusted Platform Module [10]. For the sake of concision, we will only discuss the TEM component referred as the attestation handler in this section that is directly related to this paper.

The attestation handler implements the security-assurance and validation mechanism that certify to the requesting entity (e.g. Service Provider: SP) that the smart card's state is as it was at the time of a third party evaluation and stated by the evaluation certificate [11]. An evaluation certificate is a cryptographically signed certificate issued by an evaluation body, and the respective card manufacturer places it on the platform. The evaluation certificate will certify a unique signature key pair of the Smart Card Manufacturer (SCM). The SCM will use the signature key to issue certificates to the manufactured smart cards that conform to the evaluated product (see figure 3). A point to note is that at present Common Criteria (CC) [12] or any other evaluation scheme, for that matter, does not provide any such service but proposals presented in [11] and [13] can be utilised.

The process initiated by the attestation handler validates both the hardware and software state of the platform. It is a two-part mechanism: tamper-evidence and reliability assurance. To make a smart card tamper-resistant, the respective SCM implements hardware based tamper protections. The tamper-evidence process verifies whether the implemented tamper-resistant mechanisms are still in place and effective. The reliability assurance process verifies that the software part of the smart card platform is not been tampered/modified. For the description of the TEM and implementation of the attestation handler see [14].

## 4   Application Acquisition and Contractual Agreement Framework

In this section, we detail the security and operational goals for the Application Acquisition and Contractual Agreement protocol (ACAP) that facilitates application installation/deletion in the CASC, and propose a protocol that meets them.

### 4.1   Security and Operational Goals

An ACAP for the CASC should meet sixteen goals stated in [14] along with the additional goals listed as below:

G17) Platform & Application User Separation (PAU) Attack: A malicious user provides access credentials of a genuine user to an SP and downloads the application on her smart card [14]. A protocol should tie a platform with its respective card-owner (user) to avoid platform & application user separation attack.

G18) Contractual Agreement: On the successful execution of the protocol, the communicating entities will mutually sign a contractual agreement. This will act as a proof that a particular application was installed on a smart card.

G19) Proof of Transaction: The smart card will notify the TSM about the application installation. Depending upon the TSM's policy, it will charge the user's account and notify the smart card to activate the application so it can execute.

For formal definition of the italicised terms in the above list, readers are advised to refer to [15]. Later, we will revisit these goals for the protocol comparison (see table 3).

## 4.2 Enrolment Phase

A Smart Card Manufacturer (SCM) will get their smart card product certified from a certification authority that would issue a Product Evaluation Certificate (PEC), as shown in figure 3. It will endorse that the platform conforms to the stated security and operational requirements [14], along with the attestation process and its effectiveness.

The SCM may deliver the smart cards to a card issuer (e.g. a TSM) that will also certify the smart card signature key pair. Now, it will have two certificates, one issued by the SCM and second by the TSM. Finally, the respective smart card will be acquired by a cardholder who will then initiate the ownership acquisition process, which would generate a user signature key pair, certified by the smart card.

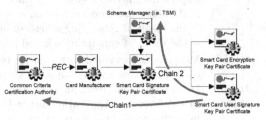

**Fig. 3.** Certificate Hierarchy in the Coopetitive Framework

There are two roots in this hierarchy (figure 3), the CC certificate authority, and the TSM. The reasons for having two separate roots are: a) to provide privacy protection to users who do not want to reveal the identity of their TSMs, and b) smart cards may not be permanently bonded with a particular TSM.

Depending upon the association of an SP with the TSM of a smart card, the appropriate chain of certificates will be provided by the smart card. If the SP is not an associate of the TSM, then the certificate chain 1 (figure 3) with the CC certification authority as a root will be used; otherwise, chain 2 will be used.

## 4.3 Proposed Protocol

Software on a mobile phone that supports the application installation process is referred as Card Application Management Software (CAMS) [16] in the UCOM. A cardholder requests the respective SP to download an application that initiates the ACAP protocol. The notation used to describe the ACAP is listed in table 1, where ACAP messages are listed in table 2 and discussed as below:

*Message 1.* The SP will initiate the ACAP by generating a random number ($N_{SP}$) and Diffie-Hellman exponential ($g^{sp}$) [19]. For computational efficiency, the SP might have a pre-computed buffer of random numbers and Diffie-Hellman exponentials. To avoid DoS attacks, the SP will compute a Session Identifier (SID) by $SID = H_{SP_k}(g^{sp}|N_{SP}|SC_{IP})$. The key ($H_{SP_k}$) used to generate the HMAC is not shared with any-other entity and $SC_{IP}$ is the current Internet Protocol (IP) address of the respective smart card. When an SP will receive a

**Table 1.** Protocol Notation

| | |
|---|---|
| $SP$ | :Denotes a Service Provider. |
| $SC$ | :Denotes a smart card. |
| $T$ | :Denotes the enrolled TSM. |
| $U$ | :Denotes a cardholder (user). |
| $App$ | :Denotes the downloaded application contents. |
| $X_i$ | :Represents the identity of an entity $X$. |
| $g^x$ | :Current Diffie-Hellman exponential $(mod\ p)$ generated by the entity $X$. |
| $C_X$ | :Signature key pair certificate of an entity $X$. |
| $N_X$ | :Random number generated by an entity $X$. |
| $A \rightarrow B$ | :Message sent by an entity $A$ to an entity $B$. |
| $X\|Y$ | :Represents the concatenation of the data items $X$, $Y$ in the given order. |
| $Sig_X(Z)$ | :Is the signature on data Z by an entity $X$ using a signature algo [17]. |
| $H(Z)$ | :Is the result of generating a hash of data Z. |
| $H_k(Z)$ | :Is the result of generating a keyed hash (HMAC) of data Z using $k$. |
| $[M]_{aK_{X-Y}}^{eK_{X-Y}}$ | :Message $M$ encrypted by the encryption key $eK_{X-Y}$ and then MAC is computed using the key $aK_{X-Y}$, shared between entities X and Y. |
| $DH_G$ | :Details the Diffie-Hellman group that is used to generate the $g^{SP}$ [18]. |
| $ALP$ | :SPs defines the Application Lease Policy (ALP) [16] that states the minimum security and operational requirements an SC has to meet to get the application lease. The application can be downloaded only after the SC satisfies the lease requirements [3]. |
| $ReqV$ | :The message sent by the respective SP to a SC requesting to provide a current state validation. |
| $CAR$ | :List of cryptographic algorithms supported by the respective SP. |
| $CAS$ | :List of cryptographic algorithms selected by the respective smart card from the CAR. |
| $ParOpt$ | :Optional parameters of the protocol messages. |
| $AppDoD$ | :An anonymised message that details the application properties (e.g. size) and it is used for charging purposes by the scheme manager. |

message from the SC, it will first verify the SID. If the SID corresponds to an open session, and it computes correctly for the stated IP address (from where the message is received), then the SP will proceed with processing the message.

*Message 2.* On receipt, the SC will first check the $DH_G$ whether support the selected group or not. If it cannot support the selected group then the smart card will sends a rejection message that lists the DH groups supported by the smart card. The SC then verifies whether it satisfy the ALP requirements. In addition to the security and operational requirements, the ALP also stipulates the required memory to install the application. The SC checks, whether it has enough available space to accommodate the requested application. If the SC cannot satisfy the ALP, it will terminate the protocol and notify the cardholder.

Otherwise, the SC will then generate a random number $(N_{SC})$ and Diffie-Hellman exponential $(g^{sc})$. It can now also generate the shared key (i.e. $DH = (g^{sp})^{sc}\ mod\ p$) and from this key, the SC will generate the session encryption $K_e = H_{DH}(N_{SP}\|N_{SC}\|0)$ and MAC key $K_a = H_{DH}(N_{SP}\|N_{SC}\|1)$. Session keys for the application download process can also be generated in the similar fashion.

**Table 2.** Application and Contractual Agreement Protocol (ACAP)

| |
|---|
| **M1.** $SP \rightarrow SC : N_{SP}\|g^{sp}\|DH_G\|ALP\|SID$ |
| **M2.** $SC \rightarrow SP : N_{SC}\|g^{sc}\|[Sign_U(SC_i\|U_i\|g^{sp}\|g^{sc}\|N_{SP}\|N_{SC}\|PEC)\|C_U]_{aK_{SC-SP}}^{eK_{SC-SP}}\|SID$ |
| **M3.** $SP \rightarrow SC : RV\|[Sign_{SP}(SP_i\|App_i\|g^{sp}\|g^{sc}\|N_{SC}\|N_{SP})\|C_{SP}\|CAR\|PO]_{aK_{SC-SP}}^{eK_{SC-SP}}$ |
| **M4.** $SC \rightarrow SP : [Sign_{SC}(SC_i\|U_i\|N_{SC}\|N_{SP}\|PO)\|CAS\|C_{SC}]_{aK_{SC-SP}}^{eK_{SC-SP}}\|SID$ |
| **M5.** $SC \rightarrow SP : [Sign_{SC}(H(App)\|SP_i\|App_i\|ALP\|SC_i\|U_i\|N_{SC}\|N_{SP})]_{aK_{SC-SP}}^{eK_{SC-SP}}\|SID$ |
| **M6.** $SP \rightarrow SC : [Sign_{SP}(H(App)\|SC_i\|U_i\|SP_i\|N_{SC}\|N_{SP}\|PO)\|C_{SP}]_{aK_{SC-SP}}^{eK_{SC-SP}}$ |
| **M7.**  $SC \rightarrow T : Card_{ID}\|[T_i\|SC_i\|U_i\|AppDoD\|N'_{SC}]_{aK_{SC-T}}^{eK_{SC-T}}\|SID_{T-SC}$ |
| **M8.**  $T \rightarrow SC : [Sign_T(T_i\|SC_i\|U_i\|N_T\|N'_{SC}\|TC\|ActApp)\|Card'_{ID}\|SID'_{T-SC}]_{aK_{SC-T}}^{eK_{SC-T}}$ |

The SC will sign the data containing the PEC (Product Evaluation Certificate) with user's signature key, then it is concatenated with the user's certificate. The entire message is encrypted and MACed, and appended to the $g^{SC}$ and $N_{SC}$.

*Message 3.* The SP will retrieve the $g^{sc}$ and calculate $DH = (g^{sc})^{sp} \bmod p$. Similar to the SC, the SP will also generate the session encryption and MAC keys.

The SP verifies the user's certificate, and the details of the cardholder listed in the user's certificate should match the SP's authenticated customer that requested the application download. This is to avoid users from installing applications for which they are not authorised (i.e. see requirement 17 in section 4.1). The SP verifies the signature and checks whether the PEC meets the minimum security-requirement set out in the SP's ALP. If it does not, the SP will terminate the protocol.

If there is no error, the SP will request (i.e. $RV$) the SC to provide a proof that it complies with the stated PEC. The SP then appends the encrypted message that contains cryptographic algorithms supported ($CAR$) by the SP (i.e. for use in application download), and an optional parameter ($PO$). The $PO$ field is used by the SP if its application also has a third party evaluation certificate that is attached the certificate with message.

*Message 4.* On receipt of the message 3, the smart card verifies whether it supports the cryptographic algorithms listed in the $CAR$. If not, then the SC will send a list of cryptographic algorithms supported by the SC. If the SP does not support any of them, it can terminate the protocol and notify the user.

Otherwise, the SC will check whether the SP's identity is included in the associated SP's list (section 4.2). If it is included, the application will be installed in the TSM's space (section 3.1). If the SP's identity is in the list, then in the response message the SC will include the TSM's identity as an optional parameter ($PO$).

The SC will then initiate the platform attestation process as discussed in section 3.2. A correct signature that includes the protocol related data (i.e. random numbers and identities) will ascertain that the smart card is still in conformance with the evaluated state. The SC also includes the list of cryptographic algorithms ($CAS$) selected from the $CAR$ list for the application download process.

Up to this point, the protocol achieves the entity authentication (e.g. SC, user, and SP), provides SC trust validation proof, and has generated session keys. For performance comparison (table 4), we refer to the message 1-4 as AKG (Authentication, Key Generation and Trust Validation) phase. After receiving the message 4, the respective SP will initiate the application download process, which is beyond the scope of this paper. However, for completeness, the communicating parties may choose one of the symmetric key-based application download protocol from the GlobalPlatform specification [20].

*Message 5.* Once the application download is completed, the SC will generate a message that acts as an SC to SP contract. The SC will generate the hash of the downloaded application and sign it with identities of the SP, downloaded application, SC, and the user.

*Message 6.* The SP verifies the $H(App)$ generated by the SC and activates the application lease to the user on the SP's server. The application lease activation does not mean that the respective SC can be used to access SP's services. The access to services is only activated at the successful conclusion of the ACAP, when the SC activates the application and it dials back home to activate the access to sanctioned services. Similarly, the SP's application is not activated on the SC; it is in the blocked (dormant) state. If the SP is not associated with the scheme TSM, then the SP will sign the message containing $H(App)$.

To activate an application, the SC requires the scheme TSM's authorisation. If the SP is associated with the TSM, it will send the identities of the SC, user, and downloaded application to the respective TSM. The TSM in reply will generate the $ActApp = Sign_T(App_i|SP_i|SC_i|Ui|N_{SP}|N_{SC})$. The $ActApp$ acts as an application activation message and it will be included in the message 6 as an optional parameter ($ParOp$). In this scenario, the last two messages will be redundant and will not be executed. This message acts as an SP to SC contract.

*Message 7.* In scenarios where the SP is not a member of the TSM, the user has to pay for the application download as per TSM policy and after this the TSM will issue the $ActApp$. The SC will request the TSM to issue $ActApp$ by sending the above message. The SC will use a one-time pseudo card identity ($Card_{ID}$) (i.e. privacy reason) so that an eavesdropper may not be able to match the $Card_{ID}$ uniquely to the $SC_i$. The SC will encrypt the message containing the identities of TSM, SC, and user. It then appends the application details ($AppDoD$) and a new random number generated by the SC. The $AppDoD$ will not have any details of the application that can help the TSM to uniquely identify either the SP or the application. It will include the memory occupied by the application, and if the TSM charges the user according to the space usage then this data will be used to calculate the charge. Finally, the SC uses the one-time $SID_{T-SC}$ that is generated in previous protocol runs with the TSM, to avoid the DoS attack on the TSM's server; . The process to generate the $Card_{ID}$ and $SID_{T-SC}$ is explained in the next message.

*Message 8.* The TSM will first verify whether the $Card_{ID}$ and $SID_{T-SC}$ corresponds to the values in its database so that it will process the transaction and charge the user's account. Afterwards, the TSM will sign the message that includes the transaction certificate of the charge performed by the TSM and the *ActApp*. The *ActApp* is generated similarly as detailed in the message 6; however, the value in the $App_i$ is a pseudo value that has no relation with the actual identity of the downloaded application. Finally, the TSM will generate the SID for the next session $SID'_{T-SC} = H_{K_T}(Card'_{ID}|T_i|SC_i)$ and $Card'_{ID} = H(T_i|SC_i|N'_{SC}|N_T)$. The TSM will store the generated $Card'_{ID}$ and $SID'_{T-SC}$ in the internal database.

After the SC receives the *ActApp*, it activates the application and notifies the cardholder about the successful outcome of the application installation, and any incurred charge. The charging mechanism for the individual transactions is on sole discretion of the respective TSM.

# 5  Analysis of the ACAP Protocol

In this section, we analyse the proposed ACAP in terms of informal analysis, mechanical formal analysis (CasperFDR), and practical implementation with performance comparison.

## 5.1  Brief Informal Analysis of the Protocol

In this section, we constantly refer to the protocol requirements and goals for the ACAP; therefore, here onward any reference to a goal or requirement number refers to the listed item in section 4.1.

As shown in the table 3, the most promising results were from the ASPeCT and JFK protocols that meet a large set of goals. The T2LS protocol [28] meets the trust assurance goal by default, but similar to SCP81 it is based on the TLS protocol, which does not meet most of the requirements. A note in favour of the SCP10, SCP81, MM, and SM protocol is that they were designed with the assumption that an application provider has a prior trusted relationship with the smart card issuer; thus implicitly trusting the respective smart card. Whereas, the proposed ACAP protocol meets all the listed goals.

## 5.2  Protocol Verification by CasperFDR

The CasperFDR approach was adopted to test the soundness of the proposed protocol under the defined security properties. In this approach, the Casper compiler [29] takes a high-level description of the protocol, together with its security requirements. It then translates the description into the process algebra of Communicating Sequential Processes (CSP) [29]. The CSP description of the protocol can be machine-verified using the Failures-Divergence Refinement (FDR) model checker [29]. The intruder's capability modelled in the Casper script for the proposed protocol is as: 1) an intruder can masquerade any entity in the network,

**Table 3.** Protocol comparison on the basis of the stated goals (see section 4.1)

| Gs | STS[21] | AD[22] | ASPeCT[23] | JFK[24] | T2LS | SCP81[25] | MM[26] | SM[27] | ACAP |
|---|---|---|---|---|---|---|---|---|---|
| G01. | * | * | * | * | * | * | −* | −* | * |
| G02. | * | * | * | * | * | * | * | −* | * |
| G03. | * | * | * | * | * | * | * | −* | * |
| G04. | * | * | * | * | * | * | | | * |
| G05. | * | * | * | * | * | * | * | −* | * |
| G06. | * | | * | * | | | * | −* | * |
| G07. | * | * | * | * | * | * | * | | * |
| G08. | * | * | * | * | * | * | * | −* | * |
| G09. | * | * | * | * | * | * | * | * | * |
| G10. | * | | * | * | * | * | | | * |
| G11. | * | (*) | +* | * | * | * | +* | +* | * |
| G12. | (*) | (*) | | (*) | (*) | (*) | | | * |
| G13. | | | | | * | −* | | | * |
| G14. | | | | * | | | | | * |
| G15. | (*) | | * | * | | | | | * |
| G16. | | | | | −* | | | | * |
| G17. | | | | | | | | | * |
| G18. | | | | | | | | | * |
| G19. | | | * | | +* | +* | +* | +* | * |

**Note:** * means that the protocol meets the stated goal, (*) shows that the protocol can be modified to satisfy the requirement, +* shows that protocol can meet the stated goal but requires an additional pass or extra signature generation, and −* means that the protocol (implicitly) meets the requirement not because of the protocol messages but because of the prior relationship between the communicating entities.

2) (s)he can read the messages transmitted by each entity in the network, and
3) (s)he cannot influence the internal process of an agent in the network.

The security specification for which the CasperFDR evaluates the network consists of: 1) the protocol run is fresh and both applications were alive, 2) the key generated by the SP and SC is not known to the intruder, 3) entities have mutually authentication and key assurance at the conclusion of the protocol, 4) long terms keys of communicating entities are not compromised, and 5) the user's identity is not revealed to the intruder. The CasperFDR tool evaluated the protocol and did not find any feasible attack(s).

### 5.3    Practical Implementation

The proposed ACAP does not provide any specific details of the cryptographic algorithms to be used during the protocol run. This choice is left to the respective SPs and smart cards. To provide a performance measure for the ACAP, we have used Advance Encryption Standard (AES) [30] 128-bit key symmetric encryption with Cipher Block Chaining (CBC) [15] without padding for both encryption and MAC operations. The signature algorithm is based on the Rivest-Shamir-Aldeman (RSA) [15] 512-bit key. We have used SHA-256 [31] for the

**Table 4.** Protocol Performance Measures (Milliseconds)

| Protocols \Phases | SSL [32] | TLS [33] | Kerberos [34] | ACAP | |
|---|---|---|---|---|---|
| | | | | Card One | Card Two |
| | 32-bit | 32-bit | 32-bit | 16-bit | 16-bit |
| AKG Phase (M1-4) | 4200 | 4300 | 4240 | 3395 | 3559 |
| Contract Phase (M5-6) | - | - | - | 1253 | 1294 |
| Charge Phase (M7-8) | - | - | - | 1407 | 1470 |
| Total (M1-8) | - | - | - | 6055 | 6323 |

hash generation by the TEM. For Diffie-Hellman key generation we used 2058-bit group with 256-bit prime order subgroup specified in the RFC-5114 [18].

The architecture of the ACAP test-bed is based upon three entities: a smart card, an SP and a TSM. The entities SP and TSM are implemented on a laptop with 1.83 GHz processor, and 2 GB of RAM, running on Windows XP. The smart card entity is implemented on a 16-bit Java Card and the implementation takes 9799 bytes of memory space. The implemented protocol was executed for 1000 iterations and time taken to complete individual iteration was recorded. The performance measures are taken from two different 16-bit Java Cards, and an average of recorded measurements for both cards is listed in table 4. For comparison, we have selected the SSL performance measured by Pascal Urien [32], TLS from Urien and Elrharbi [33], and (public key based) Kerberos by Harbitter and Menascé [34].

The rationale behind the choice of SSL and TLS for comparison lies in the GlobalPlatform's SCP81 [25], which specifies the adoption of the TSL for the NFC based mobile service architecture (i.e. TSM Framework discussed in section 2). Whereas, public key based Kerberos is suitable for the Multos application management architecture [35]. Table 4 show that the proposed protocol perform better than other listed protocols, which are either already adopted in case of the SCP81 or can be adopted in the smart card industry.

# 6   Conclusion and Future Research Directions

In this paper, we proposed a protocol referred as ACAP that provides the entity authentication, trust validation, mutual key and the contractual-agreement generation. The ACAP was then compared with existing protocols ranging from the internet-based protocols to ones that were specifically designed for the smart card environment. We have implemented the protocol and provided its performance measure. At the time of writing, authors were not aware of any other protocol that satisfies the same number of security and operational goals within the performance matrix of the ACAP.

As part of the future research direction, first we would like to provide a detailed formal analysis of the protocol. In addition, we consider that one of the important topics is how we can avoid the simulator problem and provide assurance to an SP that a smart card is a tamper-resistant, tamper-evident and a reliable device. In addition, we will look into the platform and runtime environment architecture that supports the TSM's and cardholder's space on the same device. Furthermore, we will analyse the prospects of extending the coopetitive framework to general purposes tamper-resistant devices.

# References

1. Rankl, W., Effing, W.: Smart Card Handbook. John Wiley & Sons, Inc., NY (2003)
2. Girard, P.: Which Security Policy for Multiplication Smart Cards? In: Proceedings of the USENIX Workshop on Smartcard Technology, Berkeley, CA, USA, p. 3 (1999)
3. Akram, R.N., Markantonakis, K., Mayes, K.: A Paradigm Shift in Smart Card Ownership Model. In: Apduhan, B.O., Gervasi, O., Iglesias, A., Taniar, D., Gavrilova, M. (eds.): Proceedings of the 2010 International Conference on Computational Science and Its Applications (ICCSA 2010), pp. 191–200. IEEE CS, Fukuoka (2010)
4. Framework for Smart Card use in Government, Foundation for Information Policy Research, Consultation Response (1999)
5. Near Field Communication: The Keys to Truly Interoperable Communications, NFC Forum, White Paper (November 2006)
6. NFC Trials, Pilots, Tests and Live Services around the World. Online. NFC World
7. Pay-Buy-Mobile: Business Opportunity Analysis, GSM Association, White Paper 1.0 (November 2007)
8. Java Card Platform Specification, Sun Microsystem Inc. Std. Version 3.0.1 (May 2009)
9. Multos: The Multos Specification, Online
10. Trusted Module Specification 1.2, Trusted Computing Group Std., Rev. 103 (July 2007)
11. Akram, R.N., Markantonakis, K., Mayes, K.: A Dynamic and Ubiquitous Smart Card Security Assurance and Validation Mechanism. In: Rannenberg, K., Varadharajan, V., Weber, C. (eds.) SEC 2010. IFIP AICT, vol. 330, pp. 161–172. Springer, Heidelberg (2010)
12. Common Criteria for Information Technology Security Evaluation, Common Criteria Std. Version 3.1 (August 2006)
13. Sauveron, D., Dusart, P.: Which Trust Can Be Expected of the Common Criteria Certification at End-User Level? Future Generation Communication and Networking (2007)
14. Akram, R.N., Markantonakis, K., Mayes, K.: A privacy preserving application acquisition protocol. In: Geyong Min, F.G.M. (ed.) 11th IEEE International Conference on Trust, Security and Privacy in Computing and Communications (IEEE TrustCom 2012). IEEE Computer Society, Liverpool (2012)
15. Menezes, A.J., van Oorschot, P.C., Vanstone, S.A.: Handbook of Applied Cryptography. CRC (October 1996)
16. Akram, R.N., Markantonakis, K., Mayes, K.: Application Management Framework in User Centric Smart Card Ownership Model. In: Youm, H.Y., Yung, M. (eds.) WISA 2009. LNCS, vol. 5932, pp. 20–35. Springer, Heidelberg (2009)
17. Furlani, C.: FIPS 186-3 : Digital Signature Standard (DSS), Online, National Institute of Standards and Technology (NIST) Std. (June 2009)

18. Lepinski, M., Kent, S.: RFC 5114 - Additional Diffie-Hellman Groups for Use with IETF Standards (January 2008)
19. Diffie, W., Hellman, M.E.: New Directions in Cryptography. IEEE Transactions on Information Theory IT-22(6), 644–654 (1976)
20. GlobalPlatform: GlobalPlatform Card Specification, Version 2.2, GlobalPlatform Std. (March 2006)
21. Diffie, W., Van Oorschot, P.C., Wiener, M.J.: Authentication and Authenticated Key Exchanges. Des. Codes Cryptography 2, 107–125 (1992)
22. Aziz, A., Diffie, W.: Privacy And Authentication For Wireless Local Area Networks. IEEE Personal Communications 1, 25–31 (1994)
23. Horn, G., Martin, K.M., Mitchell, C.J.: Authentication Protocols for Mobile Network Environment Value-Added Services. IEEE Transactions on Vehicular Technology 51 (March 2002)
24. Aiello, W., Bellovin, S.M., Blaze, M., Canetti, R., Ioannidis, J., Keromytis, A.D., Reingold, O.: Just Fast Keying: Key Agreement in a Hostile Internet. ACM Trans. Inf. Syst. Secur. 7 (May 2004)
25. Remote Application Management over HTTP, Card Specification v 2.2 - Amendment B, Online, GlobalPlatform Specification (September 2006)
26. Markantonakis, K., Mayes, K.: A Secure Channel Protocol for Multi-application Smart Cards based on Public Key Cryptography. In: Chadwick, D., Prennel, B. (eds.) Eight IFIP TC-6-11 Conference on Communications and Multimedia Security, pp. 79–96. Springer (September 2004)
27. Sirett, W.G., MacDonald, J.A., Mayes, K., Markantonakis, C.: Design, Installation and Execution of a Security Agent for Mobile Stations. In: Domingo-Ferrer, J., Posegga, J., Schreckling, D. (eds.) CARDIS 2006. LNCS, vol. 3928, pp. 1–15. Springer, Heidelberg (2006)
28. Dierks, T., Rescorla, E.: RFC 5246 - The Transport Layer Security (TLS) Protocol (August 2008)
29. Ryan, P., Schneider, S.: The Modelling and Analysis of Security Protocols: the CSP Approach. Addison-Wesley (2000)
30. Daemen, J., Rijmen, V.: The Design of Rijndael: AES - The Advanced Encryption Standard. Springer, Heidelberg (2002)
31. FIPS 180-2: Secure Hash Standard (SHS), National Institute of Standards and Technology Std. (2002)
32. Urien, P.: Collaboration of SSL Smart Cards within the WEB2 Landscape. In: International Symposium on Collaborative Technologies and Systems, pp. 187–194 (2009)
33. Urien, P., Elrharbi, S.: Tandem Smart Cards: Enforcing Trust for TLS-Based Network Services. In: International Workshop on Applications and Services in Wireless Networks, pp. 96–104 (2008)
34. Harbitter, A., Menascé, D.A.: The Performance of Public Key-Enabled Kerberos Authentication in Mobile Computing Applications, pp. 78–85 (2001)
35. Multos: Guide to Loading and Deleting Applications, MAOSCO, Tech. Rep. (2006)

# Permission-Based Abnormal Application Detection for Android

Jiawei Zhu[1,2,3], Zhi Guan[1,2,3,*], Yang Yang[1,2,3], Liangwen Yu[1,2,3],
Huiping Sun[1,2,3], and Zhong Chen[1,2,3]

[1] Institute of Software, School of EECS, Peking University, China
[2] MoE Key Lab of High Confidence Software Technologies (PKU)
[3] MoE Key Lab of Network and Software Security Assurance (PKU)
{zhujw,guan}@infosec.pku.edu.cn

**Abstract.** Android has become one of the most popular mobile operating system because of numerous applications it provides. Android Market is the official application store which allows users to search and install applications to their Android devices. However, with the increasingly number of applications, malware is also beginning to turn up in app stores. To mitigate the security problem brought by malware, we put forward a novel permission-based abnormal application detection framework which identifies potentially dangerous apps by the reliability of their permission lists. To judge the reliability of app's permissions, we make use of the relation between app's description text and its permission list. In detail, we use Naive Bayes with Multinomial Event Model algorithm to build the relation between the description and the permission list of an application. We evaluate this framework with 5,685 applications in Android Market and find it effective in identifying abnormal application in Android Market.

**Keywords:** Android, Abnormal Application, Permission Reliability.

## 1  Introduction

Nowadays, smartphones occupy an important position in people's daily life. They allow users to communicate, surf the Internet or have all kinds of entertainments at any place. The most common mobile operating systems used by modern smartphones include Android, iOS and Symbian. Android, which is an open source Linux-based mobile operating system distributed by Google, is one of the most popular mobile operating systems today. Because of its open architecture which is convenient to develop and debug the applications, more and more developers turn to pay attention to this rising system.

With the arising of numerous Android applications, there exists lots of app stores providing more convenient platforms for users to search and install the free and paid applications. Among all these Android app stores, Google Play Store [1] (named as Android Market originally) is the official app store for Android

---

* Corresponding author.

T.W. Chim and T.H. Yuen (Eds.): ICICS 2012, LNCS 7618, pp. 228–239, 2012.

smartphone users. A research report released by AppBrain showed that the total number of apps in Android Market was over 450,000 at the beginning of June, 2012 [2]. In Android Market, users can browse the description, application's information and the permission list in the application's main interface. For most users searching applications in the market, they usually make a decision on selecting which applications to install based on three aspects: the introductions of applications (including descriptions and application screenshots), ratings and other users' reviews.

Unlike Apple's App Store, Google has minimal involvement in Android Market. Android Market provides diverse applications not only developed by famous corporations, but also by some small companies or amateur individual developers. Once published, apps from the Android Market can only be removed by Google because of being reported malicious or their content violating terms of use. So without Google's restrict check on applications, Android Market may contain some malicious applications. For this reason, some measures should be taken to ensure the security of Android devices.

In this paper, we propose a method to analyze the potential security problem of an application in app stores. In detail, we put forward a permission-based abnormal application detection framework to mitigate the security problem in Android Market by the reliability of app's permissions. We design a detailed predicting model which is the most important part in the framework to reflect the relation between the description and the permission list of an application. With this model, we can predict the actually needed permission list of an application in Android Market based on its description.

We use 5,685 free applications in the Android Market to evaluate our permission predicting models and find that this model is effective in predicting the permission list of an application in Android Market. Besides, we apply our security framework in the detection of reliability of applications' permissions and give out a test on real malware announced by Google.

The following sections of this paper proceeds as follows. Section 2 describes the related work about Android malware detection. Section 3 overviews our framework. Section 4 describes the process of our experiment. Section 5 evaluates this model on 5,685 apps in Android Market. Section 6 applies our method on detecting the reliability of permissions and few malicious apps announced by Google and section 7 concludes.

## 2    Related Work

Smartphone security is a growing concern in recent year. Static analysis and dynamic analysis are two main approaches for the detection of malware. In Android platform, Enck et al. [3] present a dynamic tainting analysis to protect the security of users' sensitive data. They labeled the information with different types. At last, the system made a result based on the policies. They also tested this tool on 30 applications and found that 20 of these applications taking suspicious actions on users' data.

Enck et al. [4] also designed a tool to decompiled the Android executable file into Java source code to make a static analysis to identify malicious Android applications. They studied 1,100 Android applications with this method and obtained 27 finds including the leakage of phone identifiers, location information sent to advertisement servers and some specific attacks on Android OS.

Same authors [5] designed and implemented a framework to identify the dangerous applications based on their certain combinations of permissions. They designed Kirin which modified the application installer with this method to prevent the malicious applications.

Portokalidis et al. [6] utilize virtualization method to detect the security of Android applications. In detail, they put forward a method to analyze the security of applications in the remote servers which held the mirror of smartphone in the virtual environment. They implemented this system and took some analysis on the parameters of this system such as battery level and CPU utilization.

Zhou et al. [7] proposed a permission-based behavioral footprinting scheme and heuristics-based filtering scheme to detect the malware. The former compared the application with the known Android malware based on their permissions to detect the new sample of them. The latter was used to identify the unknown malicious families. The experiment was taken with 204,040 apps collected from 5 different app stores.

Burguera et al. [8] made use of k-means method with the time of system call as the features to identify the malware. The experiment was tested on two known Android malware.

## 3    Security Framework

### 3.1    Permission-Based Abnormal Application Detection Framework Overview

In this paper, we put forward a novel permission-based abnormal application detection framework in Android Market. The main point of our framework is that the description of an application is closely related to its permission list in Android platform. Here, the description of an application, which can be found in Android Market, describes the features and the functions of this application. In other word, the description information concretes the functions of the application implementing. Permission-based security model is one of the most important security measures of Android devices. Permission model is used to restrict to access to some special resources. It can also be said to restrict to take some potentially dangerous actions. If an application wants to accomplish some specific actions, it has to request the corresponding permissions. So the permission list of an application reflects the actions, or even functions of this application. For example, if an app defines the function of sharing files in its description text, this sharing files function should contain two-step actions. The first one is to find the users to be shared with the file from contact. The other is transferring the file to the selected users via network. Based on these two-step actions, this application should request READ_CONTACT and INTERNET permissions to realize its function. Therefore, we believe that the description and the permission list of an application are closely related. However, for the malicious applications, they usually hide some potentially dangerous actions which lead to their actions being not accord to the described functions.

Based on this intuitive conclusion, we provide a permission-based abnormal application detection framework to analyze the potential dangers of an app in Android Market. The detailed framework is shown in Figure 1. In this framework, the most crucial part is the model which reflects the relation between the description and the permission list. With this model, we can predict an app's normal permission list. Furthermore, after the analysis of the permission comparator, if the permission list of an app is not accord to its predicted normal permission list, we think this app is with hidden danger.

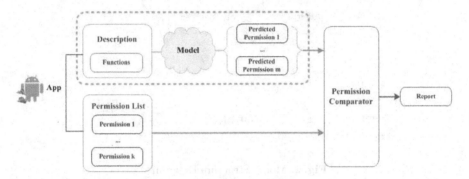

**Fig. 1.** permission-based abnormal application detection framework

In this platform, we can model the description and the permission list of an application to have a research on our security framework. In this concrete environment, we define the description and the permission list of an application as the following signs. Formally, let $p = [p_1, p_2, \ldots p_k]^T$ be the output permission list, in which $p_k \in \{0, 1\}$ denotes whether permission indexed as $k$ should be requested by an application. Let $d = (x_1, x_2, \ldots x_{|V|})$ denotes the description of an application, in which $x_i$ is the index of a word in the dictionary, $V$ is the number of words in the dictionary. Thus, our work in the next several sections is to analyze the usability of our framework in Android. More specifically, we utilize this security framework to predict the hidden dangers of an application based on its description. In our paper, we only detect the reliability of the application's permission list and view this as the criterion of the hidden dangers of the application.

## 3.2   Model Selection

Based on our research problem, we should model the relation between the description and the permission list of an application well in Android platform. In detail, we use machine learning techniques to predict the permissions of an app based on the description of this app. Here, the description which is requested to be provided by developer of this application can be found in Android Market. The basic structure diagram is shown in Figure 2. Because we use supervised learning method to model this relationship, we should collect enough training examples at first. After learning the training examples' relation between the description and permission list, the model can be used in predicting the really needed permission list of an arbitrary application.

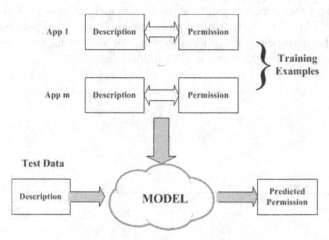

**Fig. 2.** Model Structure Diagram

We use Naive Bayes algorithm with multinomial event model [9] to classify the description of an application based on different permissions. This algorithm is a specialized version of Naive Bayes algorithm. Multinomial Naive Bayes algorithm models the words according to multinomial distribution. That is to say, it not only considers whether a word occurred or not, but also take the times of a word occurs into consideration. This algorithm is proved to have a better result than Naive Bayes algorithm in most occasions [10].

Formally, we have defined $p^{(i)} = [p_1^{(i)}, p_2^{(i)}, \ldots p_k^{(i)}]^T$ be the $i^{th}$ application's output permission list, in which $p_k^{(i)} \in \{0, 1\}$ denotes whether permission indexed as $k$ should be requested by the $i^{th}$ application. Besides, we denote $dic_1, dic_2, \ldots, dic_k$ to be the dictionary of the $k$ different permissions. let $d_k^{(i)} = (x_1^{(i)}, x_2^{(i)}, \ldots x_{|V_k|}^{(i)})$ denotes the description corresponding to the $i^{th}$ application's $k^{th}$ permission, in which $x_j^{(i)}$ is the index of a word $x_j$ occurring in $dic_k$ and $V_k$ denotes the number of words in $dic_k$. Multinomial Naive Bayes model will label the $k^{th}$ permission as 0 or 1 based on the equation:

$$p_k^{(j)*} = \arg \max_{y \in p_k^{(j)}} P(p_k^{(j)}) * \prod_i P(x_i^{(j)} | p_k^{(j)})$$

At last, the model will output a predicted real permission list of an application.

# 4 Experiment

After overviewing our framework, we will model the relation between the description and the permission list of an application in Android platform. In our work, we aim to analyze the really needed permissions of an application from the perspective of its functions. To evaluate our model built in Section 3.3, we have an experiment on the most influential application store - Android Market - to do our experiment.

## 4.1 Selection of Permissions to Be Predicted

We crawled 8,050 applications (top 350 apps in 23 categories) in April, 2011 in Android Market to get the statistics of permissions. Here, we calculate the number of 122 different kinds of permissions [11] occurring in these 8,050 applications. From this statistics, INTERNET was the most frequently requested permission. The number of this permission occurring in 8,050 apps was nearly 7,000. That is to say, most of these apps requested this permission to access internet, which shows the spread of mobile internet. There were also other permissions requested a lot by applications, such as ACCESS_COARSE_LOCATION (requested 2115 times), ACCESS_FINE_LOCATION (requested 2127 times), ACCESS_NETWORK_STATE (requested 3755 times). Except these frequently occurring permissions, nearly 100 of 122 permissions occurred only few times in these apps, which agrees with the opinion in [12]. Because many of the Google defined Android permissions are not common occurring in our dataset, we omit these uncommon permissions. In this paper, we will only focus on the permissions frequently occurring.

Based on the times occurring of different permissions in our statistics, we select the permissions which are valuable to be researched. The rule we select the permissions is as follows: we will pick up the permissions based on their occurring times (we define the times as more than 200 in this paper) in these 8,050 applications. For these permissions, we can use enough training examples to give a prediction on this kind of permissions. At last, we choose 23 common permissions to make a prediction, including ACCESS_COARSE_LOCATION, READ_CONTACTS and CALL_PHONE.

## 4.2 Dataset

Because we use a supervised learning method to make a prediction on the real permission list of an application in Android Market, we have to obtain enough training examples whose permission list is trusted to do this experiment. We crawled 8,050 applications (top 350 apps in 23 categories, including their descriptions and permission list) in Android Market in April, 2011, as discussed before. Here, we assume that these apps are all well-written and not malicious because of the top rank of these apps. So we can use these high-quality apps as training and testing examples to evaluate our model. However, some of these applications' descriptions are not written in English, so we will not use these apps to train our model. Finally, we use 5,685 apps to do this experiment. The process of the experiment is as follows.

- Step 1: Put all the words occurring in applications' descriptions into the dictionary.
- Step 2: For each different permission, we use mutual information filter to pick up the words with high mutual information to this permission to generate a new dictionary which owns words have a great influence on this permission.
- Step 3: Model to predict all 23 permissions in Multinomial Naive Bayes algorithm. Using 10-fold cross validation to test the quality of the models for different permissions.

# 5  Results

In this section, we evaluate the model with 5,685 apps in Android Market. The prediction of permissions of these apps is made by the model of different permissions. To analyze the quality of the model, we compare the real permissions requested by the applications with the predicted permissions. We analyze the result of the prediction of permissions from 2 aspects:

1. We measure the area under the ROC curve (AUC) of different permissions' models to estimate how well our method does to build the relation between the description and the permission list of an application in this problem.
2. We pick up few words which have great influence on the prediction of corresponding permissions to analyze the influence of different words on these permissions.

## 5.1  Evaluation of Model

We use 10-fold cross validation to have a test on this dataset to evaluate the proposed model's quality. At first, we get the Receiver Operating Characteristic (ROC) curves and the Area Under roc Curve (AUC) [13] form the test applications. AUC is metric to evaluate the accuracy of classifying.

Then, we list the value of AUC of 23 permissions in Table 1. From this table, we find the quality of the models predicting different permissions is fine. All of these models' AUC are above 0.8. So for the models of 23 permissions, they reasonably predict the result of permission list. What's more, 12 of 23 permissions have the AUC value greater than 0.9 such as INTERNET, RECEIVE_SMS, READ_CONTACTS. For these excellent predicted permissions, it indicates that some certain functions of an application can obviously reflect the existence of these permissions. For example, the function of making a call or sending messages can definitely correspond to the permission about call or message. For some permissions, we guess the reason why the model on these permissions does not

**Table 1.** AUC value of the model on 23 permissions

| Permission | AUC | Permission | AUC |
|---|---|---|---|
| ACCESS_COARSE_LOCATION | 0.864 | SET_WALLPAPER | 0.922 |
| ACCESS_FINE_LOCATION | 0.851 | WRITE_EXTERNAL_STORAGE | 0.913 |
| ACCESS_NETWORK_STATE | 0.806 | GET_ACCOUNTS | 0.902 |
| ACCESS_WIFI_STATE | 0.845 | GET_TASKS | 0.853 |
| CHANGE_WIFI_STATE | 0.867 | KILL_BACKGROUND_PROCESSES | 0.934 |
| INTERNET | 0.904 | WRITE_SETTINGS | 0.910 |
| READ_PHONE_STATE | 0.880 | CALL_PHONE | 0.928 |
| RECEIVE_SMS | 0.924 | SEND_SMS | 0.964 |
| READ_CONTACTS | 0.915 | WAKE_LOCK | 0.877 |
| WRITE_CONTACTS | 0.944 | VIBRATE | 0.843 |
| CAMERA | 0.909 | RECEIVE_BOOT_COMPLETED | 0.872 |
| RECORD_AUDIO | 0.898 | | |

predict so well is that some certain functions may be mapped into few possible permissions. For instance, function about connecting to the internet may relates to the internet permission or WiFi permission. We can use either of these two permissions or both of these to realize our functions. This factor may influence the accuracy of the model on these permissions to some degree. In general, this result shows that it is effective to predict the real permission list of an application based on its description. So we believe that our model is an effective model to build the relation between the description and the permission list.

## 5.2   Pick Up Influential Words

Next, we will pick up some influential words based on the parameters of the models of each permission. Here, we define the influential words with two features.

- The words should occur frequently in the description of applications. In this paper, we define the frequency as 100 according to 5,685 apps.
- The words should have dominant impact (the dominant impact in this paper is defined as that the positive/negative impact on the occurrence of a permission is as five times as the negative/positive impact on the occurrence of this permission) on positive or negative side to some certain permissions as well.

After selecting influential words based on these two features, we list the result of some of these words in Table 2.

From the words we list in Table 2, we find the result of these influential words is basically fit in with our common sense. For example, in the permissions about location, word "weather" is positive to the occurrence of ACCESS_COARSE_LOCATION, but is not positive to ACCESS_FINE_LOCATION. In contrast, word "GPS" is positive to ACCESS_FINE_LOCATION but not COARSE. For most applications, we think that

**Table 2.** Influential words according to different permissions

| Permission | Positive Words | Negative Words |
|---|---|---|
| ACCESS_COARSE_LOCATION | location, map, weather | bible, wallpaper, word |
| ACCESS_FINE_LOCATION | GPS, location, map | bible, dictionary, wallpaper |
| ACCESS_NETWORK_STATE | ringtone | dictionary, phrases |
| ACCESS_WIFI_STATE | dictionary, word | calculator, jokes, ringtone |
| CHANGE_WIFI_STATE | Wi-Fi | book, dictionary, joke |
| INTERNET | news, online, vedio, | keyboard, plugin |
| READ_PHONE_STATE | radio, ringtone, word | locate |
| RECEIVE_SMS | family, message, SMS | dictionary, image, joke |
| READ_CONTACTS | call, contact, message | dictionary, English, game |
| WRITE_CONTACTS | contact, group, message | calculator, dictionary, game |
| CAMERA | photo, picture, camera | sound, joke, dictionary |
| RECORD_AUDIO | call, record, voice | wallpaper, game, weather |
| SET_WALLPAPER | animated, wallpaper, film | calculator, call, GPS |
| WRITE_EXTERNAL_STORAGE | file, video, reader | task, widget |
| GET_ACCOUNTS | contact, registry, expense | audio, word, sports |
| GET_TASKS | lock, security, ringtone | calculator, word |
| KILL_BACKGROUND_PROCESSES | kill, running, task | dictionary, word, weather |
| WRITE_SETTINGS | alarm, lock, ringtone | book, calculator |
| CALL_PHONE | call, contact, group | file, joke, game |
| SEND_SMS | SMS, message | dictionary, sound |
| WAKE_LOCK | chat, player, radio | bible, dictionary, calculator |
| VIBRATE | alarm, battery, chat | bible, joke, word |
| RECEIVE_BOOT_COMPLETED | battery, backup, notification | calculator, dictionary |

coarse location permission is used in occasions like weather report and restaurant recommendation. So the influential words in this model are corresponding with practice. Besides this example, words such as "picture" and "photo" are positive to the CAMERA permission, which also fit in with our expectation. So the extraction of influential words from models is also basically correct from empirical analysis. From this result, we also conclude the description of an application has a strong relation with the permission list of this application. Therefore, it is a good way to make a model predicting an app's different permissions based on its description.

In addition, some words occur several times no matter as a positive word or a negative word, such as dictionary, calculator, message and location. This indicates that if this kind of words occurs in the description of an application, the model can predict the permissions correctly to a great extent. Here, we take the word "dictionary" as an instance. The word "dictionary" is positive to ACCESS_WIFI_STATE permission, but is negative to permissions about location and permissions about call and SMS. So if there is a word "dictionary" in an application, we will have a quite high probability to make a correct prediction on different permissions of this application. Therefore, the occurrence of these words greatly contributes to the quality of models. As for these influential words, most of these words, such as map, wallpaper, camera and keyboard, are directly represent one of an application's functions. It can be said the word "map" indicates that one of the application's functions is map. The similar case goes with word "wallpaper" and "keyboard". This also demonstrates the functions of an application closely relate to the actions.

# 6  Permission Comparator

## 6.1  Method to Detect Reliability of Permissions

For an application in Android Market, we define the reliability of its permissions as whether this application should request this permission from the perspective of its functions. If an app really needs a permission to accomplish its actual function, we think that the request of this permission is reliable. On the other hand, if an app requests a permission which has no relation with its description, we guess this permission is unreliable.

We can use the model mentioned in Section 3 to detect the reliability of an application's permissions. In detail, if the model which makes a prediction on the real permission list of an application predicts one of the permissions requested by an application should not occur, we believe this permission of this application is not reliable. To apply our model better in detecting the reliability of an application, we should choose a fine threshold of our model to get a higher True Positive Rate without influencing False Positive Rate too much when predicting the reliability of permissions. So from the ROC curves, we find that we can tune the thresholds of different permissions to fulfill the requirement of greater than 90% True Positive Rate and less than 30% False Positive Rate. That is to say, we can use some suitable thresholds to automatically detect the reliability of the permissions of an application. Therefore, our security framework is effective in finding the application with wrongly requested permission list in install-time permission system.

## 6.2  Test on Real Malware

After choosing a fine threshold of our model, we use this model to predict the reliability of malicious apps' permissions. Here we test this method on a real malware announced by Google.

The malware is Steamy Window, which was announced to carry Android.Pjapps code in February, 2011. A report on this malicious application by Symantec shows that this malware adds several bookmarks to the browser and sends users personal information to some certain server. Besides, it can also send some text messages and block some messages with the number of service provider [14].

In Android Market, there was a legitimate application whose name, description and screenshot were all similar with this malware but behaviors were different. The permission list of the legitimate version application is INTERNET and RECORD_AUDIO. However, the malicious application's permission list is INTERNET, RECORD_AUDIO, RECEIVE_SMS and READ_HISTORY_BOOKMARKS.

After testing this application with our model, the result is that the malicious application should not request RECEIVE_SMS permission (we didn't have a test on the permission READ_HISTORY_BOOKMARKS for the reason discussed in section 4.1). This result corresponds with the analysis report by Symantec. The RECEIVE_SMS permission in the malicious app is used to drop some messages without users' attention. So in this example, RECEIVE_SMS permission should not be added in manifest file and is disobey with the ordinary description of this application.

Besides this application, among all the applications announced malicious by Google, many of these malware conceal themselves as an existed trusted application in Android Market. However, these malware change the permission list and add some malicious functions to the ordinary applications.

After testing this malicious application with our model, we think the method predicting the reliability of permissions can also be used in mitigating the security problem of apps in some extent, especially the apps that conceal themselves as some trusted apps. For these malicious applications, some of their permissions are usually additionally added to realize the malicious activity. So we can analyze the reliability of their permission lists based on the relation between the description and the permission list.

## 7   Conclusion

In this paper, we provide a permission-based abnormal application detection framework which identify an abnormal Android app based on its description and its permission list. This novel framework consists two parts: the model which reflects the relation between the description and the permission list and the permission comparator. In detail, we use machine learning method (Naive Bayes with Multinomial Event Model) to predict the occurrence of different permissions of an application based on its description.

We evaluate our model with 5,685 applications collected from 23 different categories in official application store. The result shows that our model is able to have an accurate prediction on different permissions. Besides, we extract some words that have great influence on different permissions. Furthermore, we define the permission comparator to detect the reliability of the permission list of an application and view the permission list's reliability as the criterion of detecting application with hidden danger. After using this model to test a real malware, we find this method is effective in mitigating the security problem of Android applications, especially the malware that conceals themselves as a legitimate app.

**Acknowledgment.** This work is partially supported by the HGJ National Significant Science and Technology Projects under Grant No. 2012ZX01039-004-009, Key Lab of Information Network Security, Ministry of Public Security under Grant No.C11606, the National Natural Science Foundation of China under Grant No. 61170263.

# References

1. G. Inc., https://play.google.com/store
2. (June 5, 2012), http://www.appbrain.com/stats/number-of-android-apps/
3. Enck, W., Gilbert, P., Chun, B., Cox, L., Jung, J., McDaniel, P., Sheth, A.: Taintdroid: an information-flow tracking system for realtime privacy monitoring on smartphones. In: Proceedings of the 9th USENIX Conference on Operating Systems Design and Implementation, pp. 1–6. USENIX Association (2010)
4. Enck, W., Octeau, D., McDaniel, P., Chaudhuri, S.: A study of android application security. In: Proceedings of the 20th USENIX Security Symposium (August 2011)
5. Enck, W., Ongtang, M., McDaniel, P.: On lightweight mobile phone application certification. In: Proceedings of the 16th ACM Conference on Computer and Communications Security, pp. 235–245. ACM (2009)
6. Portokalidis, G., Homburg, P., Anagnostakis, K., Bos, H.: Paranoid android: versatile protection for smartphones. In: Proc. 26th Annual Computer Security Applications Conference (2010)
7. Zhou, Y., Wang, Z., Zhou, W., Jiang, X.: Hey, you, get off of my market: Detecting malicious apps in official and alternative android markets. In: Proceedings of the 19th Annual Network and Distributed System Security Symposium (2012)
8. Burguera, I., Zurutuza, U., Nadjm-Tehrani, S.: Crowdroid: behavior-based malware detection system for android. In: Proceedings of the 1st ACM Workshop on Security and Privacy in Smartphones and Mobile Devices, pp. 15–26. ACM (2011)
9. Lewis, D., Gale, W.: A sequential algorithm for training text classifiers. In: Proceedings of the 17th Annual International ACM SIGIR Conference on Research and Development in Information Retrieval, pp. 3–12. Springer-Verlag New York, Inc. (1994)
10. McCallum, A., Nigam, K.: A comparison of event models for naive bayes text classification. In: AAAI 1998 Workshop on Learning for Text Categorization, vol. 752, pp. 41–48 (1998)
11. G. Inc., http://developer.android.com/reference/android/Manifest.permission.html
12. Barrera, D., Kayacik, H., van Oorschot, P., Somayaji, A.: A methodology for empirical analysis of permission-based security models and its application to android. In: Proceedings of the 17th ACM Conference on Computer and Communications Security, pp. 73–84. ACM (2010)
13. Bradley, A.: The use of the area under the roc curve in the evaluation of machine learning algorithms. Pattern Recognition 30(7), 1145–1159 (1997)
14. Symantec (Februbary 28, 2011), http://www.symantec.com/connect/blogs/android-threats-getting-steamy

# Symbian Smartphone Forensics and Security: Recovery of Privacy-Protected Deleted Data

Vrizlynn L.L. Thing and Darell J.J. Tan

Digital Forensics Lab Cryptography & Security Department
Institute for Infocomm Research, Singapore
{vriz,jjdtan}@i2r.a-star.edu.sg

**Abstract.** In this paper, we discuss our proposed method to acquire privacy-protected data from Symbian smartphones running the latest OS version 9.4, S60 5th Edition, and smartphones running the prior OS version 9.3, S60 3rd Edition. We then present our reverse-engineering analysis work on the active and deleted Short Message Service (SMS) message recovery from the on-phone memory in the Symbian smartphones. We describe the encoding and format of the raw data of the SMS messages so as to achieve an automated parsing and recovery of the messages. Our experiments on various sent, received, draft and deleted messages showed that we were able to recover both the active (in its entirety) and deleted SMS messages (partially) correctly and automatically.

**Keywords:** Symbian forensics, security, memory analysis, mobile phones, smartphones, data acquisition, deleted SMS message recovery.

## 1 Introduction

As mobile phones are becoming increasingly prevalent and are constantly evolving into "smarter" devices (i.e. smartphones with higher processing power and enhanced features), capabilities to perform in-depth forensics on these devices also become essential. However, most current mobile phone forensics tools are still restricted to the acquisition and analysis of basic active files and data (i.e. logical data acquisition) on the Subscriber Identity Module (SIM), memory cards and the internal flash memory [1–7].

In the event that private application data is isolated and data-caging is in place, such security mechanisms prevent in-depth acquisition of important evidentiary data. For example, current Symbian deleted SMS recovery tools [8] have a limitation as they are only capable of recovering deleted SMS messages residing in the SIM card. SMS entries on the SIM card are marked as deleted or active. To undelete an SMS, the tools simply change the state flag in the allocation table from "free" to "in use". However, the real challenges arise when it is necessary to recover deleted SMS messages residing in the internal phone memory originally. This scenario is common due to it being a default configuration in smartphones these days (because of the memory limitation in the SIM

T.W. Chim and T.H. Yuen (Eds.): ICICS 2012, LNCS 7618, pp. 240–251, 2012.

card). Therefore, the capability to recover such deleted SMS messages to aid in forensics investigation is very important and necessary.

In this work, we focus on the recovery of deleted SMS messages from Symbian smartphones. We propose a method to conduct an in-depth evidentiary data acquisition from Symbian smartphones running the latest OS version 9.4, S60 5th Edition, and the prior OS version 9.3, S60 3rd Edition[1]. The acquisition method supports the retrieval of the relevant SMS message data from the Symbian smartphones. We also design an SMS recovery tool which accesses the associated data to reconstruct the deleted SMS messages.

Our main contributions in this work include: (i) creating our customised certificate and utility module to secure the required access to the phone, while at the same time, preserving its security protection mechanism against other softwares (ii) reverse-engineering and analysing the relevant data to support the reconstruction of deleted SMS messages, (iii) building the tool to acquire the data and reconstruct deleted SMS messages residing in the on-phone memory of Symbian smartphones, and (iv) experimenting on the smartphones which run the latest Symbian OS version 9.4, S60 5th Edition, and older OS version 9.3, S60 3rd Edition (i.e. Nokia N97 and E72, respectively). To the best of our knowledge, this is the first work on the recovery/carving of privacy protected deleted data from the Symbian smartphones since the introduction of its platform security framework in the S60 3rd Edition OS.

The rest of the paper is organised as follow. In Section 2, we present an overview of the existing work on mobile phone forensics research. We describe the in-depth acquisition and reverse-engineering experimental work with regard to the Symbian privacy-protected SMS data in Section 3. Future work is described in Section 4 and conclusions follow in Section 5.

## 2    Mobile Phone Forensics Research

In an early work [1], Willassen researched on the forensic investigation of GSM phones. The author presented the types of data of forensic relevance, which can exist on the phones, the SIM and the core network, and emphasized the need for more sound mobile forensics procedures and tools.

In [2], Casadei et al. presented their SIMbrush tool developed for both the Linux and Windows platforms. The tool relied on the PCSC library and supported the acquisition of the entire file system, including the non standard files, on the SIM. However, files with restricted read access conditions could not be extracted.

In [3], Kim et al. presented a tool to acquire the data from a Korea CDMA mobile phone's internal flash memory. The tool communicated with the phone

---

[1] S60 4th Edition does not exist and the next edition after the 3rd Edition is the 5th. Since S60 3rd Edition, Symbian phones begin to use a "hardened version" of its OS, which includes capabilities restrictions and a platform security framework. Versions prior to the 3rd and 5th Edition are not relevant to our work as forensics acquisition was technically easier [5].

through the RS-232C serial interface and was able to acquire the existing files on the phone using the underlying Qualcomm Mobile Station Modem diagnostic mode protocol.

In [4], Mokhonoana and Olivier proposed an on-phone forensic tool to acquire the active files from a Symbian OS v7 phone and store it on the removable media. Instead of interfacing with the PC connectivity services, the tool interacted with the operating system to perform a logical copy of the files. The tested phone was Sony Ericcson P800. One main limitation of the tool was that those files in use could not be copied (e.g. call logs, contacts).

In [5], Distefano et al. proposed the mobile phone internal acquisition technique on the Symbian OS v8 phones. The mobile phone data was acquired using a tool residing on the removable media, instead of the PC/mobile phone USB connection based approach. The tool utilized the Symbian S60 File Server API in the read-only mode. The authors carried out experiments comparing the tool with Paraben Device Seizure (USB connection to phone) and P3nfs (Remote access through Bluetooth). The tool took a longer time to perform the acquisition. However, it was able to acquire more data compared to the P3nfs. When compared with the Paraben Device Seizure, lesser data was acquired. However, the authors observed that the larger data size from Paraben was due to the additional information from its acquired data management.

In [6], Jansen et al. proposed a phone manager protocol filtering technique by intercepting the data between the phone and the phone manager. The objective was to address the latency in the coverage of newly available phone models by existing forensic tools. The authors also proposed an identity module programming technique, to populate the phone's SIM with reference test data, so as to provide a baseline for the validation of SIM forensic tools.

## Surveys on Existing Tools

In [9], Jansen and Ayers evaluated the state-of-the-art SIM forensic tools to understand the capabilities and limitations in their data acquisition, examination and reporting functions. The tools surveyed included Cell Seizure, GSM .XRY, MOBILedit! Forensic, TULP 2G, Forensic Card Reader, Forensic SIM, SIMCon and SIMIS. It was observed that most information such as the IMSI and SMS/EMS could be found by the tools.

In [10], Bhadsavle and Wang evaluated the effectiveness of the Paraben Device Seizure on a test data populated T-Mobile locked SIM. They determined that 100% of the test data were retrieved.

In [11], Williamson et al. studied the performance of different mobile phone forensic tools (i.e. TULP 2G, MOBILedit! Forensic, Cell Seizure and Oxygen Phone Manager) on the Nokia phones. The authors concluded that some tools failed to deliver some promised features (e.g. MD5 hash was not found in MOBILedit!, SHA1 hash was not found in Cell Seizure).

In [12], Ayers et al. conducted a comprehensive study on the current mobile phone forensic tools and presented their findings in the NIST report. The evaluated tools included the Paraben Device Seizure, Pilot-Link, GSM .XRY, Oxygen Phone Manager, MOBILedit!, BitPIM, TULP 2G, SecureView, PhoneBase2, CellDEK, SIMIS2, ForensicSIM, Forensic Card Reader, SIMCon and USIMdetective. The authors presented each tool's capabilities and limitations on a range of mobile phones, covering different operating systems, processor types, and hardware components. Some examples of the tested phones included Samsung SGH-i300, Motorola MPX220, Sony Ericsson P910a, Nokia 7610 and BlackBerry 7780.

In [7], Hoog presented the existing forensic evidence acquisition tools for the Android phone. The Android Debug Bridge (ADB) enabled interaction with the phone over the USB connection. Therefore, active files on the phone can be retrieved through the "adb pull" command. Other tools such as the Nandroid backup and Paraben Device Seizure also supported the extraction of files residing on the phone.

In [8], the SIM Manager tool attempted to recover deleted SMS messages from the SIM card. The SMS messages were stored in a file on the SIM card and each slot in the file contained an SMS. When an SMS was deleted, the slot was marked as "free". To undelete the SMS, the tool can mark the SMS slot as "in use". However, if the deleted SMS messages were stored in the internal phone memory instead, it would not be possible to recover them after deletion by using this tool.

As we can observe from the above-mentioned research, they focus on the acquisition and analysis of active files and data on the phones, with the exception of [8]. In the event of the need to recover deleted sensitive data from smartphones, it is often not possible to use the existing tools. They are either unable to perform a sufficient level of acquisition (due to privacy protection and data-caging present in smartphones) or an in-depth analysis requiring a reverse-engineering effort (due to the different encoding approaches of different OSes and applications). To support the reconstruction of deleted data, an in-depth acquisition and analysis of user data from the phones is required. In our work, we focus on designing and developing an acquisition and analysis tool for recovering deleted privacy protected data from the Symbian smartphones. Our work mainly involves obtaining a privileged access to the phone's privacy protected data in the Symbian smartphones' internal memory and subsequently reverse-engineering the acquired data for the recovery of deleted data. We describe our work using the example of deleted SMS recovery, in this paper.

## 3   Symbian Deleted SMS Recovery

The main challenge in performing an in-depth data acquisition from the internal memory of the Symbian smartphones arises from its built-in security mechanism, which prevents applications from accessing or even viewing private data of the other applications. Such data-caging mechanisms are also present in smartphones running other OSes due to the need for privacy protection as smartphones contain an increasingly substantial amount of confidential and sensitive information such as saved passwords, application configuration settings and data, emails, contacts, notes, calendar of personal and business schedules, and messages.

## 3.1  Symbian AllFiles Capability

Since Symbian S60 3rd Edition OS, the platform security architecture was put in place to restrict access to sensitive functionalities. Applications or tools without having been granted the required capability would not be able to access the restricted Symbian APIs. The AllFiles capability in Symbian allows an unrestricted read access to the entire filesystem. We describe the method to obtain this capability, as follow.

In Symbian, the loader can only run executable files from the \sys\bin directory (from any drive). However, a process with the DiskAdmin capability can access the mapdrive API that maps sub-directories to unused drive letters on the phone [13]. We obtained the DiskAdmin capability through our Symbian Developer Certificate [14]. Therefore, it becomes possible to create a sub-directory \sys\bin under any directory in the phone, place executable files in it and then map it to a new drive letter, effectively placing these executable files into the valid executable path. Details on this mapping technique can be found in [13].

In addition, to eliminate the need to integrate the above-mentioned executable file loading module into all tools and applications requiring high-level privileges, we generate a customised Symbian Authority Certificate and place it into the phone using the mapdrive API. This is achieved by triggering the Symian Certificate Store (SWICertStore) Updater, so that the phone can store our customised certificate. With this certificate residing in the phone, we are now able to sign our tool to provide it with any required high-level privilege (i.e. Allfiles capability). The main advantage of this approach is that, unlike the existing HelloOX2 hack [15], which disables the Symbian install server's security mechanism, we do not compromise the security of the phone by leaving it vulnerable to malwares. We can authorise the installation of specific tool/s by signing it with this higher authority certificate, while the phone still preserves its security mechanism to guard against other unauthorised softwares.

## 3.2  Reconstruction of Active and Deleted SMS Messages

We observed that the data that is associated with the deleted SMS messages exists in the \Private\1000484b\Mail2\Index file of the phone's internal memory. Enabled by the AlLfiles capability (in Section 3.1), this file is now exposed. We retrieved this private Index file to support our analysis. Other than this Index file, there exist several sub-folders in the \Private\1000484b\Mail2 folder. The files within these sub-folders are associated with the active SMS messages. We conducted 50 experiments to obtain the SMS test data for analysis purpose.

## Reconstruction of Active SMS Messages

Each file in the \Private\1000484b\Mail2 corresponds to an active SMS message. Based on our analysis on the data to identify and retrieve relevant information such as the contact number, the contact name, the message contents, the GMT setting and the timestamp information, we observed that each file can be consistently parsed according to the format in Table 1 to obtain its corresponding SMS message.

**Table 1.** SMS Header and Data Format

| Offset | Length | Description | Value(s) and Meaning |
|--------|--------|-------------|----------------------|
| 0 | 4 | SMS header marker | 0x683C0010 |
| 16 | 1 | SMS type | 0x04 (Incoming) or 0x08 (Outgoing) |
| 21 | 1 or 2 | Packet length | |
| +36 | 1 or 2 | SMS message length | |
| +0 | \<length\> | SMS message | |

The "offset" column in Table 1 refers to the absolute offset location within the file. A plus sign prefix, if present, represents a relative offset from the end of the previous entry.

Variable-Length Length Field

As shown in Table 1, a variable-length field is used for representing the length of the packet and message. This representation is very similar to the UTF-8 encoding, except that the lower bits were used here. If the lowest significant bit was set, the length field was extended to the following byte. Otherwise, the length field only occupied one byte. The following algorithm was designed to determine the actual packet and SMS message length.

1. Read the first "length" byte. Take note of the lowest significant bit.
2. Right-shift the byte by one bit. Assign this as the length.
3. If the lowest significant bit was set, right-shift the length by another bit. Read the next byte, left-shift it by six bits and logical OR it with the length in step 2.
4. Subtract one from the length to obtain the actual length.

The remaining data may contain an optional "sent SMS" data block (for outgoing message type only) and other essential information such as the timestamp, contact number or contact name. Table 2 shows the sent SMS data format and Table 3 shows the remaining data following either the SMS header (and message data) or the "sent SMS" data block (if present). The actual length for the contact name, contact number, SMS centre number and sender number has to be computed by dividing the provided length information by four.

Typically, the type of SMS (whether sent or received) can be determined from the message type indicator (1 byte at offset 16 as shown in Table 1). However, during our investigation, we observed a special case, which is the "PAIF message". The PAIF message is a configuration request SMS, which was sent by the

**Table 2.** Sent SMS Data Format

| Offset | Length | Description | Value(s) and Meaning |
|--------|--------|-------------|----------------------|
| +11 | 1 | Sent SMS marker | 0x01 (Data present) or 0x00 (Data not present, no need to parse further) |
| +5 | 1 | Sent flag | 0x00 (Not sent, draft SMS) or 0x01 (Sent SMS) |
| +11 | 8 | Sent timestamp | Time when SMS was sent |
| +0 | 1 | Contact number length | |
| +0 | \<length\> | Contact number | e.g. "+6512345678" |
| +0 | 1 | Contact name length | |
| +0 | \<length\> | Contact name | e.g. "Person A" |

**Table 3.** Remaining SMS Data Format

| Offset | Length | Description | Value(s) and Meaning |
|--------|--------|-------------|----------------------|
| +8 or +10 | 3 | GMT value | For GMT offset computation (+8 if sent block not present, otherwise +10) |
| +5 | 1 | SMS index entry number | Entry number (incrementally generated) |
| +3 | 8 | SMS creation timestamp | Time when SMS was created (applicable for draft and sent SMS only) |
| +2 | 1 | SMS centre number length | |
| +0 | \<length\> | SMS centre number | e.g. "+6512345678" |
| +2 | 1 | Sender number length | Only applicable for received message |
| +0 | \<length\> | Sender number | e.g. "+6587654321" (Only applicable for received message) |
| +2 | 8 | SMS received timestamp | Only applicable for received message |

smartphone to the mobile service provider automatically. Upon investigation, the header indicates a received SMS (message type = 0x04) but it contains the optional "sent SMS" data block. To handle this special scenario, we first determine the SMS message type through its type indicator byte, and then override it as a Sent SMS if the Sent SMS header block is present. Otherwise, the SMS message is deemed to be a received SMS.

For an outgoing SMS, the "Sent flag" field within the "sent SMS" data block will determine whether the SMS has been sent. If it has not been sent, it will be classified as a draft SMS. Otherwise, it will be classified as a sent SMS. The timestamp represented the date and time as the number of microseconds since midnight, January 1st, 0 AD nominal Gregorian, as mentioned in [16]. An example of an active sent SMS message is shown in Figure 1 and an active received SMS message is shown in Figure 2.

```
Offset    0  1  2  3  4  5  6  7   8  9  A  B  C  D  E  F
00000000  68 3C 00 10 68 3C 00 10  00 00 00 00 4B 8E 8D 00   h< h<    K|
00000010  09 70 0F 00 10 F5 03 04  00 00 00 1E 3A 00 10 63   p ő    : c
00000020  00 00 10 00 00 00 00 1F  3A 00 10 00 00 00 00 66   :      f
00000030  00 00 10 00 00 00 00 25  3A 00 10 AE 49 20 77 61   %: ®I va
00000040  6E 74 20 41 20 74 6F 20  64 69 73 61 70 70 65 61   nt A to disappea
00000050  72 2E 20 44 6F 6E 27 74  20 63 61 72 65 20 68 6F   r. Don't care ho
00000060  77 20 79 6F 75 20 64 6F  20 69 74 2E 20 4D 61 6B   w you do it. Mak
00000070  65 20 73 75 72 65 20 69  74 27 73 20 6E 6F 74 20   e sure it's not
00000080  6C 69 6E 6B 65 64 20 62  61 63 6B 20 74 6F 20 6D   linked back to m
00000090  65 2E 0E 20 29 34 18 00  10 1D 05 01 00 01 00 00   e.  )4
000000A0  00 02 00 01 00 00 00 00  00 00 00 00 00 00 00 A9                @
000000B0  48 5D 12 16 97 E1 00 20  38 37 36 35 34 33 32 31   H] |á 87654321
000000C0  20 50 65 72 73 6F 6E 5F  42 23 00 00 00 00 02 00    Person_B#
000000D0  00 00 02 03 08 07 00 01  00 00 00 23 00 00 00 DB            # Û
000000E0  D6 EA 0A 16 97 E1 00 02  91 2C 2B 36 35 39 36 34   Öê |á ',+65964
000000F0  30 30 30 30 31 15 00 81  20 38 37 36 35 34 33 32   00001  8765432
00000100  31 00 00 00 A0 B0 09 00  00 00 00 00 02 00 00 00   1 '
00000110  00 00 00 00 00 00 00 00  04 00 00 00 00 00 00 00
00000120  00 00 00 00 00 00 00 00  00 00 00 00 00 00 00 00
00000130  00 00 00 00 00 00 00 00  00 00 00 00 00 00 ED B0              i'
00000140  1F 10 ED 04 13 00 00 00  00 00 00 00 02 00 00 00   i
00000150  00 00 00 00 00 80 00 00  00 00 00 00 00 00 00 00   |
00000160  00 00 00 00 00 00 00 00  00 00 00 81 00 00 00 00
00000170  00 00 00 81 00 00 00 81  00 00 00 00 00 00 00 02
00000180  00 00 00 00 00 00 00 00  00 00 00 02 00 00 00 00
00000190  00 80 02 00 00 E0 01 00  00 00 00 00 00 00 00 00   | à
000001A0  00 00 00 00 00 00 00 00  00 00 00 00 00 00 00 00
000001B0  00 00 00 00 00 00 00 00  00 00 00 00 00 00 00 00
000001C0  00 00 00 00 00 00 00 00  00 00 00 00 00 00 00 00
000001D0  00 00 00 00 00 00 00 00  00 00 00 00 00 00 00 00
000001E0  00 0A B0 00 20 42 00 00  00 00 00 02 00 00 00 02   ' B
000001F0  00 00 00 00 00 00
```

**Fig. 1.** Active Sent SMS Message

```
Offset    0  1  2  3  4  5  6  7   8  9  A  B  C  D  E  F
00000000  68 3C 00 10 68 3C 00 10  00 00 00 00 4B 8E 8D 00   h< h<    K|
00000010  04 70 0F 00 10 95 04 04  00 00 00 1E 3A 00 10 63   p |    : c
00000020  00 00 10 00 00 00 00 1F  3A 00 10 00 00 00 00 66   :      f
00000030  00 00 10 00 00 00 00 25  3A 00 10 D6 4F 6B 2E 20   %: ÖOk.
00000040  44 65 70 6F 73 69 74 20  24 31 30 6B 20 74 6F 20   Deposit $10k to
00000050  41 42 43 20 62 61 6E 6B  20 61 63 63 6F 75 6E 74   ABC bank account
00000060  20 39 39 39 39 38 38 38  38 37 37 37 37 20 6E 6F    999988887777 no
00000070  77 20 61 6E 64 20 70 61  79 20 74 68 65 20 72 65   w and pay the re
00000080  73 74 20 6F 66 20 24 32  30 6B 20 61 66 74 65 72   st of $20k after
00000090  20 74 68 65 20 6A 6F 62  20 69 73 20 63 6F 6D 70    the job is comp
000000A0  6C 65 74 65 64 2E 0E 20  29 34 18 00 10 05 04 01   leted.  )4
000000B0  00 00 00 00 00 00 00 00  00 02 03 08 07 40 01 00               @
000000C0  00 00 24 00 00 00 9D 69  13 1A 16 97 E1 00 00 91   $ i |á '
000000D0  2C 2B 36 35 39 36 34 30  30 30 30 31 04 91 2C 2B   ,+6596400001 ',+
000000E0  36 35 38 37 36 35 34 33  32 31 00 00 80 E2 58 23   6587654321 |âX#
000000F0  16 97 E1 00 20 00 00 00  00 00 00 00 02 00 00 00   |á
00000100  00 00 00 00 00 00 00 00  00 04 00 00 00 00 00 00
00000110  00 00 00 00 00 00 00 00  00 00 00 00 00 00 00 00
00000120  00 00 00 00 00 00 00 00  00 00 00 00 00 00 00
```

**Fig. 2.** Active Received SMS Message

## Reconstruction of Deleted SMS Messages

We observed that each deleted SMS entry in the index file contains the start marker, "0x6A0F00102C". To extract a deleted SMS, this start marker is firstly located. The index file is parsed according to the format shown in Table 4.

**Table 4.** Deleted SMS Header and Data Format

| Offset | Length | Description | Value(s) and Meaning |
|---|---|---|---|
| 0 | 5 | SMS start marker | 0x6A0F00102C |
| 8 | 8 | Timestamp | Sent or received timestamp |
| 28 | 1 | SMS message type | 0x44 (sent or draft message) or 0x00 (received message) |
| 56 | 1 or 2 | SMS message length | |
| +0 | <length> | SMS message | |
| +0 | 1 | Contact information length | |
| +0 | <length> | Contact information | Contact number or contact name (if present in address book) |
| +2 | 8 | SMS received timestamp | Only applicable for received message |

The maximum number of bytes that each entry can hold as a deleted SMS message is observed to be 64 bytes. This is indicated by the length information of "0x0102". Therefore, if the original message is less than or equal to 64 bytes, the entire message can be recovered. Otherwise, only a partial deleted SMS is recoverable. The length information provided in the table is also of a variable length. The actual length is computed by simply dividing the provided length information by four. If the first byte is "0x01", the length information is contained in this first byte and its following byte. Otherwise, if the first byte is in the range of "0x04" to "0xFC", the length information is provided by this byte alone. In addition, no GMT setting information was provided in the index file entries for the deleted SMS messages. To retrieve the next deleted entry, a search for the next start marker is conducted and the data has to be parsed accordingly (as shown in Table 4). This procedure is repeated until no more deleted SMS start marker is found. An example of a deleted sent SMS record is shown in Figure 3 and a deleted received SMS record is shown in Figure 4.

**Further Memory Dump Investigation**

We conducted an investigation to find out if the rest of the deleted SMS message (i.e. after the 64th byte) can be retrieved from the raw data space. We developed an internal phone memory dump tool, which accessed the Symbian TBusLocalDrive API, to perform an internal phone memory dump. The dump was performed on the internal phone memory as it was the configured location to store the SMS messages. The tool required another manufacturer-approved capability, the TCB capability, which we signed using our certificate and installed on to the Symbian phones. We then made an attempt to search the entire internal phone memory dump for the non-recoverable part of the deleted SMS message contents (i.e. >64 bytes). The contents could not be found.

```
Offset     0  1  2  3  4  5  6  7   8  9  A  B  C  D  E  F
00000000  6A 0F 00 10 2C 10 00 10  86 D6 2E 12 16 97 E1 00   j    IÖ. Iá
00000010  AB 01 00 00 00 00 00 00  00 00 00 00 44 00 00 00   «          D
00000020  00 00 00 00 00 00 00 00  00 00 00 00 00 00 00 00
00000030  DA 2D 86 02 DA 2D 84 02  FC 49 20 77 61 6E 74 20   Ú-I Ú-I üI want
00000040  41 20 74 6F 20 64 69 73  61 70 70 65 61 72 2E 20   A to disappear.
00000050  44 6F 6E 27 74 20 63 61  72 65 20 68 6F 77 20 79   Don't care how y
00000060  6F 75 20 64 6F 20 69 74  2E 20 4D 61 6B 65 20 73   ou do it. Make s
00000070  75 72 65 20 69 74 27 73  20 4F 74 68 65 72 53 49   ure it's Person_
00000080  4D D8 72 20 10 3B 80 01  00 00 80 1B 00 00 83 43   BØr ;I   I   IC
00000090  00 00 00 0C 00 00 00 20  00 05 01 00 00 00 35 02                 5
000000A0  00 00 04 00 00 00 FD 09  00 00 06 00 00 00 90 06        ý
000000B0  00 00 1B 00 00 83 1C 00  00 80 42 00 00 03 9C 0A        I   IB  I
000000C0  00 00 A2 40 02 4E 00 10  00 04 10 00 00 01 02 01   o@ N
000000D0  00 00 00 00 00 00 00 00  00 01 10 00 00 00 00 10
000000E0  00
```

**Fig. 3.** Deleted Sent SMS Message

```
Offset     0  1  2  3  4  5  6  7   8  9  A  B  C  D  E  F
00000000  6A 0F 00 10 2C 10 00 10  80 E2 58 23 16 97 E1 00   j    IâX# Iá
00000010  00 00 00 00 00 00 00 00  00 00 00 00 00 00 00 00
00000020  00 00 00 00 00 00 00 00  00 00 00 00 00 00 00 00
00000030  DA 2D 89 02 DA 2D 89 02  01 02 4F 6B 2E 20 44 65   Ú-I Ú-I   Ok. De
00000040  70 6F 73 69 74 20 24 31  30 6B 20 74 6F 20 41 42   posit $10k to AB
00000050  43 20 62 61 6E 6B 20 61  63 63 6F 75 6E 74 20 39   C bank account 9
00000060  39 39 39 38 38 38 37 37  37 37 20 6E 6F 77 20 20   99988887777 now
00000070  61 6E 64 20 70 61 79 20  74 68 20 50 65 72 73 6F   and pay th Perso
00000080  6E 5F 42 84 D6 20 10 08  40 01 00 00 00 50 00 10   n_BIÖ   @    P
00000090  00 A5 40 02 48 00 10 00  02 10 00 00 21 10 12 00   ¥@ H       !
000000A0  00 00 00 00 00 00 00 00  01 10 00 00 00 00 00 00
```

**Fig. 4.** Deleted Received SMS Message

## 4 Future Work

We plan to conduct further and more thorough investigations on the persistency
of the deleted SMS messages. Our preliminary investigation results showed that
the persistency of the deleted SMS messages does not depend on factors such
as how long the phones have been left running or the active use of other applications. Instead, it depends on the messaging application. The deleted SMS
messages were observed to be undetectable after transmission of "sufficient"
multiple subsequent SMS messages (e.g. after the subsequent transmission of
ten active SMS messages, we observed that one of the deleted SMS messages
became undetectable). Another planned future work is the reconstruction of
other Symbian privacy-protected deleted application data such as the multimedia messaging service (MMS) messages, emails, notes, and other common data
types present in smartphones.

## 5 Conclusions

In this paper, we identified the need for an in-depth acquisition and analysis of
the privacy-protected data in the Symbian smartphones, which were running the
latest OS version 9.4, S60 5th Edition, as well as the prior OS version 9.3, S60 3rd

Edition. We obtained the necessary Symbian capability to access the privacy-protected data without compromising the phone's built-in security mechanism. This was achieved through the generation and installation of our customised high-level privilege certificate onto the phone through our developed mapdrive exploit.

In addition, we performed reverse-engineering on the acquired data to derive the encoding and format of the data so as to reconstruct both active and deleted SMS messages. Through our research, we also discovered the presence of a special scenario (i.e. PAIF message) and proposed the approach to handle it correctly when designing and developing our recovery tool. Our experiments on various sent, received, draft and deleted messages showed that we were able to recover both the active (in its entirety) and deleted SMS messages (up to a message length of 64 bytes) correctly and automatically.

# References

1. Willassen, S.: Forensics and the GSM mobile telephone system. International Journal of Digital Evidence 2(1), 1–17 (2003)
2. Casadei, F., Savoldi, A., Gubian, P.: Forensics and SIM cards: an overview. International Journal of Digital Evidence 5(1), 1–21 (2006)
3. Kim, K., Hong, D., Chung, K., Ryou, J.-C.: Data acquisition from cell phone using logical approach. In: Proceedings of World Academy of Science, Engineering and Technology, vol. 26 (December 2007)
4. Mokhonoana, P.M., Olivier, M.S.: Acquisition of a Symbian smart phone's content with an on-phone forensic tool. Department of Computer Science. University of Pretoria (2007)
5. Distefano, A., Me, G.: An overall assessment of mobile internal acquisition tool. In: Proceedings of the 8th Digital Forensics Research Conference (DFRWS), Digital Investigation, vol. 5(1), pp. S121–S127 (September 2008)
6. Jansen, W., Delaitre, A., Moenner, L.: Overcoming impediments to cell phone forensics. In: Proceedings of the 41st Hawaii International Conference on System Sciences (2008)
7. Hoog, A.: Android forensics, Presented at Mobile Forensics World 2009 (May 2009)
8. Dekart, Sim manager (February 2012), http://www.dekart.com
9. Jansen, W., Ayers, R.: Forensic software tools for cell phone subscriber identity modules. In: Conference on Digital Forensics, Association of Digital Forensics, Security, and Law (ADFSL) (April 2006)
10. Bhadsavle, N., Wang, J.A.: Validating tools for cell phone forensics, Southern Polytechnic State University, Technical Report CISE-CSE-08-05 (2008)
11. Williamson, B., Apeldoorn, P., Cheam, B., McDonald, M.: Forensic analysis of the contents of Nokia mobile phones. In: Proceedings of the 4th Australian Digital Forensics Conference (December 2006)
12. Ayers, R., Jansen, W., Moenner, L., Delaitre, A.: Cell phone forensic tools: An overview and analysis update, National Institute of Standards and Technology, Technical Report 7387 (March 2007)

13. Muller, B.: From 0 to 0 day on symbian - finding low level vulnerabilities on symbian smartphones. SEC Consult Vulnerability Lab Whitepaper (June 2009)

14. Nokia, Symbian signed developer certificate, `http://www.developer.nokia.com/Community/Wiki/Developer_Certificate_(Symbian_Signed)`

15. HelloOX2 Team, Helloox2 (April 2012), `http://helloox2.com`

16. Nokia, Symbian timestamp storage and manipulation (April 2012), `http://library.developer.nokia.com/index.jsp?topic=/S60_5th_Edition_Cpp_Developers_Library/GUID-35228542-8C95-4849-A73F-2B4F082F0C44/sdk/doc_source/reference/reference-cpp/Kernel_Architecture_2/TTimeClass.html`

# Detecting Encryption Functions via Process Emulation and IL-Based Program Analysis*

Ruoxu Zhao, Dawu Gu, Juanru Li, and Hui Liu

Dept. of Computer Science and Engineering
Shanghai Jiao Tong University
Shanghai, China
dwgu@sjtu.edu.cn

**Abstract.** Malware often encrypts its malicious code and sensitive data to avoid static pattern detection, thus detecting encryption functions and extracting the encryption keys in a malware can be very useful in security analysis. However, it's a complicated process to automatically detect encryption functions among huge amount of binary code, and the main challenge is to keep high efficiency and accuracy at the same time. In this paper we propose an enhanced detection approach. First we designed a novel process level emulation technique to efficiently analyze binary code, which is less resource-consuming compared with full system emulation. Further, we conduct program partitioning and assembly-to-IL(intermediate language) translation on binary code to simplify the analysis. We applied our approach to sample programs using cryptographic libraries and custom implemented version of typical encryption algorithms, and showed that these routines can be detected efficiently. It is convenient for analysts to use our approach to deal with the encrypted data within malware automatically. Our approach also provides an extensible interface for analysts to add extra templates to detect other forms of functions besides encryption routines.

**Keywords:** Encryption detection, Process emulation, Intermediate language, Binary code analysis.

## 1 Introduction

Recent years have witnessed a dramatic rise in the growth of work on automatically detecting certain algorithms in programs especially in malware. In order to solve the problem of algorithm detection, a number of approaches were proposed, and most of them are mainly heuristic[10][9][6]. However, despite an increasing interest in algorithm identification in binary programs, in particular in detecting cryptographic primitives, there still lacks systematic and convenient approaches that facilitate researchers to perform efficient detection.

---

* Supported by the National Science and Technology Major Projects 2012ZX03002011-002.

T.W. Chim and T.H. Yuen (Eds.): ICICS 2012, LNCS 7618, pp. 252–263, 2012.

We present a generic encryption function detecting approach using *Process Emulation* and *IL(intermediate language)-based Program Analysis*, which is targeted at achieving fast, convenient and extensible detection. The basic principles behind our technique are stripping unnecessary runtime information, simplifying analysis process and providing interface for new extensions. First, we designed and implemented our own process emulator to reduce the overhead brought by emulating full system environment. Then we adopted a custom defined IL to simplify analyzed program. Based on this IL, not only we designers but also other analysts could easily write a template to match certain algorithms. And finally, we combined IL-based template matching and dynamic data verification to improve the accuracy and efficiency of encryption routines identification.

Some of the contributions of this work are listed below.

- *Lightweight process emulation.* We designed process emulation, a novel emulation technique, to run a program within its host operating system, and only emulate the necessary components of a system for the program to be analyzed. This technique provides a lightweight emulation environment with fast speed while keeping fine-grained analyzing capability.
- *IL-based program transformation.* To address the issues of dynamic program pattern matching and analysis, we further extended detection method by introducing intermediate language as analyzing medium, increasing its efficiency and accuracy, and acquiring platform compatibility at the same time.
- *Flexible template matching.* We provided an open interface for analysts to write template of different algorithms in IL form. Our emulator dynamically loads templates during the detection phase and uses template to construct heuristics.
- *Template based data filtering and verification.* Traditional matching approaches may verify all runtime data, and meanwhile test huge amount of unrelated data. Our IL based analyzer first matches code fragments with templates and filters out those data of mismatching code fragments. Then, a data verifier is designed to check matched data and deploy refined input-output verification. The process not only improves verification efficiency significantly, but also reduces false positive rate to negligible level.

The rest of the paper is structured as following. Section 2 gives an overview of algorithm detection problem and related work. Section 3 describes our approach in detail. Section 4 gives concrete instance of template based encryption function detection and evaluation results. Some countermeasures to our approach are discussed in section 5 and an overview about future work is given. And section 6 concludes this paper.

## 2   Problem Statement

Encryption function detection is a problem of searching certain algorithms in programs especially in binary code. This work is based on the following assumptions: (1) The knowledge of the algorithm is obtained before detection; (2)

The implementation of the algorithm is not aimed at failing the detection deliberately. These assumptions are reasonable in the real world for the following reasons. First, it is always prudent to adopt mature encryption algorithms for the consideration of security, and these mature encryption algorithms are generally public and are tested for a long term. So we suppose that the precondition of detecting an encryption algorithm is knowing its details. Second, In most cases, the purpose of the encryption algorithms in malware is to protect malicious code and to hide sensitive data. Thus these encryption algorithms are often implemented without being obfuscated or packed in order to provide accuracy and efficiency.

Previous detection methods generally take advantage of certain properties of an algorithm as the signature. Caballero et al.[3] took advantage of the fact that encryption routines use a high percentage of bitwise arithmetic instructions. The approach of Groebert el al.[4] was based on both generic characteristics of cryptographic code and signatures for specific instances of cryptographic algorithms. Zhang et al.[12] proposed an algorithm plagiarism detection approach using critical runtime values. And Zhao et al.[13] used input-output correlation of certain ciphers to detect cryptographic data.

There are several reasons why proposing new detection techniques is necessary to current security analysis.

- Existing approaches usually use tools such as QEMU[2] and PIN[8] to trace data and instructions. And these tools don't have satisfactory performance. Actually, Groebert el al.[4] reported that for a malware analysis process the tracing took 14 hours and the analysis phase 8 hours.
- Existing approaches are not extensible. That is to say, analysts can't easily adjust these specific approaches to either adapt different implementations of algorithms or to detect new ones.
- Taking traced instructions alone as input is not enough to acquire effective heuristics. For dynamic data based detection, the main problem is how to filter out useless data according to heuristics.

In contrast to previous work in this area, the goal of our work is to design extensive, convenient and efficient detection approach. We argue that a new approach for efficient tracing is necessary. And because the data feature related to algorithm is very important for heuristics, it is suggested to combine instructions and data together to acquire powerful heuristics. What's more, a simple form of program is able to improve analyzing efficiency and help an analyst deploy her own detection. We improved the detection approach in two aspects: one is to perform a high speed program tracing using process emulation, and the other one is to translate program into IL to simplify construction of heuristics and third-party matching extension design. In addition, our approach verifies the matching result with input-output data correlation to reduce the chance of false positive, and to extract the input and output parameter(e.g., the secret key) at the same time.

# 3    Our Approach

Our approach adopts a hybrid methodology combining code characteristic matching and data input-output verification. To make dynamic analysis possible, the program we're trying to analyze is first executed in an emulation environment, and low-level runtime data is acquired in this step. Then, traced instructions are partitioned to fragments, and translated to our IL representations. For each block of program, fuzzy matching techniques which are inaccurate but fast are used with existing algorithm templates implemented in IL. And finally, dynamic data verification is conducted to identify the correct algorithm and extract parameters.

## 3.1    Process Emulation

A full-system emulator, such as Bochs[7], often emulates a set of fully functional hardware, and runs an operating system on the emulated hardware. It usually runs as a user-space process in the host operating system. A program to be analyzed runs in the emulated operating system, where non-privileged and privileged instructions are all executed in a software emulated environment.

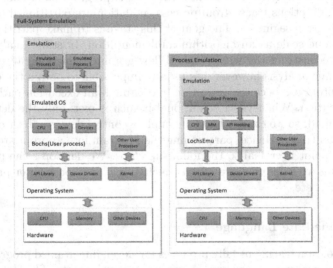

**Fig. 1.** Comparison of Full System Emulation and Process Emulation

Because of the nature of instruction emulation, full-system emulators often have a poor performance. Through actual tests, we found that Bochs emulator runs $10^2$ slower than non-emulated environment. To emulate a single instruction, we often need tens even hundreds of actual instructions, which considerably impacts the runtime performance of a full-system emulator.

In program analysis using full-system emulation, we see that the guest (emulated) operating system and the host operating system are usually the same, and the OS specific operations, such as process context switch, are trivial to our analysis. Therefore, we came up a program emulation proposal that directly emulates the target program on host operating system, which we called process emulation.

Being different from full-system emulation, process emulation directly uses the host operating system to provide OS-specific features, such as handling system API calls. This assumption requires the guest OS and the host OS to be the same. The process emulator is a user-space application that can emulate other user-space applications, where CPU instruction execution, memory management and some OS features are emulated by the process emulator, and system calls/APIs are executed by the host operating system. The comparison of full system emulation and process emulation is shown in figure 1.

One advantage of process emulation is that all system API calls are hooked by the emulator. Hence, sandboxing can be easily achieved and malware can be run directly on the emulator, preventing the malware from interfering with the real OS.

## 3.2  Program Partitioning

The first step of analysis after program tracing is program partitioning, where sequential instructions traced from process emulation are partitioned into basic blocks or program segments. The goal of this stage is to make partitioned segments the same scale as an algorithm implementation. In static analysis, it is possible to reconstruct the whole control flow graph or function call hierarchy, but in dynamic analysis however, it's usually impossible to obtain the complete image of a program, because we cannot get through all execution paths in one time of execution. Whenever a conditional branch is met, only the determined path is executed, so we cannot build a complete control flow graph through limited execution traces. Hence, partitioning the program into appropriate scale at appropriate point is crucial to the follow-up steps. We develop some partitioning algorithms with different granularity, including basic blocks, inter-procedure, procedure call, etc.

## 3.3  Intermediate Language

Dynamic program tracing usually produces low-level, fine-grained program data, including processor register values, memory access values, etc. The fact that our IL is designed to be close to machine language makes translation from tracing result to IL can be done with the lowest cost. The instruction set of our IL is highly reduced as well, which helps to increase template matching performance, and grasp primary runtime information at the same time. In this way, we build up an IL that is light-weighted, platform-compatible and easy to analyze, and is used in each step of analysis, including dynamic translation, template algorithm implementation, program matching and dynamic data verification. The structure of an IL template is shown in figure 2.

```
VAR_DESC       ::= 'var'    VAR_NAME ':' VAR_TYPE
                            (',' VAR_NAME ':' VAR_TYPE)* ;
INPUT_DESC     ::= 'input'  VAR_NAME (',' VAR_NAME)* ;
OUTPUT_DESC    ::= 'output' VAR_NAME (',' VAR_NAME)* ;


PROGRAM        ::= INSTRUCTION+ ;
INSTRUCTION    ::= UNARY_INSTRUCTION | BINARY_INSTRUCTION |
                   ASSIGNMENT_INSTRUCTION | BRANCH_INSTRUCTION |
                   CONDITIONAL_BRANCH_INSTRUCTION |
                   ARRAY_INSTRUCTION ;

UNARY_INSTRUCTION         ::= LVALUE '=' UNARY_OP RVALUE ;
BINARY_INSTRUCTION        ::= LVALUE '=' RVALUE BINARY_OP RVALUE ;
ASSIGNMENT_INSTRUCTION    ::= LVALUE '=' RVALUE ;
BRANCH_INSTRUCTION        ::= 'jmp' LABEL ;
CONDITIONAL_BRANCH_INSTRUCTION    ::=
                          'jmp' LABEL '[' RVALUE BRANCH_OP RVALUE ']' ;
ARRAY_INSTRUCTION         ::= ARRAY_GET | ARRAY_SET | ARRAY_COPY ;


VAR_TYPE       ::= int32 | int64 | array | string ;
LVALUE         ::= VAR_NAME ;
RVALUE         ::= VAR_NAME | CONSTANT ;
UNARY_OP       ::= 'length' | 'append' | 'remove' | '~' ;
BINARY_OP      ::= '+' | '-' | '^' | '&' | '|' | '*' | '/' |
                   '%' | '>>' | '<<' | '>>>' | '<<<' ;
BRANCH_OP      ::= '>' | '>=' | '<' | '<=' | '==' | '!=' ;
```

**Fig. 2.** IL Program Template

## 3.4   Assembly-to-IL Translation

In the translation step, binary instructions are translated into IL instructions. This is usually done after program partitioning, because the translation may lose information about original program context. The translation is not accurate, which means that some irrelevant information is discarded. For example, the zero flag in x86 architecture indicates if an arithmetic operation produces a zero value[5], and most of the time, we don't care if the value is zero, so the value of zero flag is discarded in the translation.

**Selection of Instructions.** Not all traced instructions are translated into IL instructions. Normally, translations are limited to these categories: arithmetic, logical, bitwise, data transferring, control-flow transferring, etc.

**Memory Access.** Data used in program execution is usually contained in memory. For almost every algorithm implementation, its input and output parameters are first stored in memory, then displayed on the screen or stored in a file. By identifying memory reading and writing, we can generate dynamic inputs and outputs of a program, and perform data verification in later stage. We treat the memory as a global array object, and memory reading and writing are translated into array getting and setting at the index specified by the address of memory access.

**Data Preservation.** The advantage of dynamic program analysis is that we have direct access to runtime data which is unavailable in static analysis. Each instruction in IL program segment has an optional field that stores its original context, including memory access values, instruction pointer, etc.

## 3.5   Template Matching

In template matching step, IL segments are matched to template IL programs using fuzzy matching techniques, and the matched segments are further verified in data verification step.

A template program is an implementation of a certain algorithm written in IL code, which can be executed in IL interpreter and has explicit input and output format. A dynamic translated IL program segment, on the other hand, contains an incomplete translation of traced instructions, and usually cannot be executed in the interpreter. Also, it contains runtime data of the original program, which is different from IL templates. Template matching is done in IL-instruction level or IL control-flow level(control flow information is contained in dynamic translated program), and is controlled by a posteriori threshold, which defines the matching accuracy.

In template matching step, efficiency is usually more important than accuracy. Previous research of data pattern matching showed that analyzing large amount of irrelevant data is the bottleneck of dynamic data analysis. Hence, the main purpose of template matching is that we can filter out most of the impossible traced result with little cost. To keep a low false-negative rate, we should only filter out the "obviously impossible" segments. Fortunately in most cases, most of the dynamic translated segments satisfy such a condition. We designed some fine-tuned template matching algorithms, including direct mapping, instruction frequency, CFG matching and scale predicting.

## 3.6   Dynamic Data Verification

In this step, all input and output data is first extracted from the program segment. We assume that all the data needed for analysis is stored in memory, and we define the input data as the memory values first referenced by memory reading, and the output data as the memory values last set by memory writing. This data is then further processed into memory chunks, according to its memory offset(address).

Next, we try to construct possible algorithm parameters from the memory chunks. We use some heuristic techniques to eliminate low-priority data, such as pointer values, all-zero (initializing) values, etc. Each possible set of parameters is in turn injected into the IL interpreter.

Then, after injection of parameters, the IL interpreter executes the template program to produce output results. Each output result is then verified in the program segment's output data, and if a matching is found, we confirm that the implementation of a certain algorithm exists in a program segment. The workflow of data verification is shown in figure 3.

We can see that we don't have to know the exact implementation of the algorithm we're trying to analyze. We just have to provide one template implementation, and the data verification will test if they are the same.

False positives are highly unlikely to happen when the input and output parameters reach a certain length, say 128-bit. We may take the AES encryption

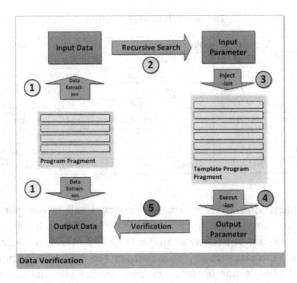

**Fig. 3.** Dynamic Data Verification

as an example. Each 128-bit input block is encrypted into an 128-bit output block, and whenever the correct 128-bit data shows up in a program segment's runtime data, we may safely say that it contains an AES encryption, because the implementation is similar to the template, which is verified in the template matching step, and the corresponding data is correct, verified in this step.

The data verification step tells us if an algorithm implementation truly exists in the original program, and extracts its corresponding parameter, completing the analysis.

## 4    Experiment and Evaluation

We choose several custom programs as well as common cryptography libraries such as OpenSSL[11] to implement cryptographic algorithms, and use them as testing programs for proof-of-concept evaluation of accuracy, effectiveness and performance. The cryptographic algorithms we use include AES(128-bit and 256-bit), RC4, MD5, SHA1 and SHA2, and the implementations of the same algorithm are different and independent. The AES implementations are from the original Rijndael implementation, OpenSSL library and Nettle[1] crypto library, the RC4 implementation is custom, and the hash functions are from OpenSSL library. A primary result of all testing programs is shown in table 1.

**Partitioning Strategy.** In experiments, we use the inter-procedure partitioning as the main program partitioning method. The basic-block partitioning can hardly satisfy the structure of template algorithms, since template algorithms often have many basic blocks and a complicated control-flow. The

**Table 1.** The Test Results

| Binary | Algorithm | Algorithm Detected | Description |
|---|---|---|---|
| aes_std.exe | AES 128-bit | aes_subkey_be | Original AES implementation |
| aes_nettle.exe | AES 128-bit | aes_subkey_le | Nettle crypto library |
| aes_ssl.exe | AES 128-bit | aes_key | OpenSSL library |
| aes256_ssl.exe | AES 256-bit | aes_key_256 | OpenSSL library |
| rc4_custom.exe | RC4 | rc4_key | Custom implementation |
| md5_ssl.exe | MD5 | md5_core | OpenSSL library |
| sha1_ssl.exe | SHA1 | sha1_core | OpenSSL library |
| sha2_ssl.exe | SHA2 | sha2_core | OpenSSL library |

procedure partitioning tracks a whole function call in one partition, which has a huge memory consumption, and is difficult to achieve an acceptable performance because of the vast amount of data. The inter-procedure partitioning satisfies all our needs, as it can get the appropriate partition scale, and the fact that it has no memory need makes the analysis can be done simultaneously with tracing.

**Matching Algorithms.** We find that complicated matching algorithms are not necessary in our analysis, and we primarily combine the instruction frequency and scale predicting as the matching algorithm. Direct mapping algorithm has complexity of $O(n^2)$, which is too slow for fast but inaccurate matching. Instruction frequency has complexity of $O(n)$, and in actual experiments it can distinguish matching program segments from other segments quite well. CFG matching algorithm is unavailable in most circumstances, since the CFG of a segment is not always available in one dynamic execution. And finally, the scale predicting turns out to be very effective. It has the complexity of $O(1)$ and can efficiently identify those segments which are too large or too small for a template program. The matching similarity is combined from all matching algorithms, and mapped to [0, 1]. We use a threshold of 0.95 in all experiments, and then the non-matching segments usually have similarity of less than 0.90. We list each of the matching similarity in table 2.

**Table 2.** Matching Results

| Binary | Algorithm | Algorithm Detected | Similarity |
|---|---|---|---|
| aes_std.exe | AES 128-bit | aes_subkey_be | 0.9650 |
| aes_nettle.exe | AES 128-bit | aes_subkey_le | 0.9713 |
| aes_ssl.exe | AES 128-bit | aes_key | 0.9610 |
| aes256_ssl.exe | AES 256-bit | aes_key_256 | 0.9574 |
| rc4_custom.exe | RC4 | rc4_key | 0.9585 |
| md5_ssl.exe | MD5 | md5_core | 0.9527 |
| sha1_ssl.exe | SHA1 | sha1_core | 0.9577 |
| sha2_ssl.exe | SHA2 | sha2_core | 0.9652 |

**Performance.** The performance evaluation includes both program emulation (tracing) and analysis. As tracing and analysis are done at the same time, we run each testing program twice, one with analysis and one without analysis. The performance result is shown in table 3. The tracing time is usually trivial in each program execution comparing to the analysis. We see that program tracing takes less than 1 second, which is much faster than whole system emulation(booting Bochs alone will take about 5 minutes, and tracing is also slower). During analysis, the dynamic data verification step is the most time-consuming one, because there's a lot of data to be verified by IL template, which is run by the IL interpreter. Improper program partitioning and template arguments can severely slow down this step, as a large segment can produce much irrelevant data, and a small length of template input argument will heavily increase the number of times in searching, thus burdening the data verification. We also tested the effectiveness of template matching, and found that analysis took 10 to 50 times longer without template matching. Besides, these is no acceleration in the IL interpreter, which also downgrade the analysis. Despite all this, the average analysis(including tracing) speed is 167 kIPS(instructions per second), which is more than 10 times faster than the previous result of 15 kIPS(excluding tracing). Such performance result is quite acceptable considering there's no optimizations in this proof-of-concept evaluation.

**Table 3.** Performance Evaluation

| Binary | Time(trace) | Time(analysis) | Time(total) | Insts | kIPS |
|---|---|---|---|---|---|
| aes_std.exe | 0.013(s) | 3.712 | 3.725 | 103,757 | 27.854 |
| aes_nettle.exe | 0.068 | 21.395 | 21.463 | 808,828 | 37.684 |
| aes_ssl.exe | 0.025 | 0.822 | 0.847 | 230,241 | 271.831 |
| aes256_ssl.exe | 0.025 | 0.847 | 0.872 | 234,680 | 269.128 |
| rc4_custom.exe | 0.051 | 1.775 | 1.826 | 459,642 | 251.720 |
| md5_ssl.exe | 0.016 | 0.422 | 0.438 | 147,256 | 336.200 |
| sha1_ssl.exe | 0.065 | 0.512 | 0.577 | 36,018 | 62.422 |
| sha2_ssl.exe | 0.011 | 0.745 | 0.756 | 57,507 | 76.067 |

# 5 Discussion

## 5.1 Countermeasures

Our method may produce false negatives when used against protected code or custom implementations of an algorithm. In these conditions, the original structure of an algorithm is sabotaged, and then failing our analysis. We discuss these conditions in details, and possible counterattacks against these conditions.

**Anti-emulation.** Malware may use anti-emulation techniques to protect from being analyzed. These techniques are usually small hacks or tricks which utilize bugs or incompleteness of the emulator. By fixing bugs and improving the completeness of emulation, we can overcome most of the anti-emulation techniques.

**Code Obfuscation.** Many malware authors use code obfuscation techniques to protect their program from being detected. Obfuscation usually transforms the instruction flow and control flow of a program, which compromise the ability of matching template algorithms in our analysis. Hence, our analysis method cannot be used against strong code obfuscation(such as VM obfuscation). However, with a few changes, we may make our analysis method invulnerable to code obfuscation. We see that data integrity can be preserved even in obfuscation, we just have to modify the partitioning and matching algorithms. The first and simplest modification is to lower the threshold of template matching. Many simple obfuscators use instruction transforms to confuse analysts, but the fundamental meaning of a program remains unchanged. As our matching is not 100% accurate, we just have to enlarge the tolerance of the similarities between a program segment and an algorithm template. To deal with strong obfuscation which usually uses virtual machine protection, we may try carefully select the representing set of instructions to be translated into IL code. For example, a virtual machine obfuscator may translate a single DIV instruction into its own VM representation. During interpretation of the VM representation, such DIV instruction will eventually be executed by the same or a similar instruction. We may select a set of instructions that are rarely used by internal logic part of a VM obfuscator, and in this way we can still use instruction frequency as a valid matching algorithm.

**Custom Implementations.** A malware author may use a non-standard version of standard algorithm. For example, one may change the constants in a cryptographic algorithm, producing a similar but different algorithm. Such modifications will bypass the data verification part of our analysis, as the detected algorithm produced a different result. This issue may be addressed by considering the constants in a algorithm as input arguments, and keeping only the computations in the algorithm templates. Some developers may break an algorithm into small parts, and such an implementation cannot be detected using a whole algorithm. We may also try split a template algorithm into small blocks, but doing so will certainly increase the running time of analysis.

## 6    Conclusion

In this paper, we presented a novel program analysis technique using process emulation and IL-based analysis which is fast and extensible. We tested the effectiveness and accuracy using custom programs implemented with common cryptographic libraries. The result showed that we could identify encryption or hashing functions within these programs, and extract the corresponding input and output data of these functions. The performance evaluation shows that program tracing and analysis could be done within acceptable time, usually less than one minute for small-scale programs, which is superior to most existing analysis techniques.

We further studied possible countermeasures against our technique, and future improvements of our technique. We showed that these countermeasures could be solved by strengthening our system and refining algorithms. We plan to develop new program matching algorithms which may concern data characteristics, and further improve the performance of our technique.

# References

1. Nettle: a low-level crypto library (last visited, 2012),
   http://www.lysator.liu.se/~nisse/nettle/
2. Bellard, F.: Qemu, a fast and portable dynamic translator. In: Proceedings of the USENIX Annual Technical Conference, FREENIX Track, pp. 41–46 (2005)
3. Caballero, J.: Binary code extraction and interface identification for security applications. Technical report, DTIC Document (2009)
4. Gröbert, F., Willems, C., Holz, T.: Automated Identification of Cryptographic Primitives in Binary Programs. In: Sommer, R., Balzarotti, D., Maier, G. (eds.) RAID 2011. LNCS, vol. 6961, pp. 41–60. Springer, Heidelberg (2011)
5. Intel. Intel 64 and ia-32 architectures software developers manual. intel,
   http://www.intel.com/products/processor/manuals 64
6. Jhi, Y.C., Wang, X., Jia, X., Zhu, S., Liu, P., Wu, D.: Value-based program characterization and its application to software plagiarism detection. In: Proceeding of the 33rd International Conference on Software Engineering, pp. 756–765. ACM (2011)
7. Lawton, K.P.: Bochs: A portable pc emulator for unix/x. Linux Journal 29es, 7 (1996)
8. Luk, C.K., Cohn, R., Muth, R., Patil, H., Klauser, A., Lowney, G., Wallace, S., Reddi, V.J., Hazelwood, K.: Pin: building customized program analysis tools with dynamic instrumentation. In: ACM SIGPLAN Notices, vol. 40, pp. 190–200. ACM (2005)
9. Oksanen, K.: Detecting algorithms using dynamic analysis. In: Proceedings of the Ninth International Workshop on Dynamic Analysis, pp. 1–6. ACM (2011)
10. Sæbjørnsen, A., Willcock, J., Panas, T., Quinlan, D., Su, Z.: Detecting code clones in binary executables. In: Proceedings of the Eighteenth International Symposium on Software Testing and Analysis, pp. 117–128. ACM (2009)
11. OpenSSL: The Open Source toolkit for SSL/TLS (last visited, 2012),
    http://www.openssl.org/
12. Zhang, F., Jhi, Y.C., Wu, D., Liu, P., Zhu, S.: A first step towards algorithm plagiarism detection (2011)
13. Zhao, R., Gu, D., Li, J., Yu, R.: Detection and analysis of cryptographic data inside software. Information Security, 182–196 (2011)

# Taint Analysis of Security Code
# in the KLEE Symbolic Execution Engine

Ricardo Corin[1,2] and Felipe Andrés Manzano[1,3]

[1] FaMAF, UNC, Argentina
[2] CONICET
[3] Binamuse, Inc.
rcorin@famaf.unc.edu.ar, feliam@binamuse.com

**Abstract.** We analyse the security of code by extending the KLEE symbolic execution engine with a tainting mechanism that tracks information flows of data. We consider both simple flows from direct assignment operations, and (more subtle) indirect flows inferred from the control flow. Our mechanism prevents overtainting by using a region-based static analysis provided by LLVM, the compiler infrastructure machine on which KLEE runs. We rigorously define taint propagation in a formal LLVM intermediate representation semantics, and show the correctness of our method. We illustrate the mechanism with several examples, showing how we use tainting to prove confidentiality and integrity properties.

## 1 Introduction

Analysis methods based on *symbolic execution* (developed initially by King [8]) have been proved to scale very well to real life code. For instance, KLEE [3], a symbolic execution engine running on top of the LLVM low-level virtual machine [9], has been used to identify subtle bugs in the popular GNU COREUTILS library, covering over 430K lines of C code.

In symbolic execution, the program is dynamically explored through all its branches looking for implementation bugs like memory manipulation errors. In order to avoid trying the entire (arbitrarily large) input space, program inputs are assumed to be symbolic variables that remain uninstantiated (but become constrained) at execution time.

Unfortunately, existing symbolic execution tools can't deal with code that uses cryptography: the search space blows up when exploring the insides of such functions, as they are specifically designed to avoid being invertible (e.g., hash or encryption operations), and hence the underlying constraint solver of the symbolic execution engine (e.g., STP [6] for KLEE) is unable to find suitable inputs in a reasonable time.

In order to cope with this problem, recent work [5] extends KLEE by introducing "symbolic" functions that replace concrete ones (e.g., a symbolic encryption function symbol replacing a OpenSSL's AES implementation), and prevent their exploration. In order to specify the behaviour of symbolic functions and allow the analysis to progress, symbolic functions are endowed with rewriting rules

T.W. Chim and T.H. Yuen (Eds.): ICICS 2012, LNCS 7618, pp. 264–275, 2012.

that detail abstractly their functional properties (e.g., that decryption inverts encryption). The advantage is that these symbolic functions can be efficiently implemented using lookup tables, enabling the symbolic execution of the whole protocol.

```
1  unsigned char K[]
2           = "SECRETSECRET";
3
4  void
5  oracle(){
6  int i;
7  unsigned char IV[256];
8  unsigned char C[256];
9  unsigned char P[256];
10
11 read(IV, 256);
12 read(C, 256);
13
14 decrypt(P, C, K);
15
16 //XOR with previous block/IV
17 for (i=0;i<256;i++)
18        P[i] ^= IV[i];
19 //Check padding..
20 if (is_valid(P))
21    write(''valid'',5);
22 else
23    write(''invalid'',7);
24 }
```

```
1  int is_valid(unsigned char * P){
2     int i;
3     //valid paddings in [1,256]
4     for (i=256-P[255];i<255;i++)
5        //all pads = pad length
6        if ( P[255] != P[i] )
7           return 0;
8     return P[255] != 0;
9  }
```

**Fig. 1.** Is this code secure?

Taint analysis [12] is a powerful method for discovering security violations. The analysis is used typically to identify dangerous flows from untrusted inputs into sensitive destinations, in order to detect, for instance, code or SQL injection attacks. This is an *integrity* property that tells whether untrusted values can reach and modify trusted placeholders. One may also be interested in the dual property of *confidentiality*, i.e., whether sensitive values can leak to untrusted sinks (e.g., whether secret information is disclosed to the network). We rely on tainting to formally justify the usage of symbolic function abstractions for replacing concrete cryptographic primitives. In order to show it is safe to perform such an abstraction, we need to reason about which information needs to be kept secret. For instance, consider an encrypted message that is sent on the network; the encryption key has been established off-band and is meant to be secret. We can only replace this encryption by a symbolic (black box) message that is totally opaque to an attacker when the key is actually verifiably secret to the attacker. That is, we can trust an eavesdropped message will not be decrypted (nor any information will deduced from it) by an attacker only if no information about the encryption key was (inadvertently) leaked by the program itself.

Let us illustrate the kind of code we wish to analyse. Consider the *oracle* C function of Figure 1. It represents a *last word oracle* used in the classic padding oracle attack [13,10]. Two 256-byte long blocks are input in lines 11 and 12, the initialization vector IV and the ciphertext C. Line 14 decrypts C into P using secret key K. Then, lines 17 and 18 xor the result with IV (since this is using CBC encryption mode for block ciphers). Finally, the padding is checked with function is_valid() in line 20. This function, shown in the right hand-side of Figure 1, checks the padding method is valid (using PKCS#5), i.e., that the last bytes are either 1, or 22, 333, and so on. This code illustrates the confidentiality concerns we are interested in analysing: Can an attacker obtain information about P from observing just the output?

As shown in [13], an attacker providing a random IV and observing the answer (that is, "valid" or "invalid" depending on the output of is_valid(P)) can infer the last byte of P. In this paper, we develop a mechanism to detect subtle leaks of information of this class. Briefly, in our analysis, the decrypted P of line 13 is secret and thus marked high (by specification), with security level H. Then, at runtime, the analysis detects information being output under a high guard (i.e., the conditional in line 19 of the result of function is_valid()). At that point our analysis would issue a security warning.

The above example illustrates our interest in detecting *all* potential leaks, including partial information. So even a 1-bit leak of P constitutes a valid attack in our setting. We aim at formal results, thus we formalize the LLVM semantics on which KLEE runs. Previous work describes the standard LLVM semantics [5], and we extend it here to model taint propagation. This enables us to show formally that tainting works as desired. More precisely, our contributions are as follows:

- We illustrate, via examples, the challenges in implementing different tainting mechanisms in the LLVM virtual machine (Section 2).
- We define three LLVM semantics to model taint propagation, each one more precise than the previous (Section 3):
  1. A basic tainting semantics for modelling direct, assignment-based flows.
  2. A more advanced tainting semantics for both direct and indirect flows arising from branching operations.
  3. A region-based tainting semantics that prevents overtainting, and is thus more precise than the previous case while still correct.
  We show security for both (2) and (3) above (Theorems 1 and 2, respectively).

Even though our development of tainting is aimed towards analysing cryptographic protocol implementations, it can of course be used in analysing regular, non-protocol code, in order to detect dangerous flows of data.

*Related Work.* To our knowledge, this is the first tainting/information flow approach specific for the LLVM virtual machine and KLEE, which combines both a working prototype and rigorous semantics with formal security results. However, of course there exist lots of work for tracking information in programming languages. First, more applied taint analyses [2]: tainting has been used for unknown vulnerability detection, automatic input filter generation, malware analysis, and test case generation (see the survey in [12] and the references therein). Second, more theoretic information flow works [11], both for static and dynamic settings, and for higher and lower level languages.

The first work we are aware on defining formal semantics for LLVM is [5]. There is more recent work [14] that also gives semantics, and focuses in mechanized formalizations of LLVM for proving intermediate optimizations correct in the Coq theorem prover.

## 2    Information Flow and Tainting in the LLVM

In order to understand the semantic rules needed to implement tainting in Section 3, in this section we consider some simple examples that illustrate the kind of issues we run into when dealing with tainting. Our examples are purposely simple, since we work at the level of LLVM IR (intermediate representation) code, which is considerably more verbose than C.

LLVM IR code is organized as a collection of function definitions, each one containing a sequence *basic blocks*. Each basic block is tagged with an entry label, to which other blocks can jump into. Basic blocks typically end when control needs to be transferred elsewhere. LLVM provides "local variables" (registers), which are identified by starting with a '%' character. Registers are used thoroughly, since they are often needed by the compilers in order to generate code that respects static single assignment (SSA), a property that simplifies LLVM's static analysis and optimizations (e.g., constant propagation). The complete LLVM language contains many instructions; in this paper we use and illustrate the main ones, like arithmetic, branching, routine call and return, and memory manipulation operations. The complete list is available elsewhere [9].

We assume given an arbitrary set of *taint levels* that we use to taint variables, be them registers or memory cells. Initially, the memory (which contains data as well as the executable code) is untainted. Tainted data is introduced from the external environment of the program, and once inside the program starts propagating through variables and memory cells during execution. We allow different sources of data, which may be potentially tainted with different levels. We model the sources as files (in the UNIX sense, so that files can also be IO devices and network connections) that the code reads from and writes to. We then assign taint levels to files. Taint levels are (partially) ordered. For simplicity, and without loss of generality, we present our examples assuming just two levels: L (for low) and H (for high), with L < H. In these examples, the experiment we run is as follows: we assume H as the taint level for the inputs from the standard input (0 in POSIX systems), and then check that the taint level of data written to the standard output (1 in POSIX systems) is L. If we ever see an output H, we declare that there is a dangerous flow, and conclude the code is insecure.

**Direct Flows.** Figure 2 shows the simplest form of information flow: an assignment that transfers taint from a source variable to another variable. On the left we see C code and on the right we show equivalent LLVM code. The C code declares two variables of one byte, of type char, named *input* and *output*. We then input a byte from the the standard input (which we assign taint level H), using function *read*. The input byte is saved on *input*. Then we assign *input* to *output*, and finally send *output* to the standard output using function *write*. It is clear that data flows from variable *input* to *output*, hence, there is a (dangerous) flow, since H data is being leaked.

On the right hand side of Figure 2 we see the LLVM IR code, which it's more verbose and complex; it uses registers as well as memory accesses, and types are explicit ($i8$ for a byte, $i32$ for 4-byte integer; the types for constants 0 and 1 are ommitted).

C variables *input* and *output* correspond to different memory locations reserved by the LLVM operation *alloca* (lines 1–2). Pointers %*input_p* and %*output* (respectivelly) reference both variables. Line 3 reads a byte into memory location pointed by %*input_p*, and line 4 loads that char into register %*input*. The relevant flow occurs at line 5, where local register %*input* is assigned a value loaded from memory using operation *load*. The memory pointer used, %*input_p*, is used in function *read* with file descriptor 1 (which has taint level H). Line 6 uses another memory operation, *store*, to save in memory the value of %*input* into memory location %*output_p*. This example shows the need to propagate taint levels both from and back memory cells into registers, something we address in the semantics developed in next section.

Being able to capture direct flows is already quite useful, and many taint techniques do just that [12], since each flow may potentially lead to a dangerous bug.

**Indirect Flows.** Figure 3 shows a more subtle flow. As we can see in the C code on the left, a H variable *input* is used to switch and assign to variable *output* different values. The effect is that at the end of execution, *output* holds the value of *input*, even though there is no direct flow from *input* to *output*. So tainting *input* would not directly taint *output*. This is a classical indirect flow arising from the control flow: *input* controls a conditional (the switch) in the code that has an impact on *output*. On the right hand side of Figure 3 we see the equivalent LLVM IR code. LLVM has a primitive switch operation as well (see line 5), so the mapping is quite direct, as each branch is implemented via jumps to entry labels of the different basic blocks (e.g., *bb0* in line 11).

The standard way of detecting these flows is to taint the control flow of the program under execution, so any following operation and its resulting memory or register modifications gets tainted with the control flow taint. In this case, the switch statement of line 5 causes the control flow to be tainted with H since we have a condition on variable *input* which is itself H. Then all following instructions inherit the taint level H, effectively tainting the result of any instruction, including the assignment to *output*. This works, but has the potential problem of overtainting, since the H level is now carried on forever, unless one can somehow turn it off at some point (see Section 3). Nevertheless, thanks to the static analysis facilities provided by the LLVM framework, we will be able to compute regions where each branch under the influence of the switch terminates and merges into a common point (*bb*256 at line 26 in the example); this information is going to be used in Section 3 to prevent overtainting, by knowing when to stop carrying the control flow taint introduced in H branches.

```
1  char input;                 1  %input_p = alloca i8
2  char output;                2  %output_p = alloca i8
3  read(H, &input, 1);         3  call i32 @read( 1, i8* %input_p, 1)
4  output = input;             4  %input = load i8* %input_p
5  write(L,&output,1);         5  store i8 %input, i8* %output_p
                               6  call i32 @write( 0, i8* %output_p, 1)
```

**Fig. 2.** Direct flow example: C code (left), LLVM IR code (right)

```
1  char input;                 1  %input_p = alloca i8
2  char output;                2  %output_p = alloca i8
3  read(H, &input, 1);         3  call i32 @read( 0, i8* %input_p, 1)
4                              4  %input = load i8* %input_p, align 1
5  switch(input){              5  switch i8 %input, label %bb256 [
6     case 0:                  6          i8 0, label %bb0
7         output = 0;          7          ...
8     case 1:                  8          i8 255, label %bb255 ]
9         output = 1;          9  bb0:
10    ...                      10 store i8 0, i8* %output_p
11    case 255:                11 br label %bb256
12        output = 255;        12 ...
13    }                        13 bb255:
14 write(L, output, 1);       14 store i8 255, i8* %output_p
                               15 br label %bb256
                               16 bb256:
                               17 call i32 @write( 1, i8* %output_p, 1)
```

**Fig. 3.** Indirect flow via conditionals example: C code (left), LLVM IR code (right)

**Pointer Arithmetic and Memory.** Figure 4 shows another subtle situation. We only show the C code for simplicity. This code copies the value of variable *input* into *output* in a special way: it initializes an array with zeroes, and then stores a 1 into the position given by *input*. Then the array is traversed until a 1 is found; while it is not 1, *output* is incremented. At the end of the loop, *output* holds the value of *input*, and this constitutes a dangerous flow since *output* is sent to the environment in line 7. Unfortunately the prevention mechanism we hinted above to deal with indirect flows in the last subsection does not work here: marking the control as H at the branch does not help in identifying this flow, as execution is not under a branch depending on *input*: the loop uses $array[0] \dots array[input - 1]$ but never reaches $array[input]$.

The problem here is in line 5: since we have a H index (*input*) accessing the array, the whole array is potentially H. If we could mark all the array as H, *output* would become tainted immediately entering the loop, and then the problem would disappear, as $array[0]$ would already be H. At the C code, we could mark the whole array as H if one element has been marked H. Unfortunately at the LLVM IR level we do not have arrays anymore, only memory cells. The conservative decision we make in our semantics in next section is to mark the *whole* memory as H, for this particular case. This can be made more precise in the future, although it is enough for our current needs. (For instance, memory reserved afterwards is unaffected.)

## 3    Taint Semantics

Our semantics is an extension of earlier work [5]. Besides that work, one can also refer to the original (informal) semantics of LLVM [9].

Semantic rules describe formally how an LLVM machine executes, i.e., how it evolves from state to state depending on the current instruction. State is represented by a tuple $\langle pc, \mathcal{M}, \mathcal{G}, fs \rangle$, where $pc$ is the program counter, $\mathcal{M}$ the memory, $\mathcal{G}$ the global identifiers, and $fs$ the stack of activation frames.

The specific details on how LLVM works for each instruction are not crucial for the understanding of this paper, though, since our addition of tainting does not change the semantics of [5], only builds on it.

**Direct Flow Semantics.** We tag LLVM registers and memory cells with taint levels H and L, and use metavariable $tl$ to range through them. Given two levels $tl_1$ and $tl_2$ we use lattice join operation $\vee$ that operates as usual: $tl_1 \vee tl_2 = L$ when $tl_1 = tl_2 = L$, and $tl_1 \vee tl_2 = H$ otherwise.

To illustrate the semantics, we show rule ADD for arithmetic addition:

$$\frac{op_\mathcal{M}(pc) = id = \textbf{add } t \, op_1, op_2 \quad v(op_1, \mathcal{L}) = (tl_1, t, v_{op_1}) v(op_2, \mathcal{L}) = (tl_2, t, v_{op_2})}{\begin{array}{c} \langle pc, \mathcal{M}, \mathcal{G}, (rslt, \mathcal{L}, ret, \mathcal{A}) :: fs \rangle \longrightarrow \\ \langle nxt_\mathcal{M}(pc), \mathcal{M}, \mathcal{G}, (rslt, \mathcal{L}\{id \rightarrow (tl_1 \vee tl_2, t, x_{op_1} +_t x_{op_2})\}, ret, \mathcal{A}) :: fs \rangle \end{array}} \text{ADD}$$

It starts by looking up the instruction pointed by the program counter $pc$, using auxiliary function $op_\mathcal{M}(pc)$ (in this rule, $op_\mathcal{M}(pc) = id = \textbf{add } t \, op_1, op_2$). This gives two operands $op_1$ and $op_2$, of type $t$. The actual values of $op_1$ and $op_2$ are looked up using auxiliary function $v()$ (the value can be either a constant with taint level L, or a local binding in $\mathcal{L}$, or a global value in $\mathcal{G}$). For $op_1$, for instance, we have $v(op_1, \mathcal{L}) = (tl_1, t, v_{op_1})$. Here we get a triple indicating the taint level $tl_1$, the type $t$, and finally the value $v_{op_1}$. (Similarly for $op_2$.) We can then update the context with the new value for identifier $id$ with triple $(tl_1 \vee tl_2, t, v_{op_1} +_t v_{op_2})$ The remaining arithmetic rules (for subtraction, multiplication, bit manipulation, and so on) are similar.

This semantics is concrete: bytes input are concrete bytes, and conditions in branching rules are deterministically evaluated. A symbolic semantics changes input values to symbolic variables, and branching rules may depend on actual assignments to the symbolic variables. A symbolic semantics of LLVM is provided in [5]; we could do it here, although for our purposes is not needed: the changes we do for tainting are completely orthogonal (under the assumption that the $pc$ is always concrete, that is, there's no dynamic code).

```
1   char array[256]={0};//256 zeros
2   char input;
3   char output;
4   read(H, &input, 1);//read a char from a H file
5   array[input]=1;
6   for(output=0; !array[output]; output++); //Count zeros
7   write(L,output,1);//write output to a L file
```

**Fig. 4.** Indirect flow via array indexing example (C code)

**Indirect Flow Semantics.** In order to account for indirect flows, we need to modify contexts and carry on a taint level of the execution. We call this the taint level of the program counter, noted by $tpc$, and add it to regular contexts: $\langle pc, tpc, \mathcal{M}, \mathcal{G}, fs \rangle$. Initially $tpc$ is L, and it evolves when H conditions are evaluated in branches. The rules of interest are conditionals (BRT) and (BRF); next we show rule (BRT):

$$\frac{op_{\mathcal{M}}(pc) = \textbf{br } c \textbf{ labelt } l_1 \textbf{ labelt } l_2 \quad v(c, \mathcal{L}) = (ts, \textbf{i1}, 1)}{\langle pc, tpc, \mathcal{M}, \mathcal{G}, (rslt, \mathcal{L}, ret, \mathcal{A}) :: fs \rangle \longrightarrow \langle l_1, tpc \vee tl, \mathcal{M}, \mathcal{G}, (rslt, \mathcal{L}, ret, \mathcal{A}) :: fs \rangle} \text{BRT}$$

Here, we can see that the condition $c$ is evaluated into a taint level $ts$, and this taint level is used to update the taint level of the program counter, which becomes $tpc \vee tl$. This is analogous in rule (BRF).

We conclude this subsection by noting that all regular direct-flow semantics have the control flow taint added in their results; for instance, the new rule ADD includes the taint level control flow $tpc$ added to the result taint level of $id$, assigning to it the taint level of $tpc \vee tl_1 \vee tl_2$.

**Analysis Methodology.** Armed with any of the above semantics, we can check integrity and confidentiality by querying the program at specific places to check the taint level of certain variables of interest.

In the following we focus on confidentiality (integrity is analogous). We let an execution trace $tr(h_1, \ldots, h_n) \to o_1, \ldots, o_k$ stand for a chain of semantic rules from the initial context (as defined in [5]), with $n$ input READ rules from H applied assigning byte $h_i$, in order. Analogously, the trace contains $k$ WRITE rules, and each output value is $o_i$, in order. (The READ and WRITE rules may be interleaved.) The output values $o_i$ come from applications of rule WRITE of Figure 3: its taint value is $tpc \lor tl$, for taint level $tl$ of the written byte joined with the control flow taint level $tpc$.

**Definition 1.** *A trace* $tr(h_1, \ldots, h_n) \to o_1, \ldots, o_k$ *is* **no-taint** *when the taint level of every* $o_i$ *is L. A program satisfies* **no-taint** *when every possible execution trace is* **no-taint**.

**Definition 2 (Attacker model).** *Our notion of security is derived from a game experiment. Assume the program is run with high inputs* $h_1, \ldots, h_n$ *chosen uniformly (i.e. randomly with uniform distribution) from the space of possible inputs* $M$. *Then, an attacker is given the outputs* $o_1, \ldots, o_k$ *of the execution trace* $tr(h_1, \ldots, h_n) \to o_1, \ldots, o_k$, *and is asked which inputs were used. We say the program is* **secure** *if the probability of guessing the inputs is* $1/|M|$ *for every trace.*

This notion of security is related to the classical definition non-interference [1]; for convenience, we took a probabilistic setting in which security is defined as a game since it simplifies the reasoning w.r.t. our byte-granulated memory and low-level machine representation.

**Theorem 1.** *If a program satisfies* **no-taint** *then it is* **secure**.

Note that its converse does not hold in general. For instance, consider the code of Figure 1 modified such that it writes "valid" instead of "invalid". In that case, all tainted outputs are the same and thus the code is actually safe, although **no-taint** is not passed. As such, this specific case must be handled manually in our current setting.

**Region-Based Semantics.** The C code of Figure 1 does not pass **no-taint**: after the for loop in is_valid(P), there is a H control flow taint $tpc$, and hence the output gets an H as well.

The first step into extending the above semantics to prevent overtainting is to construct a control flow graph. For simplicity, we assume there is a single function defined, so that there is only one sequence of basic blocks. LLVM's control flow graph is then a directed, connected graph that contains the different basic blocks of a program. It has a single start and end node, from which other nodes are reached. Control flow graphs for the examples in the paper are shown in Figure 5. In each case we can see the entry block and exit blocks.

The following are standard graph theory and compilers concepts [7]. A basic block $bb_0$ *dominates* basic block $bb_1$ when every path from the entry to $bb_1$ contains $bb_0$. Also, $bb_1$ *postdominates* $bb_0$ if every path from $bb_0$ to the exit passes trough $bb_1$. A *region* is a connected subgraph of the control flow graph that has exactly two connections to the remaining graph: an entry and an exit (this is why they are also known as single-entry-single-exit (SESE) regions). We can then characterize an SESE region by a pair of blocks: the entry and exit blocks to the region. The *entry basic block* of a region is passed through when entering the region; it is considered part of the region, and dominates all basic blocks in the region. Similarly, the *exit basic block* is passed through after leaving the region; it is not considered part of the region.

Figure 5 shows the control graphs as computed by LLVM. In the control flow graph shown in Figure 5(a), corresponding to the code of Figure 3, there are several regions: a large region containing all basic blocks with *entry* and exit *bb256* (which is *not* part of the region, and singleton blocks with entry *bbX* (for $X < 256$) and exit *bb256*. (In practice, LLVM static analysis ignores singleton regions, as they are always contained in a larger region.) In the control flow graph shown in Figure 5(b), corresponding to the code of Figure 4, there are two regions: one with entry *entry* and exit *out*, and one with entry *loop* and exit *out*.

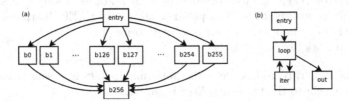

**Fig. 5.** Control flow graphs of basic blocks. (a) Graph for code of Figure 3, (b) Graph for code of Figure 4.

The important point is that control flow information (e.g., information that was added in a H branch to the control flow taint) has a region as its scope: the scope is pushed when entering a region (i.e., entering its entry basic block), and cleared (i.e., popped) once exiting the region (that is, we pass through its exit basic block), so we are free to reset the control flow taint to the previous state, since no information can be leaked anymore. In order to implement regions in the semantics, we need to add a stack of control flow taints. The rule is that whenever we enter a new region, we need to push a L value in the stack; whenever we exit, we pop the head of the stack. We use the following auxiliary function, that manipulates the stack:

$$
region(pc, s, tl) = \begin{cases} push(s, head(s) \vee tl) \\ \qquad \text{if } pc = \text{entry into new region} \\ pop(s) \quad \text{if } pc = \text{exit current region} \\ s \qquad \text{otherwise} \end{cases}
$$

This function is built using a previous pass of the code through LLVM's static analysis to compute regions. Initially, stack $s$ is empty. As we enter into new regions, we push new control flow taint levels.

The new method, called **precise-no-taint**, is similar to **no-taint** of the previous section but operates in the new semantics, and is thus more precise. We show this more precise semantics is as secure as the previous one.

**Theorem 2.** *If a program satisfies* **precise-no-taint** *then it is* **secure**.

The proof is similar to that of Theorem 1, although it now requires modularizing per region; H information that happened in a closed region in the past does not influence L outputs.

## 4   Conclusions

Tainting is an important technique to find dangerous information flows. Our addition of a dynamic tainting mechanism to KLEE is natural and complementary to the safety checks done by KLEE alone, like memory errors and overflows.

Our method can be used in isolation or coupled with previous work in order to verify code that uses cryptography; this framework is promising for analysing complex and long cryptographic protocol implementations. A longer version with more details, prototype code (as a patch to the latest KLEE distribution), and proof sketches can be found on our project website [4].

As future work, we intend to:

- Analyze larger, real-life code with subtle manipulation of sensitive data, in a similar vein to the toy example of Figure 1.
- Use the present analysis to prove secrecy of cryptographic materials like encryption keys; this will enable us to abstract away from concrete cryptographic primitives and use abstract, symbolic counterparts, as done in [5].
- Finally, we also we want to investigate more precise memory pointer tainting, as discussed in Section 2.

This work has been supported by the European Union Seventh Framework Programme under grant agreement no. 295261 (MEALS), and by the PICT-PRH 316 project.

## References

1. Barthe, G., Rezk, T.: Non-interference for a jvm-like language. In: TLDI 2005, pp. 103–112. ACM, New York (2005)
2. Brumley, D., Caballero, J., Liang, Z., Newsome, J., Song, D.: Towards automatic discovery of deviations in binary implementations with applications to error detection and fingerprint generation. In: USENIX, SS 2007, pp. 15:1–15:16. USENIX Association, Berkeley (2007)
3. Cadar, C., Dunbar, D., Engler, D.R.: Klee: Unassisted and automatic generation of high-coverage tests for complex systems programs. In: Proceedings of OSDI, pp. 209–224 (2008)
4. Corin, R., Manzano, F.: Dynamic taint analysis for the klee symbolic execution engine (extended version), http://cs.famaf.unc.edu.ar/~rcorin/kleecrypto
5. Corin, R., Manzano, F.: Efficient Symbolic Execution for Analysing Cryptographic Protocol Implementations. In: Erlingsson, Ú., Wieringa, R., Zannone, N. (eds.) ESSoS 2011. LNCS, vol. 6542, pp. 58–72. Springer, Heidelberg (2011)

6. Ganesh, V., Dill, D.L.: A Decision Procedure for Bit-Vectors and Arrays. In: Damm, W., Hermanns, H. (eds.) CAV 2007. LNCS, vol. 4590, pp. 519–531. Springer, Heidelberg (2007)

7. Johnson, R., Pearson, D., Pingali, K.: The program structure tree: Computing control regions in linear time, pp. 171–185 (1994)

8. King, J.C.: Symbolic execution and program testing. Commun. ACM 19(7), 385–394 (1976)

9. Lattner, C., Adve, V.: The LLVM language reference manual, http://llvm.org/docs/LangRef.html

10. Rizzo, J., Duong, T.: Practical padding oracle attacks. In: Proceedings of the 4th USENIX Conference on Offensive Technologies, WOOT 2010, pp. 1–8. USENIX Association, Berkeley (2010)

11. Sabelfeld, A., Myers, A.C.: Language-based information-flow security. IEEE JSAC 21(1), 5–19 (2003)

12. Schwartz, E.J., Avgerinos, T., Brumley, D.: All you ever wanted to know about dynamic taint analysis and forward symbolic execution (but might have been afraid to ask) (2010)

13. Vaudenay, S.: Security Flaws Induced by CBC Padding - Applications to SSL, IPSEC, WTLS... In: Knudsen, L.R. (ed.) EUROCRYPT 2002. LNCS, vol. 2332, pp. 534–546. Springer, Heidelberg (2002)

14. Zhao, J., Nagarakatte, S., Martin, M.M.K., Zdancewic, S.: Formalizing the llvm intermediate representation for verified program transformations. In: Proceedings of the 39th Annual ACM SIGPLAN-SIGACT Symposium on Principles of Programming Languages, POPL 2012, pp. 427–440. ACM, New York (2012)

# A Generic Approach for Providing Revocation Support in Secret Handshake[*]

Yanjiang Yang[1], Haibing Lu[2], Jian Weng[3,4,**],
Xuhua Ding[5], and Jianying Zhou[1]

[1] Institute for Infocomm Research, Singapore
[2] Dept. of Operations Management and Information Systems,
The Leavey School of Business, Santa Clara University, USA
[3] Department of Computer Science, and Emergency Technology Research Center
of Risk Evaluation and Prewarning on Public Network Security,
Jinan University, China
[4] Shanghai Key Laboratory of Integrate Administration Technologies
for Information Security, Shanghai, China
[5] School of Information Systems, Singapore Management University
{yyang,jyzhou}@i2r.a-star.edu.sg, hlu@scu.edu,
cryptjweng@gmail.com, xhding@smu.edu.sg

**Abstract.** Privacy protection and user revocation are essentially conflicting requirements in many cryptographic protocols. It is a particularly challenging problem to harmonize them in a secret handshake protocol that is geared to offering strong privacy protection on the participants' group membership in the protocol execution. In this paper, we study this problem and propose a generic approach to provide revocation support in secret handshake protocols, without sacrificing the notion of privacy preserving. The main building block of our approach is CGC (Confidential Group Communication), a primitive formulated in this paper, and we present a concrete instantiation so as to realize our generic approach.

## 1 Introduction

Users nowadays are much more concerned with individual privacy than years ago. The growing privacy awareness calls for privacy-preserving techniques that can enable users to accomplish the desired functions over the Internet without compromising their privacy. Secret Handshake (SHS) firstly introduced in [3] is one such technique. In its simplest form, a secret handshake protocol allows two

---

[*] This work was supported by the National Science Foundation of China under Grant Nos. 60903178, 61070217, 61005049, 61133014 and 61272413, the Fok Ying Tung Education Foundation under Grant No. 131066, the Fundamental Research Funds for the Central Universities under Grant No. 21610204, the Guangdong Provincial Science and Technology Project under Grand No. 2010A032000002, and the Opening Project of Shanghai Key Laboratory of Integrate Administration Technologies for Information Security under Grand No. AGK2011003.

[**] Corresponding author.

T.W. Chim and T.H. Yuen (Eds.): ICICS 2012, LNCS 7618, pp. 276–284, 2012.

members from the same group, each holding a membership credential, to establish a shared session key and authenticate each other, with the following two requirements. Firstly, an eavesdropper observing a handshake session learns no meaningful information about the participants, including whether they belong to the same group and whether the handshake is successful or not. Secondly, a non-member (i.e., a user not in the group) cannot pretend to be a member. Compared to other privacy-preserving entity authentication primitives, a secret handshake protocol is "affiliation-hiding" in the sense that the protocol does not reveal which group the handshake participants belong to. Since its introduction by Balfanz et. al. in [3], the notion of secret handshake has attracted enormous attention due to many interesting applications, such as private mutual authentication between two secret government agents or two private club members.

User revocation is an indispensable component for any practical secret handshake scheme. A member may leave or be evicted from a group. It is also likely that a user's secret credential is compromised. These scenarios demand the system to have a timely and effective revocation mechanism such that those members' credential should be nullified and the credential holders cannot run secret handshake protocols successfully with other group members. Despite that numerous secret handshake schemes have been proposed in the literature, including [1, 3, 4, 10, 6–9], the revocation problem is neglected in almost all of those using *reusable credentials* except in [7, 10, 9]. However, the revocation in [10, 7] requires a synchronized rekey protocol upon all users, which is unscalable and inefficient, while the solution in [9] is problematic, because the approach of credential-validity-checking does not rule out the possibility that the revoked user authenticates her counterpart first.

**Our Contributions**. In this work, propose a generic approach to provide revocation support in secret handshake protocols. In specific, we first introduce a new cryptographic primitive called CGC (Confidential Group Communication), which allows two users with the same valid group membership to establish a secret channel. User revocation is handled in CGC in a way that revoked users are excluded from accessing such a secret channel. Building on top of CGC, we then propose a generic approach to provide revocation support in secret handshake schemes, with the basic idea being to execute secret handshake in the secret channel established by CGC. Our approach does not make any changes on the underlying secret handshake protocol, thus it is applicable to all existing and future reusable credential based secret handshake schemes.

## 2 System Model

A secret handshake scheme considers a set of security-sensitive user groups operating under a global authority $\mathcal{GA}$ who is in charge of setting up global parameters. In an open network environment, e.g. the Internet, a member in a group expects to communicate with another group member in a private fashion such that they end up agreeing on a shared secret when they satisfy an agreed policy, e.g. the same group membership and/or certain attributes. Otherwise, none of them can determine her counterpart's membership information. We are interested in secret handshake supporting user revocation, where $\mathcal{GA}$ revokes a user whenever the user leaves her group voluntarily or is evicted. As a result of revocation, the revoked user is of no difference from non-members, e.g., she cannot successfully run a secret handshake with a legitimate member. The following definition is adapted from [1].

**Definition 1.** *A secret handshake scheme with revocation (SHS-R) consists of five algorithms {Setup, CreateGroup, AddMember, Handshake, Revoke} as described below.*

- *Setup: Given a security parameter $1^\kappa$, the algorithm, executed by $\mathcal{GA}$, outputs a suite of global parameters denoted as **params** which are shared by all groups.*
- *CreateGroup: Taking **params** as input, a group manager GM runs this algorithm to initialize a group's public information G and the group's secret key $sk_G$.*
- *AddMember: GM runs this algorithm with a user U requesting to join its group. Taking as input public group information G and group secret key $sk_G$, the algorithm assigns a credential $cred_U$ to U as a result of user admission.*
- *Handshake: Two players A and B run this protocol interactively with their respective private input $cred_A$ and $cred_B$. When the protocol ends, if A and B satisfy each other's handshake rules, they successfully share a common secret key, and mutually authenticate each other (if needed). For all other scenarios, the handshake fails.*
- *Revoke: When a group member U with credential $cred_U$ is revoked, GM runs this algorithm to update the group's public revocation list $\mathcal{R}$ such that $\mathcal{R} = \mathcal{R} \cup \{U, cred_U\}$, and U is excluded from the group and is a non-member.*

A SHS-R scheme must satisfy the following core security properties:

- **Correctness.** Honest members satisfying the handshake rules will always successfully complete the handshake.
- **Impersonator resistance.** An adversary not satisfying the rules of the handshake is unable to impersonate a group member and to successfully establish a shared secret with an honest group member.
- **Detector resistance.** An adversary not satisfying the rules of the handshake cannot decide whether some honest party satisfies the rules or not. *Affiliation hiding* is implicit in this property.
- **Unlinkability.** It is not feasible to tell whether two executions of the handshake protocol were performed by the same party or not, even if both of them were successful.

## 3   A Generic Approach

As shown above, there exist several secret handshake schemes using reusable credentials, but the revocation issue is not well addressed, e.g., [1, 5, 8] do not consider revocation at all, while the revocation method in [9] is not secure. In this section, we give a generic approach to provide revocation support to these secret handshake schemes. In particular our approach transforms a secret handshake scheme without revocation support into a SHS-R scheme. As such, the approach also facilitates the development of new protocols as the protocol designers are relieved from considering user revocation.

The building block of our approach is *Confidential Group Communication* or CGC, a primitive defined as an encryption scheme for a group of users, allowing group members to communicate with one another in a secret manner such that the conversation remains confidential to any non-members. In other words, CGC enables a confidential channel exclusively for all group members. As a result, each group member can send and receive messages via the channel, and only group members can access the communicated messages. Moreover, CGC revokes members such that once a member is revoked, she immediately becomes a non-member, losing the access to the channel established by other group members.

### 3.1 Confidential Group Communication

We formally specify Confidential Group Communication CGC as follows:

**Definition 2.** *A CGC scheme is defined as the following six algorithms.*

- *CGC.Setup: Given a security parameter $1^\kappa$, a global authority $\mathcal{GA}$ execute this algorithm to set up public global information params.*
- *CGC.CreateGroup: Taking params as input, a group manager GM runs this algorithm to initialize a group's public information G and the group's secret key $K_G$ .*
- *CGC.UserJoin: Taking as input group secret key $K_G$ and user identifier U, it outputs a secret member key $sk_U$. Depending on instantiations, $sk_U$ could be unique to U or a shared secret among all members.*
- *CGC.Enc: Taking as input a message m and a member key $sk_U$, it outputs a ciphertext c.*
- *CGC.Dec: Taking as input $sk_U$ and a ciphertext c, it outputs the corresponding plaintext m.*
- *CGC.Revoke: Taking as input user identifier U, GM executes this algorithm to revoke U by outputting the updated revocation list of the group. As a result of revocation, $sk_U$ is no longer useful (in performing CGC.Enc and CGC.Dec).*

We impose the following security requirements upon a CGC scheme:

• **Plaintext Secrecy.** The CGC.Enc algorithm should keep the secrecy of the encrypted plaintexts. In particular, CPA (chosen plaintext attack) security suffices for our use in this work.

• **Key Privacy.** The CGC scheme must also be *key private*, which intuitively means that it is infeasible to learn under which key a ciphertext is generated. In our setting, key privacy implies affiliation hiding, i.e., the ciphertexts do not disclose information on the group to which the ciphertexts are intended.

**An Instantiation.** We note that public-key broadcast encryption cannot directly instantiate CGC, because it cannot attain key privacy[1]. Our instantiation still needs to make use of public-key broadcast encryption, but using it for key update in case of user revocation. Specifically, we require group members to share a secret key, and instantiate the encryption algorithm by a key private symmetric key encryption scheme. The main issue at this point is how to enable the group members to update the shared secret key in case of user revocation. Our solution is to use public-key broadcast encryption, such that a new key is encrypted under the broadcast encryption. As public-key broadcast encryption supports user revocation, all group members except the revoked members can decrypt and get the new key. We stress that in this instantiation, since broadcast encryption is not directly involved in the encryption algorithm, it is not required to be key-private, thus any existing public-key broadcast encryption scheme can be used as long as it supports user revocation. The details of the instantiation are below:

- CGC.Setup: Determines a key-private symmetric key encryption scheme SE, e.g., AES-CBC , and sets $params = \langle SE \rangle$.
- CGC.CreateGroup: GM selects a secret key $SE.k_G$ for SE; also, determines a public-key broadcast encryption scheme $PBE_G$, and establishes the public key $PBE_G.pk$ and a set of user private keys $\{PBE_G.sk_i\}_i$ for $PBE_G$. Sets the group public information as $G = \langle SE, PBE_G, pub_G \rangle$, and sets the group secret key as $K_G = \langle SE.k_G, \{PBE_G.sk_i\}_i \rangle$.
- CGC.UserJoin: To enrol a user, $U$, set its member secret key $sk_U = \langle SE.k_G, PBE_G.sk_\ell \rangle$, where $PBE_G.sk_\ell$ is a un-assigned user private key of $PBE_G$.
- CGC.Enc: Given a message $m$, set the ciphertext as $c = SE.Enc(m, SE.k_G)$, where $SE.Enc(\cdot)$ is the encryption algorithm of SE.
- CGC.Dec: Given a ciphertext $c$, decrypt $c$ as $m = SE.Dec(c, SE.k_G)$, where $SE.Dec(\cdot)$ is the decryption algorithm of SE.
- CGC.Revoke: Upon revocation of user $U$, update the revocation list of $PBE_G$ to include $U$ (the revocation list is a part of $PBE_G.pk$); update $SE.k_G$ by assigning a new value, and encrypt it using the public-key broadcast encryption as $rekey\_msg = PBE_G.Enc(SE.k_G)$; publish $rekey\_msg$ in a public directory, such that group members can retrieve and decrypt it using their respective $PBE_G.sk$.

**Security.** Since the above CGC scheme relies on a key private symmetric key encryption scheme for data encryption, it straightforwardly inherits plaintext secrecy and key privacy. Thus, we have the following theorem.

**Theorem 1.** *The above instantiation is a secure CGC scheme, given that the underlying symmetric key encryption scheme SE is plaintext secret and key private.*

---

[1] As far as we know, all existing public-key broadcast encryption schemes in the literature are not key private. The key private broadcast encryption scheme in [2] is more precisely multicast encryption.

## 3.2   Our Approach

**Basic Idea.** As indicated earlier, we cannot expect to invoke explicit credential validity checking to address the revocation issue in secret handshake. Thus, our rationale is to eliminate the possibility that a revoked member can participate in a secret handshake protocol. In particular, equip a group with a CGC scheme, such that group members run the secret handshake protocol in a secret channel established by the CGC scheme. User revocation is implicitly handled by the CGC scheme, which guarantees that only group members can access the secret channel, while non-members including revoked members are excluded from the channel.

Concretely, given a (general) secret handshake scheme without revocation support $\Gamma$, we compile it into a SHS-R scheme $\Gamma'$ as follows. Exploiting a CGC scheme, e.g., the above instantiation, all group members share a secret key for a (global) symmetric key encryption scheme, and a private key for the group's public-key broadcast encryption scheme. When running $\Gamma$ with a peer, a group member encrypts the messages that she needs to send out with the symmetric key encryption; while upon receipt of a message from her peer, she decrypts the message first, and then behaves upon the decrypted message following the specification of $\Gamma$. User revocation is handled in a straightforward way by the CGC scheme.

We note that in case of user revocation, the remaining group members do not need to update their shared secret key as long as they have no plan to participate in handshakes. In other words, it suffices for a group member to update her key right before her participation in a handshake protocol. Due to the use of broadcast encryption, even if she misses some previous rekey messages, she can still get the latest key. Therefore, using the above CGC scheme in our approach allows group members to synchronize key update on the necessity basis, contrasting to [7, 10] which require strict synchronization.

Caveat. We have two comments. (1) If the original secret handshake scheme $\Gamma$ itself involves a shared secret (e.g., [5]), we make that secret a persistent quantity in $\Gamma'$, and it no longer needs to be updated in case of user revocation. (2) The approach seems not applicable to the secret handshake with dynamic matching scheme in [1], which allows groups members from certain different groups to perform handshake. In fact, the approach still works if we let the groups whose members are allowed to make handshake share a secret key.

**A Revisit.** Let us briefly examine the security of the approach. Adversaries to a secret handshake protocol include not only non-members, but also group members who do not participate the handshake or who do not satisfy the handshake rules in question. For a non-member adversary, since the CGC encryption is key private, intuitively the adversary cannot get extra information. But for a member adversary, the situation is complicated. In particular, having access to the secret channel, the adversary can see the execution of the handshake protocol (i.e., $\Gamma$). Even though the adversary cannot learn useful information from the execution of $\Gamma$ itself (as $\Gamma$ is a secret handshake protocol), a subtle vulnerability is the following: as the handshake protocol (i.e., $\Gamma$) is supposed to be executed in a secret channel, once the adversary can decide that what it sees is a handshake, then the secret channel must be established by group members of the group it belongs to. This compromises affiliation hiding.

To be concrete, suppose that the original secret handshake protocol $\Gamma$ involves a party sending out a message, which consists of a 80-bit component and a 120-bit component. If a member adversary observing an execution of $\Gamma'$ intercepts a corresponding message, and decrypts using its own secret key and gets a message of the above format, then the adversary can know that $\Gamma'$ is running between two members of its group. In this example, the attack still works even if the message of $\Gamma$ is of a single component, but with a recognizable structure, e.g., it is a timestamp.

We have to rectify this issue. Our intuition is that it is in fact not necessary to encrypt all messages of $\Gamma$, and it suffices to only encrypt the message that is essential for key establishment and mutual authentication. We observe that within all the messages sent out by a party, there must be at least one random component. Depending on specific schemes, it could be an element intended for key establishment or a randomized credential element, or even a nonce . Such random components must exist in a secret handshake protocol, due to the need to be secure against replay attacks and the need to randomize a user's credential. The characteristic of such a component is that it is a uniformly distributed element within its domain (e.g., a finite field).

Based on this observation, we revise our above approach to be such that each party, when running $\Gamma$, selects a single random component within her messages that is critical for the handshake, and encrypts with the CGC scheme. Figure 1 depicts the idea, where $m_1$ (resp. $m_2'$) is one of the essential random components

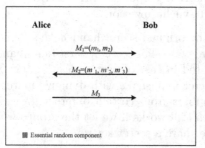
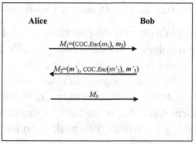

(a) Original secret handshake scheme $\Gamma$     (b) Secret handshake scheme with revocation $\Gamma'$

**Fig. 1.** Generic Approach of Transforming $\Gamma$ to $\Gamma'$

that Alice (resp. Bob) needs to send out; and only $m_1$ (resp. $m_2'$) needs to be encrypted among Alice's (resp. Bob's) messages, leaving other components intact. For this approach to work, of course we assume that the secret handshake protocol $\Gamma$ is *natural* , in the sense that during the course of $\Gamma$, there will be no other messages that de-randomize the component (e.g., the protocol does not involve the appearance of the component or its hash value in other messages). Note that if the bit length of the component to be encrypted does not match that of the encryption scheme, padding of random bits applies and the random padding will be ignored at the decryption side. Finally, it is clear that the effect of the CGC scheme for revocation remains.

**Security.** For security of our approach, we have the following theorem, and the proof can be found in the full version.

**Theorem 2.** *If $\Gamma$ is a secret handshake protocol and the CGC scheme satisfies plaintext secrecy and key privacy, then the resulting $\Gamma'$ by applying our approach on $\Gamma$ is a secret handshake protocol.*

**Comparison with [10].** The secret handshake protocol in [10] also relies on group members sharing a secret to handle user revocation. Our proposal in this work distinguishes from [10] mainly as follows. (1) First of all, [10] presents a concrete (membership-credential based) scheme, while our proposal is a generic approach intending to provide revocation support to all reusable credential based secret handshake schemes. (2) Secondly, even though both require group members to share a secret key for symmetric key encryption, there are distinctions on the way the shared secret key is used. Specifically, in [10] the participants in a handshake run Diffie-Hellman key exchange first to generate an ephemeral key, which is then XORed with the shared secret key to generate a session key, and the session key is used for symmetric key encryption. As a result, the symmetric key encryption is not necessarily key private. In contrast, the shared secret key is directly used for symmetric key encryption in our approach, thus the encryption must be explicitly key private. (3) In [10], the entire handshake session is carried out in the confidential channel established by the symmetric key encryption. But as analyzed earlier, this is not secure in our approach as we are considering *general* secret handshake where the adversary can compromise group members and can be active (in [10] such an adversary can only be passive). (4) Finally, as mentioned earlier the method in [10] requires strict synchronization for key update for group members (in case of user revocation), while our approach solves this problem and group members update the shared key on the necessity basis, due to the use of public-key broadcast encryption.

# References

1. Ateniese, G., Blanton, M., Kirsch, J.: Secret Handshakes with Dynamic and Fuzzy Matching. In: Proc. Network and Distributed System Security Symposium, NDSS 2007 (2007)
2. Barth, A., Boneh, D., Waters, B.: Privacy in Encrypted Content Distribution Using Private Broadcast Encryption. In: Di Crescenzo, G., Rubin, A. (eds.) FC 2006. LNCS, vol. 4107, pp. 52–64. Springer, Heidelberg (2006)
3. Balfanz, D., Durfee, G., Shankar, N., Smetters, D., Staddon, J., Wong, H.: Secret Handshakes from Pairing-Based Key Agreements. In: Proc. IEEE Security & Privacy, pp. 180–1966 (2003)

4. Castelluccia, C., Jarecki, S., Tsudik, G.: Secret Handshakes from CA-Oblivious Encryption. In: Lee, P.J. (ed.) ASIACRYPT 2004. LNCS, vol. 3329, pp. 293–307. Springer, Heidelberg (2004)
5. Hoepman, J.H.: Private Handshakes. In: Stajano, F., Meadows, C., Capkun, S., Moore, T. (eds.) ESAS 2007. LNCS, vol. 4572, pp. 31–42. Springer, Heidelberg (2007)
6. Jarechi, S., Kim, J., Tsudik, G.: Authenticated Group Key Agreement Protocols with the Privacy Property of Affilation-hidding. In: Proc. CT-RSA Conference (2007)
7. Jarecki, S., Liu, X.: Unlinkable Secret Handshakes and Key-Private Group Key Management Schemes. In: Katz, J., Yung, M. (eds.) ACNS 2007. LNCS, vol. 4521, pp. 270–287. Springer, Heidelberg (2007)
8. Sorniotti, A., Molva, R.: A Provably Secure Secret Handshake with Dynamic Controlled Matching. In: Gritzalis, D., Lopez, J. (eds.) SEC 2009. IFIP AICT, vol. 297, pp. 330–341. Springer, Heidelberg (2009)
9. Sorniotti, A., Molva, R.: Secret Handshakes With Revocation Support. In: Lee, D., Hong, S. (eds.) ICISC 2009. LNCS, vol. 5984, pp. 274–299. Springer, Heidelberg (2010)
10. Tsudik, G., Xu, S.: Flexible Framework for Secret Handshakes, Cryptology ePrint Archive, Report 2005/034

# An Efficient Single-Slow-Phase Mutually Authenticated RFID Distance Bounding Protocol with Tag Privacy

Anjia Yang, Yunhui Zhuang, and Duncan S. Wong

Department of Computer Science,
City University of Hong Kong, Hong Kong, China
{ayang3,yhzhuang2}@student.cityu.edu.hk, duncan@cityu.edu.hk

**Abstract.** Among the RFID distance bounding protocols in the literature, besides defending against various attacks such as impersonation, distance fraud, Mafia attack, terrorist attack, and distance hijacking, some also support mutual authentication and tag privacy protection. Due to the requirements of being lightweight, low-cost, and efficient, it is the common objective to design new RFID distance bounding protocols which require fewer message flows and less complex cryptographic operations, while maintaining or enhancing the security and privacy of the protocols. In this paper, we propose a new RFID distance bounding protocol which achieves mutual authentication, supports the untraceability of the tags, and resists all the attacks above by having only one slow transmission phase, and is more efficient and energy-saving when compared with other protocols' two slow phases. The new protocol requires the tag to evaluate a PRF function for two times only, rather than three times as in one of the most efficient mutually authenticated RFID distance bounding protocols currently available, for example, the Swiss-Knife protocol.

**Keywords:** RFID, Distance Bounding, Privacy, Mutual Authentication.

## 1 Introduction

RFID (Radio Frequency Identification) is a technology that has been widely used in our daily life. An RFID tag is a simple chip equipped with an antenna, which allows the tag to communicate with a reader. The reader needs to determine whether the tag is valid and within a legitimate distance which we call *a neighbor area* by using a distance bounding protocol. As an identification method, better than the bar code, an RFID chip makes it possible to identify non-line-of-sight objects using wireless communication technology. Nowadays, RFID chips have already been deployed in many big supermarkets such as Wal-Mart. They have also been increasingly applied to track goods or even animals and so forth. In addition, another important application of RFID is proximity-based authentication, such as the student card for entering a library, the payWave -enabled visa card for payment, and the electronic passport.

T.W. Chim and T.H. Yuen (Eds.): ICICS 2012, LNCS 7618, pp. 285–292, 2012.
© Springer-Verlag Berlin Heidelberg 2012

There have been a handful of RFID distance bounding protocols proposed recently [1–7]. Among them, various attacks have been proposed and considered in their security analysis. Five of the most commonly considered attacks are: Impersonation fraud [1], Distance fraud [1], Mafia fraud [9], Terrorist fraud [9], and Distance hijacking attack [10]. In this paper, we only consider the distance hijacking attacks in single-protocol environment defined in [10]. To mitigate Mafia fraud attack, Brands and Chaum [1] presented the first distance bounding protocol in 1993. In 2005, Hancke and Kuhn proposed a simple and efficient distance bounding protocol [2], but it cannot prevent terrorist fraud attacks. Subsequently there're some other protocols proposed. However, they either cannot prevent terrorist attacks [3–5, 7], or are not quite efficient [6]. In 2011, Avoine et al. prevented a general method to defeat terrorist frauds [8]. They made a conclusion that at least a $(3,3)$ threshold secret-sharing scheme should be used to resist terrorist frauds. Our distance bounding protocol is based on this paper.

Besides the security issue, another critical concern of RFID technology is privacy. We mainly consider the tag's privacy which suffers from traceability, which means that the adversary can distinguish whether it's the target tag that is communicating with a reader. Actually, in order to preserve the tag's privacy, many methods have been proposed [6, 11–15]. One of the most well-known methods is hash-chain based schemes [13–15], however, all of them suffer from the *de-synchronization attack* by Juels and Weis [16]. What's more, only in [6] the tag's privacy issue is considered in a distance bounding protocol.

Finally, the efficiency of a distance bounding protocol is an important concern of RFID technology, due to the tag's limited computation and storage capacities. Among the previous distance bounding protocols, only [6] has the expected properties at the same time: resistant to terrorist fraud attacks, protecting the tag's privacy, achieving mutual authentication. Nevertheless, there're four slow transmission flows in this protocol and the tag needs to compute the time-consuming pseudo-random function(PRF) for three times; what's more, the reader exhaustively searches for the tag's *ID* from its local database at each protocol run, which again reduces the efficiency. Therefore we need to design a secure efficient distance bounding protocol which protects the tag's privacy as well.

**Contribution.** We propose a new efficient RFID distance bounding protocol which achieves mutual authentication and resists all the current attacks with only single slow phase. Our protocol also preserves tag's privacy with untraceability efficiently, which can prevent the de-synchronization attack as well.

Table 1 shows a comparison between our scheme and the previous schemes. From the second column to the fourth column, we show the adversary's success probability of launching Mafia frauds, terrorist frauds and distance hijacking attacks respectively to these selected protocols. The fifth column indicates whether those protocols protect the tag's privacy, and the sixth column gives the reader's cost of providing the service of tag's privacy protection. The next column represents whether these protocols support mutual authentication. In the eighth column, we give the cost of the tag needed in each protocol, where we measure the cost as the number of computation of pseudo-random function ($PRF$), hash function ($Hash$), commitment ($com.$), symmetric key encryption ($Enc.$) and signature ($sig.$). The last column displays how many flows needed in slow phases in each protocol. Taking the limited space into account, we don't put the impersonation frauds or distance frauds in Table 1 since these two attacks are easy to be prevented and all of the protocols are resistant to them.

**Table 1.** Comparison of distance bounding protocols

| | Maf. | Terr. | Hij. | Pri. | Pri.-cost of reader | MA | Comp. of tag | No. of flows in slow phase |
|---|---|---|---|---|---|---|---|---|
| BC [1] | $(\frac{1}{2})^n$ | NO | 1 | NO | - | NO | $1com.+1sig.$ | 2 |
| HK [2] | $(\frac{3}{4})^n$ | NO | $(\frac{1}{2})^n$ | NO | - | NO | $1PRF$ | 2 |
| MP [3] | $(\frac{1}{2})^n$ | NO | $(\frac{1}{2})^n$ | NO | - | NO | $2Hash$ | 3 |
| KA [7] | $\approx(\frac{1}{2})^n$ | NO | $(\frac{1}{2})^n$ | NO | - | NO | $1PRF$ | 2 |
| Reid et al. [5] | $(\frac{3}{4})^n$ | $(\frac{3}{4})^n$ | $(\frac{1}{2})^n$ | NO | - | NO | $1PRF+1Enc.$ | 2 |
| Swiss-knife [6] | $(\frac{1}{2})^n$ | $(\frac{3}{4})^n$ | $(\frac{1}{2})^n$ | YES | $O(n)PRF$ | YES | $3PRF$ | 4 |
| Our scheme | $(\frac{3}{4})^n$ | $(\frac{3}{4})^n/(\frac{7}{8})^n$ † | $(\frac{1}{2})^n$ | YES | $O(1)PRF$ | YES | $2PRF$ | 2 |

† If the malicious tag $\mathcal{T}$ gives one of $\{r_1,r_2,r_3\}$ to the adversary $\mathcal{A}$, the success probability of $\mathcal{A}$ is $(\frac{3}{4})^n$; if $\mathcal{T}$ gives two of $\{r_1,r_2,r_3\}$ to $\mathcal{A}$, the success probability of $\mathcal{A}$ is $(\frac{7}{8})^n$.

**Outline.** We organize the remainder of this paper as follows. In Section 2, we describe our new scheme. In Section 3, we analyze the security and privacy of our protocol. Finally, we give the conclusion of this paper.

## 2   Our Protocol

As shown in Fig. 1, the tag has an identifier $ID$, an alias identifier $ID'$ which is actually used during the protocol run and is computed through a PRF function $h$ initialized with $ID' := h(ID, s)$, and a secret key $s$ that is viewed as a vector $(s_1, \ldots, s_n)$, where $n$ is a security parameter. The reader has a database, consisting of pairs of $(s, ID, TID, TID')$, where $TID$ and $TID'$ are used as the index to search the tag's $ID$, and they are initialized with $TID := h(ID, s)$ and $TID' := h(h(ID, s), s)$ respectively. Both of the tag and the reader can compute a PRF and a $(3, 3)$ threshold scheme. There are three phases in our scheme as in Fig. 1. We give the description of the protocol as follows.

**Initialization Phase**

(1) The tag generates a random nonce $N_A$ of length $n$ and transmits $N_A$ along with $ID'$ to the reader.
(2) The reader searches in the database using the index $TID$ or $TID'$. If $ID' = TID'$, the reader will update its database as shown in Fig. 1. If success, it generates a random nonce $N_B$ of length $n$ and computes a $3n$-bit sequence

$\{H\}^{3n} = f(s, N_A, N_B, ID')$ and splits it into three shares: $r_1$, $r_2$ and $v$ respectively. Furthermore, it obtains the value of $r_3$ by computing $r_3 = r_1 \oplus r_2 \oplus s$. Meantime, the reader sends $N_B$ and $v'$ to the tag. We denote by $v'$ the value of $v$ received by the tag.

(3) The tag receives $N_B$ and $v'$. It also computes the same sequence $H$ and splits it into three shares like the reader. After calculating $v$, it compares the values of $v$ and $v'$. If they are same, the protocol continues. Otherwise the protocol fails. We point out that this step can detect the failure of the protocol at an early time, which makes the protocol more efficient.

**Interactive Phase.** The interactive phase is also called the fast bit exchange phase or the critical time phase, which consists of $n$ rounds in total.

(1) The reader picks a random bit $c_i$, starts the clock and sends $c_i$ to the tag.
(2) The tag makes corresponding response $r_i$ according to both $c_i$ and $v_i$ and transmits $r_i'$ to the reader. We denote $r_i'$ by the value received by the reader.

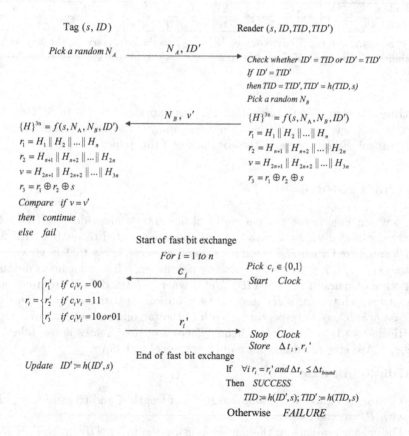

**Fig. 1.** Our distance bounding protocol

(3) Upon receiving $r_i'$, the reader stops the clock, stores $r_i'$ and the measured RTT $\Delta t_i$.

(4) Repeat the first three steps for $n$ times in total.

**Check Result Phase.** The tag updates its $ID'$ by $ID' := h(ID', s)$. The reader checks the received answers $(r_1', r_2', ...r_n')$ and the delay time $(\Delta t_1, \Delta t_2, ...\Delta t_n)$. If every response $r_i'$ matches the expected value $r_i$ and every delay time $\Delta t_i \leq \Delta t_{bound}$ where $\Delta t_{bound}$ is a given bound which indicates the tag is within the neighbor area, then the protocol succeeds and the reader also updates its database. Otherwise, the protocol fails.

***Remark 1.*** There is no fault-tolerance here, for we only consider noiseless communication. As to the noisy communication, we can use two numbers $T_1, T_2$, denoted as the number of positions for which $r_i \neq r_i'$ and $\Delta t_i > \Delta t_{bound}$ respectively. If $T_1 + T_2 > T$ where $T$ is a given threshold, then the protocol fails.

## 3   Security Analysis

We consider an active polynomial time adversary $\mathcal{A}$ who has the ability to eavesdrop, modify, inject and remove messages exchanged between all parties in the system. Furthermore, we consider a strong $\mathcal{A}$ which can also observe the result of a protocol run and even be able to observe the result of each round of a protocol run. We assume that genuine tags will not give their secret keys to attackers.

$N_A$ and $N_B$ are both randomly chosen so that they are used like a one-time pad. Actually, the presence of $N_A$ and $N_B$ are used to prevent replay attacks and also allow the reader to authenticate the tag in the result check phase, for only the tag and the reader know the shared secret key $s$, $N_A$ and $N_B$ simultaneously. Since $H$ is an output of the PRF function $f$, the adversary can't recover $s$ by decoding $H$ even if she/he can obtain part of $H$, that is $v$, which is used to allow the tag to authenticate the reader. We will give a detailed analysis on the security and privacy of our scheme as follows.

**Impersonation Fraud Resistance.** Without $s$, the adversary can generate the correct $r_i$ with probability negligibly different from $\frac{1}{2}$ since $f$ is a PRF. Thus the best the adversary can do is to guess the response randomly with success probability $\frac{1}{2}$ when receiving a challenge in each round of the fast bit exchange phase. Overall, the adversary's success probability is $(\frac{1}{2})^n$, which is negligible.

**Distance Fraud Resistance.** In this attack, the adversary can generate $r_1, r_2$, $r_3$ and $v$ and thus can get through the first slow phase easily. However, during the fast bit exchange phase, without knowing $c_i$, the adversary still needs to guess the corresponding answer $r_i$ from $\{r_1, r_2, r_3\}$ and sends it to the reader in advance in order to make the delay time measured by the reader within the bound. Therefore, at each round the success probability is $\frac{1}{2}(\frac{1}{2} \times 1 + \frac{1}{2} \times \frac{1}{2}) = \frac{3}{4}$ and after $n$ rounds, the adversary's success probability is $(\frac{3}{4})^n$, which is negligible.

**Mafia Fraud Resistance.** Again, without $s$, the adversary cannot compute the response strings $r_1$, $r_2$ and $r_3$ before the fast bit exchange phase. When carrying out a Mafia fraud attack, the attacker has two choices: using pre-ask strategy or not. Using the pre-ask strategy, the adversary slightly accelerates the clock signal provided to the tag and transmits an anticipated challenge bit $c_i'$ before the reader sends its challenge bit $c_i$. In half of all cases, the adversary will guess the right challenge bit, that is $c_i' = c_i$, and thus can get the correct value $r_i$ from the tag in advance. Afterwards, the adversary runs the fast phase with the authentic reader. In the other half of all cases, the adversary can simply reply with a guessed response bit when interacting with the reader, which will be correct with the probability of $\frac{1}{2}$. Therefore, in each round, the success probability of the adversary is $\frac{1}{2} \times 1 + \frac{1}{2} \times \frac{1}{2} = \frac{3}{4}$. If the attacker doesn't use the pre-ask strategy, she/he will have to guess the challenge bit $c_i$ with a success probability of $\frac{1}{2}$ before receiving it when executing the fast bit exchange phase with the reader. Thus we consider the adversary's success probability in each round as the maximum one, that is $\frac{3}{4}$. To sum up, the adversary can get through the whole protocol with probability of $(\frac{3}{4})^n$, which is negligible.

**Terrorist Fraud Resistance.** It's trivial to see that the malicious tag cannot give all the $r_1$, $r_2$ and $r_3$ to the attacker, for the attacker will be able to recover the secret key $s$ easily by $s = r_1 \oplus r_2 \oplus r_3$. Since $v$ is sent as plaintext in our protocol, the malicious tag can give it to the adversary directly. Hence we will consider the following two scenarios.

First, we consider the situation that the malicious tag gives $v$ and one of $r_1$, $r_2$ and $r_3$ to the attacker. Without loss of generality, we assume that it gives her/him $r_1$ and $v$. When receiving a challenge bit $c_i$, the adversary knows both $c_i$ and $v_i$, and also knows the answer when $c_i v_i = 00$. However, she/he doesn't know the value of $r_2^i$ or $r_3^i$, which means when $c_i v_i \neq 00$, she/he has to guess the value of the answer. Suppose we use $P_{k_i = j}$ to denote the probability of $k_i = j$, then the probability that the adversary replies correctly is $P_{c_i=0} \cdot (P_{v_i=0} \cdot P_{[v_i=0|c_i=0]} + P_{v_i=1} \cdot P_{[v_i=1|c_i=0]}) + P_{c_i=1} \cdot (P_{v_i=0} \cdot P_{[v_i=0|c_i=1]} + P_{v_i=1} \cdot P_{[v_i=1|c_i=1]}) = \frac{1}{2} \left( \frac{1}{2} \times 1 + \frac{1}{2} \times \frac{1}{2} \right) + \frac{1}{2} \left( \frac{1}{2} \times \frac{1}{2} + \frac{1}{2} \times \frac{1}{2} \right) = \frac{5}{8}$. Similarly, we can calculate the adversary's success probability when she/he gets $r_2$ or $r_3$ respectively. It is interesting to point out that when giving the attacker $r_3$, she/he will guess the right answer with probability of $\frac{3}{4}$. That is, the adversary can get though the protocol with a maximal probability of $(\frac{3}{4})^n$, which is negligible.

Then, we consider the situation that the malicious tag gives the adversary two of $r_1$, $r_2$ and $r_3$. With a similar analysis, we can compute the adversary's maximal success probability is $(\frac{7}{8})^n$. One interesting thing is that once passing the protocol, the adversary will know she/he has replied with all the correct responses and furthermore she/he can recover part of the secret key $s$ according to $s_i = r_1^i \oplus r_2^i \oplus r_3^i$. For example, if we assume that the malicious tag gives the adversary $\{v, r_1, r_2\}$, and the protocol run succeeds, then the adversary understands that she/he has guessed all the correct responses when the actual response should be $r_3^i$. As is shown in the protocol, there's an average probability of $\frac{1}{2}$ that the response is $r_3^i$. Hence after one successful protocol run the adversary can obtain $\lfloor \frac{1}{2} n \rfloor$ bits of $s$. We point out that the probability of recovering secret key is a conditional probability, where the condition is the adversary has passed the distance bounding protocol successfully. If the adversary's success probability is negligible, then the probability of recovering the secret key is also negligible.

**Distance Hijacking Attack Resistance.** We only consider the situation of distance hijacking attacks in single-protocol environment. To launch a distance hijacking attack in our protocol, the adversary first impersonates a reader to communicate with an exploited tag. The tag will send the preliminary information to the reader, that is $N_A$ and $ID$. Upon receiving $N_A$ and $ID$, the attacker acting as a fraudulent tag sends $N_A$ and her/his own identity $ID'$ to the authentic reader. Finally, the exploited tag will execute the fast bit exchange phase with the reader. However, the exploited tag computes $H$ with $\{H\}^{3n} = f(s, N_A, N_B, ID)$, while the authentic reader computes $H$ with $\{H\}^{3n} = f(s', N_A, N_B, ID')$, where $s'$ is the shared secret key between the attacker and the authentic reader, and the authentic reader searches $s'$ out in the database according to the attacker's identifier $ID'$. Therefore, the success probability of the adversary is $(\frac{1}{2})^n$, when the values of pseudo-random string $H$ computed by the reader and the tag are same with different inputs.

**Privacy.** As we have mentioned above, $ID'$ is initialized with $ID' := h(ID, s)$, where $ID$ is the tag's identity. Upon communicating with the reader, the tag transmits $ID'$ instead of $ID$ to the reader. What's more, the tag will update the value of $ID'$ at the end of fast bit exchange phase(see Fig. 1). Since $h$ is a PRF, if the adversary can tell if two sessions have the same tag involved, it means that it can distinguish two different outputs generated by a PRF with non-negligible probability, which is impossible. Hence our protocol supplies the property of untraceability for tags.

*Remark 2.* Our protocol prevents the de-synchronization attack by using both $TID$ and $TID'$. When launching a de-synchronization attack, the adversary either prevents the tag updating $ID'$, for example by modifying $v'$ sent from the reader to the tag, or prevents the reader updating $TID$ and $TID'$ in the check result phase, for example by tampering the value of response bits sent from the tag to the reader so that the protocol will fail. It's not difficult to see no matter the adversary stops the tag or the reader from updating its data, the value of $ID'$ sent by the tag will always be equal to either $TID$ or $TID'$. That is, the tag is always synchronized with the reader.

## 4   Conclusion

In this paper, we proposed a new efficient mutually authenticated distance bounding protocol that is resistant to all the current attacks. Our protocol also protects privacy of tags through an anonymous method, which achieves untraceability and prevents de-synchronization attacks. To our best knowledge, it is the most efficient method to provide the untraceability for the tag in RFID distance bounding protocols.

# References

1. Brands, S., Chaum, D.: Distance Bounding Protocols. In: Helleseth, T. (ed.) EU-ROCRYPT 1993. LNCS, vol. 765, pp. 344–359. Springer, Heidelberg (1994)
2. Hancke, G., Kuhn, M.: An RFID Distance Bounding Protocol. In: 1st International Conference on Security and Privacy for Emerging Areas in Communications Networks, pp. 67–73. IEEE Computer Society (2005)
3. Munilla, J., Peinado, A.: Distance bounding protocols for RFID enhanced by using void-challenges and analysis in noisy channels. In: Wireless Communications and Mobile Computing, vol. 8, pp. 1227–1232. Wiley Interscience, Hoboken (2008)
4. Tu, Y.J., Piramuthu, S.: RFID Distance Bounding Protocols. In: 1st International EURASIP Workshop in RFID Technology, Vienna, Austria (2007)
5. Reid, J., Nieto, J.G., Tang, T., Senadji, B.: Detecting Relay Attacks with Timing-Based Protocols. In: Proc. of the 2nd ACM Symposium on Information, Computer, and Communications Security - ASIACCS 2007, pp. 204–213. ACM, New York (2007)
6. Kim, C.H., Avoine, G., Koeune, F., Standaert, F.X., Pereira, O.: The Swiss-Knife RFID Distance Bounding Protocol. In: Lee, P.J., Cheon, J.H. (eds.) ICISC 2008. LNCS, vol. 5461, pp. 98–115. Springer, Heidelberg (2009)
7. Kim, C.H., Avoine, G.: RFID Distance Bounding Protocols with Mixed Challenges. IEEE Trans. on Wireless Communications 10(5), 1618–1626 (2011)
8. Avoine, G., Lauradoux, C., Marin, B.: How Secret-sharing can Defeat Terrorist Fraud. In: Proc. of the 4th ACM Conference on Wireless Network Security - WiSec 2011, pp. 145–156 (2011)
9. Desmedt, Y.: Major security problems with the 'unforgeable' (Feige)- Fiat- Shamir proofs of identify and how to overcome them. In: SecuriCom 1988, 6th World-wide Congress on Computer and Communications Security and Protection, SEDEP Paris, pp. 15–17 (1988)
10. Cremers, C., Rasmussen, K.B., Capkun, S.: Distance Hijacking Attacks on Distance Bounding Protocols. In: IEEE Symposium on Security and Privacy- S&P 2012, pp. 113–127. IEEE Computer Society, Los Alamitos (2012)
11. Juels, A., Rivest, R.L., Szydlo, M.: The Blocker Tag: Selective Blocking of RFID Tags for Consumer Privacy. In: 8th ACM Conference on Computer and Communications Security -CCS 2003, pp. 103–111. ACM (2003)
12. Weis, S.A., Sarma, S.E., Rivest, R.L., Engels, D.W.: Security and Privacy Aspects of Low-Cost Radio Frequency Identification Systems. In: International Conference on Security in Pervasive Computing -SPC 2003, pp. 201–212 (2003)
13. Ohkubo, M., Suzuki, K., Kinoshita, S.: Cryptographic Approach to "Privacy-Friendly" Tags. In: RFID Privacy Workshop (2003)
14. Henrici, D., Muller, P.: Hash-based Enhancement of Location Privacy for Radio-Frequency Identification Devices using Varying Identifiers. In: 2nd IEEE Annual Conference on Pervasive Computing and Communications Workshops (2004)
15. Paise, R., Vaudenay, S.: Mutual Authentication in RFID: Security and Privacy. In: ACM Symposium on Information, Computer and Communications Security – ASSIACCS 2008, pp. 292–299. ACM (2008)
16. Juels, A., Weis, S.A.: Defining strong privacy for RFID. ACM Trans. on Information and System Security 13(1) (2009)

# Exploring Mobile Proxies
# for Better Password Authentication

Nitesh Saxena[1] and Jonathan Voris[2]

[1] University of Alabama at Birmingham
saxena@cis.uab.edu
[2] Columbia University
jvoris@cs.columbia.edu

**Abstract.** Traditional textual password authentication techniques have numerous well documented security and usability flaws, yet have seen near universal deployment due to their desirable efficiency properties. As a result, many users who may prefer alternative authentication approaches are forced to use passwords or PINs on a daily basis due to a lack of control over third party servers. This work explores the use of a mobile device as a proxy for password management in an attempt to improve remote password authentication without making changes to remote servers.

A universal proxy-based authentication framework is presented which allows users to employ a method of their own choice to authenticate locally to their mobile devices (e.g., biometrics or graphical passwords). The framework is also compatible with many communication channels between the mobile proxy and local terminal (e.g., Bluetooth or audio). To demonstrate the practicality of this general framework, a concrete implementation using an "out-of-band" audio channel, called PIN-Audio, is also provided. While existing password management solutions may provide a reasonable level of security for commonplace services, PIN-Audio is recommended for a user-friendly deployment for security critical applications, such as online banking.

**Keywords:** User Authentication, Passwords, Mobile Devices.

## 1 Introduction

The goal of user authentication is to ensure that only legitimate users are granted access to a computer system while all others are restricted. User authentication can be achieved by establishing credentials between a user and a system, and having users demonstrate that they possess them whenever they wish to access the system. Authentication is one of the most widely studied problems in the realm of computer security. This is due both its fundamental nature, as few security guarantees can be made for a system which allows unauthorized access, as well as the frequency and wide variety of settings in which it takes place.

While many innovative authentication techniques have been proposed, historical and economic factors have stymied the adoption of these novel methods in

T.W. Chim and T.H. Yuen (Eds.): ICICS 2012, LNCS 7618, pp. 293–302, 2012.
© Springer-Verlag Berlin Heidelberg 2012

practice. Updating an entire system of computers to use an alternate approach might be costly and time consuming. As such, despite the great theoretical advancements made in this domain, the vast majority of computer systems are left using basic passwords as their primary form of authentication. Recent developments in mobile devices, such as cell phones, can be utilized to help address this issue. The past decade has seen the emergence of smarter and cheaper mobile phones that have both the computational power and user interfaces necessary to support a wide variety of potential new authentication techniques. Furthermore, phone usage habitats have evolved alongside this technology to the point where some people consider their mobile devices to be more important than their wallets [12].

This paper proposes a way in which mobile phones can be used to place users in control of what authentication method they use. Updating a single mobile phone is far more cost effective than altering an entire computer system; indeed, most cell phone users are already accustomed to installing new applications and software. As a result, this would allow users to select the authentication method that works best for them rather than waiting for a less likely event that the operators of a remote service (that needs authentication) updates their system with a more suitable mechanism.

The core improvement detailed in this work is a framework for providing more secure authentication without necessitating any changes be made to remote servers. The technique is referred to as "proxy-based authentication". The basic concept is to provide users with a mobile proxy for authentication to a local terminal, which in turn authenticates users to a remote service. Rather than forcing users to remember passwords themselves, leading to short and predictable passwords, passwords will be stored in the portable device, allowing them to be long and fully randomized.

While phone based password management software has been previously proposed, our innovation lies in the automated transfer of credentials from the mobile appliance to the terminal. Furthermore, previous portable password managers again restrict users to standard PIN or passphrase techniques for authentication to the mobile proxy. In contrast, proxy-based authentication allows users to select whichever technique they are most comfortable with for authenticating to the proxy phone. This opens up the possibility for utilizing novel authentication technology that is best suited for mobile hardware without forcing service providers to make any alterations to their systems.

## 2   Related Work

A vast majority of remote services that are available today utilize password-based authentication. In the absence of action on behalf of service providers, attempts have been made to improve the security and usability of authentication while preserving backward compatibility with passphrases. This section briefly outlines previous solutions of this kind, which are known as *password managers*.

Password managers are programs that accept weak passwords as input and output passphrases that are considered to be strong. This is accomplished by using a computing device to generate strong passwords rather than humans themselves, who behave poorly when asked to create passphrases of sufficient entropy. The appliance can then store the secure passwords that have been generated and output them to its user whenever he or she requires access. Password management software is divisible into three broad categories: desktop, remote, and portable managers.

Desktop password management systems store passwords directly on the terminal that is used to authenticate to remote hosts. High profile examples of programs in this category include Mozilla Firefox [9] and RoboForm by Siber Systems [13]. In contrast, remote managers such as LastPass, developed by the corporation of the same name [8], and Mozilla Weave [10] use one or more non-local servers to keep track of passphrases. The third class of managers utilize auxiliary mobile hardware like cell phones as a password bank. Sperle's KeePassMobile for J2ME enabled devices [5] and OI Safe for the Android platform by OpenIntents UG [11] both fall into this category.

All of these solutions utilize a master password to protect the numerous passwords which they store, therefore increasing usability but having no effect on security. Beyond this, each manager category has its own set of shortcomings. Desktop managers offer no portability for people who use more than a single terminal to authenticate to remote servers. That is, since these programs use the terminal itself as a password repository, they do not provide a mechanism for retrieving these passwords when a different terminal is in use.

While remote managers do allow for use from numerous terminals, they force users to place trust in the system of a third party service provider. This branch of passphrase managers operate by encrypting individual passwords with a master value prior to storing them remotely. They are therefore vulnerable to an offline dictionary attack in the event that these remote machines are compromised. Furthermore, if one computer is used to store passwords for more than one user, an adversary will be able to recover passwords belonging to several users by compromising a single machine. As a final drawback, remote managers are often proprietary, allowing their operators keep the precise details behind how passwords are treated after they leave a user's system guarded as a secret.

In contrast, it is easier to place trust in a portable manager as it can be managed locally by users themselves rather than relying on an external entity to do so [1]. It is also more difficult to eavesdrop on authentication with portable devices due to the small form factor of mobile hardware. Unfortunately, existing mobile password managers suffer from poor usability by requiring that the long and random passwords stored on the portable appliance be manually copied to the authentication terminal. This also provides malicious entities with a potential opportunity for observing the password entry. Such an attack could be accomplished either through casual non-technical attacks like shoulder surfing or sophisticated attacks such as Balzarotti, Cova, and Vigna's video based technique [6] or the audio logging technique introduced by Zhuang, Zhou, and Tygar [7].

# 3    Secure Authentication Framework from the Client Side

## 3.1    Threat Model

Before delving deeper into the details of the proxy-based authentication framework, it is necessary to establish the capabilities attributed to adversaries in our system as well as which devices are trusted with which pieces of data. The parties involved in this system are a human user U, a mobile device M, a local terminal T, and a remote server S. In order to provide increased security, rather than placing the burden of generating and remembering a password on U, a password is assumed to be pre-established between M and S.

While U is responsible for recalling the credentials used to authenticate to M, U need not remember or even be aware of the password shared between M and S. It can therefore be as long and random as dictated by the security needs of the application in question rather than the memory and security knowledge of a human user. Whenever U would usually authenticate to S through T, U instead authenticates to M. M reacts by retrieving the encrypted password for S from secure, tamper-resistant storage. This secure storage medium is available on many portable appliances. Only when U authenticates to M is the password corresponding to S unlocked. Next, M authenticates to T, encrypts the passphrase for S and transmits it to T.

If M and T were to share a traditional high bandwidth wireless channel such as WiFi or Bluetooth, this could be utilized to efficiently transmit the encrypted PIN. Doing so would have a unfavorable impact on the framework's universality, usability, and security, however. Along the same lines, since wireless channels are not physically authenticatable, they would leave the channel vulnerable to man-in-the-middle attacks on the framework. For these reasons OOB channels are recommended over conventional wireless channels for forming the secure communication link from M to T. Adversaries are assumed to be capable of eavesdropping on, but not modifying, transmissions over an OOB channel.

In this system, T, S, and M are all trusted with knowledge of the password, but it is only permanently stored in an encrypted form on M. T transmits password values to S without storing them, while S need only store the value produced by hashing password values with a weakly collision resistant hash function. While it is natural that S and M share this secret value, T's awareness of the secret is undesirable. This is because it would be beneficial to be able to authenticate to S using Ts that are public or may be compromised. Unfortunately, T's knowledge of the secret password is a necessary consequence of avoiding any server side changes in this proxy-based authentication framework. If changes to the server were permitted, T could instead blindly pass the encrypted password through to S who would then be delegated the responsibility of decrypting it and recovering the plaintext secret. A third party could perform the same service, but this presents similar and perhaps deeper security challenges to those incurred by trusting T.

## 3.2 Design

The proxy-based authentication framework is comprised of two overall components. First, a phase occurs where U authenticates to M. This is followed by a phase where the M authenticates itself to T instead of U doing so directly.

**User-to-Phone Authentication.** The authentication primitive that U selects to access M is critical to the framework as a whole both in terms of security and usability. The method used to secure M will unlock all of the passwords it stores, so it must be as resilient to attack as possible. Adding to its importance, using a mobile proxy burdens users by requiring them to interact with an additional device, so the authentication mechanism put into effect must be as usable as possible. Biometric authentication is a good match for these needs and adapts more easily for use on portable devices than for use in alternative settings, such as remote servers.

**Phone-to-Terminal Authentication.** Prior to using this proxy-based authentication framework to authenticate to a given service, users must first initialize M and T. This process need only be carried out once for each T U wishes to authenticate through. The rest of the initialization step depends on the time of channel in use. If M and T share compatible interfaces for a conventional wireless channel, this channel must be bootstrapped by establishing a shared key. Previous work on this topic, also known by "device pairing," can be used to achieve this.

If an OOB channel is to be used in place of an in-band wireless channel as discussed in Section 3.1, a suitable channel must first be selected based on the transmitters and corresponding receivers available on T and M. Since a bidirectional channel is needed, M and T must be equipped with both complementary input and output interfaces. One possibility is to form an audio channel using microphones and speakers. This particular OOB channel is particularly promising due to the ubiquity of these interfaces and is explored in more detail in its own section, 4.

Finally, a shared secret must be established between M and T. Once a given M and T have been properly initialized, the next required step is for M to authenticate to T. This can be executed immediately following the initialization phase when it is required by using particular a particular combination of M and T for the first time. The authentication protocol can be accomplished by using the keys established in the initialization phase to execute any challenge-response (C-R) authentication protocol of the user's choosing.

The difference between the distinct initialization and registration phases should be noted. The initialization phase is required whenever a new M and T are to be used in conjunction with each other. The registration phase, on the other hand, is required whenever a new S is used with M for the first time or when U wishes to refresh the password used to authenticate to S. After initializing, M can register with any number of Ss, after which M can skip directly to the authentication phase when using this service in the future.

### 3.3    Framework Security Guarantees

In this section the security implications of the proxy-based authentication framework are explored. In Section 3.1, it was established that M, S, and T are all trusted with the password used to authenticate to S. Let $p$ bits be the length of the shared password and $k$ bits be the size of the key by U to authentication to M. Additionally, assume for the sake of simplicity that both M and S have a policy in effect restricting U to $q$ authentication attempts.

Given these values, an adversary has at most a $q/2^p$ chance of success by bypassing M completely and simply attempting to pose as U by guessing passwords and sending them to S for verification. If the attacker compromises the M's tamper-proof hardware and is able to copy the contents M, but is not able to bypass M's access control mechanisms, he or she will have $2^k$ key possibilities to try in order to gain access to M's data, implying a $q/2^k$ probability of success for this attack. If an adversary instead compromises S, he or she will only be able to recover the weakly collision resistant hashes of the passwords stored on S, since S is assumed to store these values in lieu of saving the passwords themselves.

If a malicious entity was able to gain access to both M and S, he or she could perform a brute force attack to recover the password corresponding to S by performing $2^k$ hash operations at worst. The most direct attack on this framework would involve recovering the secret U uses to authenticate to M as well as compromising M, in which case all the passwords on M could be unlocked, breaking the security of the framework entirely. If reasonable parameters are selected, such as $p = k = 80$ and $q = 3$, proxy-based authentication achieves computational security against all adversaries except the one who is able to both compromise M and learn the secret to authenticate to M.

## 4    Illustrative Instantiation Using an Audio Codec

In this segment of the paper, we discuss PIN-Audio, a practical implementation of the theoretical proxy-based authentication framework introduced in Section 3. It is possible to use a conventional wireless channel as a communication link between M and T was mentioned. Due to the universality, security, and usability issues involved, it may not always be possible or desirable to use such a channel. Fortunately, M and T will always feature some other forms of output interfaces. In scenarios where M and T share corresponding input and output interfaces, these can be used to construct an OOB channel instead. This section proposes the use of an audio channel as a basis for transmissions from T to M and vice versa. In essence, a C-R protocol adhering to the framework established in Section 3.2 will be executed over this audio channel. While any authentication mechanism can be used by U to access M, we opted to use a standard PIN based approach. A pictorial representation of this concrete version of proxy-based authentication is provided in Figure 1.

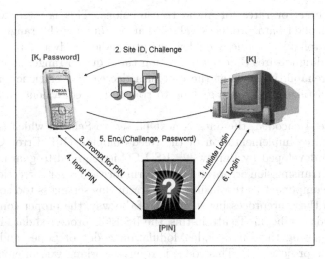

**Fig. 1.** Authenticating to a Remote Server Using a Mobile Proxy and an Audio Channel

## 4.1  Design and Implementation

In order to support this authentication system it is necessary to install new software on T and M. T requires a password client application while a password server program is needed by M. Recall, however, that no modifications of S need to be made in order to accommodate PIN-Audio. In this implementation the initialization phase was assumed to already be completed. That is, a pre-shared symmetric key was simply copied on to M and T at installation time. In practice, this can be achieved by performing a Diffie-Hellman key exchange over the audio channel as described in Section 3.2. This technique does handle both the registration and authentication steps required to access a remote service, though. Both of these phases proceed as per the framework outlined in Section 3.2.

**Device Setup.** Before proceeding with the implementation, specific devices had to be chosen to fit all of the players involved in the proxy-based authentication framework provided in Section 3.1. A desktop computer was selected for T as would be the case in a practical implementation. Rather than actually using a cell phone as M, however, a simulated proof-of-concept prototype was developed using a laptop computer. With built in microphones and speakers, these devices had all the hardware necessary to serve the roles of T and M respectively. Thus, a password server application was designed for the laptop and a password client application was crafted for the desktop. Since no changes to it were necessary, S was left out of this simulation.

**Construction of a Robust Audio Channel.** Data is encrypted prior to transmission. The resultant ciphertext is used as input to a Base64 encoder in order to facilitate transfer via audio. Base64 was selected because this encoding leads to lower error rates for audio transmissions. This is owed to the fact that byte encoded data produces values that are outside the range of sounds that can be reliably produced on low quality audio hardware. In contrast, a Base64 encoding ensures that data is within the required range. unfortunately, this higher reliability comes at the cost of a decrease in efficiency, as Base64 encoded data takes 1.33 times as long to transmit as equivalent data under a byte encoding.

Once Base64 encoded, the data is next passed to Schifra, which is a robust and open source implementation of the Reed-Solomon (RS) Error Correcting Code (ECC) developed by Partow [2]. RS ECC is required to guard the audio data against transmission errors and to perform forward error correction. This is a necessary component as retransmitting data in this setting is too costly to be viable. With these preprocessing steps out of the way, the proper conversion of data to sounds can begin. To attain this, the RS ECC processed data is encoded on last time using the Pulse-Code Modulation codec of Lopes and Aguiar's Digital Voices project [3,4]. This codec is robust, working well in environments with high levels of ambient noise, as well as usable, since it uses a pleasant "Soprano Flute" sound as a basis for its transmissions. A start marker or "initial hail sequence" and end indicator or "stop sequence" are employed in order to detect the beginning and end of the audio based data transmissions.

Intuitively, once encoded the audio data is sent through the originating computer's speakers and received by the destination device's microphone. The decoding process at the recipient's end is the inverse of the encoding process. In order to provide security, it is only necessary to encrypt the data being sent from M to T. Leaving the channel from T to M open will impact the protocol's privacy, however, since T's responses contain an identifier of the S that U wishes to access. In order to achieve privacy as well as security the link from T to M can be encrypted as well. This implementation opted for security as well as privacy by encrypting transmissions in both directions.

**Desktop Password Client Application.** The password client program developed for T can be divided into five main components: a keyboard listener, an active window handler, an encryption/decryption and encoding/decoding engine, an audio codec engine, and a key thrower. The keyboard listener comes into play first. When U presses the keyboard shortcut associated with the password client (for PIN-Audio, the F8 key was used in this capacity) this portion of the program triggers the application.

The software's active window handler then checks if the window that is currently active is a web browser. If this is the case, it extracts the name of the web site that is currently active in the browser. Note that while PIN-Audio only supports authentication to web sites through a browser, the proxy-based authentication framework can be extended to support authentication to any remote server S. Next, the client generates a 80 bit long random nonce and concatenates it with the specified request type and S's identifier. Possible options for the request type are login, registration, and password change. The two engine segments are then called upon to encrypt and encode this data as detailed in Section 4.1, which is played through T's speakers.

Once T has finished its audio transmissions, it shifts to its listener component to wait for the start sequence of the response from M's password server program. When this special value is detected, T's application captures audio until it notices the designated stop sequence value. This acquired audio is decrypted and decoded again using the process provided in Section 4.1. Finally, if the nonce that was initially sent by T matches the nonce M sent back to it, the software's key thrower places the transmitted password in the correct field of the web site that is currently being viewed.

**Laptop Password Server Application.** The password server for our laptop M was written in Java, with the exception of Schifra, Partow's C++ RS ECC implementation. Just as with the desktop password client, the laptop server executed this code through a shell. Further, the encryption, decryption, encoding, and decoding processes all occur in the same fashion as T's client program as it is laid out in Section 4.1. As soon as M's server application starts it begins listening for the unique audio start sequence. When this has been detected the program decodes the received audio and asks U to authenticate to M by entering his or her PIN. After authenticating, M requests that U confirm the request sent by T. If U accepts, M reacts as dictated by the transmitted request type. If the solicitation is for registration, a password of the minimum length deemed secure for the application at hand is generated uniformly at random. The passphrase is then encrypted and stored. If a login type request is received, an existing password corresponding to S is retrieved from the phone's memory. Irrespective of the request type, M always concludes by transmitting the proper passphrase over the audio channel.

### 4.2   Implementation Security Guarantees

PIN-Audio utilizes a 4 decimal digit PIN for user-to-phone authentication. Assuming that 4 decimal digits are equivalent to 15 bits, the chance of success for an attack scenario where M alone is compromised becomes $\frac{q}{2^{15}}$ at best. This contrasts with the security offered by conventional user selected passwords, which can be guessed with a maximum probability of $\frac{q}{|D|}$ where $D$ is the dictionary containing all of U's possible password choices. PIN-Audio clearly offers better security in cases where $|D| < 2^{15}$. Compromising S in place of M would yield an attacker no advantage when PIN-Audio is in use. This is also an improvement over normal passwords, which can be recovered by launching a dictionary attack on a compromised S. Like the general framework, PIN-Audio offers no real security in the scenario where both M and S were compromised, though. This is due to the fact that a malicious entity could recover the password for S by performing at worst $2^{15}$ hash operations.

# 5   Conclusion

This paper presented a mobile proxy-based framework for authenticating to remote servers. This system leverages a personal, portable device in a novel manner by using it as an intermediary between a user and the authentication terminal used. This provides the possibility of performing both secure user-to-phone authentication and cryptographic phone-to-terminal authentication. Most critically, it can be readily utilized by users in search of stronger security without requiring any changes be made to existing server architectures. While the manual transfer of shorter, less secure passwords offered by alternative mobile password managers may be sufficient for less sensitive applications, PIN-Audio is recommended for authentication to online services, such as banking, that demand high levels of security.

**Acknowledgments.** This work is supported, in part, by the NSF grant CNS-1209280. The authors also thank Md. Borhan Uddin for his work on the audio codec used in the implementation of PIN-Audio.

# References

1. Karole, A., Saxena, N., Christin, N.: A Comparative Usability Evaluation of Traditional Password Managers. In: Rhee, K.-H., Nyang, D. (eds.) ICISC 2010. LNCS, vol. 6829, pp. 233–251. Springer, Heidelberg (2011)
2. Partow, A.: Schifra Reed-Solomon Error Correcting Code Library (2010), http://www.schifra.com
3. Lopes, C.: Digital Voices (2003), http://www.ics.uci.edu/~lopes/dv/dv.html
4. Lopes, C., Aguiar, P.: Acoustic Modems for Ubiquitous Computing. In: Pervasive Computing (2003)
5. Sperle, C.: KeePassMobile (2010), http://www.keepassmobile.com
6. Balzarotti, D., Cova, M., Vigna, G.: ClearShot: Eavesdropping on Keyboard Input from Video. In: Symposium on Security and Privacy (2008)
7. Zhuang, L., Zhou, F., Tygar, J.: Keyboard Acoustic Emanations Revisited. In: Conference on Computer and Communications Security (2005)
8. LastPass Corporation. LastPass Password Manager (2010), https://lastpass.com
9. Mozilla Corporation. Firefox Browser (2010), http://www.mozilla.com/firefox
10. Mozilla Corporation. Weave Sync. (2010), http://labs.mozilla.com/projects/weave
11. OpenIntents UG. OpenIntents Safe (2009), http://www.openintents.org/en/node/205
12. Kim, R.: The World's a Cell-phone Stage. In: The San Fransisco Chronicle (2006), http://www.sfgate.com/cgi-bin/article.cgi?f=/c/a/2006/02/27/BUG2IHECTO1.DTL
13. Siber Systems. RoboForm Password Manager (2010), http://www.roboform.com

# On Security of Universal Hash Function Based Multiple Authentication

Aysajan Abidin

Department of Electrical Engineering, Linköping University, Linköping, Sweden
aysajan@isy.liu.se

**Abstract.** Universal hash function based multiple authentication was originally proposed by Wegman and Carter in 1981. In this authentication, a series of messages are authenticated by first hashing each message by a fixed (almost) strongly universal₂ hash function and then encrypting the hash value with a preshared one-time pad. This authentication is unconditionally secure. In this paper, we show that the unconditional security cannot be guaranteed if the hash function output for the first message is not encrypted, as remarked in [1]. This means that it is not only sufficient, but also necessary, to encrypt the hash of every message to be authenticated in order to have unconditional security. The security loss is demonstrated by a simple existential forgery attack. The impact of the attack is also discussed at the end.

**Keywords:** $\epsilon$-Almost Strongly Universal hash functions, multiple authentication, unconditionally secure, Quantum Key Distribution.

## 1 Introduction

Since its first introduction by Wegman and Carter [11] in 1979, Universal hash functions have been extensively studied over the years. They have diverse applications from cryptography to computer science to coding theory. In cryptography, they can be used for, among others, constructing unconditionally secure message authentication codes (MACs). There has been various Universal hash function constructions for authentication by Wegman and Carter, Stinson, and others [3, 5, 6, 8, 9, 12, 14–16, 18, 20–24].

Typical use of Universal hash functions, more accurately $\epsilon$-Almost Strongly Universal₂ ($\epsilon$-ASU₂) hash functions, in MACs is such that a one-time key (used to identify a hash function in the family) is used to authenticate one message; because two uses of the same key may reveal the key through the message-tag pairs. In this sense, this version of the Wegman-Carter authentication is similar to the one-time pad (OTP). Hence, the key consumption rate of the authentication in this scheme is usually quite high. In this paper we focus on another proposal by Wegman and Carter [24] that uses a fixed $\epsilon$-ASU₂ hash function (identified by a fixed key), followed by OTP encryption of the hash function output, so that the hash function can be reused. This scheme is also called counter-based multiple authentication [1] when the OTPs preshared between Alice and Bob can be

T.W. Chim and T.H. Yuen (Eds.): ICICS 2012, LNCS 7618, pp. 303–310, 2012.
© Springer-Verlag Berlin Heidelberg 2012

identified by counters. The key consumption rate of this scheme asymptotically approaches the tag length.

**Contribution.** This short paper addresses a simple existential MAC forgery attack when the universal hash function based multiple authentication is used as remarked in [1]. In its original proposal in [24], Wegman and Carter proposed to apply the OTP to the hash of every message that is exchanged. In [1], however, the authors stated that it is not necessary to apply the OTP to the hash of the initial message. As we will see later in Section 3, not using the OTP in the initial round, or in any other round for that matter, will result in the adversary being able to forge the correct tag for his/her chosen message without knowing the authentication key at all. The attack is very simple and straightforward, and also very cheap in terms of computation and storage depending on the properties of the underlying hash function family. But the impact can be deep if such authentication is used in, for example, Quantum Key Distribution (QKD).

## 2    Background

**Definitions.** First, some definitions are in order. In what follows, we let $\mathcal{M}$ and $\mathcal{T}$ be finite sets, and $\mathcal{H}$ a class of hash functions from $\mathcal{M} \to \mathcal{T}$.

**Definition 1.** *A class $\mathcal{H}$ is **Universal$_2$ (U$_2$)**, if there exists at most $|\mathcal{H}|/|\mathcal{T}|$ hash functions $h \in \mathcal{H}$ such that $h(m_1) = h(m_2)$, for any two distinct $m_1, m_2 \in \mathcal{M}$. If there are at most $\epsilon|\mathcal{H}|$ hash functions instead, the class $\mathcal{H}$ is $\epsilon$-**Almost Universal$_2$ ($\epsilon$-AU$_2$)**.*

**Definition 2.** *A class $\mathcal{H}$ is **XOR Universal$_2$ (XU$_2$)** if there exists at most $|\mathcal{H}|/|\mathcal{T}|$ hash functions $h \in \mathcal{H}$ such that $h(m_1) = h(m_2) \oplus t$, for any two distinct $m_1, m_2 \in \mathcal{M}$ and any $t \in \mathcal{T}$. If there are at most $\epsilon|\mathcal{H}|$ hash functions instead, the class $\mathcal{H}$ is $\epsilon$-**Almost XOR Universal$_2$ ($\epsilon$-AXU$_2$)**.*

**Definition 3.** *A class $\mathcal{H}$ is **Strongly Universal$_2$ (SU$_2$)** if (a) the number of hash functions in $\mathcal{H}$ that takes an arbitrary $m_1 \in \mathcal{M}$ to an arbitrary $t_1 \in \mathcal{T}$ is exactly $|\mathcal{H}|/|\mathcal{T}|$, and (b) the fraction of those functions that also takes an arbitrary $m_2 \neq m_1$ in $\mathcal{M}$ to an arbitrary $t_2 \in \mathcal{T}$ (possibly equal to $t_1$) is $1/|\mathcal{T}|$. If the fraction in (b) instead is at most $\epsilon$, the class $\mathcal{H}$ is $\epsilon$-**Almost Strongly Universal$_2$ ($\epsilon$-ASU$_2$)**.*

Here we note that SU$_2$ is the optimal case, corresponding to $1/|\mathcal{T}|$-ASU$_2$, since $\epsilon \geq 1/|\mathcal{T}|$ [21]. Also, note that ASU$_2$ families are AXU$_2$ and AU$_2$, and that AXU$_2$ families are AU$_2$; however, the reverse is not true.

**Definition 4.** *A hash function $h$ from $\mathcal{M} \to \mathcal{T}$ is called **XOR-linear** if, for any two $m, m' \in \mathcal{M}$, $h(m \oplus m') = h(m) \oplus h(m')$. Similarly, a family $\mathcal{H}$ is called XOR-linear if any hash function $h \in \mathcal{H}$ is **XOR-linear**.*

**Unconditionally Secure MAC.** Unconditionally secure authentication theory was first developed by Simmons in [19] and later by Wegman and Carter in [11,24]. Wegman and Carter proposed using the classes of $\epsilon$-ASU$_2$ hash functions for unconditionally secure MAC constructions. The application of $\epsilon$-ASU$_2$ hash functions to construct provably unconditionally secure MACs is straightforward. In these constructions, Alice and Bob share a secret key $k$ to identify a hash function $h_k$ in a family $\mathcal{H}$ of $\epsilon$-ASU$_2$ hash functions from $\mathcal{M} \to \mathcal{T}$. When Alice wants to send a message $m$ to Bob, she computes $t = h_k(m)$ and sends it along with $m$. Upon receiving $m$ and $t$, Bob checks the authenticity of $m$ by computing $h_k(m)$ using his share of the key and comparing it with $t$. If $h_k(m)$ and $t$ are identical, then Bob accepts $m$ as authentic; otherwise, he rejects it. If Eve tries to impersonate Alice and sends $m'$ without knowing the key $k$, that is, without knowing $h_k$, the best she can do is to guess the correct tag for $m'$. The probability of success in this case is $P_1 = 1/|\mathcal{T}|$. If Eve waits and intercepts a message-tag pair $(m, t)$ from Alice and substitutes $m$ with $m'$, then the probability $P_2$ of guessing the correct tag $t'$ for $m'$ is at most $\epsilon$ ($\geq 1/|\mathcal{T}|$). In other words, even seeing a valid message-tag pair does not increase Eve's success probability above $\epsilon$. Therefore, by using a family of $\epsilon$-ASU$_2$ hash functions with suitably chosen $\epsilon$, one can achieve unconditionally secure message authentication. Practical applications require not only $\epsilon$ to be small but also the length $l$ of the key $k$ identifying a hash function in $\epsilon$-ASU$_2$ family to be as small as possible.

The most attractive property of unconditionally secure MACs is that the security does not depend on any computational complexity assumptions, as is the case for other MAC schemes like CBC-MAC based on AES or HMAC based on SHA. Also, in terms of speed, Universal hash function based MAC such as UMAC is much faster than its counterparts. Unconditional security, however, comes at a price: the key consumption. This is because the key cannot be reused; repeated use of a key may reveal the whole key through the message-tag pair. For this reason, Wegman and Carter proposed in [24] an efficient and effective way to resolve this by proposing to encrypt the hash function output with an OTP in order to reuse the same key many times. In particular, their proposal is as follows. Alice and Bob share a secret but fixed hash function $h \in \mathcal{H}$ and a series of keys $K_i$, $i = 1, 2, \cdots$, of length $\log |\mathcal{T}|$ to be used as OTP to encrypt the output of $h$. Then a series of messages $m_i$, $i = 1, 2, \cdots$, can be authenticated by using $h(m_i) \oplus K_i$ as the authentication tag. An efficient way to implement this is to use a counter $c$ that is incremented by 1 after each message transmission. In this case, the authentication tag for a message $(c, m_c)$ is computed as

$$t = h(m_c) \oplus K_c, \quad , c = 1, 2, \cdots . \tag{1}$$

This counter-based multiple authentication scheme is provably unconditionally secure. It has also been stated in [1] as a remark that in this scheme the OTP in the initial round can be omitted, since in the authors' own words "it is not necessary". That is, for the first message $m_1$, $h(m_1)$ can be sent as is. So with this small revision the above scheme becomes as follows: The authentication tag for a message $(c, m_c)$ is now computed as

$$t = \begin{cases} h(m_1), & c = 1, \\ h(m_c) \oplus K_{c-1}, & c = 2, 3, \cdots. \end{cases} \tag{2}$$

We will see in the next section that this new scheme is not secure in general and there may exist a very simple MAC forgery attack in this case.

**Related Work.** Different variants of the above scheme were proposed after Wegman and Carter's original proposal, such as stateful mode by Shoup [18] and computationally secure version by Brassard [10] and so on. The stateful mode by Shoup [18] is also referred to as Wegman-Carter-Shoup (WCS) authentication. The security bounds for the WCS scheme were improved by [4]. The security of these schemes for various Universal hash function families were studied in Black and Cochran [7] and Handschuh and Preneel [13]. They have demonstrated that for some families of Universal hash functions a single forgery is enough to find another forgery and for many families a few successful forgeries lead to efficient key recovery.

## 3   The Attack

In this section, we show that the scheme in (2) is not in general secure and present a simple existential forgery attack that exploits the structure of the hash function family used. In particular, if the underlying hash function family is for example XOR-linear, then the attack is straightforward. And there exists (A)SU$_2$ families of hash functions that are XOR-linear, e.g., the SU$_2$ family $\mathcal{H}_3$ in [24].

Let us first note that for (1) to be (unconditionally) secure, $h$ (or $\mathcal{H}$) at least needs to be AXU$_2$ [15]. So, for (2) to be secure, the subset $\mathcal{H}_{m \mapsto t}$ of $\mathcal{H}$ that Eve identifies after seeing the first message-tag pair $(m, t)$ should be AXU$_2$. We will now see shortly that this requirement does not necessarily be satisfied even when $\mathcal{H}$ is SU$_2$, the strongest family of all Universal$_2$ hash function families.

As described in (2), the first message $(1, m_1)$ is sent along with the authentication tag $t_1 = h(m_1)$ from Alice to Bob. Eve intercepts the three-tuple $(1, m_1, t_1)$ and identifies the set $\mathcal{H}_{m_1 \mapsto t_1} := \{f \in \mathcal{H} : f(m_1) = t_1\}$. Note that $|\mathcal{H}_{m_1 \mapsto t_1}| = |\mathcal{H}|/|\mathcal{T}|$ by Definition 3(a). So, at the end of the first round, from Eve's point of view, the (fixed) secret hash function $h$ is taken from $\mathcal{H}_{m_1 \mapsto t_1}$ instead of $\mathcal{H}$. If, for any two distinct $m, m' \in \mathcal{M}$ and any $t \in \mathcal{T}$,

$$|\{f \in \mathcal{H}_{m_1 \mapsto t_1} : f(m) \oplus f(m') = t\}| \leq \epsilon |\mathcal{H}_{m_1 \mapsto t_1}|, \tag{3}$$

then the scheme in described by (2) is secure, since this would mean that $\mathcal{H}_{m_1 \mapsto t_1}$ is $\epsilon$-AXU$_2$. Here, $\epsilon$ is Eve's success probability when attacking the system. The definitions of (A)SU$_2$ hash functions, however, does not guarantee that (3) holds. In fact, $|\{f \in \mathcal{H}_{m_1 \mapsto t_1} : f(m) \oplus f(m') = t\}|$, for some distinct $m, m' \in \mathcal{M}$ and $t \in \mathcal{T}$, could be as large as $|\mathcal{H}_{m_1 \mapsto t_1}|$. If this is the case, then there is a very simple existential forgery attack that Eve can use to attack the authentication.

In particular, in the second round, Alice sends $(2, m_2, t_2)$, where $t_2 = h(m_2) \oplus K_1$, to Bob. Eve intercepts the three-tuple $(2, m_2, t_2)$ and searches for $m_E$ such that $f(m_2) \oplus f(m_E) = t$ is fixed by all $f \in \mathcal{H}_{m_1 \mapsto t_1}$. And then, she sends $(2, m_E, t \oplus t_2)$ to Bob, since

$$h(m_E) \oplus K_1 = h(m_E) \oplus h(m_2) \oplus t_2 = t \oplus t_2. \tag{4}$$

From the above discussion, we naturally arrive at the following theorem about the security of the scheme in (2).

**Theorem 1.** *Let AUTH be the authentication described in (2) where the secret hash function $h$ is chosen from an $ASU_2$ family $\mathcal{H}$. Then, the success probability of an adversary $A$ attacking AUTH is only upper bounded by the trivial bound 1, that is,*

$$P_{AUTH}^{success}(A) \leq 1. \tag{5}$$

*Proof.* Suppose that $(1, m_1, t_1)$ with $t_1 = h(m_1)$ is the first message-tag pair and the message number that Alice has sent to Bob. By intercepting the three-tuple, $A$ identifies $\mathcal{H}_{m_1 \mapsto t_1} := \{f \in \mathcal{H} : f(m_1) = t_1\}$. Now, the proof follows directly from the fact, for some distinct $m, m' \in \mathcal{M}$ and $t \in \mathcal{T}$,

$$|\{f \in \mathcal{H}_{m_1 \mapsto t_1} : f(m) \oplus f(m') = t\}| \leq |\mathcal{H}_{m_1 \mapsto t_1}|. \tag{6}$$

It might seem that the computational complexity of the attack is huge at first sight, since identifying the set $\mathcal{H}_{m_1 \mapsto t_1}$ requires an exhaustive search. But, Eve does not need exhaustive search if she knows the structure of the underlying hash function family $\mathcal{H}$. Consider as an example the case when $\mathcal{H}$ is XOR-linear. As mentioned earlier, there are (A)SU$_2$ hash function families that are XOR-linear. In this case, Eve simply observes the first three-tuple $(1, m_1)$ with $t_1 = h(m_1)$ from Alice to Bob, and saves a copy of $m_1$ and $t_1$ in her memory. Then in the second round, she intercepts $(2, m_2, t_2)$ with $t_2 = h(m_2) \oplus K_1$, and replaces it with $(2, m_E, t_1 \oplus t_2)$ where $m_E = m_1 \oplus m_2$. Eve now knows that $m_E$ will be accepted as authentic, because the hash function $h$ is XOR-linear and then

$$h(m_E) \oplus K_1 = h(m_1 \oplus m_2) \oplus K_1 = h(m_1) \oplus h(m_2) \oplus K_1 = t_1 \oplus t_2. \tag{7}$$

Upon receiving $(2, m_E, t_1 \oplus t_2)$, Bob verifies the authenticity of $m_E$ by computing $h(m_E) \oplus K_1$ and comparing it with $t_1 \oplus t_2$. As we have just seen, the correct tag for $m_E$ is $t_1 \oplus t_2$. In the subsequent rounds, Eve uses the same strategy to forge the MAC for a new message chosen similarly to $m_E$ above. In general, at the $i$-th round, Eve replaces the three-tuple $(i, m_i, t_i)$ that she intercepted with $(i, m_1 \oplus m_i, t_1 \oplus t_i)$.

Note that this attack is very simple and that Eve does not need to know the actual secret key that is being used. All she needs to do is store the initial message and tag pair from the initial three-tuple. Even if there does not exist $m_E \in \mathcal{M}$ such that $f(m_2) \oplus f(m_E) = t$ is fixed by all $f \in \mathcal{H}_{m_1 \mapsto t_1}$, Eve can choose a message $m_E$ for which $f(m_2) \oplus f(m_E)$ is fixed by majority of $f \in \mathcal{H}_{m_1 \mapsto t_1}$ and still have a high probability of success. It all depends on the structure and properties of the underlying hash function family used in the authentication. Therefore, we stress that when the counter-based multiple authentication scheme is used it is very important to encrypt the hash function output of every message that is to be exchanged. And Wegman and Carter were right to propose to encrypt the hash of every message. After all, since both (1) and (2) require asymptotically the same amount of secret key, one does not sacrifice much by masking the hash of every message, should this authentication be used.

## 4    Impact

We now discuss the impact of the existence of the straightforward attack presented in the previous section in the context of Quantum Key Distribution (QKD). First, let us briefly recall what QKD is and why authentication is needed in QKD.

QKD, first proposed by Bennett and Brassard in 1984 [2], is a provably secure (or universally composably secure) key agreement technique that consist of two parts: quantum transmission over a quantum channel and classical postprocessing over a classical public channel. In QKD, the legitimate users first exchange quantum signals over the quantum channel to generate a raw key. Then, they agree on a shared secret key from the raw key by performing a joint postprocessing by communicating on public channel. QKD is proven to be unconditionally secure, provided that the public channel is immutable; see, for example, [17]. If the public channel is not not authentic, QKD is, like any other key agreement protocol, susceptible to a man-in-the-middle attack. Therefore, authentic public communication channel is a must. Moreover, to guarantee unconditional security of QKD an unconditionally secure authentication is needed.

The standard choice for authentication in QKD is the Wegman-Carter type of authentication, based on $\epsilon$-ASU$_2$ hashing. To kick-start the authentication, the legitimate parties use preshared secret key. In the first round the users use the pre-shared key, which is long enough to authenticate the messages exchanged in this round. In the following rounds, a part of the key generated in the previous rounds is used for subsequent authentication. Therefore, the key-consumption rate of the authentication directly affects the key output rate of QKD, and so one needs an authentication with less key-consumption rate. Moreover, in QKD no limit is put on Eve's computational power and memory.

When the authentication in (2) is used in QKD, only $h$ is preshared by Alice and Bob. The OTP key in the second round is a portion of the QKD generated key in the first round, and the OTP key in the third round is a portion of the QKD generation in the second round, and so on. So, the OTP keys are not, and need not be, preshared by Alice and Bob. Now in the first round, Eve identifies $\mathcal{H}_{m_1 \mapsto t_1}$ and searches for $m_E$ such that $f(m_2) \oplus f(m_E) = t$ is fixed by all or most of $f \in \mathcal{H}_{m_1 \mapsto t_1}$. If the attack is successful, then Eve breaks the QKD in this round and as a consequence learns the QKD generated key, and thus the OTP key $K_2$ used in the next round. We stress here that the success probability is in general quite high. So in the next round Eve will know $h(m_3) = t_3 \oplus K_2$, and together with the knowledge of $h(m_1)$ she will be able to find $h$. Therefore, the consequence of not masking the hash value of the first message can be serious, at least, in QKD.

## 5  Solution

As we have seen in Section 3, masking the hash function output of every message with an OTP is both necessary and sufficient for unconditional security of the authentication scheme under review. One might, however, wonder whether there are other solutions than to encrypt the hash of the first message in scheme (2). We answer this question in the negative if one aims for unconditional security, unless one uses another unconditionally secure encryption than OTP. Since the attack exploits the fact that the hash value is known for the first message message, masking the hash value of the first message, or any other message for that matter, is necessary.

## 6  Conclusion

We have reviewed the universal hash function based multiple authentication. We pointed out that masking the hash value of every message is not only sufficient but also necessary to guarantee security. Furthermore, we presented an existential forgery attack. The attack is straightforward and exploits the property of the underlying hash functions. The impact of the attack is also discussed in the context of QKD.

**Acknowledgements.** The author would like to thank the anonymous reviewers for their valuable comments, and also Jan-Åke Larsson for his useful comments.

## References

1. Atici, M., Stinson, D.R.: Universal Hashing and Multiple Authentication. In: Koblitz, N. (ed.) CRYPTO 1996. LNCS, vol. 1109, pp. 16–30. Springer, Heidelberg (1996)
2. Bennett, C.H., Brassard, G.: Quantum cryptography: Public key distribution and coin tossing. In: Proc. IEEE Int. Conf. Comput. Syst. Signal Process, Bangalore, India, pp. 175–179 (1984)
3. Bernstein, D.J.: The Poly1305-AES Message-Authentication Code. In: Gilbert, H., Handschuh, H. (eds.) FSE 2005. LNCS, vol. 3557, pp. 32–49. Springer, Heidelberg (2005)
4. Bernstein, D.J.: Stronger Security Bounds for Wegman-Carter-Shoup Authenticators. In: Cramer, R. (ed.) EUROCRYPT 2005. LNCS, vol. 3494, pp. 164–180. Springer, Heidelberg (2005)
5. Bierbrauer, J., Johansson, T., Kabatianskii, G., Smeets, B.: On Families of Hash Functions via Geometric Codes and Concatenation. In: Stinson, D.R. (ed.) CRYPTO 1993. LNCS, vol. 773, pp. 331–342. Springer, Heidelberg (1994)

6. Black, J.: Message authentication codes. Ph.D. thesis, University of California Davis, USA (2000)
7. Black, J., Cochran, M.: MAC Reforgeability. In: Dunkelman, O. (ed.) FSE 2009. LNCS, vol. 5665, pp. 345–362. Springer, Heidelberg (2009), http://dx.doi.org/10.1007/978-3-642-03317-9_21
8. Black, J., Halevi, S., Krawczyk, H., Krovetz, T., Rogaway, P.: UMAC: Fast and Secure Message Authentication. In: Wiener, M. (ed.) CRYPTO 1999. LNCS, vol. 1666, pp. 216–233. Springer, Heidelberg (1999)
9. den Boer, B.: A simple and key-economical unconditional authentication scheme. J. Comp. Sec. 2, 65–72 (1993)
10. Brassard, G.: On computationally secure authentication tags requiring short secret shared keys. In: Chaum, D., Rivest, R.L., Sherman, A.T. (eds.) CRYPTO, pp. 79–86. Plenum Press, New York (1982)
11. Carter, L., Wegman, M.N.: Universal classes of hash functions. J. Comput. Syst. Sci. 18, 143–154 (1979)
12. Halevi, S., Krawczyk, H.: MMH: Software Message Authentication in the Gbit/Second Rates. In: Biham, E. (ed.) FSE 1997. LNCS, vol. 1267, pp. 172–189. Springer, Heidelberg (1997)
13. Handschuh, H., Preneel, B.: Key-Recovery Attacks on Universal Hash Function Based MAC Algorithms. In: Wagner, D. (ed.) CRYPTO 2008. LNCS, vol. 5157, pp. 144–161. Springer, Heidelberg (2008), http://dx.doi.org/10.1007/978-3-540-85174-5_9
14. Krawczyk, H.: LFSR-Based Hashing and Authentication. In: Desmedt, Y.G. (ed.) CRYPTO 1994. LNCS, vol. 839, pp. 129–139. Springer, Heidelberg (1994)
15. Krawczyk, H.: New Hash Functions for Message Authentication. In: Guillou, L.C., Quisquater, J.-J. (eds.) EUROCRYPT 1995. LNCS, vol. 921, pp. 301–310. Springer, Heidelberg (1995)
16. Rogaway, P.: Bucket Hashing and Its Application to Fast Message Authentication. In: Coppersmith, D. (ed.) CRYPTO 1995. LNCS, vol. 963, pp. 29–42. Springer, Heidelberg (1995)
17. Shor, P.W., Preskill, J.: Simple proof of security of the bb84 quantum key distribution protocol. Phys. Rev. Lett. 85, 441–444 (2000)
18. Shoup, V.: On Fast and Provably Secure Message Authentication Based on Universal Hashing. In: Koblitz, N. (ed.) CRYPTO 1996. LNCS, vol. 1109, pp. 313–328. Springer, Heidelberg (1996)
19. Simmons, G.J.: A survey of information authentication. Proceedings of the IEEE 76(5), 603 (1988)
20. Stinson, D.R.: Universal Hashing and Authentication Codes. In: Feigenbaum, J. (ed.) CRYPTO 1991. LNCS, vol. 576, pp. 74–85. Springer, Heidelberg (1992)
21. Stinson, D.R.: Combinatorial techniques for universal hashing. J. Comput. Syst. Sci. 48, 337–346 (1994)
22. Stinson, D.R.: On the connections between universal hashing, combinatorial designs and error-correcting codes. Congressus Numerantium 114, 7–27 (1996)
23. Stinson, D.R.: Universal hash families and the leftover hash lemma, and applications to cryptography and computing. J. Combin. Math. Combin. Comput. 42, 3–31 (2002)
24. Wegman, M.N., Carter, L.: New hash functions and their use in authentication and set equality. J. Comput. Syst. Sci. 22, 265–279 (1981)

# A New Variant of Time Memory Trade-Off on the Improvement of Thing and Ying's Attack

Zhenqi Li[1], Yao Lu[2], Wenhao Wang[2], Bin Zhang[2], and Dongdai Lin[2]

[1] Institute of Software Chinese Academy of Sciences, Beijing, China
[2] The State Key Laboratory of Information Security
Institute of Information Engineering, Chinese Academy of Sciences, Beijing, China
{lizhenqi,luyao,wangwenhao,zhangbin,ddlin}@is.iscas.ac.cn

**Abstract.** In this paper, we present a rigorous evaluation of Thing and Ying's attack (TY attack) [11] along with practical implementations. We find that the cryptanalysis time of their attack is too high to be practical. We also propose a more general time memory trade-off by combining the distinguished points strategy with TY attack. Both theoretical analysis and experimental results show that our new design can save about 53.7% cryptanalysis time compared to TY attack and can reduce about 35.2% storage requirement compared to the original rainbow attack.

**Keywords:** time memory tradeoff, cryptanalysis, rainbow attack.

## 1 Introduction

A basic problem in symmetric-key cryptology is the computation of preimages or inversion of one-way functions. There are two straightforward ways (suppose the function has an $n$-bit input): first one can perform an exhaustive search over an average of $2^{n-1}$ values until the target is reached. A second solution is to precompute and store $2^n$ input and output pairs in a table. If one then needs to invert a particular value, one just looks up the preimage in the table, so inverting requires only a single table lookup. Both methods will be impractical if $n$ becomes larger. Cryptanalytic time memory trade-off (TMTO) is a technique that comes between these two extremes. It inverts a one-way function in time shorter than the exhaustive search method, using a storage smaller than the table lookup method.

Since the first TMTO algorithm was proposed by Hellman [6], many of its extensions [5,3,1] and variants [9,7,2,8,4] have appeared. In 2009, Thing and Ying proposed a new TMTO [11] for password recovery. Compared to the traditional rainbow table, it has higher success probability and lower storage requirements. In this paper, we present a rigorous evaluation on the performance of TY attack along with practical implementations, we find that it has high cryptanalysis time. Combining the *distinguished point* (DP) [5] strategy with TY attack, we design a new variant of TMTO, which is a general framework not only applicable to password crack but also to cryptanalysis of cryptosystems. We also make a comparison between our new design and TY attack. Experimental results show

T.W. Chim and T.H. Yuen (Eds.): ICICS 2012, LNCS 7618, pp. 311–320, 2012.

that new design can save about 53.7% cryptanalysis time compared to TY attack and can reduce about 35.2% storage requirement compared to original rainbow attack.

The paper is organized as follows. In Section 2, some basic TMTO methodologies are provided, followed with the analysis of TY attack. Formal definitions and algorithms of our new design are given in Section 3. Section 4 identifies the performance evaluation and experimental results. Finally, conclusions are in Section 5.

## 2   Time-Memory Trade-Off Methodology and Analysis of TY Attack

### 2.1   Time-Memory Trade-Off Methodology

Let $f$ be a one-way function, given output $y$ ($y \in Y$), the trade-off target is to recover the corresponding preimage $x$ ($x \in X$) satisfying $f(x) = y$, where $X$ and $Y$ are the input space and the output space respectively. In the *offline* stage of Oechslin's TMTO [9], we randomly choose $m$ starting points: $SP_0, SP_1, ..., SP_{m-1}$ ($SP_i \in X$, $0 \le i \le m - 1$) and iteratively compute $SP_i$ for $t$ times by using a compound function: $F_j = R_j \circ f$, where $R_j$ is called *reduction* function or *mask* function which maps $Y$ to $X$, $1 \le j \le t$ and $\circ$ denotes function composition. The *offline* computation is as follows.

$$
\begin{aligned}
SP_0 &= x_{0,0} \xrightarrow{F_1} x_{0,1} \xrightarrow{F_2} x_{0,2} \cdots \xrightarrow{F_t} x_{0,t} = EP_0 \\
SP_1 &= x_{1,0} \xrightarrow{F_1} x_{1,1} \xrightarrow{F_2} x_{1,2} \cdots \xrightarrow{F_t} x_{1,t} = EP_1 \\
&\ \vdots \\
SP_{m-1} &= x_{m-1,0} \xrightarrow{F_1} x_{m-1,1} \cdots \xrightarrow{F_t} x_{m-1,t} = EP_{m-1}
\end{aligned}
$$

we only store $(SP_0, EP_0), (SP_1, EP_1), ..., (SP_{m-1}, EP_{m-1})$ in a table called rainbow table and sort the table with respect to ending points. In the *online* stage, we firstly apply $R_t$ to $y$ and look up the result in the ending points of the table. If we find a matching ending point, we know how to rebuild the chain using the corresponding starting point and locate $x$. If we don't find a match, we try if we find it by applying $R_{t-1}, F_t$ to see if the preimage was in the second last column of the table. Then we try to apply $R_{t-2}, F_{t-1}, F_t$, and so forth.

### 2.2   Analysis of TY Attack

The basic idea of TY attack is similar to rainbow attack. The difference lies in their table structures. Suppose $h$ is a hash function which is often used to password encryption. The precomputation of the $i$-th table is as follows.

$$x^i \xrightarrow{h} \quad H \qquad \xrightarrow{R_1} x^i_{1,1} \xrightarrow{F_2} x^i_{1,2} \cdots \xrightarrow{F_t} x^i_{1,t}$$

$$H+1 \xrightarrow{R_1} x^i_{2,1} \xrightarrow{F_2} x^i_{2,2} \cdots \xrightarrow{F_t} x^i_{2,t}$$

$$H+2 \xrightarrow{R_1} x^i_{3,1} \xrightarrow{F_2} x^i_{3,2} \cdots \xrightarrow{F_t} x^i_{3,t}$$

$$\vdots \qquad\qquad \vdots$$

$$H+k \xrightarrow{R_1} x^i_{k+1,1} \xrightarrow{F_2} x^i_{k+1,2} \cdots \xrightarrow{F_t} x^i_{k+1,t}$$

where $H$ is the hash value of $x^i$ and $F_j = R_j \circ h$ $(1 \le j \le t)$. It only store one starting point of $x^i$ and $k+1$ ending points for the $i$-th table. $k$ is a constant value to control the table size. The *online* analysis is the same to that of rainbow attack. When a match is found in the table, it is easy to rebuild the corresponding $H+d$ $(0 \le d \le k)$ by using the matched chain index and the stored $x^i$, then locate the possible preimage.

In [11], Thing et al. said that the optimal value of $k$ is $2m-2$, where $m$ is number of chains in rainbow table. In this way, storage usage can be maximum and only one table is computed in the *offline* stage. It can save 50% storage requirement in comparison to rainbow table. However, we found that it requires higher cryptanalysis time which makes it to be impractical in real world applications. In traditional TMTO, we often sort the precomputed table and the searching time in a sorted table is often ignored. But in TY attack, hash value of the second column increased in order and sorting will break this order, thus disturbing the correctness of the attack. Searching in an unsorted table will greatly increase the *online* cost. *Online* time comparisons between TY attack and rainbow attack are listed in Table 1.

**Table 1.** *Online* time complexity comparison

| Attack | Rainbow attack | TY attack |
|---|---|---|
| Parameters | $(m,t,r)$ | $(k,t,r)$ |
| Function calculation | $O(\frac{t^2}{2})$ | $O(\frac{t^2}{2})$ |
| Table look-up | $O(t)$ | $O(t)$ |
| Comparison of each table look-up | $O(log(m))$ | $O(k+1)$ |

From table 1, given $N = 2^{24}, m = 2^{15}, t = 2^9, r = 1$ for rainbow attack and $N = 2^{24}, k = 2m-2 = 2^{16}-2, t = 2^9, r = 1$ for TY attack, table look-up of TY attack needs totally $t(k+1) = 2^{25} - 2^9 \approx 2^{25}$ comparisons, which is slightly larger than brute force comparisons of $2^{24}$. The *online* performance comparisons[1] among rainbow attack, TY attack and brute force attack are given in Table 2.

---

[1] We randomly generate 500 integers in the searching space $\{i|0 \le i \le 2^{24} - 1, i \in \mathbf{Z}\}$ and calculate their digest values by using MD5. Inversion of each digest value is done by rainbow attack, TY attack and brute force attack.

**Table 2.** Experimental results of the *online* time complexity comparison

|  | Rainbow attack | TY attack | Brute force attack |
|---|---|---|---|
| $(m,t,r)\|(k,t,r)\|N$ | $(2^{15}, 2^9, 1)$ | $(2^{16} - 2, 2^9, 1)$ | $2^{24}$ |
| Average cryptanalysis time | | | |
| to success | 1.86 sec | 7.59 sec | 14.70 sec |
| to failure | 2.58 sec | 15.18 sec | - |
| total | 2.22 sec | 9.83 sec | 14.70 sec |
| Average function calculations | | | |
| to success | 43505 | 74978 | 4499522 |
| to failure | 174654 | 215898 | - |
| total | 110391 | 116549 | 4499522 |
| Average false alarms | | | |
| to success | 52 | 139 | - |
| to failure | 256 | 497 | - |
| total | 156 | 245 | - |

From Table 2, the average function calculations (total) of TY attack is almost the same to that of rainbow attack as we just expected in Table 1, but it takes more cryptanalysis time than rainbow attack in all cases, since the cost of table look-up dominates the total *online* cost. In failure case, TY attack takes more time than brute force attack.

In the meantime, Ying and Thing themselves also found the existing drawback of TY attack and proposed a sorting method [12] to improve the performance of the recovery process. The basic idea is to add some tags to each ending point and sort the ending points in the usual alphabetical order. These tags can be used to derive the corresponding initial hash value, which correctly solve the sorting problem. However, the revised attack can only be applied to password cracking scenario and the existence of these reserved tags will add difficulties in designing the index algorithm. They also did not present any experimental comparisons between their improved version and original rainbow attack but only gave a theoretical estimation of 23% reduction in storage requirement, which seems to be lack of convincing.

## 3   A New Design

In this section, we propose a new variant of TMTO by combining DP strategy with TY attack. It is a general framework and can be applied not only to password cracking but also to the cryptanalysis of cryptosystem.

## 3.1   *Offline* Stage

In the *offline* stage, we choose a constant value $X$ (i.e., $X = 0$) and compute $k_1 \times k_2$ starting points through $H(X + i) + j$ ($0 \le i < k_1$, $0 \le j < k_2$). Then, we choose $t_{max}$ different evaluation function: $F_1, F_2, ..., F_{t_{max}}$, where $F_k = R_k \circ h$, $1 \le k \le t_{max}$ and $R_k$ is the *reduction* function. We iteratively compute the $(i, j)$-th chain through $X_{i,k}^j = F_k(X_{i,k-1}^j)$, $X_{i,0}^j = (H(X + i) \oplus j) \bmod N$, $1 \le k \le t_{max}$. The chain stops when the most significant $|k_2|^2$ bits of some $X_{i,k}^j$ is found to be $j$ or the current chain length exceeds $t_{max}$. If the chain stops in the latter case, we discard it. The *offline* stage can be shown as follows.

$$
\begin{aligned}
SP_0^0 &= H(X+0) \oplus 0 \xrightarrow{F_1} \circ \xrightarrow{F_2} \cdots \xrightarrow{F_{t_0^0}} (0 \parallel R_0^0) = EP_0^0 \\
SP_1^0 &= H(X+1) \oplus 0 \xrightarrow{F_1} \circ \xrightarrow{F_2} \cdots \xrightarrow{F_{t_1^0}} (0 \parallel R_1^0) = EP_1^0 \\
&\;\;\vdots \\
SP_{k_1-1}^0 &= H(X+k_1-1) \oplus 0 \xrightarrow{F_1} \circ \xrightarrow{F_2} \cdots \xrightarrow{F_{t_{k_1-1}^0}} (0 \parallel R_{k_1-1}^0) = EP_{k_1-1}^0
\end{aligned}
$$

$$
\begin{aligned}
SP_0^1 &= H(X+0) \oplus 1 \xrightarrow{F_1} \circ \xrightarrow{F_2} \cdots \xrightarrow{F_{t_0^1}} (1 \parallel R_0^1) = EP_0^1 \\
SP_1^1 &= H(X+1) \oplus 1 \xrightarrow{F_1} \circ \xrightarrow{F_2} \cdots \xrightarrow{F_{t_1^1}} (1 \parallel R_1^1) = EP_1^1 \\
&\;\;\vdots \\
SP_{k_1-1}^1 &= H(X+k_1-1) \oplus 1 \xrightarrow{F_1} \circ \xrightarrow{F_2} \cdots \xrightarrow{F_{t_{k_1-1}^1}} (1 \parallel R_{k_1-1}^1) = EP_{k_1-1}^1
\end{aligned}
$$

$$
\vdots
$$

$$
\begin{aligned}
SP_0^{k_2-1} &= H(X+0) \oplus (k_2-1) \xrightarrow{F_1} \circ \xrightarrow{F_2} \cdots \xrightarrow{F_{t_0^{k_2-1}}} (k_2-1 \parallel R_0^{k_2-1}) = EP_0^{k_2-1} \\
SP_1^{k_2-1} &= H(X+1) \oplus (k_2-1) \xrightarrow{F_1} \circ \xrightarrow{F_2} \cdots \xrightarrow{F_{t_1^{k_2-1}}} (k_2-1 \parallel R_1^{k_2-1}) = EP_1^{k_2-1} \\
&\;\;\vdots \\
SP_{k_1-1}^{k_2-1} &= H(X+k_1-1) \oplus (k_2-1) \xrightarrow{F_1} \circ \xrightarrow{F_2} \cdots \xrightarrow{F_{t_{k_1-1}^{k_2-1}}} (k_2-1 \parallel R_{k_1-1}^{k_2-1}) = EP_{k_1-1}^{k_2-1}
\end{aligned}
$$

---

[2] For all $\parallel$ in this paper, $|\alpha|$ means the binary length of integer $\alpha$.

For each chain, we only store:

$$S[0,0] = \{R_0^0, l_0^0, 0\} \qquad\qquad 0 < l_0^0 \leq t_{max}$$
$$S[1,0] = \{R_1^0, l_1^0, 1\} \qquad\qquad 0 < l_1^0 \leq t_{max}$$
$$\vdots$$
$$S[i,j] = \{R_i^j, l_i^j, i\} \qquad\qquad 0 < l_i^j \leq t_{max}$$
$$\vdots$$
$$S[k_1 - 1, k_2 - 1] = \{R_{k_1-1}^{k_2-1}, l_{k_1-1}^{k_2-1}, k_1 - 1\} \quad 0 < l_{k_1-1}^{k_2-1} \leq t_{max}$$

where $R_i^j$ $(0 \leq i \leq k_1 - 1, 0 \leq j \leq k_2 - 1)$ is the rest $(n - |k_2|)$ bits of the ending point in the $(i,j)$-th chain, $l_i^j$ is the length of the $(i,j)$-th chain and $n = |EP_i^j|$.

All these chains have different lengths and can be split into groups of size $k_2$ according to their definition of DP. We sort each DP group with respect to $R_i^j$ and store them in $k_2$ tables indexed by their DP definition, which is also equal to $j$ of the starting points and also to the most significant $|k_2|$ bits of ending points.

Let $d_1 = |k_1|$, $d_2 = |k_2|$, $l = |t_{max}|$ and $n = |N|$, then $|S[i,j]| = |R_i^j| + |l_i^j| + |i| = n - d_2 + l + d_1$ bits. We have $k_1 \times k_2$ starting points, thus the storage requirement is $M = P \times k_1 \times k_2 \times (n - d_2 + l + d_1)$ bits, where $P$ $(0 < P \leq 1)$ is the proportion of chains which meet a predefined DP before their length reach $t_{max}$. More details of $P$ is given in the next section.

## 3.2  *Online* Stage

Give $Y$ (ciphertext in block ciphers and MACs, key stream segment in stream ciphers, hash value in password encryptions, etc), to lookup the preimage (secret key in block ciphers and MACs, internal state in stream ciphers, password in password encryptions, etc), we proceed in the following manner: First we apply $R_{t_{max}}$ to the ciphertext $Y$ and get $Y_0 = R_{t_{max}}(Y)$, $Y_0$ is now a DP for some definition of DP. The value of the most significant $|k_2|$ bits of $Y_0$ is corresponding to a table in which the most significant $|k_2|$ bits of each ending point equals to that of $Y_0$. Then, we look up the rest $n - |k_2|$ bits in this table as follows.

$$\begin{cases} R_i^j \overset{?}{=} (rest \ (n - |k_2|) \ bits \ of \ Y_0) \\ l_i^j \overset{?}{=} t_{max} \end{cases} \tag{1}$$

If both equations succeed, then a match is found and we get the corresponding index $i$ stored in the match $S[i,j]$ and compute $X_{i,t_{max}-1}^j$ from the starting point $(H(X + i) \oplus j) \bmod N$, where $j$ is the value of the most significant $|k_2|$ bits of $Y_0$. Then we check whether $X_{i,t_{max}-1}^j$ is the preimage or a *false alarm*.

If either equation of (1) fails, then we apply $R_{t_{max}-1}, F_{t_{max}}$ to Y as $Y \overset{R_{t_{max}-1}}{\longrightarrow} Y_1 \overset{F_{t_{max}}}{\longrightarrow} Y_0$ and check $Y_0$ and $Y_1$ separately. Provided that we have computed $Y$ iteratively for $k$ times and $1 \leq k \leq t_{max}$:

$$X \overset{R_{t_{max}-(k-1)}}{\longrightarrow} Y_{k-1} \overset{F_{t_{max}-(k-2)}}{\longrightarrow} Y_{k-2} \cdots \overset{F_{t_{max}}}{\longrightarrow} Y_0. \tag{2}$$

We search each $Y_q (0 \leq q \leq k - 1)$ in a corresponding DP table and check

$$\begin{cases} R_i^j \overset{?}{=} (rest \ (n - |k_2|) \ bits \ of \ Y_q) \\ l_i^j \overset{?}{=} t_{max} - q \end{cases} \tag{3}$$

if both equations succeed, then a match is found. $X_{i,t_{max}-q}^j$ can be computed from the starting point $(H(X + i) \oplus j) \ mod \ N$ by iteratively doing the computation from $F_1$ to $F_{t_{max}-q-1}$. Then we check whether $X_{i,t_{max}-q}^j$ is a *false alarm* or the preimage. If no match is found or *false alarm* occurred, then we set $k \leftarrow k + 1$ and repeat the process above until $k > t_{max}$. It is easy to know that new design needs $O(\frac{t_{max}^2}{2})$ function calculations and $O(\frac{t_{max}^2}{2})$ table look-ups, each table look-up only needs $log_2 |k_1|$ comparison because of the sorted ending points.

## 3.3   The Selection of $t_{max}$

The main modification caused by the introduction of DP is the variable chain length. Therefore, the selection of $t_{max}$ has a great influence on the performance of the new design. Let $k = |k_2|$, $n = |N|$ and $P_1(t)$ be the probability that a DP is reached in less than $t$ iterations. Let $P_2(t)$ be the probability that no DP is reached in less than $t$ iterations. Thus $P_1(t) = 1 - P_2(t)$ and we can easily get $P_2(t) = \prod_{i=0}^{t-1}(1 - \frac{2^{n-k}}{2^n - i})$. An approximate expression can be obtained knowing that $i \ll 2^n$. By fixing $i$ to $\frac{t-1}{2}$, we have $P_2(t) \approx (1 - \frac{2^{n-k}}{2^n - \frac{t-1}{2}})^t$. Finally, we have $P_1(t) \approx 1 - (1 - \frac{2^{n-k}}{2^n - \frac{t-1}{2}})^t$, thus the probability to reach a DP in less than $t_{max}$ iterations is $P_1(t_{max})$ which is also the $P$ we defined in Section 3.3. According to [10], The average chain length of a DP table is $\bar{t} = 2^k = k_2$. Given $N = 2^{24}$, $k_1 = 2^8$, and $k_2 = 2^8$, the theoretical and experimental results of $P_1(t_{max})$ are listed in Table 3.

**Table 3.** The value of $P_1(t_{max})$

| $t_{max}$ | Theoretical result | Experimental result |
|---|---|---|
| $1.0 \times 2^8$ | 63.28% | 63.26% |
| $1.5 \times 2^8$ | 77.75% | 77.56% |
| $2.0 \times 2^8$ | 86.25% | 86.43% |
| $2.5 \times 2^8$ | 91.83% | 91.90% |
| $3.0 \times 2^8$ | 95.05% | 95.13% |

[a] $(N, k_1, k_2) = (2^{24}, 2^8, 2^8)$

From Table 3, we see that the larger $t_{max}$ is, the higher $P_1(t_{max})$ will be. However, larger $t_{max}$ also leads to higher time complexity in the *online* stage as described in Section 3.3. Therefore, $t_{max}$ should not be too large or too small.

## 4    Performance Evaluation and Experimental Results

In this section, we present a rigorous evaluation on the performance of our new design correspond with experimental results (the analysis of success probability can be found in the full version).

### 4.1   *Online* Time Complexity Comparison

Given $N = 2^{32}$, common parameters of TY attack are $(k, t, r) = (2 \times 2^{20} - 2, 2^{12}, 1)$ and common parameters of new design are $(k_1, k_2, t_{max}) = (455, 2^{12}, 2 \times 2^{12})$. These chosen parameters can assure that both attacks have the same storage requirement and TY attack has the optimal table structure. Experimental results are listed in Table 4.

**Table 4.** Experimental results of the *online* comparison

| $(k_1, k_2, t_{max}) \| (k, t, r)$ | New design | TY attack |
|---|---|---|
| | $(455, 2^{12}, 2^{13})$ | $(2^{21} - 2, 2^{12}, 1)$ |
| | Average cryptanalysis time | |
| to success | 3 min, 23.10 sec | 7 min, 17.74 sec |
| to failure | 6 min, 7.11 sec | 16 min, 46.89 sec |
| total | 4 min, 31.00 sec | 9 min, 45.72 sec |
| | Average function calculations | |
| to success | 4,393,370 | 4,772,551 |
| to failure | 15,470,394 | 13,971,075 |
| total | 12,206,927 | 7,164,167 |
| | Average false alarms | |
| to success | 548 | 1153 |
| to failure | 1388 | 4099 |
| total | 896 | 1919 |

The experimental results show that the average function calculations of our new design is higher than TY attack, but it can save 53.7% cryptanalysis cost, since it needs less table look-ups and occurs less false alarms than TY attack.

### 4.2   Storage Requirement Comparison

In this part, the basic consumption is that all these attacks have the same precomputation time. Therefore, given $N = 2^{24}$, the common parameters for these attacks and the storage space comparison are listed in Table 5 (more details can be found in the full version).

**Table 5.** Storage space comparison

| Attack | Rainbow attack | New design | TY attack |
|---|---|---|---|
| $(m,t,r)|(k_1,k_2,t_{max})|(k,t,r)$ | $(2^{15},2^9,1)$ | $(2^6,2^9,2^{10})$ | $(2^{15},2^9,1)$ |
| Entries | $2^{15}$ | $0.8643 \times 2^{15}$ | $2^{15}+2$ |
| Entry size | 48-bit | 31-bit | 24-bit |
| Experimental result | 256 KB | 166 KB | 161 KB |

$N = 2^{24}$

The storage medium is '.txt' file and we put each entry in a single line to the file. Results in Table 5 show that our new design can save about 35.2% storage requirement compared with rainbow attack, TY attack can save about 37.1% storage requirement compared with rainbow attack. For more details and further discussion, please refer to the full version.

## 5   Conclusion

In this paper, we present a rigorous analysis on the performance of TY attack and find that it has higher precomputation time and its *online* attack time is no better than brute force attack. Therefore, TY attack is an impractical attack even though it has higher success probability and lower storage requirement than rainbow attack. By combining the DP strategy with TY attack, we propose a new variant of TMTO, which is a general framework and can be applied not only to password cracking, but also to cryptanalysis of cryptosystems. Evaluations of the performance show that our new design has higher success probability than rainbow attack and has slightly lower success probability than TY attack under the basic assumption that all these three attacks use the same storage space. It can save about 53.7% cryptanalysis time compared with TY attack and can save about 35.2% storage requirement compared with original rainbow attack. The amount of storage requirement we have saved is slightly lower than that of TY attack (37.1%), but we achieved a great improvement on the cryptanalysis time, making our new design to be a practical TMTO which can well be used in the storage limited applications.

## References

1. Avoine, G., Junod, P., Oechslin, P.: Characterization and improvement of time-memory trade-off based on perfect tables. ACM Transactions on Information and Systems Security 11(4), Article 17 (2008)
2. Biryukov, A., Mukhopadhyay, S., Sarkar, P.: Improved Time-Memory Trade-Offs with Multiple Data. In: Preneel, B., Tavares, S. (eds.) SAC 2005. LNCS, vol. 3897, pp. 110–127. Springer, Heidelberg (2006)
3. Biryukov, A., Shamir, A.: Cryptanalytic Time/Memory/Data Tradeoffs for Stream Ciphers. In: Okamoto, T. (ed.) ASIACRYPT 2000. LNCS, vol. 1976, pp. 1–13. Springer, Heidelberg (2000)

4. Dinur, I., Dunkelman, O., Keller, N., Shamir, A.: Efficient Dissection of Composite Problems, with Applications to Cryptanalysis, Knapsacks, and Combinatorial Search Problems. Cryptology ePrint Archive. Report 2012/217 (2012)
5. Denning, D.: Cryptography and Data Security, p. 100. Addison-Wesley (1982)
6. Hellman, M.: A Cryptanalytic Time-Memory Trade-Off. IEEE Transactions on Information Theory 26(4), 401–406 (1980)
7. Hong, J., Jeong, K.C., Kwon, E.Y., Lee, I.S., Ma, D.: Variants of the Distinguished Point Method for Cryptanalytic Time Memory Trade-Offs. In: Chen, L., Mu, Y., Susilo, W. (eds.) ISPEC 2008. LNCS, vol. 4991, pp. 131–145. Springer, Heidelberg (2008)
8. Hong, J., Sarkar, P.: New Applications of Time Memory Data Tradeoffs. In: Roy, B. (ed.) ASIACRYPT 2005. LNCS, vol. 3788, pp. 353–372. Springer, Heidelberg (2005)
9. Oechslin, P.: Making a Faster Cryptanalytic Time-Memory Trade-Off. In: Boneh, D. (ed.) CRYPTO 2003. LNCS, vol. 2729, pp. 617–630. Springer, Heidelberg (2003)
10. Standaert, F.X., Rouvroy, G., Quisquater, J.J., Legat, J.D.: A Time-Memory Tradeoff Using Distinguished Points: New Analysis & FPGA Results. In: Kaliski Jr., B.S., Koç, Ç.K., Paar, C. (eds.) CHES 2002. LNCS, vol. 2523, pp. 593–609. Springer, Heidelberg (2003)
11. Thing, V.L.L., Ying, H.M.: A novel time-memory trade-off method for password recovery. Digital Investigation 6, S114–S120 (2009)
12. Ying, H.M., Thing, V.L.L.: A Novel Rainbow table sorting method. In: Proceedings of the 2nd International Conference on Technical and Legal Aspects of the e-Society, CYBERLAWS 2011 (2011)

# Applying Time-Memory-Data Trade-Off
# to Plaintext Recovery Attack

Zhenqi Li[1], Bin Zhang[2], Yao Lu[2], Jing Zou[2], and Dongdai Lin[2]

[1] Institute of Software Chinese Academy of Sciences, Beijing, China
[2] The State Key Laboratory of Information Security
Institute of Information Engineering, Chinese Academy of Sciences, Beijing, China
{lizhenqi,zhangbin,luyao,zoujing,ddlin}@is.iscas.ac.cn

**Abstract.** In this paper, we propose a new attack for block ciphers by applying the well known time-memory-data (TMD) trade-off to plaintext recovery attack (PRA), thus creating two new schemes: TMD-PRA-I and TMD-PRA-II. Compared with the traditional trade-off attacks, these two schemes possess several robust properties which can greatly increase the success probability and enhance the process of analysis. We also evaluate the performance of our schemes by applying them to several block ciphers like DES, Triple-DES, Skipjack and AES. Results show that they have favourable performance especially when the key size is larger than the block size, which gives us a reminder that PRA based on TMD trade-off should be considered when designing a new cryptographic scheme.

**Keywords:** time-memory trade-off, time-memory-data trade-off, plaintext recovery attack.

## 1 Introduction

Many cryptanalytic problems can be solved in theory using an exhaustive search in the key space, but are still hard to solve in practice because each new instance of the problem requires to restart the process from scratch. The basic idea of a time-memory trade-off (TMTO) is to find a trade-off between the exhaustive search and the exhaustive storage. It carries out an exhaustive search once for all such that following instances of the problem become easier to solve.

The technique of TMTO was firstly introduced by Hellman [8] in 1980. It is a *chosen plaintext* attack which applies TMTO to the one-way function mapping the keyspace to the cipherspace by encrypting a fixed known message using a block cipher. Since then, many of its extensions[7,5,10] and variants[4,1,6] have appeared. All these TMTOs focus on inverting a one-way function at a single data point. Biryukov and Shamir [3] stated that multiple data can be combined with Hellman's tradeoff, resulting in a time-memory-data (TMD) trade-offs for stream ciphers. Later, Biryukov and Mukhopadhyay [2] found that the usual TMD tradeoff attack on stream ciphers can be considered to be a time-memory-key trade-off (BS-TMD) attack on block ciphers. This attack applies to the situation where the goal of the attacker is to obtain one out of many possible keys.

T.W. Chim and T.H. Yuen (Eds.): ICICS 2012, LNCS 7618, pp. 321–330, 2012.

In this paper, we attempt to shift the attack target of the traditional TMTO from key recovery to plaintext recovery for block ciphers and observe a potential one-way function which maps plaintext space to ciphertext space, thus proposing a new application of TMTO by applying TMD trade-off to plaintext recovery attack (PRA). Compared with the traditional TMD attack, we prove that the precomputed tables in the new application have several robust properties (i.e. no false alarms and no merges), which can greatly increase the success probability and accelerate the process of attack. Through the comparison with BS-TMD attack on several specific block ciphers (i.e. DES, Triple-DES, Skipjack and AES), we found that our new attack is appropriate for an infrequently changing key scenario and has better performance when key size is larger than block size. It should be classified to the *fixed key* attacks which prove to be more practical than the *variable key* attacks which BS-TMD attack belongs to. Furthermore, our results show that it does not make sense to increase the key size without a corresponding increase of the block size.

The paper is organized as follows. Some basic TMD methodologies are given in Section 2. We present the formal definitions and algorithms of our new schemes in Section 3. Section 4 identifies the coverage rate and trade-off complexity of our new schemes. Performance evaluation is provided in Section 5. Conclusions are in Section 6. Before we proceed, we give the general notations of the parameters below:

- $N$ : denotes the searching space.
- $m$ : denotes the number of chains in a single table.
- $t$ : denotes the chain length.
- $r$ : denotes the number of tables.
- $f$ : denotes a one-way function.
- $P$ : denotes the plaintext space.
- $C$ : denotes the ciphertext space.
- $K$ : denotes the key space.
- $T$ : denotes the time complexity in the *online* stage.
- $M$ : denotes the memory requirement of trade-off method.
- $D$ : denotes the size of ciphertexts the attacker have obtained.
- $E$ : denotes the time complexity in the *offline* stage.

## 2    Time-Memory-Data Trade-Off Methodology

The encryption algorithm of a block cipher can be treated as an one-way function $f_p = f(\cdot, p)$ maping $K$ to $C$, where $p$ is a fixed known plaintext. Given some ciphertext $c \in C$, the goal of the attacker is to invert this function to get the corresponding encryption key, while keeping the complexity as low as possible. The BS-TMD attack consists of two stages: an one-time *offline* stage followed by an *online* stage. In the *offline* stage, a set of tables are prepared covering $N/D$ of the domain points. We randomly choose $m$ distinct keys $k_1^0, k_2^0, ..., k_m^0$ and compute each key iteratively by using a compound function $F_i = r_i \circ f_p$, where $r_i$ is called reduction function which maps $C$ to $K$ and $\circ$ means function composition. The precomputation of the $i$-th $(1 \leq i \leq r)$ table is as follows.

$$SP_1^i = k_1^0 \xrightarrow{F_i} k_1^1 \cdots \xrightarrow{F_i} k_1^t = EP_1^i$$
$$SP_2^i = k_2^0 \xrightarrow{F_i} k_2^1 \cdots \xrightarrow{F_i} k_2^t = EP_2^i$$
$$\vdots \qquad\qquad\qquad\qquad \vdots$$
$$SP_m^i = k_m^0 \xrightarrow{F_i} k_m^1 \cdots \xrightarrow{F_i} k_m^t = EP_m^i$$

where $SP_j^i$ and $EP_j^i$ represent the starting point and the ending point in the $j$-th chain of the $i$-th table respectively, $k_j^s$ is the domain point (key), $1 \leq j \leq m, 0 \leq s \leq t$. We only store $(SP_1^i, EP_1^i), (SP_2^i, EP_2^i),...,(SP_m^i, EP_m^i)$ and sort these pairs with respect to ending points.

In the *online* stage, we look for the pre-image in all the tables for each data point $c_j$ $(1 \leq j \leq D)$. This process is similar to Hellman's TMTO. The complexity of the *online* analysis requires a total of $t$ applications of $f_p$ and $t$ table look-ups for each table and each data point. In order to minimize the waste of table coverage due to birthday collisions, the proper choice of $m$ and $t$ would typically satisfy $N = mt^2$ and $N/D$ domain points need to be covered. Therefore, we need $r = t/D$ tables of each size $m \times t$ corresponding to different functions $F_i$ $(1 \leq i \leq r)$. Hence memory requirement is $M = rm = mt/D$ entries and the *online* cost for all the $D$ data points is $T = t \times t/D \times D = t^2$, resulting in a tradeoff formula $N^2 = TM^2D^2$, $1 \leq D^2 < T$, $E = N/D$. More details can be found in [3,2].

## 3   Apply Time-Memory-Data Trade-Off to PRA

In this section, we will describe the details of our new attacks and propose two PRA schemes of TMD-PRA-I and TMD-PRA-II based on TMD attack. First, we will propose some basic assumptions here.

Generally speaking, encryption algorithm of a block cipher can be treated as a one-way function. Given the encryption key $k$, plaintext $x$ and the corresponding ciphertext $y$, we have $f(k, x) = y$. $f$ is one-to-one mapping, that is to say when $k$ is fixed, given any plaintext $x \in P$, we can only get one ciphertext $y \in C$ satisfying $f(k, x) = y$ and given any ciphertext $y \in C$, there is only one preimage $x \in P$ satisfying $f^{-1}(k, y) = x$. We always denote $f$ as the keyed one-to-one mapping $f(k, \cdot)$ hereafter.

We assume that the attacker can access to an encryption oracle $O_f$ of the block cipher. He can query any plaintext to $O_f$ and $O_f$ will return the corresponding ciphertext. Given $D$ ciphertexts which are the results of the different plaintexts encrypted by a block cipher under a fixed key, his target is to recovery these plaintexts as more as possible. We also assume that the size of plaintext space is same to that of ciphertext space, namely $|P| = |C| = N = 2^n$ ($n$ is the block size).

## 3.1   TMD-PRA-I

TMD-PRA-I directly treats the encryption oracle as the iterative function $F$ to precompute a ciphertext table which is different from the classic key table in traditional TMTO. We randomly choose $m$ distinct plaintexts: $c_1^0, c_2^0, ..., c_m^0$ in $P$ and precompute as follows.

$$
\begin{aligned}
SP_1 &= c_1^0 \xrightarrow{F} c_1^1 \xrightarrow{F} c_1^2 \cdots \xrightarrow{F} c_1^t = EP_1 \\
SP_2 &= c_2^0 \xrightarrow{F} c_2^1 \xrightarrow{F} c_2^2 \cdots \xrightarrow{F} c_2^t = EP_2 \\
&\vdots \qquad\qquad\qquad\qquad\qquad\qquad \vdots \\
SP_m &= c_m^0 \xrightarrow{F} c_m^1 \xrightarrow{F} c_m^2 \cdots \xrightarrow{F} c_m^t = EP_m
\end{aligned}
$$

We only store $(SP_1, EP_1), (SP_2, EP_2),..., (SP_m, EP_m)$ and sort these pairs with respect to the ending points. The *online* stage is similar to the procedure of Hellman's TMTO. However, we will prove that no *false alarm* will occur in the process of the *online* analysis in TMD-PRA-I.

**Proposition 1.** *If $f$ is an one-to-one mapping and $|P| = |C| = N$, no false alarm will occur in the process of online analysis in TMD-PRA-I.*

*Proof.* Suppose that a *false alarm* occurred in the *online* stage, that is to say, we have applied the iterative function $F$ to the given ciphertext $y$ for $k$ ($1 \leq k \leq t-1$) times and the *online* chain is $y \xrightarrow{F} y_1 \xrightarrow{F} y_2 \cdots \xrightarrow{F} y_k$, we find a matching ending point $EP_i = c_i^t = y_k$ ($1 \leq i \leq m$) and the *online* chain merged with the chain which we reconstruct from the corresponding starting point $SP_i = c_i^0$. Suppose the merging point is $y_q$ ($1 \leq q \leq k$) for *online* chain and $c_i^s$ ($t-k+1 \leq s \leq t$) for the reconstruted chain, thus we have $c_i^s = y_q$, that is $F(c_i^{s-1}) = F(y_{q-1})$, according to the definition of $F$, we derive $f(c_i^{s-1}) = f(y_{q-1})$ where $c_i^{s-1} \neq y_{q-1}$. In this way, ciphertext $y_q$ (or $c_i^s$) will be decrypted to two different plaintexts ($c_i^{s-1}$ and $y_{q-1}$), which is contradictious to the assumption that $f$ is an one-to-one mapping. Consequently, no *false alarm* will occur during *online* analysis.                                                          □

We can easily know that the *online* analysis time of TMD-PRA-I is same to that of Hellman's method. However, there is no *false alarm* in TMD-PRA-I, thus its performance is better, since Hellman [8] points out that the expected computation due to false alarms increases the expected computation by at most 50 percent. There may exist many overlap sectors among the chains of a single ciphertext table. To release this problem, we present another scheme in the following section.

## 3.2   TMD-PRA-II

Based on TMD-PRA-I, we introduce $t$ different permutations: $P_1, P_2, ..., P_t$ defined on ciphertext space $\{z | z \in \mathbf{Z}, 0 \leq z \leq N-1\}$ and redefine iterative function as $F_j = P_j \circ f$, $1 \leq j \leq t$. The *offline* stage of TMD-PRA-II is as follows.

$$SP_1 = c_1^0 \xrightarrow{F_1} c_1^1 \xrightarrow{F_2} c_1^2 \cdots \xrightarrow{F_t} c_1^t = EP_1$$
$$SP_2 = c_2^0 \xrightarrow{F_1} c_2^1 \xrightarrow{F_2} c_2^2 \cdots \xrightarrow{F_t} c_2^t = EP_2$$
$$\vdots \qquad\qquad\qquad\qquad \vdots$$
$$SP_m = c_m^0 \xrightarrow{F_1} c_m^1 \xrightarrow{F_2} c_m^2 \cdots \xrightarrow{F_t} c_m^t = EP_m$$

In this way, the chain will not enter into a loop and overlap sectors among different chains will not exist. There may exist collisions among chains, but these collisions will not lead to merges or loops. The *online* stage is similar to the rainbow attack [10]. The total number of calculations we have to make is thus $\frac{t(t-1)}{2}$ which is half as much as TMD-PRA-I. In the rainbow table, *merge* only occur when collisions occurred in the same column and collisions of different columns will not lead to *merge*. We will prove that there is no *merge* even if collisions occurred in the same column of the ciphertext table.

**Proposition 2.** *If $f$ is an one-to-one mapping and $|P| = |C| = N$, then no merge will occur in the ciphertext table of TMD-PRA-II.*

*Proof.* please see the details of the proof in the full version.    □

Proposition 2 states that ciphertext table of TMD-PRA-II is born to be a *perfect table*, which needs no additional computations to deal with the merged chains. Hence it has higher coverage rate than rainbow table. Collision of different columns may occur, but it only leads to a cross point instead of *merge*. Based on Proposition 2, we can easily get a corollary:

**Corollary 1.** *If $f$ is an one-to-one mapping and $|P| = |C| = N$, no false alarm will occur in the process of the online analysis in TMD-PRA-II.*

Corollary 1 states that TMD-PRA-II is more efficient than the rainbow attack in the *online* stage, since it need no additional computations to due with false alarms.

## 4    Success Probability and Trade-Off Complexity

In this section, we will present a rigorous analysis on the time complexities, memory requirements and success probabilities of TMD-PRA-I and TMD-PRA-II respectively.

### 4.1    Success Probability of TMD-PRA-I

The ciphertext table of TMD-PRA-I is a matrix of $m \times t$. For each $0 \le k < t$, let $m_k^I$ denote the number of distinct entries appearing in the $k$-th column, which has not appeared in any of the previous columns and $\overline{H}_k = \{c_i^j | 1 \le i \le m, 0 \le j \le k\}$ denotes the set of distinct ciphertexts in the sub matrix of $m \times k$. Therefore, $m_k^I = |\overline{H}_k \setminus \overline{H}_{k-1}|$ and let $p_k^I = m_k^I/N$ denote the proportion of the distinct ciphertexts in the $k$-th column. Suppose we choose $m_0^I = m$ distinct starting points, then $p_0^I = m/N$ and the relationship between $m_{k+1}^I$ and $m_k^I$ can be written as $m_{k+1}^I = (1 - \sum_{j=0}^{k} p_j^I)m_k^I$, or equivalently $p_{k+1}^I = (1 - \sum_{j=0}^{k} p_j^I)p_k^I$. Now, we denote $s_k^I = \sum_{j=0}^{k-1} p_j^I$ and $s_1^I = p_0^I = m/N$. By the definition of $s_k^I$, the expected coverage rate of a single ciphertext table can be written as $C_I = \frac{N}{mt}s_t^I$, hence the coverage rate for all $t$ ($t \geq 1$) tables can be written as

$$C_I^* = 1 - (1 - s_t^I)^t. \tag{1}$$

Under the matrix stopping rule of $mt^2 = N$ [3], the simulation results of $C_I^*$ are listed in the Table 1.

**Table 1.** Simulation results of $C_I^*$

| $(m, t)$ | $C_I^*$ |
|---|---|
| $(2^{22}, 2^4)$ | 58.68% |
| $(2^{14}, 2^8)$ | 57.79% |
| $(2^{10}, 2^{10})$ | 57.74% |
| $(2^6, 2^{12})$ | 57.73% |

$$N = 2^{30}, mt^2 = N$$

From the Table 1, we see that the coverage rate of a single ciphertext table is approximately 86.1%, which is very close to the results of a single Hellman table [9].

## 4.2 Success Probability of TMD-PRA-II

We will create one ciphertext table with $mt$ rows and $t$ columns. For each $0 \leq k < t$, let $m_k^{II}$ denote the number of distinct entries appearing in the $k$-th column, which has not appeared in any of the previous columns. Let $p_k^{II} = m_k^{II}/N$ denote the proportion of the distinct ciphertexts in the $k$-th column. Suppose we choose $m_0^{II} = mt$ distinct starting points, then $p_0^{II} = mt/N$ and $m_k^{II}$ can be written as $m_k^{II} = (1 - \sum_{j=0}^{k} p_j^{II})mt$, or equivalently, $p_k^{II} = (1 - \sum_{j=0}^{k} p_j^{II})p_0^{II}$. Now, we denote $s_k^{II} = \sum_{j=0}^{k-1} p_j^{II}$ and $s_1^{II} = p_0^{II} = mt/N$. By the definition of $s_t^I$, the expected coverage rate of the precomputed table is $C_{II} = \frac{N}{mt^2}s_t^{II}$. Under the matrix stopping rule of $mt^2 = N$, we denote $C_R$ as the coverage rate of a single rainbow table. The simulation results of $C_{II}$ and $C_R$ are listed in the Table 2.

From Table 2, it is obvious that the success probability of TMD-PRA-II is higher than that of rainbow table, since there is no merged chains in the ciphertext table as we have specified in the proposition 3. Furthermore, success probability of TMD-PRA-II is higher that that of TMD-PRA-I (i.e. suppose $(m, t) = (2^{10}, 2^{10})$, $C_{II} = 63.23\%$ which is higher than $C_I^* = 57.74\%$), since any chain will not enter into a loop and there are no overlap sectors among chains in TMD-PRA-II.

**Table 2.** Comparison between $C_{II}$ and $C_R$

| $(m, t)$ | $C_{II}$ | $C_R$ |
|---|---|---|
| $(2^{22}, 2^4)$ | 64.39% | 56.93% |
| $(2^{14}, 2^8)$ | 63.28% | 55.64% |
| $(2^{10}, 2^{10})$ | 63.23% | 55.58% |
| $(2^6, 2^{12})$ | 63.22% | 55.56% |
| $N = 2^{30}, mt^2 = N$ | | |

## 4.3 Time Complexity of the *Online* Stage and Memory Requirement

According to the matrix stopping rule of $mt^2 = N$. Given $E = \frac{N}{D}$, we generate $r = \frac{t}{D}$ ($D \leq t$) tables, each of which contains $m$ rows and $t$ columns for TMD-PRA-I and produce one table which contains $\frac{mt}{D}$ rows and $t$ columns for TMD-PRA-II. The time complexity of the *online* stage can be divided into two parts: one for the function calculations, another for the table look-ups. According to the descriptions of the *online* stage in section 3, both function calculations and table look-ups of TMD-PRA-I are $O(t^2)$, function calculations and table look-ups of TMD-PRA-II are $O(\frac{t^2 D}{2})$ and $O(tD)$ respectively.

Memory requirement is measured by the number of entries, each of which contains one starting point and one ending point. For TMD-PRA-I, there are $m$ chains in each of the $\frac{t}{D}$ tables, the memory requirement is thus $\frac{mt}{D}$ entries. For TMD-PRA-II, there are one table which contains $\frac{mt}{D}$ chains, hence the memory requirement is also $\frac{mt}{D}$.

## 4.4 Trade-Off Curve

We assume that the function calculations dominate the *online* cost for both TMD-PRA-I and TMD-PRA-II and we will ignore the factor of two in the function calculations of TMD-PRA-II, since it does not significantly affect the analysis. The cost of table look-ups can be greatly reduced by considering the distinguished point method of Rivest [5]. From the previous analysis of Section 4.3, trade-off curves of TMD-PRA-I and TMD-PRA-II are $T_I(M_I D)^2 = N^2$ and $T_{II} M_{II}^2 D = N^2$ respectively. Therefore, trade-off curve of TMD-PRA-II is inferior to that of TMD-PRA-I. For example, given $|P| = |C| = N = 2^{48}$, we can choose $(T_I, M_I, D) = (N^{\frac{2}{3}}, N^{\frac{1}{3}}, N^{\frac{1}{3}}) = (2^{32}, 2^{16}, 2^{16})$ and $(T_{II}, M_{II}, D) = (N^{\frac{2}{3}}, N^{\frac{1}{3}}, N^{\frac{2}{3}}) = (2^{32}, 2^{16}, 2^{32})$. This indicates that TMD-PRA-II requires more ciphertexts in order to keep the same analysis cost and memory requirement as TMD-PRA-I.

## 5    Performance Evaluation

In this section, we propose a detailed evaluation on the performance of our attacks by applying them on various block ciphers. The results are listed in the following table 3.

**Table 3.** Comparisons of TMD-PRA-I on various block ciphers

| Block Cipher | $(|K|,|C|)$ | Ciphertexts(D) | Time(T) | Memory(M) | Preprocessing(E) |
|---|---|---|---|---|---|
| DES | (56,64) | $2^{16}$ | $2^{32}$ | $2^{32}$ | $2^{48}$ |
| Triple-DES | (112,64) | $2^{16}$ | $2^{32}$ | $2^{32}$ | $2^{48}$ |
| Triple-DES | (168,64) | $2^{16}$ | $2^{32}$ | $2^{32}$ | $2^{48}$ |
| Skipjack | (80,64) | $2^{16}$ | $2^{32}$ | $2^{32}$ | $2^{48}$ |
| AES | (128,128) | $2^{32}$ | $2^{80}$ | $2^{56}$ | $2^{96}$ |
| AES | (192,128) | $2^{32}$ | $2^{80}$ | $2^{56}$ | $2^{96}$ |
| AES | (256,128) | $2^{32}$ | $2^{80}$ | $2^{56}$ | $2^{96}$ |
| Any block cipher | (k,n) | $2^{n/4}$ | $2^{n/2}$ | $2^{n/2}$ | $2^{3n/4}$ |
| Any block cipher | (k,n) | $2^{n/3}$ | $2^{2n/3}$ | $2^{n/3}$ | $2^{2n/3}$ |

The results of the Table 3 show that the complexity and efficiency of TMD-PRA-I only depend on the block size instead of the key size. We also present comparisons between our attacks and BS-TMD attack proposed by Biryukov et al [2]. The comparison results are listed in the Table 4, 5 and 6.

**Table 4.** Trade-off attacks on 112-bit key Triple-DES

| Attack | Data Type | Data(D) | Time(T) | Memory(M) | Preprocessing(E) |
|---|---|---|---|---|---|
| TMD-PRA-I | FK[a] | $2^{16}$ | $2^{32}$ | $2^{32}$ | $2^{48}$ |
| TMD-PRA-I | FK | $2^{24}$ | $2^{20}$ | $2^{30}$ | $2^{40}$ |
| BS-TMD | VK[b] | $2^{16}$ | $2^{80}$ | $2^{56}$ | $2^{96}$ |
| BS-TMD | VK | $2^{24}$ | $2^{64}$ | $2^{112}$ | $2^{88}$ |

[a] Denotes the set of ciphertexts which are the results of different plaintexts encrypted by a block cipher under a *fixed key*.
[b] Denotes the set of ciphertexts which are the results of a known plaintext encrypted by a block cipher under *various keys*.

Compared with DES, the advantage of our attack becomes more apparent when applied to Triple-DES with 112-bit key and 168-bit key respectively. The similar results also can be found in the Table 4 and 6. When the key size is larger than the block size, the performance of TMD-PRA-I is explicitly superior to that of BS-TMD. Consequently, it does not make sense to increase the key size without a corresponding increase of the block size when designing a new block

**Table 5.** Trade-off attacks on 128-bit key AES

| Attack | Data Type | Data(D) | Time(T) | Memory(M) | Preprocessing(E) |
|--------|-----------|---------|---------|-----------|------------------|
| TMD-PRA-I | FK | $2^{24}$ | $2^{92}$ | $2^{58}$ | $2^{104}$ |
| TMD-PRA-I | FK | $2^{32}$ | $2^{80}$ | $2^{56}$ | $2^{96}$ |
| BS-TMD | VK | $2^{24}$ | $2^{92}$ | $2^{58}$ | $2^{104}$ |
| BS-TMD | VK | $2^{32}$ | $2^{80}$ | $2^{56}$ | $2^{96}$ |

**Table 6.** Trade-off attacks on 192-bit key AES

| Attack | Data Type | Data(D) | Time(T) | Memory(M) | Preprocessing(E) |
|--------|-----------|---------|---------|-----------|------------------|
| TMD-PRA-I | FK | $2^{32}$ | $2^{84}$ | $2^{54}$ | $2^{96}$ |
| TMD-PRA-I | FK | $2^{48}$ | $2^{60}$ | $2^{50}$ | $2^{80}$ |
| BS-TMD | VK | $2^{32}$ | $2^{120}$ | $2^{100}$ | $2^{160}$ |
| BS-TMD | VK | $2^{48}$ | $2^{96}$ | $2^{96}$ | $2^{144}$ |

cipher. However, when the key size is same to the block size, the complexities of TMD-PRA-I and BS-TMD are identical (Table 5 shows this case). In this scenario, our preference would be BS-TMD attack, since it can recovery an encryption key instead of a plaintext. Evaluation results of TMD-PRA-II are similar to TMD-PRA-I, please see more details in the full version (also including further discussions and observations).

## 6    Conclusion

In this paper, we attempt to shift the targets of the traditional time-memory-data trade-off from key recovery to plaintext recovery for block ciphers, thus proposing a new attack by applying the time-memory-data trade-off to plaintext recovery attack. Two attack schemes of TMD-PRA-I and TMD-PRA-II have been constructed and several vigorous properties have been proved. Compared with the traditional time-memory-data trade-offs, new schemes possess higher success probability and efficiency benefitting from these properties. We also evaluate the performance of our new schemes by applying them to several block ciphers, resulting in a better performance than BS-TMD when the key size is larger than the block size. Consequently, we believe that this target shifting is valuable and it does not make sense to increase the key size without a corresponding increase of the block size when designing a new block cipher.

## References

1. Avoine, G., Junod, P., Oechslin, P.: Characterization and improvement of time-memory trade-off based on perfect tables. ACM Transactions on Information and Systems Security 11(4), Article 17 (2008)

2. Biryukov, A., Mukhopadhyay, S., Sarkar, P.: Improved Time-Memory Trade-Offs with Multiple Data. In: Preneel, B., Tavares, S. (eds.) SAC 2005. LNCS, vol. 3897, pp. 110–127. Springer, Heidelberg (2006)
3. Biryukov, A., Shamir, A.: Cryptanalytic Time/Memory/Data Tradeoffs for Stream Ciphers. In: Okamoto, T. (ed.) ASIACRYPT 2000. LNCS, vol. 1976, pp. 1–13. Springer, Heidelberg (2000)
4. Borst, J., Preneel, B., Vandewalle, J.: On the time-memory tradeoff between exhaustive key search and table precomputation. In: de With, P., van der Schaar-Mitrea, M. (eds.) The Proceedings of the 19th Symposium on Information Theory in the Benelux, Veldhoven, The Netherlands, pp. 111–118 (1998)
5. Denning, D.: Cryptography and Data Security, p. 100. Addison-Wesley (1982)
6. Dinur, I., Dunkelman, O., Keller, N., Shamir, A.: Efficient Dissection of Composite Problems, with Applications to Cryptanalysis, Knapsacks, and Combinatorial Search Problems. Cryptology ePrint Archive. Report 2012/217 (2012)
7. Fiat, A., Naor, M.: Rigorous time/space tradeoffs for inverting functions. In: Proceedings of the 23th Annual ACM Symposium on Theory of Computing (STOC 1991), pp. 534–541. ACM Press, New Orleans (1991)
8. Hellman, M.: A Cryptanalytic Time-Memory Trade-Off. IEEE Transactions on Information Theory 26(4), 401–406 (1980)
9. Ma, D., Hong, J.: Success Probability of the Hellman Trade-Off. Information Processing Letters 109, 347–351 (2009)
10. Oechslin, P.: Making a Faster Cryptanalytic Time-Memory Trade-Off. In: Boneh, D. (ed.) CRYPTO 2003. LNCS, vol. 2729, pp. 617–630. Springer, Heidelberg (2003)

# Comparison between Side-Channel
# Analysis Distinguishers

Houssem Maghrebi, Olivier Rioul, Sylvain Guilley, and Jean-Luc Danger

Institut Mines-Télécom, Télécom-ParisTech, CNRS LTCI (UMR 5141)
{houssem.maghrebi,olivier.rioul,
sylvain.guilley,jean-luc.danger}@telecom-paristech.fr

**Abstract.** Side-channel analyses allow to extract keys from devices whatever their length. They rely on tools called "distinguishers". In this paper, we intend to compare two generic distinguishers *per se*: we provide a characterization environment where all the implementation details are equal, hence a fair comparison.

In the field of distinguishers that use a model, the notion of equivalence between distinguishers has already been studied in some seminal works [6, 13]. However, no such work has been carried out for generic distinguishers, that work on observable values distributions rather than on their values themselves. In this paper, we set up simulations that aim at showing experimentally that two generic distinguishers are different. Then, we develop a theory to actually prove that one distinguisher is better than the other.

**Keywords:** Information Theoretic (IT) metrics, Probability/Cumulative Density Function (PDF/CDF), Kolmogorov-Smirnov Analysis (KSA), Inter-class Kolmogorov-Smirnov Analysis (IKSA), Masking.

## 1 Introduction

Smart cards play a crucial role in many security systems. These devices typically operate in hostile environments and, therefore, the data they contain might be relatively easily compromised. For example, their physical accessibility sometimes allows a number of very powerful attacks against their implementation. During the last decade, side-channel attacks in general, and power analysis attacks in particular, have shaken the belief in the security of smart cards. Kocher *et al.* showed in their pioneering article [10] that a smart card that is unprotected against power analysis attacks can be broken without difficulty. The core idea of side-channel attacks is to compare some key-dependent predictions of the physical leakages with actual measurements, in order to identify which prediction (or key) is the most likely to have given rise to the measurements. In practice, it requires both to be able to model the leakages with a sufficient precision in order to build the predictions, and to have a good comparison tool, thereafter referred to as a *distinguisher*, to efficiently extract the keys.

In 2008, Mutual Information Analysis (MIA) [7] has been proposed as a new side-channel distinguisher. MIA aims at genericity in the sense that it is expected

T.W. Chim and T.H. Yuen (Eds.): ICICS 2012, LNCS 7618, pp. 331–340, 2012.

to lead to successful key recoveries with as little assumptions as possible about the leaking devices it targets. Previous works [14, 19, 23] demonstrated that the estimation of probability density functions for these key-dependent models is of decisive importance to the performance of MIA in practice.

The authors of [19] suggested an alternative distinguisher that do not require explicit density estimation: the Kolmogorov-Smirnov test. It is a non-parametric statistical test to distinguish between distributions by computing the absolute difference between their cumulative distribution. Reference [24] explores the effectiveness and efficiency of the Kolmogorov-Smirnov Analysis (KSA) in the context of SCA and compare it to the MIA in a number of relevant scenarios ranging from unprotected to masked implementations.

All the distinguishers listed above compare the key-dependent predictions of the physical leakages *versus* actual measurements. Our approach in this paper consists in comparing the conditional leakages between themselves (pairwise) in order to efficiently recover the secret key. We name this approach *"inter-class"*. We provide a methodology to fairly compare two SCA distinguishers based on simulations.

The remainder of this article is organized as follows. The definition of the state-of-the-art and inter-class metric is given in section 2. This section contrasts the principle of inter-class metrics with other metrics. In section 3, a fair framework to evaluate and compare distinguishers is given. We applied this methodology to compare the KSA and the inter-class KSA (*aka* IKSA). These theoretical results are then validated by simulations in section 4. Section 5 concludes the paper and gives some perspectives for future works.

**Our Contributions**

This paper presents three novel contributions. First, we propose the notion of "inter-class" metrics, which allows to build a new distinguisher for SCA aimed to be efficient when exploiting several kinds of leakages. The originality of this new test is that it does a pairwise comparison between the key-dependent leakage classes. Second, we apply this notion to the Kolmogorov-Smirnov test which yield the Inter-class Kolmogorov-Smirnov Analysis (IKSA). In order to compare two SCA distinguishers, we propose a simulation-based "fair" framework which takes into account the different errors of estimation tools used in simulation process. Third, we present several experiments to compare IKSA to KSA using this framework, where simulated attacks are performed against unprotected and protected AES with Boolean masking. Attacks' simulation in section 4 confirm that the IKSA compares favorably to KSA and that IKSA is non-equivalent to KSA, even when masking is applied to ensure some protection.

## 2    Mutual and Inter-class Distinguishers

### 2.1    Notations

We use capital letters, like $Z$, to denote a random variable (RV), calligraphic letters, like $\mathcal{Z}$, to denote its support (set of possible values), and lowercase letters, like $z$, for its realizations. The expectation of $Z$ is denoted by $\mathbb{E}[Z]$. The Hamming weight of $z$ is written as $HW(z)$. We use the following notations.

- $X$: a RV that represents the leakage (*e.g.* the measured current drawn by a cryptographic device);
- $K$: the cryptographic key;
- $Z$: the input or the output of the cryptographic device (*i.e.* its plaintext or ciphertext);
- $Y = \psi(Z, K)$: a sensitive variable used internally, that depends both on $Z$ (known by the attacker) and $K$ (unknown by the attacker). We assume that this sensitive variable $Y$ can be computed exhaustively from $K$ by the attacker and that it causes the leakages; put differently, when the key guess is correct, $X$ and $Y$ are dependent.

Side-channel analysis consists in estimating whether $X$ and $Y$ are dependent for every key guess, *i.e.*, for every value $K = k$. The analysis is said to be *sound* if the greatest dependence is obtained for the correct value of the key, noted $k^\star$. In this case, the key can be extracted successfully from the device. In practice, the values taken by $X$ are noisy, because they consist in physical measurements and because the link between $X$ and $Y$ is imperfect (it might involve other variables, yielding algorithmic noise). Therefore, many couples $(X, Y)$ are required for the $2^n$ estimations (for each value of $K$) to find the correct key, where $n$ is the bit-width of $K$.

## 2.2    Inter-class Notion

Distinguishers can be defined based on the analysis of values or of distributions.

- Examples of distinguishers based on values: DPA [10], CPA [5], stochastic [16], DCA [1].
- Distinguishers based on distributions: MIA [2], KSA [24], *etc.*

The distinguishers based on values can be considered weaker than those based on distributions. A justification is that there exist some distributions (*e.g.* the log-normal distribution) that are not uniquely determined by their moments. Distinguishers based on distributions are referred to as *information-theoretic* and have been acknowledged as more generic.

Several "distances" $D(\,\cdot\,;\,\cdot\,)$ are known to measure the dependency between two distributions, such as Kullback-Leibler (KL) divergence, Hellinger distance, or Kolmogorov-Smirnov (KS) distance. In the sequel, we focus on KS test, because it has been investigated recently and constitutes an interesting competitor to the (already much discussed) mutual information based attacks.

The distance between distributions $D(\,\cdot\,;\,\cdot\,)$ is used to build distinguishers in two different ways:

1. (marginal-to-conditional approach) $D(X|Y; X)$, which yields the KSA distinguisher,
2. (inter-class approach) $D(X|Y; X|Y')$, where $Y'$ is an independent copy of $Y$, which yields its inter-class counterpart, called IKSA.

# 3   Comparison Methodology

## 3.1   Frameworks

In this section, we analyze previous comparison frameworks, highlight possible limitations and motivate for a new setting. The first proposed evaluation framework is [17] basically suggests to use a leakage metric to quantify the maximal chance that an optimal attacker would have to extract secrets. This metric represents a vulnerability analysis, for an attacker might not be able to turn the leakage into a successful attack. For the comparison of attacks, *i.e.* of distinguishers, [17] suggests metrics like $o$-th order success rate (with $o \in [\![1, 2^n]\!]$) or guessing entropy. In another framework [23, 24], the distance to the nearest rival is employed; it is the same definition as previously termed "Correlation Contrast" in [3]. Many other metrics can be invented, such as the signal (distinguisher expected value for the correct key $k^\star$) to noise (distinguisher variance over incorrect keys $k \in \mathbb{F}_2^n \backslash \{k^\star\}$) ratio [8] or the norm-2 of the characterized coefficients in a stochastic profiling [9].

Recent analyses [23] suggest pitfalls in the evaluation methodologies for distinguishers. Errors can arise from many sources:

- **Estimation Bias:** the estimator does not converge to the correct value. For instance, the MIA with few bins for the PDF estimation can have a square bias significantly larger than its variance.
- **Estimation Algorithm:** it can approximate the data. Whatever the kernels used in PDF constructions [14], the binning of the observed side-channel reduces its accuracy.
- **Success Rate Error:** it is a random variable, that has its own variance.
- **Sampling Errors:** the random variables are not drawn a sufficient number of times and thus do not obey to their law. As a rule of thumb, estimations are incorrect if a discrete RV has been measured a fewer number of times than the size of its set of possible values.

In the sequel, we intend to compare KSA [24] and IKSA on a fair basis.

## 3.2   The Kolmogorov-Smirnov as SCA Distinguisher

In a first stage of the SCA attack, an adversary has to estimate the leakage probability density functions (PDFs) for different key-dependent models. In a second stage, this adversary has to test the dependence of these models with actual measurements. The problem of modeling a PDF from random samples of a distribution is a well studied problem in statistics, referred to as PDF estimation. A number of solutions exist, ranging from simple histograms to kernel density estimation [7, 14] or data clustering [20].

Interestingly, an explicit PDF estimation is not always necessary and there also exist statistical tools to compare two PDFs directly from their samples. The Kolmogorov-Smirnov (KS) test is typical of such non-parametric distinguishers.

In the context of SCA, the KSA test has been mentioned first in [19] as a non-parametric statistical test to distinguish between distributions. Then, [24] explores the effectiveness and efficiency of the Kolmogorov-Smirnov Analysis (KSA) and compare it with the Mutual Information Analysis (MIA). It is mainly used as a one-sample test where it allows the comparison of the frequency distribution of a sample to some known distribution, such as a Gaussian distribution, it can also be used as a two-sample test. As a two-sample test KSA distance compares the distributions of values in the two data vectors $X_1$ and $X_2$ of length $n_1$ and $n_2$, respectively. The null hypothesis for this test is that $X_1$ and $X_2$ have the same distribution. The alternative hypothesis is that they have different distributions. The KSA distance is a simple measure which is defined as the maximum value of the absolute difference between two cumulative distribution functions (CDFs): $D_{\mathrm{KSA}} = \sup_{x \in \mathcal{X}} |F_{X_1}(x) - F_{X_2}(x)|$, where $F_{X_1}$ and $F_{X_2}$ are the empirical CDFs (*aka* ECDFs). By definition a (univariate) ECDF is a step function. It is the proportion of observed values of a RV, that are less than or equal to some value. We can write it as: $F_X(x) = \frac{1}{N} \sum_{i=1}^{N} I_{x_i \leq x}$. In this formula, the tuple $\{x_i\}_{i \in [\![1,N]\!]}$ denotes the values realized by the RV $X$. The function $I$ is an indicator, which is equal to one when the enclosed expression is true, and zero otherwise. Like MIA, the KSA distinguisher measures the maximum distance between the leakage (measurements) $X$ and the hypothesis-dependent conditional observations $X \mid Y$:

$$D_{\mathrm{KS}} = \mathbb{E}_Y \sup_{x \in \mathcal{X}} \left| F_X(x) - F_{X|Y}(x) \right| . \tag{1}$$

The KSA returns the largest difference when the key is correct, *i.e.* when $k = k^\star$.

In contrast to KSA, IKSA consists in comparing the conditional leakages between themselves, pairwise. The Inter-class KSA distinguisher can write as:

$$D_{\mathrm{IKSA}} = \frac{1}{2} \cdot \mathbb{E}_{Y,Y'} \sup_{x \in \mathcal{X}} \left| F_{X|Y}(x) - F_{X|Y'}(x) \right| , \tag{2}$$

where $Y'$ is an independent copy of $Y$. The $1/2$ factor makes up for double counts $((Y, Y') \leftrightarrow (Y', Y))$.

### 3.3   Increasing the Fairness of the Estimations

We try here to eliminate or at least bound the errors listed in Sec. 3.1.

- The KS distance is shown to be unbiased by the Glivenko-Cantelli theorem [22], (and furthermore there is a uniform convergence). This is never true for entropy estimators (for instance, all the estimation methods presented in [14] are biased).
- We use an estimation algorithm that keeps the data unchanged (see Eqn. (1) and (2)); Our estimation for KSA is the same as that of Whitnall, Oswald and Mather [24].
- We quantity the success rate error. An upper bound of the variance of the success rate error is shown below to behave as $1/\sqrt{N}$, where $N$ is the number of experiments (also called "number of queries" in [17]).

– We consider attacks with a noise large enough for the success rate to be well
below 100% for a number of queries smaller than the size of its definition
set.[1]

## 3.4 Bounding the Success Rate

Let $S_i$ denote i.i.d. Bernoulli variables that take binary values in $\{0,1\}$ with
probabilities $p$ and $1 - p$, where $p$ is the success probability. The success rate
is defined as $SR = \frac{1}{N} \sum_{i=1}^{N} S_i$ and has expectation $\mathbb{E}[SR] = p$, i.e., $SR$ is an
unbiased estimator of the success probability. According to the strong law of
large numbers the success rate converges to $p$ almost surely: $SR \xrightarrow{a.s.} p$. In
addition, $\mathbb{E}[SR] = p$, i.e. $SR$ is an unbiased estimator of the success rate. Now,
the standard deviation of $SR$ is easily computed:

$$\sigma(SR) = \sqrt{\frac{1}{N^2} \cdot N \cdot \sigma^2(S_j)} = \sqrt{\frac{p \cdot (1-p)}{N}} \ . \tag{3}$$

Thus, the estimation error on the success rate is maximized when $p$ is close to
$1/2$, and is minimized when $p$ is almost equal to 0 or 1.

In practice, one wishes to compare the success rates of two distinguishers
by examining the values of intermediate $p$ (i.e. $p \approx 1/2$). Note that there is a
uniform majoration $\sigma(SR) \leqslant \frac{1}{2\sqrt{N}}$, but the error bars can be a function of $p$
and $N$. The criterion for analyzing experiments will be that errors bars never
overlap. Otherwise (see Fig. 1 for $N = 10$), more experiments must be done,
so as to reach a situation such as Fig. 1 for $N = 200$. The exact number of
experiments depends on the distinguishers to be relatively characterized. The
closer they are in success rate, the more experiments are required.

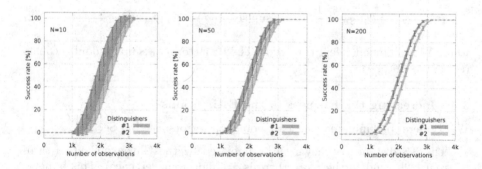

**Fig. 1.** Examples of success rates errors (Eqn. (3)) for various numbers of experiments

---

[1] For instance, it can be seen in Fig. 2 that for the unprotected (resp. Boolean masked)
AES, the number of traces to recover the key successfully with probability $> 80\%$ is
about $2,000$ (resp. $70,000$), which is significantly greater than the number of possible
plaintexts (i.e. $2^n = 256$) for $\sigma \geqslant 8$.

# 4    Simulation Results

In this section, we perform several attack experiments to compare KSA and IKSA. Our methodology allows to observe how the different attacks behave against unprotected reference and a masking scheme, and to compare their resistance for different noise's standard deviations.

In what follows, we consider a model in which the leakage variable $X$ is expressed as a deterministic leakage function $\phi$ of the intermediate variable $Y$ with an independent additive noise $N$.

*Target Leakage:* We list hereafter the leakages we consider and the underlying leaking variables:

- $1^{st}$-order leakage of an unprotected implementation: $X = \phi(Y) + N$;
- $2^{nd}$-order leakage of $1^{st}$-order Boolean masking scheme [18]: $X = \phi(Y \oplus M) + \phi(M) + N$, where the mask $M$ is a uniformly distributed RV.

The leakage measurements have been simulated as samples of the random variables $X$ with $\phi = HW^2$ and assuming an additive white Gaussian noise $N \sim \mathcal{N}(0, \sigma^2)$. For both attacks, the sensitive variable $Y$ was chosen to be an AES S-box output of the form $S(Z \oplus k^\star)$, where $S : \mathbb{F}_2^8 \to \mathbb{F}_2^8$ is SubBytes, $Z$ is uniformly distributed over $\mathbb{F}_2^8$, and represents a varying plaintext byte and $k^\star \in \mathbb{F}_2^8$ represents the key byte to recover.

*Side-Channel Distinguishers:* We apply KSA and IKSA such as described in previous sections. The guess key $k$ is tested by estimating $D_{\text{KSA}}(X; \hat{\phi}(Y(k)))$ and $D_{\text{IKSA}}(X; \hat{\phi}(Y(k)))$, respectively, where $\hat{\phi}$ is the prediction function. We select the Hamming weight function as prediction function in our simulations.

*Attack Simulation Results:* For each investigated context, we compute the first-order success rate of the attacks, over a set of 200 independent experiments for several noise standard deviation values. For comparison purposes, we compute the same metric for other univariate distinguishers: MIA, DPA [4], CPA, VPA [11] and 2O-CPA [21]. Figure 2 summarizes the number of leakage measurements required to observe a success rate of 90% in retrieving $k^\star$ for those SCA attacks. This figure is the compilation of success rates curves obtained for different values of the noise standard deviation (see examples in Fig. 3).

The results presented in Fig. 2 show the significant gain of number of measurements needed induced by IKSA compared to KSA attack. Our new distinguisher compares favorably to KSA: the IKSA attack outperforms the KSA attack when targeting the unprotected implementation or even when the Boolean masking scheme is used for the protection. As expected, CPA performs well in both scenarios since the dependency between the leakage and the model is linear. But,

---

2 Assuming Hamming weight leakage model is realistic for implementations on simple microcontrollers [12].

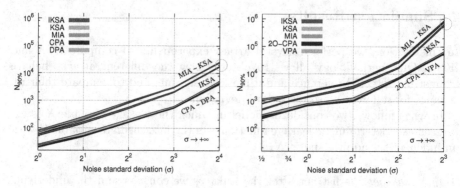

**Fig. 2.** Evaluation of $N_{90\%}$, the number of messages to achieve a success rate greater than 90%, according to the noise standard deviation when attacking unprotected (*left*) and Boolean masking (*right*) AES implementation

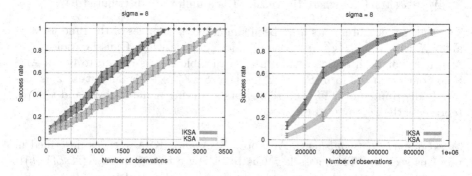

**Fig. 3.** Success rate of both IKSA and KSA distinguishers when attacking one substitution box of an unprotected AES (*left*) and of a Boolean masking scheme (*right*)

we like to stress that we focus in this paper only on information-theoretic distinguishers which are generic.

In [13], a notion of asymptotic equivalence (noted "$\sim$") for side-channel distinguishers is introduced: two distinguishers are said *equivalent* if the number of traces to overcome a given success rate (say 90%) decreases when the noise variance increases. For example, the likelihood and the Pearson correlation are equivalent in this sense. A look at $N90\%$ curves in Fig. 2 shows that other univariate distinguishers exhibit a similar equivalence law:

- DPA $\sim$ CPA on an unprotected implementation (*left*);
- 2O-CPA $\sim$ VPA on a first-order masked implementation (*right*);
- KSA $\sim$ MIA on both implementations (already proved in [24]).

However, *IKSA and KSA are not equivalent*. The difference between IKSA and KSA $\sim$ MIA is materialized in Fig. 2 as a circle in cyan color. To the best of our knowledge, it is the first time that two distinguishers that do not become equivalent in the sense of [13] are put forward. Incidentally, we note that this conclusion could not have been derived mathematically under the usual Gaussian approximation, because under this approximation equivalence holds as $\sigma \to +\infty$. This tends to show that the mutual and inter-class approaches are of a different kind, even in a mono-variate context.

## 5   Conclusions and Perspectives

In this paper, we have introduced the new "inter-class" concept to distinguish between various partitionings. We applied this concept to the Kolmogorov-Smirnov distance, resulting in IKSA. We also proposed a simulation-based fair framework to compare the two distinguishers KSA and IKSA. Our framework takes in account the different sources of errors estimations. We used this framework to compare KSA to IKSA using the success rate metric. Security metrics are clearly in favor of IKSA even when the implementation is unprotected or protected using a first-order Boolean masking countermeasure (with a linear leakage model).

An interesting question for the future work is to give a theoretical proof of the soundness of the distinguishers. Also, we endeavour to find a mathematical explanation why IKSA outperforms KSA for usual leakage functions.

## References

1. Batina, L., Gierlichs, B., Lemke-Rust, K.: Differential Cluster Analysis. In: Clavier, C., Gaj, K. (eds.) CHES 2009. LNCS, vol. 5747, pp. 112–127. Springer, Heidelberg (2009)
2. Batina, L., Gierlichs, B., Prouff, E., Rivain, M., Standaert, F.-X., Veyrat-Charvillon, N.: Mutual Information Analysis: a Comprehensive Study. J. Cryptology 24(2), 269–291 (2011)
3. Benoît, O., Peyrin, T.: Side-Channel Analysis of Six SHA-3 Candidates. In: Mangard, S., Standaert, F.-X. (eds.) CHES 2010. LNCS, vol. 6225, pp. 140–157. Springer, Heidelberg (2010)
4. Bévan, R., Knudsen, E.W.: Ways to Enhance Differential Power Analysis. In: Lee, P.J., Lim, C.H. (eds.) ICISC 2002. LNCS, vol. 2587, pp. 327–342. Springer, Heidelberg (2003)
5. Brier, E., Clavier, C., Olivier, F.: Correlation Power Analysis with a Leakage Model. In: Joye, M., Quisquater, J.-J. (eds.) CHES 2004. LNCS, vol. 3156, pp. 16–29. Springer, Heidelberg (2004)
6. Doget, J., Prouff, E., Rivain, M., Standaert, F.-X.: Univariate side channel attacks and leakage modeling. J. Cryptographic Engineering 1(2), 123–144 (2011)
7. Gierlichs, B., Batina, L., Tuyls, P., Preneel, B.: Mutual Information Analysis. In: Oswald, E., Rohatgi, P. (eds.) CHES 2008. LNCS, vol. 5154, pp. 426–442. Springer, Heidelberg (2008)
8. Guilley, S., Hoogvorst, P., Pacalet, R.: Differential Power Analysis Model and some Results. In: Kluwer (ed.) Proceedings of WCC/CARDIS 2004, Toulouse, France, pp. 127–142 (August 2004), doi:10.1007/1-4020-8147-2_9
9. Heuser, A., Schindler, W., Stöttinger, M.: Revealing side-channel issues of complex circuits by enhanced leakage models. In: Rosenstiel, W., Thiele, L. (eds.) DATE, pp. 1179–1184. IEEE (2012)

10. Kocher, P.C., Jaffe, J., Jun, B.: Differential Power Analysis. In: Wiener, M. (ed.) CRYPTO 1999. LNCS, vol. 1666, pp. 388–397. Springer, Heidelberg (1999)
11. Maghrebi, H., Danger, J.-L., Flament, F., Guilley, S.: Evaluation of Countermeasures Implementation Based on Boolean Masking to Thwart First and Second Order Side-Channel Attacks. In: SCS, Jerba, Tunisia, November 6-8, pp. 1–6. IEEE (2009), doi:10.1109/ICSCS.2009.5412597
12. Mangard, S., Oswald, E., Popp, T.: Power Analysis Attacks: Revealing the Secrets of Smart Cards. Springer (December 2006) ISBN 0-387-30857-1, http://www.springer.com/, http://www.dpabook.org/
13. Mangard, S., Oswald, E., Standaert, F.-X.: One for All - All for One: Unifying Standard DPA Attacks. Information Security, IET 5(2), 100–111 (2010) ISSN: 1751-8709; Digital Object Identifier: 10.1049/iet-ifs.2010.0096
14. Prouff, E., Rivain, M.: Theoretical and Practical Aspects of Mutual Information Based Side Channel Analysis. In: Abdalla, M., Pointcheval, D., Fouque, P.-A., Vergnaud, D. (eds.) ACNS 2009. LNCS, vol. 5536, pp. 499–518. Springer, Heidelberg (2009)
15. Rogaway, P. (ed.): CRYPTO 2011. LNCS, vol. 6841, pp. 2011–2031. Springer, Heidelberg (2011)
16. Schindler, W., Lemke, K., Paar, C.: A Stochastic Model for Differential Side Channel Cryptanalysis. In: Rao, J.R., Sunar, B. (eds.) CHES 2005. LNCS, vol. 3659, pp. 30–46. Springer, Heidelberg (2005)
17. Standaert, F.-X., Malkin, T.G., Yung, M.: A Unified Framework for the Analysis of Side-Channel Key Recovery Attacks. In: Joux, A. (ed.) EUROCRYPT 2009. LNCS, vol. 5479, pp. 443–461. Springer, Heidelberg (2009)
18. Standaert, F.-X., Rouvroy, G., Quisquater, J.-J.: FPGA Implementations of the DES and Triple-DES Masked Against Power Analysis Attacks. In: FPL. IEEE, Madrid, Spain (August 2006)
19. Veyrat-Charvillon, N., Standaert, F.-X.: Mutual Information Analysis: How, When and Why? In: Clavier, C., Gaj, K. (eds.) CHES 2009. LNCS, vol. 5747, pp. 429–443. Springer, Heidelberg (2009)
20. Veyrat-Charvillon, N., Standaert, F.-X.: Generic Side-Channel Distinguishers: Improvements and Limitations. In: Rogaway [15], pp. 354–372
21. Waddle, J., Wagner, D.: Towards Efficient Second-Order Power Analysis. In: Joye, M., Quisquater, J.-J. (eds.) CHES 2004. LNCS, vol. 3156, pp. 1–15. Springer, Heidelberg (2004)
22. Wellner, J.A.: A Glivenko-Cantelli theorem and strong laws of large numbers for functions of order statistics. Ann. Statist. 5(3), 473–480 (1977)
23. Whitnall, C., Oswald, E.: A Comprehensive Evaluation of Mutual Information Analysis Using a Fair Evaluation Framework. In: Rogaway [15], pp. 316–334
24. Whitnall, C., Oswald, E., Mather, L.: An Exploration of the Kolmogorov-Smirnov Test as a Competitor to Mutual Information Analysis. In: Prouff, E. (ed.) CARDIS 2011. LNCS, vol. 7079, pp. 234–251. Springer, Heidelberg (2011)

# Acceleration of Composite Order Bilinear Pairing on Graphics Hardware

Ye Zhang[1,*], Chun Jason Xue[2], Duncan S. Wong[2],
Nikos Mamoulis[3], and Siu Ming Yiu[3]

[1] Pennsylvania State University, USA
yxz169@cse.psu.edu
[2] City University of Hong Kong, Hong Kong
{jasonxue,duncan}@cityu.edu.hk
[3] University of Hong Kong, Hong Kong
{smyiu,nikos}@cs.hku.hk

**Abstract.** Recently, composite-order bilinear pairing has been shown to be useful in many cryptographic constructions. However, it is time-costly to evaluate. This is because the composite order should be at least 1024bit and, hence, the elliptic curve group order $n$ and base field become too large, rendering the bilinear pairing algorithm itself too slow to be practical (e.g., the Miller loop is $\Omega(n)$). Thus, composite-order computation easily becomes the bottleneck of a cryptographic construction, especially, in the case where many pairings need to be evaluated at the same time. The existing solution to this problem that converts composite-order pairings to prime-order ones is only valid for certain constructions. In this paper, we leverage the huge number of threads available on Graphics Processing Units (GPUs) to speed up composite-order pairing computation. We investigate suitable SIMD algorithms for base/extension field, elliptic curve and bilinear pairing computation as well as mapping these algorithms into GPUs with careful considerations. Experimental results show that our method achieves a record of 8.7ms per pairing on a 80bit security level, which is a 20-fold speedup compared to the state-of-the-art CPU implementation. This result also opens the road to adopting higher security levels and using rich-resource parallel platforms, which for example are available in cloud computing. For example, we can achieve a record of $7 \times 10^{-6}$ USD per pairing on the Amazon cloud computing environment.

## 1 Introduction

A bilinear pairing $\hat{e} : \mathbb{G} \times \mathbb{G} \to \mathbb{G}_T$ is said to be over a composite-order group if the order $\mathbb{G}$ and $\mathbb{G}_T$ is composite. Pairings with this property are commonly used in recent cryptographic constructions, specifically in functional encryption schemes, e.g., [2,5,7]. On the other hand, evaluating a pairing over a composite-order group is much more expensive compared to its prime-order counterpart. To achieve the

---

* Part of this work was done while the author was with the University of Hong Kong.

T.W. Chim and T.H. Yuen (Eds.): ICICS 2012, LNCS 7618, pp. 341–348, 2012.
© Springer-Verlag Berlin Heidelberg 2012

same 80bit (AES) security level, the composite order should be at least 1024 bit to be difficult to factorize, while a much smaller prime order (e.g., 160bit) is enough. As a result, the underlying finite field, elliptic curve operations and the pairing evaluating algorithm itself become much slower. An estimation [3] shows that the composite-order pairing would be 50x times slower than its prime-order counterpart. Thus, composite-order pairing computation easily becomes the bottleneck of a cryptographic construction, especially in cases where multiple such pairings need to be evaluated at the same time (e.g., decryption algorithm in the scheme [5]). Furthermore, one typical scenario of functional encryption schemes is the outsourced database scenario where the database server needs to decrypt the whole encrypted data with particular decryption key that embeds the query predicate. As a result, the database needs to evaluate mass amount of composite-order parings as fast as possible.

There are some efforts to address this problem. Freeman [3] proposed a method that can convert a scheme constructed with a composite-order pairing to a prime-order pairing construction with the same functionality. However, Freeman's method is not black-box; it is only valid for certain cryptographic constructions. [8] points out that some schemes inherently require composite-order groups and cannot be transformed mechanically by using Freeman's method.

In this paper, we leverage the huge number of threads available on GPUs (Graphics Processing Units) to speed up the composite-order bilinear pairing computation. The proposed method considers parallelism both within and between pairings. To compute a pairing, we use a block of threads, while we concurrently run many blocks to compute many pairings in parallel. We first implemented 32bit modular addition, subtraction and multiplication on each thread. Addition, subtraction and multiplication operations on finite field $\mathbb{F}_q$ are conducted on a block of threads via Residue Number System (RNS) [6]. Multiplication and square operations on extension field $\mathbb{F}_{q^2}$ and addition and double operations on an elliptic curve are implemented upon $\mathbb{F}_q$ operations, which in turn are based on a block of threads. Putting all together, the bilinear pairing algorithm [1] is implemented upon the $\mathbb{F}_q$ operations, $\mathbb{F}_{q^2}$ operations, and the elliptic curve operations. Compared to the existing work, our method is transparent and generic to cryptographic schemes. It can serve for all cryptographic schemes constructed in composite-order pairings.

To the best of our knowledge, this work is the first on evaluation of bilinear pairings over composite-order group on graphics card hardware. Porting the existing CPU-version code into the GPU is not trivial, due to the different levels of parallelism provided by CPUs and GPUs. As a result, we need to find and implement the optimized parallel (e.g., SIMD-fashion) algorithms for GPU that evaluate arithmetic operations on base field, extension field, elliptic curve, and the bilinear pairing algorithm itself. Different design decisions were made compared to the CPU code. For example, $\mathbb{F}_q$ operations in our implementation is done by a block of threads via RNS instead of the serialized method on CPU. Due to RNS, we had to seek the formulas that can minimize the number of modular reductions. Moreover, the multiplication inverse in the proposed implementation needs to be avoided which motivates us to choose a projective coordinate system to represent elliptic curve points and to postpone the final powering operation back to CPU. The experimental results show that the proposed method achieves a 20-fold speedup on a 80bit security level, compared to the state-of-the-art implementation [9] for CPUs. Specifically, it achieves a record of 8.7ms per pairing on average, which is comparable with prime-order group pairings.

The rest of this paper is organized as follows. The arithmetic operations and algorithms are presented in Section 2. Section 3 discusses the implementation considerations on mapping the algorithms. The experimental results are shown in Section 4.

## 2    Arithmetic Operations

We employ Barreto et al.'s algorithm [1] to evaluate bilinear pairing. Its details (including the algorithm to evaluate $g_{U,V}$) can be found in the full version [11] of this paper, which is also specifically designed for the composite-order pairing. We note that we choose Barreto et al.'s algorithm because the flow of computations in it only depends on the system parameters but not on the input points. Therefore, their algorithm fit well with SIMD fashion of GPUs.

The arithmetic operations required by Barreto et al.'s algorithm are the operations in the extension field $\mathbb{F}_{q^2}$ and the elliptic curve $E(\mathbb{F}_q)$ which are in turn based on operations in the base field $\mathbb{F}_q$. Specifically, given $a, b \in \mathbb{F}_{q^2}; P, Q \in E(\mathbb{F}_q)$, we consider $a \times b$, $a^2$, $P + Q$ and $2P$ operations.

The multiplication inverse in $\mathbb{F}_q$ is expensive in our GPU implementation, which motivates us to avoid it. However, there are two occasions which may require multiplication inverse. One is in the addition and double operations of $E(\mathbb{F}_q)$. This can be avoided by using a projective coordinate system to represent elliptic curve points and we do so. The second one is in the final powering of bilinear pairing. However, we identify that the final powering is not a bottleneck of the whole system. In fact, through the experiments, we find that the final powering is 500+ times faster than the Miller's loop on the CPU. Therefore, we can leave the work of final powering (and therefore multiplication inverse in $\mathbb{F}_q$) to the CPU.

Furthermore, cryptographic constructions may only require the result of a product of bilinear pairings [5]. In this case, we can calculate the multiple pairings result (without the final power) on the GPU, then multiply them and do the single final powering to get the result. In this way, the cost to compute the final powering would be even ignored.

### 2.1    Base Field Operations

Motivated by the feasibility of performing fast and parallelized operations on multi-core graphics hardware, we choose to represent the base field elements of $\mathbb{F}_q$ in Residue Number System (RNS). In RNS, an $n$-length vector $\boldsymbol{a} = (a_1, a_2, ..., a_n)$ is chosen such that $\gcd(a_i, a_j) = 1$ for all $i \neq j$ and $q < A$ where

$A = \prod_{i=1}^{n} a_i$ is called the dynamic range of $\boldsymbol{a}$. For any $x$, $0 \leq x \leq q$, it can be represented uniquely in RNS as $\langle x \rangle_a = (x \bmod a_1, x \bmod a_2, \ldots, x \bmod a_n)$, and recovered uniquely in the form of $x \bmod A$ due to the Chinese Remainder Theorem.

The purpose of using RNS is to break down some basic arithmetic operations that include $\odot \in \{+, -, \times\}$ to small pieces which can be parallelized and computed using the multiple cores of the GPU. That is, $\langle x \rangle_a \odot \langle y \rangle_a = ((x_1 \odot y_1) \bmod a_1, \ldots, (x_n \odot y_n) \bmod a_n)$ where $\langle x \rangle_a = (x_1, \ldots, x_n)$ and $\langle y \rangle_a = (y_1, \ldots, y_n)$. Note that division (and therefore multiplication inverse in $\mathbb{F}_q$) and comparison in RNS are non-trivial and usually avoided from using as they do not offer speed advantage over conventional methods.

It is known that the multiplication operation on $\mathbb{F}_q$ can be done in RNS using the RNS Montgomery multiplication algorithm (see [6]). But there are few papers dealing with addition and subtraction on $\mathbb{F}_q$ in RNS. If we see the RNS Montgomery multiplication algorithm as the first step to compute multiplication (the second step is the mod $q$ operation), we can find a uniform way to handle addition and subtraction in RNS as well. Basically, given two elements $a, b \in \mathbb{F}_q$, we calculate addition $a + b$, subtraction $a - b$ and multiplication $a \times b$ without any modular operations. The result may grow up; when it becomes larger than a threshold, we employ an explicit modular reduction (i.e., $\bmod q$) to bring back the result to the allowed range again. This idea makes the operations in base field $\mathbb{F}_q$ simple and clear. Moreover, since the first step addition, subtraction and multiplication are cheap in RNS, this method allows us to fully focus on the most expensive part; that is, the second step: modular reduction.

To perform modular reduction, we employ the Montgomery Modular Reduction algorithm in RNS. **Algorithm 1** shows the algorithm (derived from [6, Alg. 3], as we discussed). In the algorithm, the dynamic ranges of bases $\boldsymbol{a}$ and $\boldsymbol{b}$ are denoted as $A$ and $B$, respectively. Also note that the output of **Algorithm 1** is $sB^{-1}(\bmod q)$ where the component $B^{-1}$ should be removed in the conventional way of using the Montgomery Multiplication algorithm (see [6]).

---

**Algorithm 1.** Montgomery Modular Reduction in Residue Number Systems [6]

---

**Input:** $\langle s \rangle_{a \cup b}$.
**Output:** $\langle w \rangle_{a \cup b}$, where $w < 2q$ and $w \equiv sB^{-1} \pmod{q}$.
**Ensure:** $\gcd(B, q) = 1$, $\gcd(A, B) = 1$, $4q \leq B$ and $2q \leq A$.

1 $\langle t \rangle_b \leftarrow \langle s \rangle_b \cdot \langle -q^{-1} \rangle_b$ $\qquad \langle t \rangle_{a \cup b} \Leftarrow \langle t \rangle_b$
2 $\langle u \rangle_a \leftarrow \langle t \rangle_a \cdot \langle q \rangle_a$
3 $\langle v \rangle_a \leftarrow \langle s \rangle_a + \langle u \rangle_a$
4 $\langle w \rangle_a \leftarrow \langle v \rangle_a \cdot \langle B^{-1} \rangle_a$ $\qquad \langle w \rangle_a \Rightarrow \langle w \rangle_{a \cup b}$
5 **return** $\langle w \rangle_{a \cup b}$

---

The symbol $\Rightarrow$ (or $\Leftarrow$) represents a base extension algorithm [10,4]. Given an RNS representation $\langle x \rangle_c$, this algorithm outputs $\langle x \rangle_d$ for $d \neq c$. The two base extensions $\langle t \rangle_{a \cup b} \Leftarrow \langle t \rangle_b$ and $\langle w \rangle_a \Rightarrow \langle w \rangle_{a \cup b}$ are the most computationally expensive parts of **Algorithm 1**.The following theorem (whose proof is given in the full version [11]) states the correctness of **Algorithm 1**.

**Theorem 1.** *For any integer $s$ such that $0 \le s < \alpha q^2$, **Algorithm 1** outputs $w$ such that $0 \le w < 2q$ if $B > \alpha q$ and $A > 2q$.*

Therefore, when the result of $a\{+, -, \times\}b$ grows beyond threshold $\alpha q^2$, we can reduce it back to $w < 2q$. Furthermore, we can control parameter $\alpha$, such to trade off between the number of reductions and the number of threads; a larger $\alpha$ results a larger threshold, but $B > \alpha q$ will be larger as well, requiring a larger number of bases to represent.

## 2.2 Extension Field Operations

Given an element $a \in \mathbb{F}_{q^2}$, $a$ can be written as $x + iy$ where $x, y \in \mathbb{F}_q$ and $i^2 = -1$. The multiplication $a \times b$ :

$$a \times b = (x_1 + iy_1)(x_2 + iy_2) = (x_1 x_2 - y_1 y_2) + i(x_1 y_1 + x_2 y_2)$$

which requires two reductions with four cheap multiplications and two cheap additions in RNS. Since the number of reductions meets with the lower bound (two), we do not resort to more advanced methods (e.g., Karatsuba multiplication). Similarly, squaring $a^2$ requires two reductions as well.

$$a^2 = (x_1^2 - y_1^2) + i2x_1 y_1$$

## 2.3 Elliptic Curve Operations

As we discussed, we adopt the Jacobian projective coordinate system for representing points in elliptic curve to avoid multiplication inverse in $\mathbb{F}_q$. A point $P = (X, Y, Z)$ in Jacobian projective coordinates can be mapped to $(\frac{X}{Z^2}, \frac{Y}{Z^3})$ in affine coordinates. As we will often use $Z^2$, we store $Z^2$ in the coordinates as well and we call this modified Jacobian coordinates: $(X, Y, Z, Z^2)$. To make the addition formula simpler, $Q$ is also given in affine coordinates $(X_2, Y_2)$.

As in the previous section, we are interested to find patterns like $\sum A_i B_i$ in operations, to minimize the number of modular reductions. The refined formulas to compute addition and double in $E(\mathbb{F}_q)$ are shown in Table 1 provided that $P = (X_1, Y_1, Z_1, Z_1^2)$ and $Q = (X_2, Y_2)$.

# 3  Implementation and Analysis

In this section, we discuss how the previous presented algorithms are mapped to CUDA programming model. In CUDA programming model, programmers can define the block size for their own kernel function. The block size defines how many threads are within each block. CUDA guarantees that threads in the same block can communicate and will execute on the same physical SM (streaming Multiprocessors). A detailed description on SM can be found in the full version.

**Table 1.** $E(\mathbb{F}_q)$ Operations

| $2(X_1, Y_1, Z_1, Z_1^2)$ | $(X_1, Y_1, Z_1, Z_1^2) + (X_2, Y_2)$ |
|---|---|
| $Y_1^2$ | $H = X_2 Z_1^2 - X_1$ |
| $S = 2Y_1^2 X_1$ | $e_0 = Y_2 Z_1$ |
| $M = (Z_1^2)^2 + 3X_1^2$ | $r = Z_1^2 e_0 - Y_1$ |
| $X_3 = T = M^2 - 2S$ | $H^2 = (H)^2$ |
| $Y_3 = -MT + MS - 8(Y_1^2)^2$ | $X_3 = (r)^2 - (HH^2) - 2X_1 H^2$ |
| $Z_3 = 2Y_1 Z_1$ | $e_1 = -X_3 + X_1 H^2$ |
| $Z_3^2 = (Z_3)^2$ | $e_2 = Y_1 H$ |
| | $Y_3 = e_1 r - e_2 H^2$ |
| | $Z_3 = Z_1 H$ |
| | $Z_3^2 = (Z_3)^2$ |

In this paper, we consider 1024/2048 bit composite order (w.r.t. 80/112bit security levels). As the word length in GPU is 32 bits, we need at least 32/64 bases to represent a 1024/2048bit number in RNS. In fact, the least number we can choose is 33/65. To complete Montgomery modular reduction (Algorithm 1), we need additional 32/64 bases. Moreover, we employ Shenoy's base extension algorithm which requires one more base. Therefore, for the 80bit security level, we need 33+33+1=67 bases to represent a singel element in $\mathbb{F}_q$. Specifically, each $\mathbb{F}_q$ element is mapped to a block of 67 threads. For each thread, a 32bit unsigned integer (UINT32) is used to represent the element (under the particular base of that thread).

We don't consider parallelism within the operations in the $\mathbb{F}_{q^2}$ and $E(\mathbb{F}_q)$, as our goal is to compute as many as possible pairings at one time (a typical goal in the server setting). Therefore, we simply represent $\mathbb{F}_{q^2}$ elements to be a vector $(x, y)$ where $x, y$ are UINT32. Similarly, we represent $P = (x, y, z, z^2)$ in $E(\mathbb{F}_q)$ (x, y, z are UINT32). Therefore, each block handles eactly one pairing calculation. This grid/block arrangements also simplify the design.

The base field operations include $a+b \mod m, a-b \mod m$ and $a \times b \mod m$ where $a, b < m$ and $m < 2^{32}$. For example, to compute $a + b \mod m$, there are two cases: $a + b < m$ and $m \leq a + b < 2m$. In the second case, we have to output $a + b - m$ and therefore we need test whether $a + b < m$ or not. However, this case handling, depending on the input values, causes a branch divergence on GPU. In the full version [11] of this paper, we present methods to minimize the divergence for all the base field operations.

GPU also provides some memory to use. Some of it can be accessed only within a thread; some can be shared among threads of the same block. Some may have special (1D/2D) caches. We have to carefully choose which memory to use to achieve an optimized performance. To allocate memory, the basic idea is that we (try to) store all variables to the register file of their threads such that the access time to them can be ignored. For the inter-thread data generated in the modular reduction algorithm, we use shared memory to store it, as the content in a register file can be only used within one thread. Moreover, we also store 67 (and 131) bases and those one-dimensional precomputed values in the constant memory to facilitate its 1D cache. Although the time for the fist access to them is large (400-600 cycles), the overall access time could be small as the algorithms and their threads fetch them frequently. For example, in each algorithm, the first thing is to load the associated base of that thread to the register. We also store the 2D array of the base extension algorithm to the texture memory so that we can benefit from the spatial locality and the 2D cache of the texture memory. Through the CUDA profiler's report, we verified that we indeed exploit caching well and the cache-hit rate is very high.

## 4  Experimental Results

The experiments were conducted on NVIDIA GeForce GTX 285, GTX 480 and Amazon EC2 Cloud [1] (equipped with two Tesla M2050). Specifically, GTX 285, 480 and EC2 have 240, 480 and 448x2 cores separately where each with 1.476GHz, 1.4GHz and 1.15GHz clock. Moreover, GTX 285, 480, EC2 also have 1GB, 1.5GB and 3GBx2 graphical memory on board. Their CUDA versions are 1.3 (GT200), 2.0 (Fermi) and 2.0 (Fermi).

We incorporate Amazon EC2 cloud because it is a popular way to instantiate the outsourced database scenario that requires mass evaluation of composite-order bilinear pairings. We study the real price paid to the EC2 cloud to evaluate each pairing. For comparison, we also choose Pairing-Based Cryptography (PBC) library version 0.5.11 (built upon GMP library[2] version 5.0.1) as the benchmark that runs on Intel Core 2 E8300 CPU at 2.83GHz and 3GB memory. GMP library is designed to be as fast as possible with highly optimized assembly code. Through the experiments, we choose random points $P, Q \in E(\mathbb{F}_q)$ as the input to evaluate $\hat{e}(P, Q)$.

We compare the running time on CPU and GPUs. The results are shown in Fig. 1. The GPUs method seems not to have advantage when the number of pairings is small ($< 32$), as the hardware is not fully occupied. With the number becoming larger, the speedup in running time increases. This indicates that the GPUs method is especially suitable for the case that multiple composite-order pairings should be evaluated at the same time.

Specifically, in the 80bit security level, GTX 285, M2050 (Amazon EC2) and GTX 480 achieve a running time of 17.4ms, 11.9ms and 8.7ms per pairing respectively, which is 9.6, 14.3 and 19.6 times faster respectively compared to the state-of-the-art CPU implementation (171.1ms per pairing). We note that this result has been comparable with prime-order pairing implementation on CPU (see the dashed lines in Fig. 1), where both A and D179 [9] pairing are for 80bit security and A is the fastest. With 2.1 USD charged per hour, 11.9ms on Amazon EC2 also means that the cost to compute a single pairing is as low as $(2.1 \times 11.9)/(60 \times 60 \times 1000) = 7 \times 10^{-6}$ USD.

---

[1] http://aws.amazon.com/ec2/

[2] http://gmplib.org/

348     Y. Zhang et al.

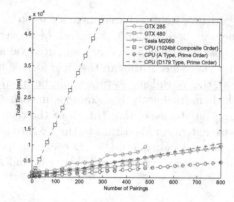

**Fig. 1.** Running Time on different GPUs and CPU (80bit Security Level)

# References

1. Barreto, P.S.L.M., Kim, H.Y., Lynn, B., Scott, M.: Efficient Algorithms for Pairing-Based Cryptosystems. In: Yung, M. (ed.) CRYPTO 2002. LNCS, vol. 2442, pp. 354–368. Springer, Heidelberg (2002)
2. Boneh, D., Goh, E., Nissim, K.: Evaluating 2-DNF Formulas on Ciphertexts. In: Kilian, J. (ed.) TCC 2005. LNCS, vol. 3378, pp. 325–341. Springer, Heidelberg (2005)
3. Freeman, D.: Converting Pairing-Based Cryptosystems from Composite-Order Groups to Prime-Order Groups. In: Gilbert, H. (ed.) EUROCRYPT 2010. LNCS, vol. 6110, pp. 44–61. Springer, Heidelberg (2010)
4. Harrison, O., Waldron, J.: Efficient Acceleration of Asymmetric Cryptography on Graphics Hardware. In: Preneel, B. (ed.) AFRICACRYPT 2009. LNCS, vol. 5580, pp. 350–367. Springer, Heidelberg (2009)
5. Katz, J., Sahai, A., Waters, B.: Predicate Encryption Supporting Disjunctions, Polynomial Equations, and Inner Products. In: Smart, N.P. (ed.) EUROCRYPT 2008. LNCS, vol. 4965, pp. 146–162. Springer, Heidelberg (2008)
6. Kawamura, S., Koike, M., Sano, F., Shimbo, A.: Cox-Rower Architecture for Fast Parallel Montgomery Multiplication. In: Preneel, B. (ed.) EUROCRYPT 2000. LNCS, vol. 1807, pp. 523–538. Springer, Heidelberg (2000)
7. Lewko, A., Okamoto, T., Sahai, A., Takashima, K., Waters, B.: Fully Secure Functional Encryption: Attribute-Based Encryption and (Hierarchical) Inner Product Encryption. In: Gilbert, H. (ed.) EUROCRYPT 2010. LNCS, vol. 6110, pp. 62–91. Springer, Heidelberg (2010)
8. Meiklejohn, S., Shacham, H., Freeman, D.: Limitations on Transformations from Composite-Order to Prime-Order Groups: The Case of Round-Optimal Blind Signatures. In: Abe, M. (ed.) ASIACRYPT 2010. LNCS, vol. 6477, pp. 519–538. Springer, Heidelberg (2010)
9. PBC Library. The pairing-based cryptography library, http://crypto.stanford.edu/pbc/
10. Szerwinski, R., Güneysu, T.: Exploiting the Power of GPUs for Asymmetric Cryptography. In: Oswald, E., Rohatgi, P. (eds.) CHES 2008. LNCS, vol. 5154, pp. 79–99. Springer, Heidelberg (2008)
11. Zhang, Y., Xue, C.J., Wong, D.S., Mamoulis, N., Yiu, S.: Acceleration of composite order bilinear pairing on graphics hardware. Full Version

# Evaluating the Effect of Tolerance on Click-Draw Based Graphical Password Scheme

Yuxin Meng[1] and Wenjuan Li[2]

[1] Department of Computer Science,
City University of Hong Kong, Hong Kong, China
`yuxinmeng@ieee.org`
[2] Computer Science Division, Zhaoqing Foreign Language College,
Guangdong, China,
`wenjuan.anastatia@gmail.com`

**Abstract.** To enhance graphical passwords, we have developed a system of click-draw based graphical password scheme (named CD-GPS) that combined current graphical password techniques and evaluated its performance with human users. In real settings, we identify that the effect of tolerance is a key factor affecting the usability of our scheme, however, we have not explored its specific effect in our previous work. In this paper, we therefore conduct a user study to investigate the effect of tolerance on creating and confirming the click-draw based graphical passwords. In particular, we conduct two experiments with totally 60 participants in the user study. The results show that accurate memory and reproduction for the CD-GPS scheme can be significantly reduced when the tolerance is greatly decreased (e.g., $12 \times 12$ pixels). In the end, we further discuss how to select an appropriate tolerance for the scheme of CD-GPS in real deployment.

**Keywords:** Graphical Password, Authentication, Usable Security, Click Draw, Tolerance Evaluation, Human Factors.

## 1 Introduction

User authentication is the process to verify whether a user is allowed to access to a particular system or resource. Traditionally, alphanumeric passwords (or called *text-based passwords*) is a widely used method in authenticating users, however, the alphanumeric passwords have some drawbacks with regard to both usability and security [1,2]. For instance, currently, a secure text-based password should be 8 characters or longer, random with upper-case, lower case characters and special characters. This kind of passwords is meaningless and it is hard for human users to remember so that users are more likely to choose simple and short password instead [1]. These usability problems can be translated directly into security problems [3].

To mitigate the drawbacks of the alphanumeric passwords, graphical passwords have been proposed as an alternative to the text-based passwords. The psychology studies [4,6] showed that human brain was better at remembering and recognizing images than text. Moreover, several studies [8,5] also reported positive results that users were

T.W. Chim and T.H. Yuen (Eds.): ICICS 2012, LNCS 7618, pp. 349–356, 2012.

able to remember their graphical passwords accurately after long periods of time. Generally, graphical passwords can be classified into three categories in terms of the input types [15]: click-based graphical passwords, choice-based graphical passwords and draw-based graphical passwords. The click-based graphical passwords (e.g., [9], [11]) require a user to click on an object or element of an image, the choice-based graphical passwords (e.g., [12], [13]) require a user to select a group of images in an ordered sequence, and the draw-based graphical passwords (e.g., [16], [20]) require a user to draw some secrets on an image for authentication.

However, there are still some intrinsic limitations regarding to each category of the above graphical password schemes (e.g., 'hot-spot' issue [17]). Relevant security studies about graphical passwords can be found in [7], [14] and [19]. In our previous work [10], we proposed and developed a click-draw based graphical password scheme (called *CD-GPS*) with the purpose of better enhancing the graphical passwords by combining the above three techniques. In real applications, we notice that the effect of tolerance is a key factor affecting the usability of the scheme.

In this paper, we therefore conduct another user study to investigate the effect of tolerance on creating and confirming the *CD-GPS* passwords. In the scheme of *CD-GPS*, with different values of $N$, an image can be divided into different tolerance sizes. In particular, we performed two experiments with totally 60 participants. By analyzing the experimental results, we find that accurate memory and reproduction for the scheme of *CD-GPS* can be significantly reduced when the tolerance size is greatly decreased. For a pixel tolerance of about $12 \times 12$ (the corresponding value of $N$ is 32), it is extremely hard for users to reproduce their graphical passwords accurately since a lot of click errors are occurred. Based on the results of user study, we point out that an appropriate value of $N$ should be smaller than 32.

The rest of this paper is organized as follows: in Section 2, we introduce background information of the *CD-GPS* scheme; Section 3 details our experimental methodology; the user study and relevant results are described in Section 4; finally, Section 5 concludes our work.

## 2    Background

In our previous work [10], we proposed and developed a prototype of click-draw based graphical password scheme (called *CD-GPS*) aiming to better enhance the graphical passwords in both usability and security. There are mainly two steps in the scheme: *image selection* and *secret drawing*.

Generally, in the first step of *image selection*, users are required to select some images from an image pool in a story ordered sequence. Story memorization can help users to better remember their selected images and ordered sequence [12]. Then, users are required to further select one or several images for drawing their secrets. In the step of *secret drawing*, the *CD-GPS* scheme divides an image into a $N \times N$ table with appropriate pixel tolerance. Users are required to click-draw their secrets, that is, using a series of clicks to construct their secrets (e.g., a digital number, a letter).

In our developed example system, the image pool contains 10 everyday images (e.g., images of cartoon characters, images of landscape, etc).

**Table 1.** The values of $N$ and the relevant smallest tolerance sizes

| Value of $N$ | Tolerance size (pixel) | Size in $cm^2$ |
|---|---|---|
| 20 | $18.75 \times 18.75$ | 0.45 |
| 24 | $15.6 \times 15.6$ | 0.39 |
| 32 | $11.7 \times 11.7$ | 0.27 |

- In the first step, users are required to select 4 images out of the image pool and remember the sequence like a story, then users should further choose 1 image for click-drawing their secrets.
- In the following step, the example system set $N = 16$ and divided an image into a $16 \times 16$ table with 256 clickable squares. Thus, the smallest pixel tolerance is $23 \times 23$. Users can click-draw their secrets by clicking a series of clickable squares within the $16 \times 16$ table.

The previous user study showed that participants preferred our scheme with respect to both security and usability, and satisfied with this pixel tolerance of $23 \times 23$ with a high success rate of creation, confirmation and login respectively.

## 3  User Study

In this section, we first introduce several tolerance sizes that are evaluated in the user study and we then give an in-depth description of the experimental methodology.

### 3.1  Tolerance Size

The example system used in this user study is the same as in [10] so that all the images have the pixel size of $500 \times 375$. As described above, the system will divide an image into a $N \times N$ table in the step of *secret drawing* (the system used a technique of floating tolerance in balancing the table). Thus, the value of $N$ can greatly affect the tolerance size of a clickable square. For instance, in our previous work, we set $N = 16$, therefore, the pixel size of the smallest clickable square of an image is $23 \times 23$. Our previous user study showed that participants were comfortable with this tolerance size.

In the user study, referred to the work [18], we set $N$ to three different values such as 20, 24 and 32. In general, a bigger value of $N$ means a smaller tolerance size of clickable squares. The values of $N$ and corresponding tolerance sizes are described in Table 1. Three values of $N$ (e.g., 20, 24 and 32) are selected because they are respectively increased by one-quarter, one-half and one compared to the value of 16 that we used in our previous work. With the increase of $N$, the pixel tolerance is respectively decreased to $18.75 \times 18.75$, $15.6 \times 15.6$ and $11.7 \times 11.7$.

### 3.2  Experimental Methodology

We conducted an in-lab user study which consisted of two experiments (named *Experiment1* and *Experiment2*) with totally 60 participants those who were interested in our

**Table 2.** Participants' information in the two experiments respectively

| Demographic | Male | Female |
|---|---|---|
| *Experiment1* | 12 | 8 |
| *Experiment2* | 23 | 17 |

work. All participants are university students with diverse backgrounds (e.g., 20 under-graduate and 40 graduate students) and 20 participants (8 females and 12 males) joined our previous studies. In total, 25 participants are female while the remaining 35 partic-ipants are male. In addition, 28 of them are from the department of computer science (not security related major) and the others are from other science and management ma-jors. All the participants are regular computer and web users, and ranged in age from 19 to 35 years.

Before the experiments, we gave an in-depth description of the *CD-GPS* scheme, introduced our objectives of the user study and showed them how to use the example system. Each participant could finish 2 practice trials to get familiar with the example system before the real trials. To investigate the effect of tolerance on creating and con-firming the click-draw based graphical passwords, we divided the participants into two experiments as below:

- *Experiment1*: This experiment involved 20 participants (by means of random selec-tion) and only required all participants to click-draw their secrets on the same image (an image of cartoon characters that was very popular in our previous study). Each participant should create and confirm up to 5 *CD-GPS* passwords corresponding to the three tolerance sizes respectively.
- *Experiment2*: This experiment involved the remaining 40 participants and all these participants were required to regularly use the two steps (image selection and se-cret drawing) to create and confirm their *CD-GPS* passwords. Similar to the *Ex-periment1*, each participant should complete 5 *CD-GPS* passwords for the three tolerance sizes respectively.

The detailed participants' information is shown in Table 2. For the *Experiment1*, we at-tempt to explore the effect of tolerance to users on creating and confirming their graph-ical passwords on the same image. On the other hand, in the *Experiment2*, we aim to investigate the effect of tolerance on the regular use of the *CD-GPS* scheme and identify the minimum affordable pixel tolerance.

For each experiment, we later gave a set of questions to all participants and collected their feedback about the tolerance sizes. Ten-point Likert scales were used in each question where 1-score indicates strong disagreement and 10-score indicates strong agreement. We denoted 5-score as the statement "It is hard to say" for a participant.

## 4   Results and Analysis

In this section, we describe the results of the two experiments (*Experiment1* and *Exper-iment2*) and analyze the participants' feedback.

**Table 3.** The success rate of *CD-GPS* creation and confirmation in the *Experiment1* for the three tolerance sizes

| Success Rate | 18.75 × 18.75 pixels | 15.6 × 15.6 pixels | 11.7 × 11.7 pixels |
|:---:|:---:|:---:|:---:|
| Creation | 88/100 (88%) | 80/100 (80%) | 73/100 (73%) |
| Confirmation | 85/100 (85%) | 75/100 (75%) | 65/100 (65%) |

**Table 4.** Several questions and relevant scores in the *Experiment1*

| Questions | Score (average) |
|:---|:---:|
| 1. I could easily create a password with the pixel tolerance of 18.75 × 18.75 | 8.5 |
| 2. I could easily create a password with the pixel tolerance of 15.6 × 15.6 | 8.0 |
| 3. I could easily create a password with the pixel tolerance of 11.7 × 11.7 | 7.1 |
| 4. I could easily confirm my password with the pixel tolerance of 18.75 × 18.75 | 8.5 |
| 5. I could easily confirm my password with the pixel tolerance of 15.6 × 15.6 | 7.8 |
| 6. I could easily confirm my password with the pixel tolerance of 11.7 × 11.7 | 7.1 |

## 4.1 Experiment1

In this experiment, each participant should create and confirm 5 *CD-GPS* passwords. Totally 100 trails have been recorded during the experiment. The success rates for these two phases are shown in Table 3. The success rate in the phase of *Creation* means that participants created their passwords without restarting while the success rate in the phase of *Confirmation* means that participants confirmed their passwords without restarting and failed attempts. In Table 3, it is easily visible that the success rate is greatly dropped down with the decrease of the tolerance size (i.e., from 88% to 73% in the phase of *Creation*, from 85% to 65% in the phase of *Confirmation*). The main reason is that by reducing the tolerance sizes, participants were hard to accurately remember and reproduce their secrets. For instance, click errors could be significantly increased.

After the experiment, we gave relevant questions to participants and collected their feedback. The questions and average scores are presented in Table 4. The average scores are simply average values calculated by the feedback of all participants. In Table 4, it is easily visible that participants were satisfied with the pixel tolerance of 18.75 × 18.75 since the questions of No.1 and No.4 received a high average score of 8.5 respectively. With regard to the other two tolerance sizes of 15.6 × 15.6 and 11.7 × 11.7, the average scores were greatly decreased. During the experiment, most participants reflected that they considered the pixel tolerance of 15.6 × 15.6 was still fine but it was very difficult for them to use the CD-GPS scheme if the pixel tolerance was only 11.7 × 11.7. Therefore, the experimental results show that by increasing the value of $N$, users could suffer from the problem of drawing reproduction especially when the pixel tolerance is decreased to 11.7 × 11.7.

## 4.2 Experiment2

The *Experiment2* involved the remaining 40 participants and each participant should complete 5 *CD-GPS* passwords. Each trial contains two phases: *Creation* and *Confirmation*. In this experiment, we attempt to investigate the effect of tolerance on affecting the regular use of *CD-GPS*.

**Table 5.** The success rate of *CD-GPS* creation and confirmation in the *Experiment2* for the three tolerance sizes

| Success Rate | $18.75 \times 18.75$ pixels | $15.6 \times 15.6$ pixels | $11.7 \times 11.7$ pixels |
|---|---|---|---|
| *Creation* | 188/200 (94.0%) | 173/200 (86.5%) | 156/200 (78.0%) |
| *Confirmation* | 179/200 (89.5%) | 166/200 (83.0%) | 140/200 (70.0%) |

**Table 6.** Several questions and relevant scores in the *Experiment2*

| Questions | Score (average) |
|---|---|
| 1. I could easily create and confirm a password in the tolerance of $18.75 \times 18.75$. | 8.3 |
| 2. I could easily create and confirm a password in the tolerance of $15.6 \times 15.6$. | 7.2 |
| 3. I could easily create and confirm a password in the tolerance of $11.7 \times 11.7$. | 6.5 |
| 4. I prefer the pixel tolerance of $18.75 \times 18.75$ in CD-GPS scheme. | 9.4 |
| 5. I prefer the pixel tolerance of $15.6 \times 15.6$ in CD-GPS scheme. | 8.2 |
| 6. I prefer the pixel tolerance of $11.7 \times 11.7$ in CD-GPS scheme. | 5.7 |

Up to 200 trials have been recorded during this experiment. The success rates for these two phases are shown in Table 5. It is easily visible that participants can achieve a high success rate (94% for the phase of *Creation* and 89.5% for the phase of *Confirmation*) with the pixel tolerance of $18.75 \times 18.75$. The same as the *Experiment1*, the success rate was quickly decreased when the pixel tolerance was reduced to $15.6 \times 15.6$ and especially to $11.7 \times 11.7$. For the pixel tolerance of $11.7 \times 11.7$, the succuss rates were only 78% and 70% for the phases of Creation and Confirmation respectively. Most patricians indicated that it was very difficult for them to click on the correct clickable squares with the pixel tolerance of $11.7 \times 11.7$ so that many click errors were occurred. These click errors cost most participants a lot of time in click-drawing their secrets again, which was unaffordable for a regular user.

After the experiment, we also gave relevant questions to all participants and collected their feedback. The questions and average scores are described in Table 6. For the No.1 question, the average score of 8.3 showed that most participants were satisfied with the pixel tolerance of $18.75 \times 18.75$. The scores of the No.2 question was 7.2 while the No.3 question only obtained a score of 6.5 which indicated that the pixel tolerance of $11.7 \times 11.7$ was not suitable in real deployment.

By comparing the scores in the No.4, No.5 and No.6 questions, we can find that most participants preferred the pixel tolerance of $18.75 \times 18.75$ (obtaining a very high score of 9.4) in that they can easily and accurately create and confirm their *CD-GPS* passwords. In addition, participants also gave a score of 8.2 for the No.5 question which indicated that they felt the pixel tolerance of $15.6 \times 15.6$ was still affordable in actual application. The low score of 5.7 for the No.6 question showed that the pixel tolerance of $11.7 \times 11.7$ was not appropriate in real settings.

On the whole, the experimental results indicate that the value of $N$ should be smaller than 32. The usability of *CD-GPS* scheme will be greatly reduced when using a small pixel tolerance of around $11.7 \times 11.7$.

## 4.3   Discussion

Based on the two experiments, we can find that determining an appropriate value of $N$ in the *CD-GPS* scheme is very crucial. To select an appropriate value, we should make a balance between usability and security.

*Usability.* This factor is very important according to our experimental results. In addition, some previous work [3,18] has shown that a lot of usability problems tended to translate directly into security problems. Therefore, in the scheme of *CD-GPS*, we should first ensure that users can use the scheme comfortably. For a comfortable and convenient graphical password scheme, users are more likely to create more secure passwords. The above two experiments showed that it was not comfortable to users if the value of $N$ reached 32, so that a smaller value of $N$ (i.e., smaller than 32) should be used in real settings.

This is another important factor for a graphical password. By safeguarding the usability, a more secure graphical password scheme is desirable. In terms of our previous work [10], the password space of the *CD-GPS* scheme can be greatly enlarged by increasing the value of $N$. Take $N = 16$ as an example, the password space of *CD-GPS* is $5.34 \times 10^{18}$ with 6 clicks on the selected image, which is very larger than the text-based passwords with 8 characters over a 64-character alphabet (the password space is $2.81 \times 10^{14}$). The calculation of the password space can be referred to our previous work [10]. Therefore, we believe that the value $N$ of 16, 20 and 24 can provide large enough password space in real settings.

Overall, the value of $N$ should be smaller than 32 and can be selected according to the specific work environment. For example, if a very high security level is desirable (i.e., in a bank), we can select the value of $N$ to 24. On the other hand, in a regular environment, we can choose the value of $N$ to 16 or 20.

## 5   Concluding Remarks

In this paper, we mainly attempt to investigate the effect of tolerance on creating and confirming the click-draw based graphical passwords. We conducted two experiments (*Experiment1* and *Experiment2*) with totally 60 participants. From the experimental results, we find that accurate memory and reproduction for the scheme of *CD-GPS* can be significantly reduced when the pixel tolerance is greatly decreased (e.g., $11.7 \times 11.7$ pixels). With this small tolerance size, users cannot accurately click on the right clickable squares. By balancing both usability and security, we find that an appropriate value of $N$ should be smaller than 32. The value of 16, 20 and 24 can all provide suitable properties in the aspect of both usability and security.

Our work is mainly conducted by means of the click-draw based graphical password scheme. Future work could include conducting another user study with larger and more varied participants to validate our results, and exploring more specific values of $N$. In addition, future work could also include investigating the effect of tolerance on other click-related graphical password schemes and identifying the relationships.

**Acknowledgments.** We thank all the participants for their hard work in our user study and all anonymous reviewers for their valuable comments.

# References

1. Brown, A.S., Bracken, E., Zoccoli, S., Douglas, K.: Generating and Remembering Passwords. Applied Cognitive Psychology 18, 641–651 (2004)
2. Yan, J., Blackwell, A., Anderson, R., Grant, A.: Password Memorability and Security: Empirical Results. IEEE Security and Privacy Magazine 2(5), 25–31 (2004)
3. Klein, D.: Foiling the Cracker; A Survey of, and Improvements to Unix Password Security. In: Proceedings of the USENIX Security Workshop, pp. 83–86 (1990)
4. Shepard, R.N.: Recognition Memory for Words, Sentences, and Pictures. Journal of Verbal Learning and Verbal Behavior 6, 156–163 (1967)
5. De Angeli, A., Coventry, L., Johnson, G., Renaud, K.: Is a Picutre Really Worth a Thousand Words? Reflecting on the Usability of Graphcial Authentication Systems. International Journal of Human Computer Studeies 63(2), 128–152 (2005)
6. Nelson, D.L., Reed, U.S., Walling, J.R.: Picture Superiority Effect. Journal of Experimental Psychology: Human Learning and Memory 3, 485–497 (1977)
7. Gołofit, K.: Click Passwords Under Investigation. In: Biskup, J., López, J. (eds.) ESORICS 2007. LNCS, vol. 4734, pp. 343–358. Springer, Heidelberg (2007)
8. Paivio, A., Rogers, T.B., Smythe, P.C.: Why are Pictures Easier to Recall than Words? Psychonomic Science 11(4), 137–138 (1976)
9. Blonder, G.E.: Graphical Passwords. United States Paten 5559961 (1996)
10. Meng, Y.: Designing Click-Draw based Graphical Password Scheme for Better Authentication. In: Proceedings of 7th IEEE International Conference on Networking, Architecture, and Storage (NAS 2012), pp. 39–48 (2012)
11. Wiedenbeck, S., Waters, J., Birget, J.C., Brodskiy, A., Memon, N.: PassPoints: Design and Longitudinal Evaluation of a Graphical Password System. International Journal of Human-Computer Studies 63, 102–127 (2005)
12. Davis, D., Monrose, F., Reiter, M.K.: On User Choice in Graphical Password Schemes. In: Proceedings of USENIX Security Symposium, pp. 151–164. USENIX Association, Berkeley (2004)
13. Passfaces (accessed by May 20, 2012), http://www.realuser.com/
14. Nali, D., Thorpe, J.: Analyzing User Choice in Graphical Passwords. Technical Report. Careton University (2004)
15. Jali, M., Furnell, S., Dowland, P.: Quantifying the Effect of Graphical Password Guidelines for Better Security. In: Camenisch, J., Fischer-Hübner, S., Murayama, Y., Portmann, A., Rieder, C. (eds.) SEC 2011. IFIP AICT, vol. 354, pp. 80–91. Springer, Heidelberg (2011)
16. Jermyn, I., Mayer, A., Monrose, F., Reiter, M.K., Rubin, A.D.: The Design and Analysis of Graphical Passwords. In: Proceedings of USENIX Security Symposium, pp. 1–14. USENIX Association, Berkeley (1999)
17. Thorpe, J., van Oorschot, P.C.: Human-Seeded Attacks and Exploiting Hot-Spots in Graphical Passwords. In: Proceedings of 16th USENIX Security Symposium, pp. 1–16. USENIX Association, Berkeley (2007)
18. Wiedenbeck, S., Birget, J.C., Brodskiy, A., Memon, N.: Authentication using Graphical Passwords: Effects of Tolerance and Image Choice. In: Proceedings of Symposium on Usability Privacy and Security (SOUPS), pp. 1–12 (2005)
19. Dirik, A.E., Memon, N., Birget, J.C.: Modelling User Choice in the Passpoints Graphical Password Scheme. In: Proceedings of Symposium on Usability Privacy and Security (SOUPS), pp. 20–28 (2007)
20. Dunphy, P., Yan, J.: Do Background Images Improve "Draw A Secret" Graphical Passwords? In: Proceedings of ACM Conference on Computer and Communiation Security (CCS), pp. 36–47 (2007)

# Robust Evidence Detection of Copy-Rotate-Move Forgery in Image Based on Singular Value Decomposition

Liu Yong[1,2], Huang Meishan[1,2], and Lin Bogang[1,2]

[1] College of Mathematics and Computer Science of Fuzhou University, Fuzhou, 350108, China
[2] Key Lab of Information Security of Network Systems, Fuzhou, 350108, China
{553761346,562444526}@qq.com, linbg95@163.com

**Abstract.** Region Copy-Move forgery, in which a part of the image is copied and then pasted to another part of the same image. Some important goals and sensitive objects can be hidden imperceptibly; this forgery is at the rather important position in a variety of forensic technology research. But the literatures published merely are confined without geometric distortion. And some algorithms focus on the special forgery's model. In order to improve the accuracy of the current algorithms, a new detection is proposed by constructing the circles rather than the traditional ways which were based on the square. The seven characterizes are constructed according to singular value decomposition. Using main rotation angle based on the radial moment and the proportion of constraint remove the error mark. Finally the dictionary-ordering method is applied to save the time-consuming. The experiment shows that this newly characteristic can locate the area where was tampered.

**Keywords:** Blind image forensics, Rotation invariant, Singular value decomposition, Radial moment, Copy-Rotate-Move Forgery.

## 1    Introduction

With the wide application of powerful digital image processing software, such as Photoshop .It has been becoming easier to create forgeries from one or more images. The effective algorithm must be researched and applied to judge whether the image has been modified. Meanwhile the current researches focus on the passive authentication, which also called blind forensic, is the method to make authentication without any help of the auxiliary information.

In recent years, some scholars have started to develop passive techniques for detecting various methods of image forgeries. Fridrich proposed several statistical methods for detecting forgeries based on pattern noise of cameras' sensor[1,2] Popecu and Farid presented method based on color filter interpolation and re-sampling[3,4]. Luo gave a proper model for region-duplication forgery, where the seven features are calculated for four basic constraints of region-duplication forgery, including two connectivity regions and two un-intersection regions [5].

The methods mentioned above have a limitation, when the copy region is rotated, the manner choosing square image blocks will fail because of dislocation. We propose a

T.W. Chim and T.H. Yuen (Eds.): ICICS 2012, LNCS 7618, pp. 357–364, 2012.

new manner matching the blocks based on the circle. Singular value decomposition is used to extract the image blocks' characteristic.

The rest of the paper is organized as follows. In section 2, the new forgery model is introduced. The mechanism of feature extraction and the detection method are presented in detail in Section 3. In section 4, some experimental results and the corresponding analysis is presented. Finally, we concluded in Section 5.

## 2    Proposed Model

It is known that we can hardly find the two same parts in one natural image. However when the regions-rotate-duplication happened, two or more similar parts must be existed, although it hardly is seen by naked eyes.

Before the model is given, two hypotheses are introduced in advance.

1. The copy region must be the no-holes and connected.
2. The copy region and paste region have no public set, and their Euclidean distance also is greater than the certain value.
3. The model of Copy-rotate-duplication is given as follows

$$F(x, y) = \begin{cases} I(x, y) & (x, y) \notin R_c \\ T(I(x - \Delta x, y - \Delta y)) * h(x, y) + n(x, y) & (x - \Delta x, y - \Delta y) \notin R_o \end{cases} \tag{1}$$

Here, T denotes the transform matrix of copy regions, $(\Delta x, \Delta y)$ denotes the translation value, $h$ denotes the fuzzy operation and fuzzy core, and $n$ is the noise and other operations. Our aim is to search the $R_c$ and $R_o$ in one image.

## 3    Proposed Detection Scheme

### 3.1    Preprocessing

Gaussian pyramid is a common decomposition way often used in image processing, the technique involves creating a series of mage which are weighted down using a Gaussian average and scaled down, when the technique is used multiple times. it creates a stack of successively smaller images, with each pixel containing a local average that corresponds to a pixel neighborhood on a lower level of the pyramid. Fig 2 gives the illustration about Gaussian pyramid decomposition.

Let the original image be $I_0$, which is taken as the zero level, the $I_i$ level image of Gaussian pyramid can be obtained by making the $I_{i-1}$ level image convoluted by a window function $w(m, n)$ with low-pass characteristics, and doing the down sampling after the convolution. The process can be described as:

$$I_i = \sum_{i=-w}^{i=w} \sum_{j=-w}^{j=w} w(m,n) I_{i-1}(2*w+m, 2*w+n) \tag{2}$$

Here, the window function w is also called the weight function or generation kernel, whose size is usually chosen as $5*5$. The Gaussian pyramid decomposition can reduce the complexity of the detection algorithm.

## 3.2   Definition and Characteristics of SVD

Definition: $A_{m*n}$ is a matrix (assume $m \geq n$), the matrix $U_{m*n}$, $V_{m*n}$ and diagonal matrix $\Im_{m*n}$ can satisfies the following equation. $A = U\Im V^T$, where $\Im = diag(\lambda_1, \lambda_2, \ldots, \lambda_k, 0, 0, 0).(\lambda_1 \geq \lambda_2 \geq \ldots \geq \lambda_k)$, $U = (U_1, U_2, \ldots, U_m)$, $V = (V_1, V_2, \ldots, V_m)$ and $\lambda_i^2 (i = 1, 2, \ldots k)$ is the Eigen values of the matrix $AA^T$ and $A^T A$, $\lambda_i$ is called the singular of $A$. For any real matrix $A$, $\lambda_1 \geq \lambda_2 \geq \ldots \geq \lambda_k$. In singular value decomposition, diagonal matrix $\Im_{m*n}$ is unique.

**Proposition 1:** Assume that there are two real matrixes $A_{m*n}, B_{m*n} \in R^{m*n}$, their singular values are $\lambda_i' \geq \lambda_2' \geq \ldots \geq \lambda_n', \lambda_1'' \geq \lambda_2'' \geq \ldots \geq \lambda_n''$ respectively, for any unitarily invariant norm on $R^{m*n}$ satisfies

$$\|diag(\lambda_1'' - \lambda_1', \lambda_2'' - \lambda_2', \ldots, \lambda_n'' - \lambda_n')\| \leq \|B - A\| \tag{3}$$

Because singular value has a good stability, it is not sensitive to noise and lighting condition for grayscale change.

**Proposition 2:** For element orthogonal matrix, such as $Q = I - 2VV^T$, where $I$ denotes the unit matrix, $V$ is a real vector, whose length is 1 and dimensions is $n$. For rotate operation, the rotation transform matrix can decompose multiplication with two orthogonal matrixes. For the real matrix $A$, rotating it means that $A*P$, P is an orthogonal matrix.

$$(PA)(PA)^T = p(AA^T)P^T \tag{4}$$

Where $P^T = P^{-1}$, because $AA^T$ and $P(AA^T)P^T$ have a same Eigen values. Therefore we can say the singular value is robust for rotation.

**Proposition 3:** Translation is equivalent to replacing two rows or columns, exchanging the $ith$, $jth$ of matrix means multiplying the following matrix on the left of A,

$$I_{i,j} = I - (e_i - e_j)(e_i - e_j)^T \tag{5}$$

Where $e_i$ and $e_j$ denote the $ith$ and $jth$ rows of matrix respectively. After translation, A became $I_{i,j}A$, meanwhile $I^T_{i,j} = I_{i,j} = I^T_{j,i}$. The characteristic equation of matrix $((I_{i,j})A(I_{i,j}A)^T)$ is as following:

$$\left| (I_{i,j}A)(I_{i,j}A)^T - \lambda I \right| = 0 \qquad (6)$$

$\left| I_{i,j}AA^T I^T_{i,j} - \lambda I \right| = \left| I_{i,j} \right| \times \left| AA^T - \lambda I_{i,j} I^T_{i,j} \right| \times \left| I_{i,j} \right| = \left| AA^T - \lambda I \right|$。 We can conclude that singular value is also robust for translation. Singular value decomposition possesses some variances on algebra and geometry. It not only provides a theoretical basis of image as an algebraic feature, but also for the copy-rotate-duplication detection.

### 3.3    Rotation Estimation Based on the Radial Moment

In copy-duplication detection, copy region and paste region have the same translation direction, many papers proposed several methods based on the main translation vector. While In copy-rotate-duplication detection, those methods almost failed. In this paper, according to the fact that the blocks in paste region have the same rotate parameters relative to the copy region, calculating the rotate parameter using the radial moment. Definition of radial moment:

$$\psi(k,p,q,l) = \int_{r=0}^{\infty} \int_{\theta=0}^{2\pi} r^k \cos^p \theta \sin^q \theta e^{il\theta} g(r,\theta) dr d\theta \qquad (7)$$

where $(r,\theta)$ denotes polar coordinates of image pixels, $g(r,\theta)$ presents the distribution of brightness in image. $k,p,q,l$ must be integers, and $p,q$ are non-negative.

Assume $\alpha$ is the angle of rotation of image and $s$ is the scale factor, the polar coordinates will be:

$$r' = s*r, \theta' = \theta + \alpha \qquad (8)$$

The raw image and rotated image meet:

$$\psi'_{k,d} = s^{k+l} e^{ikd} \psi_{k,d} \qquad (9)$$

While in computing, $s = 1$, We can easily get the information about rotation parameter.

### 3.4    Forgery Detection

Firstly, the doubtful image is decomposed by Gaussian pyramid, and the produced sub-image is in low frequency is chosen to overcome the possible distortion. Then the sub-image is divided into many circle blocks overlapping each other, the features of singular values are extracted from the circle blocks, used as the matching features. The dictionary sort is applied to reduce complexity of researching space. We use a main rotation angle to remove the mistaking blocks. Finally the morphology is used to fill the hole-regions. Area radio is helpful to improve the accurate of algorithm. The detailed steps of algorithm are as follows:

1. Note regarding color images: In both Extra and Robust Match, if the analyzed image is a color image, before proceeding with further analysis, it is first converted to a gray image using the standard formula $I = 0.299R + 0.587G + 0.114B$, where $I_{m*n}$ denotes the image, its size is $m * n$.

2. The image $I'_{a*b}$ is decomposed by Gaussian pyramid, $a = \lfloor m/2^i \rfloor b = \lfloor n/2^i \rfloor i = 1,2,.., \min(\lfloor \log 2^m \rfloor \lfloor \log 2^n \rfloor)$.

Suppose the size of the slider window is $r * r$. In actual detection, the size of forgery area is usually bigger than windows' size, considering the time-consuming and accuracy of algorithm. The step of slider windows is $r/2$, the numbers of blocks are $N = (2a/r - 1) * (2b/r - 1)$.

3.The features are extracted by singular value decomposition of each image block, and the singular value vector is construct, which is denoted by $X = (x_1, x_2, \ldots x_r)$.

4. The all eigenvectors are stored in the matrix A, and the rows of A are lexicographically sorted as before. Then we compute the similarity of the two neighboring Eigenvectors. It can be measured by the Euclidean distance $d_{i,j}$.

$$d_{i,j} = \sqrt{\frac{\sum_{k=0}^{n} (x_{ik} - x_{jk})^2}{n}} \tag{10}$$

$x_{ik}, x_{jk}$ denotes the different eigenvectors respectively, and $n$ is the dimension of the eigenvector.

5. According to the experience threshold. $d_{opt}$ Thus, the algorithm also looks at the mutual positions of each block pair and outputs a specific block pair only if there are many other matching pairs in the same mutual position (the have the same rotate angle). Towards this goal ,if consecutive rows are found, the algorithm stores the positions of the matching blocks in a separate list(for example, the coordinates of the upper left pixel of a block can be taken as its position)and increments a rotation angle counter $C$ ,the rotation angle $\theta$ between the two matching blocks is calculated by the radial moment. Then round $\theta$ to the integer and compute $sum(\theta) = sum(\theta) + 1$. The main rotate angle must be the maximum value of $sum$ in all angles, calibrate the neighboring image blocks which meet the above conditions. Finally the holes doubtful region is filled by morphology, such as dilate and erosion.

6. Compute the area of each the connected region, all the regions is sorted by the size of the regions, the result is denoted by $S$, where $S = (s_1, s_2, \ldots, s_N)$, $N$ is a number of regions. We calculate the radio of two consecutive regions.

$$\rho_i = \frac{s_i}{s_{i+1}} \tag{11}$$

The copy-rotate-duplication must be hold below condition: $\exists \rho_k, \forall \rho_l, \rho_k < \rho_l, k \neq l, k, l \in (1, N)$, where $k$ is the index of the copy-rotate-duplication region.

# 4 Experimental Results

## 4.1 Effectiveness of Algorithm

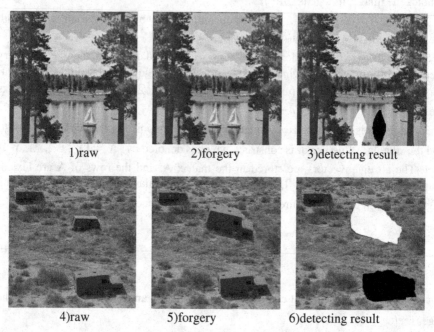

Fig. 1. Detection result of Copy Move Forgery regions

In the first part of this section, we apply the method to several examples. An experimental version of the proposed method was implemented in Matlab. Here test images have resolution of 512*512. Parameters of the method were set $r = 8$, $d = 1.25$, $N = 7$. In all experiments, the mean of additive Gaussian noise is zero and intensity levels are in the range $0 - 255$. The raw images are shown in Fig 1 1(row) and 4(row) respectively. The respective forgery images are shown in Fig 1 2(forgery) and 5(forgery). Outcomes of the method are shown in Fig 1 3(detecting result) and 6(detecting result).

## 4.2 Comparison with Relative Literatures

Compared to [1, 3, 6], the proposed method uses a more information about rotation. Proposed approaches literatures are not robust for the rotation operation. Meanwhile, the larger number of image blocks need more time and memory.

Table 1 show that our method proposed a new detection algorithm based on the Gaussian pyramid decomposition and singular value decomposition. The radial moment also plays a very important role in the proposed method, the main rotation angle

**Table 1.** Comparison result of reference' approaches with proposed approaches

| algorithm | Eigenvectors | Number blocks | dimension | rotation |
|---|---|---|---|---|
| Fridrich | DCT&quantizet ion | 255025 | 64 | no |
| Farid | PCA | 255025 | 32 | no |
| Wu q | DWT&SVD | 62001 | 8 | no |
| Our method | GPD&SVD | 3969 | 7 | yes |

firstly used to remove the mismatch blocks. Thanks to the important characteristic of singular value decomposition, it provides a theoretical basis of image as algebraic features. Meanwhile its uniqueness and stability also provide a theoretical basis for the copy-rotate-duplication detection. Experiment shows that the proposed method is robust for additive Gaussian noise and retouching, locating the forgery regions accurately.

# 5    Conclusion

Our proposed does not work well in the copy-scale-duplication cases. All the literatures based on the overlapping blocks hardly detect this forgery. In recent days, a method called SIFT and its improved versions have been introduced to detect this forgery [7, 8, 9, 10], which base on the pixels matching. While this method still has some faults since not all forgery regions are full of feature points and eigenvectors have high dimensions, and the process of matching need much more time. In addition, the image segment and region growing will be applied .These also increase the difficulty of detection. Facing the various forgery methods, it is hard to detect with one or two methods, we must depend on the synthesized method. Our future work is to focus on the new detection for copy-scale-duplication.

# Reference

[1]  Fridrich, A.J., Soukal, B.D., Mukluks, A.J.: Detection of Copy-Move forgery in digital images. In: Proceedings of Digital Forensic Research Workshop, pp. 5–8 (August 2003)

[2]  Lukas, J., Fridrich, Goljan, M.: Digital camera identification from sensor pattern noise. IEEE Transaction on Information Forensics and Security 1(2), 205–214 (2005)

[3]  Popescu, A.C., Farid, H.: Exposing digital forgeries in color filter array interpolated images. IEEE Transaction on Signal Processing 53(10), 3948–3959 (2005)

[4]  Popescu, A.C., Farid: Exposing digital forgeries by detecting duplicated image regions. Department of Computer Science, Dartmouth College, Technical Report TR 2004-515, Dartmouth College, USA (2004)

[5]  Luo, W.Q.: Robust Detection of region duplication forgery in digital image. In: Conf.-pattern Recognition, ICPR 2006, pp. 746–749 (2006)

[6] Wu, Q.: Detection of Copy Forgery Regions in the Image Based on Wavelet and Singular Value Decomposition. Journal of Chinese Computer Systems 4(29), 730–733 (2008)

[7] Lian, S.G., Zhang, Y.: Multimedia forensics for detection forgeries. In: Peter, S., Mark, S. (eds.) Handbook on Communications and Information Security, pp. 801–820. Springer (2010)

[8] Ye, S.M.: Detecting digital image forgeries by measuring inconsistencies of blocking artifact. In: Conf. Multimedia and Expo., pp. 12–15. IEEE Internet (2007)

[9] Pan, Y.P.: Detecting image region duplication using SIFT features. In: Conf-acoustics Speech and Signal Processing, pp. 1706–1709 (2010)

[10] Irene, A.: Geometric tampering estimation by means of a SIFT-based forensic analysis. In: Conf-acoustics Speech and Signal Processing, pp. 1702–1705 (2010)

# Cookie-Proxy:
# A Scheme to Prevent SSLStrip Attack

Sendong Zhao[1,*], Ding Wang[1], Sicheng Zhao[2], Wu Yang[1], and Chunguang Ma[1]

[1] College of Computer Science and Technology, Harbin Engineering University,
Harbin City 150001, China
[2] School of Computer Science and Technology, Harbin Institute of Technology,
Harbin City 150001, China
zhaosendong@hotmail.com

**Abstract.** A new Man-in-the-Middle (MitM) attack called SSLStrip poses a serious threat to the security of secure socket layer protocol. Although some researchers have presented some schemes to resist such attack, until now there is still no practical countermeasure. To withstand SSLStrip attack, in this paper we propose a scheme named Cookie-Proxy, including a secure cookie protocol and a new topology structure. The topology structure is composed of a proxy pattern and a reverse proxy pattern. Experiment results and formal security proof using SVO logic show that our scheme is effective to prevent SSLStrip attack. Besides, our scheme spends little extra time cost and little extra communication cost comparing with previous secure cookie protocols.

**Keywords:** Secure Cookie Protocol, MitM, Defending against SSLStrip, SSL, Proxy Pattern, SVO logic.

## 1 Introduction

Recently, a new Man-in-the-Middle (MitM) attack called SSLStrip [1] is introduced at the Blackhat conference by Moxie Marlinspike in 2009. It attacks secure socket layer protocol, the most widely applied security mechanism which makes secure communication established between two parties over the Internet. Most seriously, this attack exploits user's browsing habits, rather than a technical pitfall in the protocol, to strongly defeat the SSL security. At a high level, the SSLStrip allows adversaries to insert themselves in the middle of a valid SSL connection. The user believes that they have a true SSL connection established, while the adversary has the ability to view the user's Web traffic in clear-text [1].

Owing to the serious damage of SSLStrip attack, some computer science researchers have paid much attention to prevent SSLStrip attack. Nick Nikiforakis *et al.* [2] presented a method to avoid the SSLStrip attack using browser's history information. A scheme with cue information is proposed by Shin and Lopes [3], which relies on web user's active exploration. Fung and Cheung [4] put forward a

---

* Corresponding author.

T.W. Chim and T.H. Yuen (Eds.): ICICS 2012, LNCS 7618, pp. 365–372, 2012.

defending mechanism based on JavaScript code. Nevertheless, these suggestions only indicate ways to avoid a SSLStrip attack but not how to actively stop it. The cookie is a technical means to keep HTTP connection state, and it also can be used to save user's information [5]. When users relink the same Web server, browser will read the cookie information and send it to the Web site. Thus, the cookie should have the capability to check whether the HTTP connection is secure or not. Therefore, the cookie can be utilized to defend against SSLStrip attack. Some researchers have put forward some secure cookie protocols. Fu *et al.* [6] proposed a Web authentication scheme which mainly uses secure cookie as an authentication token. It uses cookie to store the authentication token with client. However, it has the following three flaws: it does not provide a high-level confidentiality; cookie replay attacks can be easily implemented on it; it is inefficient and non-scalable to defend against volume attacks. To overcome these weaknesses, Liu *et al.* [7] proposed a secure cookie protocol by improving Fu's scheme. Pujolle *et al.* [8] put forward a secure cookie protocol which implements a reverse proxy patterns [9]. Unluckily, these secure cookie protocols are both vulnerable to SSLStrip attack.

The remainder of this paper is organized as follows: In section 2, we propose a new scheme to prevent SSLStrip attack, followed by relative experiment, performance analysis, formal security analysis and comparison with previous schemes in section 3. Conclusion and the future work are discussed in section 4.

## 2   The Proposed Cookie-Proxy Scheme

In this section we propose a new scheme to defend against SSLStrip named Cookie-Proxy, including a secure cookie protocol and a new topology structure using a proxy pattern and a reverse proxy pattern [9]. To the best of our knowledge, this is the first time to defend against SSLStrip using secure cookie protocol. The notations of this paper are explained in Table 1.

**Table 1.** Notation

| Symbol | Description |
|--------|-------------|
| $sk$ | Server Key of SSGP |
| $h(\bullet)$ | Hash function |
| $E_{key}(M)$ | Encrypt M using key $key$ |
| $Sig_{key}(M)$ | Sign M using key $key$ |
| $HMAC_{key}(M)$ | Keyed-hash message authentication code of M with key $key$ |
| $\|$ | String concatenation operation |

### 2.1   A New Topology Structure

The topology structure mainly contains a secure LAN guaranteed proxy (SLGP) and a secure server guaranteed proxy (SSGP), as shown in Fig. 1. It is clear to see that SLGP and SSGP are implemented on the gateway of client LAN and server Ethernet, respectively. To facilitate presentation, we assume that the LAN of clients is a secure LAN, which means that there are no attacks such as ARP spoofing attack, DNS spoofing attack and so on. This assumption can guarantee the absolute security of the client LAN.

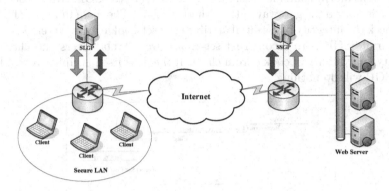

**Fig. 1.** The topology of our scheme

## 2.2    Our Secure Cookie Protocol

The secure cookie protocol shown in Table 2 is implemented between SLGP and SSGP. The cookie protocol implemented between the client and the server is still the commonly used cookie protocol [10]. The SLGP and the SSGP reconstruct commonly used cookie protocol and get the new form shown in Table 2. Recall that $ks$ denoting the private key of SSGP for signature. $SN$ denotes secure note of cookie, whose value is either 'Secure' or 'Unsecure'. $ESN=Sig_{ks}(h(SN \parallel CID))$. $CID$ is a random digit for each cookie. $k=HMAC_{sk}(username\|expires)$. $HMAC_k=HMAC_k(username\|expires\|data\|CID\|SN)$.

**Table 2.** Our secure cookie protocol

| Set-cookie Header | | | | | | | |
|---|---|---|---|---|---|---|---|
| username | expires | $E_k(data)$ | $SN$ | $CID$ | $ESN$ | $HMAC_k$ | optional |
| **Cookie Header** | | | | | | | |
| username | expires | $E_k(data)$ | | $SN$ | | $HMAC_k$ | optional |

In our secure cookie protocol, there are some new attributes comparing with Liu's secure cookie protocol. $SN$ denotes whether the HTTP connection is on SSL protocol (HTTPS) or not. If the value of $SN$ is 'Secure', the connection is on SSL protocol and vice versa. The client browser will not upload cookie to the server as a request if the value of $SN$ is secure and the protocol type of request URL is not HTTPS. The server will not return a login web page [10]. If the SSLStrip forges a login web page to SLGP, the SLGP will find and drop it. As a result, the client must send a request again. $ESN$ is the signature of $h(SN \parallel CID)$ using private key $ks$.

## 2.3   The Mechanism of Cookie-Proxy Scheme

On client-side, the data from outside of the secure LAN is sent to SLGP. After processing, the data is sent to the gateway of the LAN again. On server-side, the data from inside and outside of server Ethernet is sent to SSGP. After processing, the data is sent to the gateway of the Ethernet again. The main function of SLGP is to check the integrity of essential attributes of set-cookie from server. The main function of SSGP is to reconstruct set-cookie from Web servers and check the integrity and validity of cookie from client. If the data itself is cipher-text, SLGP and SSGP will do nothing.

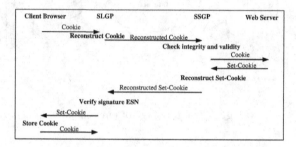

**Fig. 2.** The mechanism of Cookie-Proxy Scheme

According to Fig. 2, the operating mechanism of our scheme can be summarized as follows:

**Step 1.** Client sends request to server.

**Step 2.** SSGP receives cookie and checks its integrity and validity. Then, SSGP reconstructs the cookie and sends it to server.

**Step 3.** Server receives the request data and generates a set-cookie. Then send it to SSGP.

**Step 4.** SSGP reconstructs the set-cookie. Then send the modified set-cookie to client-side again.

**Step 5.** SLGP receives set-cookie and verifies the signature $ESN$. If the signature is not valid, drop the packet.

**Step 6.** SLGP send the set-cookie to client. The client receives the set-cookie and stores it in disk or RAM.

**Step 7.** Client sends request again with a new cookie.

**Step 8.** Go to Step 2.

In the above mechanism, SLGP should check whether set-cookie has $SN$ or not. If not, SLGP drops this response packet. SLGP applies public key of SSGP to $SN$ as a signature verification key verifies $ESN$ as the message signed with the corresponding private key $ks$ if the value of field $SN$ is 'Unsecure'. If the signature is not valid, the response packet will be dropped.

Our scheme is composed of a secure cookie protocol, a SLGP and a SSGP. In order to achieve adequate security, all the components of our secure scheme are indispensable.

## 3    Experiment and Analysis

In this section, we analyze Cookie-Proxy scheme with an experiment and a formal proof, and then evaluate our scheme with other relevant schemes.

### 3.1    Experiment

In experiment, we utilize at least four computers and two routers to build our experimental platform, shown in Fig.1. Four computers are used as client, web server, SSLGP and SSGP respectively and two routers are deployed on client LAN and server LAN. Procedures running on client, SLGP and SSGP are based on the processes discussed in section 2. An adversary as a MitM can be of any computer in the Internet between SLGP and SSGP in Fig.1. Therefore, a computer is deployed between SLGP and SSGP to simulate the SSLStrip. The procedure running on simulated SSLStrip is in accordance with the process shown in Fig.3.

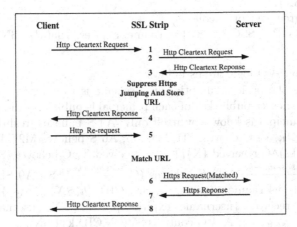

**Fig. 3.** The attack process of SSLStrip as MitM between client and server

To evaluate our scheme, five groups of experiment are conducted separately. On client-side, we use IE, FireFox, Oprea, Safari and Chrome as Web browser successively. The result of our scheme defending against SSLStrip attack is that our scheme can defend against SSLStrip attack effectively in all the five browsers.

### 3.2    Performance Analysis

Two HAMC operations and one verifying signature operation are added to our scheme, compared with traditional cookie protocols. HAMC operation is a kind of hash operation and the verifying signature operation is a modular exponentiation operation. The extra time of our scheme is composed of the consumption of two hash operations, a modular exponentiation operation and two symmetric cryptographic operations. In the process of protocol interaction, no extra

data transmission consumption is added to our scheme compared with traditional cookie protocol. Therefore, the total extra cost incurred by our scheme is
$0.385(0.273 + 2 \times 0.026 + 2 \times 0.03)$ms according to [11]. Although our scheme
needs some extra time, it improves the security when using HTTPS.

### 3.3 Security Analysis

In this section we present a formal analysis of the security properties of our
new scheme, including the following five services: authentication, confidentiality,
integrity, anti-replay and anti-SSLStrip attack. The SVO logic [12] analysis of
our scheme is as follows:

**M1:** $C \to$ SLGP$\to$ SSGP$\to$ S: $C_i$
**M2:** S$\to$ SSGP: username, expires, data, SN
**M3:** SSGP$\to$ SLGP: username, expires,$\{data\}_k$, SN, $[h(SN)]_{ks^{-1}}$,$\{$username,
   expires, data, SN$\}_k$
**M4:** SLGP$\to$ C: username, expires,$\{data\}_k$, SN, $\{$username, expires,
   data, SN$\}_k$
**M5:** Key agreement protocol
**M6:** C$\to$ SLGP$\to$ SSGP$\to$ S: $\{$username, expires, $\{data\}_k$, SN, $\{$username,
   expires, data , SN$\}_k\}_{session-key}$

The premises of SVO logic are as follows:

A1 indicates the basic assumption, the scheme is running in unsecure environment; A2 indicates public key of each principal is public; A3 indicates private
key of each principal is known by itself only; A4 S believes fresh(k); A5 S believes fresh(CID); A5 C control M1/M4/M5; A6 S believes M2/M4/M6; A7 C
believes PK(S,ks)∧C received $\{X\}_{ks^{-1}}$∧C received X⊃C believes (S said X); A8
C believes (C$\xleftarrow{session-key}$ S), S believes (C$\xleftarrow{session-key}$ S); A9 SLGP believes
SLGP received $\{$username, expires, $*_1$, SN, CID, $[h(SN)]_{ks^{-1}},*_2\}$; A10 SSGP
believes SSGP received $\{$username, expires, $\{data\}_k$, SN, $\{$username, expires,
data , SN$\}_k \}_{session-key}$; A11 C controls SV(SN|CID,ks,ESN).

The goals are as follows:

**G1:** S believes (C said (username, expires, data)∧S believes (username, ex-
   pires, data)) By A5, A10, A8, MP
**G2:** S believes C says (username, expires, data) By A10, A8, A6, A4,Ax3,
   Nec, MP
**G3:** C believe S says SN By A9, A11, A5, MP

Authentication: In our scheme, the server can get the cookie from client, in which
every field is the original value by using detection of SSGP. So the server can
authenticate the client exactly. Obviously, the set-cookie reconstructed by SSGP
is hardly to forge. G1 denotes the authentication of our scheme. Above all, the
server can verify the validity of the client easily and accurately.

Confidentiality: In our scheme, SSGP encrypts data field in set-cookie. By
this way, the data is invisible to client. Thus, the confidentiality is provided in
our new scheme.

Integrity: If adversaries have modified the field $SN$ of set-cookie from server or deleted this set-cookie fields, SLGP will check the integrity of domain items, and verify signature $ESN$. If there are any abnormalities, SLGP will drop the whole response packet. The goal G3 ensures this process.

Anti-replay: Obviously, in our scheme each cookie has its unique HMAC. If an adversary replays a cookie as a request to the server, SSGP will detect it and drop it. Also, G2 denotes the anti-repay of our scheme.

Anti-SSLStrip: The core of SSLStrip attack is to make users not recognize what the connection should be, HTTP or HTTPS. Nevertheless, our secure cookie protocol has mandatory fields: $SN$ and $ESN$. The SLGP will check these fields, so the client will definitely know what the connection should be. For this reason, our scheme can defend SSLStrip attack. Also, the goal G3 ensures that MitM cannot modify the field $SN$.

### 3.4   Comparison of Relevant Cookie Protocols

In this section, we compare our scheme with the other relevant cookie protocols. Without loss of generality, the digit fields are all recommended to be 128-bit long, while the string fields are all 1024-bit long in protocols. Let $T_H$, $T_E$, $T_I$ and $T_S$ denote the time complexity for hash function, exponential operation, inverse operation and symmetric cryptographic operation. Typically, time complexity associated with these operations can be roughly expressed as $T_E \approx T_I > T_S \geqslant T_H$ [11].

**Table 3.** Comparison with relevant schemes

| Item | Ours | Fu *et al.* [6] | Liu *et al.* [7] | Pujolle *et al.* [8] |
|------|------|------|------|------|
| Extra time cost | $T_E + 2T_H + 2T_S$ | $T_H$ | $2T_H + 2T_S$ | $2T_H + 6T_S$ |
| Extra communication cost | 2560 bit | 256 bit | 2304 bit | 2432 bit |
| Authentication | Yes | Yes | Yes | Yes |
| Confidentiality | Yes | No | Yes | No |
| Integrity | Yes | No | No | No |
| Anti-replay | Yes | No | Yes | Yes |
| Anti-SSLStrip | Yes | No | No | No |

From Table 3, we can conclude that our scheme spends not so much extra time cost and extra communication cost, but it gets the ability of withstanding SSLStrip attack and the integrity of protocol comparing with other cookie protocols.

## 4   Conclusion

Our contributions in this paper are twofold. Firstly, we elaborate on the drawbacks of state-of-the-art secure cookie protocols. Secondly, we present a Cookie-Proxy scheme to defend against SSLStrip attack. The evaluation shows the effectiveness of our scheme. However, due to the serious damage of SSLStrip attack, the cost of resisting against this attack is inevitably high. In the future, we will focus on improving the deploy-ability of our scheme and reducing security requirement of client LAN.

**Acknowledgement.** This paper is funded by the International Exchange Program of Harbin Engineering University for Innovation-oriented Talents Cultivation.

# References

1. Callegati, F., Cerroni, W., Ramilli, M.: Man-in-the-middle attack to the https protocol. IEEE Security Privacy 7(1), 78–81 (2009)
2. Nikiforakis, N., Younan, Y., Joosen, W.: HProxy: Client-Side Detection of SSL Stripping Attacks. In: Kreibich, C., Jahnke, M. (eds.) DIMVA 2010. LNCS, vol. 6201, pp. 200–218. Springer, Heidelberg (2010)
3. Shin, D., Lopes, R.: An empirical study of visual security cues to prevent the sslstripping attack. In: Proceedings of the 27th Annual Computer Security Applications Conference, ACSAC 2011, pp. 287–296. ACM, New York (2011)
4. Fung, A.P.H., Cheung, K.W.: Sslock: sustaining the trust on entities brought by ssl. In: Proceedings of the 5th ACM Symposium on Information, Computer and Communications Security, ASIACCS 2010, pp. 204–213. ACM, New York (2010)
5. Liu, A., Kovacs, J., Gouda, M.: A secure cookie scheme. Computer Networks 56(6), 1723–1730 (2012)
6. Fu, K., Sit, E., Smith, K., Feamster, N.: Dos and donts of client authentication on the web. In: Proceedings of the 10th Conference on USENIX Security Symposium, SSYM 2001, vol. 10, pp. 19–35. USENIX Association, Berkeley (2001)
7. Liu, A., Kovacs, J., Huang, C.T., Gouda, M.: A secure cookie protocol. In: Proceeding of 14th International Conference on Computer Communications and Networks, ICCCN 2005, pp. 333–338 (October 2005)
8. Pujolle, G., Serhrouchni, A., Ayadi, I.: Secure session management with cookies. In: Processing of 7th International Conference on Information, Communications and Signal, ICICS 2009, pp. 1–6 (December 2009)
9. Sommerlad, P.: Reverse proxy patterns. In: European Conference on Pattern Languages of Programming, EuroPLoP 2003 (2003)
10. Barth, A.: HTTP State Management Mechanism, IETF Internet-Draft (2010), https://datatracker.ietf.org/doc/draft-ietf-httpstate-cookie/
11. Wang, D., Ma, C., Weng, C., Jia, C.: Cryptanalysis and Improvement of a Remote User Authentication Scheme for Resource-Limited Environment. Journal of Electronics & Information Technology (in press, 2012)
12. Syverson, P., Van Oorschot, P.: A unified cryptographic protocol logic. Technical report, DTIC Document (1996)

# Detecting and Preventing ActiveX API-Misuse Vulnerabilities in Internet Explorer⋆

Ting Dai, Sai Sathyanarayan, Roland H.C. Yap, and Zhenkai Liang

School of Computing
National University of Singapore
{daiting,sathya,ryap,liangzk}@comp.nus.edu.sg

**Abstract.** ActiveX is used to build reusable software components in Microsoft Windows. It is widely used by many Windows applications, such as Internet Explorer and Microsoft Office. As general-purpose components, ActiveX controls expose methods to applications, which may be used in ways unexpected by the ActiveX designer, leading to malicious activities. We call such misuse of ActiveX methods – *ActiveX API misuse vulnerabilities*. In this paper, we present a solution which identifies and prevents API misuse of ActiveX controls in Internet Explorer. We construct models to represent normal functionality of ActiveX methods, and identify ActiveX API misuse by identifying the methods that can reach dangerous (system) APIs. We then develop a technique for Internet Explorer to prevent the use of dangerous ActiveX methods. We evaluated our approach on six real-world ActiveX controls. We are able to identify and prevent ActiveX API misuse in these controls. Our approach is effective in detecting ActiveX API misuse and has negligible overhead for preventing attacks.

## 1 Introduction

ActiveX is Microsoft technology to build reusable software components on the Microsoft Windows platform. It is widely used by many Windows applications, including Microsoft Office, Windows Media Player, and Internet Explorer (IE), allowing the applications to use the functionality embedded in ActiveX controls. IE allows methods in ActiveX controls to be accessed from web pages. ActiveX controls in IE are native binaries running with the same privilege of the IE process, thus giving web pages the ability to run native code in the operating system.[1]

Since ActiveX controls are general-purpose components, they often contain more functionality than what is needed by the applications using them. The methods of an ActiveX control may be used in unintended ways. For example, the Snapshot Viewer ActiveX control (installed with Microsoft Office) can be leveraged by malicious web pages in IE to create or overwrite files. Due to the complexity of the Windows system, even if users are aware of the functionality of such ActiveX controls, they may not be able to foresee how the functionality is used. We call this class of vulnerabilities *API*

---

⋆ This work has been supported by a DRTech grant R-394-000-054-232.

[1] The Windows Update ActiveX Control in Windows XP and Visual Studio (Windows 7) uses IE to apply Microsoft updates.

T.W. Chim and T.H. Yuen (Eds.): ICICS 2012, LNCS 7618, pp. 373–380, 2012.
© Springer-Verlag Berlin Heidelberg 2012

```
<script language='JavaScript'>
//Create Activex Object with ProgID
var obj = new ActiveXObject("snpvw.Snapshot Viewer Control.1");
// invoke method SnapshotPath, CompressedPath, ...
obj.SnapshotPath = "c:\\TestSnapshot.snp";
obj.CompressedPath = "c:\\TestSnapshot-compressed.snp";
obj.PrintSnapshot("True");
</script>
```

**Fig. 1.** A JavaScript code snippet using Microsoft Office Snapshot Viewer ActiveX Control in IE

*misuse*: an API of a software component, such as ActiveX, is misused by programs in ways unexpected by the API designer. We remark that this class of attacks is caused by misuse of an API rather than a case of misused user authority as in the confused-deputy problem.

Existing ActiveX security mechanisms are insufficient to prevent API-misuse attacks. IE's ActiveX security is based on trust. IE trusts ActiveX controls installed locally in the Windows system, except those blocked by compatibility flags in the registry (*killbits*). For remote ActiveX controls, the user provides a white list of trusted sites and permit remote ActiveX control from the white list. For untrusted ActiveX controls, IE asks the user for permission to use the control. In addition, IE implicitly trusts the control as it only initializes and utilizes the ActiveX interfaces where the *Safe for Initialization* and *Safe for Scripting* properties are implemented by the control. Once vulnerability in an ActiveX control is known, the typical solution is to completely block it but that means that all the functionality performed by the control in IE is lost.

In this paper, we develop a solution to identify and prevent API-misuse vulnerabilities in ActiveX controls. Our approach consists of an offline detection phase and an online prevention phase with proxy-based filtering. In the detection phase, we represent the normal functionality of the ActiveX control in a graph model which gives the reachability of ActiveX methods during program execution. This model is generated through dynamic analysis on standard test cases. We then identify API misuse by analyzing the access paths in the model which lead to dangerous APIs. In the prevention phase, we create a proxy to intercept every ActiveX method invocation in IE and block dangerous ActiveX methods. We are able to identify six real-world documented API-misuse vulnerabilities, of which, three are from Microsoft. Our prevention mechanism has low overheads and blocks dangerous methods while preserving other functionality compared with existing solutions.

## 1.1 A Motivating Example

We show the API misuse problem with a real-world example. The Microsoft Office Snapshot Viewer ActiveX Control is a component of Microsoft Office Access 2003. It is locally installed by default. Thus, is trusted by IE to generate print previews of Office documents.

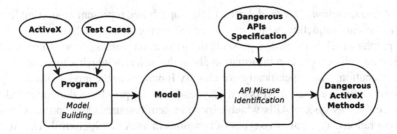

**Fig. 2.** Overview of our approach on API-misuse detection

The SnapshotPath and CompressedPath methods of the ActiveX are to specify the path of the snapshot file to be displayed in the Snapshot Viewer. Fig. 1 shows a typical usage of the control. It renders a print preview of the snapshot file TestSnapshot.snp and also saves the compressed version of the file. This ActiveX control can be exploited to allow an attacker to download remote files to the local file system or overwrite local files. The attacker invokes SnapshotPath with http://malicious.com/payload.exe to silently download the payload and invokes CompressedPath with c:\\clickme.exe to save the malicious payload to the local file system.

Such API misuse vulnerabilities are accomplished through the normal functionality in ActiveX controls. Unlike malware, this type of vulnerability is hard to detect because the program behavior is not malicious by itself. Instead, it is a "misuse" of standard or inherent functionality because of the complexity of the operating systems. Hence, we need a systematic approach to detect API misuse vulnerabilities in ActiveX controls.

## 2    API-Misuse Detection and Prevention

In this section, we describe the design of our approach. Given an ActiveX control, we aim to identify and prevent the API-misuse vulnerability in it. We assume we have the knowledge and test cases performing normal functionality of the ActiveX control. This can be obtained from software examples or software documentation. Vulnerabilities such as memory-error exploits are orthogonal and not in our scope.

### 2.1    ActiveX API-Misuse Vulnerability Detection Phase

In this phase, we identify API-misuse vulnerabilities by building a simple model and analyzing the model as shown in Fig. 2. We first build models to represent the normal functionality of ActiveX methods. This step takes an ActiveX control and test cases invoking the methods in the ActiveX control as the inputs. The output is a model consisting of all function calls in the execution of the program. We analyze the model by searching for a path from ActiveX methods to dangerous APIs. This step takes the model and a dangerous APIs specification as inputs. It outputs a list of vulnerable methods that may result in API misuse.

*Model Representation.* Our model uses a call graph-based representation. A node in the graph represents a function, which may be called during execution. Every directed edge in the graph (which is labeled) represents the invocation from a caller to a callee function. The edge labels contain information about the order, in which a function is called during execution. More specifically, we classify functions in the model into four types. *Dangerous APIs* are a set of APIs that may lead to more privileges than intended for a web page such as system APIs which expose system resources, e.g., process creation or file operations. There are two types of functions in an ActiveX control. The ActiveX functions that are defined as the scriptable interfaces are the exposed APIs in the ActiveX control, which we call *ActiveX methods*. We call the rest of the functions in the ActiveX control as *ActiveX inner functions*. The functions which are neither ActiveX methods, inner functions nor a dangerous APIs are called *other functions*.

The goal of the model is to gather information on the functionality of an ActiveX control and show the APIs an ActiveX method can reach through paths which represent potential sequences of function calls. There are two types of paths to dangerous APIs in the model. A *direct access path* of an ActiveX method $m$ is when function $m$ called from a webpage has a path to a dangerous API. There may be ActiveX inner and other functions along that path, such that $m$ is in the path and there are no ActiveX methods or ActiveX inner functions in the sub-path from root node to $m$. An *indirect access path* through ActiveX inner function $f$ is a path from the root node to dangerous APIs such that $f$ is in the path and there are no ActiveX methods or inner functions in the sub-path from root node to $f$. An example of an indirect access path is as follows, suppose IE calls a callback function $f$ which is an inner function in the ActiveX control, this means that no ActiveX method has been called although an earlier call of some ActiveX method may have returned the address of $f$. In summary, our model defines API-misuse of an ActiveX method $m$ as either a direct access path from $m$ to a dangerous API or an indirect access path from ActiveX inner function $f$ caused by a ActiveX method $m$ (these may be a set).

*Model Building.* The goal of this step is to extract the model of an ActiveX control from execution of several test cases. The test cases are meant to be representative of the normal functionality of an ActiveX control. The model is then extracted by instrumenting the execution of the program (IE) running various (standard) test cases.

Direct access paths are straightforward to detect. The challenge is to correlate an ActiveX method to an indirect access path. We modify the model by adding pseudo edges, once an indirect access path is found at an ActiveX inner function $f$. A conservative approach is to add pseudo edges from every ActiveX method in the corresponding ActiveX control to node $f$. More accurate dynamic or static analysis could be used to reduce the set of pseudo edges from $m$ but such analysis is necessarily conservative. As static or dynamic analysis can be challenging in the multi-threaded Windows environment which also has the possibility of kernel callbacks.[2] Instead, we chose a simple approach which is to add pseudo edges from the ActiveX methods which were executed prior to the indirect access path.

---

[2] Non-local control flow transfers where the Windows kernel calls code in the program, somewhat analogous to signals in Unix but are not due to exceptions.

*API-misuse Identification.* We identify the API misuse in the ActiveX control by searching for access paths in the model. First, we predefine several categories of (system) APIs as dangerous APIs in the model, e.g., file, process creation and library loading APIs. These system APIs allow access to system resources which are normally not exposed to scriptable ActiveX interfaces in IE. ActiveX methods which can have API misuse are found by checking whether an access path exists from the ActiveX methods in the test cases to the dangerous APIs.

## 2.2  Proxy-Based ActiveX API-Misuse Vulnerability Prevention Phase

To prevent API misuse vulnerability in ActiveX interfaces, we propose a fine-grained proxy-based solution blocking only dangerous ActiveX methods rather than the whole control. We intercept every ActiveX method invocation in the browser and reject any invocation of methods in a blacklist at run time. This blacklist is either generated by our detection phase or defined by users. Rejected methods raise an E_ACCESSDENIED exception, i.e. *General Access Denied* exception used in Windows to block access to certain functionality. The advantage of the exception mechanism is that it does not affect the use of other methods in the browser, thus, the user can still interact with a webpage in IE using ActiveX controls as long as dangerous methods are not needed. Additional policies can allow specified trusted webpages to still use methods in the blacklist.

# 3  Implementation

We have prototyped our approach on Microsoft Windows XP SP2. Our API-misuse detection tool is a PIN tool [1] to collect the function call/return control flow which is then subsequently analyzed to build the model and find API-misuse paths.

In order to track control flow in the program executable and ActiveX binaries which are dynamically loaded, we instrument all binaries during execution. Our PIN tool is an adaptation from [2], which keeps track of how function call and return control flow happens during execution.

To make it more efficient to search for the ActiveX method corresponding to an indirect access path, we use a testing strategy which tests one ActiveX method at the time where possible. This assumes that there is a causal relationship between the single ActiveX method $m$ and any inner function $f$ found in an indirect access path. This can be extended to allow more than one ActiveX method in the test case, in which case, the assumption becomes more relaxed since the causal relation may or may not hold.

In some cases, an ActiveX method can expose objects of another ActiveX to IE, giving a web page the complete access to all methods in the exposed control. This is a more dangerous type of API misuse which is similar to dynamic library loading. To identify this type of API misuse, we apply heuristics to analyze the library loaded by an ActiveX method to identify whether an ActiveX method controls which library to load by specifying an argument – this is a form of data dependency checking.

**Table 1.** Number of methods with critical access paths in six ActiveX controls

| ActiveX Controls | Total methods | file operation | library loading | process creation | access paths |
|---|---|---|---|---|---|
| MS ADODB Stream | 26 | 2 | 0 | 0 | 2 |
| MS RDS DataSpace | 3 | 0 | 1 | 0 | 1 |
| MS Office Snapshot Viewer | 27 | 2 | 3 | 0 | 3 |
| Chilkat Crypt | 159 | 2 | 1 | 0 | 2 |
| InstallShield Update Service | 14 | 6 | 3 | 3 | 8 |
| Zenturi ProgramChecker | 23 | 9 | 4 | 0 | 9 |

# 4   Evaluation

We evaluated our approach on six real-world ActiveX controls in IE6 SP2: *Microsoft ADODB Stream* (ADODB), *Microsoft RDS DataSpace* (RDS), *Microsoft Office Snapshot Viewer* (Snapshot), *Chilkat Crypt* (Chilkat), *InstallShield Update Service* (Install-Shield) and *Zenturi ProgramChecker* (Zenturi). All ActiveX controls have exploits in the Metasploit framework, and have documented functionality except for InstallShield and Zenturi.

## 4.1   Effectiveness of API-Misuse Vulnerability Detection

Our evaluation uses test cases constructed from user manuals and MSDN library in JavaScript or VBScript for the documented ActiveX controls. For the two ActiveX controls without documentation, we created simple test cases where the parameters to ActiveX methods are initialized to fixed values according to their type. We defined the following three types of dangerous APIs in our evaluation: file operations (NtCreateFile and NtWriteFile), process creation (NtCreateProcessEx), and library loading (LoadLibraryExW).

Table 1 shows the results of testing the ActiveX controls. For each control, we list the total number of the exposed methods and number of the exposed methods that have API-misuse access paths found. The access paths are further broken down according to whether they involve file, library or process APIs. Some methods may have multiple access paths, so totaling the number of access paths in individual categories may exceed the total number of methods with access paths. We were successful in detecting API misuses in all six controls which have known API-misuse vulnerabilities and exploits in Metasploit. We identified 25 access paths in total of which seven are indirect access paths which employ callbacks. We now discuss three representative cases in our evaluation.

The Snapshot Viewer ActiveX Control has 27 methods that are available to IE. The generated model has 4963 nodes. We identified three methods have access paths to the system APIs. The SnapshotPath and CompressedPath methods specify the path to the snapshot file to be displayed in the Snapshot Viewer. We found both have access paths to NtCreateFile and NtWriteFile with a local or remote URL as the Path. With a local URL, CompressedPath has a direct access path to NtCreateFile and NtWriteFile. With a remote URL, SnapshotPath has an indirect access path to the same APIs and we identified the callback functions used in the indirect access path. Other than file operations, `PrintSnapshot` together with the previous methods also has a direct access path to `LoadLibraryExW`.

For the ADODB Stream ActiveX control, we found two methods have direct access paths to `NtCreateFile`: (i) the `SaveToFile` method saves the binary contents of a *Stream* object to a file; and (ii) `LoadFromFile` loads the contents of an existing file into a *Stream* object. We detected the API-misuse vulnerability with the `SaveToFile` method, which has the same direct access path as in the Metasploit sample attack. In Windows, `NtCreateFile` is required to open a file, so `LoadFromFile` is a false positive.

For the RDS DataSpace ActiveX Control, we found that the `CreateObject` method can load any library and create the object registered in the local system through access paths to `LoadLibraryExW`. In the sample exploit, `CreateObject` is used to create objects, from other disabled vulnerable ActiveX controls in IE. It is interesting that this attack bypasses the checking mechanism for preventing certain ActiveX controls from being loaded in IE. The newly created vulnerable object can be further exploited to achieve remote code execution. This exploit has the same access path to `LoadLibraryExW` found in the test case we analyzed. This is also the vulnerability reported in Microsoft advisory `MS06-014` where the killbit checking of IE is bypassed to allow a blocked library to load.

### 4.2   Performance Evaluation

To evaluate detection performance, we selected 27 test cases from Office Snapshot Viewer ActiveX control. Each method is tested separately in a new IE process. The total time for testing with instrumentation is 1174 seconds (43.5 seconds/test case). The total time for building the model and checking for API-misuse access paths is 264 seconds (9.8 seconds/test case). Although our prototype is not an optimized implementation, it already offers reasonable performance for off-line dynamic analysis.

Our proxy-based prevention mechanism is effective and efficient with negligible overhead. In fact, we target methods that are not in our blacklist with 12 test cases from three ActiveX controls. The overheads range from 0.01% to 1.7%.

## 5   Related Work

Existing work in ActiveX security mainly focus on memory vulnerabilities in ActiveX controls. Dromann and Plakosh [3] proposed an automated fuzzing system to detect security flaws in ActiveX controls. Its target is memory-related vulnerabilities, instead of API-misuse vulnerabilities. Song et al. [4] proposed an approach to detect malicious exploitation of vulnerable ActiveX controls to prevent drive-by download attacks. The prototype prevention is integrated into IE with ActiveX hooking, using similar techniques as our proxy to block dangerous methods in ActiveX controls.

On a broader problem domain, there are solutions to detect attacks using system-level attack graphs generated by dynamic analysis. For example, Backtracker [5] identifies the files or processes that cause an attack through dependencies between these files and processes in a system-level dependency graph. As another example, Martignoni et al. [6] perform data-flow analysis to identify high-level actions from system calls.

Our approach is also related to solutions to detect security vulnerabilities using model checking. Schneider [7] proposed security automata for defining security properties and prevent the illegal actions in the system. MOPS [8] detect attacks by checking the reachability of a state that violates the desired security goal in a model. Both Sheyner et al. [9] and Jha et al. [10] construct attack graphs for model checking to detect safety violation in the system.

## 6    Conclusion

In this paper, we present a system to detect and prevent ActiveX API misuse vulnerabilities in IE. Our system detects potential ActiveX API misuse in an ActiveX control used by IE. Our method can also be easily adapted to other applications using ActiveX. We also provide a prevention mechanism which blocks the use of dangerous ActiveX methods. The results are promising, as we are able to detect all API misuse vulnerabilities in the six real-world ActiveX controls and can block the vulnerable ActiveX methods. The cost of the detection is reasonable and the overhead of the prevention mechanism is negligible.

## References

1. Luk, C., Cohn, R., Muth, R., Patil, H., Klauser, A., Lowney, G., Wallace, S., Reddi, V., Hazelwood, K.: Pin: Building Customized Program Analysis Tools with Dynamic Instrumentation. In: ACM SIGPLAN Conf. on Programming Language Design and Implementation, pp. 190–200 (2005)
2. Wu, Y., Yap, R., Ramnath, R.: Comprehending Module Dependencies and Sharing. In: ACM/IEEE Intl. Conf. on Software Engineering, pp. 89–98 (2010)
3. Dormann, W., Plakosh, D.: Vulnerability Detection in ActiveX Controls through Automated Fuzz Testing (2008), http://www.cert.org/archive/pdf/dranzer.pdf
4. Song, C., Zhuge, J., Han, X., Ye, Z.: Preventing Drive-by Download via Inter-Module Communication Monitoring. In: ACM Symp. on Information, Computer and Communications Security, pp. 124–134 (2010)
5. King, S., Chen, P.: Backtracking Intrusions. ACM Trans. on Computer Systems 23(1), 51–76 (2005)
6. Martignoni, L., Stinson, E., Fredrikson, M., Jha, S., Mitchell, J.: A Layered Architecture for Detecting Malicious Behaviors. In: Lippmann, R., Kirda, E., Trachtenberg, A. (eds.) RAID 2008. LNCS, vol. 5230, pp. 78–97. Springer, Heidelberg (2008)
7. Schneider, F.: Enforceable Security Policies. ACM Trans. on Information and System Security 3(1), 30–50 (2000)
8. Chen, H., Wagner, D.: MOPS: an Infrastructure for Examining Security Properties of Software. In: ACM Conf. on Computer and Communications Security, pp. 235–244 (2002)
9. Sheyner, O., Haines, J., Jha, S., Lippmann, R., Wing, J.: Automated Generation and Analysis of Attack Graphs. In: IEEE Symp. on Security and Privacy, pp. 273–284 (2002)
10. Jha, S., Sheyner, O., Wing, J.: Two Formal Analyses of Attack Graphs. In: IEEE Computer Security Foundations Workshop, pp. 49–63 (2002)

# Endpoint Mitigation of DDoS Attacks
# Based on Dynamic Thresholding

Daewon Kim, Byoungkoo Kim, Ikkyun Kim, Jeongnyeo Kim, and Hyunsook Cho

Cyber Convergence Security Research Department
Electronics and Telecommunications Research Institute
218 Gajeong-ro, Yuseong-gu, Daejeon, 305-700, Korea
{dwkim77,bkkim05,ikkim21,jnkim,hscho}@etri.re.kr

**Abstract.** Socially and economically, the distributed denial-of-service (DDoS) attacks have been serious threats in the cyber world. Despite of many researches, current defense methods can be vulnerable to the DDoS attacks of unknown traffic pattern to avoid the methods. That is because most of the defense policies configured for the methods are fixed thresholds that were mainly determined by the learning of traffic volume. To overcome the problem caused by the fixed thresholds, we introduce the endpoint mitigation method based on the dynamic thresholding of DDoS defense policies according to the usage changes of system resources. We focused on the fact that the usage changes of system resources show the abnormal statuses of server if the failure/delay of service is occurred by the DDoS attacks that have not been blocked by current defense thresholds. The proposed method detects the server overload as measuring the usage changes of system resources and automatically adjusts current defense thresholds in conjunction with the strength of usage change. As the result, the service problem caused by the DDoS attacks can be gradually mitigated by the automatic threshold controlling of our method.

**Keywords:** cyber threat, network security, distributed denial-of-service attack, intrusion detection system, intrusion prevention system.

# 1   Introduction

Internet services have been rapidly developed enough to cover most of our lives [1], [2]. However, these important internet services are always exposed to various attacks millions time a day [3]. The recent attacks are mainly focused on financial and political demands [4], [5]. To achieve these goals, the attackers use the distributed denial-of-service (DDoS) attacks with the zombie PCs which have been infected with malicious codes due to security vulnerabilities. Although many researches [6] to enhance security vulnerabilities have been studied, new vulnerabilities are still being discovered and new malwares are still being propagated to infect new zombie PCs. In recent, the DDoS attack that caused extensive damage to South Korea mobilized approximately 150,000 zombie PCs [7].

To prevent the servers from DDoS attacks, various DDoS defense methods have been researched. These works can be divided into the ways to change current network

T.W. Chim and T.H. Yuen (Eds.): ICICS 2012, LNCS 7618, pp. 381–391, 2012.

infrastructure [8], [9] and the ways to maintain the infrastructure [10], [11], [12]. The formers to modify network protocols or network configurations are effective for the defense of DDoS attack. However, the methods are difficult to spread the technology because they need to change current network environments. After all, the latters to maintain current network environments are leading research trends on the defense of DDoS attack. A research trend recently appeared is visualization techniques [14]. However, the techniques have a disadvantage that the information for visualization has to be sampled due to the performance problem.

The researches [10], [11], [12] to maintain current network environments learn the traffic patterns of normal and attack, and configure their defense policies as the differences of analyzed traffic patterns. After that, they compare the measurement result of incoming traffic to the defense policies configured in advance. However, the defense policies with fixed thresholds based on the learned traffic patterns may pass many attack packets if weak policies. On the other hand, if strong policies, the fixed thresholds may block many normal packets. As the reason, current DDoS defense systems cannot arbitrarily apply the strong policies to prepare for new DDoS attacks of the future with unknown traffic patterns. Because of this limitation, new DDoS attacks to circumvent the policies of fixed thresholds will be continuously appeared, and the denials of service by the new attacks will be repeated as well.

In order to solve the problem of defense policy with the fixed threshold, our method monitors the usage changes of server resources such as CPU, memory and network session, and automatically controls current thresholds depending on the strength of usage change whenever the resource usages show abnormal patterns. That is possible because service troubles can be detected with the abnormal usage patterns of server resources. Finally, if any defensive action leads the abnormal usages of server resources to the normal usages, the server service will be stabilized. In the paper, our method gradually and automatically adjusts the fixed thresholds for the defense mechanisms, which are embedded in some security systems, as applying the analysis results of current abnormal resource usages.

The rest of the paper is structured as follows. In Section II, we briefly introduce the overview for the automatic control of DDoS defense thresholds, and Section III describes the detailed operations of our method. In Section IV, the paper introduces the *SecureNIC* which is a FPGA-based network interface card for endpoint DDoS defense and presents the experiment results that our prototype program automatically adjusts the thresholds of defense mechanisms embedded in the *SecureNIC*. Finally, we conclude the paper in Section V.

## 2     The Overview

Fig. 1 shows the operation overview of our method under DDoS attacks. In Fig. 1, (1) when unknown DDoS attacks are incoming into the server via the *SecureNIC*, (2) if the embedded defense mechanisms are applying the policies with wrong thresholds or the *SecureNIC* has not defense mechanisms to detect the new attack traffic patterns, (3) the DDoS attacks flow into the server without some attack detection. (4) The server has service troubles by the attack packets and the service troubles are measured with various server usages such as CPU, memory, and network session. The proposed method analyzes the measured resource usages and (5) depending on the results, the method adjusts current defense thresholds or triggers new defense mechanism being prepared. The prepared defense mechanism means the defense method that is more effective if it is activated only in cases of some special attacks. (6) By the proposed method, next attack packets are gradually blocked through the changes of defense thresholds and the activation of prepared defense mechanism. (7) Finally, the server status is stabilized and the service troubles are disappeared as well.

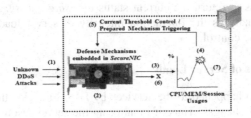

**Fig. 1.** The overview

# 3    Endpoint Mitigation of DDoS Attacks Based on the Dynamic Thresholding

## 3.1    The Types of Server Loads

Fig. 2 shows the typical server loads that can be occurred as time passes. In Fig. 2, the server load means the current usage ratio (%), which is max 100%, of resources that have direct impacts on the server service. In our prototype program, it includes the usage ratios of CPU, memory, and network session. Additionally, as a service-wide, it can include the usage ratios of PPS, BPS, and SYN_RECV for each protocol and port. Large server load means that the values of these usage ratios are high.

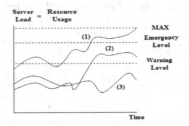

**Fig. 2.** The typical server loads

Like Fig. 2, normal server loads can be classified into the three types of (1) *rising*, (2) *surging*, and (3) *vibrating*. For the classification, the level configuration of resource usage ratios is required. From the perspective of DDoS attacks, the case of *rising* means that the attack transfers a small amount of traffic at a low speed to avoid the threshold policies of DDoS defense mechanisms. On the other hand, the case of *surging* means that the attack transfers a large amount of traffic at a high speed in a short time to paralyze the server with the weak DDoS defense policy. From the perspective of a server, the cases of *rising* and *surging* have a high probability that the service troubles will be occurred and on the other hand, the *vibrating* will be occurred routinely.

Therefore, on the endpoint to mitigate the service troubles caused by DDoS attacks, our method analyzes the changes of server load and detects the cases of *rising* and *surging*. After that, the method automatically controls the thresholds of current defense mechanisms to return the current status of *rising* and *surging* to the normal *vibrating*. It also analyzes the fluctuation intensity of server load to determine the strength of automatic control.

## 3.2    The Analysis of Server Loads

If some troubles are happened to the services by DDoS attacks, the resource usages will show abnormal changes. Thus, if monitoring the server resources, we can determine whether the service troubles are occurred or not. In the paper, based on the fact, the method of paper periodically monitors the resource usage ratios of CPU, memory, and network session to determine whether the services are going smoothly. For example, in the case of TCP web service, for reliable service to users, the service has normally the maximum concurrent TCP session number depending on the performance of server system. As monitoring the current usage ratio of TCP sessions, the method in advance can detect the overload statuses causing service failures.

Excepting for the cases targeting the vulnerable codes of operating system and service program among various DDoS attacks, most of DDoS attacks use the attack techniques with the excessive or irregular service requests to occur the service failures of target server. For example, if the 100 percent utilization of resources is monitored, the service troubles on the server can be detected in advance. Our method periodically monitors the usage ratios of resources and detects the service troubles. Then, the method controls the thresholds of defense policies depending on the change strength of resource usages. Therefore, our method can respond to the new and unknown attacks that are pointed to the shortcomings of existing methods based on the learned traffic volumes.

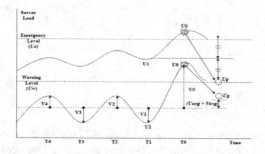

**Fig. 3.** Detection and threshold control

Fig. 3 shows the detection of service troubles depending on the server loads, which are the resource usages. If the resource usages in normal situation exceed the emergency level percentage $Ue$, in general the administrator extends the service performance with the upgrades and replacements of current systems. Therefore, if the service is smoothly dealing with the service requests of normal users, current usage ratio $U0$ will not exceed $Ue$, except for special situations. In contrast, if $U0$ often exceeds $Ue$ by attacks, it means that the server will be out of service soon. Eventually, if $U0$ exceeds $Ue$ as the cases of *rising* and *surging* on the server loads, the adjustments of current defense thresholds will be needed at $T0$. (*Emergency Detection: if $U0 > Ue$*).

On the other hand, if $U0$ exceeds the warning level percentage $Uw$, the additional analysis about usage changes is required to finally determine whether the services has troubles by attacks because this can even occur to normal situations. Our method has individual FIFOs (First-In First-Out) on each resource to save, on every second, the usage ratio $U$ of maximum $n$ number. The average usage ratio $Uavg = \frac{\sum_{i=0}^{i=n-1}|Ui|}{n}$ and the average usage variations $Vavg = \frac{\sum_{i=0}^{i=n-1}|Vi|}{n}$ are calculated for each resource on every period. The *Warning Detection* can determine the *surging* type attack. (*Warning Detection: if $(U0 > Uw)$ and $(U0 > Uavg)$ and $(V0 > Vavg)$*). The reason that current surged $U0$ needs to be compared to $Uavg$ and $Vavg$ is for excluding the surge cases of usage changes that can often happen under normal situations.

### 3.3    The Load Measurement of Internal Processes

In the cases of CPU and Memory, the server overload can be temporarily occurred by the internal processes unrelated to the services for external users. For example, under the condition that the attack traffic does not flow into the server, the server can be overloaded by the programs for server maintenance such as log managements. When adjusting the defense thresholds in this situation, the normal user traffic can be blocked by the *SecureNIC*. To avoid the problem, if the server overload is detected as *Warning* or *Emergency*, it is necessary to determine whether the cause of overload is the internal processes or not.

To do this, our method sorts the processes in descending order of CPU and MEM usages. After that, the decision is given by

$$If \ \frac{\sum_{i}^{Np} Up_i}{U0} > Uint, Not \ Attack \ and \ No \ Threshold \ Control$$

**Where:** $Np$ = the process number to be selected; $Up_i$ = the CPU or MEM usage (%) of $i$-th process; $Uint$ = the set usage to be compared.

### 3.4    The Selection of Defense Threshold to Be Adjusted

If the service troubles occurred by external attack traffic are detected by analyzing the resource usages, the analysis to find the cause of theses troubles is worked to determine how to defend the attacks. By the analysis, our method determines which policies should be adjusted among the defense mechanisms mounted to the *SecureNIC*. The work uses the traffic statistics of each defense mechanism. Each of the defense mechanisms has individual thresholds for blocking the attacks, and the incoming traffic that exceeds the threshold is blocked. As mentioned earlier, if the server overload situation occurs by normal service requests, the administrator will upgrade the system performance. Thus, assuming that the server performance is enough for accepting all normal service requests, if the service troubles happen in situation that each of the defense mechanisms is normally working with each threshold, the reasons of troubles can be consider as three cases.

The first is the case that the service trouble occurs under the situation blocking the attack traffic over the threshold. The second is the case that the service trouble occurs by the attack traffic under the threshold, and the third is the case that the defense mechanism is none for responding the attacks. The point that the resource usage of server is abnormally increasing means that any kinds of traffic volumes are unusually increasing. Therefore, the method of this paper selects the defense mechanism closest to each threshold among traffic statistics related to each defense mechanism and adjusts its threshold stronger. Through this analysis, in the cases of first and second the proposed method can mitigate the service trouble with the adjustment of policy threshold, and in the case of third, the method can activate the prepared defense mechanism.

### 3.5    The Threshold Control for Attack Defense

If the defense mechanism to be adjusted is selected, our method adjusts the threshold for strengthening the attack response. The purpose of threshold adjustment is to stabilize the abnormally overloaded usages through the gradual blocking of specific traffic determined as attacks. The existing defense methods fail to block the attack traffic when the defense threshold was wrong, and the server service may be out of control because there is no time to fundamentally analyze the attack traffic such as the generation of defense rule and signature. Therefore, the large damage will be happened economically and socially because the server needs a lot of time to recover the service.

On the other hand, the proposed method, by controlling the defense thresholds, manages gradually the server load to avoid the out-of-control service during the attacks are continued. The first reason that the gradual threshold adjustment is required is because the majority of normal users may be blocked by the strong threshold adjustment at a time, and the second is because the method is no need to adjust the defense threshold by force if the server performance is available apart from the attack traffic that is incoming.

Fig. 3 represents the example to determine the strength of threshold adjustment according to the resource usage change of *rising* and *surging*. In the case of *rising* type the attack traffic increases slowly and in the future we can expect the slow increasing of server load. Thus, without the strong threshold adjustment, our approach precisely controls the current defense threshold for simply deviating from the emergency level. When the server load exceeds the emergency level, our method adjusts the current threshold to come $U0$ to $Ug$. New threshold $Pn$ is shown to Eq. (1).

$$Pn = \frac{P0 \times \{U0 - 2 \times (U0 - U1) \times Ru\}}{U0} \quad \text{Eq. (1)}$$

**Where:** $P0$ = current threshold value; $Ru$ = constant ratio that reflects the difference of $U0$ and $U1$ (If $Ru > 1$, weak adjustment).

In the case of *surging* type the attack traffic increases rapidly. Thus, in the future we can expect the rapid increasing of server load, and if there is no defense for that situation, the server will be out-of-control soon. With the strong threshold adjustment, it is necessary to urgently stabilize the current server load to the average server load. When the server load rapidly exceeds the warning level, our method adjusts the current threshold to come $U0$ to $Ug$. New threshold $Pn$ is shown to Eq. (2).

$$Pn = \frac{P0\times(Uavg+Rv\times Vavg)}{U0} \quad \text{Eq. (2)}$$

*Where:* $Vavg$ = average usage variation; $Uavg$ = average usage (%); $Rv$ = constant ratio that reflects $Vavg$ (If $Rv > 1$, weak adjustment).

## 3.6    Attack Mitigation

Although our approach adjusted the thresholds to stabilize the server overload, the server load may not be reduced in contrary to our prediction. The first reason is because the current usage $U0$ for determining new threshold $Pn$ and the current threshold $P0$ applied already to the defense mechanism are not proportional relation. Therefore, this case can fail to decrease the usage because the attacks were not blocked as much as the expected through the threshold adjustment. The second reason is due to the wrong selection of defense mechanism although the cause analysis of service trouble was performed. The third is the case that there is no defense mechanism for blocking the attacks. The reason that the subsequent attack mitigation is required, even after the current threshold was adjusted by our method, is because the additional defense is needed for the first and second situation to stabilize the server load even except for the third case.

To reduce current overload, our approach firstly adjusts the threshold of defense mechanism selected by the cause analysis to the new threshold $Pn$ determined by Eq. (1) and Eq. (2). After the threshold changing, if the server load is reduced or maintained by monitoring the load at the next time, the threshold adjustment of selected defense mechanism is considered as a success. On the other hand, after the threshold changing, if the server load is increased, our method adjusts the thresholds of all mechanisms embedded in the *SecureNIC* because the reason of adjustment failure is one among the above first and second. At this time, our method decreases the thresholds of all defense mechanisms to 10% rather than conforming to Eq. (1) and Eq. (2). Such the processes of subsequent defenses are lasted until the server overload is released. In the situation of subsequent defense, if the server load is decreased under the warning level, our method considers as the termination of attack situation, and returns all thresholds to their original thresholds.

## 3.7    The Selection and Continuous Block of Attack Traffic

The purpose of proposed method is to mitigate the damage of out-of-service caused by an overload condition due to the attacks. The proposed method cannot choose and block only attacks. The reason that the method has not the detailed functions is because the work implemented by software aggravates the server load on the endpoint system. To complement this problem, the *SecureNIC* includes an intelligent IP-based ACL (access control logic) which are based on the arrival time gap of request packets between the attack and normal traffic.

If the thresholds by detecting the server overload are adjusted, the attack and normal traffic that excesses the thresholds are blocked, and then the remote IP addresses are registered to the ACL list. In general, the requests by attack programs are transferred automatically and quickly, and the requests by normal users are transferred manually and slowly. Using the fact, in the first step, if the packet of ACL-registered IP address flows into the *SecureNIC* within the block time of one second, it is blocked as requests of attack program and the block time of the ACL entry is doubled as the consideration of attack IP. If the packets of ACL-registered IP address do not flow into the *SecureNIC* within the block time, the IP address is deleted from the ACL as the consideration of normal user IP.

# 4     Experiments

## 4.1     SecureNIC

Our method has been implemented to the management software for controlling the host-based DDoS defense network interface card, which is the *SecureNIC* in Fig. 4. It is a NIC developed for the DDoS defense of host-level server and includes one giga bit NIC function that supports both the optic and RJ-45 with DDoS defense function. With Xilinx FPGA (Field Programmable Gate Array), the *SecureNIC* supports the SYN proxy function for the defense of attacks related to TCP session, the DDoS defense function of network and application level, and various ACL functions.

**Fig. 4.** The SecureNIC

Our implementation in the management software monitors the usage ratios (%) of CPU, memory, and service session in the *SecureNIC*-installed server and automatically adjusts the thresholds of defense mechanisms based on the hardware security logics in the *SecureNIC* against the attacks of TCP ESTABLISHED flooding [13], UDP/ICMP flooding, HTTP GET flooding, and so on. We demonstrate the effectiveness of our mechanism through a representative experiment because the way to adjust the thresholds is similar to each of the defense mechanisms on the hardware security logics.

## 4.2     The Mitigation of TCP ESTABLISHED Flooding Attack

The *SecureNIC* blocks most of the abnormal behaviors related to TCP session with the SYN Proxy feature on FPGA. However, the SYN Proxy cannot response the attacks exhausting the resource of TCP ESTABLISHED session [13]. Every second, our implementation monitors the usage ratio (%) of current ESTABLISHED number to maximum allowable ESTABLISHED number. If the usage ratio shows abnormal patterns, our method sends RST packets to the attack hosts for disconnecting the ESTABLISHED sessions in order of a large number of ESTABLISHED per IP address.

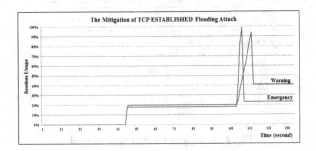

**Fig. 5.** Experiment of TCP established flooding attack

The number to disconnect the ESTABLISHEDs is *P0 – Pn*. In Section III.E, *P0* is the maximum allowable service session number and *Pn* is the allowable service session number to be adjusted. The difference of threshold adjustment compared to other defense mechanisms is the point that *Pn* is not applied to new threshold and the attack IPs are forced to ACL on FPGA to block the traffic of attack IPs.

Fig. 5, on the *SecureNIC*, shows the experimental results of session defense function in our approach. The environment is as follows:

- Apache web server in CentOS 5.6.
- The maximum allowable TCP ESTABLISHED number is set to 1000.
- The emergency level is 99% and the warning level is 89%.
- The normal average ESTABLISHED number is about 200 from 47 to 105 seconds. The attack is started from 106 seconds.

In the case of *Emergency*, the ESTABLISHED attack for exhausting the service session resource was performed with full speed of attack tool and only in 2 seconds the session usage ratio became 100%. When the usage ratio exceeded 99%, our method disconnected the attack sessions to be the previous normal average ratio of about 20%. In the case of *Warning*, we increased about 200 ESABLISHED sessions with the attack tools every second. That means that the average usage ratio also increases. At the time of 113 seconds, our method detected 95% session usage and disconnected the attacks sessions to be the measured average usage of about 40% because it was matched to the condition of warning level detection.

### 4.3    The Load Analysis Log of Internal Processes

Fig. 6 presents a part of log file saved by our program of the *SecureNIC* operated in a real web hosting server. From the log, when the CPU average usage (*USAGE_AVG*) is 5%, the warning (*CPU_STATUS_WARNING*) is detected with the current usage

91%. The top CPU usage processes except for the service process *httpd* used about 74%. *Uint* had been 50%, our program did not adjust the thresholds because the total usage ratio of top processes usage occupied 81% of current usage 91% load.

```
[2011-08-30_04-02-09.308406]
--------------------------------------------------------------------------------
| CPU Usage | MEM Usage | SERVICE(00080 port) Usage | SESSION_NUM | SYN_RECV_NUM |
--------------------------------------------------------------------------------
|     091%  |      033% |    001% (00005/00500)     |     00005   |        00002 |
--------------------------------------------------------------------------------
---------------------------------------------------------------------------
| GCMB GET cnt | PARB UDP cnt | PARB ICMP cnt |      NIC rx |      NIC tx |
---------------------------------------------------------------------------
|  00005/04000 |  00001/02000 |   00000/02000 |          64 |          62 |
---------------------------------------------------------------------------
[DETECTION] CPU_STATUS_WARNING by usage 91%.
[INFO] USAGE_AVG : 5 USAGE_VAR_AVG : 1
Total CPU(91%). Top 8 process CPU(74%).
Internal process CPU overload percentage(81%).
     PID                              PROCESS    CPU
----------------------------------------------------
    8548                               (perl)    37%
    8549                               (perl)    29%
    8547                                (cat)     7%
    1843                         (kjournald)     1%
       9                     (ksoftirqd/2)       0%
       8                     (migration/2)       0%
       7                      (watchdog/1)       0%
     273                          (kswapd0)      0%
```

**Fig. 6.** The log of internal process load

## 5 Conclusion

Most of the existing DDoS Defense systems determine large thresholds to reduce the false alarms of normal situation because their systems apply the defense thresholds of fixed type. It means that under the thresholds the probability of successful attack is high as well. To solve the problem, we focused on the fact that the service troubles can be detected from the usage ratios of system resources.

Based on the fact, we developed the *SecureNIC* and the management software which includes the method of paper. Finally, in the paper we suggested the automatic threshold adjustment method of DDoS defense mechanisms embedded in the *SecureNIC* of server system through the analysis of current server loads. The effectiveness of our method was presented with the automatic control experiment of *SecureNIC* developed by our project team.

## References


1. Internet World Stats. Internet Growth Statistics, `http://www.internetworldstats.com/emarketing.html`
2. The Internet Economist. The Internet Economy 25 years After.com, `http://www.itif.org/files/2010-25-years.pdf`
3. Symantec. Internet Security Threat Report-Volume XV, `http://eval.symantec.com/mktginfo/enterprise/white_papers/b-whitepaper_internet_security_threat_report_xv_04-2010.en-us.pdf`
4. Cisco. Cisco 2010 Annual Security Report, `http://www.cisco.com/en/US/prod/collateral/vpndevc/security_annual_report_2010.pdf`

5. Symantec. Symantec's monthly state of spam report (October 2008),
   `http://eval.symantec.com/mktginfo/enterprise/other_resources/`
   `b-state_of_spam_report_10-2008.en-us.pdf`
6. Lee, J.-H., Sohn, S.-G., Chang, B.-H., Chung, T.-M.: PKG-VUL: Security Vulnerability Evaluation and Patch Framework for Package-Based Systems. ETRI Journal (2009)
7. Hauri. 7.7 DDos Virus Report, `http://www.maxoverpro.org/77DDoS.pdf`
8. Liu, X., Yang, X., Xia, Y.: NetFence: Preventing Internet Denial of Service from Inside Out. In: ACM SIGCOMM (2010)
9. Argyraki, K., Cheriton, D.: Scalable Network-layer Defense Against Internet Bandwidth-Flooding Attacks. ACM/IEEE ToN 17(4) (2009)
10. Carl, G., Kesidis, G., Brooks, R.: Denial-of-Service Attack-Detection Techniques. IEEE Internet Computing 10, 82–89 (2006)
11. Vijayasarathy, R., Raghavan, S., Ravindran, B.: A system approach to network modelling for DDoS detection using a Naive Bayesian classifier. In: Communication Systems and Networks, COMSNETS (2011)
12. Yu., S., Zhou, W., Dross, R., Jia, W.: Traceback of DDoS Attacks Using Entropy Variations. IEEE Transactions on Parallel and Distributed Systems 22 (2011)
13. The Open Web Application Security Project. OWASP HTTP Post Tool,
    `https://www.owasp.org/index.php/OWASP_HTTP_Post_Tool`
14. Chang, B.-H., Jeong, C.: An Efficient Network Attack Visualization Using Security Quad and Cube. ETRI Journal (2011)

# Parameter Pollution Vulnerabilities Detection Study Based on Tree Edit Distance

Yan Cao, Qiang Wei, and Qingxian Wang

National Digital Switching System Engineering & Technological R&D Center,
Zhengzhou, China
vspyan@hotmail.com, funnywei@163.com,
wqx2008@vip.sina.com

**Abstract.** A new web attack pattern called HTTP Parameter Pollution has been presented in recent years. The harm and detection method about HPP has become a hot topic in the field of web application security. In the paper, we started with analyzing the HPP attack pattern, researched on the necessary conditions and the potential harm of attack, pointed that the determination of parameter precedence is a prerequisite for the implementation and testing of such attacks, and proposed determination method for parameter priority based on tree edit distance to provide the necessary support for HPP vulnerabilities detection. As well as, we developed different detection methods for the difference of parameters between URL and the page. Finally the detection system for HPP vulnerability was realized, and some vulnerabilities have been discovered in real world.

**Keywords:** Web security, Parameter pollution, Parameter precedence, Vulnerability detection, Edit distance.

## 1 HTTP Parameter Pollution Attacks

HPP(HTTP Parameter Pollution attacks) was put forward first by Stefano Di Paola and Luca Carettoni in 2009[1]. Many well-known sites, such as Google, Yahoo, are found to have this vulnerability. HPP itself belongs to vulnerability of input validation. HPP along with XSS (Cross Site Scripting)[2], parameter tampering[3], SQL injection[4], in essence, dues to the lack of input validation. Through exploiting HPP vulnerability, attackers can modify the HTTP hard-coded parameters, change the behavior of Web applications, access or use the uncontrollable variables, as well as bypass input validation checks and WAF (Web Application Firewall Web Application Firewall) rules.

### 1.1 Priority of Parameter Selection

We focus on the type of HPP attack in the paper, which transfering the input information using URL results in. According to the syntax of the URL, "?" is the end of the

T.W. Chim and T.H. Yuen (Eds.): ICICS 2012, LNCS 7618, pp. 392–399, 2012.

file address to access, followed by the parameters passed to the server. Different parameters separated by "&". The variable name is before "=", and the parameter values is after "=". As follows:

?Username=jybox&pwd=password
?Do=&id=12

In order to avoid ambiguous when passed parameter contains special characters, a special character needs encoded in hexadecimal, as %hh. For example, if the parameters passed contain "?", and identifier "?" isolate the file addresses and parameters, "?" must be encoded for transmission, expressed as %3F.

When some parameters with identical name but different values, such as *example.pl?id=1&id=2&id=3*, the parameter *id* passing for three different values, it is need to study pre-conditions of HPP attacks that how the application deal with these. That is parameter priority.

Generally, there are three different ways which web application to deal with such issues in:

- Extract the first value as a parameter value. As *id = 1*.
- Extract the last value as the value of the parameter. As *id = 3*.
- Extract all values passed to the parameter as a list. For example, when the HTML page uses the Checkbox object to represent the form of a check box, several parameters with identical name but different values need be passed. To support this function, list of all the parameters as an array is passed in the majority of the programming language.

It is no unified standard to process the parameters with identical name but different values in different programming languages. Whatever method to choose, that is not HPP vulnerability. However, if the web application developer ignores such issues, it is likely for an attacker to exploit combining with a variety of ways. How the different parameter priorities impact HPP attack will be explained below.

## 1.2   HPP Attack

HPP can be described that given the existing legal parameter *p* and malicious parameters *p'*, if the *p'* together with the URL encoding *hh%* of the parameter separator are injected together *p*, becoming the new input parameters *p%hhp'*, and the application doesn't check legality of the parameter *p* and filter, *p'* would be accepted by the application and the attacker's intent would be achieved.

The following is to take an example for describing the actual process of HPP attack.

Scenario: there is one election web site URL: http://host/election.jsp?poll_id=4568, containing two candidates called White and Green. The URL of the election passes a single parameter *poll_id*. The server might use the following code:

ID = Request.getParameter ("pool_id")
href_link = "vote.jsp? poll_id =" + ID + "& candidate = xyz"
Two new links *Link1* and *Link2*:
Link1: <a href="vote.jsp?poll_id=4568&candidate=white"> Vote for Mr.White </ a>
Link2: <a href="vote.jsp?poll_id=4568&candidate=green"> Vote for Mrs.Green </ a>

Through these two links, the users can vote for two candidates.

When processing parameter *pool_id* did, server doesn't check necessarily, so *pool_id* can become an exploitable parameter. An attacker creates a new parameter injection URL, as follows:

http://host/election.jsp? poll_id = 4568% 26candidate% 3Dgreen

At this point, decoded *pool_id* is *4568&candidate=green*. Thus two election links are generated, as follows:

Link 1': <a href = vote.jsp? Pool_id = 4568 & **candidate = green** & candidate = the white> Vote for Mr. White </ a>

Link 2': <a href = vote.jsp? pool_id = 4568 & **candidate = green** & candidate = green> Vote for Mrs. Green </ a>

*Request.getParameter* (candidate) in JSP only takes the first value when encounter some parameters with identical name but different values (determined by the priority of parameters). Therefore, whichever link the user clicks on, Green would be eventually elected. This is a complete instance of HPP attacks.

In this paper, we begined with analysis of HPP attacks, studied on attack conditions and testing methods, and pointed out the important influence of the parameters priority of HPP attack, and proposed the method for determining priority of the parameters based on the HTML tree edit distance. As well as more sound and viable solution about the HPP vulnerability detection was given.

## 2     System Architecture

According to the characteristics of HPP attacks, HPP vulnerability detection system based on tree edit distance was designed, consisting of five modules, namely web crawling module, HTML parsing module, parameters priority determination module, vulnerability scanning module and page response comparison module, as shown in Fig. 1.

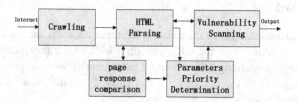

**Fig. 1.** HPP vulnerability detection system

The main function of each module is represented as follows:

- **Web crawling module** traversals web sites following the HTTP protocol, automatically extracts the hierarchy of the web sites, adds a URL link to the web's hierarchy to find these pages containing the passed parameters which can be browsed and interacted. From efficiency considerations, crawling depth is 3-layer.

- **HTML parsing module** obtains web pages from the web crawling module, of which DOM structure is parsed, and extracts all the links in the page and text and the URL of the form.
- **Parameters priority determination module** determines the response behavior of pages which receive some parameters with identical name but different values, in order to determine the parameter priority (see 3.1).
- **Vulnerability Scanning module** according to the parameter priority passed, injectes URL-encoded test parameters into the existing parameters in the page in the query string, checks whether there exist injected test parameters in link element of the response page, and action and hidden domain of form element, in order to detect whether there is the HPP vulnerability (see 3.2).
- **Page response comparison module** by HTML tree edit distance algorithm, determines whether the two pages are equivalent, to provide the basis for the parameters priority determination (see 3.1).

# 3    Key Algorithms and Technology

From Section 1, it can be drawn that the parameters priority determination is a prerequisite for HPP vulnerability detection. Parameters priority determination based on tree edit distance is the main contributions. Parameters priority determination and HPP vulnerability detection are represented in this section.

## 3.1    Parameters Priority Determination Based on Tree Edit Distance

Different web applications pass parameters with identical name but different values in different ways. This impact on the HPP attack has been discussed in Section 1. This section describes the problem to determine the parameters priority based on tree edit distance.

### A.    A Parameter Priority to Determine Algorithm

In this paper, the parameters priority determination method requires that one parameter need be transferred for three times. For example, the value *orgin* at the 1st get the server response page *P1*, 2nd with value *new* get page *P2*, and 3rd with value *orgin* and *new* to get page P3. As follows:

P1: pptest.php?par1=origin
P2: pptest.php?par1=new
P3: pptest.php?par1=origin&par1=new

By comparison among the three response pages, the parameters priority is determinated. The specific algorithm is shown in Fig. 2.

Parameter priority determination algorithm is explained as follows:

1: If the page *P1* and *P2* are equal, indicating that the identical parameter was transferred with both different values , and web application makes the same response, at this point, it is unable to determine the parameters priority.

2: If the page *P2* and *P3* are equal, indicating that web applications accepts the last value, selection strategy on some parameters with identical name but different values is to take the last value.

3: If the page *P1* and *P3* are equal, indicating that web applications accepts the first value, selection strategy on some parameters with identical name but different values is to take the first value.

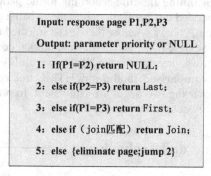

**Fig. 2.** Parameter priority determination algorithm

4: If the page *P1, P2, P3* are pair wise unequal, it is suspect that web application to accept all of the parameter values. Then the two values are connected into new string by a comma or space character string. And the new string is compared with page P3 strings. If be equal, it shows that web application can accept all of the parameter values.

5: If the page *P1, P2, P3* are pair wise unequal and web application does not accept all of the parameter values, it is possible that the page containing dynamic content result in the response page being not equal. At this point, the dynamic information contained in the response page should be disposed of first. Then go back to Step 2 of the algorithm.

Page equivalen means that the application made the same response to various requests. So, this paper realized comparison between pages based on tree edit distance algorithm.

## B.    Comparison Algorithm between Pages Based on Tree Edit Distance

HTML tree edit distance is used to quantify the similarity of the structure bewtween both pages. Edit distance, also known as Levenshtein distance, usually is used for similarity calculation between two strings[5].

Through parsing hierarchical tag structure, any HTML can be converted to an HTML DOM tree. Each node is identified corresponding to its HTML tag name. Each data object in HTML document can also be converted into a tree. Therefore, web page can be extracted into into HTML tree, and degree of similarity can be calculated between both pages by the tree edit distance.

HTML tree edit distance algorithm proposed in this paper improved on the STEDM algorithm[6]. Because the tree edit distance operations such as insertion, remove, and replacement, are on leaf node, the performance is enhanced.

**Definition 1. HTML Tree Node Mapping:** given tree *T1* containing *n1* nodes and tree *T2* containing *n2* nodes, mapping set *M (i, j)* between both trees satisfies *(i1, j1 is), (i2, j2)* with the following conditions:

(1) *i1 =i2* if and only if *j1=j2*.
(2) If *T1[i1]* is on the left of the *T1[i2], the T2[j1] is* on the *left* of *T2[j2]*.
(3) If the *T1[i1]* is the ancestor of *T1[i2], T2[j1]* is the ancestor of *T2[j2]*.

**Definition 2. The Tree Edit Distance:** If the tree *T1* is converted to tree *T2*, the tree edit distance *Dis(T1, T2)* is the number of operations for two trees to convert. As follows:

$$Dis(T1, T2)=Rep\times |R| +DEL\times|D|+Ins\times|I|$$

Among them, *Rep, Del, Ins* respectively represent operations of replace, delete, insert. HTML tree edit distance algorithm shown in Fig. 3:

```
Input: tree T1, T2
Output: edit distance dist
M is the number of T1's childnodes
N is the number of T2's childnodes
C1i is set of t1[i] deriving nodes
C2j is set of t2[j] deriving Nodes
Dis(T1, T2)
{
    for i = 1 to m
    for j = 1 to n
    {
      if (t1[i]==t2[j]) dist=0;
      else
      {
        if (t1[i] is leaf node)
        dist= dist+R*1+I*|C2j|;
        else if (t2[j] is leaf node);
        dist= dist+ R*1+D*|C1i|;
        else if(t1[i] and t2[j] aren't leaf
        node)
        dist=dist+Dis(t1[i], t2[j]);
      }
    }
    return dist;
}
```

**Fig. 3.** The HTML tree edit distance algorithm

By *Dist = the dist * (m + n) / 2 * mn* normalized, the range of the tree edit distance is [0,1]. From manual testing, if the edit distance of web pages is less than 0.15, they can be considered equal. If the edit distance is more than 0.8, they can be considered unequal. Ranging from 0.15 to 0.8, similarity between them needs to be further analyzed manually.

## 3.2    HPP Vulnerability Scanning

In this paper, the HPP vulnerabilities of the web application are detected, through injecting the URL-encoded test parameters into known legal parameters and detecting behavior of the response page. If in link element of the response page, and action and hidden domain of form element, the injected test parameters are found out, it is considered that the page contains HPP vulnerability. The detection process is shown in Fig. 4.

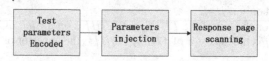

**Fig. 4.** HPP vulnerability scanning process

For example, the test parameter is encoded into *%26testparameter%3Dtp*, which is injected into the existing legal parameters *parameter=lp*. Then elements and domain on the answer page are scanned to serach for *&testparameter=tp*. If the test parameter exists and the parameter *lparameter* can be contaminated, the measured page contains HPP vulnerability.

Parameters in the pages and URL are not identical, so three situations should be discussed as follows:

- If parameters exist in the URL and the page, they can be injected directly to test.
- If parameters exist in the URL but not page, page may rename the parameters in the URL. So it is feasible to search the corresponding renamed parameters in the page and re-injection test.
- If parameters exist in the page and but not URL, the parameters should be explicitly place in URL and used for re-injection test.

## 4    Experiment

According to technical method in the paper, the HPP vulnerability detection system was designed to experimental test.

In order to verify the validity of the system on the HPP vulnerability detection, the system scanned for shopping, education, government, and search engine sites and found HPP vulnerabilities in the real Internet environment.

Take an example of HPP vulnerability on a search engine site. Fig. 5 is the normal search results page after entering the keyword *result*. Fig. 6 shows the page after the parameter *area* injected the test string into *area=0%to26kw%3Dtest*. Then the pages are the same as one before injected. However, when select Page 2 of the search results, as shown in Fig. 7, this should show search result with the key words *result*. But the page shown search result with a test parameter *test* instead. It is shown that through injecting the parameter *area* into the test string, due to selecting the last value of the priority strategy, the server accepted the parameter *test*, and achieved the purpose of polluting parameter *area*, to detect HPP vulnerability. In testing, the parameter *page* in URL is the same effect of pollution as *area*, but the parameters *do* and *src* are not.

There is a certain false rate in the system. Because after the test parameters were injected, it was accepted as a new parameter, it did not reach the effect of polluting other parameters. For axample, the parameter *%26test%3Dtp* injected into *lparameter=lp*, becames a new parameter *lparameter=lp%26test%3Dtp*, instead of *lparameter=lp&test=tp*. New parameter assignment resulting in page error is mistaken for HPP vulnerability. The system need be improved in the future.

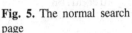

**Fig. 5.** The normal search page

**Fig. 6.** The page after the injection parameters

**Fig. 7.** The page after the pollution parameters

# 5    Conclusion

Nowadays, web application has been widely applied. Increasingly complex interactions and the dynamic characteristics strengthen the function and role of Web applications, but it also brings many new security issues. Traditional SQL injection, XSS and other web attacks are still continuing today, and the new attack and web vulnerability mode will still continue to appear. Although HPP vulnerability exists soon, its harm should raise people's concern and attention.

We studied on determine method for the priority of parameters based on the HTML tree edit distance. From analysis on the characteristics of parameter in the URL and page, HPP vulnerability detection solution was proposed. Finally, HPP vulnerability detection system was designed and realized. The effectiveness of the parameters priority determination has been verified by the experiment and HPP vulnerabilities has been discovered in real world.

# References

1. Carettoni, L., di Paola, S.: HTTP Parameter Pollution (EB/OL) (May 2009),
   http://www.owasp.org/images/b/ba/
   AppsecEU09_CarettoniDiPaola_v0.8.pdf
2. Rafail, J.: Cross-Site Scripting Vulnerabilities (EB/OL) (May 27, 2008),
   http://www.cert.org/archive/pdf/cross_site_scripting.pdf
3. Prithvi, B., Timothy, H., Nazari, S., et al.: NoTamper: Automatic Blackbox Detection of Parameter Tampering Opportunities in Web Applications. In: Computer and Communications Security, CCS (2010)
4. Chapela, V.: Advanced SQL Injection (EB/OL) (April 11, 2005),
   http://www.owasp.org/images/7/74/Advanced_SQL_Injection.ppt
5. Bille, P.: A survey on tree edit distance and related problems. Theoretical Computer Science 1(3), 217–239 (2005)
6. Yang, W.: Identifying Syntactic Differences Between Two Programs. Software-Practice and Experience 21(7), 739–755 (1991)

# A Privacy-Preserving Path-Checking Solution
# for RFID-Based Supply Chains

Wei Xin, Huiping Sun, Tao Yang, Zhi Guan*, and Zhong Chen

Institute of Software, EECS, Peking University, Beijing, China
MoE Key Lab of High Confidence Software Technologies (PKU)
MoE Key Lab of Network and Software Security Assurance (PKU)
{xinwei,sunhp,ytao,guanzhi,chen}@infosec.pku.edu.cn

**Abstract.** In this paper, we focus on designing of path-checking protocols to verify the valid paths in supply chains. By inputting a valid path, the reader at the check point is able to verify whether the tags have passed through the valid path or not. we propose a path-checking solution based on sequential aggregate message authentication codes. For security and privacy considerations, we add mutual authentication into path-checking protocols. In order to save resources, we use SQUASH as message authentication codes which is considered to be suited for RFID systems. Finally, we do some security and privacy analysis.

**Keywords:** Supply chains, path-checking, privacy-preserving, sequential MACs.

## 1 Introduction

Radio Frequency Identification (RFID) technology represents a fundamental change in the information technology infrastructure. It is a non-contact, automatic identification technology that uses radio signals to identify, track, sort and detect a variety of objects including people, vehicles, goods and assets without the need for direct contact.

To track and trace RFID-based products in supply chains recently has seen growing interests from both academic research and industrial practices. The tags are attached to some products and go through a special path in a supply chain. The path consists of a list of steps. Typically, we need to guarantee that the products pass through the right path as it was supposed to for quality assurance. The path-checking process can be described as follows. At the beginning, the issuer($I$) do preparations for tags, while attaching a tag $T_i$ to a product. $T_i$ then pass through a series of steps and will be marked at each one of readers. In the end, the *checker* will interact with the tags being able to verify whether, according to some data stored in the tags, they go through the valid path. The goal of an adversary in such a scheme is to either produce a phony tag or make a genuine tag which followed a different path that passes the verification of the checking reader. Meanwhile, an adversary should not be able to trace and recognize tags during the flow steps in the supply chain.

The rest of the paper is organized as follows. In section 2, we introduce the related work concerning RFID privacy and path-checking issues in RFID systems. Section 3

---

* Corresponding author.

T.W. Chim and T.H. Yuen (Eds.): ICICS 2012, LNCS 7618, pp. 400–407, 2012.

describes informally the proposed scheme in supply chain. Sections 4 demonstrates security and privacy analysis. And finally, section 5 concludes.

## 2  Related Work

### 2.1  RFID Privacy

RFID privacy is one of the areas which are most discussed in recent years. Without lose of generality, there are two notions of privacy in RFID system: the first one is commonly known as tag *anonymity*. That is, an adversary $\mathcal{A}$ should not be able to disclose the identity of tags he reads from or writes into. The second notion is called *untraceability*: an adversary $\mathcal{A}$ should not be able to trace or track the person(product) attached with tags by a fake reader. There is a special untraceability named *forward untraceability* (also known as forward privacy), that is, an adversary capturing the tags secret information cannot correlate the tag with its responses before the last complete protocol run with a valid reader [1].

A great number of privacy-preserving RFID protocols have been proposed in the literature, Juels offers a survey of much of this work in [2]. Tag *anonymity* corresponds to anonymization protocol, one trivial approach is proposed by Sarma named hash-lock[3], using meta-ID instead of real ID. Later, Weis [4]improved hash-lock to randomized hash-lock identification scheme. *Untraceability* implies that the tag response differently upon receiving the same request. The approach to reach *untraceability* is either based on the pseudorandom numbers or the random noise. Most existing protocols are based on the former primitive, while the HB family protocols [5–7] are based on the latter named LPN(Parity with Noise) problem. The Ohkubo-Suzuki-Kinoshita protocol (OSK) [8] made forward privacy possible, the scheme relies on the use of two one-way hash functions. Variants of the OSK scheme proposed in [9], making it resistant to replay attacks. An further improvement to the OSK [10] was proposed by Berbain using a pseudorandom number generator and a universal family of hash functions, moreover, they provided a provable secure proof under standard model. Recently, Ma [11] gave a simpler one of [10] using tags only equipped with pseududorandom generator.

### 2.2  Path-Checking Scheme

The first RFID path-checking scheme in supply chain was introduced by Ouafi, the process consists of three sequential phases: namely initialization phase, update phase, and verification phase. In initialization phase, readers in the supply chain and tags are initialized with some security parameters. When the tag starts to pass through readers in supply chain, the tag will come to update phase being written into some path information. When the tag is passing by the reader $v_i$, the path information in the tag will refresh to $s_i$. Suppose the path that the tag has passed is $\nu = \{v_0, ..., v_n\}$, so $s_n$ is the last status of the tag. At last, the tag enters into verification phase checking whether the tag passed through a valid path, it is determined by whether $s'_l$ equals $s_n$, $s'_l$ is the valid path status previously stored in the *checker*. Assume $\nu' = \{v'_0, ..., v'_l\}$ is the valid path, $s'_l$ can be computed as follows:

$$s_0' = id$$

$$......$$

$$s_l' = H_t(s_{l-1}', H_l'(x_l', id, extract(s_{l-1}')))$$

In NDSS 2011, Blass [12] proposed another protocol named TRACKER for the purpose of object genuineness verification. The process of the TRACKER can be described as follows. At the beginning, the tag is assigned with the state value $S^0$, when the tag passes by $reader_i$ in the supply chain, $reader_i$ update the value $S^{i-1}$ into $S^i$ by $F_i$, $S^i = F_i(S^{i-1})$. At last, by inputting the the current state $S^n$, the *checker* will output a valid path $(v_0...v_l)$ if the tag passes the verification, otherwise output 0 which implies the tag fails to pass the verification. TRACKER's main idea is to encode valid paths in a supply chain with polynomials, the great advantage of TRACKER is that it does not require any computational complexity on the tag, only 80 bytes of storage.

Both Ouafi's and Blass's protocols suffer from impersonate attacks, their approaches do not provide authentication for the reader and the tag. An adversary can write anything he wants to the tag in order to break the path-checking scheme. As for path coding, Ouafi's construction uses two hash functions which can be further reduced, moreover, it did not give security proof. Blass's path encoding was based on polynomials, whether the path encoding polynomials are unforgeable or not have not been fully proved. For the reasons above, we put forward our proposal.

### 2.3 Sequential Aggregate Message Authentication Codes

Aggregate message authentication codes(MACs) was proposed by Katz et al. [13] allow the aggregation of multiple MACs on messages, which was generated by distinct senders, such that the size of the aggregates was the same as a single MAC. They proved that if the underlying MAC scheme is existentially unforgeable under an adaptive chosen-message attack and is deterministic, then the aggregate message authentication code generated by computing the XOR of every individual MAC values is secure. These MACs are especially suited for resource-constrained devices as RFID tags. As a result, verification of an aggregated tag can be carried out by any verifier that shares all secret keys with the participating senders.

In an aggregate MAC scheme, the aggregation can be performed by same parties in different order. In contrast, in a *sequential* aggregate MAC schemes, each sender gets as additional input an aggregate-so-far $\sigma'$ and transforms that tag into a new aggregate $\sigma$ which includes the authentication of a message of his choice.

## 3    Proposed Scheme

The main purpose of our scheme is to combine authentication and path recording primitive to solve path-checking issues in the RFID based supply chain. Our authentication protocol is based on Ma's proposal [11] using only pseudorandom number generator as its cryptographic primitive, we extend the protocol from one way tag authentication protocol to mutual authentication protocol. Taking into account that not only the tag but also the reader constraints in resources, we use SQUASH[14] algorithm as MAC in the reader, which is regarded as more efficient and memory-saving than most of the existing MAC primitive. The idea of sequential aggregate MAC is based on Eikemeier's scheme [15].

## 3.1 Pseudorandom Number Generators

A pseudorandom generator is a deterministic algorithm that receives a short truly random seed and stretches it into a long string that is pseudorandom. Stated differently, a pseudorandom generator uses a small amount of true randomness in order to generate a large amount of pseudorandom.

Let $g : \{0,1\}^{\kappa} \rightarrow \{0,1\}^{2\kappa}$ and $g = (g_1, g_2)$. $g_1$ and $g_2$ respectively map the input of $g$ to the first $n$ output bits of $g$ and the last $n$ output bits of $g$. We take $g$ as the pseudorandom generator in the tag.

## 3.2 SQUASH Algorithm

In 2008, Adi Shamir [14] presented SQUASH algorithm, a message authentication code which is based on the one-way function $c = m^2 \bmod n$ coming from the Rabin cryptosystem, performs very well on benchmarks. Moreover, it offers some kind of provable security based on the hardness of factoring large integers. To make it secure, the binary length of $n$ must be at least 1000 bits long and is recommended to use Mersenne numbers or the more general Cunningham project numbers whose factorization remains unexplored till now. In our scheme, we use the SQUASH as a MAC algorithm for recording path information.

## 3.3 Description of the Our Scheme

Each tag has two variants $S$ and $P$, $S$ stands for the state of the tag, $P$ stands for the path information written by readers in the supply chain. $P$ is initialized to $IV$ by the issuer. $S$ and $P$ change when passing through readers in the supply chain. For better understanding of our scheme, we use the following definitions:

- a supply chain $G = (V, E)$ consisting of vertices $V$ and edges $E$.
- pseudorandom number generator $g : \{0,1\}^{\kappa} \rightarrow \{0,1\}^{2\kappa}$
- a set $T$ of different tags
- a set $S_1$ of possible states for the tags
- a set $S_2$ of possible path information stored in the tags
- a set $K$ of possible keys stored in reader
- a set $R$ of possible random numbers generated by the readers
- a set of $\nu$ valid paths
- issuer $I$ and checker $C$, issuer $I$ is represented in G by the only vertex without incoming edges $v_0$, $C$ is a checkpoint, which will check for tag $T_i$'s path validity.
- A valid path $P_{valid_i}$ is a special path which $C$ will eventually check products for. There may be up to $\nu$ multiple different valid paths $\{P_{valid_0}, ..., P_{valid_l}\}$ in a supply chain. A valid path $P_{valid_i} = \{v_0, ..., v_l\}$, $v_0$ represents issuer $I$, $v_l$ represents a checkpoint.

- a database DB behind each reader to store tuples $(S, IV)$ of each tag, $S$ stands for the current state of the tag, $IV$ stands for the initial path information stored in the tag
- a MAC function using SQUASH algorithm in the reader.
- a function CHECK $: S_2 \times \nu \times R^l \to \{0, 1\}$, assume $\nu_i = \{v_0, ..., v_l\}$, $\{v_0, ..., v_l\}$ represent different readers in set $\nu_i$, the keys of which can be denoted as $\{K_0, ..., K_l\}$ respectively, $R^l$ represents random numbers generated by $\{v_1, ..., v_l\}$. The CHECK function determine that the tag has passed the path $\nu_i$ or not.

We divide the process of our theme into three basic phases as follows:

**Initialization Phase.** The issuer writes the initial state $S$ and path information $P_0 = IV$ to each tag, and store the tuples $(S, IV)$ for each tag in a database, $S$ and $IV$ are random numbers, different tags have different values of $S$ and $IV$.

**Authentication and Update Phase.** This phase consists of two different parts, an authentication protocol $A_1$ and a path computing method $A_2$. $A_1$ can be described as follows, every tag has its unique initial state $S$, the pseudorandom number generator $g$ can be denoted as $g(S) = (g_1(S), g_2(S))$ for the input of $S$, we use a secret $k$ to denote the second part of $g(S)$, i.e. $g_2(S)$. Upon receiving a challenge $r_i$ from $reader_i$, the tag derives two values, a new secret $k = g_2(S)$ and a new state $S = g_1(S)$. Then, the tag authenticates to the reader by replying $c_1 = g_1(r_i \oplus k)$, $c_2 = k \oplus P_{i-1}$. $P_{i-1}$ stands for the path information stored in the tag before encountering $reader_i$. $reader_i$ verifies the answer of the tag by searching its DB: for each tag in the system, the reader fetches the last known state $S'$, for $j = 1$ to $\omega$, computes $c_1' = g_1(r_i \oplus g_2^j(S'))$, $\omega$ is used for solving asynchronous issues between the tag and the reader. If $c_1 = c_1'$, then the tag passes the authentication and the reader update the DB of $S'$ to $g_1^j(S')$, let $k' = g_2^j(S')$, the reader computes $P_{i-1}$ by $c_2 \oplus k'$. In response, the reader computes new path information $P_i$ and returns to the tag $g_2(r_i \oplus k')$ and $k' \oplus r_i \oplus P_i$. Upon receiving the messages from the reader, the tag do the judgement that whether $g_2(r_i \oplus k) = g_2(r_i \oplus k')$, if true, the reader will pass the authentication and the tag store the random number $r_i$ and updates the path information from $P_{i-1}$ to $P_i$, otherwise the tag does not do the updating.

$A_2$ mainly contains the computing primitive of path information. Assume $\nu_i = \{v_0, ..., v_l\}$ is the path that the tag passed by, The corresponding $l + 1$ keys of the readers are $\{K_0, ..., K_l\}$. $P_i$ represents path information written by a reader in $\nu_i$, $id_i$ represents $id$ of the reader $v_i$, and $r_i$ represents the random numbers generated by $v_i$. In this paper, we are considering sequential MACs based on Eikemeier's scheme[15] to encode path information, $\{P_0, ..., P_l\}$ can be computed as follows:

$$P_0 = IV$$

$$P_i = id_i \parallel MAC(K_i, r_i \parallel P_{i-1})$$

$$......$$

$$P_l = id_l \parallel MAC(K_l, r_l \parallel P_{l-1})$$

MAC is a function using SQUASH algorithm computed by the reader. Fig.1 illustrates the authentication and update phase interacting with reader $v_i$.

**Verification Phase.** The *checker* executes the CHECK function to ensure that the tag has passed through the valid path. The checker first read random numbers stored in the tag, then verify the path information $P_l$ as Algorithm 1. Assume that the valid path input is $\nu_{valid_i} = \{v'_0, ..., v'_l\}$, the corresponding $l' + 1$ keys and identities of the readers are $\{K'_0,...,K'_l\}$ and $\{id'_0,...,id'_l\}$. The the initial and the last path information stored in the tag is $IV$ and $P_l$ respectively. The CHECK function can be described in Algorithm 1:

---

**Algorithm 1.** The CHECK function

---

$P_0 = IV$
**for** $i = 1$ to $l'$ **do**
    $P'_i = id'_i \parallel MAC(K'_i, r_i \parallel P'_{i-1})$;
**end for**
**if** $P'_l == P_l$ **then**
    output 1
**else**
    output 0
**end if**

---

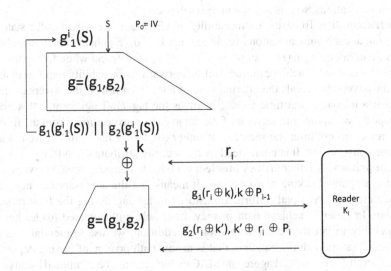

**Fig. 1.** Authentication and update phase in our scheme

## 4 Scheme Analysis

### 4.1 Security Analysis

The main security threat comes from two different aspects, one is that an adversary creates a fake tag passing the authentication of the legitimate reader. The success probability of this attack has been proved to be upper-bounded by negligible probability $\epsilon$ in

Ma's paper. Another threat is that an adversary forges a tag's valid path information to deceive the *checker* in the supply chain. State differently, we have to achieve the goal that if the verification of tag $T_i$'s path information $P_{T_i}$ by CHECK function returns 1, then $T_i$ must have gone through the valid path $P_v$ in the supply chain.

From Eikemeier's work, we know that, assuming $t$ be the number of parties and $Q$ denote the number of aggregation queries, each of $L$ parties at most, the probability that an adversary breaks the our sequential aggregate MAC scheme is bounded by $3t(Q + 1)^2 L^2 \epsilon$, $\epsilon$ stands for the probability of breaking the underlying MAC. Since SQUASH algorithm remains unexplored, the security of our construction is guaranteed.

## 4.2  Performance and Privacy

- **Hardware Performance.** Note that only a PRNG is used in the tag, according to [11], it is required to an overall gate count of less than 2000 gate equivalents (GE) for hardware implementations of PRNG. From the Serge's thesis [16], SQUASH requires less than 3000 GE. Thereby, both PRNG and SQUASH are suited for constrained resources RFID system.
- **Anonymity.** Tag anonymity means that an adversary is not able to get the real identity of the tag by eavesdropping the communications between the reader and the tag. In our scheme, the real identity of the tag is not used in the process of the communications, so it is an anonymous scheme.
- **Untraceability.** To ensure untraceability of RFID tags, we refreshes the state $S$ of the tag at each authentication exchange, then $k = g_2(S)$ changes accordingly, as a result, either $c_1 = g_1(r_i \oplus k)$ or $c_2 = k \oplus P_{i-1}$ is different when facing the same challenge, so as to achieve untraceability. Forward untraceability requires that even if the adversary reveals the internal state of a tag $T_i$ at time $t$, the adversary cannot tell if a transaction at time $t' < t$ involves the tag $T_i$. To guarantee this privacy property, we update the secret $k$ of the tag at each conversation. From the time $t$ of secret $k$ can not infer the secret $k'$ at time $t'$, if $t' < t$ and $t$ and $t'$ are not at the same conversation. It is guaranteed by the security attribute of PNRG.
- **Path privacy.** Another privacy problem we have to consider is path privacy which exists in path-checking protocol only. It means that the adversary can not get the concrete path from path information stored in the tag during the flow in supply chain. In order to achieve path privacy, first, only authenticated reader have the capability to get the path information. In addition, we use sequential aggregate MACs to store path information, that is to say, path privacy of the tag depends on the security of sequential aggregate MACs which can not be computed by adversary without the keys of the readers.

## 5  Conclusion

In this paper, we propose a privacy-preserving solution to solve path-checking problems in RFID-based supply chain. The main idea is to combine authentication and path-checking together. We extend Ma's protocol and take sequential aggregate MACs as path-checking primitive. From the security and privacy analysis we can see that the proposed solution achieve the purpose of privacy-preserving and effective path-checking.

**Acknowledgments.** This work is partially supported by the HGJ National Significant Science and Technology Projects under Grant No. 2012ZX01039-004-009, Key Lab of Information Network Security, Ministry of Public Security under Grant No.C11606, the National Natural Science Foundation of China under Grant No. 61170263.

# References

1. Alomair, B., Clark, A., Cuellar, J., Poovendran, R.: Scalable RFID Systems: a Privacy-Preserving Protocol with Constant-Time Identification. In: DSN 2010. IEEE Computer Society, Chicago (2010)
2. Juels, A.: RFID Security and Privacy: A Research Survey. IEEE Journal on Selected Areas in Communications 24(2), 381–394 (2006)
3. Sarma, S., Weis, S., Engels, D.: Radio-Frequency Identification: Security Risks and Challenges. Cryptobytes, RSA Laboratories 6(1), 2–9 (2003)
4. Weis, S., Sarma, S., Rivest, R.: Security and privacy aspects of low-cost radio frequency identification systems. In: Hutter, D., Müller, G., Stephan, W., Ullmann, M. (eds.) Security in Pervasive Computing. LNCS, vol. 2802, pp. 201–212. Springer, Heidelberg (2004)
5. Hopper, N.J., Blum, M.: Secure Human Identification Protocols. In: Boyd, C. (ed.) ASIACRYPT 2001. LNCS, vol. 2248, pp. 52–66. Springer, Heidelberg (2001)
6. Juels, A., Weis, S.: Authenticating Pervasive Devices with Human Protocols. In: Shoup, V. (ed.) CRYPTO 2005. LNCS, vol. 3621, pp. 293–308. Springer, Heidelberg (2005)
7. Bringer, J., Chabanne, H., Emmanuelle, D.: HB$^{++}$: a Lightweight Authentication Protocol Secure against Some Attacks. In: IEEE International Conference on Pervasive Services, Workshop on Security, Privacy and Trust in Pervasive and Ubiquitous Computing – SecPerU 2006. IEEE Computer Society, Lyon (2006)
8. Ohkubo, M., Suzuki, K., Kinoshita, S.: Cryptographic Approach to "Privacy-Friendly" Tags. In: RFID Privacy Workshop. MIT, Massachusetts (2003)
9. Avoine, G., Dysli, E., Oechslin, P.: Reducing Time Complexity in RFID Systems. In: Preneel, B., Tavares, S. (eds.) SAC 2005. LNCS, vol. 3897, pp. 291–306. Springer, Heidelberg (2006)
10. Berbain, C., Billet, O., Etrog, J., Gilbert, H.: An efficient forward private rfid protocol. In: ACM Conference on Computer and Communications Security, pp. 43–53 (2009)
11. Chang-She, M.: Low cost rfid authentication protocol with forward privacy. Chinese Journal of Computers 34(8) (2011)
12. Blass, E.O., Elkhiyaoui, K., Molva, R.: Tracker: Security and privacy for rfid-based supply chains. In: NDSS (2011)
13. Katz, J., Lindell, A.Y.: Aggregate Message Authentication Codes. In: Malkin, T. (ed.) CT-RSA 2008. LNCS, vol. 4964, pp. 155–169. Springer, Heidelberg (2008)
14. Shamir, A.: SQUASH – A New MAC with Provable Security Properties for Highly Constrained Devices Such as RFID Tags. In: Nyberg, K. (ed.) FSE 2008. LNCS, vol. 5086, pp. 144–157. Springer, Heidelberg (2008)
15. Eikemeier, O., Fischlin, M., Götzmann, J.F., Lehmann, A., Schröder, D., Schröder, P., Wagner, D.: History-Free Aggregate Message Authentication Codes. In: Garay, J.A., De Prisco, R. (eds.) SCN 2010. LNCS, vol. 6280, pp. 309–328. Springer, Heidelberg (2010)
16. Zhilyaev, S.: Evaluating a new MAC for current and next generation RFID. Master's thesis, University of Massachusetts Amherst (2010)

# Efficient Attribute Proofs in Anonymous Credential Using Attribute-based Cryptography*

Yan Zhang and Dengguo Feng

Institute of Software, Chinese Academy of Sciences, Beijing, China
{janian,feng}@is.iscas.ac.cn

**Abstract.** As an important property of anonymous credential, attribute proof allows user to prove the possession of attributes issued by the issuing authority anonymously. In this paper, we introduced the notation of Attribute-based signature into anonymous credential to propose an anonymous credential with constant complexity attribute proof. Compared with other constant complexity pairing based schemes, our scheme could support more types of attribute relations while the public parameter is much shorter.

**Keywords:** Attribute-based, anonymous credential, attribute proof, efficient.

## 1 Introduction

Along with the widely applied electronic identification and requirements of user privacy, anonymous credential has become a research focus of authentication technology these days. Besides the basic anonymity, attribute proof plays an important role in anonymous credential systems, too. By using anonymous attribute proof, user could make an attestation to the verifier that certain attributes were issued to his credential without disclosing his identity.

In current anonymous credentials, the attribute proof usually use the proof of knowledge algorithms, however, the computational complexity and length of attestation of these schemes were linearly related to the number of attributes contained in the proof. To solve this problem, Camenisch and Gross proposed an efficient coding method and extended the CL anonymous credential with it to significantly improve the efficiency of anonymous attribute proofs in 2008 [4]. In 2011, Amang Sudarsono et al. proposed a similar scheme in Pairing-Based anonymous credentials [5].

By using relevant technologies like accumulators, both two schemes mentioned above can achieve constant complexity of finite attributes(attribute values select from a small sized finite-set, for example: gender, nationality, age etc.) proofs,

---

* Supported by the National Natural Science Foundation of China under Grant No. 91118006; The National High-Tech Research and Development Plan of China under Grant Nos. 2011AA01A203, 2012AA01A403; The Opening Project of Key Lab of Information Network Security of Ministry of Public Security (The Third Research Institute of Ministry of Public Security) under Grant No. C11604.

T.W. Chim and T.H. Yuen (Eds.): ICICS 2012, LNCS 7618, pp. 408–415, 2012.

which make the attribute attestation significantly efficient. Unfortunately, although the two schemes could improve the efficiency of proof, there are still some drawbacks. In the first scheme, the computational complexity was linearly related to the total number of the finite attributes. The scheme of [5] could achieve computational complexity independent with attributes' number, but the size of its public parameters was very long so it is hard to apply in resource limited environment.

Attribute-based Signatures(ABS) [1][2], which is an extension of Identity-based signature proposed by Maji et al. in 2008 [1], gives us a new idea to build efficient attributes proofs in anonymous credential. In ABS, the user's secret key contains some attribute information, which makes the signature be verified to be generated by a user holds certain attributes, while hiding the identity of the true generator. For user-anonymity and attribute attestation were already contained in the signature scheme, it can be extended into anonymous credentials with efficient attribute proofs. Furthermore, by using ABS, the attribute proof scheme could support some complex attribute-based policy which is hard to realize in common anonymous credentials. Although ABS could only support binary attribute values, we can transform the finite attributes into multiple binary attributes to solve this problem.

## 1.1   Our Contributions

In this paper, we propose an anonymous credential system with constant complexity attribute proof using attribute-based signature. Our main idea is to use an ABS secret key as an attribute-based token and bind string attributes with it. The proof of finite-attributes could be extracted with the sign protocol of ABS schemes and we can use knowledge proofs to prove the string attributes.

Compared with scheme [4] and [5], our scheme has following advantages: First, by using ABS, our scheme can support proofs of threshold relation, which can be extend to general predicates, which makes our scheme more flexible to using in the attribute-based access control system. Secondly, for threshold predicates, the computational complexity is independent with the total number of the possible finite attributes, which is an advantage to [4]. Finally, for the problem of oversized public parameters in [5], our scheme significantly reduces the size of user data, which is about only 1/30 to 1/300 of scheme [5].

## 2   Preliminaries

### 2.1   Bilinear Pairings

First, we review the notion of bilinear parings, let $\mathbb{G}$ and $\mathbb{G}_T$ be cyclic groups of the prime order $p$, where $g$ is a generator of $\mathbb{G}$.

If there exists a mapping $e : \mathbb{G} \times \mathbb{G} \to \mathbb{G}_T$ with following properties, then we call $e$ a bilinear pairing.

**Bilinearity:** $e(g^a, h^b) = e(g, h)^{ab}$ for all $g, h \in \mathbb{G}, a, b \in \mathbb{Z}_p$;

**Non-dengeneracy:** There exist $g \in \mathbb{G}$ such that $e(g,g) \neq 1$, in other words, the map does not send all pairs in $\mathbb{G} \times \mathbb{G}$ to the identity in $\mathbb{G}_T$.

**Computability:** There is an efficient algorithm to compute $e(g_1, g_2)$ for all $g_1, g_2 \in \mathbb{G}$.

## 2.2  Assumptions

Our scheme is based on a new assumption we called q-HPDH, the proof of its security under generic group can be found in our full paper:

**Definition 1 (q-HPDH).** In a prime order group $\mathbb{G}$ with order $p$, the q-Hidden-Polynomial-Diffie-Hellman (q-HPDH) problem is, given a tuple $(g, g^x, g^{x^2}, \ldots, g^{x^q})$ where $x \in \mathbb{Z}_p, g \in \mathbb{G}$ and distinct $(c_1, c_2, \ldots, c_{q+1}) \in \mathbb{Z}_p$, to compute a tuple $g^r, g^{r \cdot \prod_{i=1}^{q+1}(x+c_i)}$ for some hidden value $r \neq 0$.

Moreover, the following assumptions are used in our anonymous credential scheme:

**Definition 2 (q-SDH [7]).** In a prime order group $\mathbb{G}$ with order $p$, the q-Strong-Diffie-Hellman (q-SDH) problem is, given a tuple $(g, g^x, g^{x^2}, \ldots, g^{x^q})$ where $x \in \mathbb{Z}_p, g \in \mathbb{G}$, to compute $c, g^{1/(x+c)}$.

**Definition 3 (q-HSDH [9]).** In a prime order group $\mathbb{G}$ with order $p$, the q-Hidden-Diffie-Hellman Exponent(q-HSDH) problem is, given a tuple $(g, h, g^x, (g^{1/(x+b_1)}, u^{b_1}, v^{b_1}), \ldots, (g^{1/(x+b_q)}, u^{b_q}, v^{b_q}))$ where $x \in \mathbb{Z}_p, g, h \in \mathbb{G}$, to compute $(g^{1/(x+b)}, u^b, v^b)$ for some $b$ distinct from $b_i (i = 1, \ldots, q)$.

**Definition 4 (q-TDH [8]).** In a prime order group $\mathbb{G}$ with order $p$, the q-Triple-Diffie-Hellman Exponent(q-TDH) problem is, given a tuple $(g, g^x, g^y, (c_1, g^{1/(x+c_1)}), \ldots, (c_q, g^{1/(x+c_q)}))$ where $x, y \in \mathbb{Z}_p, g \in \mathbb{G}$, to compute $g^{rx}, g^{ry}, g^{rxy}$ for some $r$.

## 2.3  BBS+ Signature

In this paper, we adopt the BBS+ signature proposed in [7] to issue the string attributes for user. This scheme is proposed as following:

Setup. Select bilinear groups $\mathbb{G}, \mathbb{G}_T$ with prime order $p$ and a bilinear map $e$. Randomly select $g, g_0, h_1, \ldots, h_L \in \mathbb{G}$.

KeyGen. Select $x \in \mathbb{Z}_p$ and compute $Y = g^x$. The secret key is $x$ and the public key is $(p, \mathbb{G}, \mathbb{G}_T, e, g, g_0, h_1, \ldots, h_L, Y)$.

Sign. Given message $M_1, \ldots, M_L \in \mathbb{Z}_p$, randomly select $w, r \in \mathbb{Z}_p$ and compute $A = (\prod_{1 \leq j \leq L} h_j^{M_j} \cdot g_0^r \cdot g)^{1/(x+w)}$. The signature is $(A, w, r)$.

**Verify.** Given the signatures $(A, w, r)$ on message $M_1, \ldots, M_L$, check $e(A, Y g^w)$
$= e(\Pi_{1 \leq j \leq L} h_j^{M_j} \cdot g_0^r \cdot g, g)$.

The BBS+ signature is proved to be unforgeable against adaptively chosen message attack under the q-SDH assumption.

## 2.4  F-Secure BB Signature

We also adopt F-secure BB signature proposed in [8] in our scheme. This scheme is proposed as following:

**Setup.** Select bilinear groups $\mathbb{G}, \mathbb{G}_T$ with prime order $p$ and a bilinear map $e$. Select $h, \tilde{h} \in \mathbb{G}$.

**KeyGen.** Select $\tilde{x}, \hat{x} \in \mathbb{Z}_p$ and compute $\tilde{Y} = h^{\tilde{x}}, \hat{Y} = h^{\hat{x}}$. The secret key is $(\tilde{x}, \hat{x})$ and the public key is $(p, \mathbb{G}, \mathbb{G}_T, e, g, h, \tilde{Y}, \hat{Y})$.

**Sign.** Given message $m \in \mathbb{Z}_p$, randomly select $\mu \in \mathbb{Z}_p - \{\frac{\tilde{x}-m}{\hat{x}}\}$ and compute $S = h^{1/(\tilde{x}+m+\hat{x}\mu)}, T = \hat{Y}^\mu, U = \hat{h}^\mu$. The signature is $(S, T, U)$.

**Verify.** Given the signatures $(S, T, U)$ on message $M$, check $e(S, \tilde{Y} h^m T) = e(h, h)$ and $e(\tilde{h}, T) = e(U, \hat{x})$.

Besides the normal unforgeablity, this signature system has a property called F-security defined as below: Define bijection $F$ as $F(M) = (h^M, \tilde{h}^M)$ for Message $M$. The F-security of this signature means that no adversary can output a tuple $(F(M), \sigma)$ where $\sigma$ is a valid signature on $M$ unless he previously obtained a signature on message $M$. The F-security of FBB signature above can be proved under the q-HSDH and q-TDH assumptions.

## 2.5  Proofs of Knowledge

To prove the string attributes and achieve non-transferability we adopt zero-knowledge proofs of knowledge(POKs) on representations. By using this, the prover can prove the knowledge of a representation that for some $C, g_1, g_2, \ldots, g_n \in G$, he knows $x_1, \ldots, x_n$ satisfy the equation $C = g_1^{x_1} \cdots g_n^{x_n}$, to simplify the description, we denote this proof as $POK\{(x_1, \ldots, x_n) | C = g_1^{x_1} \cdots g_n^{x_n}\}$. Moreover, the POKs can be extended to prove multiple exponents equal. For prime-order groups which we used in this paper, there exists a knowledge extractor which can extract these quantities from a successful prover.

# 3  Scheme Construction

## 3.1  Anonymous Credential with Efficient Attribute Attestation

By using the signature schemes mentioned above and attribute-based cryptography, we propose an anonymous credential scheme with efficient attribute attestation, the concrete scheme are defined as follow:

**Setup.** Let $\mathbb{G}$ and $\mathbb{G}_T$ be cyclic groups of the prime order $p$, where $g$ is a generator of $\mathbb{G}$. $e : \mathbb{G} \times \mathbb{G} \to \mathbb{G}_T$ be a bilinear mapping from $\mathbb{G}$ to $\mathbb{G}_T$. First, choose $n$ as the maximum number of attributes in single threshold supported by the system, then randomly select a number $\omega_i \in \mathbb{Z}_p^*$ for each probably used attribute, furthermore, $n-1$ additional dummy attributes $d_i$ are chosen from $\mathbb{Z}_p^*$ as well, these dummy attributes would never be issued.

Secondly, randomly select $g_0, g_F, h_0, h_1, \ldots, h_L, h, \widehat{g}, \widehat{h} \in \mathbb{G}$, $L$ is the number of string attributes. Finally, the public parameters are defined as
params=$\{ \ \mathbb{G}, \mathbb{G}_T, e, g_0, g_F, h_0, h_1, \ldots, h_L, h, \widehat{g}, \widehat{h}, \Omega = \{\omega_i\}, \mathbb{D} = \{d_j\} \ \}$.

**IssuerGen.** To generate the key pair of issuer ,firstly randomly choose $x, x_0, \widetilde{x}, \widehat{x} \in \mathbb{Z}_p^*$ and compute $Y_0 = g^{x_0}, \widetilde{Y} = g^{\widetilde{x}}, \widehat{Y} = g^{\widehat{x}}, g^x, g^{x^2}, \ldots, g^{x^{2n-1}}, h^x, h^{x^2}, \ldots, h^{x^{n-1}}$. The issuer secret key is $isk = \{x, x_0, \widetilde{x}, \widehat{x}\}$ and public key is $ipk = \{Y_0 = g^{x_0}, \widetilde{Y} = g^{\widetilde{x}}, \widehat{Y} = g^{\widehat{x}}, (g^x, g^{x^2}, \ldots, g^{x^{2n-1}}), (h^x, h^{x^2}, \ldots, h^{x^{n-1}})\}$.

**CreIssue.** Suppose the user has some secret infomation $f$, the corresponding public key is $F = g_F^f$, the finite attributes contain in the credential is $\Omega_u$, as well as $L$ string attributes $M_1, \ldots, M_L$. The issuer proceeds as follow:

1. Check the validity of $F$ and all attributes.

2. Randomly choose a token $g_u = g^u \in \mathbb{G}$ and compute $U_i = g_u^{1/(x+\omega_{U_i})}$ for each finite attribute $\omega_{U_i}$.

3. Use F-secure BB signature with secret key $\widetilde{x}, \widehat{x}$ to generate a signature on message $u$, the signature is defined as $\sigma_{FBB} = (S, T, U) = (g^{1/\widetilde{x}+u+\widehat{x}\mu}, \widehat{Y}^\mu, \widehat{h}^\mu)$, additionally, issuer computes $h_u = \widehat{h}^u$.

4. Use the BBS+ Signature scheme with secret key $x_0$ to sign string attributes $M_1, \ldots, M_L$ together with $f$ and $u$, the signature is $\sigma_{BBS} = (A, w, r) = ((Fg^u \prod_{j=1}^L h_j^{M_j} g_0^r g)^{1/(x_0+w)}, w, r)$.

5. Output the credential $cre = g_u, U_i, S, T, U, h_u, A, w, r$.

**AttributeProve.** When user wants to prove that he has a valid credential which contains string attributes $\{SA\} = S_1, \ldots, S_j$ and his finite attributes satisfied with the predicate $\Upsilon = (t, \mathbb{A})$, which is a $(t, k)$threshold for an attributes set $\mathbb{A}(1 \le t \le k = |\mathbb{A}| \le n)$ he proceeds as follow:

1. Firstly choose a subset $\Omega_u'$ he owns that $\Upsilon(\Omega_u') = 1$, where $\Omega_u' \subseteq \mathbb{A} \cap \Omega_u$ and $|\Omega_u'| = t$. Then select the first $n+t-k-1$ attributes from $\mathbb{D}$, for $t \le k$, the size of this set is less than $n-1$, denote it as $\mathbb{D}_{n+t-k-1}$.

2. By using the aggregate algorithm in [6],it is possible to compute

$$A_1 = g_u^{\frac{1}{\prod_{\omega_{U_i} \in \Omega_u'} (x+\omega_{U_i})}}$$

Then, for $|\mathbb{D}_{n+t-k-1} \cup (\mathbb{A} \setminus \Omega_u')| = (n+t-k-1) + (k-t) = n-1$, user could use $(g, g^x, g^{x^2}, \ldots, g^{x^{n-1}}), (h, h^x, h^{x^2}, \ldots, h^{x^{n-1}})$ to compute

$$A_2 = g^{\prod_{\omega \in \mathbb{D}_{n+t-k-1} \cup (\mathbb{A} \setminus \Omega_u')} (x+\omega)}, \quad A_3 = h^{\prod_{\omega \in \mathbb{D}_{n+t-k-1} \cap (\mathbb{A} \setminus \Omega_u')} (x+\omega)}$$

. 3. Then randomly choose $r, s \in \mathbb{Z}_p^*$ and output the proof as $\Pi = (\pi_1, \pi_2, \pi_3, \pi_4) = (A_1^{rs}, A_2^r, A_3^r, g_u^s)$.

4. Randomly select $\rho_\pi, \rho_A, \rho_S, \rho_T, \rho_U, \rho_H \in \mathbb{Z}_p^*$ and compute commitments $C_\pi = g_u \widehat{g}^{\rho_\pi}, C_A = A \widehat{g}^{\rho_A}, C_S = S \widehat{g}^{\rho_S}, C_T = T \widehat{g}^{\rho_T}, C_U = U \widehat{g}^{\rho_U}, C_H = h_u \widehat{g}^{\rho_H}$.

5. Then randomly select $\rho_w, \rho' \mathbb{Z}_p^*$, sets $\alpha = \rho_A w, \zeta = \rho_S \rho_\pi$ and $\xi = \rho_S \rho_T$. Compute auxiliary commitments $C_w = g^w \widehat{g}^{\rho_w}, C_{\rho_S} = g^{\rho_S} \widehat{g}^{\rho'}$ and set $\rho_\alpha = \rho_w \rho_A, \rho_\zeta = \rho' \rho_\pi, \rho_\xi = \rho' \rho_T$.

6. Finally, the user sends $\Pi, C_\pi, C_A, C_S, C_T, C_U, C_H, C_w, C_{\rho_S}$ to the verifier and use proofs of knowledge on representations to generate the following proofs and send it to the verifier:

$$POK(\rho_\pi, \rho_A, \rho_S, \rho_T, \rho_U, \rho_H, \rho_w, \rho', \alpha, \zeta, \xi, s, r, w, f, M_k):$$

$$e(C_A, Y_0) e(\prod_{1 \le k \le j, M_k \in \{SA\}} h_k^{M_k} g, g)^{-1} = \{\prod_{1 \le k \le j, M_k \notin \{SA\}} e(h_k, g)^{M_k}\}$$

$$e(g_F, g)^f e(C_A, g)^{-w} e(\pi_4, g)^{1/s} e(g_0, g)^r e(\widehat{g}, Y_0)^{\rho_A} e(\widehat{g}, g)^\alpha \quad (1)$$

$$e(C_S, \widetilde{Y} C_\pi C_T) e(g, g)^{-1} = e(\widehat{g}, \widetilde{Y} C_\pi C_T)^{\rho_s} e(C_S, \widehat{g})^{\rho_\pi + \rho_T} e(\widehat{g}, \widehat{g})^{-\zeta - \xi} \quad (2)$$

$$e(\widehat{h}, C_T) e(C_U, \widehat{Y})^{-1} = e(\widehat{h}, \widehat{g})^{\rho_T} e(\widehat{g}, \widehat{Y})^{-\rho_U} \quad (3)$$

$$e(\widehat{h}, C_\pi) e(C_H, g)^{-1} = e(\widehat{h}, \widehat{g})^{\rho_\pi} e(\widehat{g}, g)^{-\rho_H} \quad (4)$$

$$C_\pi = \pi_4^{1/s} \widehat{g}^{\rho_\pi} \quad (5)$$

$$C_w = g^w \widehat{g}^{\rho_w}, 1 = C_w^{\rho_A} g^{-\alpha} \widehat{g}^{-\rho_\alpha} \quad (6)$$

$$C_{\rho_S} = g^{\rho_S} \widehat{g}^{\rho'}, 1 = C_{\rho_S}^{\rho_\pi} g^{-\zeta} \widehat{g}^{-\rho_\zeta}, 1 = C_{\rho_S}^{\rho_T} g^{-\xi} \widehat{g}^{-\rho_\xi} \quad (7)$$

**Verify.** After receiving the attribute attestation from the user, verifier verifies the correctness of the proofs of knowledge above at first. Then the verifier checks the following equation:

$$e(\pi_4, \pi_2) = e(\pi_1, g^{\prod_{\omega \in \mathbb{D}_{n+t-k-1} \cup \mathbb{A}} (x + \omega)})$$

and

$$e(\pi_2, h) = e(\pi_3, g)$$

if all of the above are correct, accept the attestation, otherwise, reject it.

## 3.2 Security Results

**Privacy.** In the Attribute Prove procedure, the verifier receives following messages: $(\Pi, C_\pi, C_A, C_S, C_T, C_U, C_H, C_w, C_{\rho_S})$, for the commitments $C_\pi, C_A, C_S, C_T, C_U, C_H, C_w, C_{\rho_S}$, which is randomized by $\rho_\pi, \rho_A, \rho_S, \rho_T, \rho_U, \rho_H, \rho_w, \rho'$ and the zero knowledge property of $POKs$, these values contain no extra information about the user and is unlinkable. Then we consider the values in $\Pi$, for randomly chosen $r$ and $s$, the value of $\pi_1$ and $\pi_4$ are uniformly distributed in group $\mathbb{G}$. Furthermore, when $\pi_1$ and $\pi_4$ are determined, the value of $\pi_2$ and $\pi_3$ are uniquely determined by threshold parameter $n, k$ and attributes in set $\mathbb{A}$, which is only dependent with the predicate $\Upsilon$, contains no information about user attributes and identity, too. From the above analysis, we can see that our scheme has full privacy and unlinkablity for user identity and attributes.

**Unforgeabilty.** For the unforgeability, we have the following theorem:

**Theorem 1.** The Attribute attestation protocol is a proof of knowledge of a modified BBS+ signature $(A, w, r)$ on secret $f$, string type attributes $M_1, \cdots, M_L$, and the finite type of attributes is unforgeable under q-HPDH assumption.

**Proof.** The proof of Theorem 1 is described in our full paper.

## 4   Efficiency Results

In this section, we will compare the efficiency of our system with the pairing based system using accumulators in [5]. We use the same environment in [5] which described a common eID system, here is the parameter setting:

$L$: the total number of string attribute types. $\tilde{L}$: the total number of finite attribute types. $n$: the total number of finite attribute values. $k$: the number of attributes referenced in a proof. In addition, our system uses the following parameters: $N$: the upper limit of threshold parameter the system supports. According to paper [5], in an eID system, an approximate value of those parameters are $L = 5, \tilde{L} = 40, n = 1000$ to $10000$ and $k = 10$, for there is no $N$ in that scheme, we set it to 20, which is sufficient for normal attribute-based access control.

### 4.1   Computational and Communication Complexity

According to paper [5], we consider the computational complexity based on the number of exponentiations and pairings. Both our scheme and the scheme in [5] can achieve computational complexity independent with the total number of finite attribute types $\tilde{L}$, which is an advantage to scheme [4]. Although our scheme takes some more exponentiations than [5] for the proof of AND relation, but this is because our scheme is designed for the general threshold predicate with complexity independent to the type of predicate.

Then we compare the communication complexity of the attributes proof. The proof length in both our scheme and [5] are independent with the number of finite attributes in the predicate. For AND relation, our scheme has 3 more group components than scheme [5], which is roughly equal, but in the situation of any other relations, our scheme is more efficient. The concrete results can be found in our full paper.

### 4.2   Storage Data Size

For scheme [5] there was a main problem that for each probably used attribute in the system, the user has to store a tuple of corresponding public parameters, from the discussion of [5], this part of data consists with about 6000 to 60000 elements and would take a space of 200KB to 2MB. For common used eID cards, this size is too large. When $L = 5, \tilde{L} = 40, n = 1000, k = 10, N = 20$, the total user data size of our scheme, which contains public parameters and user credentials, contains about 120 group elements. Compared with 6000 to 60000 elements in [5], our scheme can save more than 97 percents storage cost in user device.

## 5   Conclusion

In this paper, we considered a new way to build anonymous credentials with efficient anonymous attributes proofs using Attribute-based signature and proposed a concrete anonymous credential scheme. By using this new construction idea, our scheme could realize constant complexity attribute proofs while support more flexible threshold relations. Furthermore, our scheme solves the problem of the oversized public key in [5]. Finally, our scheme could be extended to support general attributes predicates, which are hard and inconvenient to realize in common anonymous credentials.

## References

1. Maji, H., Prabhakaran, M., Rosulek, M.: Attribute based signatures: Achieving attribute privacy and collusion-resistance (2008), http://eprint.iacr.org/2008/328
2. Maji, H., Prabhakaran, M., Rosulek, M.: Attribute-Based Signatures. In: Kiayias, A. (ed.) CT-RSA 2011. LNCS, vol. 6558, pp. 376–392. Springer, Heidelberg (2011)
3. Camenisch, J., Lysyanskaya, A.: Dynamic Accumulators and Application to Efficient Revocation of Anonymous Credentials. In: Yung, M. (ed.) CRYPTO 2002. LNCS, vol. 2442, pp. 61–76. Springer, Heidelberg (2002)
4. Camenisch, J., Gross, T.: Efficient attributes for anonymous credentials. In: ACM-CCS 2008, pp. 345–356 (2008)
5. Sudarsono, A., Nakanishi, T., Funabiki, N.: Efficient Proofs of Attributes in Pairing-Based Anonymous Credential System. In: Fischer-Hübner, S., Hopper, N. (eds.) PETS 2011. LNCS, vol. 6794, pp. 246–263. Springer, Heidelberg (2011)
6. Delerablbee, C., Pointcheval, D.: Dynamic Threshold Public-Key Encryption. In: Wagner, D. (ed.) CRYPTO 2008. LNCS, vol. 5157, pp. 317–334. Springer, Heidelberg (2008)
7. Boneh, D., Boyen, X., Shacham, H.: Short Group Signatures. In: Franklin, M. (ed.) CRYPTO 2004. LNCS, vol. 3152, pp. 41–55. Springer, Heidelberg (2004)
8. Belenkiy, M., Chase, M., Kohlweiss, M., Lysyanskaya, A.: P-signatures and Noninteractive Anonymous Credentials. In: Canetti, R. (ed.) TCC 2008. LNCS, vol. 4948, pp. 356–374. Springer, Heidelberg (2008)
9. Boyen, X., Waters, B.: Full-Domain Subgroup Hiding and Constant-Size Group Signatures. In: Okamoto, T., Wang, X. (eds.) PKC 2007. LNCS, vol. 4450, pp. 1–15. Springer, Heidelberg (2007)

# F⁵P⁵: Keyword Search over Encrypted Data with Five Functions and Five Privacy Assurances

Huimin Shuai[1,2] and Wen Tao Zhu[1]

[1] State Key Laboratory of Information Security
Institute of Information Engineering, Chinese Academy of Sciences, Beijing, China
[2] Graduate University of Chinese Academy of Sciences, Beijing, China
hmshuai@is.ac.cn, wtzhu@ieee.org

**Abstract.** Breaches of data security and privacy have prompted concerns about data outsourcing. Encryption is an ideal solution, yet searching over encrypted data is a challenging task. Traditional data retrieval no longer hold, so searchable encryption (SE) techniques rise in response. Most of the related efforts are narrowly focused and problem-specific. None of them has *simultaneously* achieved the five keyword search functions (F⁵): *fuzzy, multi-keyword,* and *ranked search* as well as *keyword addition/removal* and *instantaneous search revocation,* together with the five privacy preserving requirements (P⁵): *keyword privacy, index privacy, token privacy, search pattern privacy,* and *access pattern privacy.* In this paper, a full-featured approach called F⁵P⁵ is presented, which achieves F⁵ and P⁵ simultaneously. Analysis and experiments show that F⁵P⁵ is secure and privacy preserving, and provides high-precision search results and is efficiency in terms of computation and storage.

**Keywords:** Data outsourcing, security, privacy, searchable encryption.

## 1 Introduction

Data outsourcing promises an economic paradigm of data sharing such as Dropbox. Despite of all the hype, this paradigm deprives data owners of direct control over outsourced data and prompts concerns about potential data breaches on the service provider (SP) side. Searchable encryption (SE) is an ideal solution to protecting sensitive data, yet searching over encrypted data without touching the plaintext is a challenging task, which requires that the index for each encrypted file be elaborately encrypted in a searchable way. Many efforts have been made. However, none of them has *simultaneously* achieved the five keyword search functions (F⁵): *fuzzy, multi-keyword,* and *ranked search* as well as *keyword addition/removal* and *instantaneous search revocation,* together with the five privacy preserving requirements (P⁵): *keyword privacy,*

* This work was supported by the National Natural Science Foundation of China under Grants 60970138 and 61272479, and also by the Strategic Priority Research Program of Chinese Academy of Sciences under Grant XDA06010702.

T.W. Chim and T.H. Yuen (Eds.): ICICS 2012, LNCS 7618, pp. 416–426, 2012.

Table 1. Overview of related work regarding F$^5$ and P$^5$

| Scheme | Fuzzy search | Multi-keyword search | Ranked search | Keyword +/- | Search revo-cation | Keyword privacy | Index privacy | Token privacy | Search pattern privacy | Access pattern privacy |
|---|---|---|---|---|---|---|---|---|---|---|
| [1] | ✗ | ✗ | ✓ | ✗ | ✗ | ✓ | ✓ | ✓ | ✗ | ✗ |
| [2] | ✗ | ✓ | ✓ | ✗ | ✗ | ✓ | ✓ | ✓ | ✓ | ✓ |
| [3] | ✓ | ✗ | ✗ | ✓ | ✗ | ✓ | ✓ | ✓ | ✗ | ✗ |
| [4] | ✓ | ✓ | ✗ | ✓ | ✗ | ✓ | ✓ | ✓ | ✗ | ✗ |
| F$^5$P$^5$ | ✓ | ✓ | ✓ | ✓ | ✓ | ✓ | ✓ | ✓ | ✓ | ✓ |

*index privacy*, **token privacy**, **search pattern privacy**, and **access pattern privacy**. To simultaneously achieve F$^5$ and P$^5$ (F$^5$+P$^5$), big surgeries to the underlying algorithms of the previous proposals are required. An overview of the widely referenced related work is illustrated in Table 1.

The rest of the paper is organized as follows. Section 2 is related work. Preliminaries are given in Section 3. Section 4 presents the construction of F$^5$P$^5$. Security and privacy analysis is presented in Section 5. Section 6 is performance evaluation. Section 7 concludes this paper.

## 2    Related Work

**Multi-Keyword Search.** Multi-keyword search enables users to search by specifying keywords of interests, and [2] achieved this by leveraging coordinate matching [5] which uses the number of queried keywords that appear in a file (i.e., the number of keywords that are hit) as the measurement of similarity between a file and a query. In [2], the similarity score is the inner product of the searchable index ($SI$) and searchable token ($ST$), both of which are binary vectors recording the existence of the predefined keyword in a file or in a query. Nevertheless, the similarity scores are coarse in [2], as binary vectors only indicate existence or not. Suppose files $F$ and $F'$ contain keyword $w$; yet, the number of times that $w$ appears in $F$ is larger than that in $F'$. In [2], both $F$ and $F'$ will be returned to users with the same similarity score; users need to decrypt the files and conduct certain manual postprocess to obtain the more related one by themselves. Our F$^5$P$^5$ modifies coordinate matching by changing binary bits in $SI$ into weight information of corresponding keywords, which is typically the number of times that the keyword appears in a file. The SP, by doing the modified coordinate matching, will get fine-grained similarity scores.

**Ranked Search.** The SP returns top-$k$ files as search results according to certain scoring mechanism, without ever touching any sensitive information, which has been achieved by [1] and [2]. However, the order preserving symmetric encryption in [1] only supports single and exact keyword search where search pattern privacy and access pattern privacy cannot be protected. In [2], two $(n+1) \times (n+1)$ matrices ($M_1, M_2$) corresponding to $n$ predefined keywords are used to encrypt $SI$; keyword addition/removal will result in corresponding changes to the size of ($M_1, M_2$), so the data owner has to re-generate all $SI$.

**Fuzzy Search.** Fuzzy search aims to tolerate various typos and representation inconsistencies in different searching inputs, yet even two words that are close to each other would no longer be so after the cryptographic transformation. This has been coped with in [3], [4] via building a fuzzy keyword set ($Fuz$). However, they did not achieve search pattern privacy and access pattern privacy due to the underlying algorithms. Besides, storage cost of $Fuz$ is another problem. Edit distance $ed(w_1, w_2)$ is introduced which is the number of operations[1] required to transform word $w_1$ to $w_2$ [3], [4]. The storage cost of $Fuz$ is $\mathcal{O}(t^{ed})$ for a keyword with length $t$ and edit distance $ed$ in [3]. In [4], both data owners and users are required to construct bloom filters according to every possible distance $ed' \leq ed$. So, the storage cost is even larger than [3], considering both the data owner and the user sides. We construct $Fuz$ by leveraging an information retrieval technique [8] and the storage cost of $Fuz$ has been reduced to $\mathcal{O}(t^2)$ per keyword with length $t$ without requiring users to specify appropriate edit distance.

**Keyword Addition/Removal.** Suppose $W$ is the predefined keyword set and a new file, characterized by some new keywords $W'(W' \not\subseteq W)$, needs to be outsourced. $W'$ must be added into $W$ for further search. Also, sometimes some keywords need to be withdrawn from $W$. Previously, [3] and [4] have tackled this, yet they are inherently incapable of fulfilling F⁵+P⁵. In [1] and [2], keyword addition/removal will result in re-encryption of all $SI$.

**Search Revocation.** It is preferable that the data owner may invoke a user's search ability immediately, which is known as instantaneous search revocation. Previously, [6] achieved this, but a look-up table is introduced, which is inflexible and has not been widely adopted. So far, none of the methods without look-up table has achieved search revocation due to the limit of the underlying algorithm.

## 3   Preliminaries

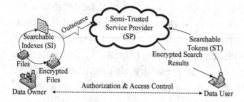

**Fig. 1.** Architecture of F⁵P⁵

**Table 2.** Fuzzy keyword set for "cate"

| Permuterms | Prefixes | | | |
|---|---|---|---|---|
| /cate | /c | /ca | /cat | /cate |
| e/cat | e/ | e/c | e/ca | e/cat |
| te/ca | te/ | te/c | te/ca | |
| ate/c | ate/ | ate/c | | |

**System Model.** We follow a typical architecture for data outsourcing as shown in Fig. 1. Three entities are involved: data owner $O$, data user $U$, and the SP. $O$ has a collection of files $F$ to be outsourced. $O$ extracts predefined keywords $W$ from $F$. $O$ builds $SI$ for each file in $F$ and encrypts the file with a symmetric cipher $E(\cdot)$. $SI$ is attached to $E(F)$ and $(SI, E(F))$ are outsourced to the SP.

---

[1] The operations include changing, deleting, and inserting characters into a word.

Each user $U$ will be granted a searchable key $(SK)$ by $O$. $U$ specifies keywords of interest and generates $ST$ with $SK$. Then, $U$ sends $ST$ to the SP. The SP evaluates the $ST$ over each $SI$ and returns the ranked top-$k$ files without decrypting $E(F)$. We assume the authorization between $O$ and $U$ has been appropriately established by separate cryptographic techniques. The search ability of $U$ can be revoked by $O$, which is called search revocation. Any user $U$ with a valid $SK$ has the same ability to search. Issues such as selection of $E(\cdot)$, symmetric key agreement, and access control, are not within the scope of this paper. We only focus on searchable encryption, which is consistent with previous work [1], [2].

**Threat Model.** Any user with a valid $SK$ can search over the *entire* dataset, which makes collusion of users meaningless, as the collusion will not provide a greater search ability. The SP is "honest-but-curious" who could be the potential adversary, which is consistent with previous work [1], [2], [6]. The SP will honestly follow the protocol, but it is curious to guess or infer underlying information based on what it knows. To meet high safety standard as [2], in addition to $SI$, $ST$, encrypted files and the search results, we assume the SP has some additional background information about the encrypted files.

**Fuzzy Keyword Set.** We construct the fuzzy keyword set $Fuz$ by leveraging the method in [8]. First, for keyword $w = c_1c_2...c_t$ with $t$ characters, add "/" to the end: $w = c_1c_2...c_t/$. Then, by rotating $t$ times $w$ we get $t$ permuterms: $(/c_1c_2...c_t, c_t/c_1c_2...c_{t-1}, ..., c_2...c_{t-1}/c_1)$. To illustrate, the permuterms for "cate" is: $(/cate, e/cat, te/ca, ate/c)$. Each permuterm is expanded to get all its prefixes. The prefixes of "/cate" are $(/c, /ca, /cat, /cate)$. Note that a valid prefix must contain "/" and at least one character. Namely, "/" of "/cate" and "e" of "e/cat" are invalid. Table 2 summarizes $Fuz$ for "cate". Each keyword with length $t$ will generate $t$ permuterms and each permuterm has up to $t$ prefixes. So the storage cost of $Fuz$ is up to $\mathcal{O}(t^2)$, which yields a better performance than that in [3].

## 4   Construction of F⁵P⁵

**Setup.** First, data owner $O$ extracts predefined keywords $W = (w_i, 1 \leq i \leq d)$ from the files $F = (F_j, 1 \leq j \leq l)$ and builds $Fuz_i$ for $w_i$, $Fuz = (Fuz_i, 1 \leq i \leq d)$. Second, $O$ finds a large prime $p$ with $||p||$ bits² and picks $g \in_R [2, p-1]$, $g^{-1} \cdot g \equiv 1 \bmod p$. Third, $O$ creates a truncated normal distribution $TN(\mu, \sigma^2)$ within the interval $[\mu - 3\sigma, \mu + 3\sigma]$, where $\mu, \sigma \in \mathbb{Z}^+$, $\mu - 3\sigma > 0$, and $||\mu|| < \frac{||p||}{4}$. Then, $O$ randomly picks $2d$ secret integers $(r_q \in \mathbb{Z}^+, 1 \leq q \leq 2d)$ and computes:

$$R = (R_q = g^{r_q} \bmod p, 1 \leq q \leq 2d), \ R^{-1} = (R_q^{-1} = g^{-r_q} \bmod p, 1 \leq q \leq 2d).$$

**Index Generation.** For $F_j \in F$, $O$ calculates the number of times that $w_i \in W$ appears in $F_j$: $N_{j,i}$, $N_j = (N_{j,i}, 1 \leq i \leq d)$. Then, a $d$-dimension vector $\theta_j$ is generated for $F_j$, where each entry $\theta_{j,i}$ is constructed as: $\theta_{j,i} = aN_{j,i}$, if $N_{j,i} \neq 0$; else $\theta_{j,i} = a'$. Here, $a = x_1^{a_1} x_2^{a_2}...x_e^{a_e}$, $||a|| < \frac{||p||}{4}$ is a large integer for enlarging

---

² We use $|| \cdot ||$ to denote the number of bits in $\cdot$.

$N_{j,i}$. $a' = x_1^{a_1'} x_2^{a_2'} ... x_e^{a_e'}$ is a small integer as dummy weight. Subsequently, based on $\theta_j$, a $2d$-dimension vector $\alpha$ will be generated. Each entry $\alpha_i$ is set as:

$$\alpha_i = \theta_{j,i} + \theta_{j,i+1}, \quad \alpha_{i+d} = \theta_{j,i} - \theta_{j,i+1}, \ 1 \leq i \leq d.$$

$O$ randomly picks $d$ integers ($m_i, 1 \leq i \leq d$) according to $TN(\mu, \sigma^2)$ and rounds $m_i$ to its closest integer. The searchable index $SI_j$ for $F_j$ is generated as:

$$SI_j = (m_1 \alpha_1 R_1, , ..., m_d \alpha_d R_d, m_1 \alpha_{d+1} R_{d+1}, ..., m_d \alpha_{2d} R_{2d}) \bmod p.$$

Then, $O$ randomly picks $v \in \mathbb{Z}^+$ and publishes $(p, 2v\mu^2)$. Finally, $O$ encrypts $F_j$ as $E(F_j)$ and outsources $((SI_j, E(F_j)), 1 \leq j \leq l)$ to the SP. The secret parameters: $(g, W, R, a, a', v, N_j, 1 \leq j \leq l)$ are secretly held by $O$.

**Searchable Key Generation.** $O$ sends each authorized user the same searchable key: $SK = (Fuz, \mu, \sigma^2, R^{-1})$. $SK$ is only sent once.

**Token Generation.** User $U$ searches by specifying a set of keywords and generating a searchable token $ST_u$ with $SK$. Note that the keywords of interests may not exactly match the predefined keywords in $W$. To support fuzzy search, certain pretreatment should be conducted. Suppose "cate" is a fuzzy keyword. $U$ will go through $Fuz$ to get the most possible keywords in $W$ for "cate".

1. Deletion. Delete some characters of "cate". We illustrate by deleting one character: $(ate, cte, cae, cat)$. By adding "/" before each word, we get $H = (/ate, /cte, /cae, /cat)$. For each $h \in H$, if there exists $w \in Fuz_i$ satisfying $h = w$, $i$ is added into $Pos$.

2. Insertion. Insert some characters into "cate": $(*cate, c*ate, ca*te, cat*e, cate*)$. Three transformations should be conducted.
   - Prefix transformation. Wildcards like $c_1 c_2 ... c_t *$ are translated into $/c_1 c_2 ... c_t *$.
   - Suffix transformation. Wildcards like $*c_1 c_2 ... c_t$ are translated into $c_1 c_2 ... c_t /*$.
   - Pre/Suffix transformation. $c_1 ... c_i * c_j ... c_t$ are translated into $c_j ... c_t / c_1 ... c_i *$.

   Finally, we get $H = (cate/*, ate/c*, te/ca*, e/cat*, /cate*)$. For each $h \in H$, if there exists $w \in Fuz_i$ such that $w$ is a prefix of $h$, $i$ is added into $Pos$.

3. Substitution. Change one character to another: $(cat*, ca*e, c*te, *ate)$. After the same transformations, we get: $H = (/cat*, e/ca*, te/c*, ate/*)$. For each $h \in H$, if there exists $w \in Fuz_i$ such that $w$ is a prefix of $h$, add $i$ to $Pos$.

After the same pretreatment for all the fuzzy keywords, we get $(w_i, i \in Pos)$. With $Pos$, a $d$-dimension vector $\eta$ will be generated, where each entry $\eta_i$ is constructed as: $\eta_i = b$, if $i \in Pos$; else, $\eta_i = b'$. $b = x_1^{b_1} x_2^{b_2} ... x_t^{b_t}, ||b|| < \frac{||p||}{4}$ is a random large integer chosen by $U$ for enlarging the actual query entries. $b' = x_1^{b_1'} x_2^{b_2'} ... x_t^{b_t'}$ is a small random integer called dummy query. A $2d$-dimension vector $\beta$ is generated where each entry is constructed as:

$$\beta_i = \eta_i + \eta_{i+1}, \ \beta_{i+d} = \eta_i - \eta_{i+1}, \ 1 \leq i \leq d.$$

$U$ randomly picks $d$ integers ($n_i, 1 \leq i \leq d$) according to $TN(\mu, \sigma^2)$ and rounds $n_i$ to its closest integer. The searchable token $ST_u$ is constructed as:

$$ST_u = (n_1 \beta_1 R_1^{-1}, ..., n_d \beta_d R_d^{-1}, n_1 \beta_{d+1} R_{d+1}^{-1}, ..., n_d \beta_{2d} R_{2d}^{-1}) \bmod p.$$

**Query.** $U$ sends $ST_u$ to the SP. The SP evaluates $ST_u$ over each $SI_j$ as:

$$SI_j \cdot ST_u \bmod p = [\Sigma_{i=1}^d m_i n_i(\theta_{j,i} + \theta_{j,i+1})(\eta_i + \eta_{i+1})$$
$$+ \Sigma_{i=1}^d m_i n_i(\theta_{j,i} - \theta_{j,i+1})(\eta_i - \eta_{i+1})] \bmod p$$
$$= 2\Sigma_{i=1}^d (m_{i-1} n_{i-1} + m_i n_i)\theta_{j,i}\eta_i \bmod p,$$

where we set $m_0 = m_d, n_0 = n_d$. Since $p$ is a large prime, the results can be simplified as $SS_j = 2\Sigma_{i=1}^d(m_{i-1}n_{i-1} + m_i n_i)\theta_{j,i}\eta_i$. The SP gets the final similarity scores by computing:

$$SS_j/2v\mu^2 = (2/v)\Sigma_{i=1}^d \theta_{j,i}\eta_i(m_{i-1}n_{i-1} + m_i n_i)/2\mu^2.$$

Files will be ordered according to the similarity scores in a descending way and top-$k$ files will be returned. Here, $(m_{i-1}n_{i-1} + m_i n_i)/2\mu^2$ are interference elements whose expectation is: $E(m_{i-1}n_{i-1} + m_i n_i)/2\mu^2 = (E(m_{i-1})E(n_{i-1}) + E(m_i)E(n_i))/2\mu^2 = 1$. The slight fluctuation of similarity scores due to the interference elements is a tradeoff between access pattern privacy and search precision. Experiments later shows that this is a practice-friendly tradeoff.

**Keyword Addition/Removal.** Suppose $F_{l+1}$ is the new file needs to be outsourced, which introduces a new keyword $w_{d+1}$. First, $O$ builds $Fuz_{d+1}$ for $w_{d+1}$. Second, $O$ randomly picks $r_{2d+1}, r_{2d+2}$ and generates $R_{2d+1}, R_{2d+2}$ as in **Setup**. Third, $O$ re-picks $m_d'$ and randomly chooses $m_{d+1}$ as in **Index Generation**. Last, for each $F_j$, $O$ sets $\theta_{j,d+1} = a'$ and re-encrypts $SI_{j,d}, SI_{j,2d}$ as:

$$SI_{j,d} = (\theta_{j,d} + \theta_{j,d+1})m_d'R_d \bmod p, \quad SI_{j,2d} = (\theta_{j,d} - \theta_{j,d+1})m_d'R_{2d} \bmod p.$$

Two new entries $SI_{j,d+1}, SI_{j,2d+2}$ will be inserted into $SI_j$:

$$SI_{j,d+1} = (\theta_{j,d+1} + \theta_{j,1})m_{d+1}R_{2d+1} \bmod p,$$
$$SI_{j,2d+2} = (\theta_{j,d+1} - \theta_{j,1})m_{d+1}R_{2d+2} \bmod p.$$

Next, $O$ generates $SI_{l+1}$ for $F_{l+1}$ as it did in **Index Generation**. Finally,

$$((SI_{j,d}, SI_{j,2d}, SI_{j,d+1}, SI_{j,2d+2}, j \in [1,l]), (SI_{l+1}, E(F_{l+1})))$$

will be sent to the SP and $(Fuz_{d+1}, R_{2d+1}^{-1}, R_{2d+2}^{-1}, d+1)$ will be sent to users. Sometimes, certain predefined keywords $w_z$ needs to be removed due to deletion of some files. In such cases, $O$ re-picks $m_{z-1}'$ and updates $SI_{j,z-1}, SI_{j,z+d-1}$:

$$SI_{j,z-1} = (\theta_{j,z-1} + \theta_{j,z+1})m_{z-1}'R_{z-1} \bmod p,$$
$$SI_{j,z+d-1} = (\theta_{j,z-1} - \theta_{j,z+1})m_{z-1}'R_{z+d-1} \bmod p.$$

Update message $(z, SI_{j,z-1}, SI_{j,z+d-1}, 1 \le j \le l)$ will be send to the SP. The SP deletes $SI_{j,z}, SI_{j,z+d}$ and updates $SI_{j,z-1}, SI_{j,z+d-1}$. $U$ updates $SK$ as $SK = (Fuz \backslash Fuz_z, \mu, \sigma^2, R^{-1} \backslash R_z^{-1})$.

**Search Revocation.** F$^5$P$^5$ achieves search revocation by updating pivotal information. First, $O$ re-picks $(r_q' \in \mathbb{Z}^+, 1 \le q \le 2d)$ as it did in **Setup** and generates two update keys respectively for the SP and all unrevoked users:

$$UK_{sp} = (g^{r_q'-r_q} \bmod p, 1 \le q \le 2d), \quad UK_u = (g^{r_q-r_q'} \bmod p, 1 \le q \le 2d).$$

The SP updates $SI_j$ with $UK_{sp}$: $SI_{j,q} = SI_{j,q} \cdot g^{r'_q - r_q} \bmod p$. Unrevoked user $U$ updates $SK$ with $UK_u$: $R_q^{-1} = R_q^{-1} \cdot g^{r_q - r'_q} \bmod p$.

# 5 Security and Privacy

## 5.1 Security

We prove the security of $F^5P^5$ in two scenarios. First, the SP guesses with $SI$, $ST$, and background knowledge. Additionally, the SP guesses with $ST \triangle SI$, which is a binary relation: $ST \triangle SI = (m_q n_q \alpha_q \beta_q, 1 \leq q \leq 2d)$, $m_i = m_{i+d}, 1 \leq i \leq d$.

**Theorem 1.** Alone with the $SI$, $ST$, and the background knowledge, $F^5P^5$ is secure as long as the entries of $SI$ or $ST$ are indistinguishable to the SP.

**Proof.** Since $m_q, \alpha_q, n_q, \beta_q \in [2, p-1]$, $1 \leq q \leq 2d$, $SI$ and $ST$ can be uniformly denoted as $S = (g^{S_1}, ..., g^{S_{2q}}) \bmod p$. The SP guesses by picking $g' \in_R [2, p-1]$ and $S'_q$ such that $(g')^{S'_q} = g^{S_q}$. Since the choice of $g$ and $S_q$ are out of the SP's sight, it cannot verify whether $g' = g$. Namely, the entries in $SI$ and $ST$ are indistinguishable to SP. Thus, $F^5P^5$ is secure according to Theorem 1.

**Theorem 2.** In addition to what the SP knows in Theorem 1, $F^5P^5$ is secure if the SP decomposes $ST \triangle SI$ with a negligible advantage.

**Proof.** According to the construction of $SI$ and $ST$, $a'$ is a divisor of $\alpha_q$: $a'|\alpha_q$. Also, $b'|\beta_q$. If the SP decomposes $m_q n_q \alpha_q \beta_q$, it decomposes $m_q n_q a' b'$. We set:

$$m_q = x_1^{m_{q1}} x_2^{m_{q2}} ... x_y^{m_{qy}}, n_q = x_1^{n_{q1}} x_2^{n_{q2}} ... x_y^{n_{qy}}, a' = x_1^{a'_1} x_2^{a'_2} ... x_y^{a'_y}, b' = x_1^{b'_1} x_2^{b'_2} ... x_y^{b'_y}.$$

The probability that the SP decomposes $m_q n_q a' b'$ is:

$$\varepsilon = 1 / [(m_{q1} + n_{q1} + a'_1 + b'_1 + 1) \cdot (m_{q2} + n_{q2} + a'_2 + b'_1 + 2) ... (m_{qy} + n_{qy} + a'_y + b'_y + 1)].$$

The number of divisors ($y$) can be large enough as long as $p$ is large enough, so $\varepsilon$ is negligible and $F^5P^5$ is secure according to Theorem 2.

## 5.2 Privacy

**Keyword Privacy.** Which keywords are being queried must not be divulged. In $F^5P^5$, the SP cannot speculate which keywords are being queried from $ST$ without $SK$. Keyword privacy has been achieved.

**Index Privacy.** The SP should not deduce any sensitive information from $SI$ and its associated encrypted file. In $F^5P^5$, $SI$ are indistinguishably encrypted without deterministic relationship due to the random $m_i$ and $r_i$, so the SP cannot deduce any underlying information even if it knows background information.

**Token Privacy.** The SP should not have the ability to generate a valid $ST$ based on previously ones received from users. In $F^5P^5$, the entries within a single $ST$ are indistinguishably generated thanks to $n_i, r_i$. Among different $ST$, there is no

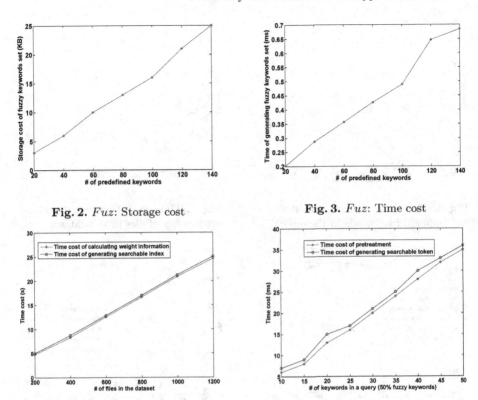

**Fig. 2.** *Fuz*: Storage cost

**Fig. 3.** *Fuz*: Time cost

**Fig. 4.** Time cost of generating *SI*

**Fig. 5.** Time cost of generating *ST*

deterministic relationship thanks to the random choice of $b, b'$. Namely, the SP cannot make up a valid *ST* from previous ones to search by itself.

**Search Pattern Privacy.** Search pattern is the information that can be derived when the SP knows two arbitrary searches are performed for the same keywords. In F⁵P⁵, the random $b, b'$ makes *ST* indistinguishable even if two *ST* involve the same keywords, so search pattern privacy is preserved.

**Access Pattern Privacy.** Access pattern refers to search result sequence. Private information retrieval (PIR) [7] could solve this but it is inefficient. In F⁵P⁵, result sequence fluctuates slightly due to the interference elements, even if the same keywords have been queried. Namely, an "as-strong-as-possible" access pattern privacy is provided, which is consistent with previous work [2].

# 6   Performance Analysis

We implement F⁵P⁵ on a Windows 7 Server (Intel Core(TM) Processor 3.00GHz) with a real-world dataset the same with [2]: the Enron Email Dataset [9].

**Fuzzy Keyword Set Generation.** Time and storage costs of building *Fuz* depend directly on the cardinality of $W$: $|W|$. For the first time, we reduce

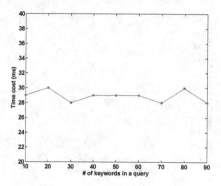

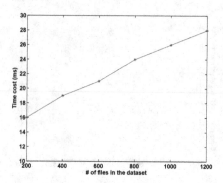

**Fig. 6.** Time cost of query with different number of keywords in the query

**Fig. 7.** Time cost of query with different number of files in the dataset

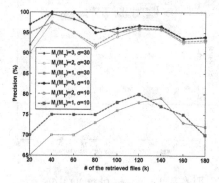

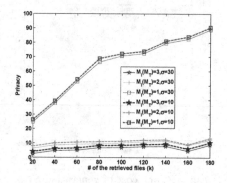

**Fig. 8.** Precision

**Fig. 9.** Privacy

the storage cost to $\mathcal{O}(t^2)$ per keyword with length $t$. Fig. 2 is the storage cost according to different $|W|$, where 25KB is required when $|W| = 140$. In Fig. 3, only 0.68 milliseconds are required when $|W| = 140$. Note that building $Fuz$ is a one-time operation before data outsourcing.

**Index Generation.** Generation of $SI$ involves calculating weight information and encryption. Fig. 4 is the evaluation of generating $SI$ where $|W| = 140$. 25.1 seconds are required to build searchable indexes for 1200 files, which is an improvement compared with previous work.

**Token Generation.** Generation of $ST$ involves pretreatment of keywords and encryption. Fig. 5 evaluates the generation of $ST$. In Fig. 5, the time cost is almost linear with the number of queried keywords, where 21 milliseconds are required for 30 keywords (15 fuzzy keywords). Pretreatment accounts most of the time and encryption only consumes a small part.

**Query.** Fig. 6 is evaluation of time cost according to different number of keywords ($|F| = 1200$, $|W| = 140$). The time cost keeps almost constant (approximate 29 milliseconds) no matter how many keywords in the query, which it is a desirable feature and has not been achieved in most related researches except

[2]. Fig. 7 is evaluation according to different dataset sizes. 21 milliseconds are required to query among 600 files, which is almost negligible.

**Precision and Privacy.** The adoption of interference elements involves a trade-off between search precision and access pattern privacy. We follow the same definition as [2]: precision, $Pre_k = k'/k$, where $k'$ is the number of files that exist in the real top-$k$ files; privacy, $Pri_k = (\sum pri_j)/k$, where $pri_j = |Rank_j - Rank'_j|$ is the rank perturbation of $F_j$. $Rank_j$ is the rank of $F_j$ in the retrieved top-$k$ files and $Rank'_j$ is its rank in real top-$k$ files. $M_{SI}$ ($M_{ST}$) is the magnitude difference between $a$ and $a'$ ($b$ and $b'$). We set $M_{SI} = M_{ST}$ for convenience. Fig. 8 is evaluation of precision and Fig. 9 is evaluation of privacy ($|F| = 1200$, $|W| = 140$), where large choice of $M_{SI}(M_{ST})$ will result in high precision and low privacy. So, $M_{SI}(M_{ST})$ is a balance parameter between precision and privacy. Precision in F$^5$P$^5$ is around 95% with approximate 5 privacy ($M_{SI} = M_{ST} = 3$), compared with 90% precision and 0.08 privacy in [2]. Namely, F$^5$P$^5$ provides higher precision and better privacy assurance. Also, the slight impact of $\sigma$ indicates that the interference elements have done a good job of making $SI$ and $ST$ undistinguishable without reducing precision.

# 7   Conclusion

We have proposed a full-fledged searchable encryption scheme called F$^5$P$^5$ which simultaneously achieves the five keyword search functions (F$^5$) and the five privacy preserving requirements (P$^5$). Thorough analysis shows that F$^5$P$^5$ is secure and privacy preserving. Experiments based on a real-world dataset show that F$^5$P$^5$ performs well in terms of both computation and storage with high precision of search results. As for our future work, we will explore how to assign different search abilities to different users.

# References

1. Wang, C., Cao, N., Li, J., Ren, K., Lou, W.: Secure Ranked Keyword Search over Encrypted Cloud Data. In: IEEE 30th International Conference on Distributed Computing Systems, pp. 253–262 (June 2010)
2. Cao, N., Wang, C., Li, M., Ren, K., Lou, W.: Privacy-preserving Multi-keyword Ranked Search over Encrypted Cloud Data. In: 30th IEEE Conference on Computer Communications, pp. 829–837 (March 2011)
3. Li, J., Wang, Q., Wang, C., Cao, N., Ren, K., Lou, W.: Fuzzy Keyword Search over Encrypted Data in Cloud Computing. In: 29th IEEE Conference on Computer Communications, pp. 1–16 (March 2010)
4. Chuah, M., Hu, W.: Privacy-aware Bedtree Based Solution for Fuzzy Multi-keyword Search over Encrypted Data. In: 31st International Conference on Distributed Computing Systems Workshops, pp. 273–281 (June 2011)
5. Witten, I.H., Moffat, A., Bell, T.C.: Managing gigabytes: Compressing and Indexing Documents and Images. Morgan Kaufmann Publishing (May 1999)

6. Curtmola, R., Garay, J.A., Kamara, S., Ostrovsky, R.: Searchable Symmetric Encryption: Improved Definitions and Efficient constructions. In: 13th ACM Conference on Computer and Communications Security, pp. 79–88 (November 2006)
7. Ishai, Y., Kushilevitz, E., Ostrovsky, R., Sahai, A.: Cryptography from Anonymity. In: 47th IEEE Symposium on Foundations of Computer Science, pp. 239–248 (Otctober 2006)
8. Salton, G.: Automatic Text Processing, the Transformation, Analysis and Retrieval of Information by Computer. Addison-Wesley, MA (1989)
9. Cohen, W.W.: Enron email dataset, http://www.cs.cmu.edu/~enron/

# Location Privacy Policy Management System

Arej Muhammed[1], Dan Lin[1], and Anna Squicciarini[2]

[1] Department of Computer Science
Missouri University of Science & Technology
{aamcq9,lindan}@mst.edu
[2] Information Sciences & Technology
Pennsylvania State University
asquicciarini@ist.psu.edu

**Abstract.** As location-based services become more and more popular, concerns are growing about the misuse of location information by malicious parties. In order to preserve location privacy, many efforts have been devoted to preventing service providers from determining users' exact locations. Few works have sought to help users manage their privacy preferences; however management of privacy is an important issue in real applications. This work developed an easy-to-use location privacy management system including functions of policy composition, policy conflict detection and policy recommendation.

**Keywords:** Location privacy, policy management.

## 1 Introduction

With the advance of mobile devices and positioning systems, location-based services (LBSs) have become prevalent. While enjoying the convenience brought by LBSs, consumers have begun worrying about their location privacy due to the very nature of LBSs which typically require the disclosure of the users' locations. Undesired exposure of location information may render users an easy target of criminal behaviors. For example, kidnappers could take advantage of LBSs to acquire a target's daily travel route.

Many efforts [7, 8, 10] have been devoted to preventing service providers from knowing users' exact locations. However, few works [13–15] have sought to help users manage their privacy preferences, which is yet an important issue in real applications and at the core of the success of these applications. Several exploratory studies [3, 5] have shown that most users are concerned about their location privacy, but when they are actually facing the location-based services, they either give up their privacy concerns or totally abandon the services. The main reasons behind such behavior are summarized as follows: (i) lack of understanding about the privacy implications of their behavior; (ii) lack of a proper method for them to control privacy options; (iii) overhead introduced by privacy protections. For example, existing access control policies like XACML [16] aim to cover a wide range of needs of access control for various applications, which are too complicated to be manipulated by non-expert end-users and contain functions that may not be necessary in location-based services. The complexity of general access control policies is also the main cause of the management overhead that has been shown to hinder the adoption of location privacy protection mechanism by the end users.

T.W. Chim and T.H. Yuen (Eds.): ICICS 2012, LNCS 7618, pp. 427–434, 2012.

To cope with the above issues, in this work, we present an overview of an easy-to-use location privacy policy management system. We define a succinct yet expressive policy language tailored for location privacy protection. We propose algorithms for detecting policy redundancy, policy conflict and policy merging that ensure the consistency of the access right being granted as well as efficient policy evaluation. We develop a policy recommendation function that generates recommended policies based on users' basic requirements in order to reduce user's burden.

The rest of the paper is organized as follows. Section 2 reviews related work. Section 3 presents the proposed policy management system. Finally, Section 4 concludes the paper.

## 2   Related Work

There have been extensive efforts on location anonymization in order to prevent service providers from knowing end-users' exact locations [1, 2, 6, 7, 9–11]. There are few works on location privacy policy management. Snekkeness [15] is one of the earliest researchers to identify the concepts for formulating personal privacy policies. Smailagic et al. [14] proposed a privacy model which specifies location privacy using set theory and rules. Myles et al. [12] developed a middleware service to allow location-based applications to use multiple location positioning systems. A recent related work is by Sadeh et al. [13] who developed an application, namely PeopleFinder, to enable cell phone and laptop users to selectively share their locations with others. Unlike existing works, our proposed system considers more policy management related tasks such as policy composition assistance, policy redundancy and conflict detection.

In addition, it is worth noting that location privacy policies are relevant but different from the concept of location-based access control (e.g., [4]) in the sense that location data plays different roles.

## 3   Location Privacy Policy Management System

The Location Privacy Policy Management System (LPPM) system is installed at user side, such as users' smart phones. We assume that users subscribe to location-based service providers who are allowed to know each user's location. We also assume that users may have created groups of contacts (e.g., family, friends) for their use of installed location-based services. The group information will be leveraged by the LPPM system to simplify the specification of the location privacy policy.

Figure 1 illustrates the framework of the LPPM system. When a user adds a new contact to his/her installed location-based service application, the LPPM system takes the profile of the new contact (such as his/her relationship with the user, hobbies, etc.) and invokes the recommendation module to generate a candidate privacy policy for the user's consideration. If the user is satisfied with the recommended policy, the policy will be inserted into the policy repository and may be merged with other policies for storage efficiency as well as evaluation efficiency. If the user modifies the recommended policy, the revised policy will be checked by the policy conflict detection module before inserting to the policy repository.

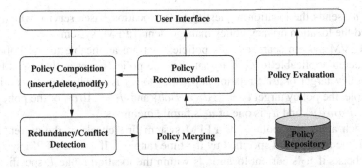

**Fig. 1.** Overview of the LPPM System

When someone (say Jack) sends a request to a location-based service provider to ask for his friend (Bob)'s location, the service provider will direct the request to Bob's mobile device. Bob's LPPM system checks the stored location privacy policies to see if Jack is allowed to view Bob's location. The decision is then forwarded back to the service provider. If Jack is granted the access right, the service provider will display Bob's current location on Jack's device. Otherwise, Jack will receive a message that his request is denied.

### 3.1 Location Privacy Policy

We define a policy language (as shown in Definition 1) that is able to specify the common components and requirements that are related to location privacy concerns.

**Definition 1.** *A location privacy policy P consists of the following components:*

- *$U$, $E$ specify the policy target which are defined by a set of user IDs and roles. $U/E$ excludes users in $E$ from $U$.*
- *$T$ is a Boolean expression on the time $t$, the day $d_1$ and the date $d_2$, which is the time when a location request is received.*
- *$L$ specifies a set of policy owner's locations which are defined by either ranges of location coordinates, or semantic locations.*
- *$G$ specifies the granularity of the location disclosure in a five scale system: exact location, district, city, state, country.*

*$P\langle U/E, T, L, G \rangle$ specifies that users in $U$ but not $E$ are allowed to view the policy owner's location at granularity $G$ if the policy owner is within the region $L$ during the time period defined by $T$.*

A user can define one location privacy policy for an individual user or a group of users. The access to the policy owner's location will be granted only when the policy is satisfied. Otherwise, the location request will be denied. The policy evaluation consists of the following four steps:

1. User $u_1$ wants to query user $u_2$'s location and $u_1$ composes a location request in the form of $Q : \langle RID = u_1, QID = u_2 \rangle$, where $RID$ is the requester's ID and QID is the user being queried.

2. User $u_1$ sends the location request $Q$ to the location-based service which has installed the location privacy policy management (LPPM) system.
3. The LPPM system searches $u_2$'s policies that are applicable to $u_1$. Policies are considered applicable to $u_1$ if $u_1$ satisfies the policy target in that $u_1$ is listed in the policy target or $u_1$'s relationship (role) to $u_2$ is specified in the policy. For example, the policy target $U = \{Alice, Bob\}$ and $u_1 = Alice$, or the policy target $U = \{Family\}$ and $u_1$ is one of $u_2$'s family members.
4. For each applicable policy, the LPPM system first checks if the current time is within the time period specified by the time range $T$. If so, the LPPM system further checks if $u_2$'s current location is within the location range $L$ specified in the policy. To check the location, the LPPM system will convert the semantic locations (such as a name of a company) defined in the policy into location coordinates to be compared to $u_2$'s current location coordinates. If the location check is also satisfied, the access to $u_2$'s location will be granted to $u_1$, and the policy evaluation stops. Otherwise, the LPPM system continues to evaluate the remaining applicable policies. If none of the applicable policies are satisfied, $u_1$'s request to view $u_2$'s location will be denied, i.e., $u_1$ will not be able to know $u_2$'s current location.

For example, suppose that Bob allows his colleagues to know his exact location only when he is in the company during work hours from 8am to 5pm on weekdays. To achieve this, Bob can use the following policy: $P_1\langle\{Colleague\}, (8am < t < 5pm)$ AND $(d_1 = \{Mon, .., Fri\}), companyLoc, exactLoc\rangle$. Given $P_1$, if one of Bob's colleagues, Jack, is looking for Bob for a meeting at 10am and Bob is in the company at that time, Jack will be able to view Bob's location according to the policy. If Jack wants to know where is Bob at 12pm while Bob is at lunch outside the company, Jack will not be able to see Bob's location in this case.

As another example, assume that Bob usually allows his family members to know his locations according to the following policy: $P_2\langle\{Family\}, Anytime, Anywhere, exactLoc\rangle$. One day, Bob needs to shop for a gift for one of his family members, say Alice. In order to surprise her, Bob may want to block Alice from knowing his locations by temporarily changing the policy $P_2$ to $P_2'\langle\{Family\}/\{\textbf{Alice}\}, Anytime, Anywhere\rangle$. $P_2'$ excludes Alice from the policy target and hence Alice request to viewing Bob's location will be denied.

## 3.2 Policy Maintenance

For a given new policy, it is important to check if the access right granted by the new policy has already been included in some existing policies. If so, it is unnecessary to insert the new -redundant- policy. For example, suppose that Alice is Bob's family member. A new policy says that Alice is allowed to view Bob's location anytime on Saturday: $P_4\langle\{Alice\}, d1 = \{Saturday\}, Anywhere, exatLoc\rangle$; while there is an existing policy which says that family members are allowed to view Bob's location anytime during weekend: $P_3\langle\{Family\}, d1 = \{Weekend\}, Anywhere, exatLoc\rangle$. It is obvious that $P_4$ is covered by the existing policy $P_3$ and does not need to be inserted to the system. Policy redundancy is formalized as follows.

**Definition 2.** *(Policy Redundancy) Let* $P_i\langle U_i/E_i, T_i, L_i, G_i\rangle$ *be a new policy composed by user* $u$, *and* $S_p$ *be a set of existing policies belonging to the user* $u$. $P_i$ *is redundant if there exists a policy* $P_j\langle U_j/E_j, T_j, L_j\rangle \in S_p$, *and* $\{U_j/E_j\} \supseteq \{U_i/E_i\}$ *and* $T_j \supseteq T_i, L_j \supseteq L_i$ *and* $G_j = G_i$.

Based on Definition 2, we can see that $P_4$'s target, time constraint and location range are all subsets of that of the existing policy $P_3$, and they are specifying at the same location disclosure granularity, hence, $P_4$ is redundant.

If the above policy $P_4$ is slightly modified to $P_4'$ which specifies a different location disclosure granularity: $P_4'\langle\{Alice\}, d1 = \{Saturday\}$, Anywhere, **city**$\rangle$, $P_4'$ is not considered redundant but conflict with $P_3$. This is because $P_4'$ does not allow Alice to see Bob's exact location but only the city of the location, while $P_3$ allows family members including Alice to see Bob's exact locations. In a nutshell, the conflict may occur when the new policy grants access to a user which is denied by an existing policy, or vice versa. Its formal definition is the following.

**Definition 3.** *(Policy Conflict) Let* $P_i\langle U_i/E_i, T_i, L_i, G_i\rangle$ *be a new policy composed by user* $u$, *and* $P_j\langle U_j/E_j, T_j, L_j, G_j\rangle$ *be an existing policy belonging to the user* $u$. $P_i$ *conflicts with* $P_j$ *if one of the following conditions is satisfied:*

- $E_j \bigcap U_i \neq \emptyset$ *and* $T_j \bigcap T_i \neq \emptyset$ *and* $L_j \bigcap L_i \neq \emptyset$;
- $E_i \bigcap U_j \neq \emptyset$ *and* $T_j \bigcap T_i \neq \emptyset$ *and* $L_j \bigcap L_i \neq \emptyset$.

After passing the policy redundancy and conflict check, a new policy will be considered whether it can be merged with existing policies. Merging related policies not only helps enhance the presentation of policies to users but also improves the efficiency of policy management and evaluation since fewer policies need to be checked given a location request.

Before the formal definition, let us first exam an example when two policies can be merged. Policy $P_7$ states that Jack is allowed to view Bob's location on Monday when Bob is at Chicago: $P_7\langle\{Jack\}$, d1=Monday, Chicago, exactLoc$\rangle$, and another policy specifies that Alice is allowed to view Bob's location when Bob is at Chicago: $P_8\langle\{Alice\}$, d1=Monday, Chicago, exactLoc$\rangle$. $P_7$ and $P_8$ has the same location, time constraints and location disclosure granularity, but only differ in the policy targets. $P_7$ and $P_8$ can then be merged into one policy $P_m\langle\{Jack, Alice\}$, d1=Monday, Chicago, exactLoc$\rangle$. In general, two policies can be merged if they are specified at the same location disclosure granularity and have only one different component. The following definition summarizes the scenarios when two policies can be merged.

**Definition 4.** *Two policies* $P_i\langle U_i/E_i, T_i, L_i, G_i\rangle$ *and* $P_j\langle U_j/E_j, T_j, L_j, G_j\rangle$ *can be merged if they satisfy one of the following conditions:*

- *Two policies have the same policy targets, time constraints, i.e.,* $U_i/E_i = U_i/E_i$, $T_i = T_j$, *and* $G_i = G_j$.
- *Two policies have the same policy targets and location constraints, i.e.,* $U_i/E_i = U_i/E_i$, $L_i = L_j$ *and* $G_i = G_j$.
- *Two policies have the same time constraints and location constraints, i.e.,* $T_i = T_j$, $L_i = L_j$, *and* $G_i = G_j$.

*The result of the policy merge will be:* $P_m\langle(U_i\bigcup U_j)/(E_i\bigcup E_j), (T_i\bigcup T_j),$ $(L_i\bigcup L_j), G_i\rangle$.

## 3.3   Policy Recommendation

The policy recommendation is based on the analysis of the privacy level of the existing policies. The privacy level dictates visibility of a user's location on a level hierarchy. The less the visibility of the user's location, the higher the privacy level is. In order to quantify the visibility level, we consider the following parameters:

- $N_u$: denotes the total number of contacts of the policy owner.
- $N_p$: denotes the number of contacts specified in the policy target.
- $D_t, D_{d_1}, D_{d_2}$: denote the range of the time constraint in the policy.
- $Space$: denotes the total area that covers the policy owner's recorded locations.
- $G_d$: maps the location disclosure granularity to numbers to quantify their visibility level: exactLoc, district, city, state, country are represented as number 1, 2, 3, 4, 5 respectively.

By comparing each policy component with its corresponding domain (i.e., all possible values that the policy component may have), we define the privacy level $PL$ as follows:

**Definition 5.** *The privacy level $(PL_p)$ of $P$ is defined as the weighted sum of the ratio between each component value and its domain, where $w_u$, and $w_t$ and $w_l$ are the weights.*

$$PL = w_u \frac{N_u - N_p}{N_u} + w_t (1 - \frac{D_t}{24} \cdot \frac{D_{d_1}}{7} \frac{D_{d_2}}{12}) + w_l (1 - \frac{D_L}{Space} \frac{1}{G_d})$$

The privacy level $PL$ consists of three parts. The first part is the total number of users in the policy compared to the total number of contacts of the policy owner. If the policy owner allows more users to view his/her locations, that means the privacy owner has lower level of privacy concerns, and hence the value of $\frac{N_u - N_p}{N_u}$ will be smaller. The second part of $PL$ considers the time constraints in terms of hours, days and date. The longer the time that the policy owner's locations are disclosed, the lower the privacy level will be. The last part of the $PL$ integrates the effect of both the range of the space and the disclosure granularity. The larger the range of the locations and the finer the granularity, the lower the privacy level will be. Finally, the weight values are used for the need to adjust the impact of each component if any prior knowledge is available. By default, the weight values are equal for all components.

We now proceed to introduce the process of policy recommendation which includes three phases: (1) a preparation phase, (2) a policy generation phase and (3) the finalization phase.

**Phase 1:** The preparation phase aims to build the knowledge base. The LPPM system needs to have a few policies input by the users to be used as the base of the recommendation. For the first few policies, the LPPM system groups them based on the relationship between the policy target and the policy owner. In other words, policies regarding the same role of users will be placed in the same group. For example, if Alice and Jack are Bob's family members, the policies regarding Alice, Jack, and family members, will be in the same group. The reason of such grouping is that individuals usually maintain different rules for different types of contacts. For instance, the privacy policies for family members may usually allow the disclosure of the exact locations while the privacy policies for colleagues may just allow the disclosure of locations at city level. Next, in each group, the policies are further classified into three categories: low, medium, and high, according to their privacy levels. In particular, let $max(PL)$ denote the maximum $PL$ of all existing policies of a user. If a policy's privacy level is lower than $\frac{max(PL)}{3}$, the policy is considered to have low privacy protection level. If a policy's privacy level is greater than $\frac{2 \cdot max(PL)}{3}$, the policy is assigned a high privacy protection level. The remaining policies are at the medium level.

**Phase 2:** With the aid of the knowledge base, the second step is to generate the recommendation policy based on the user input. When a user needs a policy for a certain scenario, the user just needs to input part of the information that he/she knows and desired privacy level. The LPPM system will fill in the remaining information. The LPPM system requires the users to specify at least two items when using the recommendation system: (1) the desired privacy protection level; (2) either the policy target or the locations to be protected.

In the first case when the user input the policy target and privacy level, the LPPM system will conduct the following steps. First, the LPPM system locates the group of policies which contain the same role of the input policy target. For example, Bob indicates that he would like to assign a medium level privacy policy to his new friend Tim. This input contains information about the privacy level, the role of the policy target (i.e., "friend"). The LPPM system will search the policy repository to find the group of policies for "friends". Within the retrieved policies, the LPPM system further looks for policies of user requested privacy level, e.g., medium level. Among the qualifying policies, the one with highest $PL$ value will be selected. Finally, the LPPM system customizes the policy target to include the information from user input, e.g., the friend's name (i.e., Tim).

In the second case when the user input the locations to be protected and the desired privacy level, the LPPM system will search all the existing policies to find the ones at the required privacy level. Then, the LPPM system replaces the locations in the identified policies to the user input. For example, Bob wants to set up location privacy policies with high level protection when he is traveling at Chicago. The LPPM system finds that there are three policies at high level which are specified for family, friends and colleagues respectively. These three policies will be customized by modifying the locations to "Chicago" and present to Bob for review.

**Phase 3:** Finally, after the user decides the policies to be added to the system, the LPPM system will compute the privacy level of the newly inserted policies and store them for the future use. Note that it is possible that no matching policy is found by the recommendation function. In that case, the user needs to compose the policy by himself.

# 4   Conclusion

We developed a location privacy policy management system. The system supports an easy-to-understand yet expressive policy language. The system also automatically detects policy conflict whenever there is a policy update. Moreover, the system generates recommended policies based on existing privacy policies so that users do not need to compose entire policy for every new friend. In the future, we plan to implement a prototype in smart phones to further verify the practical value of the proposed system.

# References

1. Bamba, B., Liu, L., Pesti, P., Wang, T.: Supporting anonymous location queries in mobile environments with privacygrid. In: Proceeding of the 17th International Conference on World Wide Web, pp. 237–246 (2008)
2. Chow, C.Y., Mokbel, M.F., Liu, X.: A peer-to-peer spatial cloaking algorithm for anonymous location-based service. In: Proceedings of the 14th Annual ACM International Symposium on Advances in Geographic Information Systems, pp. 171–178 (2006)
3. Cvrcek, D., Kumpost, M., Matyas, V., Danezis, G.: A study on the value of location privacy. In: Proc. of the ACM Workshop on Privacy in Electronic Society, pp. 109–118 (2006)
4. Damiani, M.L., Bertino, E., Silvestri, C.: Spatial domains for the administration of location-based access control policies. Journal of Network and Systems Management 16(3), 277–302 (2008)
5. Danezis, G., Lewis, S., Anderson, R.: How much is location privacy worth. In: Fourth Workshop on the Economics of Information Security (2005)
6. Gedik, B., Liu, L.: Protecting location privacy with personalized k-anonymity: Architecture and algorithms. IEEE Transactions on Mobile Computing 7(1), 1–18 (2008)
7. Ghinita, G., Kalnis, P., Skiadopoulos, S.: Prive: anonymous location-based queries in distributed mobile systems. In: Proceedings of the 16th International Conference on World Wide Web, pp. 371–380 (2007)
8. Gruteser, M., Grunwald, D.: Anonymous usage of location-based services through spatial and temporal cloaking. In: Proceedings of the 1st International Conference on Mobile Systems, Applications and Services, pp. 31–42 (2003)
9. Lin, D., Bertino, E., Cheng, R., Prabhakar, S.: Location privacy in moving-object environments. Transactions on Data Privacy 2(1), 21–46 (2009)
10. Mokbel, M.F.: Towards privacy-aware location-based database servers. In: 22nd International Conference on Data Engineering Workshops. Proceedings, p. 93 (2006)
11. Mokbel, M.F., Chow, C.Y., Aref, W.G.: The new casper: query processing for location services without compromising privacy. In: Proceedings of the 32nd International Conference on Very Large Data Bases, pp. 763–774 (2006)
12. Myles, G., Friday, A., Davies, N.: Preserving privacy in environments with location-based applications. IEEE Pervasive Computing 2(1), 56–64 (2003)
13. Sadeh, N., Hong, J., Cranor, L., Fette, I., Kelley, P., Prabaker, M., Rao, J.: Understanding and capturing people's privacy policies in a mobile social networking application. Personal and Ubiquitous Computing 13(6), 401–412 (2009)
14. Smailagic, A., Kogan, D.: Location sensing and privacy in a context-aware computing environment. IEEE Wireless Communications 9(5), 10–17 (2002)
15. Snekkenes, E.: Concepts for personal location privacy policies. In: Proceedings of the 3rd ACM Conference on Electronic Commerce, pp. 48–57 (2001)
16. OASIS Standard. Extensible access control markup language (XACML). version 2.0 (2005)

# Privacy Protection in Social Networks Using $l$-Diversity

Liangwen Yu[1,2,3], Jiawei Zhu[1,2,3], Zhengang Wu[1,2,3], Tao Yang[1,2,3], Jianbin Hu[1,2,3,*], and Zhong Chen[1,2,3]

[1] Institute of Software, School of EECS, Peking University, China
[2] MoE Key Lab of High Confidence Software Technologies (PKU)
[3] MoE Key Lab of Network and Software Security Assurance (PKU)
{yulw,zhujw,wuzg,ytao,hjbin,chen}@infosec.pku.edu.cn

**Abstract.** With the increasing popularity of online social networks, such as twitter and weibo, privacy preserving publishing of social network data has raised serious concerns. In this paper, we focus on the problem of preserving the sensitive attribute of the node in social network data. We call a graph $l$-diversity anonymous if all the same degree nodes in the graph form a group in which the frequency of the most frequent sensitive value is at most $\frac{1}{l}$. To achieve this objective, we devise an efficient heuristic algorithm via graphic $l$-diverse partition and also use three anonymous strategies(AdjustGroup, RedirectEdges, AssignResidue)to optimize the heuristic algorithm. Finally, we verify the effectiveness of the algorithm through experiments.

**Keywords:** socail network, privacy preserving, data publishing, $l$-diversity.

## 1 Introduction

Nowadays, online social network sites, such as facebook, twitter and weibo, have received dramatic interest, more and more people join in various social networks. People use online social networks to share data, which produce lots of social network data. If this data is directly exposed to researchers, it will cause the privacy disclosure, which leads us to study how to effectively anonymize so as to protect sensitive information in social networks while maximizing the social network's utility analysis.

Anonymous methods for relational data have been widely studied. $k$-anonymity [1],$l$-diversity[2],$(a, k)$-anonymity[3],$t$-closeness[4],anatomy[5] are models for anonymizing relational data. As there are some relationships between the individuals in social networks, anonymizing social network data is different from anonymizing relational data. Anonymous approaches for social network data should consider attacks from network's topological structure. Privacy in social networks has begun to receive attention recently, and practical approaches are yet to be devised.

---

* Corresponding author.

T.W. Chim and T.H. Yuen (Eds.): ICICS 2012, LNCS 7618, pp. 435–444, 2012.

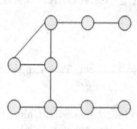

| Id | Degree | Sensitive Attribute |
|----|--------|---------------------|
| 1 | 1 | Heart Disease |
| 2 | 1 | Heart Disease |
| 3 | 1 | Flu |
| 4 | 2 | Cancer |
| 5 | 2 | Heart Disease |
| 6 | 2 | Flu |
| 7 | 3 | Cancer |
| 8 | 3 | Cancer |
| 9 | 3 | Cancer |

**Fig. 1.** A 3-degree anonymous graph and a table of nodes' sensitive attribute

Most of the previous works on protecting the node re-identification and sensitive relationship in social networks. In real social networks, however, nodes are usually associated with the sensitive attribute, such as disease information. For example, figure 1 shows a 3-degree anonymous graph[1] and a table of nodes' sensitive attribute. Consider an adversary knows that Bob's degree is 3. As there are three nodes with degree 3 in figure 1, we can conclude that Bob has a disease of cancer even if we can't ascertain which node is associated with Bob.

$l$-diversity[2] is an anonymous model for preserving the sensitive attribute in data publishing. It is first proposed in relational data, requiring at least $l$ "well-represented" values in every equivalence group. Moreover, anatomy[5] proposes a simple $l$-diversity which requires the frequency of the most frequent sensitive value in every equivalence group is at most $\frac{1}{l}$. Regarding social network data, [6, 7]have studied $l$-diversity, but there are certain shortcomings. Tai et al.[6] doesn't restrict the frequency of sensitive attribute, so it couldn't prevent probabilistic inference attack. Zhou and Pei[7] doesn't have a systematic introduction to $l$-diversity, the algorithm in [7] is not efficient and experiments are tested only on synthetic datasets. In this paper, we set nodes' sensitive attribute as the sensitive information. Based on the $k$-degree anonymity[8], we propose an anonymous approach that applies the simple $l$-diversity[5] in every equivalence group. As the anonymizing social network data is much more complicated than anonymizing relational data, we propose a heuristic algorithm in our anonymous approach.

In this work, we make the following contributions:

1. We propose a graphic $l$-diversity anonymous model for privacy preserving in social network data, which could protect node re-identification as well as node's sensitive attribute.
2. We devise three anonymous strategies, and propose a heuristic algorithm which transforms original social network data $G$ to anonymous social network data $G^*$ that obeys the graphic $l$-diversity anonymity.
3. We evaluate our approach on real datasets and synthetic datasets.

The remainder of the paper is organized as follows. Section 2 gives the problem definition. Section 3 introduces three anonymous strategies. Section 4 presents

---

[1] The number of nodes, which have the same degree in the graph, is at least 3.

the anonymous algorithm. Section 5 reports the experimental results. Section 6 presents the related work. Section 7 concludes the paper.

## 2  Problem Definiton

In this paper, a social network is modeled as an undirected simple graph $G(V, E, S)$, where $V$ stands for the node set, $E$ stands for the edge set and $S$ stands for the node's sensitive attribute set. Each node is associated with a sensitive attribute.

**Definition 1 ($l$-diversity).** *An equivalence class is said to have $l$-diversity if there are at least $l$ "well-represented" values for the sensitive attribute. A table is said to have $l$-diversity if every equivalence class of the table has $l$-diversity.*

Definition 1 presents $l$-diversity in relational data, and [2, 5] give some interpretations of the term "well-represented" in it: distinct $l$-diversity, entropy $l$-diversity, recursive $(c,l)$-diversity and simple $l$-diversity. We applies simple $l$-diversity in our approach for the following reasons: (1) Distinct $l$-diversity doesn't prevent probabilistic inference attacks; (2) Entropy $l$-diversity is too restrictive sometimes; (3) Recursive $(c,l)$-diversity mainly aims at countering background knowledge attack which rules out some possible values in sensitive attribute, and parameters $c$ and $l$ are difficult to set for users.

**Definition 2 (graphic $l$-diversity).** *A graph $G(V, E, S)$ is graphic $l$-diversity if all the same degree nodes in the graph form a group in which the frequency of the most frequent sensitive value is at most $\frac{1}{l}$.*

**Definition 3 (anonymization cost).** *Given an original network $G$ and its anonymous version $G^*$, the anonymization cost in $G^*$ is defined as*

$$Cost(G, G^*) = |E(G^*)| - |E(G)|$$

Anonymization cost is a measure to evaluate the information loss. In our approach, we almost keep the number of nodes unchanged and restrict the graph modification to edge additions, that is, graph $G^*$ is constructed from $G$ by adding a minimal set of edges. Furthermore, we use the statistical network measures to verify the utility of anonymous graph $G^*$. These statistics include average path length and clustering co-efficient.

## 3  The Anonymous Strategies

### 3.1  The AdjustGroup Method

To construct an $l$-diversity graph, we first enable all the nodes in the group have the same degree by adding edges after $l$-diversity partition is done.

The first step is to set a target degree for the group. For a group g, we sort the nodes in the degree descending order and set the target degree of $g$ to be the largest degree. All the nodes in $g$ need to have the same target degree. For

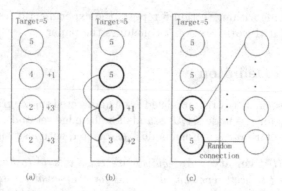

**Fig. 2.** The AdjustGroup method

example, in figure $2(a)$, the target degree of the group is 5. The number beside each node is the degree this node needs to be increased. All these numbers form a number sequence in ascending order. The second step is to create edges between nodes in the group. Based on the number sequence, we increase the nodes' degree in turn. If the nodes in the number sequence and there is no edge between them, we create one edge and update the number sequence. For example, in figure $2(b)$, two edges are created between nodes in the group, and the number sequence (1, 3, 3) is transformed into (1, 2). In the third step, we randomly create edges between nodes in the group and nodes ungrouped if there is no existing edge between them in the original graph. The quantity of random edge additions is equal to the sum in the number sequence. In figure $2(c)$, three edges are randomly created, and all the nodes in the group reach the target degree 5.

The second step in the AdjustGroup method is to decrease anonymization cost. For example, in figure 2, if we skip the second step directly to the third step, the number of edge additions will be increased from 5 to 7. Moreover, the target degree of the created new group is more likely to be increased, which may also cause the increment of anonymization cost.

## 3.2   The RedirectEdges Method

To construct an $l$-diversity graph, when the nodes form a new group, the AdjustGroup method enables all the nodes in the new group have the same target degree. For the node $v$ with the largest degree in the new group, if the degree of $v$ has already been increased using AdjustGroup method, the anonymization cost is certainly enlarged. To further reduce the anonymization cost, we propose the RedirectEdges method to avoid the above case, by redirecting the existing add edge set $\{e_1, e_2, \ldots, e_n\}$ to the edge set $\{e_1', e_2', \ldots, e_m'\}$ where $m \leq n$.

The RedirectEdges method allows us to reduce the degree of $v$ without changing the nodes' degree in any group which has been anonymized. Therefore, let $R_v$ denote the set of edges that should be redirected away from $v$ and $N_v$ denote the set of nodes besides $v$ that are associated with the edges in $R_v$. We first

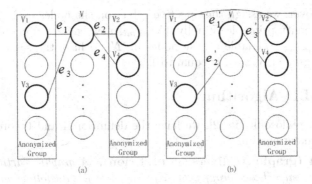

**Fig. 3.** The RedirectEdges method

create edges between the nodes in $N_v$, and all the nodes could be used only once. Further, residue nodes in $N_v$ randomly created one edge with the nodes ungrouped in the graph. However, if some of the residue nodes have relationships with all the ungrouped nodes, we link them back to $v$. For example, in figure 3(a), the redirected edges set $R_v$ is $\{e_1, e_2, e_3, e_4\}$ and the associated nodes set $N_v$ is $\{v_1, v_2, v_3, v_4\}$. In figure 3(b), we first create an edge $e_1'$ between $v_1$ and $v_2$, and then randomly create edges between $\{v_3, v_4\}$ and ungrouped nodes. Because $v_4$ has relationships with all the ungrouped nodes, only one new edge $e_2'$ is created and $v_4$ links back to $v$ again. After proposing the RedirectEdges method, the existing add edge set $\{e_1, e_2, e_3, e_4\}$ is transformed into the edge set $\{e_1', e_2', e_3'\}$.

## 3.3 The AssignResidue Method

The degree distribution of the social network follows a power law, which means that the majority of the nodes have small degree and a few nodes have significantly high degree. As the GLD algorithm first processes the high degree node, the nodes of the last group $N_{last}$ usually have the same 1 degree and no processing is needed. If not, the anonymous approach on $N_{last}$ is different from the one of other groups. First, the size of $N_{last}$ is $(n \pmod{l} + l)$. Moreover, we couldn't directly apply the AdjustGroup method on $N_{last}$, because there is no remaining nodes and the third step in AdjustGroup couldn't cover this special situation.

We specially process the $N_{last}$ in the following steps. First, we apply the previous two steps in AdjustGroup on $N_{last}$, which output the number sequence. After that, we set the sum in number sequence as $d$ and create a special $l$-diversity group $N_{special}$ whose size is determined by $d$.

$$|N_{special}| = \begin{cases} d, & if\, d \geq l \\ d + |N_{last}|, & if\, d < l \end{cases}$$

As the special group $N_{special}$ satisfies $l$-diversity principle, $|N_{special}|$(the number of nodes in $N_{special}$) must be equal to or more than $l$. If $d$ is equal to or more than $l$, we create $d$ new nodes in $N_{special}$. Otherwise, $|N_{special}|$ is equal to $d$ plus

$|N_{last}|$. Moreover, we assign the sensitive values on the nodes in $N_{special}$ on the basis of $l$-diversity principle. Finally, $|N_{special}|$ new edges are created between $N_{last}$ and $N_{special}$ to enable all the nodes in $|N_{last}|$ have the same degree and the nodes' degree in $N_{special}$ is equal to 1.

## 4   The GLD Algorithm

Following the philosophy in [2], we have the definition 4 and theorem 1 which are similarly mentioned in [5, 7].

**Definition 4 (graphic $l$-diversity partition).** *A graphic partition with $m$ groups is $l$-diversity, if each group $g_j$ ($1 \leq j \leq m$) satisfies the following conditions.*

---

**Algorithm 1.** Graphic $l$-Diversity (GLD) Algorithm

---

**Input:** An original graph $G(V, E, S)$ and the parameter $l$.
**Output:** The anonymous network $G^*(V^*, E^*, S)$, which is graphic $l$-diversity.

1: $G^* \leftarrow G$, $LastNode \leftarrow \phi$;
2: sort $v_i \in V(G)$ as $NodeList$ in the degree descending order;
3: **while** NodeList$\neq \phi$ **do**
4:    $SeedNode \leftarrow NodeList.head()$;
5:    **repeat**
6:       $LastNode \leftarrow SeedNode$;
7:       **RedirectEdges**($SeedNode$);
8:       update $NodeList$;
9:       $SeedNode \leftarrow NodeList.head()$;
10:    **until** $SeedNode = LastNode$
11:    remove the $SeedNode$ from $NodeList$;
12:    **if** $NodeList.size() \geq 2l - 1$ **then**
13:       $AnonymousGroup \leftarrow$ **Partition**($NodeList$) $\cup \{SeedNode\}$;
14:       **AdjustGroup**($AnonymousGroup$);
15:       update $NodeList$;
16:    **else**
17:       let $AnonymousGroup$ contain the remaining nodes in $NodeList$ with $SeedNode$;
18:       remove the remaining nodes from $NodeList$;
19:       **AssignResidue**($AnonymousGroup$);
20:    **end if**
21: **end while**
        **Function:** Partition($NodeList$)
22: $S \leftarrow \phi$;
23: put $v_i \in NodeList$ in buckets and node's sensitive value in each bucket is the same;
24: let $S$ contain $l$ - 1 the largest degree nodes respectively from $l$ - 1 different buckets whose sensitive values are different from the one to $SeedNode$ and remove them from $NodeList$;
25: **while** not exist a graphic $l$-diversity partition for $NodeList$ **do**
26:    find the largest degree node $v$ from bucket of the most frequent sensitive value;
27:    find the smallest degree node $v'$ in $S$ and the sensitive value of $v'$ is different from $v$, replace $v'$ with $v$, and place $v'$ back into $NodeList$;
28: **end while**

---

*(1)All the nodes in $g_j$ have the same degree; (2)Let c be the most frequent sensitive value in $g_j$, and $freq_j(c)$ be the number of nodes in $g_j$ with the sensitive value c; then $\frac{freq_j(c)}{|g_j|} \leq \frac{1}{l}$ where $|g_j|$ is the size (the number of nodes) of $|g_j|$.*

**Theorem 1.** *A graphic l-diversity exists, if and only if the graph $G(V, E, S)$ satisfies the following condition. At most $\frac{n}{l}$ nodes in G are associated with the same sensitive value, where n is the number of nodes in G.*

As shown in algorithm 1, the input of GLD is a original graph $G$ and a parameter $l$, and the output is an $l$-diversity graph $G^*$ for publishment. GLD first maintains a list *NodeList* of nodes in the degree descending order. At each iteration, we select the first node *SeedNode* in the *NodeList*. We repeatedly perform RedirectEdges to decrease the degree of *SeedNode* by redirecting added edges, then update *NodeList* and *SeedNode*, until the *SeedNode* keeps unchanged(lines 5-10). We remove the *SeedNode* from the *NodeList*. If the size of *NodeList* is at least $2l$ - 1, we apply Partition function in selecting $l$ - 1 the largest degree nodes which have unique sensitive values different from the one to *SeedNode* on the basis of the remaining nodes in *NodeList* satisfy the graphic $l$-diversity partition. Let a set *AnonymousGroup* contain *SeedNode* and above $l$ - 1 nodes. We apply AdjustGroup in making all the nodes in *AnonymousGroup* have the same degree, and update the *NodeList*. If the size of *NodeList* is less than $2l$ - 1, let *AnonymousGroup* contain the remaining nodes in *NodeList* and remove them from *NodeList*. We perform AssignResidue to enable the residual nodes in *AnonymousGroup* have the same degree via creating a special group sometimes. The GLD algorithm ceases when there is no node left in *NodeList*.

## 5   Experimental Results

In this section, we evaluate the performance of the proposed GLD algorithm on one real dataset and one synthetic dataset.

**ca-CondMat:** This dataset shows a Condense Matter collaboration network which is built from the scientific collaborations between authors' papers from January 1993 to April 2003(http://snap.stanford.edu/data/ca-CondMat.htm). It contains 23,133 nodes and 186,936 edges. An undirected edge is created if two authors co-authored a paper. Due to the lack of sensitive attribute in ca-CondMat, we apply the METIS graph partition tool in deriving the group identification and set it as the sensitive attribute.

**Synthetic Dataset:** We also use the software Pajek to generate a graph with scale-free property. The default number of nodes in synthetic dataset is 5000. In order to assign a sensitive value to each node in the graph, we assign a random integer in the range [0,100] to each node on the basis of theorem 1.

In this experiment, We study the utility of anonymous graphs from average path length and clustering co-efficient. We compare our approach with $k$-degree anonymity[8] and other $l$-diversity methods[6, 7]. Figure 4 shows the average path length of anonymous graphs for $k, l = 4, 6, 8, 10, 12, 14$. As the graph modification is restricted to edge additions in these anonymous approaches, the average path length is trending downwards. Comparing the four anonymous approaches separately with the original one, we can see the result of $k$-degree[8] is the best, but it can't protect nodes' sensitive attribute. The result of $l$-diversity in this paper is close to that of $k$-SDA[6], and our approach can also prevent probabilistic inference attack. The $l$-diversity(1 neighborhood)[7] loses some utility for protecting 1 neighborhood isomorphism, and its result is the lowest. Figure 5 shows the clustering co-efficient of anonymous graphs. The clustering co-efficient is trending upwards in the two graphs. Moreover, we can find that clustering co-efficient is stable in our approach when $l = 12, 14$. The reason is that we create some new nodes in AssignResidue. Similar to average path length, our approach loss little utility in the clustering co-efficient, and it can protect nodes' sensitive attribute from probabilistic inference attack. Generally, all these observations verify that graphic $l$-diversity model could acceptably capture main features of the social network.

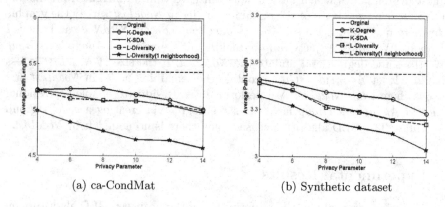

(a) ca-CondMat                    (b) Synthetic dataset

**Fig. 4.** Average path length

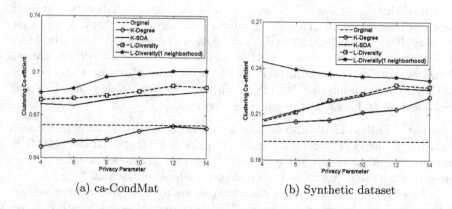

(a) ca-CondMat                    (b) Synthetic dataset

**Fig. 5.** Clustering co-efficient

# 6   Related Work

The problem of privacy protection in social networks is first proposed in [9], where the authors demonstrate that the naive anonymization strategy which replaces all identifiers of individuals with randomized integers is not sufficient by both active and passive attacks.

In anonymizing social network data, there are two categories: clustering-based approaches and graph modification approaches. The clustering-based methods[10–13] cluster nodes and edges into groups and anonymize a subgraph into a super-node. In this way, the details about individuals can be hidden properly. [10] propose anonymizing a graph by partitioning the nodes and summarizing the graph at partition level. Zheleva and Getoor[11] focuses on the case where there are multiple types of edges but only one type of nodes, and applies clustering-based method in protecting relationships disclosure. Cormode et al.[12] focuses on the problem of anonymizing bipartite graphs. Based on [12], Bhagat et al.[13] further constructs a model of the rich interaction graph, and proposes three approaches in protecting users' rich interaction.

The graph modification methods[6–8, 14–16] anonymize a graph by modifying edges and nodes in a graph. Hay et al.[15] proposes an approach that obeys a rule of random edge additions and deletions in anonymizing the graph, this method can effectively resist some kinds of attacks but suffers a significant cost in utility. Liu and Terzi[8] first introduces the $k$-anonymity model from the relational data to the social network data, and proposes $k$-degree anonymity to protect each individual in a group consisting of at least $k$ nodes of the same degree. Zhou and Pei[14] proposes the stronger model that each individual in a group consisting of at least $k$ nodes sharing 1-neighbourhood isomorphism. Zou et al.[16] proposes a $k$-automorphism model that each individual in a group consisting of at least $k$ nodes without any structural difference. [6, 7] based on different models apply $l$-diversity in protecting nodes re-identification and nodes' sensitive attribute.

# 7   Conclusions

In this paper, we consider the $l$-diversity in anonymizing the social network data. We present a heuristic algorithm which could transform the original graph $G$ to an $l$-diversity $G^*$ via the three anonymous strategies(AdjustGroup, RedirectEdges, AssignResidue). Our experiments, based on two datasets and several utility measures, show that our algorithm can effectively produce $l$-diversity graph that have acceptable utility.

**Acknowledgment.** This work is partially supported by the HGJ National Significant Science and Technology Projects under Grant No. 2012ZX01039-004-009, Key Lab of Information Network Security, Ministry of Public Security under Grant No.C11606, the National Natural Science Foundation of China under Grant No. 61170263.

# References

1. Sweeney, L., et al.: k-anonymity: A model for protecting privacy. International Journal of Uncertainty Fuzziness and Knowledge Based Systems 10(5), 557–570 (2002)
2. Machanavajjhala, A., Kifer, D., Gehrke, J., Venkitasubramaniam, M.: l-diversity: Privacy beyond k-anonymity. ACM Transactions on Knowledge Discovery from Data (TKDD) 1(1), 3 (2007)
3. Wong, R., Li, J., Fu, A., Wang, K.: (a,k)-anonymity: An enhanced k-anonymity model for privacy, preserving data publishing. In: KDD, vol. 6, pp. 754–759 (2006)
4. Li, N., Li, T., Venkatasubramanian, S.: t-closeness: Privacy beyond k-anonymity and l-diversity. In: IEEE 23rd International Conference on Data Engineering, ICDE 2007, pp. 106–115. IEEE (2007)
5. Xiao, X., Tao, Y.: Anatomy: Simple and effective privacy preservation. In: Proceedings of the 32nd International Conference on Very Large Data Bases. VLDB Endowment, pp. 139–150 (2006)
6. Tai, C., Yang, D., Yu, P., Chen, M.: Structural diversity for privacy in publishing social networks. In: Proc. of SDM (2011)
7. Zhou, B., Pei, J.: The k-anonymity and l-diversity approaches for privacy preservation in social networks against neighborhood attacks. Knowledge and Information Systems 28(1), 47–77 (2011)
8. Liu, K., Terzi, E.: Towards identity anonymization on graphs. In: Proceedings of the 2008 ACM SIGMOD International Conference on Management of Data, pp. 93–106. ACM (2008)
9. Backstrom, L., Dwork, C., Kleinberg, J.: Wherefore art thou r3579x?: anonymized social networks, hidden patterns, and structural steganography. In: Proceedings of the 16th International Conference on World Wide Web, pp. 181–190. ACM (2007)
10. Hay, M., Miklau, G., Jensen, D., Towsley, D., Weis, P.: Resisting structural re-identification in anonymized social networks. Proceedings of the VLDB Endowment 1(1), 102–114 (2008)
11. Zheleva, E., Getoor, L.: Preserving the Privacy of Sensitive Relationships in Graph Data. In: Bonchi, F., Malin, B., Saygın, Y. (eds.) PInKDD 2007. LNCS, vol. 4890, pp. 153–171. Springer, Heidelberg (2008)
12. Cormode, G., Srivastava, D., Yu, T., Zhang, Q.: Anonymizing bipartite graph data using safe groupings. Proceedings of the VLDB Endowment 1(1), 833–844 (2008)
13. Bhagat, S., Cormode, G., Krishnamurthy, B., Srivastava, D.: Class-based graph anonymization for social network data. Proceedings of the VLDB Endowment 2(1), 766–777 (2009)
14. Zhou, B., Pei, J.: Preserving privacy in social networks against neighborhood attacks. In: IEEE 24th International Conference on Data Engineering, ICDE 2008, pp. 506–515. IEEE (2008)
15. Hay, M., Miklau, G., Jensen, D., Weis, P., Srivastava, S.: Anonymizing social networks. Computer Science Department Faculty Publication Series, p. 180 (2007)
16. Zou, L., Chen, L., Özsu, M.: K-automorphism: A general framework for privacy preserving network publication. Proceedings of the VLDB Endowment 2(1), 946–957 (2009)

# Selling Power Back to the Grid in a Secure and Privacy-Preserving Manner

Tat Wing Chim[1], Siu Ming Yiu[1], Lucas Chi Kwong Hui[1], Victor On Kwok Li[2], Tin Wing Mui[1], Yu Hin Tsang[1], Chun Kin Kwok[1], and Kwun Yin Yu[1]

[1] Department of Computer Science
[2] Department of Electrical and Electronic Engineering
The University of Hong Kong, Pokfulam Road, Hong Kong
{twchim,smyiu,hui}@cs.hku.hk, vli@eee.hku.hk,
{twmui,yhtsang,ckkwok,kyyu2}@cs.hku.hk

**Abstract.** Smart grid facilitates a customer to sell unused or self-generated power back to the grid. This not only helps the power operator to reduce power generation, but also brings customers a means of getting revenue. However, the process of power selling induces two security problems, namely authentication and privacy-preservation. Like other messages, a customer's request messages for power selling should be properly authenticated to avoid various attacks. At the same time, the customer's privacy such as daily electricity usage pattern should be properly protected. In this paper, we propose a secure and privacy-preserving protocol to make this possible. Basically, authentication is done by means of anonymous credentials. Even in the reconciliation phase, the power operator only knows how much power a customer has uploaded to the grid but cannot know when the customer has done so. We evaluate our scheme to show that it is effective.

**Keywords:** smart grid, power selling, authentication, privacy-preservation, anonymous credential, blind signature.

## 1 Introduction

Smart grid is the next generation power grid. It integrates information and communication technology with power generation and distribution technologies. Its basic function is to facilitate the power operator to adjust the amount of power generated based on customers' demands. It ensures that customers' demands are satisfied while excess electricity generation can be avoided. This in turn can help protect the environment by reducing air pollutants emitted from the power generation process (especially those by fossil-fuel generators).

In the old days, power transmission is always one-way (i.e. from power grid to customers). The other way (i.e. from customers back to power grid) is impossible. However, the introduction of smart grid changes this picture. Selling power back to the power grid becomes common in U.S. and European countries [1]. The mechanism is in fact beneficial to both the power operator and the customers. The power operator

T.W. Chim and T.H. Yuen (Eds.): ICICS 2012, LNCS 7618, pp. 445–452, 2012.

can "recycle" customers' unused or self-generated power so that it can reduce the amount of power generated and thus lower the expenses. The customers can obtain revenue by selling power. Suppose a customer owns an electric vehicle. Due to differential pricing of electricity, the customer can charge up the battery in his electric vehicle during the low tariff hours, and sell the electricity back to the grid during the high tariff hours. In some countries, to encourage citizens to build renewable generation facilities such as wind mills and solar panels, the government dictates that the utility company has to buy electricity from the customers at a given tariff.

Basically, when a customer wants to sell power back to the grid, he/she has to first make a request with the amount of power to be uploaded to the control center. The control center then authenticates and approves the request. After that, the customer starts uploading power to the grid. As the power transmission system and the communications system are independent of each other, one may ask how the control center can ensure that the customer really upload the amount of power agreed in the request. To facilitate such checking, the smart meter in the customer's home has to be upgraded so that it can measure bi-directional power transmission (i.e. from grid to customer and from customer back to grid). The mechanism of power uploading and how a smart meter can measure bi-directional power transmission are out of the scope of this paper.

This paper focuses on the security and privacy issues in the communications involved in power selling between the control center and smart meters. Two security problems, namely authentication and privacy-preservation are addressed. Like other messages, a customer's request messages for power uploading should be properly authenticated. Otherwise, an attacker can generate numerous fake request messages so as to affect the power operator's decision about power generation. At the same time, the customer's privacy such as daily electricity usage pattern should be properly protected. If a criminal obtains this information, the family is susceptible to being burglarized. Thus we propose a secure and privacy-preserving protocol to resolve both problems. Basically, authentication is done by means of anonymous credentials (analogous to tickets). A customer first generates a set of credentials and blinding factors. The customer "blinds" the credentials and then requests the control center to sign them using the control center's private key. Interested readers may refer to our previous work [13] for details about the blind signature technique. When the customer wants to sell power to the grid, he/she will send an appropriate number of credentials (to represent the amount of power to upload) to the control center anonymously. In the reconciliation phase, the control center computes the number of used credentials to estimate how much power the customer has agreed to upload to the grid (but cannot know when the customer has done so), and then compares this value with the smart meter measurement. If the values are comparable, payment will be made to the customer accordingly. We evaluate our scheme to show that it is effective.

The rest of the paper is organized as follows: related work is summarized in Section 2. The system model and the security requirements are described in Section 3. Our scheme is presented in Section 4. The analysis of our scheme is given in Section 5. Finally, Section 6 concludes the paper.

## 2    Related Work

The smart grid project was started by the European Union in 2003 [6]. At about the same time, the U.S. Electric Power Research Institute started the IntelliGrid Project [7] and the US DOE also initiated the Grid 2030 project [8]. In early 2010, NIST released a report [5] which describes the potential components and cyber security issues of the smart grid system. As such, smart grid research and development is an important engineering trend in most developed and developing countries.

Two recent works [9] and [10] elaborate the importance of a smart grid especially with the consideration of renewable energy resources. They propose a communication-oriented smart grid framework. New requirements of the communication architecture and possible security problems of the smart grid system are also identified.

Some major security problems have been pointed out and studied in [3] and [4]. On the communication between the control center of the power grid and the smart meter, it is proved that a statistical analysis approach cannot protect the system from false data injection attack [11]. It would also be infeasible for the smart grid system to adopt this approach since the system will need to handle a large amount of data in real time, but the control center of the smart grid system only has a few seconds to respond.

Some solutions have been proposed in [12], [13], [14] and [15]. All these works provide user authentication. The schemes proposed in [12] and [13] even provide some level of user privacy preservation. [12] assumes that the power operator is fully trusted and can know the electricity usage pattern of all customers. [13] does not allow the power operator to know the electricity usage pattern of any customer. Their work also adopts anonymous credentials as in our scheme. However, their use of credentials with many different values causes huge burden to both the control center as well as the communications network during the registration phase. Nevertheless, none of the works address the power selling issue.

## 3    System Model and Security Requirements

Following [12] and [13], we assume that a smart gird network can be simplified into three basic layers to form a hierarchical structure. At the top level, there is a control center maintained by the power operator. At the second level, there are substations in the distribution network and each substation is responsible for the power supply of an area. At the lowest level, there are smart meters which are placed at the homes of the customers.

Smart meters should send requests to the control center when they want to sell power back to the grid. The control center can be a single server located inside the power plant or be distributed servers located at different geographical locations for load-balancing purposes and to avoid single point of failure. The communication channels from the smart meters to the control center and from the substations to the control center may be the Internet which is public and is always considered unsafe.

We aim at designing a system to resolve the following security problems:

a) Message authentication: Every request message sent by any smart meter should be checked to confirm that it is from a valid user. Authentication is the basis of the system. Without it, anyone can abuse or attack the system easily.

b) Identity privacy preservation: The real identity of the customer during the requesting phase should be unknown to everyone, including the power operator to protect the privacy of customers.

c) Request message confidentiality: The amount of power to be sold to the grid by any smart meter should not be known by any third party in order to protect the privacy of the customers.

d) Traceability: The total amount of power to be uploaded by each customer in a certain period of time should be known by the power operator (i.e. its control center) so that it can compare this value with the smart meter measurement and to arrange payment to the customer accordingly.

## 4    Details of Our Scheme

In our scheme, we assume that any smart meter can communicate with the control center via a secure communications channel. That is, every message transmitted is encrypted (say using AES encryption) and third parties cannot read the contents without the key concerned. The basic idea of our scheme is to make use of the blind signature technique for the control center to sign credentials on behalf of customers. In this way, when a customer presents a credential anonymously (without any information about the customer's identity provided), the control center cannot tell which customer is making the request, yet it can verify the signature to confirm that it is from a valid customer because only a valid customer can request for blind signatures. At the end of each month, each customer sends the unused credentials back to the control center to evaluate the amount of power he has agreed to sell so far. Next let us describe our scheme in details.

### A    Setup Phase

During system startup, the control center assigns itself an RSA public and private key pair for signing credentials. The public key is assumed to be known by everyone while the private key is only known by the control center.

Whenever a new smart meter is registered, it will be assigned a unique identity for identification purpose and a secret value for authentication purpose (details of their usage will be discussed later). Also a shared key between the smart meter and the control center, $sk$, will be established.

### B    Registration Phase

At the beginning of each month, the registration phase will be carried out. *This phase is not anonymous.* Customers need to be authenticated using their real identities in this phase. For this purpose, the smart meter submits its identity and secret value to the control center (via a secure channel) to authenticate itself. This phase continues with the following steps:

**Step 1:** Each customer, with the help of the smart meter, sends credential signing requests to the power operator. Each credential $C_i$ is of the format: (*CID, date of issuance, V*). Recall that *CID* is a unique[1] (it has been shown in [13] that the probability of collision is low if its size is properly set) credential identifier for each credential and *V* indicates that by presenting a credential, one agrees to upload *V* credits of power to the grid.

**Step 2:** For each credential the smart meter needs, $n$ credentials with $n$ different *CID*s and blinding factors, where $n$ is pre-determined by the control center, are generated. Among them, the control center requests the customer to open $(n-1)$ of them for verification purpose.

**Step 3:** If the information in all the "opened" credentials is valid, the control center signs the remaining one. Otherwise, it requires the customer to re-submit its request. Recall that the blinded version of credential $C_i$ constructed by the customer is in the format $B_i = (C_i F_i^e) \bmod n$, where $F_i$ is the blinding factor. For each signed credential, the control center assigns each blinded credential $B_i$ a unique blinded credential identity, $BID_i$ and stores $BID_i$, $B_i$ together with the customer's identity into a list $L_1$ in its local database. Finally, the control center transmits $BID_i$ and its signature on $B_i$ (i.e. $(C_i^d F_i) \bmod n$) back to the customer.

**Step 4:** The smart meter extracts the control center's signature, $C_i^d \bmod n$, on the credential by multiplying the inverse of the blinding factor $F_i$ to the received signature.

**Step 5:** The smart meter repeats Steps 2 to 4 above until all credentials required have been signed.

**Step 6:** The smart meter stores BIDs and blinding factors of all signed credentials locally.

**Step 7:** The control center calculates and records the number of credentials that it has signed so far into its local database.

**Step 8:** The smart meter of the customer stores these signed credentials properly for later usage. Since a smart meter can be considered as a tamper-proof device, we assume that the stored signed credentials cannot be modified by an outsider easily.

## C    Power Selling Phase

This phase can be executed at any time during the month when the smart meter of a customer finds that it has excess power to sell back to the grid. To protect the privacy of the customer, *this phase is anonymous*. Customers do not have to authenticate themselves in this phase and the validity of the customer is represented by the anonymous credentials made in the registration phase.

When the customer wants to sell power back to the power grid, the smart meter randomly picks and sends an appropriate amount of credentials to represent the

---

[1] It has been shown in [12] that the collision probability of *CID*s can be very low if the size of *CID* is properly set.

amount of power uploading agreed. In our design, the value of each credential $V$ is expressed in terms of credits such that the power operator can impose different weights on power sold at different times. For example, a customer can get more revenue if he/she sells power during peak hours. Without loss of generality, assume that the current weight is $R$ credits for each unit of power sold. If a customer wants to sell $T$ units of power, the smart meter has to submit $\lfloor TR/V \rfloor$ credentials to the control center. The control center then verifies its own signature on each credential. It then checks whether the credential identifier $CID$ has been used previously and whether *date of issuance* is up to date. To facilitate the former checking, the control center maintains another list $L_2$ to store all used $CID$s. This list will also be used in the reconciliation phase. A used credential will be considered as invalid. Otherwise, the control center includes this new $CID$ into $L_2$ and broadcasts the list to all customers as an acknowledgement. In this way, a customer can know that its power selling request has been approved by the control center. Each smart meter maintains a list $L_3$ to record $BID$s and the corresponding blinding factors of credentials in all approved power selling instances.

For each used credential $C_i$, the smart meter generates a keyed hash on the identity of the blinded credential, $BID_i$, together with the random blinding factor used, $F_i$. The key used here is the shared key, $sk$, established between the customer and the control center in the setup phase. That is, the keyed hash is of the format $h_{sk}(BID_i, F_i)$. All these keyed hash values are stored into a list $L_4$. Both lists $L_3$ and $L_4$ will be used in the reconciliation phase.

## D    Reconciliation Phase

After a certain time period (e.g. at the end of a month), the reconciliation phase will be carried out. Similar to the registration phase, *this phase is not anonymous*. Customers need to be authenticated using their real identities in this phase.

Assume that a customer has used $n$ credentials for which the $BID$s and the corresponding blinding factors are recorded in the list $L_3$ in the smart meter. The list $L_4$ stores $n$ keyed hash values accordingly.

In the reconciliation phase, the smart meter sends the list $L_4$ to the control center. Upon receiving $L_4$, the control center randomly picks $m$, where $m < n$, entries from $L_4$ to form a sub-list $L_5$. The control center then challenges the smart meter to reveal entries in $L_5$ by providing the $m$ $BID$s and the $m$ blinding factors concerned. Upon receiving the response, the control center re-computes $m$ keyed hash values with the received $BID$s and blinding factors to see whether they are the same as those listed on $L_5$. On the other hand, the control center also checks whether the $BID$s actually belong to that particular customer by checking their existence in list $L_1$ in its local database. If both checking pass, for each pair of $BID_i$ and $F_i$, the control center tries to use the blinding factor $F_i$ to "open" the blinded credential $B_i$ with identifier $BID_i$ (i.e. to compute $C_i = (B_i / F_i^e) \bmod n$). This is possible because all blinded credentials have been stored in list $L_1$ during the registration phase. After obtaining the actual credential $C_i$ which is of the format $C_i = (CID_i, date\ of\ issuance, V)$, the control center checks whether $CID_i$ has been used by checking its existence in the list $L_2$. If all the $m$ opened credentials are valid, the control center assumes that the remaining $(n - m)$ unopened credentials are also valid. The control center then trusts that the customer has sold $nV$ credits of power to the grid during the month, and later offers payments to the customer.

# 5    Security Analysis

In this section, we evaluate our scheme according to the security requirements listed in Section 3:

   a)   Message authentication: During the registration phase, a customer needs to authenticate himself/herself using the private key signature before requesting any signing of credentials. So when the customer presents the signed credentials during the power selling phase, he/she proves himself/herself authenticated.
   b)   Identity privacy: Customers only reveal their identities during the registration and the reconciliation phases. During the power selling phase, when the customer presents the credentials, the control center only knows whether the credential is from a valid user or not. Due to the properties of the blind signature, the credential identity is only known by the owner. The credentials do not reveal the identities of the customers.
   c)   Request message confidentiality: As we mentioned earlier, we assume that a smart meter communicates with the control center via a secure channel. Therefore, the amount of power to be sold agreed by any smart meter cannot be known by any third party. Confidentiality of the request message is preserved.
   d)   Traceability: During the registration phase, a customer needs to present his/her identity (i.e. not anonymous) to obtain signed anonymous credentials. In the reconciliation phase, a customer again needs to present his/her identity to the control center. Therefore, the total amount of power requested by each particular customer in a certain period of time (say a month) can be known by the control center. The control center can then properly offer payments to the customer at the end of the billing period.

# 6    Conclusion

In this paper, we focused on how to facilitate a customer to sell power back to the power grid in a secure and privacy-preserving manner. We proposed a secure and privacy-preserving protocol to solve the problem. Basically, we adopted the technique of anonymous credentials for authentication. These credentials are generated by the customer but are blindly signed by the control center. Also based on our design, even in the reconciliation phase, the power operator only knows how much power a customer has sold to the grid but cannot tell when the customer has done so. We evaluated our scheme using security analysis to show that it is effective. In the future, we will investigate the tradeoff between privacy preservation and traceability statistically, suggest how to set the proportion of credentials that the control center should choose for challenging in the reconciliation phase, and study other security problems in smart grid.

**Acknowledgement.** This research is supported in part by the HKU RCGAS Small Project Funding under Grant No. 201109176206, the Collaborative Research Fund of the Research Grants Council of Hong Kong under Grant No. HKU10/CRF/10, the General Research Fund from the Research Grants Council of the Hong Kong Special Administrative Region, China under Project No. RGC GRF HKU 713009E and the NSFC/RGC Joint Research Scheme under Project No. N_HKU 722/09.

# References

1. Networx: Guide to Selling Power Back to the Grid, http://www.networx.com/article/guide-to-selling-solar-geothermal-and
2. Khurana, H., Hadley, M., Lu, N., Frincke, D.A.: Smart-Grid Security Issues. IEEE Security and Privacy Magazine 81–85 (2010)
3. The Smart Grid Interoperability Panel Cyber Security Working Group: Second Draft NISTIR 7628 Smart Grid Cyber Security Strategy and Requirements (2010)
4. Office of the National Coordinator for Smart Grid Interoperability: NIST Special Publication 1108: NIST Framework and Roadmap for Smart Grid Interoperability Standards, Release 1.0 (2010)
5. SmartGrids: European SmartGrids Technology Platform: Vision and Strategy for Europe's Electricity Networks of the Future. In: European Commission, Directorate-General for Research, Sustainable Energy Systems, EUR 22040 (2006)
6. Electric Power Research Institute: Intelligrid, http://intelligrid.epri.com/
7. US Department of Energy: Grid 2030: A National Vision for Electricity's Second 100 Years (2003)
8. Wen, M.H.F., Leung, K.C., Li, V.O.K.: Communication-oriented Smart Grid Framework. In: Proceedings of the IEEE SmartGridComm 2011 (2011)
9. Li, V.O.K., Wu, F.F., Zhong, J.: Communication requirements for Risk-Limiting Dispatch in Smart Grid. In: Proceedings of the IEEE Workshop on Smart Grid Communications (2010)
10. Liu, Y., Ning, P., Reiter, M.K.: False Data Injection Attacks against State Estimation in Electric Power Grids. In: Proceedings of the CCS 2009, pp. 21–32 (2009)
11. Chim, T.W., Yiu, S.M., Hui, Lucas C.K., Li, V.O.K.: PASS: Privacy-preserving Authentication Scheme for Smart Grid Network. In: Proceedings of the IEEE SmartGridComm'11 (2011).
12. Cheung, J.C.L., Chim, T.W., Yiu, S.M., Hui, L.C.K., Li, V.O.K.: Credential-based Privacy-preserving Power Request Scheme for Smart Grid Network. In: Proceedings of the IEEE GLOBECOM 2011 (2011)
13. Fouda, M.M., Fadlullah, Z.M., Kato, N., Lu, R., Shen, X.S.: Towards a Light-weight Message Authentication Mechanism Tailored for Smart Grid Communications. In: Proceedings of the First International Workshop on Security in Computers, Networking and Communications, pp. 1018–1023 (2011)
14. Fouda, M.M., Fadlullah, Z.M., Kato, N., Lu, R., Shen, X.S.: A Lightweight Message Authentication Scheme for Smart Grid Communications. IEEE Transactions on Smart Grid 2(4), 675–685 (2011)

# A Key Sharing Fuzzy Vault Scheme

Lin You[1], Mengsheng Fan[1], Jie Lu[2], Shengguo Wang[2], and Fenghai Li[3]

[1] College of Comm. Engr., Hangzhou Dianzi Univ., Hangzhou 310018, China
[2] Zhejiang Wellcom Technology Co., Ltd, Hangzhou 310012, China
[3] The Key Lab. of Information Assurance Technology, Beijing 10072, China

**Abstract.** Based on the classical fuzzy vault and the Diffie-Hellman key exchange scheme, a key sharing fuzzy vault scheme is proposed. In this fuzzy vault scheme, the two users cooperatively build their shared fuzzy vault with a shared key hidden in it using their own biometric features, and they can respectively use their biometric features to unlock the fuzzy vault to get their shared key without running the risk of disclosure of their biometric features later. The security of our scheme is based on the security of the classical fuzzy vault scheme and and the discrete logarithm problem in a given finite group.

**Keywords:** Fuzzy Vault, Diffie-Hellman key exchange, Finite group, Biometrics, Polynomial interpolation.

## 1 Introduction

In a cryptosystem, one of the most important procedure is to securely store the secret key. Generally, the secret key is stored in the user's computer, a smart card or other storage medias by using a password for accessing, but it will run the risks that the storage medias be lost or stolen, or the password will suffer from the exhaustive search attack. A better way is to use the user's biometric features as the access control measure, while the user's biometric feature or secret key may also be disclosed if his biometric template and key are separately stored. Therefore, to ensure their safety simultaneously, the user's biometric feature and secret key should be completely blended into one set or a data. A classical solution is the fuzzy vault proposed by Juels and Sudan in 2002 [1]. In their fuzzy vault scheme, they used the user's unique set to blend his secret into a vault based on Reed-Solomon codes, and the user can recover his secret by providing a set that overlaps largely with the original set. Even if an attacker can get the vault he cannot obtain the the user's secret or the information about the set.

Diffie-Hellman key exchange scheme is a key cryptographic protocol, but how to safely store the shared key between the users is also a thorny problem. In order to produce a shared key between two parties and protect it from being illegally exposed, based on the ideals of the original fuzzy vault and the Diffie-Hellman key exchange scheme, a fuzzy vault scheme for the secret key exchange is proposed in this work. The security of this fuzzy vault scheme is based on both a polynomial reconstruction problem and a discrete logarithm problem.

T.W. Chim and T.H. Yuen (Eds.): ICICS 2012, LNCS 7618, pp. 453–460, 2012.

In the following Section 2, the classical fuzzy vault scheme is introduced. Then, our key sharing fuzzy vault scheme is proposed in Section 3 and its security analysis is given in Section 4. Finally, some concluding remarks are presented in Section 5.

## 2   The Classical Fuzzy Vault Scheme

The classical fuzzy vault scheme was invented by Juels and Sudan in 2002 and was revised in 2006 [2]. Essentially, the fuzzy vault is a scheme for the secure protection of one's secret (value or key) by the use of his some private message set which generally comes from his unique biometrics. A fuzzy vault is composed of two algorithms, one is called the locking algorithm, and the other is called the unlocking algorithm, as the following Fig. 1 and Fig. 2 shown, respectively.

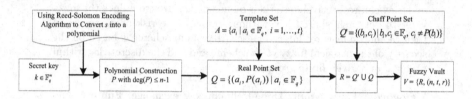

**Fig. 1.** Juels & Sudan's Fuzzy Vault Scheme–Locking Algorithm

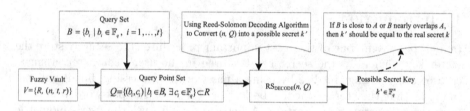

**Fig. 2.** Juels & Sudan's Fuzzy Vault Scheme–Locking Algorithm

A fuzzy vault scheme includes two public parameters, one is a finite field $\mathbb{F}_q$ with $q$ a power of a prime, and the other is a Reed-Solomon decoding algorithm (denoted as $\text{RS}_{\text{DECODE}}$ for short). The most practical choice for $\text{RS}_{\text{DECODE}}$ is the Reed-Solomon decoding algorithm based on Newton's interpolation [3] or the Lagrange interpolation polynomial. The following two algorithms for the fuzzy vault scheme comes originally from the revised work of Juels and Sudan [2] except for some minor changes. The security of this scheme is based on a polynomial reconstruction problem.

### 2.1   Locking Algorithm

INPUT: Parameters $n$, $t$, and $r$ such that $n \leq t \leq r \leq q$, a pre-selected secret
key $k \in \mathbb{F}_q^n$, a set $A = \{a_i\}_{i=1}^t$ with $a_i \in \mathbb{F}_q$ being distinct.
OUTPUT: A fuzzy vault $V = \{R, (n, r, q)\}$ with $R$ being a set of points $\{(x_i, y_i)\}_{i=1}^r$ such that $x_i, y_i \in \mathbb{F}_q$ and all $x_i$ being distinct.

1. $X, R, V \leftarrow \varnothing$;
2. $P \leftarrow k$, that is, $k$ is block-encoded into the coefficients of a polynomials of degree $n$ in $\mathbb{F}_q$;
3. For $i = 1$ to $t$ do
    - $(x_i, y_i) \leftarrow (a_i, P(a_i))$;
    - $X \leftarrow X \bigcup \{x_i\}$;
    - $R \leftarrow R \bigcup \{(x_i, y_i)\}$;
    for $i = t + 1$ to $r$ do
    - $x_i \in_U \mathbb{F}_q \backslash X$;
    - $X \leftarrow X \bigcup \{x_i\}$;
    - $y_i \in_U \mathbb{F}_q \backslash \{P(x_i)\}$;
    - $R \leftarrow R \bigcup \{(x_i, y_i)\}$.
4. Output $R$ or $V = \{R, (n, r, q)\}$.

In order not to leak information about the order in which the $x_i$ are chosen, the set $R$ should be output in a pre-determined order, e.g., the points in $R$ may be arranged in order of ascending $x$-coordinates, or else in a random order. Note that the chaff points in the locking algorithm should be selected so as to intersect neither the set $A$ nor the polynomial $P$ is for the security consideration. Generally, the set $V$ combining the set $R$ and the triple vector $(n, r, q)$ is called a fuzzy vault.

## 2.2 Unlocking Algorithm

INPUT: A fuzzy vault $V$ comprising a parameter pair $(n, r, q)$ such that $n \leq r \ll q$ and a set $R$ of $r$ points with their two coordinations in $\mathbb{F}_q$. A query set $B = \{b_i\}_{i=1}^t$ with $b_i \in \mathbb{F}_q$.
OUTPUT: An element $k' \in \mathbb{F}_q^n \bigcup \{\text{`null'}\}$.

1. $Q \leftarrow \varnothing$;
2. For $i = 1$ to $t$ do
    - If there exists some $y_i \in \mathbb{F}_q$ such that $(b_i, y_i) \in R$, set $Q \leftarrow Q \bigcup \{(b_i, y_i)\}$;
    - Set $k' \leftarrow \text{`null'}$ if $Q$ has less than $n$ points;
    - Otherwise, set $k' \leftarrow \text{RS}_{\text{DECODE}}(n, Q)$;
3. Output $k'$.

Suppose that the fuzzy vault $V$ is created by Alice and Bob tries to unlock $V$ to recover the secret key $k$. Bob has to use his set $B$ to determine the codeword that encodes the secret key $k$ to get a possible secret key $k'$. Since the set $A$ specifies the $x$-coordinates of "correct" points that lie on the polynomial $P$. Thus, if $B$ is close to $A$, then $B$ will identify a large majority of these "correct" points. Any divergence between $B$ and $A$ will introduce a certain amount of error. However, this noise may be removed by means of a Reed-Solomon decoding algorithm provided that there is sufficient overlap.

The most convenient and unique features to the user is his biometric feature set, such as the fingerprint features, iris features, retinal features and etc. In 2005, Uludag and $et$ $al.$ [4] proposed a fingerprint-based fuzzy vault. One can also use our other biometric features to construct fuzzy vault schemes.

# 3   A Key Sharing Fuzzy Vault Scheme

The most popular and classical key sharing scheme is the Diffie-Hellman key exchange scheme [5] which is a specific method for sharing a secret key between two parties, and it is one of the earliest practical examples of secret key exchange or secret key scheme implemented within the field of cryptography. The Diffie-Hellman key exchange method allows two parties that have no prior knowledge of each other to jointly establish a shared secret key over an insecure communications channel. This established shared (secret) key can later be used in any symmetric key algorithm.

In practical applications, the multiplicative group $G$ is generally chosen to be a multiplicative group $\mathbb{F}_q^*$ with $q$ a power of a prime. To increase its security strength, we can set up the key sharing scheme on an elliptic curve rational point group or a hyperelliptic curve Jacobian group since the discrete logarithm problem is much harder than the discrete logarithm problem in the multiplicative group of a Galois field.

In this section, we will put out a novel fuzzy vault scheme for secret key sharing scheme based on the classical fuzzy vault and a multiplicative group, here we denote this scheme as KSFV scheme.

We suppose that Alice and Bob want to establish a shared secret key for their future cryptographic applications by using their biometric features, such as their fingerprint features, then they agree on a finite multiplicative group $G = \mathbb{F}_q^*$ with $q$ a power of a large prime and a cyclic subgroup $< g >$ of $G$ with $g$ an element of some large prime order $p$. Here, $G$, $q$, $g$ and $p$ are assumed to be public parameters.

## 3.1   Locking Algorithm

INPUT: A finite multiplicative group $G = \mathbb{F}_q^*$ with $q$ a prime power and one of its cyclic subgroup $H =< g >$ of large prime order $p$; Positive integers $n$, $s$, $t$, $r_A$ and $r_B$ satisfying $n \leq min\{s,t\} \leq s+t \leq r_A, r_B \ll p$ ; All these parameters are made public.

OUTPUT: $V = \{R_{AB}, (p, g, n)\}$, where $R_{AB}$ is a set composed of much more than $n$ points with their coordinations in $\mathbb{F}_q^*$.

1. $X, \bar{X}, R, R_A, R_B, V \leftarrow \emptyset$;
2. Alice and Bob extract their private biometric features $A = \{a_i\}_{i=1}^s$ and $B = \{b_j\}_{j=1}^t$, respectively;
3. Convert $a_i$ and $b_j$ ($i = 1, \ldots, s, j = 1, \ldots, t$ ) into the elements in $\{2, \ldots, p-1\}$. For convenience, they are still respectively represented as $a_i$ and $b_j$ which are supposed to be different from each others, and the corresponding sets are still respectively denoted as $A$ and $B$.
4. Alice randomly selects a select key $a \in \{2, \ldots, p-1\}$, computes $g^a$ and sends it to Bob;
5. For $i = 1, \ldots, s$, Alice compute $g^{a_i} (\triangleq \alpha_i)$ and sends the results to Bob;

6. Bob randomly selects a select key $b \in \{2, \ldots, p-1\}$, computes $g^b$ and sends it to Alice;
7. For $j = 1, \ldots, t$, Bob computes $g^{b_j} (\triangleq \beta_j)$ and sends the results to Alice;
8. Alice and Bob compute $(g^b)^a$ and $(g^a)^b$, respectively;
9. For each fixed $j \in \{1, \ldots, t\}$, Alice computes $(\beta_j)^{a_i}$ and set it to $\alpha_{j,i}$ for $i = 1, \ldots, s$;
10. For each fixed $i \in \{1, \ldots, s\}$, Bob computes $(\alpha_i)^{b_j}$ and set it to $\beta_{i,j}$ for $j = 1, \ldots, t$;
11. For $i = 1, \ldots, s$ and $j = 1, \ldots, t$, set $\gamma_{i,j} = \alpha_{i,j}$ (Obviously, we have $\alpha_{j,i} = g^{a_i b_j} = \beta_{i,j}$);
12. $k \leftarrow g^{ab}$ (Since $(g^b)^a = g^{ba} = g^{ab} = (g^a)^b$, $k$ can be regarded as Alice and Bob's shared key);
13. Alice and Bob, respectively, set $P(x) \leftarrow k$. That is, $k$ is block-encoded into the coefficients of a polynomial of degree $n$ in $\mathbb{F}_p[x]$;
14. Alice does the following steps:
    (a) For $j = 1$ to $t$, $i = 1$ to $s$ do
        - $(x_{i+j}, y_{i+j}) \leftarrow (\gamma_{i,j}, P(\gamma_{i,j}))$;
        - $X \leftarrow X \bigcup \{x_{i+j}\}$;
        - $R \leftarrow R \bigcup \{(x_{i+j}, y_{i+j})\}$;
    (b) For $l = s + t + 1$ to $r_A$ do
        - $x_l \in_U <g> \backslash X$;
        - $\bar{X} \leftarrow \bar{X} \bigcup \{x_l\}$;
        - $y_l \in_U <g> \backslash \{P(x_l)\}$;
        - $R_A \leftarrow R \bigcup \{(x_l, y_l)\}$.
    (c) Alice sends $R_A$ to Bob.
15. In the meantime, Bob does the similar steps to generate $R_B$ with the same real point set $R$ and $r_B - (s + t)$ chaff pints. $R_B$ is sent to Alice;
16. Set $R_{AB} = R_A \bigcup (R_B \backslash R)$. (Note that $R_{AB} = (R_A \bigcup R_B) \backslash R = R_B \bigcup (R_A \backslash R)$);
17. Output $V = \{R_{AB}, (p, g, n)\}$.

The output $V$ is regarded as the key sharing fuzzy vault owned by both Alice and Bob. If one of them wants to restore the shared key $k$, he/she can independently use his/her own biometrics to restore the possible shared sky $k'$ by the following "Unlocking Algorithm".

## 3.2    Unlocking Algorithm

INPUT: A finite multiplicative group $G = \mathbb{F}_q^*$ and one of its cyclic subgroup $<g>$ of large prime order $p$; Alice and Bob's biometric sets $A' = \{a_i'\}_{i=1}^{s'}$ and $B' = \{b_j'\}_{j=1}^{t'}$ with $a_i', b_j' \in \{2, \ldots, p-1\}$, respectively; A set $V = \{R_{AB}, (p, g, n)\}$ satisfying that $n \leq s', t' < s' + t' \ll p$, and the all points in $R_{AB}$ are in $\mathbb{F}_p^* \times \mathbb{F}_p^*$.
OUTPUT: An element $k' \in \mathbb{F}_p^* \bigcup \{'null'\}$.

1. $Q \leftarrow \emptyset$;
2. If Alice and Bob want to recover the shared key $k$, they do the following:

(a) For $i = 1$ to $s'$, Alice computes $g^{a'_i}$ ($\triangleq \alpha'_i$) and send $\alpha'_i$ to Bob;

(b) For $j = 1$ to $t'$, Bob computes $g^{b'_j}$ ($\triangleq \beta'_j$) and send $\beta'_j$ to Alice;

(c) For each fixed $j \in \{1, \ldots, t'\}$, Alice computes $(\beta'_j)^{a'_i}$ and set it to $\beta'_{i,j}$ for $i = 1, \ldots, s'$;

(d) For each fixed $i \in \{1, \ldots, s'\}$, Bob computes $(\alpha'_i)^{b'_j}$ and set it to $\alpha'_{i,j}$ for $j = 1, \ldots, t'$;

(e) Alice does the following:

   i. If there exists some $y \in \mathbb{F}_q^*$ such that $(\alpha'_{i,j}, y) \in R_{AB}$, do
      – $(x_{i+j}, y_{i+j}) \leftarrow (\alpha'_{i,j}, y)$;
      – $Q \leftarrow Q \bigcup \{(x_{i+j}, y_{i+j})\}$.

   ii. $k' \leftarrow \text{RS}_{\text{DECODE}}(n, Q)$ (For example, one can apply Newton's interpolation polynomial or Lagrange interpolation polynomial to get a possible key $k'$ if $Q$ has no less than $n$ points. );

   iii. $k' \leftarrow$ 'null' if $Q$ has less than $n$ points.

(f) $k' \leftarrow \text{RS}_{\text{DECODE}}(n, Q)$ or 'null'.

3. Similarly, Bob can do the similar steps as Alice does to recover the possible shared key $k'$.

4. Output $k'$.

The locking algorithm and unlocking algorithm can be described as the following Fig.3 and Fig.4, respectively. Here, the used biometrics are supposed to be the users' fingerprints and Lagrange interpolation polynomial is used for the Reed-Solomon decoding algorithm.

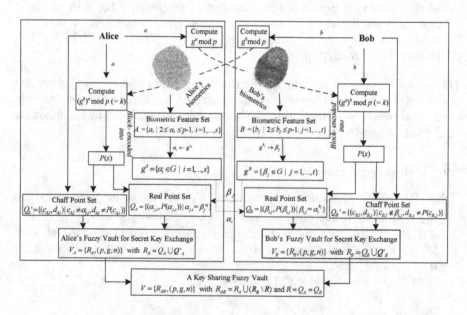

**Fig. 3.** KSFV-Locking Algorithm

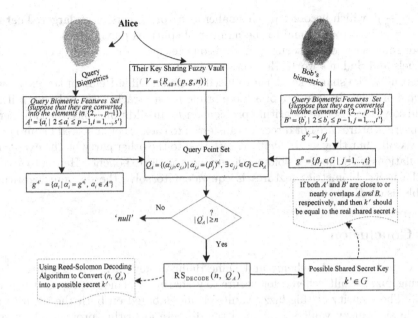

**Fig. 4.** SKFV-Unlocking Algorithm (for Alice)

If Alice and Bob can provide their biometric sets $A'$ and $B'$ that are respectively close to or sufficiently overlap $A$ and $B$, that is, if both of their biometric sets $A'$ and $B'$ contain no less than $n$ "correct" biometric features, then they will recover their real shared key $k$ successfully. Otherwise, they will fail to recover a right shared key.

According to Guruswami and Sudan's polynomial reconstruction algorithm [6], if the query set $Q$ contains at least $\min\{\sqrt{ns'}, \sqrt{nt'}\}$ "correct" or real points, then there exists a polynomial time algorithm to reconstruct the correct polynomial $P(x)$, and it follows that the real shared key $k$ can be recovered successfully.

## 4  Security Analysis

From the construction of our KSFV scheme, one can see that its security is based on both the security of the classical fuzzy vault scheme and the discrete logarithm problem (DLP).

Firstly, the security of our KSFV construction depends on the number of chaff points $r_A + r_B - 2(s+t)$ in the target set $R_{AB}$ of the total points $r_A + r_B - s - t$. The greater the number of such points, the more noise there is to conceal the real polynomial $P(x)$ from an attacker. As many chaff points are added to $R_{AB}$, there will be a set of many spurious polynomials that look like $P(x)$. In the absence of additional favorable information, the probability, that an attacker can obtain the real polynomial is $\binom{s+t}{n+1} / \binom{r_A+r_B-s-t}{n+1}$ or $\prod_{i=0}^{n-1} \frac{s+t-i}{r_A+r_B-s-t-i}$. Since both $r_A$ and $r_B$ are taken much larger than $n$ and $s+t$, the probability is approximate to $(\frac{s+t}{r_A+r_B})^n$ which becomes much smaller as $r_A$ or $r_B$ gets much larger. That is, the security is proportional to the number of spurious polynomials.

For some more detail security analysis on the classic fuzzy vault, one can refer to Juels and Sudan's work (the section 4 in [2]).

Secondly, the shared key $k$ is produced based on Diffie-Hellman key exchange scheme on a cyclic group $H$ of a large prime $p$, an attacker can only get $k$ if he could solve the discrete logarithm problem on $H$. In addition, since the two users' biometric features are not directly transferred to each other or stored in our novel fuzzy vault, but they are hiddenly transferred to the other party by the exponent calculations with the user's biometric numbers as the exponents. Hence, to access to the users' biometrics features is equivalent to solve the discrete logarithm problems on $H$.

## 5    Conclusion

Based on fuzzy vault scheme and Diffie-Hellman key exchange scheme, a key sharing fuzzy vault scheme for secure key sharing scheme is proposed in this work. The security of this fuzzy vault scheme is based on both the security of the classical fuzzy vault scheme and the discrete logarithm problem. This key sharing fuzzy vault scheme is just a detailed model but it will be simulated for fingerprints in our future work. In addition, similar to our method, a key sharing fuzzy vault scheme for the multiparty secret sharing protocol can also be set up.

**Acknowledgments.** This work is partially supported by the Research Projects of Zhejiang Natural Science Foundations (No.R10900138) and The Key Laboratory of Information Assurance Technology (KJ-11-05).

## References

1. Juels, A., Sudan, M.: A fuzzy vault scheme. In: IEEE International Symposium on Information Theory (ISIT), p. 408. IEEE Press, Lausanne (2002)
2. Juels, A., Sudan, M.: A fuzzy vault scheme. Designs, Codes, and Cryptography 38(2), 237–257 (2006)
3. Sorger, U.K.: A New Reed-Solomon Code Decoding Algorithm Based on Newton's Interpolation. IEEE Transactions on Information Theory 39(2), 358–365 (1993)
4. Uludag, U., Pankanti, S., Jain, A.K.: Fuzzy Vault for Fingerprints. In: Kanade, T., Jain, A., Ratha, N.K. (eds.) AVBPA 2005. LNCS, vol. 3546, pp. 310–319. Springer, Heidelberg (2005)
5. Diffie, W., Hellman, M.: New directions in cryptography. IEEE Transactions on Information Theory 22(6), 644–654 (1976)
6. Guruswami, V., Sudan, M.: Improved deconding of Reed-Solomon and Algebraic-Geometric codes. IEEE Transactions on Information Theory 45(6), 1757–1767 (1999)

# A New Version of McEliece PKC
# Based on Convolutional Codes

Carl Löndahl and Thomas Johansson

Dept. of Electrical and Information Technology, Lund University,
P.O. Box 118, 221 00 Lund, Sweden
{carl,thomas}@eit.lth.se

**Abstract.** This paper presents new versions of the McEliece PKC that use time-varying convolutional codes. In opposite to the choice of Goppa codes, the proposed construction uses large parts of randomly generated parity-checks, presumably making structured attacks more difficult. The drawback is that we have a small but nonzero probability of not being successful in decoding, in which case we need to ask for a retransmission.

## 1 Introduction

The original McEliece construction proposed by McEliece [14] in 1978 is an asymmetric encryption scheme using a family of error correcting codes. McEliece proposed a construction based on Goppa codes, and this original construction remains unbroken today. A few years later, Niederreiter [15] proposed a different scheme and proposed to use generalized Reed-Solomon codes. It can be shown that if one uses Goppa codes then Neiderreiter PKC is equivalent to McEliece PKC. It was also shown by Sidelnikov and Shestakov [16] that the choice of generalized Reed-Solomon codes is insecure (in both cases). There has been many proposals of modified schemes, mostly by replacing the Goppa codes by another family of codes, e.g. LDPC codes [2] or codes for the rank metric [6]. Interestingly, most of these proposals have turned out to be insecure and the choice of Goppa codes is still the standard solution.

A motivating factor for studying McEliece PKC is that the cryptosystem is a candidate for *post-quantum cryptography*, as it is not known to be susceptible to attacks using quantum computers. There have also been modifications of McEliece PKC with proved formal security (CCA2-secure), some of which are presented in [7]. Attempts on improving the rate of the system by using a subset of the message bits as error vectors have been done. Some approaches appear in [17]. We should also note that there have been many attempts to build other public key primitives based on coding theory. There exist an signature scheme by Courtois, Finiasz and Sendrier [5] from 2001 and an interesting hash function FSB by Augot, Finiasz and Sendrier [1].

Several versions of McEliece, for example, using quasi-cyclic or quasi-dyadic codes have been attacked in structural attacks [8]. Faugère et. al. [8] give the basic setting of structural attacks using *algebraic attacks*. In this approach, the

T.W. Chim and T.H. Yuen (Eds.): ICICS 2012, LNCS 7618, pp. 461–470, 2012.
© Springer-Verlag Berlin Heidelberg 2012

problem of reconstructing the secret matrix is formulated as the problem of solving a specific overdefined algebraic system, and it applies to any alternant code (among them Goppa codes). Even though the attack is currently not successful against Goppa codes, as the system is too difficult to solve, we do not know what improvements will come in the future.

This paper presents a new version of the McEliece PKC that uses convolutional codes. The first construction is based on tail-biting time-varying convolutional codes. The second construction uses a block code to set the starting state for the convolutional code. A large part of the code is constructed by randomly generating parity-checks for a systematic convolutional code. The new proposal allows for flexible parameters and efficient decoding. The drawback is that we have a nonzero probability of not being successful in decoding, in which case we need to ask for a retransmission. In opposite to the choice of Goppa codes, the first proposed construction uses large parts of randomly generated parity-checks, and presumably, this makes structured attacks more difficult. This is the main contribution of the construction. All parity-checks are randomly generated and of low weight, but not too low. Algebraic attacks applied to our system are unlikely to be successful, as well as attacks using Sendrier's support splitting algorithm.

The paper is organized as follows. In Section 2, we introduce the original McEliece construction. In Section 3, we then give a basic introduction to convolutional codes. The suggested constructions based on time-varying convolutional codes are given in Section 4. In Section 5 we investigate the security. Section 6 presents two examples.

## 2    The Original McEliece Construction

Let us start by giving a short overview of the original McEliece construction of a public key encryption scheme.

Let $G$ be a $k \times n$ generator matrix for a code $\mathcal{C}$ capable of correcting $e$ errors, $P$ a $n \times n$ random permutation matrix and $S$ a $k \times k$ non-singular matrix. We require an efficient decoding algorithm associated with $\mathcal{C}$. The sizes of these matrices are public parameters, but $G$, $P$ and $S$ are randomly generated secret parameters. Furthermore, $G$ is selected from a large set of possible generator matrices, say $G \in \mathcal{G}$, where the generator matrices in $\mathcal{G}$ all allow a very computationally efficient decoding procedure. Also, $P$ is selected among all permutations and $S$ is selected among all non-singular matrices. Then, preprocessing, encryption and decryption can be described in the following three steps.

A key issue is the selection of a set of easily decodable codes, from which we select $G$. The original suggestion was to use all binary Goppa codes for some fixed code parameters. This is a large enough set of possible codes and they can all be decoded assuming a fixed number of errors.

In the paper by McEliece [14], parameters $(n, k, e) = (1024, 524, 50)$ were proposed. These parameters, however, do not attain the promised security level in [14] due to advances in attacks, see e.g. [11], [13] and [3]. Bernstein, Lange and Peters proposed $(n, k, e) = (1632, 1269, 34)$ in [4].

---

**McEliece PKC**

1. Alice randomly chooses a triple $(S, G, P)$ as her secret key. She constructs the product $SGP = \hat{G}$, which is the public key. Now Alice publishes $\hat{G}$.
2. Bob encrypts a message $\mathbf{m}$ by computing the vector $\mathbf{c}' = \mathbf{m}\hat{G}$, using Alice's public key $\hat{G}$. He then adds a randomly generated error vector $\mathbf{e}$ of weight $e$ to form the ciphertext, $\mathbf{c} = \mathbf{c}' + \mathbf{e}$.
3. Alice decrypts the ciphertext by computing $\hat{\mathbf{c}} = \mathbf{c}P^{-1}$ and uses the efficient decoding algorithm to decode $\hat{\mathbf{c}}$ to $\hat{\mathbf{m}}$. Finally, the plaintext $\mathbf{m}$ is given by $\mathbf{m} = \hat{\mathbf{m}}S^{-1}$.

---

# 3 Convolutional Codes and Its Decoding

The underlying idea of this paper is that we can use convolutional codes to construct a McEliece PKC. A convolutional code $\mathcal{C}$ is a subclass of error-correcting codes where $b$-bit information symbols are transformed into $c$-bit symbols. The ratio $R = b/c$ is called the *rate* of the code. An information sequence $\mathbf{u}$ is transformed into a codeword sequence $\mathbf{v}$ via $\mathbf{u}G = \mathbf{v}$.

For a *time-invariant* or *fixed* convolutional code $\mathcal{C}$, $G$ is a matrix such that

$$G = \begin{bmatrix} G_1 & G_2 & \cdots & G_m & & & \\ & G_1 & G_2 & \cdots & G_m & & \\ & & G_1 & G_2 & \cdots & G_m & \\ & & & \ddots & \ddots & & \ddots \end{bmatrix},$$

and where $G_i$ is a $b \times c$ matrix and with zeroes in the empty spaces. The current output is a linear combination of the current information symbol and the $m - 1$ previous ones, where $m$ is the *memory* of the code. The submatrices of each row are the same as the previous row, but shifted one step. If this property is not satisfied, it is called a *time-variant* code, where $G$ is

$$G = \begin{bmatrix} G_{1,1} & G_{1,2} & \cdots & G_{1,m} & & & \\ & G_{2,1} & G_{2,2} & \cdots & G_{2,m} & & \\ & & G_{3,1} & G_{3,2} & \cdots & G_{3,m} & \\ & & & \ddots & \ddots & & \ddots \end{bmatrix},$$

and all the $G_{ij}$ matrices may be different.

A convolutional code sequence may be infinite, but in our application it is terminated. For this, we use a *tail-biting* construction, i.e. starting the encoder in the same state as it will stop after encoding all information blocks. The code will have a generator matrix of the form

$$G = \begin{bmatrix} G_{1,1} & \cdots & \cdots & G_{1,m} & & & \\ & \ddots & \ddots & & \ddots & \ddots & \\ & & \ddots & & \ddots & \ddots & G_{i,m} \\ G_{i+1,m} & & & & \ddots & \ddots & \vdots \\ \vdots & \ddots & & & & \ddots & \vdots \\ G_{L,2} & \cdots & G_{L,m} & & & & G_{L,1} \end{bmatrix} . \tag{1}$$

This is now an $(n, k)$ linear block code. Optimal decoding of convolutional codes can be done by the Viterbi algorithm, having complexity $\mathcal{O}\left(2^{mb}k\right)$. An alternative is to use *sequential decoding*, e.g. the stack algorithm. We refer to [10] and [12] for a detailed description.

# 4    A New Construction Based on Convolutional Codes

Our basic idea is that we would like to replace the Goppa code used in McEliece by a convolutional code that can be efficiently decoded. However, this basic approach suffers from two problems that we need to deal with.

The first problem is that a usual convolutional code as used for error correcting purposes has a somewhat limited memory. This is necessary if we would like to have optimal (ML) decoding through, e.g., the Viterbi algorithm. As an example, a rate $R = 1/2$ convolutional code with a memory of 20 would mean that we will have parity checks of low weight. This would be a security problem, as one can try to recover the low weight parity checks and through this also recover the structure of the secret code. The solution we propose here is to use convolutional codes with large memory, but to use a sequential decoding procedure instead of Viterbi decoding. Using, e.g., the stack algorithm we can use codes with much larger memory. This will remove the very low weight parities in the code. Still leaving low weight parity checks, but if the weight is not very small, the complexity of finding them will be too large.

The second problem is that a convolutional code usually start in the all zero state. This means that the first code symbols that are produced will again allow very low weight parity checks, giving security problems. As we cannot allow the identification of low weight parity checks, we need to modify this. A similar problem may occur when we terminate the code.

The solution that we propose is to use so-called tail-biting to terminate the code, giving tail-biting trellises in decoding. This would work quite straightforward if we had a small trellis size and were using Viterbi decoding. But for a large memory size and sequential decoding it is not immediate how tail-biting could be used, as one has to go through all possible states at some starting point in the circular trellis. Another approach to solve this problem is to use a block code to set the starting state. We have examined this approach also.

## 4.1    The McEliece PKC Based on a Tail-Biting Convolutional Code

The scheme works as usual McEliece, with a different way of generating the secret matrix $G$ as well as a different decoding procedure for the decryption process. The secret generator matrix will have the characteristics of the one appearing in (1), i.e., it has a cyclic diagonal structure with $m$ matrices $G_{i,j}$ in each column and row. We also set the code $G$ to be systematic, see Algorithm 1 for a detailed description.

---

**Algorithm 1. (Precomputation)**

---

1. Choose parameters: code length $n$, rate $R = b/c$, memory $m$ giving $2^{bm}$ possible states, and a minimum weight $l$ for all parity checks, where $l$ should be around $bm/2$. Also, a value $l'$, corresponding to the minimum number of ones in a row in $G$ could be specified.
2. Write up a generator matrix as (1) in systematic form, i.e., choose $G_{i,1} = (IJ_{i1})$ and $G_{i,j} = (0J_{i,j})$, for $2 \leq j \leq m$, where $J_{i,1}$ is chosen to give the code spanned by $G_{i,1}$ maximal minimum distance and $J_{i,j}$, for $2 \leq j \leq m$, is chosen randomly.
3. Run a test to verify that all parity check positions, or sums of them, have weight at least $l$. Also check that every information symbol appears in at least $l$ parity checks. If this is not the case, go to Step 2.
4. We have now created the secret matrix $G$. Create the public key matrix as usual, i.e., randomly choose $(S, P)$, $P$ permutation and $S$ non-singular, and compute $SGP = \hat{G}$, and publish $\hat{G}$.

---

Assuming that we receive a word $\mathbf{c}$ with $e$ errors, how do we correct them, knowing $G$? A problem when decoding this structure is that we have to guess a starting state at some time instance and then perform the sequential decoding. With many possible starting states this increases the complexity of decoding. We assume that we use the stack algorithm as decoding algorithm and put a number of possible starting states on the stack in the beginning. An advantage is that this part of the decoding can be easily parallelized by starting decoding at different time instances.

We now describe a basic approach for decoding. Compute $\hat{\mathbf{c}} = \mathbf{c}P^{-1}$. Start the decoding at any time $t$. On the stack we then put a set $S$ of possible states, which would be formed from the $mb$ received information symbols in $\hat{\mathbf{c}}$ just before time $t$. Since these symbols may be perturbated by the error vector, we put all states reachable by $e'$ errors on the stack, where $e'$ is fixed by the decoding algorithm. The expected number of errors in an interval of $mb$ symbols is $emb/n$.

If decoding is unsuccessful we can try a different starting point $t$. If the correct state has been established, and decoding is successful, we will get the correct weight of the error vector. As the weight is assumed to be known, this is a way of knowing that decoding was successful.

A description of a basic decoding procedure is given in Algorithm 2.

---

**Algorithm 2. (Decoding in tail-biting construction)**

---

**Input**: Codeword sequence $\hat{\mathbf{c}}$

1. Write $\hat{\mathbf{c}} = (\mathbf{c}_1, \mathbf{c}_2, \ldots \mathbf{c}_{n/c})$, where $\mathbf{c}_i = (\mathbf{u}_i, \mathbf{p}_i)$ is a $c$ bit vector and $\mathbf{u}_i$ is the systematic part.

2. Choose a random starting point $t$ and put $(\mathbf{u}_{t-m}, \mathbf{u}_{t-m+1}, \ldots, \mathbf{u}_{t-1})$ (index modulo $n/c$), together with all other vectors with at most distance $e'$ from it as starting states in $\mathcal{S}$. Run the stack algorithm until time $t$ is reached again. If decoding was successful, return the decoded sequence. Otherwise, do this item again.

3. If many starting points $t$ have been tried without success, ask for retransmission.

---

## 4.2   Finding a List of Good Starting States

Finding the correct starting state is the major complexity cost in decoding. To be able to decode correctly, we need the correct starting state in $\mathcal{S}$, but we also do not want $\mathcal{S}$ to be too large as this gives a high decoding complexity. As mentioned, we can use different starting points $t$, and hope that one of them will have a set $\mathcal{S}$ including the correct starting state. We can even put sets $\mathcal{S}$ from many different starting points on the same stack.

In order to decrease the size of $\mathcal{S}$, we propose to use not only $mb$ bits to form the set $\mathcal{S}$, but to use $mb + m'c$ consecutive bits from $\mathbf{c}$, where we now have $(m+m')b$ information bits but can also use $m'(c-b)$ parity checks. Deciding that we include all such length $mb + m'c$ with at most $e'$ errors as possible starting states, this corresponds exactly to finding all codewords in a $(mb+m'c, (m+m')b)$ linear code with weight at most $e'$.

## 4.3   A Modified Construction

Our construction based on tail-biting convolutional codes has a simple description and it has a good portion of randomness in its construction, making it a desirable construction. One problem however, is the first part of the decoding, i.e., finding the correct starting state before starting the efficient stack algorithm. For constructions with security level around $2^{80}$, this can be done with reasonable complexity. But the complexity of this process grows exponentially with the security level measured in bits.

In order to solve this problem we propose a modified construction, using only polynomial complexity to get the starting state. Our second construction uses a small block code for setting a starting state and then a larger convolutional code for the remaining part of the code. The original code is generated by the generator matrix of the form

$$G = \begin{bmatrix} \boxed{\begin{array}{c} G_B \end{array}} & \\ \boxed{\phantom{xx}} & G_C \end{bmatrix}, \tag{2}$$

where $G_B$ is a block code (we propose a Goppa code to be used), $G_C$ is a random time-varying systematic convolutional code as in the first tail-biting construction with memory $m = k$ and white areas represent all zeroes.

The block code $G_B$ is an $(n_B, k_B)$ linear code with efficient decoding of up to $t_B$ errors. We suggest it to be a classical Goppa code. Since the number of errors in the first $n_B$ positions can be higher than the block code can correct, we note that a decoding error might occur here. It is given by

$$\mathbf{Pr}\left[\text{more than } t_B \text{ errors in block code}\right] = \sum_{x > t_B}^{e} \frac{\binom{n_B}{x}\binom{n_C}{e-x}}{\binom{n}{e}}. \tag{3}$$

With suitable parameters this probability can be made very low. An important issue is that we need to have a dimension $k_B$ of the code larger than the number of bits in memory $mb$. This again comes from the fact that we cannot allow low weight codewords in the dual code. As the block code generally will have more parity-check symbols per information symbol that leads to an expected existence of codewords with weight lower than in the convolutional code. So we require, no codewords of weight less than $l$ in the dual code of $G_B$.

We then use as before a rate $b/c$ convolutional code $G_C$. Since the leftmost $k_B$ information bits are assumed to be already known (if the block decoding is successful), we do not need to decode these using the sequential decoding procedure.

## 5    Analysis of the Security of the Proposed Scheme

First, let us give the complexity formulas for Stern's algorithm [9]. The complexity of finding a codeword of weight $w$ using Stern's algorithm, with algorithm parameter $p$, is given by $W/P$, where $W$ and $P$ is defined below. The probability $P$ of an iteration being successful is

$$P = \frac{\binom{w}{2p}\binom{n-w}{k-2p}\binom{2p}{p}}{\binom{n}{k}\binom{n-k-w+2p}{l}4^p\binom{n-k}{l}} \tag{4}$$

and each such iteration performs

$$W = (n-k)^3/2 + k(n-k)^2 + 2lp\binom{k/2}{p} + 2p(n-k)\binom{k/2}{p}^2/2^l \tag{5}$$

bit operations.

There are two standard approaches to attack McEliece PKC. One is to try to recover the plaintext from a received ciphertext, whereas the second approach is a structural attack where we try to recover the structure of the secret generator matrix.

**Plaintext Recovery.** Recovery of the plaintext from a ciphertext is best done by so-called information set decoding algorithms. The simplest form of information set decoding appeared in McEliece's original paper from 1978 [14]. The idea is to select $k$ out of $n$ columns and hope that no errors occur in these positions in the received ciphertext. Numerous papers on information set decoding have been published. The algorithms currently attaining the lowest attack complexity are described in [11], [13] and [3].

**Structural Attacks.** In a structural attack we try to recover the structure of the code. In our case the only deviation from a random code is the convolutional code structure in terms of low weight parity checks. In fact, in precomputation we specified the weight of parity checks to be no less than $l$.

We expect that a structural attack would need to recover parity checks of weight $l$, and sketch the difficulty of this problem. It is well known that all parity checks form codewords of the dual code.

One should also observe that we have a large number of low weight parity checks (codewords in the dual code). This decreases the complexity of finding one of them when running Stern's algorithm, as the probability of being successful in one iteration increases with the number of existing low weight vectors. In our case, parity checks are created from $mb$ bits in memory and $c$ additional bits. For example, there are then at least $2^{c-b-1}$ parity checks of weight $(mb+c)/2$ or less. But in the precomputation creating the generator matrix, we can keep track of how many low weight vectors we have and make sure that the complexity of finding any of them is high enough.

# 6   Example

For security level around $2^{80}$, we propose the following set of parameters. Use parameters $(n, k, e, m) = (1800, 1200, 45, 12)$ with rate $R = 20/30$. We will have a security of $2^{81}$ against decoding attacks, measured by Stern's algorithm, see (4) and (5). We get a security level of $2^{78.4}$ with the best known algorithms [11]. In the construction phase, we set $l = 125$, i.e., every parity check should have a weight no less than 125. This is achievable as every parity check has $240 + 30$ positions where it can be nonzero. The complexity of finding a weight 125 vector in the dual code using Stern's algorithm is roughly $2^{87}$. As this complexity is decreased by the number of low weight vectors, we need to keep track of the number of low weight vectors in the code to guarantee a complexity of about $2^{80}$ for finding such a low weight parity check.

For the decoding, we keep $mb = 240$ bits as our starting state. Fixing a starting time $t$, the expected number of errors in these 240 information symbols is 6. We include another 40 information symbols from just before time $t - m$ and the corresponding 20 parity checks that is computed from these $240 + 40$ information symbols. We also split the 240 symbols in two halves.

Our assumption is now that we have at most 1 error in the added 60 symbols and at most 3 errors in each of the halves of the state.

We then generate two tables of all parity check syndromes that up to 3 errors can generate, in total less than $2^{19}$ entries in each table. One table is expanded with adding to every entry the 61 syndromes that the additional 60 information symbols created, giving $2^{25}$ entries. Merging the two tables, knowing that the syndrome must be zero, gives $2^{24}$ surviving states. Now, taking the next 30 information symbols and starting sequential decoding, quickly takes the correct state to the top of the stack. If we are unsuccessful, pick a new $t$.

The probability that our assumption about errors is correct is about 0.25, so the expected total decoding complexity is about $2^{25}/0.25 = 2^{27}$. By assuming fewer errors, the expected decoding complexity can be further decreased.

### 6.1   Continuing the Example with the Modified Construction

Considering the same example but with a block code to fix the initial state as described in Subsection 4.3.

Pick as $G_B$ a Goppa code of length $n_B = 1020$, dimension $k_B = 660$ and with capabability of correcting 36 errors. Let the convolutional code have rate $R = 20/30$ and run 25 information blocks. End the code with 30 additional parity checks. This gives rise to a full code of length $1020 + 25 \cdot 30 + 30 = 1800$ and dimension $k = 660 + 25 \cdot 20 = 1160$.

The decoding step first decodes the Goppa code. For a $n_B = 1020$ code we expect that algorithms with complexity $\mathcal{O}\left(n^2\right)$ are still the best choice. There are algorithms with better asymptotic performance, but they are useful only for excessively large $n_B$. So we expect say $2^{20}$ steps for this part. Decoding the convolutional code is then done in much less time than $2^{20}$ steps. Overall, this gives a faster decoding than standard McEliece, requiring close to $2^{22}$ steps.

With 45 inserted errors, the probability that we get a decoding error can be found to be around $2^{-12}$, see (3).

## References

1. Augot, D., Finiasz, M., Sendrier, N.: A Family of Fast Syndrome Based Cryptographic Hash Functions. In: Dawson, E., Vaudenay, S. (eds.) Mycrypt 2005. LNCS, vol. 3715, pp. 64–83. Springer, Heidelberg (2005)
2. Baldi, M.: LDPC Codes in the McEliece Cryptosystem: Attacks and Countermeasures. In: NATO Science for Peace and Security Series – D: Information and Communication Security. LNCS, vol. 23, pp. 160–174 (2009)
3. Becker, A., Joux, A., May, A., Meurer, A.: Decoding Random Binary Linear Codes in $2^{n/20}$: How $1 + 1 = 0$ Improves Information Set Decoding. In: Pointcheval, D., Johansson, T. (eds.) EUROCRYPT 2012. LNCS, vol. 7237, pp. 520–536. Springer, Heidelberg (2012)

4. Bernstein, D.J., Lange, T., Peters, C.: Attacking and Defending the McEliece Cryptosystem. In: Buchmann, J., Ding, J. (eds.) PQCrypto 2008. LNCS, vol. 5299, pp. 31–46. Springer, Heidelberg (2008)

5. Courtois, N., Finiasz, M., Sendrier, N.: How to Achieve a McEliece-Based Digital Signature Scheme. In: Goos, G., Hartmanis, J., van Leeuwen, J. (eds.) ASIACRYPT 2001. LNCS, vol. 2248, pp. 157–174. Springer, Heidelberg (2001)

6. Delsarte, P.: Bilinear forms over a finite field. Journal of Combinatorial Theory, Series A 25, 226–241 (1978)

7. Engelbert, D., Overbeck, R., Schmidt, A.: A summary of McEliece-type cryptosystems and their security (2007)

8. Faugère, J.C., Otmani, A., Perret, L., Tillich, J.-P.: Algebraic Cryptanalysis of McEliece Variants with Compact Keys. In: Gilbert, H. (ed.) EUROCRYPT 2010. LNCS, vol. 6110, pp. 279–298. Springer, Heidelberg (2010)

9. Stern, J.: A Method for Finding Codewords of Small Weight. In: Wolfmann, J., Cohen, G.D. (eds.) Coding Theory and Applications. LNCS, vol. 388, pp. 106–113. Springer (1989)

10. Johannesson, R., Zigangirov, K.S.: Fundamentals of Convolutional Coding. IEEE Series on Digital and Mobile Communication. IEEE Press (1999)

11. Johansson, T., Löndahl, C.: An improvement to Stern's algorithm, internal report (2011), http://lup.lub.lu.se/record/2204753

12. Lin, S., Costello, D.J.: Error Control Coding, 2nd edn. Prentice-Hall, Inc. (2004)

13. May, A., Meurer, A., Thomae, E.: Decoding random linear codes in $\tilde{O}(2^{0.054n})$. In: Lee, D.H., Wang, X. (eds.) ASIACRYPT 2011. LNCS, vol. 7073, pp. 107–124. Springer, Heidelberg (2011)

14. McEliece, R.J.: A public-key cryptosystem based on algebraic coding theory. DSN Progress Report 42–44, 114–116 (1978)

15. Niederreiter, H.: Knapsack-type crytosystems and algebraic coding theory. Problems of Control and Information Theory 15(2), 157–166 (1986)

16. Sidelnikov, V.M., Shestakov, S.O.: On the insecurity of cryptosystems based on generalized Reed-Solomon codes. Discrete Mathematics and Applications 2(4), 439–444 (1992)

17. Sun, H.M.: Improving the Security of the McEliece Public-Key Cryptosystem. In: Ohta, K., Pei, D. (eds.) ASIACRYPT 1998. LNCS, vol. 1514, pp. 200–213. Springer, Heidelberg (1998)

# Flexible Attribute-Based Encryption

Seiko Arita*

Graduate School of Information Security,
Institute of Information Security, Japan
`arita@iisec.ac.jp`

**Abstract.** In this paper, we propose a notion of *flexible attribute-based encryption*. Flexible attribute-based encryption is a variant of ciphertext-policy ABE, which allows one to *loosen* a decryption policy underlying a given ciphertext, if one knows some system-wide trapdoor information, without knowing its underlying plaintext message. We give a concrete construction of the flexible attribute-based encryption that satisfies indistinguishability under the loosening operation, based on the construction of ciphertext-policy ABE given by Bethencourt, Sahai and Waters.

**Keywords:** Attribute-based encryption, Ciphertext-policy, Loosening operation.

## 1 Introduction

A notion of attribute-based encryption (ABE) was first proposed by Sahai and Waters [13], in which, a message $m$ is encrypted to a ciphertext $c$ under some predicate $f$, and a user with credential $X$ can decrypt the ciphertext $c$ if and only if the predicate $f$ is satisfied by the user's credential $X$: $f(X) = 1$. The concept of ABE was further clarified by Goyal, Pandey, Sahai, and Waters [6]. They proposed two complementary forms of ABE: Key-Policy ABE and Ciphertext-Policy ABE. In this paper, we focus on Ciphertext-Policy ABE, in which attributes are used to describe users' credentials and formulas over these attributes are attached to the ciphertext by the encrypting party.

The first construction of Ciphertext-Policy ABE was given by Bethencourt, Sahai, and Waters [4]. Its security is proved under the generic bilinear group with random oracle model. (We call the model which uses both the generic bilinear group and random oracle the generic bilinear group with random oracle model.) Waters [15] gives a construction of ABE which can be proved under the standard model in a selective manner. Lewko, Okamoto, Sahai, Takashima, and Waters [10] and Okamoto and Takashima [12] give fully secure constructions of ABE in the standard model.

---

\* Supported by MEXT-Supported Program for the Strategic Research Foundation at Private Universities, 2011-2013.

T.W. Chim and T.H. Yuen (Eds.): ICICS 2012, LNCS 7618, pp. 471–478, 2012.
© Springer-Verlag Berlin Heidelberg 2012

On a while, ABE has been applied in building a variety of secure systems [14,5,2]. One of major problems in these applications is that ABE-based systems tend to lack flexibility. A ciphertext once produced under decryption policy $f$ never can be decrypted under a more loosened policy $\mathbf{or}(f, \Delta f)$ (if $f$ is not satisfied) by the definition of security of ABE (of course). However, in reality, the degree of privacy of information is never fixed: yesterday's secret is not necessary secret of today. Even if some information is very restrictive (described as policy $f$) to be accessed at this moment of time, the same information gradually can be made more and more accessible (described as policy $\mathbf{or}(f, \Delta f)$) as time goes by.

*Our contribution.* In this paper, we propose a notion of *flexible attribute-based encryption*. Flexible attribute-based encryption is a variant of ciphertext-policy ABE, which allows one to *loosen* a decryption policy underlying a given ciphertext, if one knows some system-wide trapdoor information, without knowing its underlying plaintext message. More precisely, suppose a given ciphertext $c$ was generated by encrypting a plaintext $m$ under a decryption policy $f$. The flexible attribute-based encryption enables a "loosening operation" that, given $\Delta f$ and some system-wide trapdoor information $\gamma$, converts the ciphertext $c$ into a more nonrestrictive version of ciphertext $c'$ which encrypts the same plaintext $m$ under the loosened policy $\mathbf{or}(f, \Delta f)$, without knowing the message $m$ itself. Users having attributes that satisfy (only) the appended policy $\Delta f$ now can decrypt the ciphertext $c'$ to know the message $m$. Here we note that the trapdoor information $\gamma$ is independent of individual policies or ciphertexts.

As one of applications of such flexible attribute-based encryption, we can consider an integration of cloud storage services. Suppose two storage services $A$ and $B$ are going to integrate into one storage service. Suppose, by policy mapping, that encrypted files $C_{f_A}$ under policy $f_A$ in service $A$ now should be decrypted also by entities satisfying policy $f_B$ in service $B$. The authenticated operator in service $A$ with trapdoor $\gamma$ can use the loosening operation against those $C_{f_A}$ to get new encrypted files $C_{\mathbf{or}(f_A, f_B)}$ that can be decrypted also by entities satisfying policy $f_B$ in service $B$.

We will see that there is a subtlety over security concerning such loosening operations and then we will define two notions of security of flexible attribute-based encryption, *indistinguishability under loosening operation* and *indistinguishability under loosening key*.

We also give a concrete construction of the flexible attribute-based encryption that satisfies the indistinguishability under loosening operation and the indistinguishability under loosening key, based on the construction of ciphertext-policy attribute-based encryption given by [4]. Its security proof is given in the generic bilinear group with random oracle model.

*Related works.* The concept of our flexible attribute-based encryption is similar to the attribute-based proxy re-encryption [7,9,8].

In the attribute-base proxy re-encryption, one can generate re-encryption key $rk_{f_1 \to f_2}$, and by using the key $rk_{f_1 \to f_2}$, a ciphertext $c_{f_1}$ for policy $f_1$ can be re-encrypted into a ciphertext $c_{f_2}$ for policy $f_2$. To generate such re-encryption key $rk_{f_1 \to f_2}$, the secret key $sk_{f_1}$ for policy $f_1$ is required. On a while, in our flexible ABE, all ciphertexts can be "loosened" using the single (system-wide) trapdoor information $\gamma$ (which is independent of individual policies).

## 2    A Notion of Flexible Attribute-Based Encryption

*A flexible attribute-based encryption scheme* is a tuple of five PPT algorithms Setup, Enc, Ext, Dec and Loosen.

Algorithm Setup generates a public parameter $par$, a master secret $mk$ and a trapdoor information $lk$ for loosening, given a security parameter $1^k$: $(par, mk, lk) \leftarrow$ Setup$(1^k)$. Algorithm Enc encrypts a given message $m$ to a ciphertext $c$ under a given decryption policy represented as a Boolean formula $f$: $(f, c) \leftarrow$ Enc$(par, f, m)$. Algorithm Ext generates a secret key $d$ for a given attribute set $as$, using the master secret $mk$: $(as, d) \leftarrow$ Ext$(par, mk, as)$. Algorithm Dec decrypts a ciphertext $(f, c)$ by using a secret key $d$ for an attribute set $as$ to obtain a resulting plaintext $m$. The plaintext $m$ may be a special symbol $\perp$ indicating a decryption error if something is wrong: $m/\perp \leftarrow$ Dec$(par, (f, c), (as, d))$. By using the dedicated trapdoor information $lk$, algorithm Loosen loosens a decryption policy of a given ciphertext $(f, c)$ so that more entities, that satisfy some added policy $\Delta f$, can also decrypt the ciphertext $c$, resulting a new ciphertext $(\text{or}(f, \Delta f), c')$: $(\text{or}(f, \Delta f), c') \leftarrow$ Loosen$(par, lk, (f, c), \Delta f)$.

*Correctness requirement.* Under any valid setup information $(par, mk, lk)$ $(\leftarrow$ Setup$(1^k))$, if one encrypts any message $m \in$ Message$(k)$ under any decryption policy $f \in$ Policy$(k)$ to a ciphertext $(f, c)$, then it must be decrypted to the original plaintext $m$ as Dec$(par, (f, c), (as, d)) = m$, if the secret key $(as, d)$ $(\leftarrow$ Ext$(par, mk, as))$ is generated for some attribute set $as$ that satisfies the decryption policy $f$.

If the ciphertext $(f, c)$ is loosened by a policy $\Delta f$ to a new ciphertext $(\text{or}(f, \Delta f), c')$ as $(\text{or}(f, \Delta f), c')$ $\leftarrow$ Loosen$(par, lk, (f, c), \Delta f)$, then the resulting ciphertext $c'$ must be decrypted to the original plaintext $m$ as Dec$(par, (\text{or}(f, \Delta f), c'), (as', d')) = m$, even if the attribute set $as'$ satisfies the appended policy $\Delta f$ (or $f$).

*Regarding security under loosening operations.* Before defining security in a formal way, here we consider some aspects regarding security of such attribute-based encryption that gives loosening operations to users.

First of all, the loosening operation should be performed by some entity with possession of the trapdoor information $lk$ without knowing the underlying message. This will be captured in the security condition named 'indistinguishability under loosening key'.

Another point is a more subtle one. Suppose an adversary $A$ obtains a ciphertext $c^*$ of a plaintext $m$ under a policy $f = A$ or $B$ or $C$. It is plausible that $A$

manages to construct a ciphertext $c'$ of the same plaintext $m$ (without knowing $m$ itself) under a more restricted policy $f' = A$ or $B$, based on the ciphertext $c^*$. Then, $A$ can use the loosening operation on $c'$ to get another ciphertext $c''$ also of the same plaintext $m$ but under a loosened policy $f'' = A$ or $B$ or $D$ and then $A$ could know the underlying plaintext $m$ of the original ciphertext $c^*$ by using a corrupt key $d_D$ of the added attribute $D$ against the ciphertext $c''$.

That scenario means that a victim's ciphertext $c^*$ can be corrupted even if $c^*$ itself has never been processed under loosening operations. (Off course, if the attribute-based encryption has CCA-security, that type of attack based on malleability can be avoided. However, at the same time we lose the loosening operations, too.)

We will require that loosening operations for $c'$ different from $c^*$ should never affect the security of $c^*$, in the security condition named 'indistinguishability under loosening operation'.

# 3    Security of Flexible Attribute-Based Encryption

To define security of a flexible attribute encryption scheme, we describe two games using the framework of code-based games [3]. In the framework, a game $\mathbf{Game}_A$ is executed with an adversary $A$ as follows. First, **Initialize** executes, and its outputs are the inputs to $A$. Then $A$ executes, its oracle queries being answered by the corresponding procedures of $\mathbf{Game}_A$. When $A$ terminates, its output becomes the input to the **Finalize** procedure. The output of the latter is called the output of the game.

## 3.1    Indistinguishability under Loosening Operation

Let $\mathsf{FABE}$ = $(\mathsf{Setup}, \mathsf{Enc}, \mathsf{Ext}, \mathsf{Dec}, \mathsf{Loosen})$ be a flexible attribute encryption scheme. Let $A$ be an arbitrary PPT adversary against $\mathsf{FABE}$. Our game $\mathbf{Game}_{A,\mathsf{FABE}}^{ind-lso}(k)$ uses the following **Initialize** and **Finalize** procedures:

**procedure Initialize:**
$b \xleftarrow{\$} \{0,1\}$
$(par, mk, lk) \leftarrow \mathsf{Setup}(1^k)$
return $par$.

**procedure Finalize** $(b')$:
return $b' \overset{?}{=} b$.

The game uses procedures **Extract**, **LR** and **Loosen** to answer oracle queries from $A$:

**procedure Extract** $(as)$:
assert$(f^*(as) = \mathsf{false})$
$(as, d) \leftarrow \mathsf{Ext}(par, mk, as)$
return $(as, d)$.

**procedure Loosen** $((f, c), \Delta f)$:
assert$((f, c)\,!= (f^*, c^*))$
$(f', c') \leftarrow \mathsf{Loosen}(par, lk, (f, c), \Delta f)$
return $(f', c')$.

**procedure LR** $(f^*, m_0, m_1)$:
assert$(f^*(as) = \mathsf{false})$ for $as$'s submitted to **Extract**
$(f^*, c^*) \leftarrow \mathsf{Enc}(par, f^*, m_b)$
return $(f^*, c^*)$.

In the above, "assert($f^*(as)$ = false)" means that one must check whether the condition $f^*(as)$ = false holds or not if $f^*$ already defined, and abort if it does not hold, or else continue. Similar for "assert($(f,c)!= (f^*,c^*)$)".

**Definition 1.** *A flexible attribute encryption scheme* FABE *is said to be* indistinguishable under loosening operation (IND-LSO) *if for an arbitrary PPT adversary A its advantage* $\mathbf{Adv}^{ind-lso}_{A,\mathsf{FABE}}(k) := |\Pr[\mathrm{Game}^{ind-lso}_{A,\mathsf{FABE}}(k) = 1] - 1/2|$ *is a negligible function in* $k$.

### 3.2  Indistinguishability under Loosening Key

Our game $\mathbf{Game}^{ind-lsk}_{A,\mathsf{FABE}}(k)$ uses the following **Initialize** and **Finalize** procedures:

| **procedure Initialize:** | **procedure Finalize** ($b'$): |
|---|---|
| $b \stackrel{\$}{\leftarrow} \{0,1\}$ | **return** $b' \stackrel{?}{=} b$. |
| $(par, mk, lk) \leftarrow \mathsf{Setup}(1^k)$ | |
| **return** $(par, lk)$. | |

Note that **Initialize** returns a trapdoor information $lk$ for loosening operation as well as parameter $par$ (and adversaries $A$ will know $lk$ as well as $par$). The game uses procedure **LR** to answer oracle queries from $A$:

> **procedure LR** ($f^*, m_0, m_1$):
> $(f^*, c^*) \leftarrow \mathsf{Enc}(par, f^*, m_b)$
> **return** $(f^*, c^*)$.

**Definition 2.** *A flexible attribute encryption scheme* FABE *is said to be* indistinguishable under loosening key (IND-LSK) *if for an arbitrary PPT adversary A its advantage* $\mathbf{Adv}^{ind-lsk}_{A,\mathsf{FABE}}(k) := |\Pr[\mathrm{Game}^{ind-lsk}_{A,\mathsf{FABE}}(k) = 1] - 1/2|$ *is a negligible function in* $k$.

Note that since $A$ has now loosening key $lk$, $A$ can trivially decrypt the challenge ciphertext if $A$ had access to **Extract**-oracle.

## 4  Concrete FABE Scheme

**Definition 3.** *A function* $F : \{0,1\}^* \rightarrow \{0,1\}^{2N}$ *is said to be* $N$-lineardependency resistant *if for any* $n \leq N$ *any PPT algorithm A is not able to generate any* $n$ *distinct strings* $x_1, \ldots, x_n$ *with function values* $F(x_1), \ldots, F(x_n)$ *that are linearly dependent (as vectors over* $Z_2$*) except with a negligible probability.*

A hash function $F : \{0,1\}^* \rightarrow \{0,1\}^{2N}$ is $N$-linear-dependency resistant in the random oracle model with respect to $F$.

We construct a concrete flexible attribute encryption scheme based on the attribute encryption scheme of [4]. In the followings, $\sharp \mathrm{Leaf}(f)$ denotes a number of leaf nodes of a given binary formula $f$. $(\rho, M) \leftarrow \mathrm{LSS}(p, f)$ denotes a transformation to convert a Boolean formula $f$ into a linear secret sharing scheme defined by a share-generating matrix $M$ over prime $p$ (with corresponding secret-restoring coefficients $(\omega_i)_i$) with an assignment function $\rho$ from the rows of matrix $M$ to the universe of attributes. For its details we refer to [11]. Predicate $\mathrm{IsDH}(g, g_1, g_2, g_3)$ means the tuple $(g, g_1, g_2, g_3)$ is a Diffie-Hellman tuple, i.e., $g_3 = g_2^a$ for $a$ satisfying $g_1 = g^a$. For vectors $a = (a_1, \ldots, a_n)$ and $b = (b_1, \ldots, b_n)$, their inner product is written as $a \cdot b = \sum_{i=1,\ldots,n} a_i b_i$.

---

Setup $(1^k, N(k))$:

$(g, p, e) \leftarrow \mathsf{GenGrp}(1^k)$

Select $F (= F_1 \cdots F_{2N}) : \{0,1\}^* \rightarrow \{0,1\}^{2N}$

$\alpha, \beta, \gamma_1, \ldots, \gamma_{2N} \xleftarrow{\$} Z_p$

$h = g^\beta, w = e(g,g)^\alpha, u_1 = g^{\gamma_1}, \ldots, u_{2N} = g^{\gamma_{2N}}$

Return $par = (g, h, w, F, u_1, \ldots, u_{2N})$, $mk = (\beta, g^\alpha)$ and $lk = \gamma := (\gamma_1, \ldots, \gamma_{2N})$.

/* $(u_1, \ldots, u_{2N})$ defines a hash function $\mathcal{H}(S) = u_1^{F_1(S)} \cdots u_{2N}^{F_{2N}(S)}$ */

---

Enc $(par, f, m)$:

Assert $n := \sharp\mathrm{Leaf}(f) < N$

$(\rho, M) \leftarrow \mathrm{LSS}(p, f)$ /* Let dimension of $M$ be $n \times l$ */

$s, r_2, \ldots, r_l \xleftarrow{\$} Z_p, s_i = M_i \cdot (s, r_2, \ldots, r_l)$ $(i \in [1..n])$

$c_0 = m w^s, c_1 = g^s, c_2 = h^s, c_3 = (g^{s_i})_{i \in [1..n]}, c_4 = (\mathcal{H}(\rho(i))^{s_i})_{i \in [1..n]}, c_5 = \mathcal{H}(f, c_0, \ldots, c_4)^s$

Return $(f, c = (c_0, \ldots, c_5))$.

---

Ext $(f, mk, as)$:

$r \xleftarrow{\$} Z_p, r_a \xleftarrow{\$} Z_p$ $(a \in as)$

$d_1 = g^{(\alpha+r)/\beta}$

$d_2 = (g^r \mathcal{H}(a)^{r_a})_{a \in as}, d_3 = (g^{r_a})_{a \in as}$

Return $d = (as, d_1, d_2, d_3)$.

Dec $(par, (f, c), (as, d))$:

$(\rho, M) \leftarrow \mathrm{LSS}(p, f)$

$I = \rho^{-1}(as)$ and compute the constants $\{\omega_i\}_{i \in I}$

$\kappa = \prod_{i \in I}\{e(c_{3,i}, d_{2,\rho(i)})/e(c_{4,i}, d_{3,\rho(i)})\}^{\omega_i}$

Return $\kappa c_0 / e(d_1, c_2)$.

---

Loosen $(par, lk, (f, c), \Delta f)$:

Loosen the policy $f$ to $f' = \mathrm{or}(f, \Delta f)$

Assert $n := \sharp\mathrm{Leaf}(f') < N$ and $\mathrm{IsDH}(g, \mathcal{H}(f, c_0, \cdots, c_4), c_1, c_5)$

$(\rho, M) \leftarrow \mathrm{LSS}(p, f')$ /* Let dimension of $M$ be $n \times l$ */

Let $g^s = c_1$ and $r_2, \ldots, r_l \xleftarrow{\$} Z_p$ /* We don't know the value of $s$ */

Compute $g^{s_i} = g^{M_i \cdot (s, r_2, \ldots, r_l)}$ for $i \in [1..n]$ and set $c_3' = (g^{s_i})_{i \in [1..n]}$

/* The knowledge $g^s$ is enough to compute $g^{s_i}$ */

$c_4' = (g^{s_i(\gamma \cdot F(\rho(i)))})_{i \in [1..n]}, c_5' = (c_1)^{\gamma \cdot F(f', c_0, c_1, c_2, c_3', c_4')}$

Return $c' = (f', c_0, c_1, c_2, c_3', c_4', c_5')$.

---

We can prove the following theorems regarding security of the FABE scheme (the proofs are in the full version [1]).

**Theorem 1.** *The FABE scheme with parameter $N = N(k)$ is indistinguishable under loosening operation in the generic bilinear group model, under the assumption that the function $F$ is $(N + 1)$-linear-dependency resistant.*

**Theorem 2.** *The FABE scheme is indistinguishable under loosening key in the generic bilinear group model.*

## 5    Conclusion

We proposed a notion of flexible attribute-based encryption, that allows one to loosen a decryption policy underlying a given ciphertext. We gave a concrete construction of such flexible attribute-based encryption that is provably secure in the generic bilinear group model.

## References

1. Arita, S.: Flexible Attribute-Based Encryption (2012),
   http://lab.iisec.ac.jp/~arita/pdf/fabe.pdf
2. Badenand, R., Benderand, A., Springand, N., Bhattacharjee, B., Starin, D.: Persona: An online social network with user defined privacy. In: ACM SIGCOMM (2009)
3. Bellare, M., Rogaway, P.: The Security of Triple Encryption and a Framework for Code-Based Game-Playing Proofs. In: Vaudenay, S. (ed.) EUROCRYPT 2006. LNCS, vol. 4004, pp. 409–426. Springer, Heidelberg (2006)
4. Bethencourt, J., Sahai, A., Waters, B.: Ciphertext-Policy Attribute-Based Encryption. In: SP 2007, pp. 321–334. IEEE Computer Society (2007)
5. Bobba, R., Fatemieh, O., Khan, F., Gunter, A.K.C.A., Khurana, H., Prabhakaran, M.: Attribute-based messaging: Access control and confidentiality. ACM Transactions on Information and System Security (TISSEC) 13(4)
6. Goyal, V., Pandey, O., Sahai, A., Waters, B.: Attribute-based encryption for fine-grained access control of encrypted data. In: ACM Conference on Computer and Communications Security, pp. 89–98 (2006)
7. Guo, S., Zeng, Y., Wei, J., Xu, Q.: Attribute-based re-encryption scheme in the standard model. Wuhan University Journal of Natural Sciences 13(5), 621–625 (2008)
8. Ibraimi, L., Asim, M., Petkovic, M.: An Encryption Scheme for a Secure Policy Updating. In: SECRYPT 2010, pp. 399–408 (2010)
9. Liang, X., Cao, Z., Lin, H., Shao, J.: Attribute Based Proxy Re-encryption with Delegating Capabilities. In: ASIACCS 2009, pp. 276–286 (2009)
10. Lewko, A., Okamoto, T., Sahai, A., Takashima, K., Waters, B.: Fully Secure Functional Encryption: Attribute-Based Encryption and (Hierarchical) Inner Product Encryption. In: Gilbert, H. (ed.) EUROCRYPT 2010. LNCS, vol. 6110, pp. 62–91. Springer, Heidelberg (2010)
11. Lewko, A., Waters, B.: Decentralizing Attribute-Based Encryption. In: Paterson, K.G. (ed.) EUROCRYPT 2011. LNCS, vol. 6632, pp. 568–588. Springer, Heidelberg (2011)

12. Okamoto, T., Takashima, K.: Fully Secure Functional Encryption with General Relations from the Decisional Linear Assumption. In: Rabin, T. (ed.) CRYPTO 2010. LNCS, vol. 6223, pp. 191–208. Springer, Heidelberg (2010)
13. Sahai, A., Waters, B.: Fuzzy Identity-Based Encryption. In: Cramer, R. (ed.) EUROCRYPT 2005. LNCS, vol. 3494, pp. 457–473. Springer, Heidelberg (2005)
14. Traynor, P., Butler, K.R.B., Enck, W., McDaniel, P.: Realizing massive-scale conditional access systems through attribute-based cryptosystems. In: NDSS (2008)
15. Waters, B.: Ciphertext-Policy Attribute-Based Encryption: An Expressive, Efficient, and Provably Secure Realization. In: Catalano, D., Fazio, N., Gennaro, R., Nicolosi, A. (eds.) PKC 2011. LNCS, vol. 6571, pp. 53–70. Springer, Heidelberg (2011)

# Non-interactive Dynamic Identity-Based Broadcast Encryption without Random Oracles

Yanli Ren, Shuozhong Wang, and Xinpeng Zhang

School of Communication and Information Engineering,
Shanghai University,
Shanghai 200072, China
{ryl1982,shuowang,xzhang}@shu.edu.cn

**Abstract.** A dynamic broadcast encryption (DBE) is a broadcast encryption (BE) scheme where a new user can join the system anytime without modifying preexisting user decryption keys. In this paper, we propose a non-interactive dynamic identity-based broadcast encryption (DIBBE) scheme that is fully secure without random oracles. The PKG does not need to execute any interactive operation with the user during the lifetime of the system. The ciphertext is of constant size, and the public key size is linear in the maximal number of receivers for one encryption. This is the first non-interactive DIBBE scheme which is fully secure without random oracles, and it is collusion resistant for arbitrarily large collusion of users.

## 1 Introduction

Broadcast encryption (BE) scheme [1] allows a broadcaster to encrypt a message to an arbitrarily designated subset $S$ of users who are listening to a broadcast channel. A BE scheme is said to be fully collusion resistant when, even if all users that are not in S collude, they can by no means infer information about the broadcast message [6]. A dynamic broadcast encryption (DBE) is a BE scheme in which the total number of users is not fixed in the setup phase and a new user can join the system anytime without modifying preexisting user decryption keys.

Identity-based (ID-based) encryption [2] is a cryptosystem where the public key can be represented as an arbitrary string. A private key generator (PKG) uses a master secret key to issue private keys for users based on their identities. Many ID-based schemes have been proposed, but practical schemes were not found until the work of Boneh and Franklin [9] in 2001. Their identity-based encryption (IBE) scheme was based on efficiently computable bilinear maps, but it is only provably secure in the random oracle model. Since 2001, several schemes have been introduced [3,7,10]. There are mainly two security definitions: full security and selective-ID security, and the selective-ID security is weaker than full security.

T.W. Chim and T.H. Yuen (Eds.): ICICS 2012, LNCS 7618, pp. 479–487, 2012.
© Springer-Verlag Berlin Heidelberg 2012

In 2007, Sakai et al. proposed an identity-based broadcast encryption (IBBE) scheme with constant size ciphertext and private key [11]. The user can join the system anytime without generating new decryption keys for preexisting users. The scheme is only provably secure in the random oracle model. Delerablee proposed another dynamic IBBE scheme [5], where the ciphertext and private key are also of constant size, and the public key is of size linear to the maximal value of the set of receivers. The scheme only achieves selective-ID security in the random oracle model. Gentry et al. proposed several IBBE schemes [8], one of which is dynamic, but it only achieves sublinear size ciphertext in the standard model, or constant size ciphertext in the random oracle model. Boneh et al. described a dynamic IBBE scheme in 2008, which is only selective-ID secure without random oracles [4]. Zhao et al. presented another dynamic IBBE scheme, which is fully secure without random oracles [12]. However, the PKG needs to execute multiple interactive operations with each user in the extract phase, which is not efficient in practice if there are a lot of users in the system. Currently, there is no non-interactive DIBBE scheme available that is fully secure without random oracles.

**Our Contributions.** In this paper, we solve the open problem raised in [5] and propose a non-interactive DIBBE scheme that is fully secure without random oracles. The scheme has constant size ciphertexts and a tight reduction based on the $q$-wABDHE assumption. To the best of our knowledge, this is the first non-interactive DIBBE scheme that is fully secure without random oracles. Moreover, our DIBBE scheme is collusion resistant for arbitrarily large collusion of users.

## 2    Definitions

Below, we review the definition of a symmetric bilinear map and the security model for a DIBBE system. We also discuss the complexity assumption on which our system is based.

### 2.1    Symmetric Bilinear Map

Let $p$ be a large prime number, $G_1$ and $G_2$ be two groups of order $p$, and $g$ be a generator of $G_1$. $e : G_1 \times G_1 \to G_2$ is a symmetric bilinear map, which has the following properties [3,9,10]:

(1)Bilinearity: For all $u, v \in G_1$ and $a, b \in Z_p$, $e(u^a, v^b) = e(u, v)^{ab}$.
(2)Non-degeneracy: $e(g, g) \neq 1$.
(3)Computability: There exists an efficient algorithm to compute $e(u, v)$, $\forall u, v \in G_1$.

## 2.2   Complexity Assumption

Our scheme is based on decisional weaker augmented bilinear Diffie-Hellman exponent (wABDHE) assumption. The detailed definition is as follows: Given a vector of $2q + 2$ elements

$$(g', (g')^{\alpha^{q+2}}, \ldots, (g')^{\alpha^{2q}}, g, g^{\alpha}, \ldots, g^{\alpha^q}, Z) \in G_1^{2q+1} \times G_2$$

to decide whether $Z = e(g', g)^{\alpha^{q+1}}$.

An algorithm $A$ that outputs $w \in \{0, 1\}$ has advantage of $\varepsilon$ in solving the decision $q$-wABDHE problem if

$$|Pr[A(g', (g')^{\alpha^{q+2}}, \ldots, (g')^{\alpha^{2q}}, g, \ldots, g^{\alpha^q}, e(g', g)^{\alpha^{q+1}}) = 0]$$
$$-Pr[A(g', (g')^{\alpha^{q+2}}, \ldots, (g')^{\alpha^{2q}}, g, \ldots, g^{\alpha^q}, Z) = 0]| \geq \varepsilon,$$

where the probability depends on the random choice of $g, g' \in G_1, \alpha \in Z_p^*, Z \in G_2$, and the random bits consumed by $A$. We refer to the distribution on the left or right as $P_{wABDHE}$ or $R_{wABDHE}$.

We say that the decision $(t, \varepsilon, q)$-wABDHE assumption holds in $G_1, G_2$ if no $t$-time algorithm has advantage of at least $\varepsilon$ in solving the decision $q$-wABDHE problem in $G_1, G_2$.

## 2.3   Security Model

In this section, we define full security against an chosen plaintext attack (IND-ID-CPA) for a non-interactive DIBBE scheme. It is executed by the following game between an adversary $A$ and a challenger $B$.

**Setup.** The challenger runs $Setup(\lambda, m)$ algorithm to obtain a public key $PK$ and sends it to $A$.

**Phase 1.** The adversary $A$ adaptively issues queries.

Joinging query ($ID_i$): $A$ sends $ID_i$ to $B$. The challenger runs $Join$ algorithm on $ID_i$ and returns $A$ a decryption key $d_{ID_i}$.

**Challenge.** $A$ sends $(S^*, K_0, K_1)$ to $B$, where the identities in $S^*$ have not been executed the joining query in Phase 1.

The challenger randomly chooses $w \in \{0, 1\}$ and runs algorithm $Encrypt$ to obtain $(Hdr^*, K_w)$. It then gives $Hdr^*$ to adversary $A$.

**Phase 2.** $A$ adaptively issues joining query ($ID_i$), where $ID_i \notin S^*$.

**Guess.** Finally, the adversary outputs a guess $w' \in \{0, 1\}$ and wins the game if $w' = w$.

We call the adversary $A$ in the above game an IND-ID-CPA adversary. The advantage of $A$ is defined as $|Pr[w' = w] - \frac{1}{2}|$.

**Definition.** A non-interactive DIBBE system is $(t, \varepsilon, q)$ IND-ID-CPA secure if all $t$-time IND-ID-CPA adversaries making at most $q$ joining queries have advantage of at most $\varepsilon$ in winning the above game.

# 3   The Proposed DIBBE Scheme

We present a non-interactive DIBBE scheme with constant size ciphertext which is fully secure without random oracles. The system makes use of the hybrid encryption paradigm (KEM-DEM) where the broadcast ciphertext only encrypts a symmetric key used to encrypt the broadcast contents.

## 3.1   Setup

Given security parameter $\lambda$ and an integer $m$, the maximal size of the set of receivers for one encryption, two groups $G_1, G_2$ of order $p$ are constructed. $e : G_1 \times G_1 \to G_2$ is a symmetric bilinear map and $g$ is a generator of $G_1$. The PKG randomly chooses $l_0 \in G_1, \alpha, \beta, c \in Z_p^*$, and computes $k_0 = g^{\alpha\beta}, \mathrm{f}(x) = cx$. Finally, the public parameters are $(\mathrm{f}(x), g, g^\alpha, \ldots, g^{\alpha^m}, l_0, l_0^\alpha, \ldots, l_0^{\alpha^m}, k_0, k_0^\alpha, \ldots, k_0^{\alpha^m})$ and $\alpha, \beta$ are the master secret keys of PKG.

## 3.2   Join

To an $\mathsf{ID}_i \in Z_p^*$, the PKG randomly chooses $r_i \in Z_p^*, h_i \in G_1$, and sets

$$d_{1,i} = (h_i g^{r_i})^{\frac{1}{\alpha\beta(\alpha - ID_i)}}, d_{2,i} = r_i, d_{3,i} = (l_0^{f(r_i)} h_i)^{1/\alpha\beta}, lab_i = \{h_i, h_i^\alpha, \ldots, h_i^{\alpha^m}\},$$

so the corresponding private key is $d_{ID_i} = (d_{1,i}, d_{2,i}, d_{3,i}, lab_i)$.

## 3.3   Encrypt

For a set $S$, randomly choose $s \in Z_p^*, K \in G_2$, and compute

$$c_1 = k_0^{s \cdot \prod_{i \in S}(\alpha - ID_i)}, c_2 = (g^\alpha)^{-s}, c_3 = e(g, g)^{-s}, c_4 = K \cdot e(g, l_0)^s.$$

The ciphertext is $(Hdr, S)$, where $Hdr = (c_1, c_2, c_3, c_4)$. Then $K$ is used to encrypt the message.

## 3.4   Decrypt

The receiver of $S$ with identity $\mathsf{ID}_i$ decrypts

$$[e(c_1, d_{1,i})e(c_2, h_i g^{d_{2,i}})^{A_{i,S}(\alpha)}]^{\overline{\prod_{j \in S}^{j \neq i}(-ID_j)}} c_3^{d_{2,i}} = e(g, h_i)^s,$$

$$[e(c_1, d_{3,i})e(c_2, l_0^{f(d_{2,i})} h_i)^{B_{i,S}(\alpha)}]^{\frac{1}{\prod_{i \in S}(-ID_i)}} = e(g, l_0^{f(r_i)} h_i)^s,$$

$$[e(g, l_0^{f(r_i)} h_i)^s / e(g, h_i)^s]^{\frac{1}{f(d_{2,i})}} = e(g, l_0)^s, c_4 / e(g, l_0)^s = K,$$

where $A_{i,S}(\alpha) = \frac{1}{\alpha} [\prod_{j \in S}^{j \neq i} (\alpha - \mathsf{ID}_j) - \prod_{j \in S}^{j \neq i} (-\mathsf{ID}_j)]$,

$B_{i,S}(\alpha) = \frac{1}{\alpha} [\prod_{i \in S} (\alpha - \mathsf{ID}_i) - \prod_{i \in S} (-\mathsf{ID}_i)]$.

## 4   Analysis of the DIBBE Scheme

In this section, we analyze security of the DIBBE scheme and compare the proposed scheme with the previous ones.

### 4.1   Security

We now prove that the DIBBE scheme achieves IND-ID-CPA security under the $q$-wABDHE assumption without random oracles.

**Theorem 1.** Assume that the $(t', \varepsilon', q)$-wABDHE assumption holds in $G_1, G_2$, then the DIBBE scheme is $(t, \varepsilon, q - 1)$ IND-ID-CPA secure for $t = t' - O(t_{exp} \cdot mq), \varepsilon = \varepsilon' + 1/p, q \geq 2m$, where $m$ is the maximal size of the set of receivers for one encryption and $t_{exp}$ is the average time required to exponentiate in $G_1$ respectively.

*Proof.* Assume $A$ is an IND-ID-CPA adversary as described in Section 2.3, then we can construct an algorithm $B$ that solves the $q$-wABDHE problem as follows. At the beginning of the game, $B$ is given

$$(g', (g')^{\alpha^{q+2}}, \ldots, (g')^{\alpha^{2q}}, g, g^\alpha, \ldots, g^{\alpha^q}, Z) \in G_1^{2q+1} \times G_2$$

to decide whether $Z = e(g', g)^{\alpha^{q+1}}$.

**Setup.** $B$ randomly chooses $E(x) = \sum_{j=0}^{m-1} b_{0,j} x^j, \beta \in Z_p^*$ and sets

$$F(x) = x E(x) + b_0, \mathsf{f}(x) = \frac{1}{b_0} x, k_0 = g^{\alpha\beta}, k_0^\alpha = g^{\alpha^2\beta}, \ldots, k_0^{\alpha^m} = g^{\alpha^{m+1}\beta},$$
$$l_0 = g^{F(\alpha)}, l_0^\alpha = g^{\alpha F(\alpha)}, \ldots, l_0^{\alpha^m} = g^{\alpha^m F(\alpha)}, \text{ where } b_{0,j}, b_0 \in Z_p^*.$$

In fact, $B$ can compute the parameters as follows:

$$l_0 = g^{b_0} \prod_{j=0}^{m-1} (g^{\alpha^{j+1}})^{b_{0,j}} = g^{\sum_{j=0}^{m-1} b_{0,j} \alpha^{j+1} + b_0} = g^{\alpha E(\alpha) + b_0} = g^{F(\alpha)},$$
$$l_0^\alpha = g^{b_0 \alpha} \prod_{j=0}^{m-1} (g^{\alpha^{j+2}})^{b_{0,j}} = g^{\sum_{j=0}^{m-1} b_{0,j} \alpha^{j+2}} g^{b_0 \alpha} = g^{\alpha F(\alpha)}, \ldots,$$
$$l_0^{\alpha^m} = g^{b_0 \alpha^m} \prod_{j=0}^{m-1} (g^{\alpha^{j+m+1}})^{b_{0,j}} = g^{\sum_{j=0}^{m-1} b_{0,j} \alpha^{j+m+1}} g^{b_0 \alpha^m} = g^{\alpha^m F(\alpha)}.$$

$B$ sends $(\mathsf{f}(x), g, g^\alpha, \ldots, g^{\alpha^m}, l_0, l_0^\alpha, \ldots, l_0^{\alpha^m}, k_0, k_0^\alpha, \ldots, k_0^{\alpha^m})$ to $A$ as the public parameters. Note that the public keys are randomly distributed and indistiguishable from the real scheme for the adversary since $E(x), b_0$ and $\beta$ are randomly chosen.

**Phase 1.** The adversary $A$ adaptively issues queries.

Joining query $\langle \mathsf{ID}_i \rangle$: $A$ sends $\mathsf{ID}_i$ to $B$. $B$ randomly chooses

$$C_i(x) = \sum_{j=0}^{m-2} b_{i,j} x^j, D_i(x) = x(x - \mathsf{ID}_i) C_i(x) + b_i,$$

where $b_{i,j}, b_i \in Z_p^*$, and computes $d_{ID_i} = (d_{1,i}, d_{2,i}, d_{3,i}, lab_i)$ as below:

$$d_{1,i} = (g^{C_i(\alpha)})^{\frac{1}{\beta}}, d_{2,i} = -D_i(\mathsf{ID}_i) = -b_i,$$
$$d_{3,i} = (g^{-\frac{b_i}{b_0} E(\alpha) + (\alpha - ID_i) C_i(\alpha)})^{\frac{1}{\beta}}.$$
$$lab_i = \{h_i = g^{D_i(\alpha)}, h_i^{\alpha} = g^{\alpha D_i(\alpha)}, \ldots, h_i^{\alpha^m} = g^{\alpha^m D_i(\alpha)}\}.$$

Now we need to show that the adversary can compute $d_{ID_i}$ as follows.

$$d_{1,i} = (\prod_{j=0}^{m-2} g^{b_{i,j} \alpha^j})^{\frac{1}{\beta}} = (g^{\sum_{j=0}^{m-2} b_{i,j} \alpha^j})^{\frac{1}{\beta}} = (g^{C_i(\alpha)})^{\frac{1}{\beta}},$$
$$d_{2,i} = -\tilde{I}D_i(ID_i - \mathsf{ID}_i)C_i(x) - b_i = -b_i = -D_i(\mathsf{ID}_i),$$

$$d_{3,i} = (\prod_{j=0}^{m-1} g^{-\frac{b_i}{b_0} b_{0,j} \alpha^j} \cdot \prod_{j=0}^{m-2} g^{b_{i,j}(\alpha - ID_i) \alpha^j})^{\frac{1}{\beta}}$$
$$= (g^{-\frac{b_i}{b_0} E(\alpha) + (\alpha - ID_i) C_i(\alpha)})^{\frac{1}{\beta}},$$

$$h_i = g^{b_i} \prod_{j=0}^{m-2} (g^{\alpha^{j+2}} g^{-ID_i \alpha^{j+1}})^{b_{i,j}} = g^{\alpha(\alpha - ID_i) \sum_{j=0}^{m-2} b_{i,j} \alpha^j} g^{b_i} = g^{D_i(\alpha)},$$
$$h_i^{\alpha} = g^{b_i \alpha} \prod_{j=0}^{m-2} (g^{\alpha^{j+3}})^{b_{i,j}} (g^{\alpha^{j+2}})^{-ID_i b_{i,j}} = g^{\alpha D_i(\alpha)},$$

$$\cdots\cdots,$$

$$h_i^{\alpha^m} = g^{b_i \alpha^m} \prod_{j=0}^{m-2} (g^{\alpha^{j+m+2}})^{b_{i,j}} (g^{\alpha^{j+m+1}})^{-ID_i b_{i,j}} = g^{\alpha^m D_i(\alpha)}.$$

It is a valid private key, because

$$d_{1,i} = (g^{C_i(\alpha)})^{\frac{1}{\beta}} = g^{\frac{D_i(\alpha) - b_i}{\alpha \beta (\alpha - ID_i)}} = g^{\frac{D_i(\alpha) - D_i(ID_i)}{\alpha \beta (\alpha - ID_i)}} = (h_i g^{d_{2,i}})^{\frac{1}{\alpha \beta (\alpha - ID_i)}},$$
$$d_{2,i} = -D_i(\mathsf{ID}_i) = -ID_i(ID_i - \mathsf{ID}_i)C_i(x) - b_i = -b_i,$$
$$d_{3,i} = (g^{(-\frac{b_i}{b_0})(F(\alpha) - b_0) + D_i(\alpha) - b_i})^{\frac{1}{\alpha \beta}} = g^{\frac{(-\frac{b_i}{b_0})F(\alpha) + D_i(\alpha)}{\alpha \beta}} = (l_0^{f(d_{2,i})} h_i)^{\frac{1}{\alpha \beta}}.$$
$$lab_i = \{h_i = g^{D_i(\alpha)}, h_i^{\alpha} = g^{\alpha D_i(\alpha)}, \ldots, h_i^{\alpha^m} = g^{\alpha^m D_i(\alpha)}\}.$$

We conclude that $d_{1,i}, d_{2,i}, d_{3,i}, h_i$ are random distributed for the adversary since $E(x), b_0, \beta, C_i(x), b_i$ are randomly chosen. Thus, $d_{ID_i}$ is randomly distributed and indistiguishable from the real scheme for the adversary because of the randomness of $E(x), b_0$ and $C_i(x), b_i, \beta$.

**Challenge.** $A$ sends $(S^*, K_0, K_1)$ to $B$, where the identities of $S^*$ have not been executed the joining query in Phase 1.

$B$ randomly chooses $K_w, w \in \{0,1\}$, and sends $Hdr^*$ to $A$, where

$$c_1^* = (g'^{\alpha^{q+2}})^{\beta} \prod_{i \in S^*} (\alpha - ID_i), c_2^* = (g')^{-\alpha^{q+2}}, c_3^* = Z^{-1},$$
$$c_4^* = K_w \cdot Z^{b_0} \cdot e(g'^{\alpha^{q+2}}, g^{E(\alpha)}), Hdr^* = (c_1^*, c_2^*, c_3^*, c_4^*, S^*).$$

Let $s^* = \log_g g' \cdot \alpha^{q+1}$. If $Z = e(g', g)^{\alpha^{q+1}}$,

$$c_1^* = (g^{s^*\alpha})^\beta \prod_{i \in S^*}(\alpha - ID_i) = (k_0^{s^*})^{\prod_{i \in S^*}(\alpha - ID_i)},$$
$$c_2^* = (g')^{-\alpha^{q+2}} = (g^\alpha)^{-s^*}, \quad c_3^* = e(g', g)^{-\alpha^{q+1}} = e(g, g)^{-s^*},$$
$$c_4^* = K_w \cdot e(g'^{\alpha^{q+1}}, g^{F(\alpha)}) = K_w \cdot e(g, l_0)^{s^*}.$$

Since $\log_g g', \alpha$ are uniformly random, $s^*$ is uniformly random, and so $Hdr^*$ is a valid and appropriately-distributed challenge to A.

**Phase 2.** $A$ adaptively issues joining query $(ID_i)$, where $ID_i \notin S^*$.

**Guess.** $A$ submits a guess $w' \in \{0, 1\}$. If $w' = w$, $B$ outputs 0 (indicating that $Z = e(g', g)^{\alpha^{q+1}}$); else, it outputs 1.

**Probability Analysis:** When $Z$ is sampled from $P_{wABDHE}$, $Hdr^*$ is a valid ciphertext for the randomness of $s^*$, $A$ can guess $w' = w$ with probability $1/2 + \varepsilon'$. When $Z$ is sampled from $R_{wABDHE}$, $c_4^* = K_w \cdot Z^{b_0} \cdot e(g'^{\alpha^{q+1}}, g^{E(\alpha)})$. Since $g', Z, b_0, E(x)$ are uniformly random, $c_4^*/K_w$ is random for the adversary except probability $1/p$, and so $A$ can only guess $w' = w$ with probability $1/2 + 1/p$.

**Time Complexity:** Each joining query requires $O(m)$ exponentiations in $G_1$. Since $A$ makes at most $q - 1$ such queries, $t' = t + O(t_{exp} \cdot mq)$.

In the reduction, $B$'s success probability and time complexity are the same as that of $A$, except for additive factors depending on $p$ and $q$ respectively. So, the DIBBE system has a tight security reduction without random oracles. This completes the proof for Theorem 1.

## 4.2   Comparison

In this section, we compare the known DIBBE schemes in Table 1.

**Table 1.** Comparison among DIBBE schemes

| Scheme | Non-Interactive | Random oracles | Security model | Public key size | Ciphertext size | Decrypt time | Pairing |
|:---:|:---:|:---:|:---:|:---:|:---:|:---:|:---:|
| [5] | yes | yes | sID | $O(m)$ | $O(1)$ | $O(m)$ | 2 |
| [11] | yes | yes | ID | $O(m)$ | $O(1)$ | $O(m)$ | 2 |
| [4] | yes | no | sID | $O(m)$ | $O(1)$ | $O(m)$ | 2 |
| [8] | yes | no | ID | $O(\sqrt{m})$ | $O(\sqrt{m})$ | $O(m)$ | 2 |
| [12] | no | no | ID | $O(m)$ | $O(1)$ | $O(m)$ | 2 |
| Ours | yes | no | ID | $O(m)$ | $O(1)$ | $O(m)$ | 4 |

In Table 1, "sID, ID" denote "selective-ID" and "adaptive-ID" security model respectively, and $m$ represents the maximal number of receivers for one encryption.

From Table 1, we conclude that the scheme in [5] and [11] are provably secure in the random oracle model, and the scheme of [4] is selective-ID secure without random oracles. In [8,12], the scheme only achieves sublinear size ciphertext or the PKG needs to interact with each user for many times though the schemes are fully secure without random oracles. Our scheme is non-interactive with constant size ciphertext and also fully secure without random oracles. Thus, the proposed scheme has stronger security than that of the previous ones without decreasing the efficiency.

## 5    Conclusion

In this paper, we construct a non-interactive dynamic IBBE scheme with constant size ciphertexts, which achieves full security without random oracles. The PKG does not need to execute any interactive operation with each user. The security reduction is based on decision $q$-wABDHE assumption, it remains an open problem to construct a fully secure non-interactive DIBBE scheme based on a more natural assumption, which has a tight reduction without random oracles.

**Acknowledgement.** This work was supported by the Natural Science Foundation of China (61202367, 61073190, 60832010), and the Research Fund for the Doctoral Program of Higher Education of China (20113108110010).

## References

1. Fiat, A., Naor, M.: Broadcast Encryption. In: Stinson, D.R. (ed.) CRYPTO 1993. LNCS, vol. 773, pp. 480–491. Springer, Heidelberg (1994)
2. Shamir, A.: Identity-Based Cryptosystems and Signature Schemes. In: Blakely, G.R., Chaum, D. (eds.) CRYPTO 1984. LNCS, vol. 196, pp. 47–53. Springer, Heidelberg (1985)
3. Waters, B.: Efficient Identity-Based Encryption Without Random Oracles. In: Cramer, R. (ed.) EUROCRYPT 2005. LNCS, vol. 3494, pp. 114–127. Springer, Heidelberg (2005)
4. Libert, B., Vergnaud, D.: Towards Black-Box Accountable Authority IBE with Short Ciphertexts and Private Keys. In: Jarecki, S., Tsudik, G. (eds.) PKC 2009. LNCS, vol. 5443, pp. 235–255. Springer, Heidelberg (2009)
5. Delerablee, C.: Identity-Based Broadcast Encryption with Constant Size Ciphertexts and Private Keys. In: Kurosawa, K. (ed.) ASIACRYPT 2007. LNCS, vol. 4833, pp. 200–215. Springer, Heidelberg (2007)
6. Delerablee, C., Paillier, P., Pointcheval, D.: Fully Collusion Secure Dynamic Broadcast Encryption with Constant-Size Ciphertexts or Decryption Keys. In: Takagi, T., Okamoto, T., Okamoto, E., Okamoto, T. (eds.) Pairing 2007. LNCS, vol. 4575, pp. 39–59. Springer, Heidelberg (2007)

7. Gentry, C.: Practical Identity-Based Encryption Without Random Oracles. In: Vaudenay, S. (ed.) EUROCRYPT 2006. LNCS, vol. 4004, pp. 445–464. Springer, Heidelberg (2006)
8. Gentry, C., Waters, B.: Adaptive Security in Broadcast Encryption Systems (with Short Ciphertexts). In: Joux, A. (ed.) EUROCRYPT 2009. LNCS, vol. 5479, pp. 171–188. Springer, Heidelberg (2009)
9. Boneh, D., Franklin, M.: Identity-Based Encryption from the Weil Pairing. In: Kilian, J. (ed.) CRYPTO 2001. LNCS, vol. 2139, pp. 213–229. Springer, Heidelberg (2001)
10. Boneh, D., Boyen, X.: Efficient Selective-ID Secure Identity-Based Encryption Without Random Oracles. In: Cachin, C., Camenisch, J.L. (eds.) EUROCRYPT 2004. LNCS, vol. 3027, pp. 223–238. Springer, Heidelberg (2004)
11. Sakai, R., Furukawa, J.: Identity-Based Broadcast Encryption, http://eprint.iacr.org/2007/217
12. Zhao, X., Zhang, F.: Fully CCA2 Secure Identity-Based Broadcast Encryption with Black-Box Accountable Authority. Journal of Systems and Software 85, 708–716 (2012)

# A Comparative Study of Malware Family Classification

Rafiqul Islam and Irfan Altas

School of Computing and Mathematics,
Charles Sturt University, NSW, Australia
{mislam,ialtas}@csu.edu.au

**Abstract.** In this paper, we present a comparative study of conventional malware family classification techniques and identifiy their limitations. In our study, we investigate three different feature set, function length frequency and printable string information as static features and Application Programming Interface (API) calls and API parameters as dynamic features. In our classification process, we used some of well-known machine-learning algorithms by invoking WEKA libraries. We made a comparative analysis and conclude that the independent features are not good enough to defence against current as well as future malware.

**Keywords:** malware, classification, static, dynamic.

## 1   Introduction

The Internet has rapidly become an integral part of everyday life and our reliance on it is expected to continue to grow. However, its rapid adoption has also left it susceptible to misuse and abuse. Over the last decade, researchers have adopted a diversity of solutions in order to control malware. Much research has been conducted on developing automatic malware classification systems using data mining and machine-learning approaches [1, 2, 3, 4, 5, 6, 7, 8 and 10]. All classification approaches taken in the literature can basically be categorized into two types: (i) based on static features of the (unpacked) executable file [9, 10, 11, 12] and (ii) based on dynamic features of the (packed) executable file [13, 14, 15].

In this paper, we investigate performance of malware family classification based on the independent feature set by running our experiments on a set of executable files collected over 8 year period (2003 to 2010). Our empirical evidences indicate that the performance of earlier collected malware executable are better compared to later collected malware executable with the same feature set.

In Section 2, we discuss related work in this area. In Section 3, we describe our experimental setup and we present our classification method using machine learning technique in section 4. Section 5 presents the experimental results. In section 6, we describe the limitations of feature selection. In Section 7, we draw conclusions.

T.W. Chim and T.H. Yuen (Eds.): ICICS 2012, LNCS 7618, pp. 488–496, 2012.
© Springer-Verlag Berlin Heidelberg 2012

## 2    Related Work

Conventional malware detection and classification systems are based on static features extracted from executables by reverse-engineering process. For instance, the authors in [4], introduced the static feature extraction process based on three different types of feature: Portable Executable (PE); byte-sequence n-grams; and string features. The string features are based on text strings that are encoded in program files [17]. The string feature outperforms other two techniques in [4]. The authors of [10] used only printable string information contained within the executables because they noted that an obfuscated file usually does not have any strings consisting of words or sentences; packers encode almost all of the strings as nonprintable or random characters. In [12 and 16], the authors used the n-gram technique to deal with two classification problems: 1) classification between clean and malicious executables, and 2) classification of executables as a function of their payload.

In other studies, operational code (OpCode) has been used as static information to calculate the cosine similarity between two PE executables. For example, sequence frequencies [5], sequences and permutations [18] and critical instruction sequences [19] are used for differentiating between malware binaries. In a similar but slightly different method, the authors of [18] examined the OpCode frequency distribution to differentiate between malicious and clean code. However, the OpCode approach is not always feasible because some executable files cannot be disassembled properly [20]. Some researchers have also used function-based feature extraction [7 and 17], where functions are extracted from malware binaries and used to produce various attributes to identify the file.

In [22], the authors executed malware files to generate lists of API calls and then calculated the similarity between two API call sequences by using a similarity matrix. The run-time execution of malware files to generate usable information has also been used in the following papers: maximal common sub-graph detection by capturing system calls during the execution [21]; runtime behaviour in the form of sequenced events with canonical format [24]; sample of rootkits that use inline function hooking [23]. In [13], the authors introduce a malware detection technique combining two different dynamic features (from spatial and temporal information) available in run-time API. The authors of [25] proposed an automated tool running in a virtual environment to extract API call features from executables and apply pattern recognition algorithms and statistical methods to differentiate between cleanware and malware. In all of these cases, the methods give good classification accuracy but at the cost of high computational complexity.

## 3    Experimental Setup

### 3.1    The Data Set

The malware executables that we used in our experiment are based on our previous experiment [10 and 25], which are collected from CA's VET Zoo [www.ca.com.au]. The total numbers of malware executables used in our experiments are 2398. Table 1 presents the family wise number of malware executables and their corresponding number of instances used in the experiment.

**Table 1.** Experimental dataset showing old and new families

| Type | | Family | Number of Executables | Number of Instances |
|---|---|---|---|---|
| Malware | Trojan | Bambo | 44 | 5100 |
| | | Boxed | 178 | 56662 |
| | | Alureon | 41 | 7635 |
| | | Robknot | 78 | 10411 |
| | | Clagger | 44 | 4520 |
| | | Robzips | 72 | 6549 |
| | Worms | SillyDl | 439 | 56933 |
| | | Vundo | 80 | 1660 |
| | | Frethog | 174 | 28042 |
| | | SillyAutorun | 87 | 9965 |
| | Virus | Gamepass | 179 | 23730 |
| | | Bancos | 446 | 89554 |
| | | Adclicker | 65 | 11637 |
| | | Agobot | 283 | 216430 |
| | | Looked | 66 | 36644 |
| | | Emerleox | 75 | 61242 |
| | | Banker | 47 | 12112 |
| Total | | | **2398** | **638826** |

## 3.2   Static Feature Vectors

We unpacked each of the 2398 malware files by means of a command line anti-virus engine same as our existing process [10 and 25]. Thus we were able to unpack the malware executables in batch mode in order to speed up the unppacking time. From the unpacked files, we then extracted the desired static features and passed the information to our automated classification system as illustrated in Fig.1.

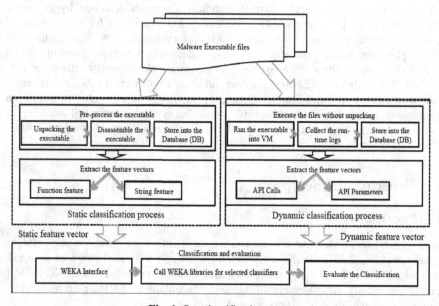

**Fig. 1.** Our classification process

### 3.3 Dynamic Feature Vectors

After running all the executable files and logging the Windows API calls we extract API features, comprising API function names and parameters, from the log files and again construct a global list that is samiliar to our existing process in [25]. Here, we treat the functions and parameters as separate entities as they may separately affect the ability to detect and identify the executable as illustrated in Fig. 1.

Fig. 2 describes the file in execution. A vector representation of the log data extracted after emulation is used in the classification. After running all the executable files in our sample set and logging the Windows API calls we extract the strings from the log files and again construct a global string list, same method as our previous work [25]. The strings extracted include API function names and parameters passed to the functions.

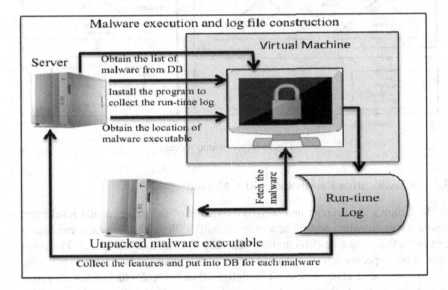

**Fig. 2.** Execution process of the files

## 4 Machine Learning Techniques

In the current literature, many publications apply a machine learning approach to malware classification. Machine learning algorithms used in this area include association classifiers, support vector machines, decision tree, random forest and Naive Bayes [16, 17 and 25].

Our analysis of the literature on classification algorithms and our preliminary testing led to the choice of four algorithms to use in our present classification work: support vector machine (SVM), decision tree (DT), random forest (RF) and instance-based (IB1) along with boosting techniques. These algorithms represent the spectrum of major classification techniques available based on differing approaches to the classification.

# 5     Experiment

In our test, we do the following three independent tests using each feature set; a) FLF test, b) PSI test and c) Dynamic test. The Fig. 3 shows our experimental process.

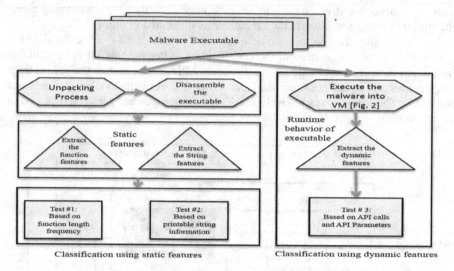

**Fig. 3.** Experimental process

## 5.1     Classification Results Using FLF Method

Table 2 shows the average and weighted average of the experimental results for the function length feature according to meta-classifier. We use three statistics: false positive (FP), false negative (FN) and the accuracy of detection rate (Acc). The performance of our experimental study shows that meta-RF gives the best average performance compared to other classifiers. As it is higlighted in Table 2, old families, in particular Boxed, emerleox, looked give better results than new families such as Adclicker, Banker, SillyDI do.

## 5.2     Classification Results Using PSI Method

Table 3 shows the average classification results of the PSI method based on the our data set. Meta-RF is, again, the best performer among the classifiers. The classifier SVM displays lowest accuracy in both the FLF and PSI methods as indicated in Tables 2 and 3. One reason for this would be that SVM is designed to handle data sets with a large feature space. Both feature sets for FLF and PSI are relatively small in our test (20 and an average of 448 respectively), which may also explain why the SVM result is better in the PSI test. However, some families (agobot, alureon, robzips, looked, emerleox etc. higlited in Table 3) show better performance compared to others, in particular *ropzips* shows 100% accuracy for some classifiers, which is significant.

**Table 2.** Classification results using FLF method

| Family | Meta Classifier | | | | | | | | | | | |
|---|---|---|---|---|---|---|---|---|---|---|---|---|
| | SVM | | | IB1 | | | DT | | | RF | | |
| | FP | FN | Acc | FP | FN | Acc | FP | FN | Acc | FP | FN | Acc |
| Adclicker | 0.51 | 0.1 | 69.17 | 0.26 | 0.17 | 78.33 | 0.3 | 0.26 | 71.67 | 0.18 | 0.2 | 80.83 |
| Bancos | 0.41 | 0.08 | 75 | 0.22 | 0.12 | 82.62 | 0.17 | 0.15 | 83.31 | 0.14 | 0.12 | 86.93 |
| Banker | 0.47 | 0.17 | 67.5 | 0.3 | 0.33 | 68.75 | 0.22 | 0.62 | 57.5 | 0.22 | 0.32 | 72.5 |
| Frethog | 0.35 | 0.04 | 79.71 | 0.17 | 0.1 | 86.18 | 0.11 | 0.10 | 89.42 | 0.15 | 0.07 | 88.53 |
| Gamepass | 0.54 | 0.13 | 65.88 | 0.19 | 0.25 | 77.65 | 0.21 | 0.34 | 72.36 | 0.11 | 0.17 | 85.88 |
| SillyAulorun | 0.77 | 0.11 | 55.63 | 0.32 | 0.2 | 73.75 | 0.32 | 0.33 | 66.88 | 0.21 | 0.25 | 76.86 |
| SillyDl | 0.58 | 0.11 | 65 | 0.31 | 0.27 | 70.35 | 0.47 | 0.26 | 63.14 | 0.3 | 0.24 | 72.56 |
| Vundo | 0.41 | 0.07 | 75.63 | 0.2 | 0.24 | 78.13 | 0.15 | 0.21 | 81.88 | 0.12 | 0.12 | 87.5 |
| clagger | 0.1 | 0.05 | 92.5 | 0 | 0 | 100 | 0.15 | 0.07 | 88.75 | 0 | 0.05 | 97.5 |
| agobot | 0.01 | 0.17 | 90.54 | 0.07 | 0.04 | 94.64 | 0.04 | 0.05 | 95 | 0.03 | 0.03 | 96.25 |
| alureon | 0.05 | 0.27 | 83.75 | 0.2 | 0.05 | 87.5 | 0.1 | 0.12 | 88.75 | 0.07 | 0.05 | 93.75 |
| bambo | 0.22 | 0.15 | 81.25 | 0.25 | 0.13 | 81.25 | 0.47 | 0.22 | 65 | 0.12 | 0.05 | 91.25 |
| boxed | 0.04 | 0.02 | 96.18 | 0.04 | 0.02 | 96.77 | 0.01 | 0.03 | 97.94 | 0.02 | 0.03 | 96.77 |
| emerleox | 0.01 | 0.01 | 98.57 | 0.04 | 0.01 | 97.14 | 0.07 | 0.01 | 95.72 | 0.01 | 0.01 | 98.57 |
| looked | 0.05 | 0.01 | 96.67 | 0.01 | 0.02 | 98.33 | 0.03 | 0.03 | 96.67 | 0.03 | 0.03 | 96.67 |
| robknot | 0 | 0.15 | 92.14 | 0.15 | 0.04 | 90 | 0.05 | 0.04 | 95 | 0.04 | 0.04 | 95.72 |
| robzips | 0.15 | 0 | 92.14 | 0.01 | 0 | 99.29 | 0.01 | 0 | 99.29 | 0.01 | 0 | 99.28 |
| Avg | 0.27 | 0.09 | 81.11 | 0.16 | 0.12 | 86.01 | 0.16 | 0.17 | 83.01 | 0.1 | 0.1 | 89.27 |

**Table 3.** Classification results using PSI method

| Family | Meta Classifier | | | | | | | | | | | |
|---|---|---|---|---|---|---|---|---|---|---|---|---|
| | SVM | | | IB1 | | | DT | | | RF | | |
| | FP | FN | Acc | FP | FN | Acc | FP | FN | Acc | FP | FN | Acc |
| Adclicker | 0.28 | 0.38 | 66.67 | 0.28 | 0.28 | 71.67 | 0.2 | 0.35 | 72.5 | 0.25 | 0.28 | 73.33 |
| Bancos | 0.1 | 0.13 | 88.19 | 0.17 | 0.13 | 84.21 | 0.11 | 0.14 | 87.16 | 0.11 | 0.13 | 88.29 |
| Banker | 0.37 | 0.37 | 62.5 | 0.3 | 0.4 | 65 | 0.37 | 0.42 | 60 | 0.25 | 0.35 | 70 |
| Frethog | 0.26 | 0.21 | 76.47 | 0.12 | 0.11 | 87.65 | 0.14 | 0.04 | 90.59 | 0.1 | 0.14 | 87.65 |
| Gamepass | 0.28 | 0.26 | 72.36 | 0.19 | 0.21 | 79.41 | 0.21 | 0.26 | 76.48 | 0.17 | 0.21 | 80.88 |
| SillyAutorun | 0.22 | 0.27 | 75.01 | 0.2 | 0.26 | 76.88 | 0.17 | 0.33 | 74.38 | 0.11 | 0.26 | 81.25 |
| SillyDl | 0.38 | 0.33 | 64.31 | 0.28 | 0.32 | 69.55 | 0.29 | 0.31 | 70 | 0.26 | 0.3 | 71.62 |
| Vundo | 0.01 | 0.37 | 80.63 | 0.22 | 0.2 | 78.75 | 0.07 | 0.32 | 80 | 0.22 | 0.23 | 76.87 |
| clagger | 0.05 | 0.07 | 93.75 | 0.02 | 0.05 | 96.25 | 0 | 0.07 | 96.25 | 0 | 0.05 | 97.5 |
| agobot | 0.01 | 0.05 | 96.79 | 0.04 | 0.04 | 95.37 | 0.02 | 0.02 | 97.5 | 0.01 | 0.03 | 98.03 |
| alureon | 0 | 0.07 | 96.25 | 0.02 | 0.07 | 95 | 0.02 | 0.02 | 97.5 | 0.05 | 0.07 | 93.75 |
| bambo | 0.02 | 0.02 | 97.5 | 0.02 | 0.12 | 92.5 | 0 | 0.05 | 97.5 | 0.03 | 0.05 | 96.25 |
| boxed | 0.01 | 0.04 | 97.06 | 0.01 | 0.04 | 97.35 | 0.01 | 0.04 | 97.36 | 0.02 | 0.05 | 96.17 |
| emerleox | 0.01 | 0.01 | 98.57 | 0.02 | 0.01 | 97.87 | 0 | 0.09 | 95.72 | 0 | 0.01 | 99.28 |
| looked | 0 | 0.01 | 99.17 | 0 | 0.01 | 99.17 | 0.01 | 0 | 99.17 | 0 | 0.01 | 99.16 |
| robknot | 0.02 | 0.01 | 97.86 | 0.03 | 0.05 | 95.71 | 0.01 | 0.04 | 97.15 | 0.01 | 0.02 | 97.85 |
| robzips | 0 | 0 | 100 | 0 | 0 | 100 | 0.01 | 0 | 99.29 | 0 | 0 | 100 |
| Avg | 0.11 | 0.15 | 86.06 | 0.11 | 0.13 | 87.19 | 0.09 | 0.14 | 87.58 | 0.09 | 0.12 | 89.01 |

## 5.3    Classification Results Using the Dynamic Method

Table 4 shows that the accuracy for the dynamic method across all classifiers is better than the FLF and PSI tests have for each meta-classifier. Once again, meta-RF achieves highest accuracy. It is also obvious from table 4 that *Robknot* shows 100% accuracy in dynamic test. However, the *Robzips* shows accuracy around 99% which is less than PSI test. Therefore, it is clear from our dynamic test that API features can detect highest rate of excutable than any other static features. It is also demonstrated from our experiment that detection ratio of old executables is better in current feature set compared to new executables.

**Table 4.** Classification results using dynamic method

| Family | Meta Classifier | | | | | | | | | | | |
|---|---|---|---|---|---|---|---|---|---|---|---|---|
| | SVM | | | IB1 | | | DT | | | RF | | |
| | FP | FN | Acc | FP | FN | Acc | FP | FN | Acc | FP | FN | Acc |
| Adclicker | 0.21 | 0.25 | 76.67 | 0.28 | 0.217 | 75 | 0.11 | 0.3 | 79.17 | 0.21 | 0.25 | 76.67 |
| Bancos | 0.12 | 0.11 | 88.07 | 0.14 | 0.1 | 88.18 | 0.13 | 0.12 | 87.27 | 0.09 | 0.1 | 90.23 |
| Banker | 0.4 | 0.22 | 68.75 | 0.33 | 0.375 | 65 | 0.45 | 0.3 | 62.5 | 0.47 | 0.27 | 62.5 |
| Frethog | 0.06 | 0.07 | 92.94 | 0.11 | 0.071 | 90.88 | 0.04 | 0.11 | 92.06 | 0.02 | 0.1 | 93.53 |
| Gamepass | 0.11 | 0.14 | 87.06 | 0.17 | 0.147 | 84.12 | 0.15 | 0.21 | 82.06 | 0.17 | 0.11 | 85.59 |
| SillyAutorun | 0.23 | 0.16 | 80 | 0.28 | 0.162 | 78.13 | 0.23 | 0.22 | 76.88 | 0.18 | 0.16 | 82.5 |
| SillyDl | 0.21 | 0.31 | 73.49 | 0.263 | 0.235 | 75.12 | 0.28 | 0.31 | 69.77 | 0.21 | 0.22 | 78.61 |
| Vundo | 0.03 | 0.08 | 93.75 | 0.162 | 0.075 | 88.13 | 0.06 | 0.08 | 92.5 | 0.05 | 0.11 | 91.88 |
| Clagger | 0 | 0.02 | 98.75 | 0 | 0.025 | 98.75 | 0.02 | 0.02 | 97.5 | 0 | 0.05 | 97.5 |
| Agobot | 0.01 | 0.01 | 98.75 | 0.025 | 0.006 | 98.44 | 0.01 | 0.01 | 98.75 | 0.01 | 0.01 | 98.28 |
| Alureon | 0.07 | 0.07 | 92.5 | 0.15 | 0.075 | 88.75 | 0.12 | 0.02 | 92.5 | 0.15 | 0.1 | 87.5 |
| Bamboo | 0.01 | 0.01 | 98.33 | 0.067 | 0.033 | 95 | 0.03 | 0.03 | 96.67 | 0.05 | 0.05 | 95 |
| Boxed | 0.02 | 0.01 | 98.22 | 0.032 | 0.029 | 96.97 | 0.01 | 0.01 | 98.57 | 0.01 | 0.02 | 97.68 |
| Emerleox | 0.04 | 0.07 | 94.29 | 0.071 | 0.043 | 94.29 | 0.04 | 0.04 | 95.72 | 0.04 | 0.1 | 92.86 |
| Looked | 0.01 | 0.01 | 98.33 | 0.083 | 0 | 95.84 | 0.05 | 0.03 | 95.83 | 0.05 | 0.03 | 95.83 |
| Robknot | 0 | 0 | 100 | 0 | 0 | 100 | 0.02 | 0 | 98.57 | 0 | 0 | 100 |
| Robzips | 0.01 | 0 | 99.29 | 0.043 | 0 | 97.86 | 0.02 | 0 | 98.57 | 0.01 | 0 | 99.28 |
| Avg | 0.09 | 0.09 | 90.54 | 0.12 | 0.09 | 88.85 | 0.1 | 0.1 | 89.15 | 0.1 | 0.09 | 90.01 |

Fig. 4 shows the comparative results of the accuracy of the above methods based on our data set. From the figure, classifier-by-classifier, the dynamic method outperforms the other methods. It is also noted from figure 4 that the classifier RF shows better performance than the other three do. However, the SVM shows comparable performance in dynamic test than other two tests as SVM can handle large data set which we mentioned earlier.

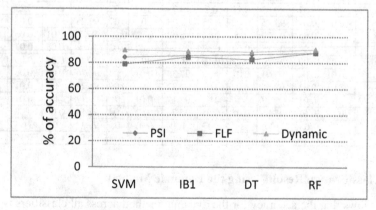

**Fig. 4.** Comparison of accuracy of three different tests

# 6    Limitations

While static techniques are widely used for malware detection and classification, they have some major drawbacks [26]. First, they are often used to find a malware 'signature' or identity, which requires a human expert and can take more time than it is available to stop an attack. Secondly, the static feature approach can be easily bypassed by obfuscation methods.Thus, the inability of the static feature approach to accurately detect new forms of malicious executables shifted the focus of virus research to the determination of features that can identify malicious behaviour as a process instead of by means of a unique signature.

Dynamic analysis is time consuming as each malware sample must be executed for a certain time period and its actions logged all within a controlled environment to ensure that it cannot infect an active platform. This controlled virtual environment is quite different from a real runtime environment and the malware may act in different ways in the two environments resulting in an inaccurate picture of the malware in the logs. Additionally, some malware behavior is triggered only under certain conditions (via a specific command or interaction with a human, for example) and this cannot be picked up in the virtual environment. Nevertheless,it has been suggested that dynamic extraction is a necessary complement to static techniques as it is significantly less vulnerable to code obfuscating transformations [12].

# 7    Conclusion

The results of Section 5 along with figures indicate that the Random Forest machine learning technique is best equipped to classify our data. Considering the results of Section 5, we conclude that the age (as measured by when the executable file was first collected) of the malware used has an impact on the test results. Since our classification method is less effective on the latest malware executables as compared to the older files in our library. This demonstrates that malware continues to evolve and to deploy advanced anti-detection techniques.

It is comprehensible from our investigation that the independent features are not good enough to fight against current as well as future malware. The integrated test would perform better and we will explore it in our future work.

# References

1. Bailey, M., Oberheide, J., Andersen, J., Mao, Z., Jahanian, F., Nazario, J.: Automated Classification and Analysis of Internet Malware. In: Kruegel, C., Lippmann, R., Clark, A. (eds.) RAID 2007. LNCS, vol. 4637, pp. 178–197. Springer, Heidelberg (2007)
2. Gurrutxaga, I., Arbelaitz, O., Ma Perez, J., Muguerza, J., Martin, J.I., Perona, I.: Evaluation of Malware clustering based on its dynamic behaviour. In: Seventh Australasian Data Mining Conference (AusDM), pp. 163–170 (2008)
3. Jiang, X., Zhu, X.: Eye behavioral footprinting for self-propagating worm detection and profiling. Knowledge and Information Systems 18, 231–262 (2009)
4. Schultz, M.G., Eskin, E., Zadok, E., Stolfo, S.J.: Data Mining Methods for Detection of New Malicious Executables. In: Proceedings of the IEEE Symposium on Security and Privacy, pp. 38–49 (2001)

5. Stolfo, S., Wang, K., Li, J.: Towards Stealthy Malware Detection. In: Mihai, C., Somesh, J., Douglas, M., Dawn, S., Cliff, W. (eds.) Malware Detection, pp. 231–249. Springer (2007)
6. Sung, A.H., Xu, J., Chavez, P., Mukkamala, S.: Static Analyzer of Vicious Executables. In: Proceedings of the Annual Computer Security Applications Conference, pp. 326–334 (2004)
7. Tian, R., Batten, L., Versteeg, S.: Function Length as a Tool for Malware Classification. In: Proceedings of the MALWARE 2008, pp. 69–76 (2008)
8. Ye, Y., Wang, D., Li, T., Ye, D.: IMDS intelligent malware detection system. In: Proceedings of the 13th ACM SIGKDD, pp. 1043–1047 (2007)
9. Santos, I., Nieves, J., Bringas, P.G.: Semi-supervised Learning for Unknown Malware Detection. In: Abraham, A., Corchado, J.M., González, S.R., De Paz Santana, J.F. (eds.) International Symposium on DCAI. AISC, vol. 91, pp. 415–422. Springer, Heidelberg (2011)
10. Tian, R., Batten, L., Islam, R., Versteeg, S.: An Automated Classification System Based on the Strings of Trojan and Virus Families. In: MALWARE 2009, pp. 23–30 (2009)
11. Wang, C., Pang, J., Zhao, R., Liu, X.: Using API Sequence and Bayes Algorithm to Detect Suspicious Behavior. In: ICCSN, pp. 544–548 (2009)
12. Ye, Y., Li, T., Chen, Y., Jiang, Q.: Automatic malware categorization using cluster ensemble. In: Proceedings of the 16th ACM SIGKDD, pp. 95–104 (2010)
13. Ahmed, F., Hameed, H., Shafiq, Z., Farooq, M.: Using spatio-temporal information in API calls with machine learning algorithms for malware detection. In: Proceedings of the ACM Workshop on Security and Artificial Intelligence, pp. 55–62 (2009)
14. Kolbitsch, C., Comparetti, M., Kruegel, C., Kirda, E., Zhou, X., Wang, X.: Effective and efficient malware detection at the end host. In: USENIX, pp. 351–366 (2009)
15. Zhao, H., Xu, M., Zheng, N., Yao, J., Ho, Q.: Malicious Executables Classification Based on Behavioral Factor Analysis. In: IEEE International Conference on e-Education, e-Business, e-Management and e-Learning, pp. 502–506 (2010)
16. Abou-Assaleh, T., Cercone, N., Keselj, V., Sweidan, R.: N-Gram-Based Detection of New Malicious Code. In: Proceedings of the 28th Annual International Computer Software and Applications Conference, vol. 02, pp. 41–42 (2004)
17. Shabtai, A., Moskovitch, R., Elovici, Y., Glezer, C.: Detection of malicious code by applying machine learning classifiers on static features. A state-of-the-art survey, pp. 16–29. Elsevier Advanced Technology Publications, Oxford (2009)
18. Karim, M., Walenstein, A., Lakhotia, A., Parida, L.: Malware phylogeny generation using permutations of code. Journal in Computer Virology 1(1), 13–23 (2005)
19. Siddiqui, M., Wang, C., Lee, J.: Data mining methods for malware detection using instruction sequences. In: 'Proceedings of the 26th IASTED ICAIA, pp. 358–363 (2008)
20. Bilar, D.: Opcodes as predictor for malware, pp. 156–168. Inderscience Publishers, Geneva (2007)
21. Park, Y., Reeves, D., Mulukutla, V., Sundaravel, B.: Fast malware classification by automated behavioral graph matching. In: Proceedings of Annual Workshop on Cyber Security and Information Intelligence Research, pp. 45:1–45:4 (2010)
22. Wagener, G., State, R., Dulaunoy, A.: Malware behaviour analysis. Journal in Computer Virology 4(4), 279–287 (2008)
23. Lobo, D., Watters, P., Wu, X.: RBACS Rootkit Behavioral Analysis and Classification System. In: WKDD 2010, pp. 75–80 (2010)
24. Lin, J.: On Malicious Software Classification. In: International Symposium on Intelligent Information Technology Application Workshops, pp. 368–371 (2008)
25. Tian, R., Islam, R., Batten, L., Versteeg, S.: Differentiating malware from cleanware using behavioural analysis. In: MALWARE 2010, pp. 23–30 (2010)
26. Menahem, E., Shabtai, A., Rokach, L., Elovici, Y.: Improving malware detection by applying multi-inducer ensemble. Computational Statistics & Data Analysis 53(4), 1483–1494 (2009)

# A Fine-Grained Classification Approach
# for the Packed Malicious Code

Shanqing Guo[1], Shuangshuang Li[1], Yan Yu[2], Anlei Hu[3], and Tao Ban[4]

[1] School of Computer Science and Technology, Shandong University, China
[2] School of Computer Science, Nanjing University of Science & Technology, China
[3] DNSLAB, China Internet Network Information Center, Beijing, China
[4] National Institute of Information and Communications Technology, Japan
bantao@nict.go.jp, guoshanqing@sdu.edu.cn,
huanlei@cnnic.cn, yuyan@mail.njust.edu.cn

**Abstract.** Executable packing is the most common technique to evade detection by anti-virus software.Many signature-based unpackers have been presented to uncover hidden viruses,which make the signature-based anti-virus software successfully detect the packed malicious code. However,these universal unpackers are computationally expensive and scanning large collections of executables may take several hours or even days.In order to improve the computational efficiency, Machine learning techniques have recently been proven effective in solving the focused issues,but up to now,no methods can show what packing method has been used in it.In this paper we proposed a fine-grained detection method to detect whether a malicious code has been packed and which method is been used to.This method firstly extract a hex-string from the target object file and then apply a String-Kernel-Based SVM Classifier to implement the fast detection of packed malicious code.We also show that our system achieves very high detection accuracy of packed executables, so that only executables detected as packed will be sent to an universal unpacker, thus saving a significant amount of processing time.

**Keywords:** Computer Security, String-Based Kernel,Support Vector Machine, Packed Malicious Code,Computer Virus Detection.

## 1 Introduction

In these days,honeypot systems,operated in malware analysis groups,encounter with numerous of malware samples day by day.Unfortunately,large portions of such malware samples,at around 50%,are identified to be packed with PEiD tool [1]. Applying packing in malware can degrade the effectiveness of signature-based AV scanners,for it has no choice but to create a separate signature. Therefore, It is very significant to develop an efficient automated approach to identify packers and uncover hidden codes from so huge volumes of malwares. Some universal unpackers [2, 3] have been developed, and these tools are able to detect and extract (part of) the original code from the encrypted code without specific knowledge about the encryption algorithm. However, these universal unpackers introduce a high computational overhead, and the processing time may vary

T.W. Chim and T.H. Yuen (Eds.): ICICS 2012, LNCS 7618, pp. 497–504, 2012.
© Springer-Verlag Berlin Heidelberg 2012

from tens of seconds to several minutes per executable. For example, the average time it takes to unpack a packed virus using the Renovo [3] unpacker is around 40 seconds. For this reason, we need to do some research about how to effectively distinguish the packed malicious code from the unpacked malicious code.

Machine learning techniques have recently been proven effective in solving the focused issues in this paper [4–6],but most of the existed works focus on how to detect whether a malware been packed. In this paper,based on the string-based kernel function, we proposed a fast fine-grained detection method to accurately distinguish whether a malware is packed, and if packed, what kind of packed toolkit has been used? After the packed toolkit has been identified, it can be directly sent to a special unpacking engineer to implement the hidden code extraction. Therefore, our classification system helps in improving virus detection while saving a significant amount of processing time.

The remainder of the paper is organized as follows. In Section 2 we present an overview of the related work. Section 3 introduce the Support Vector Machine(SVM) and a simple string-based kernel function.In Section 4 we briefly discuss the Portable Executable (PE) file format, and describe the features used for classifying PE executables. We then present and discuss the experimental results in Section 5,and summarize our work in Section 6.

## 2   Related Works

Although distinguishing between packed and non-packed executables is undecidable [3], several detecting methods have been proposed. The firstly proposed methods is the signature-based methods,and it also has developed many tools,like PEiD [1]. Signature-based detectors are fast and have relatively low false positives, but malware authors soon discovered that it was sufficient to use a slightly different packing algorithm each time to frustrate this kinds of regular expression matching algorithm, which make the signature-based detectors produce a high number of false negatives alerts.

The other related works is dynamic unpackers. Dynamic unpackers execute and monitor a program in memory, and detect attempts of executing dynamically decrypted code. To date, some dynamic unpackers have been proposed: Omniunpack[7], PolyUnpack[2], which try to monitors the execution of applications in memory and detects whether a PE file is packed. One important drawback of the dynamic unpackers is the performance overhead they introduce. Unfortunately, this performance overhead makes it impossible to install and run them as real-time systems on end-user machines. Therefore, [4, 8] divides the PE file into blocks of 256 bytes , and detect whether a file be packed by only computing the entropy of each block, the average, and the maximum block entropy. [9] do not limit the analysis to the PE file entropy and introduce and motivate the use of additional features that help in distinguishing between packed and non-packed executables.

To the best of our knowledge, the closest works to ours are [4, 8]. There exist many difference between [4, 8] and our works.On the one hand, our proposed method is a fine-grained classification method,which can identify which packed tools has been used by a packed malware, but [4, 8] only can detect whether a malware is packed. On the other hand, we can show that our classification approach also has a low average processing time with very low false positive and false negative rates.

## 3   String-Kernel-Based SVM Classifier

Support vector machines (SVMs) are a set of related supervised learning methods that are used for classification and regression analysis. SVM maps the data points into a high dimensional feature space, where a hyperplane or set of hyperplanes was constructed to implement the task of classification. According to the form of the error function, SVM models can be classified into distinct groups. Here, We only focus on the standard soft-margin SVM problem (C-SVM). The main task in C-SVM is to solve the following quadratic optimization problem with respect to $\alpha$:

$$\begin{aligned} &\min_\alpha \tfrac{1}{2}\alpha^T Q\alpha - 1^T\alpha \\ &Subject\ to\ y^T\alpha > 0 \quad 0 \le \alpha_i \le C, i = 1, \cdots, m \end{aligned} \tag{1}$$

Where Q is the N*N positive semi-definite kernel matrix, $Q_{ij} = y_i y_j K(x_i, x_j)$, and $K(x_i, x_j) = (x_i)^T(x_j)$ is the kernel function; and 1 is a vector of all ones.C-SVM predict the class label of a new data point x to be classified by the following decision function: $f(x) = sign(\sum_{i=1}^{m} y_i \alpha_i K(x_i, x) + b)$ Where b is a bias constant.

Traditional regular kernels for SVM work merely on numerical data, which is unsuitable for internet security where huge amount of string data is presented. Towards extending SVM for string data processing, many string-based kernel were proposed.In our implementation, we use $K = e^{\lambda d(i,j)}$ as the kernel function of the SVM for getting better results,here, $d(i,j)$ is the Levenshtein (or edit) distance [10]. Analog to the other substring kernel, the computational complexity of Levenshtein Distance is $O(\| s \| t \|)$. In the case that s and t have the same length, the complexity is $O(n^2)$.

## 4   JUMPS: JUst-in-tiMe Packer Scanning

### 4.1   Our Classification System

Figure 1 illustrates the processing procedure of our proposed system. Once a PE executable is received, our classification system performs a static analysis of the PE file and extract the first N bytes from its code section. After first N bytes were translated into a pattern vector, the obtained pattern vector representation of the PE executable is sent to the SVM classifier. If the executable is classified as packed, it will be sent to the universal unpacker for hidden code extraction, and the hidden code will then be sent to the anti-virus scanner. On the other hand, if the executable is classified as non-packed, it will be sent directly to the anti-virus

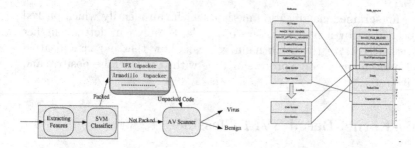

**Fig. 1.** Our Classifier System

**Fig. 2.** The layout of the packed binary Hello.exe by UPS packer

scanner. It is worth noting that the PE file classifier may erroneously label a non-packed executable as packed. In this case the universal unpacker will not be able to extract any hidden code from the received PE file. Nonetheless, this is not critical because if no hidden code is extracted, the AV scanner will simply scan the original non-packed code. The only cost paid in this case is the time spent by the universal unpacker in trying to unpack a non-packed executable. On the other hand, the PE classifier may in some cases classify a packed executable as non-packed. In this case, the packed executable will be sent directly to the anti-virus scanner, which may fail to detect the presence of malicious code embedded in the packed executable, thus causing a false negative.Figure 1 also shows that our classifier may be used to improve virus detection accuracy with low overhead, compared to a system where all the executables are directly sent to the universal unpacker.

## 4.2   Features Extraction

Lets start with a simple example,named UPX, which arguably is among the most straightforward packers in use today. Fig.2 shows how UPX packs an example program Hello.exe. When UPX compresses a PE binary, it begins by merging all of its sections into a single section, with the exception of the resource section. The combined data is then compressed into a single section of the resulting packed binary. In Fig2, the code section and data section of hello.exe is compressed and stored in the Packed Data area of section UPX1 of the resulting binary Hello upx.exe.

The resulting binary Hello upx.exe contains three sections. The first section UPX0 is entirely virtual - it contains no physical data and is simply a place-holder.It reserves the address range when Hello.exe is loaded to memory. The second section contains the Packed Data, followed immediately by the Unpacker Code. The entry point in the PE header of Hello upx.exe is changed to point directly to the Unpacker Code. The third section contains the resource data, if the original binary had a resource section, and a partial import table, which contains some essential imports from kernel32.dll as well as one imported function from every DLL used by the original binary.

From this example, we can get a fact that the packing and unpacking process is simple. The packer modifies the entry point of the original file and inserting an unpacking routine.When the compressed binary is launched, the unpacker code is firstly executed to decompress or decrypt the original code and data into the UPX0 section, actually allocated in memory and performs some tasks normally carried out by the PE loader, such as import resolution. lastly, it transfers control to the original code, for example by jumping to the so-called Original Entry Point (OEP).

Our method is basically to leverage general behavior of unpacker codes dangled in packed binaries.According to the analysis of more than thirteen different packing techniques, there exists a one - to - one correspondence between the unpacker and the packer,so the unpacker can be used to uniquely identify the packer. By analyzing the execution of a packed malicious code, it can be known that the unpacker will be firstly executed, so under the help of the AddresssOfEntrypoint in the PE Header, we can locate code section including unpacker.Here we extract it and transform it into a Hex-string as the input features of the string-kernel-based SVM classifier.

Although the packer can be very tricky by adding padding, indirect jumps, and other obfuscation methods to the PE file, it can frustrate our approach easily. In practice, we try to change the value of the N from 150 to 50, the accuracy of the classification seldom fluctuates. According to results of the experiments, we can conclude that the unpacking features can be represented by just a few bytes located by the AddressOfEntryPoint in the PE Header.

## 5  Evaluation

AS we know, the effectiveness of a classification system based on string subsequence kernel can be controlled by the free parameters, "length of a subsequence" and "weight decay parameter". In the experiments,we set decay parameter for subsequence kernel 0.9 and substring length for subsequence kernel 4.

### 5.1  Data Sets

We performed experiments on 2180 executables in PE format, including 1280 packed viruses collected from the Malfease Project dataset [11], and 900 non-packed benign executables obtained from a clean installation of Windows XP Home. Table 1 summarizes the proportion of normal executable and packed malware.

### 5.2  Experimental Procedures

SVM classifier is a supervised methods,therefore,we first applied Peid tools to some of the executables in our collection and obtained a labeled dataset, which will be used to train and test the performance of our proposed system. Next, we begin to train and test our system. The training and testing samples were

**Table 1.** Proportion of Normal Executable and Packed Malware

| Packer Name | Sample size |
|---|---|
| Unpacking Executables | 900 |
| Armadillo | 600 |
| Aspack | 180 |
| Bobsoft | 180 |
| Nspack | 40 |
| PECompact | 20 |
| Petite | 60 |
| UPX | 160 |
| Upack | 20 |
| WinUpack | 20 |

randomly drawn from the original data sets, and the number of instances in all the training data subsets were restricted with 3% percent to 15% percent for the unpacked and packed instances.In order to estimate the generalized accuracy, a 10-fold cross-validation procedure was repeated 5 times. In each of the cross-validation iteration, the training set was randomly partitioned into 10 disjoint instance subsets. Each subset was utilized once in a test set and nine times in a training set.

## 5.3    Evaluation Metrics

In the context of classification tasks, the terms true positives, true negatives, false positives and false negatives are used to compare the given classification of an item (the class label assigned to the item by a classifier) with the desired correct classification (the class the item actually belongs to). And for a class X.Based on these, we calculate four metrics that are commonly used in machine learning literature to measure per class performance,which is the Accuracy,Precision,TPR(True Positive Rate) and FPR(False Positive Rate)[12].

## 5.4    Performance

Firstly, we evaluate wether the proposed system can effectively identify the single packed executables and un-packed executables. In this expirement, each time we trained and test the proposed system with a dataset including just one type of packed malware and un-packed files. Here, we run SVM nine times on each kind of packed malware and the same un-packed files as training and test dataset with the 5% and 10% overall dataset as training samples, respectively. Then the average results are calculated. Fig.3 and Fig.4 report the performance of Jumps methods averaged in terms of TPR, FPR, Precision, and Accuracy. As represented in Fig.3 and Fig.4 , the accuracy of the proposed system is not less than 98%, and false positive is under 0.1% even with the 5% overall dataset as training samples. Therefore,it is considered that the proposed system perform well on the identification of single type of packer.

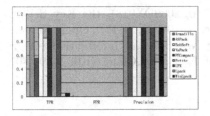

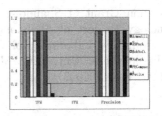

**Fig. 3.** Performance of JUMPS over 5% overall dataset as training samples

**Fig. 4.** Performance of JUMPS over 10% overall dataset as training samples

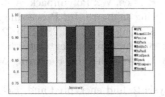

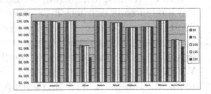

**Fig. 5.** Performance of JUMPS in detecting multi-packer

**Fig. 6.** Performance of JUMPS with different lengths of the features

In the above experiments, we take N=100 as default to test the performance of our approach. In order to test its robustness, we also evaluate its accuracy across a range from N=50 to N=150. its results were shown in Fig N.From Fig. 6, we can find that the accuracy of the classification seldom fluctuates.

## 6 Conclusions

In this paper we do not focus on the improvements in malicious code detection accuracy achieved after unpacking, Instead, we focus on the accuracy and computational cost related to the classification of packed executables into the packed and non-packed,inlcuding the identification issues of different packers . we first analysis its feature of the typical packed malicious code and described how to extract discriminant features from executable files in Portable Executable format. Then we developed the packer recognition system based on string-kernel-based SVM. The experimental results manifest that Jumps's effectiveness at detecting packed malware is excellent.

In future, we would like to evaluate our scheme on a larger dataset of packed and unpacked malicious executables for further improving the detection accuracy,and also attempt to explore the inflection point of lengths of the extracted code.Moreover,we also plan to improve our approach and applied it into the malicious code with multi-packer in the same samples.

**Acknowledgement.** Supported by Specialized Research Fund for the Doctoral Program of Higher Education (20090131120009), Outstanding Young Scientists

Foundation Grant of Shandong Province (BS2009DX018), the Key Science-Technology Project of Shandong Province(2010GGX10117), Open Research Fund from Key Laboratory of Computer Network and Information Integration In Southeast University, Ministry of Education,China (K93-9-2010-05), DNSLAB(K201206007).

# References

1. http://www.peid.info/
2. Royal, P., Halpin, M., Dagon, D., Edmonds, R., Lee, W.: Polyunpack: Automating the hidden-code extraction of unpack-executing malware. In: Proceedings of the 22nd Annual Computer Security Applications Conference, pp. 289–300 (2006)
3. Kang, M.G., Poosankam, P., Yin, H.: Renovo: a hidden code extractor for packed executables. In: Proceedings of the 2007 ACM Workshop on Recurring Malcode, WORM 2007, pp. 46–53 (2007)
4. Lyda, R., Hamrock, J.: Using entropy analysis to find encrypted and packed malware. IEEE Security and Privacy 5, 40–45 (2007)
5. Kolter, J.Z., Maloof, M.A.: Learning to detect and classify malicious executables in the wild. J. Mach. Learn. Res. 7, 2721–2744 (2006)
6. Perdisci, R., Gu, G., Lee, W.: Using an ensemble of one-class svm classifiers to harden payload-based anomaly detection systems. In: Proceedings of the Sixth International Conference on Data Mining, ICDM 2006, pp. 488–498 (2006)
7. Martignoni, L., Christodorescu, M., Jha, S.: OmniUnpack: Fast, Generic, and Safe Unpacking of Malware. In: Proceedings of the 21st Annual Computer Security Applications Conference, ACSAC 2007, Miami Beach, Florida, USA (December 2007)
8. Lyda, R., Hamrock, J.: Using entropy analysis to find encrypted and packed malware. IEEE Security and Privacy 5, 40–45 (2007)
9. Perdisci, R., Lanzi, A., Lee, W.: Classification of packed executables for accurate computer virus detection. Pattern Recogn. Lett. 29, 1941–1946 (2008)
10. Charras, C., Lecroq, T.: Sequence comparison. Laboratoire d'Informatique de Rouen et Atelier Biologie Informatique Statistique Socio-Linguistique. Universit'e de Rouen, France (1998)
11. http://malfease.oarci.net/
12. http://en.wikipedia.org/wiki/Receiver_operating_characteristic/

# Author Index

Abidin, Aysajan    303
Akram, Raja Naeem    214
Alins, Juanjo    22
Altas, Irfan    488
Arita, Seiko    471
Au, Man Ho    142, 167
Ayad, Beghdad    1

Bahig, Hatem M.    33
Ban, Tao    497
Bean, Nigel    131
Bhery, Ashraf    33

Cao, Yan    392
Chen, Xiaofeng    191
Chen, Zhong    228, 400, 435
Chim, Tat Wing    445
Cho, Hyunsook    381
Chow, Yang-Wai    10
Corin, Ricardo    264

Dai, Ting    373
Danger, Jean-Luc    331
Ding, Ning    178
Ding, Xuhua    276
Djebbar, Fatiha    1

Esparza, Oscar    22

Fan, Mengsheng    453
Felix, John    93
Feng, Dengguo    408
Fujioka, Atsushi    202

Gañán, Carlos    22
Ghorbani, Ali A.    93
Gong, Zheng    58
Gu, Dawu    178, 252
Guan, Zhi    228, 400
Guilley, Sylvain    331
Guo, Shanqing    497

Henecka, Wilko    131
Hu, Anlei    497
Hu, Jianbin    435

Hu, Lei    45
Huang, Meishan    357
Huang, Qiong    154
Huang, Xinyi    167
Hui, Lucas Chi Kwong    445

Islam, Rafiqul    488

Jia, Chunfu    191
Jing, Jiwu    105
Johansson, Thomas    461
Joseph, Charles    93

Kim, Byoungkoo    381
Kim, Daewon    381
Kim, Ikkyun    381
Kim, Jeongnyeo    381
Kwok, Chun Kin    445

Li, Fenghai    453
Li, Jin    191
Li, Jingwei    191
Li, Juanru    252
Li, Shuangshuang    497
Li, Victor On Kwok    445
Li, Wenjuan    349
Li, Zhenqi    311, 321
Liang, Zhenkai    373
Lin, Bogang    357
Lin, Dan    427
Lin, Dongdai    311, 321
Lin, Jingqiang    105
Liu, Hui    252
Liu, Joseph K.    167
Liu, Shusheng    58
Liu, Yong    357
Liu, Zongbin    105
Löndahl, Carl    461
Lu, Haibing    276
Lu, Jie    453
Lu, Yao    311, 321

Ma, Chunguang    365
Ma, Yuan    105
Maghrebi, Houssem    331

Mamoulis, Nikos    341
Manzano, Felipe Andrés    264
Markantonakis, Konstantinos    214
Mata-Díaz, Jorge    22
Mayes, Keith    214
Meng, Yuxin    349
Muhammed, Arej    427
Mui, Tin Wing    445
Muñoz, Jose L.    22

Nassr, Dieaa I.    33

Pang, Xiaoqiong    154

Qing, Sihan    119

Ren, Yanli    479
Rioul, Olivier    331
Roughan, Matthew    131

Saito, Taiichi    202
Sathyanarayan, Sai    373
Saxena, Nitesh    293
Shuai, Huimin    416
Squicciarini, Anna    427
Sun, Huiping    228, 400
Sun, Siwei    45
Susilo, Willy    10, 142, 167

Tan, Darell J.J.    240
Tang, Yajuan    70
Thing, Vrizlynn L.L.    240
Trabelsi, Zouheir    81
Tsang, Yu Hin    445

Voris, Jonathan    293

Wang, Ding    365
Wang, Libin    58
Wang, Qingxian    392
Wang, Shengguo    453
Wang, Shuozhong    479
Wang, Wenhao    311
Wang, Yang    142

Wei, Qiang    392
Weng, Jian    276
Wong, Duncan S.    10, 285, 341
Wu, Zhengang    435

Xagawa, Keita    202
Xia, Luning    105
Xin, Wei    400
Xiong, Hao    119
Xu, Jun    45
Xue, Chun Jason    341

Yang, Anjia    285
Yang, Bo    154
Yang, Tao    400, 435
Yang, Wu    365
Yang, Yang    228
Yang, Yanjiang    276
Yap, Roland H.C.    373
Yiu, Siu Ming    119, 341, 445
You, Lin    453
Yu, Kwun Yin    445
Yu, Liangwen    228, 435
Yu, Xingjie    105
Yu, Yan    497
Yuen, Tsz Hon    119, 167

Zeidan, Safaa    81
Zhang, Bin    311, 321
Zhang, Cong    119
Zhang, Echo P.    119
Zhang, Liren    81
Zhang, Xinpeng    479
Zhang, Yan    408
Zhang, Ye    341
Zhao, Ruoxu    252
Zhao, Sendong    365
Zhao, Sicheng    365
Zhou, Jianying    167, 276
Zhu, Jiawei    228, 435
Zhu, Wen Tao    416
Zhuang, Yunhui    285
Zou, Jing    321